Driving Down
Health Care Costs

STRATEGIES AND SOLUTIONS

1994

A PANEL PUBLICATION
ASPEN PUBLISHERS, INC.

Copyright © 1994

by
PANEL PUBLISHERS
A division of Aspen Publishers, Inc.
A Wolters Kluwer Company
36 West 44th Street
New York, NY 10036
(212) 790-2000

ISBN 1-56706-015-3

Printed in the United States of America

About Panel Publishers

Panel Publishers derives its name from a panel of business professionals who organized in 1964 to publish authoritative, timely books, information services, and journals written by specialists to assist business professionals in the areas of human resources administration, compensation, and benefits management, and pension planning and compliance as well as owners of small-to-medium-sized businesses and their legal and financial advisors. Our mission is to provide practical, solution-based "how-to" information to business professionals.

Panel's list of publications that are designed to assist professionals in the areas of human resources, compensation and benefits, and pension and profit-sharing includes:

Managing Employee Health Benefits
Medical Benefits
Employee Benefits Answer Book
The Americans With Disabilities Act: Revised Edition
The Family and Medical Leave Act
State by State Guide to Human Resources Law
Health Insurance Answer Book
Hiring Handbook
Sexual Harassment
Employment Law Answer Book
The Pension Answer Book
401(k) Answer Book
Individual Retirement Account Answer Book

All Panel publications are supplemented periodically to ensure that the information presented is accurate and up-to-date. If you would like to receive updates for this volume, please contact our Customer Service Department at 1-800-457-9222.

PANEL PUBLISHERS
A division of Aspen Publishers, Inc.
Practical Solutions for Business Professionals

SUBSCRIPTION NOTICE

This Panel product is updated on a periodic basis with supplements to reflect important changes in the subject matter. If you purchased this product directly from Panel Publishers, we have already recorded your subscription for this update service.

If, however, you purchased this product from a bookstore and wish to receive future updates and revised or related volumes billed separately with a 30-day examination review, please contact our Customer Service Department at 1-301-698-9342 or send your name, company name (if applicable), address, and the title of the product to:

PANEL PUBLISHERS
A division of Aspen Publishers, Inc.
A Wolters Kluwer Company

7201 McKinney Circle
Frederick, MD 21701

Preface

The 1994 edition of *Driving Down Health Care Costs* is designed to help you, the employee benefits professional, guide your corporation as the nation takes its first steps toward health care reform. Leading employers are focusing on key planning questions, including:

- What impact will various reform proposals have on employers?
- What is a realistic timetable for action?
- Most important of all, what can employers do now with their existing health benefit plans to prepare for tomorrow?

Driving Down Health Care Costs answers those questions and helps you deal with today's double digit premium increases. If you are in the trenches of health care cost control efforts, you've seen the proliferation of health care cost containment strategies. Here you'll find practical advice from the nation's leading benefits experts on your real world benefits—advice that will help you solve your real world problems. For example:

- Concerned that your cost control efforts may expose your corporation to legal problems? Find out what the courts are saying today—and what experts see for tomorrow.
- Thinking about capping mental health benefits? If you're like most employers, you'll find that that strategy could backfire. The good news is that there are ways to contain mental health costs.
- Worried about the complexities involved in point-of-service plans? Your concerns are on target. But there are steps you can take to minimize problems at point-of-service start-up, the time when most difficulties arise.
- Interested in setting up or expanding a wellness program? Find out the strategy behind the most successful programs—and learn what specific actions to avoid.

The 1994 edition of *Driving Down Health Care Costs* will help you tackle these tough issues. You'll find out what works, what doesn't, and why—from organizations that are at the forefront of health care cost control efforts. Inside, you will:

- See what measures Gannet Corporation has taken to slice health insurance claims from cumulative trauma disorders by 75 percent.
- Find out how Utah's Public Employees Health Plan combined practice guidelines, global fees, and employee education to control rising health care costs.
- Examine the strategy Continental Bank has used to hold prescription drug cost increases to under 3 percent.
- Consider the steps AT&T took *before* it designed its strategy for communicating a new flexible benefit plan while implementing potentially controversial cost control measures.
- Take a look at the cost control results Milwaukee achieved in five years of managed competition.
- Learn how Hewlett Packard saves 20 percent in dental costs using managed care and how New York City has saved millions of dollars with a second surgical opinion program.

The distinguished contributors to this edition offer proven, practical solutions to specific problems, whether you need to evaluate the effectiveness of managed care options, fine tune your self-insurance or flexible benefits plan, determine what services to demand in the changing third party administrator market, or find ways to teach your employees to be better medical care consumers.

Whether you are looking five years down the road or need an answer in five minutes, *Driving Down Health Care Costs* is a resource no benefits professional should be without.

Contributors

Donald F. Anderson, PhD, is director of Mental Health Programs at the Medical Audit Services unit of William M. Mercer, Incorporated. He is a clinical psychologist specializing in the evaluation and design of high performance managed mental health and chemical dependency programs. Dr. Anderson recently directed the first national study of the effectiveness of specialized mental health utilization review and PPO networks. He is also national coordinator of the mental health/substance abuse practice area for Mercer. Dr. Anderson was educated at the University of California, Berkeley (BA, Magna Cum Laude) and Harvard University (MA, PhD, Clinical Psychology). He served as a member of the clinical faculty at Harvard Medical School, and also as Deputy Assistant Commissioner of Mental Health for the Commonwealth of Massachusetts. Dr. Anderson's career experience has included serving as CEO of a manufacturing business in California, founding and directing a community-based mental health service program in Cambridge, Massachusetts, and administering a summer research and teaching program for severely disturbed children. Dr. Anderson is the author of multiple book chapters and articles on the subject of managed behavioral health programs, and has directed performance evaluations of such programs for many Fortune 500 companies.

Hocine Azeni is a research associate at the Massachusetts Mental Health Center in Boston.

Linn J. Baker has been director of the State of Utah's Group Insurance Department for the last 17 years. He was instrumental in developing the state's self-administered health, dental, and long-term disability programs. Most recently, he set up a statewide preferred provider network for State employees. In 1980, he served on the Governor's Cost-Containment Task Force. Since that time, he has set up several cost reduction programs within the State's health insurance program. Mr. Baker has worked closely with the State Health Department in developing "Healthy Utah," a health promotion program for employees who adopt healthier lifestyles. Mr. Baker is past president of the Utah Medical Claims Association, past president of the National State and Local Governments Benefits Association, has served on the National Advisory Committee for State Data Commissions. He served on the executive committee of the National Academy of State Health Policy and on the International Foundation's Public Employee Benefits Committee. He is also on the board of directors for the Utah Cost Management Foundation, a board member for the Scrip Card Enterprises, a member of the Governor's Fitness Council, and a member of the Health Education Advisory Council. He graduated from Weber State College with a BS in economics.

Patricia A. Ball is a research associate at the Health Outcomes Institute, a nonprofit organization guiding the development and use of health outcomes assessment technology, where she is responsible for various educational and research activities, including implementation of outcomes management systems in various health care settings. Previously, she worked with Interstudy's Center for Managed Care Research. Her experience there included maintaining a longitudinal national database of HMOs, survey design and data collection methodologies, trend analysis, and technical writing.

Judy Bauserman is a member of the Washington Resource Group of William M. Mercer, Inc.

Jeffrey L. Berlant, MD, PhD, is the chief psychiatric consultant at Medical Audit Services, a division of William M. Mercer, Incorporated. He is currently directing the Medical Audit Services quality assurance program for the CHAMPUS managed mental health demonstration project in Norfolk, Virginia. Dr. Berlant's other specialties include medical chart audits and on-site operational audits of psychiatric utilization review organizations. Dr. Berlant was educated at the University of California, Berkeley (BA, PhD, Sociology), and at the University of California, San Diego School of Medicine (MD). He is board-certified in psychiatry and in internal medicine and has held faculty positions at the University of California, Berkeley. Dr. Berlant's hospital positions have included acting director of the Behavioral Neuroscience Service at Langley Porter Psychiatric Institute, University of California, San Francisco. He has also served as director of outpatient services at Fair Oaks Hospital, Summit, New Jersey, and as medical director of psychiatric services at St. Alphonsus Regional Medical Center in Idaho.

Richard S. Betterley, CMC, is the president of Betterley Risk Consultants, Inc., a national risk management consulting firm headquartered in Worcester, Massachusetts. He is a managing director of Betterley Risk Consultants (Bermuda) Ltd. He holds a BA from Bates College and is active in a number of professional organizations, and recently served as president of the New England Chapter of the Institute of Management Consultants, Inc. He is a frequent speaker and author on risk and insurance management topics.

Louis Bodian is a Morristown, N.J. based consultant to the insurance industry.

Douglas G. Cave, PhD, is a consultant for Hewitt Associates, Newport Beach, California.

Steven P. Chase is a senior consultant in the Human Resource Advisory Group in Cooper's & Lybrand's Syracuse office. Before joining Coopers & Lybrand, he worked for another national benefits consulting firm and for a major health insurance company. Mr. Chase graduated with an AB, cum laude, from Hamilton College and is currently pursuing an MBA in finance from Syracuse University.

Amelia Chu, DSW, ACSW, is senior research associate in the Research Department, Building Service 32B-J Health Fund, New York City.

William S. Custer, PhD, is director of research at the Employee Benefit Research Institute (EBRI) in Washington, DC, where he conducts research related to employer health benefits and the health care delivery system. Dr. Custer has investigated a wide range of topics in health care, including the market for hospital services, hospital-physician relationships, Medicare's Prospective Payment System, and alternative physician payment mechanisms. He is currently directing studies of private health plan cost management incentives, the impact of health care reform proposals, and quality assessment in health care services. Before joining EBRI, Dr. Custer was an economist in the Center for Health Policy Research at the American Medical Association and was an assistant professor of economics at Northern Illinois University.

William J. Danish is A&ACG's health and welfare practice leader for the greater New York region. Before joining the company, he spent 11 years in the group and flexible benefits consulting field with two national firms, and had worked as an underwriter. A graduate of the College of Insurance, he holds a BBA with a major in insurance. He has authored several articles on the subject of health care and has been a guest lecturer on flexible benefits for the masters program at the City University of New York.

Taylor Dennen is principal of William M. Mercer, Inc., in Deerfield, Illinois.

Barbara Dickey is an associate professor in the Harvard Medical School Department of Psychiatry.

Kenneth W. Drummer is Coopers & Lybrand's national line of business leader for flexible benefits and partner-in-charge of health benefits consulting for the firm's western region. Based in San Francisco, he specializes in the design and implementation of flexible benefits programs and health benefits cost containment strategies for large employers.

John Erfut is an associate research scientist in the Worker Health Program, Institute of Labor & Industrial Relations, University of Michigan.

Allen D. Feezor has served as chief deputy commissioner of insurance with the North Carolina Department of Insurance since 1985. From 1985 to 1987 he worked in a dual capacity, serving also as executive administrator for the State Employee Health Plan, a 430,000 member health benefit plan. He is a faculty member of the National Academy for State Health Policy, a board member of the Utilization Review Accreditation Committee, and presently serves as URAC's president. He received his AB and AM from Duke University.

Ron Fontanetta is a principal at Towers Perrin specializing in group benefits. His specific areas of expertise include the design and financing of managed health care programs and the administration of group benefits. Mr. Fontanetta has published several articles on health benefit topics, including "Managed Care: Prescription for the 1990s" in *Topics in Total Compensation* and "The Health Care Connection: How One Company Put a Limit on Cost Increases" in the *Journal of Compensation and Benefits*. He has been a featured speaker at seminars sponsored by the Managed Health Care Congress, the Employers' Council on Flexible Compensation (ECFC) and The Conference Board. Before joining Towers Perrin, Mr. Fontanetta was a senior consultant at a major accounting firm, where he conducted benefit reviews for corporate clients and provided financial consulting services to hospitals. He holds a BA degree from the State University of New York at Albany, as well MBA and MPH degrees from Columbia University.

Andrea Foote is a research scientist in the Worker Health Program, Institute of Labor & Industrial Relations, University of Michigan, and director of the Worker Health Program.

Elizabeth E. Friberg has served as executive director of the Utilization Review Accreditation Commission since 1992; she was previously its director of accreditation. She was a member of the original Standards Committee developing the National Utilization Review Standards and was engaged by URAC to operationalize its Accreditation program in 1991. She is a certified clinical nurse specialist in adult psychiatric and mental health nursing. She received her master's degree from Catholic University of America in Washington, DC.

Jerry Fruetel is a provider contract administrator in the health care affairs department of Blue Cross and Blue Shield of Minnesota. He is co-chair of the select network development task force. Before joining BCBSM in 1990, he served as executive director of the Bloomington, Indiana, Heart Health Program, which received the Governor's Award for Excellence in Health Promotion during his tenure in 1988.

James L. Garcia is the director of the Health Insurance Tracking Unit at Aetna Insurance. He is a co-founder of the National Health Care Anti-Fraud Association and a past president and chairman and current member of its Board of Governors. He is also chairman of the Health Insurance Association of America's Anti-Fraud Task Force. At Aetna, he developed the strongest fraud network system in the nation, including national health care fraud task force committees in 12 states; he has been with Aetna since 1973.

John C. Garner is president of Garner Consulting, in Pasadena, California. He began his career in employee benefits in 1972. Before founding Garner Consulting he was a principal in the Los Angeles office of TPF&C. He has served as technical advisor on flexible benefits for the Family Economic Policy Task Force of the League of California Cities and County Supervisors Association of California. He has special expertise in the area of cost containment.

John A. George is the president of InterGroup Services Corporation, and has been in the managed health care field for the past eight years. Before that he served as a senior consultant with Arthur Young and Company in its health care consulting group. He has served as a vice president with the Presbyterian University Hospital in Pittsburgh, Pennsylvania. He holds a BS from Duquesne University, an MBA from the University of Pittsburgh, and an MST from Robert Morris College. He serves on the editorial board of the *Journal of the AAPPO* and is a board member of the Northeast Region of the AAPPO.

Stephen George, MD, MBA, is vice president and chief medical officer for the Group Department of Providence Life and Accident Insurance Co., in Chattanooga, Tenn. He oversees managed care development and operations, as well as medical management policy for Provident, the fourteenth largest group health insurer in the country.

Lawrence Goelman is the president and CEO of Cost Care, Inc., one of the first health care cost-management firms in the nation. A company founder, Mr. Goelman has been Cost Care's president since operations began in 1981. He received his master's degree in business administration from the University of Western Ontario and Harvard University. Before founding Cost Care, he served as corporate vice president for FHP, one of the largest health maintenance organizations in California.

Max A. Heirich is an associate research scientist in the Worker Health Program, Institute of Labor & Industrial Relations, University of Michigan, and an associate professor.

Peter A. Hinrichs is a consulting actuary for AT&T Actuarial Sciences Associates, Inc., of Piscataway, New Jersey, a national employee-benefits consulting firm.

Lori Sawyer Jenson is a claims analyst for Utah Public Employees Health Program, where she has helped develop their Designated Service Plan. She received her BA in behavioral science and health from the University of Utah, where she is currently an assistant editor for *Utah's Health: An Annual Review*. Ms. Jenson also serves on the Utah Breast Cancer Task Force.

Richard E. Johnson is managing director of William M. Mercer, Companies, Inc. in Chicago. He consults to corporate clients and labor-management trusts for both domestic and international issues. His primary consulting emphases are: total compensation planning/strategic planning, flexible compensation programs, cost-management/utilization review for health plans, medical gain sharing, and defined contribution plans (401(k) and 457). Mr. Johnson is a member of Mercer's flex and health care consulting practice group and past chair of this group. Mr. Johnson is a member of the International Foundation of Employee Benefit Plans (IFEBP), a director of the Alaska Health Cost Management Coalition, and a member of the Association of Private Pension and Welfare Plans. He is the author of three books: *Flexible Benefits—A How-To Guide* (four editions), *Flexible Benefits: What's Best for You?* published by IFEBP. He is also a contributing author to *Employee Benefits Handbook* (Health Management Strategies) and *Handbook of Health Care Human Resources Management* (Flexible Benefit Plans).

Michael B. Jones is a partner and manages the Account Management Group and health care consulting services in Hewitt Associates' East Region. He has been a consultant in the field of employee benefits and compensation for more than 27 years. He is technical advisor to the Committee on Employee Benenfits of the Financial Executive Institute, and serves on the editorial advisory board of the *Journal of Compensation and Benefits*. He is Associate of the Society of Actuaries, and enrolled actuary, and a a member of the American Academy of Actuaries. He received his BA in mathematics from Bucknell University.

Carol L. Kitchell is a senior communications consultant to AT&T. She is a member of the management, systems, and training consulting firm of M.F. Smith and Associates, Inc., in Morristown, New Jersey.

George M. Kraw is a partner in the Silicon Valley law firm of Kraw & Kraw, where his practice spans health, business, and labor law as well as civil litigation. He is a member of the California and District of Columbia bars, the American Bar Association, the Inter-American Bar Association, and the Union International des Advocats. He did his undergraduate work at the University of California at Santa Cruz and received an MA and JD from the University of California at Berkeley.

Richard Kronick, PhD, is assistant professor, Department of Community and Family Medicine, University of California, San Diego.

Joe Lamoglia is assistant editor for HRMagazine.

Thomas K. Langston, CEBS, is corporate director of employee benefits and services for the SSM Healthy Care System, St. Louis, MO.

Victoria Lavoie, BA, is coordinator of professional health services, Building Service 32B-J Health Fund, New York City.

Arthur N. Lerner is a principal with the law firm of Michaels & Wishner, PC, in Washington, DC, practicing in the fields of managed health care and health care antitrust.

John C. Lewin, MD, is director of Hawaii's Department of Health (DOH). He serves as chief health and environmental official for the state, managing an agency with 6,500 employees and an annual operating budget of more than $500 million. The Department has more than 80 statewide programs which are all centrally managed by Dr. Lewin. Under Dr. Lewin's direction are the statewide community hospitals, emergency medical services, care of the mentally ill, alcohol and substance abuse programs, environmental monitoring, comprehensive public health services, health promotion, and disease prevention. Most recently, the DOH spearheaded the new State Health Insurance Program (SHIP) which provides access to medical insurance for those not eligible under other programs and who cannot afford their own. Dr. Lewin is past president of the Association of State and Territorial Health Officials (ASTHO), the national organization of state commissioners and directors of health. He is a member of the board of directors of the Washington DC-based Public Health Foundation. Dr. Lewin is also a clinical professor of International Health at the University of Hawaii School of Public Health, and is a member of the board of directors of the Pacific Basin Health Promotion and Development Center. Before his current position, Dr. Lewin was in private practice on Maui, was the medical director of Kula Hospital, and chief of family practice at Maui Memorial Hospital.

Alfred B. Lewis is executive vice president at InterQual, Inc., a Marlborough, Massachusetts firm specializing in utilization management, network development, and quality improvement for managed care.

Jane M. Lump, principal and senior communications consultant, joined the Chicago office of William M. Mercer, Incorporated, in 1983. Since then, she has been involved in all stages of employee and organizational communication, including program planning and implementation for a broad spectrum of international benefits and human resource issues. Ms. Lump holds a BS from Ball State University and an MA from Purdue University, and is currently on the faculty of the Keller School of Management in Chicago. She was a speaker at the International Foundation's 1991 Benefit Communications Institute.

Scott J. Macey is executive vice president and general counsel for AT&T Actuarial Sciences Associates, Inc., of Piscataway, New Jersey, a national employee-benefits consulting firm.

Lewis L. Maltby is the founder and director of the American Civil Liberties Union's National Taskforce on Civil Liberties in the Workplace. He is the author of five model statutes, including a model act on lifestyle discrimination that has been enacted in states across the country. He has been an advisor to Congress, the Uniform State Law Commissioners, and the American Psychological Association on issues ranging from electronic surveillance to wrongful discharge to honesty testing. He appears regularly in print, radio, and television media as an expert on a variety of employment rights issues.

Michelle Neely Martinez is senior editor for HRMagazine.

Michelle Maynard is editor of the *Business Letter* for the Good Neighbor Alliance Corporation.

Frank B. McArdle is a partner and the manager of Hewitt Associates' Washington, DC, Research Office. He is a principal resource in Washington on matters relating to employee benefits and compensation, with nearly 20 years of experience in the field. Prior to joining Hewiit Associates in 1988, he was director of education and communications with the Employee Benefit Research Institute (EBRI) in Washington, DC. He holds a PhD from the University of Virginia and a BA from Fordham University.

Eugene G. McCarthy, MD, MPH, is medical adviser of several union health funds, including SEIU Local 32J, Transit Workers Union Local 100, Carpenters Union, and Hotel and Hospital Workers Union.

Brian T. McMahon is an associate professor and area chair of the Rehabilitation Counselor Education Program at the University of Wisconsin, Milwaukee.

Thomas W. Meagher is a consulting attorney for AT&T Actuarial Sciences Associates, Inc., of Piscataway, New Jersey, a national employee-benefits consulting firm.

Michael E. Mihlbauer earned a master's degree in health services delivery systems from the University of Wisconsin in 1978. He has held a number of HMO positions, starting out as director of patient services at Compcare, the Blue Cross plan in Milwaukee, in 1976. Mr. Mihlbauer later was the first employee and start up manager of CNA's Intergroup of Wisconsin, a position that, through acquisition, grew into CEO of Maxicare of Wisconsin. In 1983, he worked as president of MCW Physicians, Inc., a subsidiary of the Medical College of Wisconsin, where he handled contracting, marketing, and some ambulatory care management for 300 academic physicians. A 17-year veteran of managed care, Mr. Mihlbauer founded Mihlbauer and Associates six years ago. The company specializes in the health care purchasing relationship and serves providers, managed care companies, and purchasers of health care services.

Richard D. Morrison is executive director of the Virginia Board of Health Professions, an advisory commission appointed by the Governor to coordinate policy in the regulation of health professions. He holds a master's degree from the College of William and Mary and a doctoral degree from Virginia Commonwealth University. Dr. Morrison serves on the adjunct faculty of the Department of Sociology at Virginia Commonwealth University, and has taught sociology and social work at the Christopher Newport College and at William and Mary.

Dennis J. Nirtaut is vice president/manager of employee benefits for Continental Bank in Chicago, Illinois, where he is responsible for all employee benefit matters for 4,200 employees and 3,000 retirees. He is the author of the column "Ask a Benefit Manager" in *Business Insurance*, is an instructor for the American Compensation Association (ACA) teaching employee benefit classes in the benefit certification program, and serves on the education committee of the ACA.

Nicholas J. Phillips is a principal in the Human Resource Advisory Group in Coopers & Lybrand's Syracuse office. He has 16 years of experience in employee benefit plan design and financing. Before moving to Syracuse, he had worked as an actuarial and benefits consultant for Gulf & Western Industries, Inc., and American Home Products Corporation. He is an associate of the Society of Actuaries, a member of the American Academy of Actuaries, and is an Authorized Group Actuary for Coopers & Lybrand. He graduated magna cum laude from Wagner College in Staten Island, New York with a BS degree in mathematics, and from the University of Rochester with an MA in statistics.

Don R. Powell is the president of the American Institute for Preventive Medicine.

Robert P. Power, CEBS, serves as senior medical economist for Group Health Incorporated and as a consultant to insurers and managed care organizations. He holds a BA in economics from Colorado College and an MBA in insurance from the University of Minnesota. His current research interests include Medicare cost shifting and selection effects in managed care.

Anna M. Rapport, FSA, is a managing director of William M. Mercer. She is an actuary and futurist with 30 years of business experience and has a broad background in pension and benefits consulting, corporate research, and life insurance company management. Her special interest has been social and economic change and how it affects benefits and human resources management. She has published in the *Harvard Business Review*, *Inquiry*, the *Journal of Pension Planning and Compliance*, and *Compensation and Benefits Management*, for which she is a regular columnist.

Diana Reace is a consultant in Hewitt Associates' Lincolnshire, Illinois, Headquarters. She is responsible for managing all health care research activities, including those relating to employer plan design, plan experience, and health care legislation. Before joining Hewitt Associates in 1982, she attended Miami University, where she received her BA in international studies.

David R. Reimer is the director of administration for the City of Milwaukee. He is a graduate of Harvard Law School and Harvard College.

George W. Rimler is professor of management at Virginia Commonwealth University, where he is also director of the Small Business Institute. His particular academic interests lie in entrepreneurship and organizational productivity. Dr. Rimler has published many articles in practitioner and academic journals, and his book, *Small Business: Developing the Winning Management Team*, has been published in a Japanese edition.

Curtis Rooney is legislative associate for the Association of Private Pension and Welfare Plans. Prior to his current position, he was legislative analyst for the Mutual of Omaha Companies in Washington, DC. He was a Congressional Intern for former Representative James J. Florio (D-NJ) and worked for the Doorkeeper of the U.S. House of Representatives as an administrator of the Congressional Page Program. He also served as a law clerk to the General Counsel to the Clerk of the U.S. House of Representatives. Mr. Rooney received a BA from the George Washington University in Political Science in 1985 and a JD from the Catholic University School of Law in 1989.

Paul A. Ross, EdD, is Digital Equipment Corporation's corporate manager of the HIV/AIDS Program Office. Ross has held a number of senior level human resource management positions at Digital since joining the company in 1978. Before establishing the HIV/AIDS Program Office, he was personnel manager for the 4,00 Digital employees in New England and upstate New York field operations. He is the United States Commissioner on International AIDS Issues for UNESCO; chairman of the New England Corporate Consortium for AIDS Education; director of The National Leadership Coalition on AIDS; and former director and secretary of the Executive Committee of the American Society of Training and Development. Ross is also a member of the Steering Committee of the Boston AIDS Consortium, Harvard School of Public Health; the HIV Tax Check-off Advisory Board, Massachusetts Department of Public Health; and the AIDS Reference Guide Editorial Board.

Joyce E. Santora is a free-lance writer.

Michael W. Schionning is a senior consultant for Treacy & Rhodes Consultants in Solana Beach, California.

Ernest J. Sessa is the executive director of the Pennsylvania Health Care Cost Containment Council. A graduate of St. Joseph's University, he has 30 years of experience in the health care delivery field, including 13 as the administrator of the 73,000 member Benefits Trust Fund for Pennsylvania state workers. He has served as chairperson of the Pennsylvania Blue Shield Subscriber Advisory Council, as a member of he Governor's Task Force for Economic Development Partnership for the Public Sector, and on the Finance Committee of the Governor's Long Term Care Council. He is a member of the editorial board of *Compensation and Benefits Management.*

Donald E. Shrey, PhD, CRC, is an associate professor and Director of Disability Management, Department of Physical Medicine and Rehabilitation, University of Cincinnati Medical Center.

MaryAnn Stump, RN, is vice president of quality improvement for Blue Plus of Minnesota. She is co-chair of the select network development task force. She is past president of the Minnesota Healthcare Quality Professionals and a certified professional in healthcare quality (CPHQ).

Peter A. Sybinsky, PhD, is deputy director of the Hawaii State Department of Health (Health Resources Administration). Dr. Sybinsky currently coordinates the state's health care reform efforts for Governor Waihee as Healthcare Reform Manager. In this capacity Dr. Sybinsky has assisted as a member of the National Governors' Association (NGA) Task Force on Health Care, which developed NGA policy on health care reform and issued the recent report *A Healthy America: The Challenge for States.* In addition, he is responsible for managing the Department's programs of planning, health status monitoring, quality assurance, and legislation. Dr. Sybinsky also manages Hawaii's new State Health Insurance Program (SHIP)—a gap group insurance program. At various times during his tenure as deputy director, Dr. Sybinsky has also been responsible for the Department's laboratory programs, its emergency medical services program (the only statewide fully professional paramedic service in the nation), hospital and medical quality assurance program, maternal and child health, school health, and health promotion and education efforts. He holds a PhD in political science from the University of Hawaii and has taught extensively for local universities and colleges.

Tom Trabin, PhD, MSW, has over six years of program consultation and development experience, including outpatient mental health programs for hospital corporations in Missouri, Minnesota, and Utah and partial hospital programs for hospital corporations in California, Minnesota, Missouri, Texas, and Wisconsin. Dr. Trabin was the Director of Managed Care for U.S. Behavioral Health where he developed and directed core operations for major national managed care companies specializing in mental health and chemical dependency benefits and treatment. He also served as a member of the faculty at St. Mary's Graduate Institute and is currently on the Board of Directors of the California Psychological Association. After receiving a BA and MA in Philosophy, Dr. Trabin completed his PhD in psychology at the University of Minnesota. In addition, Dr. Trabin received a Masters degree from Stanford University, Graduate School of Business.

Neil J. Waldron is vice president of marketing and product development at Mass Mutual.

William K. Willson is the executive director of the Utah Community Health Plan in Salt Lake City. He previously served as director of research and development at Intermountain Health Care, and has worked as a consultant for Brighton Consulting. He holds an MA in hospital and health administration and a BBA, both from the University of Iowa.

Cindy Yoder-Brown, MSW, is EAO manager for Continental Bank, Chicago, Illinois.

Coleen W. Young is a consultant for Treacy & Rhodes Consultants in Solana Beach, California.

Contents

Introduction:
President Clinton's Health Reform Plan

To keep you current on health care reform, presented here is an abridged, verbatim account from the 239-page White House report entitled "Clinton Administration Description of President's Health Care Reform Plan: American Health Security Act of 1993." Sections reproduced here are those of greatest relevance to employers and other major purchasers of health care services. Legislation is to be presented to Congress in due course.

OVERVIEW

The American Health Security Act guarantees comprehensive health coverage for all Americans regardless of health or employment status. Health coverage continues without interruption if Americans lose or change jobs, move from one area to another, become ill or confront a family crisis.

Through a system of regional and corporate health alliances that organize the buying power of consumers and employers, the American Health Security Act stimulates market forces so that health plans and providers compete on the basis of quality, service and price.

Under the Act health plans must meet national standards on benefits, quality and access to care but each state may tailor the new system to local needs and conditions. Thus the program encourages local innovation within a national framework.

It frees the health care system of much of the accumulated burden of unnecessary regulation and paperwork, allowing doctors, nurses, hospitals and other health providers to focus on providing high-quality care.

COVERAGE

All Americans and legal residents are guaranteed access to health services in a nationally defined, comprehensive package of benefits with no lifetime limits on coverage. Categories of eligible individuals:

- American citizens
- Nationals
- Citizens of other countries legally residing in the United States
- Long-term non-immigrants

Sources of Health Coverage

A health security card provided to each eligible person entitles him or her to obtain coverage through a health plan that delivers services covered in a nationally defined, comprehensive benefit package.

Eligible individuals enroll in a health plan through a health alliance unless they are covered under government-sponsored health programs that continue, including:

- Medicare
- Military personnel covered by the Department of Defense
- Department of Veterans Affairs
- Indian Health Service

Individuals eligible for Medicaid receive coverage through regional health alliances.

All employed persons choose a health plan through a corporate or regional health alliance. Employees of firms with 5,000 or fewer workers become members of a regional alliance established to serve the area in which they reside. Employees of firms with more than 5,000 employees obtain coverage through a corporate alliance established by their employer unless the employer chooses to purchase coverage through regional alliances.

Employees of government, including federal, state, local and special-purpose agencies, obtain coverage through the regional alliance where they live. All individuals who are self-employed or not employed obtain coverage through regional alliances unless they are eligible for Medicare.

Obtaining Coverage

Individuals obtain health coverage by enrolling in a plan through a regional or corporate health alliance. The national health security card serves as proof of eligibility.

An individual eligible for cash assistance (AFDC or SSI), whether employed or unemployed, has coverage purchased from the regional alliance by the Medicaid program.

Individuals over age 65 continue to enroll in the Medicare program. The Medicare secondary payer program remains for Medicare eligible individuals who continue to work. Individuals over the age of 65 but not eligible for Medicare receive coverage through regional alliances, into which they pay premiums. Individuals who are eligible for Medicare because of disability continue to receive Medicare coverage.

Retired workers under 65 are eligible for health care coverage through regional alliances, and pay only the 20 percent share they would have paid if employed. Retirees who receive health coverage through former employers or through pension funds continue to be eligible for payment for their share of the premium from those sources.

Assurance of Coverage

It is the obligation of every eligible individual to enroll in a health plan. Anyone who does not meet the established deadline for enrollment automatically is enrolled in a health plan when he or she seeks medical care.

No health plan may cancel an enrollment until the individual enrolls in another plan.

Employer Obligation

All employers contribute to the purchase of health coverage for their employees. All employers pay 80 percent of the weighted-average premium for health insurance coverage in the regional alliances that serve their employees or in their corporate alliance. The required employer contribution in regional alliances is capped at a percentage of payroll, with lower caps for small and low-wage employers.

Firms that employ more than 5,000 workers ensure that their employees are enrolled in health plans that meet federal guidelines and report information about enrollment. Employers with more than 5,000 employees that choose to operate corporate alliances may be required to continue to pay for health insurance coverage for their terminated employees for six months following termination or may have to pay 1 percent of payroll to cover unemployed workers.

Large employers may fulfill their obligation to provide coverage by operating a program of self-insurance through a corporate alliance, contracting with a certified health plan or joining the regional alliance. If a large employer merges with a firm in the regional alliance, it may continue as a corporate alliance. If the number of employees falls below 4,800, the employer joins the regional alliance.

Individual Obligations

Families and individuals pay 20 percent of the weighted-average premium for an average cost health plan chosen through an alliance. An individual or family who chooses a less expensive plan pays less, and someone who chooses a more expensive plan pays more.

An employer also may elect to pay some or all of the employee's portion of the premium.

Self-employed and unemployed individuals are responsible for paying the family share of the premium as well as the employer share, unless they are eligible for assistance based on income.

Enforcement

The Secretary of Labor ensures that all employers fulfill the obligation to make contributions or provide coverage through a qualified health plan.

Coordination of Coverage

When an individual obtains necessary medical services outside the geographic area served by his or her regional or corporate alliance, the plan pays for care under arrangements established among alliances.

Undocumented Persons

Undocumented persons are not eligible for guaranteed health benefits. However, employers are required to pay health insurance premiums for all of their employees, regardless of immigration status.

Alliances do not share information related to health insurance premiums paid by employers with the Immigration and Naturalization Service.

GUARANTEED NATIONAL BENEFIT PACKAGE

The health benefits guaranteed to all Americans provide comprehensive coverage, including mental health services, substance-abuse treatment, some dental services and clinical preventive services.

The guaranteed benefit package contains no lifetime limitations on coverage, with the exception of coverage for orthodontia.

Medical Services Covered

Each health plan must provide coverage for the following categories of services as medically necessary or appropriate with additional limitations and cost-sharing only as specified in the American Health Security Act of 1993 or by the National Health Board. Covered health services are:

- Hospital services
- Emergency services
- Services of physicians and other health professionals
- Clinical preventive services
- Mental health and substance abuse services
- Family planning services
- Pregnancy-related services
- Hospice
- Home health care
- Extended-care services
- Ambulance services
- Outpatient laboratory and diagnostic services
- Outpatient prescription drugs and biologicals
- Outpatient rehabilitation services
- Durable medical equipment, prosthetic and orthotic devices
- Vision and hearing care
- Preventive dental services for children
- Health education classes

Exclusions

The benefit package does not cover services that are not medically necessary or appropriate, private duty nursing, cosmetic orthodontia and other cosmetic surgery, hearing aids, adult eyeglasses and contact lenses, in vitro fertilization services, sex change surgery and related services, private room accommodations, custodial care, personal comfort services and supplies and investigational treatments, except [as part of an approved research trial for an investigational treatment].

Cost-Sharing

Consumer out-of-pocket costs for health services in the comprehensive benefit package are limited, to ensure financial protection, and standardized to ensure simplicity in choosing among health plans.

Health plans use [a] standard consumer cost-sharing requirement. Health plans may offer consumers one of three cost-sharing schedules:

- Low cost-sharing: $10 co-payments for outpatient services; no co-payments for inpatient services; may offer point-of-service option with 40 percent coinsurance.
- Higher cost-sharing: $200 individual/$400 family deductibles; 20 percent coinsurance; $1,500/$3,000 maximum on out-of-pocket spending.
- Combination: Plan provides low cost-sharing if participants use preferred providers and high cost-sharing (20 percent coinsurance) if they use out-of-network providers.

NATIONAL HEALTH BOARD

The American Health Security Act creates an independent National Health Board responsible for setting national standards and overseeing the establishment and administration of the new health system by states.

The National Health Board and existing executive agencies divide responsibility for administration of the new health care system at the national level.

Responsibilities of Department of Health and Human Services

The Department of Health and Human Services continues to administer existing programs, such as Medicaid, Medicare and the Public Health Service. The Department of Health and Human Services also administers and implements those aspects of the new health care system not delegated to the National Health Board or any other federal department.

NATIONAL ADMINISTRATION

The National Health Board reviews plans submitted by the states for the implementation of the new health care system. Corporate alliances are supervised through ERISA and the Department of Labor.

STATE RESPONSIBILITIES

States assume primary responsibility for ensuring that all eligible individuals have access to a health plan that delivers the nationally guaranteed comprehensive benefit package.

State Plans

Each state submits to the National Health Board a plan for implementation of health reform, demonstrating that its health care system meets requirements under federal law. States periodically update their plans, as required by the National Health Board.

The plan also describes how the state intends to perform each of the following functions:

- Administration of subsidies for low-income individuals, families and employers
- Certification of health plans
- Financial regulation of health plans
- Administration of data collection and quality management and improvement program
- Establishment and governance of health alliances, including a mechanism for selecting members of the boards of directors and advisory boards for alliances

Establishment of Alliances

No later than January 1, 1997, each state must establish one or more regional health alliances responsible for providing health coverage to residents in every area of the state.

The state ensures that all eligible individuals enroll in a regional alliance and that all alliances offer health plans that provide the comprehensive benefit package. The state also ensures that each alliance enrolls all eligible persons in the geographic area covered by the alliance.

Alliance Size and Population

The geographic area assigned to each regional alliance must encompass a population large enough to ensure that it controls adequate market share to negotiate effectively with health plans. States may establish one, and only one, regional alliance in each area.

Guaranty Funds

Each state operates a guaranty fund to provide financial protection to health care providers and others if a health plan becomes insolvent. States may use existing guaranty fund arrangements, provided that the arrangement meets national standards.

REGIONAL HEALTH ALLIANCES

Regional health alliances assume the following responsibilities:

- Representing the interests of consumers and purchasers of health care services
- Structuring the market for health care to encourage the delivery of high-quality care and the control of costs
- Assuring that all residents in an area who are covered through the regional alliance enroll in health plans that provide the nationally guaranteed benefits

Operation of Alliances

A regional alliance may operate as a nonprofit corporation, an independent state agency or an agency of the state executive branch.

States require each alliance to provide an ombudsman to assist consumers in dealing with problems that arise with health plans and the alliance.

Enrollment

Each regional alliance enrolls all eligible persons, including low-income and nonworking persons, who reside in the geographic area it serves into a health plan that provides the comprehensive benefits.

Information

Alliances publish (or otherwise make available to consumers) easily understood, useful information, including brochures, computerized information and interactive media, that allows them to make valid comparisons among health plans. The following information must be included:

- Cost to consumers, including premiums and average out-of-pocket expenses
- Characteristics and availability of health care professionals and institutions participating in the plan
- Any restrictions on access to providers and services
- The annual Quality Performance Report, which contains measures of quality presented in a standard format

Fee-for-Service Plans

Each alliance includes among its health plan offerings at least one plan organized around a fee-for-service system. A fee-for-service system is one in which patients have the option of consulting any health provider subject to reasonable requirements. Reasonable requirements may include utilization review and prior approval for certain services but do not include a requirement to seek approval through a gatekeeper.

Balance Billing

A provider may not charge or collect from a patient a fee in excess of the fee schedule adopted by an alliance. A plan and its participants are not legally responsible for payment of any amount in excess of the allowable charge.

CORPORATE ALLIANCES

The following organizations and firms must either form corporate health alliances or join regional health alliances:

- Employers with more than 5,000 employees
- Existing plans formed pursuant to collective bargaining with more than 5,000 covered employees (or a group of plans within the same union structure) such as Taft-Hartley plans, although certain limitations apply to the ability of such plans to provide coverage to associate union members
- Plans formed by rural electric and telephone cooperatives with more than 5,000 covered employees

   The term employer is defined as it is under the ERISA statute.

Election to Form a Corporate Alliance

Large employers eligible to form corporate alliances elect to exercise that option or to purchase health coverage through a regional alliance.

   Large employers periodically have the opportunity to switch to regional alliances.

Health Plans

Corporate alliances provide health benefits to eligible employees and dependents either through a certified self-funded employee benefit plan or through contracts with state-certified health plans.

   Contracts between health plans and corporate alliances comply with the following requirements:

- Premium rates charged to the corporate alliance may be based on community rating, adjusted community rating or experience rating. For corporate alliances composed of more than one employer, such as Taft-Hartley plans and rural electric or telephone cooperatives, premium rates charged to individual employers must be community rated.
- Health plans that contract with corporate alliances must accept all eligible employees and their dependents, regardless of individual characteristics, health status, anticipated need for health services, occupation, affiliation with any person or entity (except for affiliation with another alliance or health plan).
- Health plans may not terminate, restrict or limit coverage for the nationally guaranteed comprehensive benefit package.
- Exclusions for existing medical conditions and waiting periods or riders that exclude certain individuals are prohibited.
- Health plans may not cancel coverage for eligible employees and dependents until they enroll in another health plan.

Information

Corporate alliances assure that employees have ready access to comparative information about health plans. Information is obtained through a brochure published annually. At a minimum, the brochure must include the following information about health plans:

- Cost to consumers, including premiums and average out-of-pocket expenses
- Characteristics and availability of health providers
- Restrictions on access to providers and services
- The annual Quality Performance Report for each health plan containing measures of quality presented in a standard format

Corporate alliances are responsible for assuring that employees are aware of information they may obtain from participating plans.

Choice of Plans

Each corporate alliance contracts with at least one fee-for-service health plan.

In addition to a fee-for-service plan, a corporate alliance contracts with at least two other health plans offering the comprehensive benefits.

ERISA

The American Health Security Act amends the Employee Retirement Income Security Act of 1974 (ERISA) to create a new chapter governing employee health benefit plans and modifying the current ERISA preemption section.

Requirements Related to Employee Health Benefit Plans

A new chapter or title of ERISA establishes fiduciary and enforcement requirements for employers and others sponsoring health benefit plans in corporate alliances. Current provisions of ERISA do not apply to health benefits except by specific reference. Provisions address:

- Ensuring that everyone enrolled in corporate health alliances obtains coverage providing at least the nationally guaranteed benefit package
- Establishing fiduciary requirements for employers, plan sponsors and plan fiduciaries
- Setting requirements related to information and notification made available to employees
- Ensuring compliance with national standards with respect to uniform claims form, data reporting, electronic billing and other areas
- Applying grievance and benefit dispute procedures to self-funded health benefit plans
- Establishing financial reporting requirements for self-funded health benefit plans and for corporate alliances
- Setting financial reserve requirements for self-funded health benefit plans.

The new title or chapter also sets fiduciary requirements for employers in regional alliances governing the withholding of employee contributions from wages. The Department of Labor may enter into agreements with states to enforce these requirements.

Preemption of State Laws

The ERISA preemption provision is modified to:

- Apply the preemption only with respect to employers and health benefit plans in corporate alliances
- Permit taxes and assessments on employers or health benefit plans in corporate alliances if the assessments are nondiscriminatory in nature
- Permit states to develop all-payer hospital rates or all-payer rate setting
- States also may require all payers, including health benefit plans in corporate alliances, to reimburse essential community providers.

HEALTH PLANS

Health plans provide coverage for the nationally guaranteed comprehensive benefit package through contracts with regional or corporate alliances. Only state-certified health plans are allowed to provide health insurance and benefits in regional alliances.

Enrollment

Health plans accept every eligible person enrolled by an alliance without regard to individual characteristics, health status, anticipated need for health care, occupation, affiliation with any person or entity (except affiliation with a corporate alliance or health plan).

Health plans may not terminate, restrict or limit coverage for the comprehensive benefit package for any reason, including nonpayment of premiums. They may not cancel coverage for any individual until that individual is enrolled in another health plan.

Health plans may not exclude participants because of existing medical conditions or impose waiting periods before coverage begins. Riders that serve to exclude certain illnesses or health conditions also are prohibited.

With the approval of the state, health plans may limit enrollment because of restrictions on the plan's capacity to deliver services or to maintain financial stability.

Community Rating

Health plans use community rating to determine premiums establishing separate rates to reflect family status.

Beginning in August of each calendar year, alliances negotiate premium rates with each health plan contracting for coverage through that alliance. Negotiations set individual and family premiums for each health plan within the alliance. During an annual open enrollment period, alliances publish the negotiated rates for all health plans.

Employers and employees pay a community-rated premium. However, payments to health plans by alliances are adjusted to account for the level of risk associated with individuals enrolled in plans. The adjustment is made using a formula developed by the National Health Board.

Information

Each health plan provides to the alliance and makes available to consumers and health care professionals information concerning:

- Costs
- Qualifications and availability of providers
- Procedures used to control utilization of services and expenditures
- Procedures for assuring and improving the quality of care
- Rights and responsibilities of consumers and patients

Health plans are responsible for the accuracy of information submitted and may be disqualified from participating in an alliance if information is inaccurate.

Grievance Procedure

Health plans offering coverage through both regional and corporate alliances are required to establish a benefit claims dispute procedure.

RISK ADJUSTMENT

Alliances adjust premium payments to health plans to reflect the level of risk assumed for patients enrolled in comparison to the average population in the area. The adjustment mechanism takes into account factors such as age, gender, health status and services to disadvantaged populations.

Development of Federal Model System

Nine months before the date on which states first enroll consumers in regional alliances, the National Health Board promulgates a risk-adjustment system.

Regional alliances are required to use the risk-adjustment system unless an alliance obtains a waiver from the National Board.

Integration of Workers' Compensation Insurance

Health plans provide treatment for individuals with work-related injuries covered under workers' compensation insurance.

Workers' compensation insurers (including self-funding employers) continue to be responsible for the costs of treatment based on current law and reimburse health plans for services provided. Reimbursement is based on a fee schedule or on an alternative arrangement established by alliances or negotiated between workers' compensation insurers and health plans.

Each health plan designates a workers' compensation case manager to coordinate the treatment and rehabilitation of injured workers.

A Commission on Health Benefit and Integration is created to study the feasibility and appropriateness of transferring the financial responsibility for all medical benefits (including those now covered under workers' compensation and automobile insurance) to the new health system. The Department of Labor and Department of Health and Human Services provide staff support to the Commission. The Commission reports to the President and presents a detailed plan for integration if it is recommended, on or before July 1, 1995.

BUDGET DEVELOPMENT ENFORCEMENT

The American Health Security Act organizes the market for health care and creates mechanisms to control costs through enhanced competition, consumer choice, administrative simplification, and increased negotiating power through health alliances. A national health care budget serves as a backstop to that system of incentives and organized market power. The budget ensures that health care costs do not rise faster than other sectors of the economy.

ANNUAL INCREASES

The growth in premiums in regional alliances is limited through a national inflation factor.

NATIONAL PER CAPITA BASELINE TARGET

The National Health Board calculates a national per capita premium target based on:

- Current per capita health expenditures for the guaranteed benefits package trended forward to 1996 based on projected increases in private sector health care spending.
- With adjustments for expected increases in utilization by the uninsured and underinsured and to recapture currently uncompensated care.

ENFORCEMENT OF THE BUDGET

The federal government is responsible for enforcing the health care budget.

If an alliance's anticipated weighted-average premium exceeds its per capita budget target, an assessment is imposed on each plan whose premium increase (adjusted upward to reflect the previous year's assessment) exceeds the alliance's premium inflation factor. Revenues from assessments on plans are used to reduce required employer premium contributions.

Budgets for Corporate Alliances

A large employer may operate a corporate alliance rather than purchasing health coverage through a regional alliance, provided it complies with cost-containment goals. Large employers whose health plans do not meet national spending goals are required to purchase coverage through regional alliances.

The allowed rate of growth for corporate alliance premiums is the same as the national inflation factor for regional alliances.

QUALITY MANAGEMENT AND IMPROVEMENT

National Quality Management Program

The National Quality Management Program develops the quality information and accountability program. An advisory council under the National Health Board, appointed by the President, oversees the program.

Performance Reports

The National Quality Management Program under the National Health Board develops a core set of measures of performance that applies to all health plans, institutions and practitioners. It publishes annual performance reports outlining the results of those measures for each health plan, creating a public system of accountability for quality and providing consumers with meaningful information.

It also provides annual reports to the states on the comparative performance of health plans and state quality programs. Quality reports include information on the performance of alliances and health plans on as many as 50 measures of access to care, appropriateness of care, health outcomes, health promotion, disease prevention and satisfaction with care.

It provides the results of a smaller number of quality measures for health care institutions, doctors and other practitioners if the available information is statistically meaningful. State performance reports include trends, performance on national quality measures and on goals for national performance on access, appropriateness and health outcomes.

INFORMATION SYSTEMS

Data and Information Framework

Every American receives a national health security card to assure access to needed health services throughout the United States. Much like ATM cards, the health security card allows access to information about health coverage through an integrated national network. The card itself contains a minimal amount of information.

Federal, State, Alliance and Health Plan Data Network

An electronic network of regional centers containing enrollment, financial, and utilization data is created. The network receives standardized enrollment, encounter, and related data from plans for aggregation, analysis and feedback to plans, alliances, states and the federal government.

Consumer Surveys and Public Health Surveillance

Consumer surveys of satisfaction, access to care and related measures are conducted on a plan-by-plan and state-by-state basis. The National Health Board approves a nationally standard design for the survey.

ADMINISTRATION SIMPLIFICATION

Standard Forms

By January 1, 1995, all health plans adopt a single, standard form for reimbursement according to the following classes of providers:

- The UB 92 for institutional providers
- The Standard Health Insurance Claim Form (similar to the HCFA-1500) for all noninstitutional providers except pharmacies and dentists
- HCFA 1500 for dentists
- The Universal Drug Claim Form developed by the National Council on Prescription Drug Programs for pharmacies that seek reimbursement

LONG-TERM CARE

A new long-term care program, created through Title XV of the Social Security Act, encompasses five components:

- Expanded home and community-based services
- Improvements in Medicaid coverage for institutional care
- Standards to improve the quality and reliability of private long-term care insurance and tax incentives to encourage people to buy it
- Tax incentives that help individuals with disabilities to work
- A demonstration study intended to pave the way toward greater integration of acute and long-term care

MALPRACTICE REFORM

Reform of the dispute resolution system for medical malpractice in the American Health Security Act encompasses both changes in tort law and the development of alternative approaches to resolving patients' claims against providers. Reforms are:

- Creation of alternative dispute resolution mechanisms

    Each health plan establishes an alternative dispute resolution process using one or more of several models developed by the National Health Board. Potential model systems include early offers of settlement, mediation and arbitration.

    Consumers who have a claim against a health care provider are required to submit the claim through the alternative dispute system. At the completion of the alternative dispute system, if the consumer is not satisfied with the outcome, he or she is free to pursue the complaint in court.

- Requirement for certificate of merit

    Lawsuits claiming injury from medical malpractice include submission of an affidavit signed by a medical specialist practicing in a field relevant to the claimed injury. The affidavit must attest that a specialist examined the claim and concluded that medical procedures or treatments that produced the claim deviated from established standards of care.

- Limits on attorney fees

    Attorneys' fees for malpractice cases are limited to a maximum of 33⅓ percent of an award. States may impose lower limits, as many have.

- Repeat offenders

    The Department of Health and Human Services establishes rules for public access to information contained in the National Practitioner Data Bank, which tracks health care providers who incur repeated malpractice judgments and settlements.

- Collateral sources

    New rules require reduction of the amount of any award in a medical malpractice case by the amount of recovery from other sources.
- Periodic payment of awards
- Enterprise liability demonstration project

    Federal funds support state demonstration projects to establish enterprise liability.
- Standards based on practice guidelines

    Based on a five-year program underway to determine the effect of using practice patterns in three specialty areas (anesthesia, emergency medicine and gynecology), the Department of Health and Human Services will develop a medical liability pilot program based on practice guidelines adopted by the National Quality Management Program.

MEDICARE

State Integration

The Secretary of the Department of Health and Human Services has authority to permit states to integrate Medicare beneficiaries into health alliances under specified conditions that ensure:

- Beneficiaries have the same or better coverage as standard Medicare benefits.
- Federal financial liability is not increased.

FINANCING HEALTH COVERAGE FOR THE UNDER-65 POPULATION

Contributions for Health Coverage

Payments for health coverage will be divided into two shares: contributions by individuals and families and contributions by employers.

Individuals who work less than a full year, as well as families whose members jointly have less than one full year's employer contributions, are also responsible for any unpaid employer share to the extent they have non-wage income.

Individual and Family Contributions

Each individual and family is guaranteed health coverage through the alliance in which they are enrolled. Where families have workers at firms in two different corporate alliances or in one regional and one corporate alliance, they may choose coverage through either alliance.

Alliances offer consumers a choice of health plans. All consumers receive the same schedule of premiums for enrollment.

Premiums vary according to four family types: single individual, couples without children, single-parent family, and two-parent family.

Employer contributions pay for 80 percent of the average-priced plan in the alliance for each family type.

Families and individuals pay the difference between 80 percent of the average-priced premium and the actual cost of the plan they select.

Subsidies for Low-Income Families and Individuals

Families and individuals with incomes below 150 percent of poverty in a regional alliance may apply to their alliance for help in paying their premium. The subsidy will depend on their family income and the average premium for that family type in the alliance.

Employer Contributions

The contributions of employers total 80 percent of average premiums for each family status in an alliance.

Firms in the regional alliance pay a fixed per-worker contribution for each employee according to his or her family status.

The per-worker employer contribution depends on the average number of workers per family within each family status in the alliance. For example, if two-parent families in a region have an average of 1.5 workers per family, the per-worker contribution for a two-parent family is 80 percent of the average family premium divided by 1.5. In an alliance where 80 percent of the average family premium is $3,360, the per-worker contribution is $2,240 ($3,360 per family divided by 1.5 workers per family). Thus, each employer pays a flat $2,240 premium for each family worker, and total employer contributions for all family workers cover 80 percent of family premiums.

The following chart shows the relationship between premiums and per-worker contributions in an alliance where the average individual premium is $1,800, the average family premium is $4,200, and the average number of workers per family is as listed:

Premiums and the number of workers per family will vary from one alliance region to another.

Example: Average premiums, workers per family, and premiums per worker for employers, by family status of worker.

Type of policy	Total average premium	80 percent of average premium	Average number of workers per family	Employer contribution per worker
Single individual	$1,800	$1,440	1.0	$1,440
Two-parent family	$4,200	$3,360	1.5	$2,240

Subsidies for Employers

No employer in a regional alliance will be required to pay more than 7.9 percent of payroll for health coverage annually. Firms with fewer than 50 employees will be eligible for caps varying from 3.5 to 7.9 percent of payroll, depending on the employer's average wage.

EMPLOYERS IN THE NEW SYSTEM

Regional Alliances

For each of their eligible full-time employees, employers participating in a regional alliance contribute 80 percent of the appropriate per-worker contribution for the employee's family status.

The per-worker contribution paid by the employer varies only by the alliance area in which the employee lives and the family status of the employee. There are per-worker contributions for:

- A single worker
- A couple
- A single-parent worker
- A worker with a spouse and children

Employers receive subsidies that cap total premium contributions for employees at 3.5 percent to 7.9 percent of the firm's payroll.

Contributions for employers with 50 or fewer employees are capped at a lower level, based on the average wage of the firm. Caps vary as follows:

Employers with more than 50 employees pay no more than 7.9 percent of payroll.

Small employer's average wage per full-time equivalent worker	Cap on employer contributions as a % of total payroll
Less than $12,000	3.5%
$12,000 to $15,000	3.8%
$15,000 to $18,000	4.4%
$18,000 to $21,000	5.5%
$21,000 to $24,000	6.5%
Greater than $24,000	7.9%

Corporate Alliances

For each of their eligible full-time employees, employers in corporate alliances contribute a minimum of 80 percent of the weighted-average premium among the health plans they offer to employees. The employer contribution varies according to the type of policy chosen by the worker—single, couple, single-parent family, or two-parent family.

For low-wage full-time workers in corporate alliances, the employer contributes an additional amount. If the worker earns annualized wages of $15,000 or less, the employer contributes the greater of 80 percent of the average premium or 95 percent of the premium for the lowest-cost plan available to the employee in the corporate alliance.

No subsidies are available for corporate alliance employers.

If a large employer chooses to join the regional health alliances, the rules are the same as for other employers, except that the per-worker premiums contributed by the employer are adjusted for the risk profile of its employees. Risk is measured based on the industry classification of the employer and the demographic characteristics of its workforce.

For the first four years after choosing to join regional alliances, the employer pays the greater of the community-rated per-worker premiums or its risk-adjusted per-worker premiums. The risk adjustment uses a national formula developed by the Department of Labor, but is calculated separately for each alliance area in which the firm's employees live.

The employer contribution for each regional alliance area is adjusted over the four subsequent years until it reaches the level of the community-rated per-worker premium:

- In the fifth year, the employer's payment is equal to 75 percent of the risk-adjusted employer share of the per-worker premium plus 25 percent of what the employer would pay under a community-rated per-worker premium.

- In the sixth year, the employer's payment is equal to 50 percent of the risk-adjusted employer share of the per-worker premium plus 50 percent of what the employer would pay under a community-rated per-worker premium.
- In the seventh year, the employer's payment is equal to 25 percent of the risk-adjusted employer share of the per-worker premium plus 75 percent of what the employer would pay under a community-rated per-worker premium.
- In the eighth year, the employer begins paying on the basis of community-rated per-worker premiums.

Subsidies to which an employer is entitled are similarly phased in over several years. The employer receives no subsidies in the first four years. It receives 25 percent of the subsidies to which it would normally be entitled in the fifth year, 50 percent in the sixth year, 75 percent in the seventh year, and 100 percent beginning in the eighth year.

Employer Contributions for Part-Time Employees

Regional alliances cover part-time workers, whether they work for a regional alliance or corporate alliance employer. A part-time worker who is the spouse or child of a full-time worker covered through a corporate alliance is an exception, and is instead covered through the corporate alliance.

For part-time workers, all employers—regardless of whether they participate in a regional or corporate alliance—contribute a prorated portion of the regional alliance's appropriate per-worker premium (varying by the worker's family status). The contribution is prorated based on the ratio of hours worked to a 30-hour workweek.

All employer payments for part-time workers are forwarded to the regional alliance.

Self-Employed Individuals

Self-employed people pay the employer share and the individual share of the appropriate premium (e.g., individual, couple, single-parent family, or two-parent family). Contributions are made to alliances at least quarterly.

The employer share paid by the self-employed person is equal to the amount employers contribute for workers in the alliance with the same family status. The contribution is capped as a percentage of self-employed income, using the percentage caps applied to small businesses in the alliance.

If a self-employed person also works for another employer, any amount contributed by that employer—prior to any employer subsidies—reduces the person's premium obligation as a self-employed person.

National health expenditures

Calendar years	1994	1995	1996	1997	1998	1999	2000
CBO baseline[1]	998	1,089	1,185	1,288	1,395	1,510	1,631
% of GDP[2]	15.1	15.7	16.3	16.9	17.5	18.2	18.9
% change	9.4	9.1	8.8	8.6	8.4	8.2	8.0
Reform	999	1,112	1,237	1,314	1,376	1,438	1,495
% of GDP	15.1	16.0	17.0	17.2	17.3	17.4	17.3
% change	9.4	11.3	11.2	6.2	4.7	4.5	4.0
Change in spending							
Corporate/regional alliances	0	19	71	83	86	90	93
Other new spending	1	4	13	20	25	33	38
Savings	0	0	−32	−77	−130	−195	−267

[1] CBO: Congressional Budget Office
[2] GDP: Gross Domestic Product
Note: Estimates are preliminary.

Budgetary effects of health reform (billions of dollars)

Fiscal years	1994	1995	1996	1997	1998	1999	2000
Changes in outlays for existing programs	0	−5	−28	−53	−73	−94	−123
Medicaid	0	−4	−21	−36	−46	−57	−70
Medicare	0	−2	−5	−12	−20	−30	−44
Veterans	0	0	−1	−2	−2	−2	−2
Defense Department health	0	0	0	0	0	0	−1
Federal employees health benefits	0	0	−2	−4	−5	−6	−7
New public health initiatives	0	1	3	3	3	4	4
Public health savings	0	0	−2	−2	−3	−3	−3
Added outlays for new programs	1	12	52	76	86	95	103
Long-term care (net of premiums)	0	0	3	8	13	19	25
Subsidies	0	14	58	80	86	89	92
Less state offset for Medicaid in alliances	0	−3	−10	−14	−15	−15	−16
New administrative costs	0	0	1	2	2	2	2
Start-up costs	1	1	0	0	0	0	0
Total outlay changes	1	7	24	23	13	1	−20
Receipts changes	12	15	15	18	23	26	31
Sin taxes/corporate assessment	12	15	15	15	16	16	16
Tax incentives for long-term care	0	0	−1	−1	−1	−2	−2
Expanded deduction for self-employed	0	0	−1	−2	−2	−2	−2
Effects of other taxes of the mandate	0	0	2	6	10	14	19
Deficit	−11	−8	9	5	−10	−25	−51

Note: Estimates are preliminary and do not incorporate interactive effects.

The self-employed person and his or her family are also responsible for the family share of the premium. Subsidies are provided to families whose income is below 150 percent of poverty.

All premium payments made by self-employed persons are fully tax deductible.

Nonworkers and Part-Time Workers

All part-time workers and nonworkers without a spouse working fulltime for a corporate alliance employer are covered through a regional alliance.

Nonworking and part-time single people and families make contributions based on their unearned income. Nonworkers and part-time workers pay toward the employer share and the family share of the appropriate premium for their family status.

TAX SUBSIDIES

Employer contributions toward the premium and toward cost-sharing for the nationally guaranteed comprehensive benefit package and for additional benefits phased in by the year 2000 are tax deductible to the employer and not counted as income to the employee.

Any premium payment by a self-employed person for the comprehensive benefit package is fully tax deductible.

Once alliances are established, contributions continue to be tax-preferred only if made through an alliance.

Section 125 plans (so-called "cafeteria plans") are amended to exclude employee contributions for health benefits.

Part 1

HEALTH CARE REFORMS

1. Employers and Health Care Reform

William S. Custer

Changing political tides have made it clear that health care reform is finally coming to America, and employers need to be prepared. Understanding how managed competition and other health care reform proposals differ from the current employment-based health care financing system is the first step. Employers also need to explore the likely impacts of moving toward a managed competition system, and how changes in the tax treatment of health insurance purchases and the imposition of health care system budgets—both possibilities on the horizon—are likely to affect them.

Although health care reform has been discussed for many years, it has only been since the 1990 election of Senator Harris Wofford in Pennsylvania that it became a potent enough issue to determine the outcome of political campaigns. Senator Wofford made health care reform the centerpiece of his campaign and upset the favored candidate, former U.S. Attorney General Richard Thornberg. Since then, political pollsters have found that health care reform is consistently the second most important issue on voters' minds, following only the economy. Health care reform was an important issue in the presidential election of 1992, as well as in most congressional races.

Proposals have been put forth by the President, the Conservative Democratic Forum, and the Senate Republican Health Care Taskforce, which differ considerably in philosophy, but do not differ greatly in their basic approaches to health care reform. Both parties' proposals built on the present employment-based financing system, both reformed the health insurance market, and both suggested changing the tax treatment of health insurance purchases for individuals and employees.

Proposals to reform the health care system have focused on costs and access to care. It is estimated that the United States will spend more than $900 billion on health care in 1993, while more than 36 million Americans do not have any form of health insurance.[1] Reform proposals intended to reduce health care cost inflation have attempted to correct flaws in the organization of health care financing and delivery or to place an overall cap on costs or prices. Malpractice reform, small group insurance market reform, removal of regulatory barriers to managed care, and efforts to change the tax code are all intended to address specific problems. At the other extreme are proposals for a national health care system that would create a single payer, which would essentially budget national health expenditures. Between these extremes are a number of measures that would overlay some features of set budgets on the present system by controlling prices or would reform the system but retain a public-private mix in the financing and delivery of health care services.

Since the election, the health care reform debate has focused on three broad features: implementation of managed competition, changes in the tax treatment of health insurance, and the imposition of budget caps or targets.[2] Managed competition is a term that describes a wide variety of models for reforming the health insurance market. These models have in common the creation of a sponsor who manages the competition among health insurers for enrollees.

Changing the tax treatment of health insurance is an important element of health care reform, both in extending coverage and managing the increase in health care costs. Although it is argued that these reforms will ultimately control the rate of health care cost inflation, neither managed competition nor changes in the tax treatment of health insurance is likely to significantly control costs in the short run. As a result, some have argued that budget caps should be placed on the health care delivery system at least in the short run, to limit health care cost increases immediately.

The federal government may find it difficult to reach consensus on a specific health care reform proposal, and even more difficult to implement a reform proposal in the near term. While public policy attention has been focused on national reform, individual states have moved forward in seeking their own solutions. Many states have proposed implementing the various reform proposals in their own jurisdictions. However, they face a number of barriers, including federal law, in implementing these proposals. Many policy analysts have urged the federal government to develop mechanisms to allow states to experiment with the various reform proposals before implementing them throughout the nation.

Employers attempting to provide a cost-effective health benefit need to understand the potential changes that health care reform could bring and how health care reform will affect the changes already occurring in the health care delivery system. This report begins with an examination of the basic elements of managed competition, contrasting this approach with the current employment-based health care financing system and other health care reform proposals. It includes a discussion of the likely impact of moving toward a managed competition system, changing the tax treatment of health insurance purchases, and imposing budgets on the health care system. In addition, it discusses recent state reform activity.

MANAGED COMPETITION

In the late 1970s, Stanford Professor Alain Enthoven, building on earlier efforts by a number of analysts, developed a concept known as managed competition as an alternative to the existing markets for health insurance and health care services. A number of groups have integrated Enthoven's concept into their health care reform proposals, with adaptations that fit each group's particular inclinations. The basic element of managed competition is the creation of sponsors who act as collective purchasing agents for large groups of individuals. These sponsors negotiate with insurers or health plans and then offer their subscribers a menu of choices among different insurance plans, with information on each plan's quality of care and price. Managed competition is intended to shift the market for health insurance from competition based on risk to price competition. As a result of this shift in the health insurance market, the health care services markets will also theoretically move toward price competition.

Enthoven's original proposal was called the Consumer Choice Health Plan. In that proposal and in his later writings Enthoven described a sponsor as "an agency that assures each eligible beneficiary financial coverage of health care expenses at a reasonable price."[3] The sponsor's role is to act as a broker between the beneficiaries and the health plans, negotiating with health plans on the basis of price and quality, and then offering that range of choices to individual consumers.

Many recent descriptions of managed competition use the term "health insurance purchasing cooperative" (HIPC) interchangeably with the term "sponsor." This is not strictly correct in that many managed competition proposals allow large employers to act as sponsors for their employees. HIPCs can be sponsors only for small employers and individuals, or, conversely, in some models of managed competition there is only one HIPC per region and all individuals purchase health insurance through that HIPC.

Aside from large employers, the organization of the sponsors differs from proposal to proposal. These sponsors or HIPCs could be federal, state, or local government agencies; private, not-for-profit organizations; or regulated, for-profit entities similar to public utilities. The organization of the sponsors is an important issue that needs to be addressed in implementing a managed competition model.

The terms "managed care" and "managed competition" have often been confused in the media and elsewhere. Enthoven's description of how managed competition would work contributed to this confusion because his vision of the result of managed competition built on the ideas of Dr. Paul Ellwood, Walter McLure, and others who helped create the movement toward health maintenance organizations (HMOs). Enthoven believed managed competition would lead to a health care delivery system composed of competing health plans resembling HMOs or other managed care networks with limited choices of providers. Managed competition is intended to change the health insurance market fundamentally because individuals would choose among plans on the basis of costs and quality. To the extent that this is true, it is assumed that cost-effective plans such as HMOs and other managed care plans would attract more enrollees than the more traditional insurance arrangements that offer more choice of providers and treatment sites. However, that result need not occur, nor is it fundamental to managed competition.

Under managed competition, the health insurance market would be altered by the substitution of the sponsor as a knowledgeable negotiator with health insurance plans in the place of individual consumers or employee benefit managers. The sponsor would represent a group of consumers, whether they be the employees and employee dependents of large employers or all the individuals in a geographic area. Insurers would be required to accept any individuals who purchase health coverage through the sponsor. In theory, the health insurance market would be fundamentally changed under managed competition in that insurers could no longer attempt to avoid poorer risks and would need to find ways to control the costs of providing care.

Individuals under managed competition would be offered a menu of choices of health plans and given price and quality of care information for each plan. Theoretically, they could then choose the plan whose price and quality combination most suited their preferences. Such a choice requires that insurance policies be standardized to facilitate consumer choice, consumers be given a financial stake in their choice, and quality measures be developed that consumers can use to make choices.

Managed competition proposals represent a significant departure from the current system of financing health care services. They are intended to correct many of the problems currently observed in the employment-based financing system. Policymakers have embraced managed competition as a compromise between market-based and regulatory-based approaches to health care reform. Understanding the current employer-based system is important to understanding the rationale behind these proposals and the barriers to implementing them, as well as their implications for employees, employers, providers, taxpayers, and patients. Following this section on the current

Table 1. Nonelderly and Elderly Americans with Selected Sources of Health Insurance Coverage

Source of Coverage	Total Population		Nonelderly		Elderly	
	Number (millions)	Percent- age	Number (millions)	Percent- age	Number (millions)	Percent- age
Total Population	248.7	100.0%	218.1	100.0%	30.6	100.0%
Total with Private Health Insurance	178.4	71.7	157.7	72.3	20.7	67.7
Employer coverage	150.0	60.3	139.8	64.1	10.1	33.1
Other private coverage	28.6	11.5	18.0	8.2	10.6	34.7
Total with Public Health Insurance	61.2	24.6	31.7	14.5	29.5	96.3
Medicare	32.9	13.2	3.5	1.6	29.4	96.0
Medicaid	26.8	10.8	23.9	11.0	2.9	9.5
CHAMPUS/ CHAMPVA[a]	7.1	2.9	5.9	2.7	1.2	3.8
No Health Insurance	36.6	14.7	36.3	16.6	0.3	0.9

Source: Employee Benefit Research Institute analysis of the March 1992 Current Population Survey.

Note: Details may not add to totals because individuals may receive coverage from more than one source.

[a] Includes the Civilian Health and Medical Program of the Uniformed Services and the Civilian Health and Medical Program for the Department of Veterans Affairs.

employment-based system, the issues in implementing managed competition will be examined.

FINANCING HEALTH CARE THROUGH THE WORKPLACE

Health insurance costs in the private sector are not currently distributed equally among all payers. The cost of employer-sponsored health insurance depends on the characteristics of an employer's work force, risk factors attributed to the industry, and the local health care service market. There are significant differences in average costs among industries and between large and small employers. Health insurance for small firms may cost more because of higher administrative costs and insurers' reduced ability to pool risks.

Health expenditures represent an increasingly large component of employee compensation, public budgets, and individuals' disposable income. The employer share of national health expenditures has remained virtually constant since 1980, but national expenditures for health have grown faster than income. As a result, health benefits as a percentage of compensation (averaged over all workers, whether they receive health benefits or not) have grown from 4.4 percent in 1980 to 6.4 percent in 1990.[4] Although more employers today require employee contributions to group health plan premiums than did ten years ago, and deductibles are higher and copayments more common, individual health spending as a share of adjusted personal income has increased by only 0.9 percentage points since 1965. Of course, the increase in health care as a component of total compensation means that employees bear at least some of the costs attributed to employers in the form of lower wages or lower levels of other benefits.

Employer contributions to employee health plans are not counted as taxable income to employees and are deducted from the calculation of income as a normal business expense for those employers who pay taxes. The tax preference gives employees an incentive to receive part of their income as health benefits rather than cash. It also gives them an incentive to purchase more comprehensive coverage with lower deductibles and other out-of-pocket expenditures, which has the effect of increasing the demand for health care services. Large employer health plans have a considerable cost advantage over individually purchased plans or small group plans because of lower administrative costs and the ability to avoid or reduce adverse selection.[5]

These considerations have led many to argue that tying the financing of health care to the labor market results in an inequitable distribution of both benefits and costs. Currently, 64 percent of Americans under age 65 receive health insurance through an employer-sponsored or union-sponsored plan (see Table 1). Separation from the labor market—through job loss, divorce, or death—may result in the loss of health insurance coverage. Individuals without health insurance are predominantly nonworkers, self-employed, workers in small establishments, or persons in families headed by a member of one of these groups. Moreover, if employees with health insurance coverage are reluctant to change jobs because of concern about health insurance, they may forgo opportunities that would increase their productivity.

Most health care reform proposals focus on the difficulty individuals and small groups have in obtaining health insurance at the same cost as larger groups. Small groups often face higher costs per participant because of their higher per capita administrative costs and insurance companies' limited ability to pool risks. Insurers currently price their policies on the basis of the expected risk of the individual group. If an insurer pools all the groups it insures together and charges a premium based on that total pool, some of the groups in the pool will pay higher premiums than they would if the premiums were set on their risk alone, while others will pay lower premiums. In the current health insurance market, insurers who attempt to pool risk across groups in that manner will find the lower risk groups will choose another insurer whose premiums reflect only their own risks and are therefore lower. By removing barriers that prevent insurers from pooling small groups, employment-based coverage may expand to include many of the employed uninsured in small firms and their dependents (who constitute 37 percent of the nonelderly uninsured).

INSURANCE REFORM

A number of proposals have been offered to reform the health insurance market. Although there are significant differences among these proposals, there is agreement on some basic principles:

1. Small groups should be guaranteed access to insurance;
2. Restrictions on preexisting conditions should be limited;
3. New restrictions should not be imposed when individuals change jobs or when groups change insurers;
4. Coverage should not be canceled because of high utilization of services;
5. Insurers should be required to offer coverage to all small groups (if they offer insurance to any);
6. Premium rates should be stabilized; and
7. Policies should be renewable (except for reasonable cause, such as nonpayment of premiums).

What proponents of insurance market reform disagree on are the means to achieve guaranteed access to insurance and on some of the measures needed to make such a guarantee work, including limits on premium rates and rate increases.[6]

Most proposals include some means for guaranteeing that all small groups have access to insurance and are not denied coverage based on individual characteristics. However, proponents of insurance market reform recognize that guaranteed availability alone accomplishes little unless premium rates for small groups are stabilized. Without some limits, insurers could use rating practices to raise the cost of coverage for riskier groups until the price becomes so high that these groups choose not to purchase insurance. Some proponents suggest moving toward community rating so that insurance would be offered to all small groups at fixed rates. Others would allow insurers to adjust community rates for factors such as age, sex, geographic location, and industry type (class rating). Generally, proposals would limit restrictions on preexisting conditions and medical underwriting.[7]

Premium limits are common to a wide variety of health reform proposals. These proposals would allow insurers to use medical underwriting and factors such as claims experience, health status, age, and sex to set rates, but only within permitted rate bands. Some analysts argue that mandating community rating or eliminating demographic adjustments would raise rates for many groups and create adverse selection.

Adverse selection occurs when individuals with greater health risks are disproportionately enrolled in a particular plan. Community rating limits insurers' ability to charge different premiums to groups on the basis of risk. As a result, premiums for groups that represent good health risks would rise with the implementation of community rating, while premiums for groups representing bad risks would fall. Some of the healthier individuals would choose not to purchase health insurance as a result of the premium increase, while more of those individuals who are poorer health risks would purchase health insurance. The result would be an increase in the pool's average risk, increasing premiums and potentially creating a vicious cycle that would end in an unviable health insurance market. The likelihood of this scenario actually occurring depends on the sensitivity of the demand for health insurance to changes in premiums among individuals who represent good and bad risks, and on the ability of individuals to determine their own risk status.

One mechanism for preventing adverse selection is to develop a reinsurance mechanism for health insurance. A number of proposals include measures that would encourage the creation of either public or private reinsurance pools to reduce the effects of adverse selection. These pools would permit individual insurance plans to cap the costs of the poorer risks, allowing them to offer premiums closer to those offered to good risks.

Another issue addressed by most proposals is the guarantee that group policies cannot be canceled by the insurer due to changes in the health status of individuals in the group. Many carriers currently refuse to renew high-risk groups, or only offer to renew policies at significantly higher rates. Some insurers charge low rates initially and then raise premiums substantially when small groups renew (a practice called durational rating). Small groups often change insurers frequently to avoid these increases. This process subjects small businesses to repeated medical underwriting and works against companies with less healthy employees by raising premiums even higher and constantly imposing new waiting periods for individuals with preexisting conditions. Other insurers use tiered rating to establish renewal rates for groups too small to be experience rated. Tiered rating sets renewal rates based on an analysis of each enrollee who incurred high medical expenses and the likelihood of continued high expenses. Rating practices such as these have reduced the premium rates for some small groups, but overall have increased segmentation in the small group market.[8]

Most proposals would limit annual premium increases to eliminate durational rating. Industry advocates recommend that carriers limit premium increases to the rates established for new businesses plus an adjustment factor of up to 15 percent. However, congressional bills generally do not allow for such an experience adjustment and limit renewal rates to those established for new policies.

Because nearly one-half of all uninsured workers are self-employed or working in firms with fewer than 25 employees, proposals of all types have included as part of their package a set of small group insurance market reform proposals. Small group reform advocates argue that small employers would purchase health insurance if it were offered at the right price. However, it is likely that at least some small employers would not be willing to purchase coverage in the absence of substantial federal or state subsidies.

Researchers evaluating the Robert Wood Johnson Foundation (RWJF) projects for the medically uninsured found that small employers' primary reason for not offering health insurance was the high cost of coverage; 85 percent of employers not offering insurance cited high premiums as an important reason.[9] Although the RWJF demonstration projects did not reform local small group insurance markets the way that current national proposals would, their goals are similar: to stabilize the cost of insurance to small businesses, and to distribute these costs more equitably. Previously uninsured small employers began to offer insurance to their employees during the enrollment phase of the demonstration projects. However, only 17 percent of employers who previously did not offer insurance enrolled even in the most successful RWJF project targeted at small employers.[10] If the experience of these projects is representative of national experience, small group insurance market reform may result in only a minority of small employers choosing to purchase health insurance.

The development of reinsurance markets, state risk pools, or other methods to subsidize the insurance costs for poor risks may alleviate some concerns about restrictions on premiums. However, public and private reinsurance schemes distribute the cost burden differently. If a private reinsurance market develops, the costs of providing expanded access to poorer risks will be borne by the purchasers of insurance. The premium paid by individuals and employers for health coverage will include the premium paid by insurers for the reinsurance of poorer risks. On the other hand, the burden of the costs of a public risk pool will depend on that pool's financing mechanism. Most state risk pools are now financed by state insurance premium taxes. Courts have ruled that employers who self-insure are exempt from these taxes under the Employee Retirement Income Security Act of 1974 (ERISA). As a result, the cost of risk pools is borne by individuals and employers who purchase commercial insurance. There are ways to spread the costs of the risk pool in a different manner—for example, by financing through general revenues—but most proposals do not specify any financing mechanism for reinsurance pools.

IMPLEMENTING MANAGED COMPETITION

Managed competition would fundamentally alter the health insurance market. It incorporates many elements of small group health insurance reform but goes beyond those changes to restructure the entire market. However, there are many issues that must be addressed before a managed competition model could be implemented. How these issues are resolved will determine not only the structure of the health insurance and health services markets, but also the speed and costs of the transition from our present system to a managed competition system.

Minimum Benefit Package

Defining the minimum standard benefit package is likely to be one of the most politically difficult issues in implementing any health care reform proposal. President Clinton and others have asserted that health care is a right to which all Americans are entitled, but it is the minimum standard benefit package that determines and defines that right. It will determine the costs society bears, the incomes of providers, the health of many individuals, and the attributes of a workable health care reform package.

Under most managed competition proposals, the sponsor manages competition based on the price of a standard benefit package that is considered to be the minimum to which all Americans are entitled. This package determines the tax preferences given to individuals and employers in the purchase of health insurance benefits. Determining the basic benefit package will have important consequences for the income of physicians and other health care providers and for the type of care available to Americans. The richer, more inclusive the package, the wider the range of benefits available to the individual patient, the more health care individuals will have access to, the higher the costs to private payers and taxpayers, and consequently, the greater the income to providers.

Perhaps a starting point for defining a basic benefit package would be the Medicare program, although Medicare offers a relatively poor set of benefits compared with most private health plans. Defining a basic benefit package more generous than Medicare may require changes in the Medicare program that could considerably increase the costs of health care reform to the federal government. Currently, most Medicare beneficiaries do not rely on Medicare alone; less than 13 percent of elderly Medicare beneficiaries have no supplemental coverage.

Hospital Insurance (HI), or Medicare Part A, provides benefits for inpatient hospital care, skilled nursing care, home health care, and hospice care. Beneficiaries are subject to a deductible for each hospital admission. The amount of the deductible ($676 in 1993) is generally indexed to the average cost of hospital days. If the hospital stay exceeds 60 days, the beneficiary is also subject to a copayment. HI provides no coverage after 150 days.

Supplementary Medical Insurance (SMI), or Medicare Part B, finances 80 percent of the cost of most outpatient services for Medicare beneficiaries. A wide array of physician services is covered under Medicare Part B, including visits in the home, office, and hospital. This program also finances various miscellaneous health services, including outpatient services received in hospitals and in rural health, community health, and renal dialysis centers. Part B coverage also includes physical and occupational therapy services.

Medicare provides limited coverage for extended inpatient hospital care and care received in a skilled nursing facility. It does not cover long-term care, nursing home care, or home health care that is determined to be unrelated to rehabilitation or purely custodial. In addition, Medicare does not cover prescription drugs.

The other major public program that defines benefits is the Medicaid program. While this program generally offers more generous benefits than Medicare, especially with respect to copayments, provider reimbursement under Medicaid is usually less generous. As a result, a large number of studies indicate that the care received by Medicaid recipients and by the uninsured differs markedly from that received by privately insured individuals. A recent report by the U.S. Office of Technology Assessment reviewed this literature and found that Medicaid recipients "are up to 2.5 times more likely than privately insured patients to experience potentially inadequate health services, and up to 4 times more likely to experience an adverse health outcome."[11]

The difference between the minimum benefit package and the benefits currently offered by public or private plans will determine the impact of the minimum benefit package on the health care delivery system. Currently, private plans generally include coverage for care associated with an episode of hospital care, including hospitalization, in-hospital professional care, and surgery, as well as many outpatient services. Fee-for-service plans are less likely than alternative delivery systems to offer preventive services and services that are predictable or not considered medically necessary. Deductibles are generally much lower than those faced by individuals with Medicare coverage alone, and there are often limits on an insured individual's out-of-pocket expenditures. Finally, lifetime maximum benefits for privately insured individuals are generally much higher than those offered under the Medicare program.

The comprehensiveness of the minimum benefit package obviously would affect the costs to individuals and to taxpayers. Under most managed competition models, subsidies would be provided to low-income individuals either directly or through the tax code. However, for individuals with income above a certain level, most managed competition models would alter the tax code to remove incentives to purchase health insurance. These models usually tie the tax preference to the cost of the basic benefit package. Thus, the distribution of health care costs would vary, depending on the definition of the minimum basic benefit.

Administration

Defining a minimum benefit package is only the first step in the operation of a managed competition model. Once that minimum benefit package is defined, the sponsor would also negotiate with the insurer or the health plan for packages that are richer than the basic benefit. A richer benefit package will leave less of an opportunity for insurers to offer differentiated products, while a less generous minimum benefit package might induce many individuals to purchase additional coverage. Insurers might have an opportunity to affect the characteristics of the population they insure by choosing the attributes of the plans they offer above the minimum package. Standardizing the benefit packages that insurers could offer above the minimum package might alleviate this problem.

There are several other issues in the administration of a managed competition system. These include the organization of the sponsors; the size of the market served by a sponsor, both geographically and in terms of covered individuals; and the sponsors' role in allocating risks across insurers or health plans.

One concern with managed competition models is the organization of the sponsor. Enthoven's original proposal described these sponsors as public entities, but he later broadened the definition to include large employers or any other purchasing cooperative. Other proposals have characterized the sponsors as public utilities. One proposal allows large employers to act as the sponsors for their employees and dependents and sets up nonprofit organizations (HIPCs) to act as sponsors for all others. These nonprofit organizations may have publicly appointed boards, or may simply be regulated by the states or the federal government.

The organization of the sponsor may have important consequences for local health care delivery. Publicly appointed boards may have different objectives from those of large employers or a privately organized regulated utility. If there are multiple sponsors within a single health market, these differences in objectives might present providers and insurers with unintended incentives that could thwart the goals of managed competition.

The size of the population served by each sponsor would affect both the health insurance market and the health care services market. If multiple sponsors are operating in a local health care market, insurers might be able to manipulate the system to avoid insuring the poorer risks. If avoiding insuring poorer risks is less costly than managing health care, insurers might attempt to create a niche for themselves by insuring the healthier groups.

Under a managed competition model, health plans or insurers contract with or hire providers and facilities to provide health care to the plans' enrollees. The theory of managed competition is that the competition among health plans along cost and quality dimensions will lead them to negotiating with providers to either attract cost-effective providers, or to alter the treatment patterns of providers to remove any waste or inefficient practices. To be effective, health plans have to have sufficient market power within the local health care services market to affect provider behavior, and they need the competition from other health plans to give them an incentive to exert that market power.

The size of the local market thus becomes an issue in implementing managed competition. How large a market is necessary to support competing health plans? A recent study estimated that it would take a population of 450,000 to support a single HMO that owned its own tertiary care hospital.[12] Thus, a market population of at least 1.2 million would be necessary for three completely independent health plans to compete in the same market. The authors estimate that only about 42 percent of Americans live in market areas of 1.2 million or more people. Conversely, the authors estimate that a plan with 60,000 enrollees could provide primary care and most of the specialists necessary for tertiary care, but would need to share cardiology, urology, and hospital services. Seventy-one percent of Americans live in markets with more than 180,000 people.

It is not clear how sharing facilities such as hospitals or specialists would affect competition among plans. One of the benefits of competition is the incentives provided for private entities to spend resources on research and development of cost-effective methods for delivering care. If health plans share facilities, the incentives for individual health plans to fund this research may be limited if their competitors' share the benefits. This may be less of a problem if there is public investment in the development of treatment protocols and quality measures.

The organization of the sponsors becomes crucial to assessing the mini-mum size of the market. If multiple sponsors are allowed to operate in a single market, it is conceivable that a single health plan could be negotiating with several sponsors, which could limit the sponsors' ability to negotiate.

If an individual sponsor is responsible for all care in a large enough geographic area, the sponsor could negotiate with health plans over the whole area rather than within a local market. The sponsor could then compare costs and quality across markets and apply these standards to health plans that, because of size constraints, are the sole providers in a given market. In that sense, the bids from all the plans in the sponsor's geographic area, or even bids from potential plans that have not yet entered the market, could be used to determine costs. In essence, the plan may be competing in an area larger than the market area from which the plan actually draws enrollees. The health plan would essentially be a regulated monopoly in those markets too small to sustain more than one health plan. If that is the case, the sponsor's role changes considerably, because competition among plans would no longer ensure that the plans are responsive to enrollees' needs. Moreover, given the present situation in which the organization of the health care services market varies considerably across local markets in the same state, it may well be the case that data on costs from one area may not be relevant to another.

For areas too thinly populated to support competition, the sponsor's role would become very important in determining the costs and quality of care for that market. The organization of that sponsor would be even more critical in shaping the health care system for such markets than for markets in which competition helps regulate provider and insurer behavior. One of the most important tools the sponsor and the consumer would have is the measurement of the quality of care provided by a health plan.

Defining Quality of Care

Managed competition is intended to foster competition among health plans on the basis of cost and quality, but defining and measuring health care quality are controversial and costly endeavors. Quality of care is a multidimensional concept: it can be viewed narrowly (as clinical effectiveness) or broadly (as all the attributes of medical care that patients value). The difficulty with any multidimensional concept is properly weighting the disparate components. Even if individuals agree on the attributes of care that determine its quality, they may disagree about the relative importance of each attribute.

Another important issue is determining who will develop the definition of quality used to assess health plans and providers. The measures of quality actually employed in the health care system will determine in large part the incentives faced by insurers, providers, and consumers, but the different participants in the health care delivery system have different interpretations of quality. Once a definition of quality is developed, health plans will be required to provide the sponsor with specific information that will be used to ascertain the quality of care, and the plans will then compete along the dimensions of quality defined by the system. The definition of quality may therefore be as important as the definition of a minimum benefit package in determining the overall costs of health care, the distribution of those costs, and the rate of health care cost inflation.

Distribution of Risks

In addition to defining the quality of care, definitions of the risks facing individual health plans are needed to fully implement a managed competition model. In most managed competition proposals a mechanism is provided to redistribute premium income across insurers on the basis of risks. This mechanism is intended to remove risk selection as a barrier to cost competition among insurers. Insurers of health plans that have a healthier than average enrollee population would be required to transfer some funds to plans with a less healthy population. This requirement would limit the rewards of attempting to attract a healthier population.

Several potential issues must be addressed in using this mechanism. First, over what population is the transfer to be made? If transfers are made only over local health care markets, theoretically the sponsor could administer that transfer, unless there were multiple sponsors within an area. Transfers made over a larger region might reward some insurers solely for their location if populations differ by those risk factors used to determine the transfer payment.

A second issue is deciding which factors will be used to determine the risks of each insurer's populations. These factors may introduce unintended incentives if they do not completely capture the observable differences in characteristics associated with health care services utilization across enrollee populations.

Moreover, there is a question of whether these factors should be applied prospectively—that is, without any adjustment for actual utilization—or retrospectively, after it is clear that one insured group has incurred more costs than another. In the first case, a set of demographic characteristics would be identified as risk adjusters, and an insurer who attracted a healthier group based solely on these characteristics would be required to transfer some of its premium income to another insurer whose risk profile based on these characteristics was poorer. Retrospective adjustment would transfer income based on actual utilization by plan enrollees. If prospective risk adjusters accurately predict the risks faced by the insurer, they preserve the incentive for the health plan to manage care efficiently. Because they are based on actual utilization, retrospective adjustments may be a more accurate measure of the differences in risks faced by competing health plans, but they may also mitigate the incentive to practice cost-effective medicine.

Adverse Selection and Mandated Coverage

While adverse selection among health plans may be an issue, another major issue in implementing a managed competition proposal is adverse selection for the entire system. The issue becomes a question of whether individuals or groups should be required to participate. To contain health care costs, managed competition relies on individuals to make choices among health plans on the basis of costs and quality. In order to give individuals the incentive to choose cost-effective plans, they must feel the financial consequences of their choices. Imposing increased costs on individuals by changing the tax preferences, limiting employer contributions to health plans, or changing the insurance market so that premiums are no longer based on individual risk means that some individuals may choose not to purchase health insurance. To the extent that these individuals tend to be healthier, the remaining participating population will tend to be less healthy, driving up the average costs of providing health insurance, forcing others out of the system, and potentially making the system unsustainable.

The problem of adverse selection is potentially the most important issue in reforming the health insurance market. Insurers and health plans price their products on the basis of the risks they face. As noted above, in Enthoven's model of managed competition transfers are made among health plans to avoid reward- ing plans that attract lower risk enrollees. Setting aside the important issue of how this transfer is to be implemented, the transfer alone cannot prevent the problems that adverse selection presents to the managed competition model. If individuals can opt to not purchase health benefits, poorer risks will be more likely to purchase health insurance than good risks and, at minimum, the price of these benefits will be higher than would otherwise be the case.

Mandating that all employers offer health benefits alleviates the problem somewhat. Offering health benefits through an employer lowers the transaction costs for individuals, and this may help capture more of the good risks. Never- theless, if employees can choose between cash or health benefits, an employer mandate may not completely alleviate the problem of adverse selection. That is, if employees can receive the cash equivalent of the health benefit rather than the health benefit, the good risks are more likely to opt for the cash. If employees cannot make the tradeoff between cash and health benefits, then more of the good risks are likely to opt for coverage, making the issue of adverse selection less important.

Individuals not connected to the workplace may still make their decision on whether to purchase health benefits based on their own assessment of their risks of needing health care (which is likely to be more accurate than an insurer's assessment of that individual's risks). There are two issues that make this group important to the success of a managed competition model. One is the adverse selection problem described above. It is unclear how unstable the market would be without an individual mandate, especially if those not connected to the work force constitute a greater health risk than workers. The second issue is how to provide individuals who choose not to purchase health insurance with health care should they need it. One of the criticisms of our present system is that care for the uninsured is funded by hidden subsidies and cost shifting. Without an explicit source of funds for care for those who remain uninsured, those hidden subsidies may remain.

Tax Changes

Managed competition requires that individuals share at least some of the financial consequences of their choices among health plans. As a result, most managed competition proposals change the tax code with respect to health care. Most tax-based approaches focus on limiting the exclusion of employer contributions to health insurance from workers' taxable income and expanding individual tax credits. Because no employer contributions to health insurance are currently included in employees' taxable income, proponents of this type of reform argue that neither employers nor employees have any incentive to choose the most cost-effective plan. They suggest that if contributions are limited to a maximum dollar amount or to the average cost of a basic health plan in a geographic area, employers and employees would be more likely to choose cost-effective providers. By expanding individual tax credits, advocates hope that low-income individuals would be more easily able to purchase health protection for themselves and their families.

Currently, employer contributions to health insurance are excluded from employees' taxable income. This tax preference is intended to expand access to health care by encouraging health insurance coverage. Many analysts have concluded that the tax preference leads to the purchase of too much health insurance, insulating insured individuals from the financial consequences of their health care service purchases and thereby contributing to health care cost inflation.

Changes in tax policy without other health system reforms will clearly affect the cost of health benefits and workers' income. Including the value of health benefits as taxable income reduces the total after-tax compensation of workers who receive these benefits. The reduction in compensation will depend on the worker's taxable income, with high-income workers facing the largest dollar drop if health benefits are included as taxable income. Some workers may feel that, absent the tax preference, they would rather have cash than health benefits. Employers trying to attract these workers may be less likely to offer health benefits.[13]

Removing the cost of health benefits as a tax deductible business expense for employers (but not including it as part of employees' taxable income) increases employers' labor costs. Employers may respond to such a change by reducing or dropping health benefits, reducing the provision of other benefits or cash compensation, or reducing employment. Because the cost of providing health benefits does not generally vary by income for employees within a plan, changing the tax preference in this way will increase the costs of employing high- and low-wage employees by the same dollar amount, although the percentage increase in costs for high-income workers will be less. A $3,000 increase in the cost of employing a highly skilled (and therefore high-income) worker may not reduce the demand for these workers very much, whereas the same increase in the cost of employing a less skilled worker may have a large impact on the demand for such workers.

Most large employers who offer health insurance would likely continue to offer it in the absence of a tax preference. Group insurance is less expensive than individual policies because of the costs of administration and the problem of adverse selection. Employers are thus able to provide more insurance per dollar than the employee could purchase individually. Employer-sponsored health insurance may also decrease employee turnover and increase productivity.

The ultimate effect of changes in tax policy on national health care expenditures is unclear. It is clear that, by itself, removing the exclusion from individual taxable income of an employer's contribution to health benefits would reduce the number of individuals with employer-sponsored health insurance and reduce the breadth of services for those with employer-sponsored coverage, although the magnitude of that change is unknown. Research into the relationship between tax policy and the demand for health insurance, and between insurance and the demand for health care services, suggests that the magnitude may be small. However, the impact of insurance coverage on technological advances and the quality and intensity of care are not well understood.[14] It may be that, over time, changes in health insurance induced by changes in tax policy will have profound impacts on the health care delivery system.

Global Budgets

Changing the health insurance market, mandating employer health benefits, and changing the tax code may have significant effects on the health care delivery system, but they are unlikely to reduce health care cost inflation in the near term. One of the proposals for restraining the growth in health care costs is the imposition of a budget on the amount spent on health care services. How this budget would be implemented, what services would be subject to the budget, and whether the budget would be global or limited to government purchases of health care services are issues that have not yet been addressed.

The most limited approach would be to cap the amount the federal government spends on health care. This approach would affect the Medicare and Medicaid programs at a minimum, and perhaps the federal employees' health benefits program and the veterans' health system as well. While such an approach has the benefit of controlling federal expenditures, it may exacerbate the problems faced by the health care delivery system as a whole. The history of health care cost management has demonstrated that reducing the amount an individual payer spends for care redistributes the cost burden across other payers. In the federal government's case, that redistribution will mean that some providers earn less income but also that private payers—especially those with limited market power in local health care markets, the states through the Medicaid program, and individuals without health insurance—are going to bear a substantial portion of the reduction in expenditures through cost shifting.

Placing a budget cap over the entire health care delivery system would require that price controls be implemented on the system. Without those controls, the budget cap would simply be a target. A target is distinct from a cap in that a target has no enforcement mechanism. Simply setting a target may have some benefits, but it seems unlikely that it would substantially reduce health care expenditures. One of the benefits of imposing a budget cap or a target is that the amount society wishes to spend for health care is determined by the political process rather than an informal market.

A target can be used to determine future regulatory action, for example, by triggering the imposition of price controls in the future. The issue is whether these nonbinding targets have much of an effect on individual provider behavior. If individual health care providers believe their own actions have little impact on the system as a whole, the presence of a target may not have much effect even if exceeding that target would lower reimbursement in the future.

Conversely, a budget cap implies the existence of a mechanism for enforcing that cap. That enforcement mechanism has to be the regulation of prices in the health care system. Employing a system of administered prices (i.e., prices that are determined by regulators rather than by market forces) in the health care services market as an enforcement mechanism raises a number of issues. In general, administered prices are inferior to prices determined in an efficient market because they do not necessarily reflect the underlying costs of producing a service or the demand for that service. In practice, administered prices are often used in industries characterized by monopoly power, such as public utilities. As the number of interrelated services increases, it becomes increasingly difficult to administratively set prices that accurately reflect underlying costs and demands. Setting efficient prices in the health care services market, which is currently characterized by large differences in costs determined by provider type, region, and patient type, may prove to be much more difficult. Conversely, if health care service prices do not now accurately reflect costs and demands as a result of provider monopoly power, administered prices may in fact be an improvement. Whether a system of administered prices would be an improvement over prices as currently determined depends on the mechanism used to generate regulated prices and the degree to which the fees currently charged in the health care delivery system are different from those that would be charged in an efficient market.

There are several different ways to organize the financing and delivery of care with a binding budget cap. One way is to retain a private delivery system but impose an all-payer system in which providers are reimbursed by all payers according to a common fee schedule. Another way to implement price controls is to apply Medicare's reimbursement system to the entire health care system. Medicare prospectively sets a per admission fee schedule for hospitals, adjusted for diagnosis, and a per service fee schedule for physicians. Since the Medicare population is predominately elderly, some adjustments would have to be made for diagnoses and services for younger populations, but the basic methodologies could be directly applied.

An advantage of this approach is that it eliminates price discrimination and cost shifting. Currently, there are wide differences in the prices paid by public payers, small private payers, and large private payers for health care services. It is often asserted that these price differences reflect cost shifts from public payers to private payers. To the extent that this is true, the cost of care provided to those in public programs and those who are uninsured is subsidized by higher costs in the private sector.

It has been proposed that budget caps could be imposed in a managed competition system by regulating the maximum amounts that can be charged for the basic benefit package.[15] In his campaign, President Clinton also suggested that global budgets be used in conjunction with managed competition. Conversely, Alain Enthoven has suggested that global budgets would rob managed competition of price competition, its major cost management feature.[16] Because the intention of managed competition is to develop a mechanism that would allow the market for health care services to operate efficiently, imposing price controls means that the market will not determine the allocation of health care resources.

Controlling prices alone may not be enough to control total expenditures. If providers are able to increase utilization or to recode procedures to maximize their incomes, price controls may be ineffective in the short run. To the extent that they are effective, they may affect the quality of care. Over time, the fees paid for health care services may become considerably different from those that would have been charged in the marketplace. Practice patterns in existence when the controls were developed might be frozen in place. The mix of physician specialties may not reflect the mix that would be most cost-effective or provide the highest quality of care.

President Nixon imposed wage and price controls on the health care system in the early 1970s. These controls were considered an abject failure in controlling health care cost inflation. The lifting of the controls led to rapid increases in the prices of health care services and in health care expenditures. A similar result might be avoided if budget caps are imposed in the short term until the markets for health insurance and health care services are reformed. Then market forces might restrain health care cost inflation if the caps are removed.

The arguments for or against price controls come down to a debate on the efficiency of the market for health care services and health insurance. If those two markets fail, administered prices might actually improve the allocation of resources. However, if the markets are efficient enough to represent the desires of consumers and the costs faced by providers better than regulators, administered prices result in a less efficient allocation of resources.

If the primary goal of health care reform is to contain costs in the near term, binding budget caps seem to be inevitable. No other mechanism will have as immediate an effect on health care costs. To have significant effects on health care costs, budgets must be accompanied by price controls and some constraint on utilization. Simply setting targets for health expenditures may not have much of an impact. In the short run, the excess capacity of the U.S. health care system would probably mitigate some of the adverse effects on the quality of care that many analysts have suggested would be the result of binding budget caps.

HEALTH CARE REFORM IN THE STATES

The combination of the constraints placed on federal governmental action by the budget and the significant political problems involved in reaching a consensus on the important elements of health care reform may limit the ability of the federal government to implement national health care reform in the near term. As a result, individual states may be encouraged by the federal government to continue to experiment with their own health reform programs. Many states are actively considering a variety of approaches to health care reform. These proposals vary according to the type of system used to provide health care coverage and the population covered, how the system will be financed, the types of health care services provided, and how the system will be administered. Even if individual states are able to reach a consensus on an approach to implement, most proposals still face a number of barriers in attempting to expand access or reduce health care cost inflation.

Most health care reform proposals reallocate the costs of health care services in order to expand access to care. As a result of the reallocation, some groups would face higher costs in the form of increased labor costs, higher insurance costs, or higher taxes. Therefore, state health care reform provides an incentive for employers who face higher costs to move out of the state. Of course, this is also true of national health care reform, but there are language, cultural, and technical barriers that may limit movement out of the country; these barriers are much less of a factor in movement among states. Moreover, individual states may not have a sufficient tax base to implement and sustain comprehensive health care reform measures. Finally, the interaction of state and federal law places important constraints on states' ability to regulate the health care delivery system. ERISA authority is of particular significance to state health care reform.

ERISA establishes uniform standards that employee benefit plans must follow to obtain and maintain their tax-favored status. Section 514(a) of ERISA provides that ERISA generally supersedes or preempts all state law otherwise applicable to pension and welfare plans covered by the act, with the exception of state law regulating insurance, banking, and securities. The exception covering insurance in effect allows certain indirect state regulation of insured health plans. Recent court decisions have affirmed that ERISA exempts employers who self-insure their health insurance benefits from many such state laws. Many employers choose to self-insure because they are exempt from state mandated benefit laws, which specify certain types and levels of coverage that group policies must include. Moreover, self-insured plans have been able to invoke ERISA preemption protection to avoid paying taxes on insurance premiums or taxes that fund state pools to insure poor risks. As a result, ERISA preemption has limited the states' ability to finance health care proposals. Many state reform efforts face the risk of being overturned in court because they would cause some impact to employee benefit plans. For example, a federal district court ruled in

May 1992 that ERISA preempts a New Jersey hospital rate-setting law that would have required self-insured health plans to pay surcharges to cover the costs of care provided to the poor.

More recently, fully insured plans have begun to successfully challenge the states' financing mechanisms. On February 3, 1993, a federal judge struck down a large part of New York's payment system that added surcharges to hospital bills paid by commercial insurance companies and HMOs. The surcharges were meant to be used to help nonprofit insurers, which did not have to pay the surcharges, compete more evenly with the for-profit companies. The court found that the surcharges violated ERISA because they involved the use of employee contributions to benefit funds to subsidize the health care of others. Under ERISA, employee contributions to benefit funds can be used only for the "sole and exclusive" benefit of workers and their families. This ruling has important implications for state reform efforts throughout the nation. Florida, Minnesota, and Vermont also have enacted comprehensive reform proposals that would affect private employee benefit plans.[17]

Although a number of states have implemented, or seem close to implementing, significant reform measures, many states have not seriously considered these proposals. Given the barriers facing individual states, it seems likely that most states will not take major action on health care reform in the near future without significant incentives from the federal government.

However the national debate on health care reform is resolved, the diversity across states is likely to influence the implementation of any national reform. In the absence of national reform, individual states will continue to affect their local health care delivery systems through regulation of health insurance and health providers. Employers and other purchasers of health care services who are active in more than one state are likely to find increasing diversity across local health care service markets.

CONCLUSION

There are many significant unanswered questions that must be addressed before health care reform can be implemented. These questions include:

- What health care services are all Americans entitled to as a right?
- How would the health insurance market be regulated?
- If a managed competition model were implemented, how would the sponsors be organized?
- How would their respective market areas be allocated?
- What quality of care measures would be used to evaluate health plans?
- Would employers or individuals be mandated to procure health insurance?
- How would differences in risks faced by competing health plans be rewarded?

- How would the tax treatment of health insurance change and how would these changes affect coverage, costs, and quality?
- Are global budgets desirable and what form would they take?
- Who would bear the costs of health care reform?

However these questions are ultimately addressed, it is clear that health care reform is going to have significant impacts on health care financing and delivery systems. Changes in the market for health insurance are likely to decrease the numbers of health insurers. Changes in the tax code may provide an incentive for individuals to choose more cost-effective plans, which may accelerate the growth of organized systems of care such as HMOs and other managed care networks.

Regardless of the way in which the political debate over health care reform is resolved, fully implementing these reforms is likely to be a prolonged process. Some of the reforms and their impacts will be felt immediately, but it is more likely that the issues of health care cost inflation and limited access to health care services will be with us for some time.

REFERENCES

A Foster Higgins & Co, Inc, *Health Care Benefits Survey, Report 1: Indemnity Plans,* (NY: A Foster Higgins & Co, Inc, 1992).

Congressional Budget Office, *Selected Options for Expanding Health Insurance Coverage,* (Washington, DC: US Government Printing Office, 1991).

_____, *Universal Health Insurance Coverage Using Medicare's Payment Rates,* (Washington, DC: US Government Printing Office, 1991).

Custer, William S and Jill Foley, "Health Care Reform: Tradeoffs and Implications" *EBRI Issue Brief* 125 (Employee Benefit Research Institute, Apr 1992).

Employee Benefit Research Institute. "Revising the Federal Tax Treatment of Employer Contributions to Health Insurance: A Continuing Debate," *EBRI Issue Brief* 21 (Employee Benefit Research Institute, Aug 1983).

Enthoven, Alain C, *Theory and Practice of Managed Competition in Health Care Finance* (Amsterdam: Elsevier Science Publishers BV, 1988): 82-83

Enthoven, Alain, and Richard Kronick. "A Consumer Choice Health Plan for the 1990s: Universal Health Insurance in a System Designed to Promote Quality and Economy (Part 1)" *The New England Journal of Medicine* (Jan 5, 1989): 29–37.

_____, "A Consumer Choice Health Plan for the 1990s: Universal Health Insurance in a System Designed to Promote Quality and Economy (Part 2)." *The New England Journal of Medicine* (Jan 12, 1989): 94-101.

Feldman, Roger, "Health Insurance in the United States: Is Market Failure Avoidable?" LIV *The Journal of Risk and Insurance* 2 (June, 1987): 298-313.

Feldstein, Martin S, "The Welfare Loss of Excess Health Insurance," *Journal of Political Economy* (Mar/Apr 1973): 251-280.

Gabel, Jon, and Gail Jensen, "The Price of State Mandated Benefits," *HIAA Research Bulletin* (July 1989): 2-21.

Hamermesh, Daniel S, "The Demand for Labor in the Long Run," *Handbook of Labor Economics* vol. 1 (NY: Elsevier Science Publishers, 1986).

Health Insurance Association of America, *The Case Against the Taxation of Employee Benefits* (Washington, DC: Health Insurance Association of America, 1985).

Pauly, Mark, Patricia Danzon, Paul Feldstein, and John Hoff. "A Plan for 'Responsible National Health Insurance,' " *Health Affairs* (Spring 1991): 5-25.

Rustuccia, Joseph D, *et al.* "The Appropriateness of Hospital Use," *Health Affairs* (Summer 1984): 130-138.

US Bipartisan Commission on Comprehensive Health Care. *A Call for Action, Final Report* (Washington, DC: US Government Printing Office, 1990).

US Department of Health and Human Services, Health Care Financing Administration, "National Health Expenditures, 1990," *Health Care Financing Review* (Fall 1991): 29-54.

1. Jill Foley, "Sources of Health Insurance and Characteristics of the Uninsured: Analysis of the March 1992 Current Population Survey," *Issue Brief* 133 (Employee Benefit Research Institute, Jan 1993).

2. For further discussion of other reform proposals, see William Custer and Jill Foley, "Health Care Reform: Tradeoffs and Implications," *EBRI Issue Brief* 125 (Employee Benefit Research Institute, Apr 1992).

3. Alain C Enthoven, *Theory and Practice of Managed Competition in Health Care Finance* (Amsterdam: Elsevier Science Publishers, BV, 1988).

4. US Department of Commerce, Bureau of Economic Analysis, *Survey of Current Business* Jan 1992 (Washington, DC: US Government Printing Office, 1992).

5. Adverse selection refers to differences in risk. A health insurance plan that attracts enrollees who are more likely than average to utilize health care services is said to suffer from adverse selection. Adverse selection may also be used to describe the phenomenon that the individuals most likely to need health care services are also more likely to purchase health insurance.

6. George Washington University Health Policy Forum, "Regulating Health Insurance in the Small Group Market: Proposals to Increase Availability and Affordability," *Issue Brief* 581 (Washington, DC: The George Washington University, 1991).

7. Medical underwriting refers to the practice of requiring a potential purchaser of health insurance to undergo a physical examination or submit other evidence of good health before being allowed to purchase insurance.

8. Supra note 6.

9. Catherine G McLaughlin, "The Dilemma of Affordability: Private Health Insurance for Small Businesses," prepared for the American Enterprise Institute conference, *American Health Policy: Critical Issues for Reform* (Washington, DC) Oct 3-4, 1991.

10. Id.

11. See US Congress, Office of Technology Assessment, "Does Health Insurance Make a Difference?" background paper, OTA-BP-H-99 (Washington, DC: US Government Printing Office, 1992): 2.

12. R Kronick, DC Goodman, J Wennberg, and E Wagner, "The Marketplace in Health Care Reform: The Demographic Limitations of Managed Competition," *New England Journal of Medicine* Jan 14, 1993: 148-153.

13. Mark V Pauly, "Taxation, Health Insurance, and Market Failure in the Medical Economy," *Journal of Economic Literature* June 1986: 629-675.

14. Id.

15. Paul Starr, *The Logic of Health Care Reform* (Knoxville, Tenn: Whittle Direct Books, 1992).

16. Alain C Enthoven, "The History and Principles of Managed Competition," 12 *Health Affairs* Supplement (1993): 24-48.

17. Supra note 6.

2.   Planning Today for Health Care Reform Tomorrow

Michael B. Jones   Frank A. McArdle   and Diana Reace

Employers need to begin planning now for the national health care reforms that will come to pass some time in the future. Setting long-term health care benefit goals and strategies will prepare employers as these reforms are unveiled and go into effect, a process that will likely continue through the turn of the century.

The Clinton Administration has been working for several months to develop a proposal the President can present to Congress. The closed nature of discussion throughout the development process, along with repeated delays in release of plan details, has been a frustrating experience for employees who are looking to reform efforts for help in controlling medical costs. This article focuses on ways in which employers can begin planning now for changes under national health care reform, before these changes become law. Also discussed is the use of "breakthrough thinking"—a problem-solving methodology being used by proactive employers to achieve desired outcomes under health care reform.

TIMING

The Task Force on National Health Reform, headed by Hillary Rodham Clinton, was created by President Clinton in January 1993. While this task force has officially disbanded, Ms. Clinton continues to lead the effort to develop the President's reform plans. With the release of the President's proposal in September of 1993, the earliest we are likely to see legislative language sent to Congress is late 1993 or early 1994.

28

The Democratic National Committee hopes to raise up to $37 million from corporations, labor unions, and individuals, to finance a six-month media blitz to promote the President's plan. The labor unions also have their own public education campaign planned, as do other consumer groups. Over a dozen groups have formed a nonprofit organization called the Health Project, with a stated goal "to get health reform enacted into law." Among the Health Project's members are the American Association of Retired Persons (AARP), the AFL-CIO, the American Hospital Association (AHA), the American Academy of Family Physicians, and Families USA. Launching a campaign to *defeat* Clinton's health reform proposal and instead build public support for their alternative plan are members of an ad hoc coalition that includes the American Conservative Union, United Seniors Association, and Citizens for a Sound Economy.

Advance congressional consultation may help smooth the way—at least among the Democratic leadership in Congress. But overall congressional reaction will be more complex, more partisan, and more tentative, as the Members of Congress ask for time and for hearings to weigh the impact of the reform on the constituents and to gauge the effectiveness of the campaign to sell the reform. It's likely to take a year or more for legislation to move its way through Congress. From there it will take several years to establish completely the structure for managed competition.

How long can we expect the process to take? Viewing the plan released in September by the Clinton Administration as a *starting point,* a reasonable timeline for health care reform might look something like Table 1.

In May 1993, the Congressional Budget Office noted the complexity involved with a system of managed competition: "A complex series of changes would have to be introduced progressively and refined over time. . . . It could easily take two or three years before significant changes in the functioning of the health care system began to be apparent, and it could require five or more years to establish completely the structure for managed competition. In fact, the full benefits would probably not accrue until the next century."

We are reminded by earlier experience to keep a close watch on the legislative process. To adopt a holding pattern until a health reform package is signed, sealed, and delivered could be costly to employers. But there's also a risk

Table 1. Health Care Reform Timetable		
Event	*Reasonable Timeframe for Completion*	*Projected Date*
Preparation of legislative language	4 months	1/94
Congressional passage	12 months	1/95
Purchasing cooperatives	2.5 years	6/96
Universal coverage	3.5 years	6/97
Management competition structure	3-5 years	1998-2000
Cost containment results	5-10 years	1999-2004

in adopting sweeping design changes that are not compatible with health care reform. The approach to health care reform being taken by proactive employers involves preparing themselves for a process of change that is likely to take years to complete.

BALANCING PRIORITIES

With congressional passage at least a year away and full medical cost containment results as much as ten years down the road, employers have ample opportunity to begin preparation for change under health care reform. For many employers the first step is to balance priorities for short-term and long-term health care strategies. Most employers already are having to confront the immediate question of what they want their long-term strategy to be under national health care reform. For example, some are asking themselves *whether they should enthusiastically push for the Clinton plan, oppose it, or accept it with reservations.* Others have begun an assessment of the potential financial impact on their organization, and are figuring out how they might fix problem areas.

Inevitably, some employers will choose to hold off on analysis of their long-term direction until more details are known about the health care reform plan. But many are finding that they know enough now to prepare for such an analysis, or at least to set up a matrix of possible savings and possible costs under emerging scenarios. These employers are gearing up, and in the process, establishing their own priority areas in health care reform. For example, one employer has identified these four priorities:

1. Set up an option to buy through a health insurance purchasing cooperative;
2. Preserve the current level of tax deductibility for the company;
3. Identify new financing opportunities for subsidizing care to retirees; and
4. Design a new standard benefit package that doesn't materially add to the cost of coverage under their current plan.

Priorities will vary among employers, but the process of setting priorities empowers an employer to better understand its interest in health care reform and to work for its own priorities. Another advantage of identifying priorities is that it provides a foundation for giving input to Congress and to Washington lobbyists and enables employers to identify potential allies among other employers.

THE EMPLOYER'S ROLE IN DELIVERING HEALTH CARE REFORM

For an employer, the planning process begins with deciding what role to play in providing health care to employees under national health care reform. For example, it's likely that large employers will get the opportunity to exercise a choice of whether to continue their existing plan or to move instead toward subsidizing employee purchase of coverage through a purchasing cooperative.

If given such an opportunity, what would you as an employer do? Who would make that decision? What role would employee attitudes and preferences play in that decision? And is there a process or vehicle in place within the organization to begin addressing this question today—or will one have to be created?

Some employers may be inclined to drop their health care plans, especially if it is financially advantageous to do so. Others will be reluctant to drop their plan when culture, history, or geography would encourage them to remain providers of health care coverage, assuming neutral or slightly negative financial impact. Some employers may wish to maintain their own plan for quality-of-care reasons, or because their employees expect it. But when financial indicators suggest change, and employee attitudes suggest status quo, a process will be needed for managing the decision and for creating ownership by the decision makers and affected employees.

What's the bottom line? Employers need to define in advance the criteria that would make them want to continue providing health care as well as those that would prompt them to phase it out. Within these criteria, employers will seek to balance what they think is good for their organization with what they think is good for the nation as a whole.

PREPARING FOR EMPLOYEE AND RETIREE REACTIONS

As the reform process rolls out, we can expect employees to be asking their employers whether they'll be better off under the new reform or under their current program. There will be varying levels of anxiety about what the changes mean for them, given their personal circumstances. Initial reactions will reflect confusion, uncertainty, and insecurity: *"Will I get hurt? How will reform affect me and my choice of doctors?"*

Some employers already have laid a foundation for communicating health care reform to employees and retirees. They're getting a headstart by sharing their thoughts about the proposal, and educating employees on all aspects of the situation, to supplement what's being seen and heard in the media. This helps prepare employees for becoming active in the reform debate and creates, or reinforces, an employer/employee partnership as health care reform evolves. By beginning the communication process early, employers can help employees feel more secure, while developing a win/win atmosphere for the tough decisions ahead. The diagram in Exhibit 1 summarizes the process of organizing to support employees during health care reform.

If the decision is made to use health care reform to strengthen the employer/employee relationship, employers then face the task of planning and

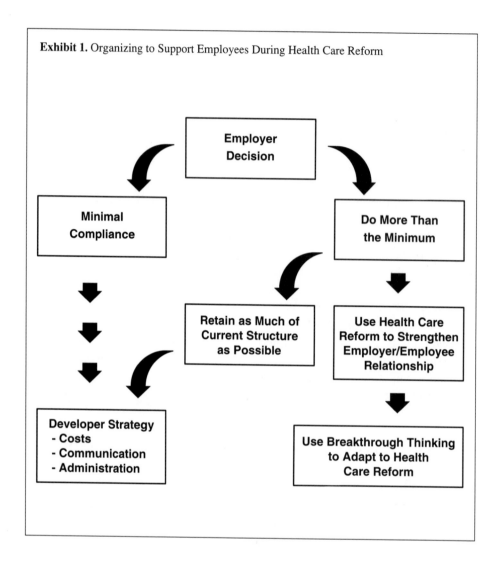

Exhibit 1. Organizing to Support Employees During Health Care Reform

implementing their strategy. The following model is being used by innovative employers to "break through" to a new level of problem solving—one in which the traditional series of linear tasks is replaced with dynamic cycles for continual improvement (see Exhibit 2). In the remaining pages of this article, each step in the cycle is discussed in the context of health care reform.

Defining Success

The first step in applying breakthrough thinking to health care reform is to define success in terms of a desired end result, and to identify the issues relative to that end result. For example, if the desired result is a definition of the human resources and financial environment that should exist after health care reform, the corresponding list of issues might include:

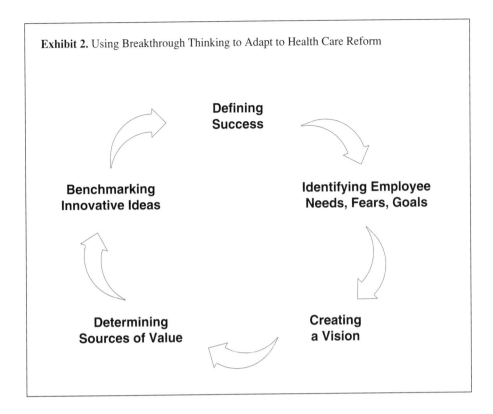

Exhibit 2. Using Breakthrough Thinking to Adapt to Health Care Reform

- What is the desired effect on employer costs?
    —Savings?
    —Break even?
    —Additional cost?
- Should the new tax structure affect the above issues?
- What is the desired effect on employees in terms of:
    —Health status?
    —Access to care?
    —Quality of care?
    —Convenience?
    —Choice?
    —Satisfaction?
- How should employees perceive the employer's role during and after the transition?

Identifying Employee Needs, Fears, and Goals

Once an employer has defined successful, post-reform health care delivery, the next step is to identify the aspects of health care reform that raise the biggest concerns from an employee perspective. Again using breakthrough thinking, the desired end result of this step might be to make employees feel as if they're part of the process, and help them understand the trade-offs necessary during the transition. Another desirable end result is to create ownership and understanding of employer goals to gain support and encourage employee action. Examples of the issues raised by these desired results include:

- What is the best way to determine employees' needs, fears, and goals with respect to health and health care reform?
    —Focus groups?
    —Surveys?
    —Study groups?
- How do we build additional employee consensus into the process?

Creating a Vision

To create a vision, the end result should encompass a clear identification of strategic directions, employer commitments, and employee responsibilities. Examples of issues that might arise during the creation of a vision include:

- How can the employer/employee "partnership" be enhanced while adapting to health care reform?
- How will the transition strategy support business needs?
- How will the transition strategy alleviate employee concerns?

Determining Sources of Value

In this step, employers want to identify and quantify opportunities, and adapt to health care reform so that the employer's return on investment of benefit dollars can be maximized. Issues here include:

- Where can employer dollars be spent most efficiently?
- What alternatives are available in each state, and how will they impact:
    —Cost?
    —Design?
    —Employee reactions?

Benchmarking Innovative Ideas

Here an employer may be seeking to create a resource or database of "best practice" solutions to aspects of health care such as cost sharing, broad-based and focused managed care, illness prevention, early intervention, equity in covering spouses and children, administration, risk pooling alternatives, and HMO management. For each potential best practice solution, an employer will want to identify its viability after reform, the cost implications, employee responsibilities, communication implications, administrative requirements, and anticipated employee reactions. Issues relevant to creating this database include:

- What kinds of benefit solutions should be considered?
  —In general?
  —In health care?
  —In transition to health care reform?
- How does the employer keep informed of transition strategies being used by other employers?
- Which employers should be considered "benchmark" employers?

Once a database of best practice solutions is available, an employer is well positioned to evaluate alternative strategies.

WHERE TO GO FROM HERE?

To summarize, there are a few key guidelines to keep in mind as the health care reform process rolls out:

- Develop a transition strategy
  —Keep employees informed
  —Develop an opportunity for employee appreciation
- Don't move *too* fast (what you see in Clinton's plan is not what ultimately will be implemented)
- Keep management informed
- Participate in business groups
  —To have input into the process
  —To keep informed of other employers' thinking
- Develop health care resources on a local level to cope with the expected local focus of health care reform
- Get tighter financial controls over HMOs in preparation for their potential use as accountable health plans

Independent of health care reform, employers need to decide where they are in the cost management continuum, and the cost implications of waiting for reform. As mentioned at the outset, the health care reform process itself will take many years to be realized in full. The cost containment effectiveness of "managed competition with a global budget" is the most questionable and uncertain piece of the entire reform proposal. Even those who assume its effectiveness say it will take five to ten years before its full effects are felt.

If strong pressure currently exists to contain costs, then this waiting period may be too expensive. If employee relations are a primary concern, then waiting may be an option. Most employers will want to ask themselves whether the projected cost increases in their current plan are tolerable in their current business or revenue environment. If not, what savings could be realized from employer cost management efforts—over one year? . . . three years? . . . five years?

Public release of the proposal is expected to raise as many issues as it answers, because it is only the start of a long process to develop the law, enact it, implement it, and see its results. In the interim, employers will be better prepared to cope with the reform process if their internal health care reform priorities are part of a longer-term human resource strategy, and they have a process in place to benchmark alternative reform proposals against their own priorities and desired outcomes.

3. Identifying the Value of Your Health Care Purchase: Pennsylvania Points the Way

Ernest J. Sessa

People are ready and willing to be good health care consumers if they are provided with the information necessary to make intelligent decisions. In Pennsylvania, a council composed of insurers, business people, public officials, health care professionals, and consumers is providing that information, with very encouraging results.

Our nation's health care system is in deep trouble and its impact on business and labor costs is dramatically increasing. *The New York Times* recently reported that health spending rose another 12 percent in 1992. Twenty-six percent of the average company's net earnings now go for medical costs, and 82 percent of employers require employees to pay for part of their family health care costs. Nearly 40 million Americans are uninsured, and many more are underinsured. We have the best health care money can buy, but more people each year cannot afford it.

Fortunately, Pennsylvania is in the forefront of a national movement to contain health care costs. Beginning in the mid-1980s, the business and labor communities in Pennsylvania joined together in an attempt to find a solution to the rising costs and diminishing access of health care. These efforts resulted in the passage of legislation forming the Health Care Cost Containment Council (HC4), which was created to introduce market-driven competition into the health care delivery system. This independent state agency collects, analyzes, and distributes to the public cost and quality related data for acute care hospitals in the commonwealth. Information on cardiac surgeons has now been reported as well. The council itself is composed of six representatives of the business community, six from organized labor, and one each from hospitals, physicians, the Blues, HMOs, commercial insurers, consumers, the Secretary of Health, Secretary of Public Welfare, and the Commissioner of Insurance.

Concerned about escalating health care costs, business and labor groups have worked together to provide the major thrust behind the council's creation and activity. Both recognize the health care issue as a growing factor in labor-management conflict. Health care benefits are now seen as the number one cause of strikes in Pennsylvania.

Pennsylvania's unique approach—choosing market competition over rate regulation—is being closely watched by other states. The underlying concept is that, just as airlines have improved their on-time performance since ratings have been published, health care providers will improve their performance when the facts about the care they give become known, which will rein in costs and improve quality for everyone. In addition, employers—the major purchasers of health care—as well as consumers will know which institutions provide high quality, cost-effective care, and can make informed selections based on this information.

This free-market approach sounds good in theory, but can it really work? The answer is an emphatic yes! In September, 1991, HC4 issued a public report that showed that St. Vincent's Hospital in Erie had significantly higher charges for open heart surgery than neighboring hospitals. In January, 1992, one week before the council's next report was released, an extraordinary thing happened. St. Vincent's announced that it was lowering its charges for coronary bypass surgery by $8,000, a savings to patients of $5 million each year.

A hospital reducing its charges? No one in Pennsylvania could remember it ever happening before. Why did it happen? Local business leaders claimed, and St. Vincent's has agreed, that the price reduction was a competitive response to HC4's public information. It shows that Pennsylvania's health care strategy is beginning to work. Competition can be effective at lowering health care costs.

In November 1992, Pennsylvania became the second state to publish information about patient death rates for surgeons who perform coronary bypass surgery. HC4 examined deaths of patients of 170 cardiac surgeons and 35 hospitals that performed bypass surgery in 1990, as well as the average amount hospitals charged for the procedure. This report names and rates each doctor and hospital. (See Exhibit 1.)

The most surprising finding of the report was that the two hospitals that charged the most for the surgery (Hospital of the University of Pennsylvania at $76,928 and Graduate Hospital at $83,851) had "more deaths than expected," while the one that charges the least (Reading Hospital at $21,063) had "fewer deaths than expected." In addition, the council noted that Allegheny General Hospital in Pittsburgh charged $47,000 for the surgery, the statewide median charge, and had "fewer deaths than expected." HC4 estimated that if all the

Exhibit 1. Hospitals Performing Coronary Artery Bypass Graft Surgery: Treatment Effectiveness and Average Charge

| Hospital | Total Patients | Patients Who Died | | Statistical Rating | Average Charge (in dollars) |
		Actual Number	Expected Range		
Hospitals with Fewer Number of Deaths than Expected					
Allegheny General Hospital	1,010	25	29.32–52.60	+	$46,704
Altoona Hospital	332	4	5.35–18.08	+	$27,333
Hahnemann University Hospital	847	26	29.44–53.49	+	$65,825
Reading Hospital and Medical Center	526	12	15.99–33.76	+	$21,063
Hospitals with Similar Number of Deaths as Expected					
Albert Einstein Medical Center	581	23	20.85–41.08	Δ	$61,971
Bryn Mawr Hospital	300	15	5.63–17.69	Δ	$49,309
Central Medical Center & Hospital	335	14	8.45–23.18	Δ	$46,544
Episcopal Hospital	285	18	8.05–21.64	Δ	$44,081
Geisinger Medical Center/Danville	323	15	3.91–15.30	Δ	$30,202
Hamot Medical Center	444	16	6.21–19.82	Δ	$34,769
Lancaster General Hospital	673	17	13.75–31.79	Δ	$24,307
Lankenau Hospital	584	25	15.57–33.74	Δ	$48,261
Medical College Hospitals/Main Clinical Campus	174	7	1.61–10.73	Δ	$56,530
Mercy Hospital of Pittsburgh	682	20	17.62–36.42	Δ	$39,002
Montefiore University Hospital	204	11	1.67–11.23	Δ	$54,479
Pennsylvania Hospital	90	1	0.72–7.79	Δ	$51,164
Polyclinic Medical Center	330	8	2.28–12.75	Δ	$39,314
Presbyterian Medical Center of Philadelphia	478	14	13.58–30.74	Δ	$42,408
Presbyterian–University Hospital	171	6	2.37–12.59	Δ	$70,089
Robert Packer Hospital	386	10	5.04–17.96	Δ	$21,246
Saint Luke's Hospital of Bethlehem	337	14	7.84–21.67	Δ	$33,245
Saint Vincent Health Center	304	11	4.10–16.25	Δ	$45,667
Shadyside Hospital	714	23	22.07–42.50	Δ	$56,015
Temple University Hospital	258	20	8.12–22.44	Δ	$65,303
Thomas Jefferson University Hospital	292	14	6.45–19.05	Δ	$52,464
University Hospital Milton S. Hershey Medical	201	6	3.27–13.44	Δ	$33,282
Western Pennsylvania Hospital	579	10	9.29–24.87	Δ	$57,569
Wilkes-Barre General Hospital	214	4	2.32–12.23	Δ	$29,746
Hospitals with Greater Number of Deaths than Expected					
Graduate Hospital	287	20	4.71–17.00	–	$83,851
Harrisburg Hospital	467	21	6.42–20.09	–	$39,587
Hospital of the University of Pennsylvania	354	33	8.50–22.38	–	$76,928
Lehigh Valley Hospital	920	46	20.67–40.69	–	$39,186
Mercy Hospital/Scranton	415	27	7.90–21.79	–	$23,885
Saint Francis Medical Center	463	31	13.26–29.03	–	$48,808
York Hospital	335	13	2.23–11.96	–	$26,334
STATEWIDE TOTAL	14,985	580			$44,649

Hospitals and Physicians may have commented on this report. Copies are available upon request.
Source: Pennsylvania Health Care Cost Containment Council, 1990 data.

hospitals that charged more reduced their prices to Allegheny's level, the annual savings would be $88 million. The council's data is repeatedly showing that you don't have to pay exorbitant charges to receive high quality medical care.

The New York State Health Department recently released its third annual listing of coronary bypass mortality rates for New York cardiac surgeons. The state found that the mortality rate was down 36 percent from the rate of the first year that the data were reported to the public, while at the same time the number of high risk operations increased. The system of collecting, analyzing, and publishing health care data appears to be working. In Pennsylvania, consumers and purchasers are using this kind of information to find the best hospitals and doctors, and to stimulate the rest to improve their performance and prices.

In addition to its impact upon business and labor costs, the council's data can help to hold down the cost of government. Through HC4, the state government, as Pennsylvania's largest insurer through Medicaid and the largest employer, will have valuable information as it struggles to contain staggering costs without compromising the quality of care that people receive.

The Council's Reports

The council publishes three primary reports that can aid purchasers, consumers, and decision makers, plus a variety of other reports.

Hospitals are required by law to provide cost and quality data to the council. Each year, the agency publishes a *Hospital Effectiveness Report* for each of nine regions. These reports combine acute care hospital records of effectiveness with average charges for services. The council measures hospital effectiveness by comparing, for each of a set of 59 medical conditions and surgeries, the hospitals' actual number of patient deaths and patients who were very ill during their first week of hospitalization to the number expected for that condition and patient age. The expected numbers are calculated from a comparative database of nearly one million patient records from similar hospitals throughout the nation.

The second set of reports are the *Small Area Analysis Reports*. The small area analysis technique highlights striking variations in the residence-based hospitalization rates for 154 surgical procedures and medical treatments, and allows for comparisons to be made between communities and counties, and to statewide averages. Small area analysis pinpoints communities where access-to-care problems may exist. This may be reflected by a higher-than-average hospitalization rate. Residents may not have access to primary care—such as that obtained from a pediatrician or general practitioner in an office visit—so instead they go to the local hospital for treatment.

Small area analysis can also indicate communities where differences in clinical judgement among physicians may exist—differences that add up over time. For example, cesarean section childbirth deliveries cost, on average, $2,200 more than vaginal deliveries. Chicago's Mt. Sinai Hospital, through a voluntary program, reduced its cesarean section rate from 17.5 percent to 11.5 percent in two years. At just this one hospital for just this one procedure, the savings were approximately $1 million.

Pennsylvania's studies have shown that in 1988, residents of northeastern Pennsylvania were 25 percent more likely to have surgery than the rest of the state. The next highest regional surgery rate was only 2 percent above the state average. We need to better understand why the rates for certain communities are so different from those of their neighbors and from the state averages. Changing these differences where appropriate can have major implications and can help to determine the real factors underlying patterns of health care spending. It shows that the volume of hospital services is as important as the individual price of those services in determining cost.

The third report is the previously mentioned *Consumer Guide to Coronary Bypass Surgery.* In reporting on the mortality rates of surgeons and hospitals performing bypass surgery, the council developed a state-of-the-art method of measuring the age, gender, and medical condition of each patient. The council's method of adjusting raw mortality figures takes the medical risk of patients into account. Since first releasing this new consumer report, the council has distributed more than 10,000 copies of it.

Management and labor now have a chance to meaningfully and objectively compare hospitals. Large companies like Hershey Foods, General Electric, and ALCOA, as well as unions like the Pennsylvania State Education Association and the Laborers' District Council of Western Pennsylvania, are using the data to make health benefits decisions that could affect thousands of employees and their families.

In Pennsylvania, the Hershey Foods Corporation, in a cooperative effort with its 6,500 in-state employees, has used the council's data to create a quality-based network of ten hospitals and 200 physicians. Hershey's goal is to bring together the quality physicians with the quality hospitals, and to establish relationships with centers of excellence for about a dozen expensive, specialized procedures such as cardiac care. Last year, a majority of Hershey's employees were enrolled in traditional indemnity plans. This year, a majority are now enrolled in "managed care." By focusing on the quality of care, Hershey estimates a 10 percent annual reduction in the company's health care costs. Other companies are expected to follow suit. At Hershey, the company and its employees recognize that quality is the key to cost containment because over the long run, quality is less expensive.

In another case, Accutrex, Inc., which employs 100 people in Washington County, Pennsylvania, used the HC4 reports to cut 13 percent from its health care bill, and managed to expand coverage to include prescription drugs and routine check-ups. Accutrex is part of an alliance of businesses in Southwest Pennsylvania that has saved $1 million in the last six months by using the council's *Hospital Effectiveness Report* for their region.

In addition to the council's public reports, HC4 offers a special opportunity to purchasers who want cost and quality information tailored to their specialized needs. HC4's Special Reports Unit can provide customized data to meet a variety of organizational goals that go far beyond the scope of the council's public reports. The council has filled more than a hundred of these special requests over the past two years, with the majority coming from Pennsylvania hospitals seeking these strategic data to improve both their internal quality assurance efforts and their competitive position.

There is a tremendous need for such medical information. Misdiagnosis, substandard or inappropriate surgery, improper drug therapies, and hospital acquired infections result in more and longer hospitalizations—and they cost more money. A 1990 Harvard Medical School study suggests that approximately 300,000 people are injured or die from medical negligence in hospitals each year. Ongoing research by the Rand Corporation found that only 56 percent of coronary bypass operations were justified, and that as many as one in three major medical and surgical procedures are not appropriate. Pennsylvania data indicate that certain surgical procedures are done more often in some communities than others; for example, in Allegheny County a woman's likelihood of having a hysterectomy is 20 percent more than the statewide average. Clearly, the human and financial costs of medical care that is of poor or questionable quality are staggering. Outcomes research is showing that for many medical conditions, there are many options, and many questions.

The issue of patient choice has also received much attention. Correctly or not, much of the public's anxiety rests on the belief that managed care organizations care only for the bottom line—that quality is sacrificed on the altar of cost containment. However, the reality is that currently, patients have only limited and, generally, anecdotal information upon which to base choices.

In states like Pennsylvania and Iowa and cities like Cleveland and St. Louis, consumers and purchasers now have access to objective, risk-adjusted data to use in identifying the most efficient, effective providers—information that gives patients real choices. Quality is not at odds with cost containment strategies, it enhances them!

If, under managed competition, managed care networks must compete on quality as well as price, purchasing groups can reassure consumers that the quality of medical care is key. Patient choice—a more informed choice—can be strengthened, not diminished.

Focusing on quality can reduce the trend toward micro-management of medicine. Instead of second-guessing doctors after the fact, consumers and purchasers of health care can use quality measurements to select quality providers up front, and then allow the providers to do their jobs.

Focusing on quality may also help avoid the perception, or the actual hard choices, of rationing. Quality providers eliminate unnecessary procedures and treatments, avoid overutilization, and promote cost efficiencies that can free up enormous resources. Avoiding care that is not medically necessary in the first instance can prevent the conscious choice of withholding essential medical care because of lack of resources in the second instance.

Unfortunately, the council has been limited in its impact upon health care cost and quality by severe budget cutbacks over the past two years. As a result, the council has been unable to expand into the area of public reports on outpatient surgeries and medical treatment. The issue of actual payments to hospitals and physicians has been left unscrutinized, as have a host of important physician specialties other than cardiac care. Previously published aggregate hospital financial reports, as well as follow-up small area analysis reports (critical to the examination of utilization of health services), have been placed on the back burner. In the future, if the council receives adequate budget appropriations, it can begin explorations into some of these important areas.

It seems clear that people are ready, willing, and able to be good health care consumers, if they have the proper informational tools. In Pennsylvania, the HC4 provides purchasers, as well as their employees and subscribers, with those tools. Never before has such information been available. Quality measurements and information about charges are the concrete data that allow purchasers to seek value when making health care decisions.

It will take time for an investment such as this to pay off fully. But accurate health care data, when used effectively, is key to controlling health care costs. As former U.S. Surgeon General and HC4 supporter Dr. C. Everett Koop wrote in a letter to U.S. News and World Report, "The only way to determine improvement in hospital and physician performance is through repeated documentation made available to the public on a continuing basis. This public and professional examination of performance is necessary no matter which direction America takes in restructuring and refinancing its health care system. In the effort to measure quality, Pennsylvania is furthest along."

4. Caring for the Uninsured and Underinsured: Hawaii's Employer Mandate and Its Contribution to Universal Access

John C. Lewin, MD   Peter A. Sybinsky, PhD

Much national debate centers around national models in which an employer mandate plays an important rule in providing for health care coverage for all Americans. Hawaii has had the nation's only health insurance employer mandate for almost 20 years, yet little is known nationally about the mandate itself or Hawaii's experience with it. This article describes the long-term effects of Hawaii's employer mandate on health care access and costs, and offers reflections on the potentials of national health care reform based on Hawaii's experience.

At least since the early 1970s, employer mandates have been a part of the policy debate on how to provide cost-effective, high-quality health care coverage for all Americans. During that decade, several administrations prepared employer mandates that, for one reason or another, were eventually rejected. However, in 1974, Hawaii enacted the Prepaid Health Care Act (PPHCA), a remarkably successful law that remains the nation's only employer mandate for health care coverage. Except for a brief period in the early 1980s, employers in Hawaii have been required to cover their employees with a standard, state-established package of health care benefits. This article describes the relationship of the PPHCA to Hawaii's overall system and outlines some health costs and outcomes that the authors believe recommend this policy to other states and the nation.

Reprinted from the *JAMA®* The Journal of the American Medical Association, May 19, 1993, Volume 269, Copyright 1993, American Medical Association.

HAWAII'S PPHCA

The keystone of Hawaii's health care reform efforts is its employer mandate, Chapter 393, Hawaii Revised Statutes, better known as the PPHCA. By significantly reducing the number of uninsured, this measure allowed Hawaii to implement a system of universal access to health care coverage in the late 1980s, making it the only state in the nation to offer such a guarantee to its people.

After 6 years of study and policy development, the PPHCA was adopted in 1974 to provide health care coverage for virtually all employees in the state. The PPHCA, enforced by Hawaii's Department of Labor and Industrial Relations, directs businesses to provide a prescribed standard and comprehensive benefits package for employees throughout the private sector. While not enthusiastically supported by the business community, the measure did have a great deal of support among unions and consumers. The PPHCA was supported by an environment already strong in employment-based health care coverage for comprehensive medical care through prepaid health plans. The major reasons for the PPHCA's passage were to protect the employees in the state from an erosion of health care coverage due to spiraling costs, evident even 18 years ago, and to add to the insured rolls those workers without coverage or with inadequate coverage.[1]

In this, the nation's first and only state-mandated benefits plan, costs are shared between the employer and the employee. The employee may be required to pay as much as 1.5% of monthly wages, up to half the premium cost. The employer pays the balance, but in all cases, at least 50% of the cost. Dependent coverage, while optional, has become the almost universal standard practice, the cost of which may be fully borne by the employer. Any employee who works more than 20 hours a week and makes at least 86.67 times the minimum hourly wage per month is eligible for prepaid health care.

Under the law, employers must provide as a minimum the basic services defined in Section-393 (Table 1). Coverage alternatives include both a fee-for-service plan and a health maintenance plan. The fee-for-service plan is the most used in Hawaii and provides a good package of diagnostic and treatment services, using copayments (usually 20%) to reduce overutilization. The health maintenance organization (HMO) model provides a generous package of benefits based on services included for a federally qualified HMO. The prescribed coverage may be purchased from any insurance provider licensed in Hawaii or provided on a self-insured basis by the employers themselves. An alternate package with fewer benefits, deductibles, and higher copayments may be substituted for the two basic plans, but then dependent coverage is required. Most employers, however, have not chosen the alternate plan.

No large state bureaucracy is needed to administer prepaid health care. A PPHCA Premium Supplementation Funds assists small employers (those with eight employees or less) who, because of economic limitations, cannot provide the required insurance, and covers employees whose employers have gone out of

Table 1.—Prepaid Health Care Benefits Based on Section 393-7, Hawaii Revised Statutes

Hospital
  Inpatient (120 d)
  Outpatient
  Emergency Department
Surgical
  Physician
  After care
  Anesthesiologist
Medical
  Necessary home, office, and hospital physician visits
  Medical/surgical consultations
  Medical care while hospitalized
Laboratory and radiology services necessary for diagnosis or treatment
  Maternity benefits (9-mo waiting period)

business or who are not in compliance with the law. During the 17 years of the program, this fund has had minimal use (a total of $85,000) has been tapped). The PPHCA is enforced by monetary penalties and a provision that the employer is responsible for all the employee's health care expenses in the event the employee is not covered by the employer, as required by law.

There are exclusions to the PPHCA. All government employees (who have their own plans or other coverage alternatives), seasonal agricultural workers (there are relatively few, and a seasonal employer must obtain a specific waiver from the state), real estate and insurance agents working on a commission, family members in small family businesses, and government assistance program recipients are not covered by the PPHCA. People with coverage as a dependent under another employer's coverage care are excused from being covered by their employer.

The prepaid health care program does not provide specifically for cost containment. However, the PPHCA has created the context required for cost containment by the health care system. The PPHCA's irreducible and broad standard benefits package, the inability under the PPHCA of insurers to reject any employed person, and the PPHCA's indirect coercion of the insurers to more effectively treat patients with chronic disease rather than reject them, and thus to use community rating, all result in a more cost-efficient system. Also, since very little bureaucracy is needed to administer the PPHCA and reporting is minimal, administrative costs created by the mandate are minimal. The healthy competition the PPHCA has fostered among the major companies for the market not only has tended to limit costs, but positions Hawaii for further marketplace competition opportunities as national health reform proceeds. Finally, the state's health planning certificate-of-need process administered by the State Health Planning and Development Agency has limited unnecessary construction, preventing the problems of overbuilding and overcapacity, which have driven up costs in many jurisdictions.

Overall health care costs in Hawaii remain well below the rest of the nation, but they still cause significant concern, increasing at double-digit rates for much of the 1980s. Nonetheless, a recent study comparing health care costs (including government expenditures such as Medicare and Medicaid) in Hawaii with those in the United States and other nations indicated that Hawaii's overall costs are lower than not only the rest of the nation (7.8% of gross state product compared with the US figure of 11.2% of gross domestic product), but also Canada (8.6%), Sweden (9.0%), the Netherlands (8.5%), and Germany (8.2%).[2]

ERISA AND PREPAID HEALTH CARE

The PPHCA was passed just months before the federal government passed the Employee Retirement Income Security Act (ERISA). While it focuses on pension plans, ERISA also contains language that preempts state employer health coverage mandates. Standard Oil Co, California, challenged the PPHCA in 1976 (*Standard Oil v Agsalud*), after the Hawaii state legislature passed a bill adding mental health and substance abuse coverage to the basic provisions of the 1974 PPHCA. The basis for this suit was ERISA preemption of the PPHCA. In 1981, the Supreme Court declined to review the lower court decisions and the PPHCA was overturned. It took special federal legislation in 1983 to allow the mandate to be reinstated by exempting Hawaii from the ERISA provision. The exemption was based on the 1974 law, which was enacted before the mental health and substance abuse amendment. While it has been reinstated, the PPHCA cannot be modified without congressional action.[3] Because of this limitation, the state cannot amend the PPHCA to reflect the changes in Hawaii's health care system since 1974. Amendments to the 18-year-old law would make sense in areas such as requiring mandatory coverage of dependents of workers, affording periodic and equitable cost-share adjustments between employers and employees, and modifying benefits to reflect improvements in clinical preventive services.

COMMUNITY RATING FOR HEALTH INSURANCE

Community rating spreads risk across an entire population. Commercial insurance practices often focus on trying to find and sell insurance to "low risk" or those without the ability to pay high rates, without insurance. Without community rating, then, an insurance market is fragmented.

Because Hawaii has such a high level of persons with health care coverage due to its employer mandate, major health care insurers (the Hawaii Medical Service Association, Honolulu, and Kaiser Permanente Medical Programs,

Table 2.—Market Share of Health Insurance Providers in Hawaii*

Provider	Market Share, %
Hawaii Medical Service Association	56.4
Kaiser Family Foundation	18.0
Other Hawaii	8.2
Commercials	7.9
Other	9.5
Total	**100.0**

*Data derived from Friedman.[3(p86)]

Table 3.—Comparative Health Maintenance Organization Family Rates, 1992*†

Organization and State	Monthly Rate, $
Kaiser,‡ Hawaii	288
Kaiser,‡ Northern California	327
Kaiser,‡ Oregon, Washington	313
Kaiser,‡ Southern California	362
Kaiser,‡ Colorado	324
Kaiser,‡ Ohio	377
Kaiser,‡ Washington, DC	386
Group Health, Minnesota, Wisconsin	449
Harvard Community Health Plan, Massachusetts	465
Columbia Free State, Maryland	574

*Comparison subject to a number of factors including potentially different benefits and varying market situations.
†Data derived from *Consumer Reports*, August 1992.[4]
‡Kaiser Foundation Health Plan

Honolulu, Hawaii) can use community rating for coverage for small employers. These rates are comparable to those enjoyed by large employers. Since Hawaii's major health insurers (both of which are nonprofit) voluntarily use modified community rating for small businesses and have such a significant market share (Table 2), rates are affordable for small business in Hawaii. Other factors, such as low inpatient utilization, contribute to the lower costs as well. As a result, fee-for-service and HMO coverage (Table 3) are well below the cost of comparable plans elsewhere in the United States.

Small businesses can purchase insurance at reasonable rates and can comply with the employer mandate without undue burden. Insurance companies cut administrative costs and can market to a large pool of businesses. Costs are low in part because everyone must play and the young and healthy must pay into the pool along with those who are in greater need of services. The requirements of the PPHCA and responsible voluntary insurance practices have provided a uniformly level field for competition.

SYSTEM'S EFFECTS

While detailed analyses on the effects of Hawaii's system have not been undertaken, observation and preliminary data suggest that the policies established in Hawaii's system and supported by medical practice patterns in Hawaii have resulted in good health outcomes and little overall negative effects. These are evident in Hawaii's health status and its successful implementation and operation of an employer mandate and a supportive insurance system.

Effects on Health Care Coverage

The effect of an employer mandate are apparent. In 1971, 11.7% of the state's population was without hospital coverage and 17.2% was without physician coverage.[5] The PPHCA dramatically reduced those figures. Numbers of people who become insured owing to the passage of the new law were not directly measured. One observer estimated that at least 46,000 people were immediately covered.[6] The Department of Health estimates that many more, mostly employees of small businesses, were brought on board, and a Department of Health study indicated that the overall state rate of uninsured was approximately 3.9% after the implementation of the PPHCA.[7] As the Medicaid caseload decreased in the early 1980s, the number in the gap group (those without health care coverage) grew to approximately 5% by 1987.[8]

Some of the remaining uninsured, such as professionals or people with high commission incomes, were able to purchase health service. Others, however, could not. In 1989, the Department of Health estimated the gap group in financial need or "medical indigence" to be about 3.5% of the population, about 35,000 people. Populations at risk in the gap group were the unemployed, some dependents of low-income parents, unemployed dependents, and part-time workers. While a few seasonal agricultural workers and other groups also remained outside the provisions of the PPHCA, their numbers were small. Neighbor island residents (those residing on islands other than Oahu) and immigrants were in the excluded groups in higher numbers, although they are not formally excluded from employer-based coverage.[9] With the remaining in-need population less than 5% of the population, a program of universal access was deemed feasible for the state.

This strategy took two forms. The first was expansion of Medicaid, largely by utilizing the options allowed in the various Omnibus Budget Reconciliation Act measures passed by Congress in the late 1980s and early 1990s. Medicaid was expanded to include pregnant women and infants, young children, elderly persons, and disabled persons. With these additions, and with significant growth in Hawaii/Medicaid's Aid to Families With Dependent children caseload, Hawaii's Medicaid program grew to more than 96,000 persons by February 1993.[10]

A second option was "gap group insurance." The State Health Insurance Program (SHIP) (Chapter 431N, Hawaii Revised Statutes) was developed for those ineligible for Medicaid. This program provides a basic benefits package, rich in prevention and primary care but limited in catastrophic benefits (under the assumption that the SHIP member can use Medicaid "spend-down" for truly catastrophic events). By February 1993, the SHIP had just under 2% of the state's population enrolled, 86% of whom are under 150% of poverty. Forty percent of the SHIP clientele are children.

Together, the SHIP and Medicaid expansions have provided more than 40,000 recently uninsured people with health care coverage. The state's unemployment rate, while increasing in 1992, remains one of the lowest in the nation. The state conducted a survey on the uninsured from January through September 1991 and reported that those who identified themselves are being uninsured totaled 3.75%.[11] This remaining group may be difficult to insure owing to mental illness, severe substance abuse, or sociocultural reasons such as immigrant status. However, it is critical to point out that once these people present to a medical facility, they receive care.

Mandated health care coverage does not eliminate all barriers to health care. By and large, Hawaii has adequate health care services for its population. However, there are provider shortages in certain areas in Hawaii (four areas on Oahu and two areas on the island of Hawaii have been designated as a "medically undeserved population" by the federal government and six other areas are in the process of obtaining federal designation). Community health centers currently serve the Oahu areas, and plans are under way to provide for the needs of the others.

Despite these delivery system problems, the PPHCA has been directly responsible for reducing the overall size of the gap roup in Hawaii, which has permitted the state to provide cost-effective coverage for the rest. Hawaii can claim universal access to health care coverage for all of its citizens.

Effects on Business

One of the principal objections to an employer mandate has been an alleged negative effect on business, particularly small business. Hawaii is a "small business" state. Table 4 shows that 97% of Hawaii's businesses employ fewer than 100 persons and account for 51% of the jobs in the state; 94% employ fewer than 50. We note that the available data do not demonstrate that the PPHCA has an adverse effect on business in Hawaii. In fact, some indirect indicators suggest that the effect may be positive.

From a small-business standpoint, the typical argument against mandated benefits is that, as business costs increase with the burden of required health insurance, marginal businesses, will fail and the growth of others will be slower.

Table 4.—Reporting Units and Employment by Size of Firm, December 1990*

Size of Firm	No. of Reporting Units	% of Total	No. of Employees	% of Total
1 to 49 employees	25,768	94	173,277	38
1 to 99 employees	26,578	97	228927	51
All employers	27,271	100	444,871	100

*Unpublished information from the Hawaii State Department of Labor and Industrial Relations.

Figure 1. Unemployment Percentages for the United States and Hawaii, 1970 through 1991. PPHCA indicates the effective date of the Pre-paid Health Care Act. Data from unpublished information from the Hawaii State Department of Labor and Industrial Relations.

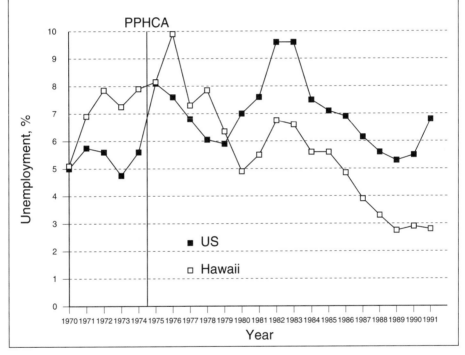

In either case, a higher than average proportion of businesses would fail and jobs would be lost. Hawaii's statistics do no bear this out. Hawaii's unemployment rate, high when the PPHCA was enacted in 1974 and throughout most of the 1970s, has shown a downward trend since 1977 (Fig. 1). While unemployment did reach a high point in the year following the PPHCA's effective date, an evaluation at the time concluded that the PPHCA had no appreciable effect on business.[6] Many factors contributed to the downward unemployment trend in the two decades following the mandate, but it is clear that the PPHCA did not have the devastating economic effect predicted. In fact, viewing job creation as another indicator, Fig 2 shows that in all but 1 year since the PPHCA's effective date more

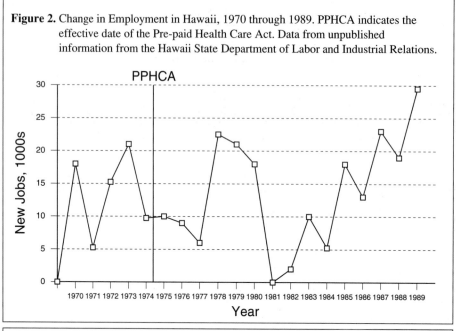

Figure 2. Change in Employment in Hawaii, 1970 through 1989. PPHCA indicates the effective date of the Pre-paid Health Care Act. Data from unpublished information from the Hawaii State Department of Labor and Industrial Relations.

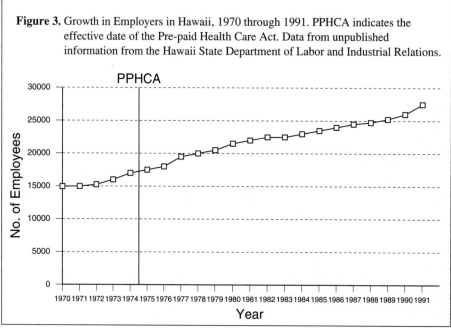

Figure 3. Growth in Employers in Hawaii, 1970 through 1991. PPHCA indicates the effective date of the Pre-paid Health Care Act. Data from unpublished information from the Hawaii State Department of Labor and Industrial Relations.

jobs have been created than have been lost. Throughout this period, Hawaii has enjoyed a general growth in employers (Fig. 3) and in jobs. In 1990, it was third highest in the nation in the per capita start-up of new businesses and about average with respect to business failures.[12]

One can actually argue that the employer mandate has been good for small businesses. Because its provisions set the basis for the continued voluntary community rating by Hawaii's major insurers, costs of health insurance for Hawaii's small businesses are relatively low. And, unlike other states, since all small businesses are part of the insurance pool, small businesses covering their workers are not paying for the uncompensated care costs of the small employers who don't. Finally, the PPHCA Premium Supplementation Fund rarely has been sued. This would suggest that little negative impact has been felt by small businesses eligible for the supplement.

Effects on Health Status

Considering that health outcomes ought to be the key objective of a health care system, Hawaii fares very well, if not the best of all states, in terms of longevity, low infant mortality, and very low premature morbidity and mortality rates for cardiovascular and pulmonary disease and cancer.[13] Two recent national analyses of the comparative health status of all 50 states, one by Northwest Life Insurance Company, Milwaukee, WI[14] and another by the American Public Health Association, Washington, DC,[15] have rated Hawaii first among all states. We believe a considerable amount of this success is attributable to direct and indirect effects of Hawaii's employer mandate over the past two decades. Historically, Hawaii's physicians and agricultural plantations emphasized outpatient care over hospitalization, an orientation that continues to the present in Hawaii's medical practice patterns. While no study of health status was undertaken over the effective period of the PPHCA, data available now support our contention.

The state's continued emphasis on ensuring access to primary care for nearly all its citizens has been a major factor in better health outcomes and improved health status for Hawaii's people. This is true despite risk populations and risk factors consistent with other urban and rural areas of the nation. On an age-adjusted basis, Hawaii has many fewer years of productive life lost owing to premature mortality due to cancer, heart disease, and overall causes (Table 5). Early access to primary care also shows up in health utilization statistics. Table 6 shows that Hawaii has 70% of the national rate of acute hospital beds per 1000 population, 90% of the national average for acute hospital utilization, 61% of the national average for surgeries, and 48% of the national rate of emergency department utilization. There is no rationing, and Hawaii has the same commitment to tertiary care and new technologies as other states. We believe the economies of lower inpatient utilization are a major source of Hawaii's lower costs.

Other hypotheses for the state's better outcomes abound. Because of a high proportion of Asian–Pacific Islanders in its population, Hawaii is purported to have a healthier "genetic stock"; in national data, Asian–Pacific Islanders appear

Table 5.—Years of Productive Life Lost (YPLL) per 100 000 due to Premature Mortality, Age Adjusted*

	Hawaii	US Population
Cancer	684	871
Heart disease	523	699
Index of YPLL, 1978	2345.3	3126.6

*Robert Worth, MD, written communication, March 1991, based on 1990 data from the Centers for Disease Control and Prevention.

to have better health status in all states. If this is so, the Asian–Pacific Islanders in Hawaii's population presumably would have better health status than Caucasians. However, analysis of recent data belies this hypothesis. As can been seen in Table 7, when age-adjusted populations of Japanese, Filipinos, Caucasians, and Hawaiians are compared (together these four groups make up 85% of Hawaii's population), Japanese, Filipinos, and Caucasians have similar status in terms of years of productive life lost per 100,000 people, with Caucasians coming out the best overall. The only group at variance from this profile are the native Hawaiians, representing 20% of the population, but with about twice the rate of productive years lost. These data suggest no major ethnic component to Hawaii's improved health status, and reveal that the category of Asian–Pacific Islander used in reporting national health statistics appears to mask the poor health status of Pacific Island peoples in Hawaii and might also be hidden in national statistics as well.

Another frequently stated hypothesis about Hawaii's good outcomes and lower health costs presumes that superior life-style choices and climate are responsible. However, Hawaii's data are not particularly noteworthy in this regard. Compared with the other states surveyed by the Centers for Disease Control and Prevention,

Table 6.—Utilization of Community Hospitals, 1991*

	Nation	Hawaii	% of US Rate
Beds per 1000 population	3.7	2.6	70
Patient days per 1000 population	884	792	89.6
Surgery per 1000 population	87.4	52.9	60.5
Emergency departments per 1000 population	351.1	168.9	48.1

*Data derived from the *Universal Healthcare Almanac*.[16]

Table 7.—Years of Productive Life Lost due to All Causes, 1990*†

By Ethnicity	Rate per 100 000 Population
Caucasians	4,894
Japanese	6,025
Filipinos	5,689
Hawaiians	10,297

*Age adjusted.
†Robert Worth, MD, written communication, March 1991, based on data from the Centers for Disease Control and Prevention.

Table 8.—Health Risk Behaviors for Hawaii and 45 States, 1990*

	% of Population	
Risk Behavior	Hawaii	Median of 45 States
No leisure activity	31.6	28.7
Sedentary life-style	62.4	58.5
Smoking	21.1	22.7
Overweight	17.7	22.7
Binge alcohol	19.4	15.2
Drink and drive	3.9	2.9
No seat belt	4.9	25.9

*Data derived from Siegel et al.[17]

Hawaii actually ranks above the median for 45 states on four of seven indications of "unhealthy" life-style; lack of leisure-time activity, sedentary lifestyle, binge alcohol drinking, and percentage of population drinking and driving (Table 8). The incidence of essential hypertension and hypercholesterolemia is higher than national averages. Life-style factors reflect Hawaii as an above-average state perhaps, but certainly do not in themselves explain Hawaii's excellent health mortality outcomes and lower costs.

While Hawaii's warm climate reduces health care expenses due to cold weather (eg, pneumonia, falls from slipping on ice), the state experiences more drowning, bodysurfing and ocean injuries, and skin cancers. Because Hawaii is a gateway from the Asia/Pacific region, it has the second highest rate of tuberculosis in the nation, and ranks among the top 10 states in per capita incidence of human immunodeficiency virus contraction.[18] It also has been calculated by the Hawaii State Department of Health to have the highest rate of hepatitis B in the nation and a high rate of Hansen's disease.

Access to basic health care appears to have been a key factor in improving the health status of Hawaii's people through the reduction of unnecessary in-

Table 9.—Comparison of Satisfaction With Health Care System in Hawaii and the Rest of the United States*

| | Hawaii | | |
Base	Hawaii's System, % (n=1000)	Nation's System, % (n=1000)	Total US, % (n=2000)
"It works as well as can be expected" or "it works fairly well, but minor changes are needed."	76	55	40
"It works badly and major changes are needed" or "it works so badly that an entirely different system is needed."	18	39	57
Not sure/refused.	6	7	3

* Data derived from the *Hawaii Health Care Survey.*[19]

patient and emergency department care. However, this analysis needs further documentation and investigation.

PUBLIC PERCEPTION OF EFFECTS

Public support for Hawaii's system is strong in the state. A recent poll conducted by Louis Harris and Associates, New York, NY, and sponsored by the Kaiser Family Foundation and the Queen Emma Foundation shows this.[19] The study was designed to be comparable to a national study conducted by the Kaiser Family foundation and the Commonwealth Fund in late 1991. The Harris pool provides a good comparative base for the perceptions of Hawaii respondents with those of the rest of the nation. In that survey, 76% of the respondents felt that Hawaii's system "works as well as can be expected" or "fairly well, but minor changes are needed," with 55% of Hawaii respondents indicating similar confidence in the nation's system. Nationally, only 40% of the respondents had a similar opinion. On the other hand, 18% of Hawaii's respondents felt the system worked badly and needed major changes or an entirely new system, as opposed to 57% of the national sample (Table 9).

Citizen confidence in Hawaii's state-based system is also evident when the respondents are asked about their choices of who should lead the health care reform effort. While 62% of the national sample looked to the federal government to lead health reform, only 48% of the people pooled in Hawaii picked the federal government to lead. In Hawaii's case, 43% chose the state to lead, compared with only 30% of the national sample.[19] Thus, while Hawaii recognizes the need for a 50-state system for true health care reform, the response of its citizens implies confidence in the directions and responsibility taken locally.

LESSONS FROM HAWAII'S EXPERIENCE

Hawaii's experience with an employer mandate injects several lessons into the national debate. As the only state with an employer mandate, Hawaii runs the risk of being termed "an outlier" or an anomaly owing to factors as diverse as its geographic location or the ethnic makeup of its people. While unique in many ways, Hawaii's overall health care system, hospital costs, provider salaries, and standards of care are not atypical among states. However, the state's commitment to universal access, community insurance rating, and primary and preventive care have paid unexpected cost-containment dividends in addition to the expected social rewards. This experience does deserve consideration by national and state policymakers.

Hawaii's experience suggests much from which the nation can benefit:

1. An employer mandate can be a powerfully effective means of increasing access, without a devastating impact on business. Several hypothetical studies based on projections and a limited number of variables have predicted that an employer mandate would result in a loss of jobs or a business slowdown.[20,21] Hawaii's actual experience suggests the opposite: Insurance rates are lower, there's a sizable reduction in uncompensated care, insurance practices are more equitable, and all employers are included. We do not believe an overall negative effect on either business or employment has occurred in Hawaii owing to the employer mandate.

2. Fair insurance practices are essential for and are supported by an employer mandate. By providing a base for community rating, Hawaii's employer mandate provided a base for the generally fair system of insurance coverage in the state. Because all employers are in the risk pool, community rates are affordable, and insurance is transportable. This provides the strong argument from Hawaii's perspective for a simple and clear, "everybody plays" mandate.

3. A broad standard benefits package, emphasizing primary, outpatient, and community care, but including a comprehensive spread of benefits extending from preventive services to inpatient and catastrophic care, is necessary to contain overall costs. Hawaii's experience supports inclusion of benefits and services that are demonstrated to be clinically and financially effective and appropriate and that collectively reduce unnecessary emergency department, in-patient, and high-technology care by design. We believe that some mental health, substance abuse, dental, and pharmaceutical drug coverage must be

included in a cost-effective, minimum-benefits package to promote cost containment through more successful primary and noninstitutional care.

4. Universal access is in itself a cost-containment strategy. Because virtually all of Hawaii's people have access to primary care coverage through the employer mandate and the state programs it has made possible, utilization of high-cost services in Hawaii is well below the rest of the nation. This leads to the lower health care costs, comparatively low small-business insurance rates, and a lower portion of gross domestic product spent on health care when the state is compared with the nation.[2] By allowing free access to primary care, a national or state health policy could decrease the use of expensive modes of care and thus decrease health costs. Universal access, then, has been our best cost-cutting tool.

5. States can be successful in health care reform. Even though a "small business" state, Hawaii has demonstrated that states can implement comprehensive health reforms when given flexibility by the federal government to design and implement these reforms. Hawaii's ERISA exemption was crucial in this reform process. Recent federal court decisions are citing ERISA to limit an ever-increasing number of incremental state-mediated reforms. For example, in New Jersey, the decision in *United Wire, Metal, and Machine Health and Welfare Fund v Morristown Memorial Hospital* overturned that state's long operating uncompensated care fund. It would seem prudent public policy to allow for careful and deliberate state experimentation through ERISA exemptions or waivers in the event the needed national reform does not happen right away.

CONCLUSION

While health care reform has increased significantly in importance to the American public in recent years, no specific health reform strategy has yet found general support by a majority of American people.[19] Hawaii offers positive and nonhypothetical experience with the nation's only employer mandate, coupled with the advantages of community insurance rating and an emphasis on primary and preventive care. Our state demonstrates and validates that this approach is a viable one for serious consideration in health care reform not only by other states, but by the nation itself as the Clinton administration and the Congress proceed to grapple with the issues involved.

The authors wish to thank the following individuals for their invaluable help in making this article possible: Mario Ramil, Orlando Wannabe, Frederick Pang, and Tomio Anzai, the Department of Labor and Industrial Relations, State of Hawaii; Cliff Cisco, Hawaii Medical Services Association; Barbara Hastings, Robert Worth, MD, Anthony Ching, Kathleen Kondo, Claire Adachi, and Annette

Perumbala, the Department of Health, State of Hawaii; and Joshua Agsalud, EdD, Office of the Governor, State of Hawaii.

References

1. Section 1, Act 210, Hawaii Session Laws, 1974.

2. Stenson RV. Comparison of health expenditures in US and Hawaii economies. *Hawaii Med J.* 1992; 51(1):14.

3. Friedman E. *The Aloha Way: Health Care Structure and Finance in Hawaii.* Honolulu: Hawaii Medical Service Association; 1993.

4. *Consumer Reports.* August 1992;57:530-531.

5. Riesenfeld SA. *Prepaid Health Care in Hawaii.* Honolulu: Legislative Reference Bureau, State of Hawaii; 1971. Report 2.

6. Van Steenwyk J, Fink R. Evaluation of Impact of Hawaii's Mandatory Health Insurance Law: A Report on the Prepaid Health Care Act. Washington, DC: US Dept of Health, Education and Welfare; 1978. Contract 299-77-0014.

7. Nakamura A, Johnson D, Oyama N, Peterson J. *Research and Statistics Report: Cost of Medical Care.* Honolulu: Dept of Health, State of Hawaii; 1981.

8. Dept of Health, State of Hawaii. *The Medically Indigent in Hawaii: A Preliminary Report to the Legislature in Response to SR 149-86, SD1.* Honolulu: Dept of Health, State of Hawaii; January 1987.

9. *Policy Working Paper: Universal Primary and Preventive Health Care for Hawaii.* Honolulu: Dept of Health, State of Hawaii; 1989.

10. Rubin W, director, Dept of Human Services. Testimony before *Hawaii State Legislature Joint House Health and Human Service Committee,* February 1993.

11. Dept of Health, State of Hawaii. *Measuring the Uninsured Population in Hawaii.* Honolulu: Dept of Health, State of Hawaii; November 1992.

12. *National Governor's Association Regional Hearings on Healthcare.* Vancouver, Wash: June 27, 1991 (testimony of M. Ramil, director of labor and industrial relations, state of Hawaii).

13. *Hawaii Health Profile, 1992.* Atlanta, Ga: US Department of Health and Human Services, Public Health Service, Centers for Disease Control and Prevention; 1992:2-5, 9.

14. *The Northwestern National Life State Health Rankings, 1991 Edition.* Milwaukee, Wis: Northwestern National Life Insurance Co; 1991.

15. *America's Public Health Report Card: A State-by-State Report on the Health of the Public.* Washington, DC: American Public Health Association; November 1992.

16. Universal Healthcare Almanac. Phoenix, Ariz: Silver and Cherner; 1993. Tables 2.2.1 and 2.14.1.

17. Siegel PZ, Brackbill RM, Frazier EL, et al. Behavioral risk factor surveillance, 1986-1990. *MMWR CDC Surveill Summ.* 1991;55(4):1-23.

18. Centers for Disease Control and Prevention. *Hawaii Health Profile—1992.* Atlanta, Ga: US Dept of Health and Human Services; 1992:20-21.

19. Kaiser Family Foundation, Queen Emma Foundation, Louis Harris & Associates. *Hawaii Health Care Survey.* New York, NY: Louis Harris & Associates; February-March, 1992.

20.   Zedlewski SR, Aos GP, Wheaton L, Winterbottom CL. *Pay or Play Employer Mandates: Effects on Insurance Coverage and Costs.* Washington, DC: Urban Institute; 1992.

21.   Swartz K. Why requiring employers to provide health insurance is a bad idea. *J Health Polit Policy Law.* 1990;15:779-792.

5.   Medicaid: States Turn to Managed Care
to Improve Access and Control Costs

State Medicaid costs have been increasing rapidly, and many states have turned to managed care programs to help reduce the growing strain Medicaid puts on their budgets and to improve health care access for Medicaid recipients. A number of studies and analyses conducted on these managed care programs have yielded interesting results on the effectiveness and cost savings of managed care.

The Medicaid program has been growing at a substantial rate. Combined state and federal program expenditures have nearly doubled since 1989, and the $119 billion cost of the program in fiscal year 1992 has now equalled the total cost of the Medicare program. At present, state Medicaid expenditures are second only to combined state costs of elementary and secondary education. The potential for managed care to control costs while improving access has appealed to many states confronting such growth in program costs.

STATES INCREASE USE OF MANAGED CARE IN THEIR MEDICAID PROGRAMS

According to the Health Care Financing Administration (HCFA), Medicaid managed care enrollment more than doubled between 1987 and 1992, and included about 3.6 million beneficiaries nationwide as of June 30, 1992. This represents about 12 percent of the total Medicaid population. Federal legislation in 1981 that permitted greater experimentation in the Medicaid program was a catalyst for states to consider managed care. However, the real stimulus for

Source: U.S. General Accounting Office. Excerpted from *Medicaid: States Turn to Managed Care to Improve Access and Control Costs* (GAO/HRD-93-46, March 17, 1993).

developing managed care programs has occurred in the last several years, as states contend with increasing growth in the Medicaid population, spiraling program costs, and limited state budgets. Thirty-six states were operating one or more managed care programs for Medicaid beneficiaries in February 1993. Another 13 states planned to implement managed care programs by January 1994.

States' Use of Managed Care

Survey data show that states participating in managed care are employing a wide variety of managed care models. These range from models that provide all health care in exchange for a prepaid set monthly fee—generally called fully capitated plans—to fee-for-service primary care case management (PCCM) programs. In PCCM programs, participating primary care physicians receive payments for each service delivered plus a case management fee to coordinate an individual's health care needs. Many arrangements fall somewhere in between. Partially capitated plans, for example, receive a fixed monthly payment per enrolled individual for a limited range of services—for example, physician services and referral care such as specialty and diagnostic services.

Managed care models seek to establish relationships between providers and beneficiaries, thereby improving access to care. States require providers to set office hours and provide 24-hour physician coverage. They also encourage or require beneficiaries to select from participating providers the one who will be responsible for coordinating their care. Common to all managed care models in the Medicaid program is the use of a primary care physician to act as a "gatekeeper" and coordinate the delivery of health care services in a cost conscious manner.

Table 1 shows the types of managed care programs and the populations targeted for managed care enrollment for each state. We found that since 1982, 17 states have established PCCM programs, seven states have established partially capitated programs, and 25 states have established fully capitated programs.

INDICATIONS OF IMPROVED ACCESS, EQUAL QUALITY, UNCERTAIN COST-SAVINGS

The key reasons that states report moving to managed care in their Medicaid programs are:

1. Their frustration with rising and uncontrolled Medicaid costs;
2. Poor access to health care for their beneficiaries; and
3. Uncertain quality of care.

One key expectation is that beneficiaries will establish long-term relationships with physicians, obtain appropriate and timely health care services, and

Table 1. Type of Managed Care Program Used and Target Population, by State

State	Managed care program	Type of program(s) Fully capitated	Partially capitated	FFS PCCM	Target population(s)[a] AFDC recipients[b]	AFDC related[c]	SSI recipients[d]	SSI related[e]	Medically needy[f]	Number enrolled[g]
Alabama	•	•			•	•				15,399
Alaska										0
Arizona	•	•			•	•	•	•		365,623
Arkansas										0
California	•	•		•	•	•	•	•	•	610,000
Colorado	•	•	•	•	•	•	•	•		127,000
Connecticut										0
Delaware										0
Florida	•	•		•	•	•	•			382,000
Georgia										0
Hawaii	•	•			•	•				3,572
Idaho										0
Illinois	•	•			•					100,000
Indiana	•	•			•					733
Iowa	•	•		•	•	•				50,000
Kansas	•	•		•	•	•	•	•	•	56,000
Kentucky	•	•		•	•	•	•			303,831
Louisiana	•	•		•	•	•	•	•	•	22,560
Maine										0
Maryland	•	•		•	•	•	•		•	300,000
Massachusetts	•	•	•	•	•	•	•	•		245,000
Michigan	•	•	•	•	•	•	•			327,265

Table 1. Type of Managed Care Program Used and Target Population, by State (continued)

State	Type of program(s)				Target population(s)[a]					Number enrolled[g]
	Managed care program	Fully capitated	Partially capitated	FFS PCCM	AFDC recipients[b]	AFDC related[c]	SSI recipients[d]	SSI related[e]	Medically needy[f]	
Minnesota	•	•			•	•	•	•	•	79,516
Mississippi										0
Missouri	•	•		•	•					36,000
Montana	•	•		•	•					49,000
Nebraska										0
Nevada	•		•		•	•	•			14,000
New Hampshire	•	•			•	•				7,700
New Jersey	•		•		•	•	•	•		18,000
New Mexico	•			•	•	•	•			90,000
New York	•	•	•	•	•	•	•	•	•	158,215
North Carolina	•			•	•	•	•	•	•	57,596
North Dakota										0
Ohio	•	•			•	•	•			147,000
Oklahoma										0
Oregon	•	•	•		•	•	•			82,877
Pennsylvania	•	•			•	•	•	•	•	220,000
Rhode Island	•	•			•	•	•	•	•	1,100
South Carolina	•	•			h	h	h	h	h	240
South Dakota										0
Tennessee	•	•			•					29,645
Texas										0
Utah	•		•		•	•	•		•	126,096

Table 1. Type of Managed Care Program Used and Target Population, by State

State	Type of program(s)			Target population(s)[a]					Number enrolled[g]
	Fully capitated	Partially capitated	FFS PCCM	AFDC recipients[b]	AFDC related[c]	SSI recipients[d]	SSI related[e]	Medically needy[f]	
Vermont									0
Virginia	•		•	•	•				32,000
Washington	•			•	•				34,596
West Virginia	•		•	•	•				59,345
Wisconsin	•			•	•				117,000
Wyoming									0
Washington, D.C.	•			•	•				14,989

[a]If a state has at least one managed care provider serving some Medicaid clients within a target population, the state is identified as serving this population through its managed care programs.

[b]AFDC includes families actually receiving cash assistance.

[c]AFDC-related is a variety of groups including pregnant women and children who are not receiving cash assistance but are eligible based on family income relative to the poverty level.

[d]SSI includes the aged, blind, or disabled that are receiving cash assistance.

[e]SSI-related includes people who meet SSI requirements except that they have too much income to qualify for SSI or supplemental payments, but too little to cover their health care costs. States can set an upper level of eligibility for the groups at up to 300 percent of the SSI financial eligibility level.

[f]Medically needy includes individuals that become eligible because they have impoverished themselves due to medical expenses.

[g]State officials provided estimates of enrollment as of December 1992, January 1993, and February 1993. Officials from Alabama, Hawaii, Indiana, Missouri, New Jersey, Tennessee, Utah, Washington, and Washington, D.C., said that enrollment data reported to HCFA in June 1992 were still relatively accurate as of February 1993.

[h]Serves only mental health recipients.

ultimately achieve improved health status. In the traditional Medicaid program, eligibility is no guarantee of services because physicians often refuse to treat Medicaid beneficiaries. In our review of studies on Medicaid managed care and interviews with officials and beneficiary advocacy groups, we found that, to date, program results are showing:

- Slight improvements overall in access to care
- Improved beneficiary satisfaction, as measured by beneficiary advocacy groups, in four of the six states
- Quality of care that is the same as traditional Medicaid fee-for-service
- Cost-savings being reported by the states

Many of the evaluations of Medicaid managed care have limitations. for example, many of the data used in the evaluations are dated, coming from the HCFA demonstrations of the early and mid-1980s. Medicaid managed care evaluations, in general, focused on either capitated arrangements or PCCM. Further, evaluations of the quality of care provided to Medicaid managed care beneficiaries have focused on one medical outcome or procedure rather than a more general review of services. The current body of research on Medicaid managed care does not provide a complete picture.

Access to Care Equal or Slightly Improved

Encouragement of managed care has been based on the premise that through managed care programs beneficiaries have better access to care and that they are more apt to obtain medical services in a timely and appropriate manner than under a traditional Medicaid fee-for-service program. There is, however, some dis-agreement about how best to assess improvements in access to care. Some experts argue that access is one component of quality care, and that measuring access alone does not address whether beneficiaries improve their health. Others argue that, compared to Medicaid beneficiaries' historically difficult time in finding physicians, their ability to even make an appointment is significant.

Debate also exists about the proper measures of access. To find out if beneficiaries have access to care, studies do not generally assess the number and availability of providers in a particular service area. Instead, they employ various proxy measures that assess provider responsiveness and beneficiaries' com-pliance with managed care rules. Studies on access also typically incorporate beneficiary and advocacy satisfaction data. Although the study findings we looked at were mixed, they generally concluded that there were or can be improvements in access when using managed care models over Medicaid's traditional fee-for-service programs.

Several studies assessing access in Medicaid managed care compared beneficiaries' experiences in managed care demonstration programs with tradi-tional fee-for-service. In 1983, HCFA funded an evaluation of Medicaid demonstrations in six states—California, Florida, Minnesota, Missouri, New Jersey, and New York. The alternative delivery systems represented by the demonstrations contained a number of features—most notably capitation, case management, limitations on provider choice, and provider competition.

One study concluded that data for beneficiaries in managed care did not show any reduction in either diagnostic testing or follow-up visits for three common ambulatory problems.[1] Another reported substantial reductions in the proportion of persons with at least one emergency room visit for adults and children in the demonstrations.[2] These findings suggest that the use of a gatekeeper can alter Medicaid beneficiaries' pattern of emergency use. However, much weaker evidence of the gatekeeper effect was shown for persons with at least one visit. Finally, in a summary of findings comparing managed care demonstration sites of fee-for-service in two states,[3] access to care was perceived by beneficiaries to be greater than that of traditional fee-for-service. However, results assessing objective measures of access including waiting times for appointments, travel time, and office wait time were mixed in one state and equivalent to fee-for-service in another.

In its 1992 annual report, the Physician Payment Review Commission reviewed the effectiveness of managed care in serving Medicaid beneficiaries and other policy options for improving their access to care.[4] Based on a review of the literature and discussions with heath care experts, commission members concluded that managed care appeared to lessen emergency room use and reduce expenditures for states and the federal government. It also noted that, on balance, the evidence showed that with an enhanced quality assurance system, greater use of managed care in Medicaid could improve access to health care for beneficiaries.

Independent reviews specifically addressing access to care were performed in four of the six states we reviewed and reported mixed results. The methodology used in most of this research typically compared access to care for medicaid managed care beneficiaries with access in traditional Medicaid fee-for-service or other insurance programs.

In a 1989 report, for example, SRI International a private research group, compared access to routine care in Arizona's Health Care Cost Containment System (AHCCCS) with the New Mexico Medicaid fee-for-service program.[5] Based on a survey of beneficiary households in 1985, the report concluded that access to routine care was better in AHCCCS. The SRI report noted, however, that AHCCCS beneficiaries reported increased difficulty in receiving emergency care.

A more recent study in Arizona evaluated access to cancer screening services for women in Medicaid managed care.[6] The study concluded that poor women receiving health care through a managed care Medicaid program received Pap smears and mammograms at the same rate as women with other types of health insurance, while the uninsured were less likely to have had either type of service.

Based on a questionnaire sent to 6,000 managed care beneficiaries, a University of Kentucky researcher measured access in the state's PCCM program—The Kentucky Patient Access and Care System (KenPAC)—in terms of timeliness of care, geographic access, and refusal of care by physicians.[7] In 1991, the client questionnaire showed that access to care had been maintained or improved over beneficiaries' previous experiences with Medicaid. A 1990 report on Michigan's capitated Clinic Plan also concluded that, overall, the plans' beneficiaries were receiving a level of access to care that was equal to that provided to Medicaid fee-for-service beneficiaries.[8]

In 1992 we studied Oregon's managed care program and reported that Medicaid beneficiaries were generally satisfied with their access to medical services.[9] We reported that the Oregon Healthcare Cost Containment Advisory Committee found that some beneficiaries had difficulty adjusting to the restrictions inherent in managed care—such as more limited use of emergency rooms—but the program had received few formal complaints. We pointed out that HCFA and the Oregon Advisory Committee indicated general satisfaction with the program and the access to services it provided. This was true despite our finding that the program's capacity had been strained at times.

Finally, evidence of improved access to care came from Medicaid beneficiary advocacy groups in four of the six states we visited. Although beneficiary advocates in Arizona, Kentucky, Minnesota, and Oregon voiced some concerns about how managed care programs operated, they nonetheless had noticed a definite improvement in access to care after the programs began. On the other hand, representatives of beneficiary advocacy groups in Michigan and New York did not believe that managed care had contributed to better access.

Quality of Care Matches Traditional Fee-for-Service

Measuring the quality of managed care is an inexact and evolving process. However, national studies and those performed in the six states show some evidence that although managed care is vulnerable to undeserving beneficiaries[10] the quality of care in Medicaid managed care programs has at least equalled that provided in traditional Medicaid fee-for-service programs. Again, studies typically focus on one or two services or treatments delivered by the health care system. Researchers and Medicaid managed care experts agree that a more comprehensive set of indicators needs to be developed before conclusions on overall quality can be made.

Several studies in 1991 and 1992 compared the level of prenatal care and actual birth outcomes among pregnant women enrolled in managed care and traditional fee-for-services programs. This is a convenient proxy measurement for quality of care because managed care tends to target the AFDC population, and there is a high demand for these services among this group. In most cases, these studies found no significant difference between managed care and fee-for-service beneficiaries, and concluded that there was no decreased quality of care provided to enrollees in managed care. However, most of the studies did find that compared to non-Medicaid groups, Medicaid beneficiaries in both types of programs fared much worse.

A 1991 study of pregnancy outcomes and prenatal care among women and infants in two managed care demonstration sites—Santa Barbara, California, and Jackson County, Missouri—concluded that there was no decrease in quality of care provided to beneficiaries in capitated Medicaid programs compared with fee-for-service programs. To reach this conclusion the study reviewed frequency of prenatal visits, mean birth weight and incidence of low birth weight, complication of pregnancy and cesarean section rates, and length of pregnancy-related hospital stays.[11]

A 1992 study that looked at pregnancy outcomes and prenatal care in Washington state found that Medicaid beneficiaries enrolled in managed care used prenatal care similarly to those in Medicaid fee-for-service, and showed equal or modestly improved birth weight distributions. However, Medicaid managed care beneficiaries showed poorer use of prenatal care and birth outcomes compared with non-Medicaid enrollees in the same plan.[12] The latter finding was also reported in a 1991 study of the Philadelphia HealthPASS managed care program.[13] However, the usefulness of the HealthPASS study was limited by several factors. For example, obstetrical care was exempted from the gatekeeper requirements out of concern that this would create a barrier to care. In addition, the authors questioned whether the results of the study could be generalized because the study focused on only one site where 40 to 50 percent of West Philadelphia residents delivered their babies.

Independent studies in the six states we reviewed compared the quality of health care services being provided to Medicaid managed care beneficiaries to those enrolled in traditional fee-for-service programs. Some compared Medicaid managed care not only to other Medicaid populations but to generally accepted medical standards for all patients in the state. These studies reported no diminution in quality for managed care beneficiaries in relation to fee-for-service enrollees, although the studies of care in Minnesota and Oregon cited a need to improve some types of care, including well-child care.

An evaluation of Michigan's Physician Sponsor Plan was conducted for fiscal years 1988 to 1990.[14] The evaluation found that ambulatory care provided through the Physician Sponsor Plan was modestly superior to such care in the state's fee-for-service Medicaid program. The Physician Sponsor Plan beneficiaries had fewer cases in which established criteria for quality were not met and a higher percentage of cases that met all of the quality criteria. In 1990, a similar evaluation was released of ambulatory care in Michigan's capitated Clinic Plan.[15] The evaluation, based on 1988 data, concluded that, in essence, there appeared to be no difference in the quality of ambulatory care provided to Clinic Plan and fee-for-service beneficiaries.

The New York State Department of Social Services, Office of Audit and Quality Control, conducted evaluations of two managed care plans in Erie County, New York.[16,17] The 1991 reports concluded that the overall quality of medical care provided to Medicaid beneficiaries in the plans exceeded the care they received before enrollment. The evaluators of both plans determined that physicians participating in the plans had a higher degree of compliance with recommended examinations and procedures for well-child care and treatment protocols for sick-child visits. The evaluation of one plan showed a higher rate of preventive adult care visits and treatment protocols for common adult illnesses. The other plan did not enroll adults. Surveys of households participating in the two plans showed that 85 percent and 93 percent of the households, respectively, indicated that quality of care was equal to or better than that encountered before enrollment.

As reported in 1991, Kentucky Medicaid beneficiary and provider surveys conducted by researchers at the University of Kentucky found that the quality of care had been maintained or improved in the state's PCCM program.[18] Over 50 percent of the beneficiaries responding to the survey reported that their health care was better, and nearly 40 percent felt it was about the same. Only 5 to 6 percent felt that the quality of their health care was worse.

After evaluating Arizona's AHCCCS program, SRI International concluded in 1989 that the quality of care, while not ideal, was generally at least as good, and in some cases better, than that provided by New Mexico's traditional fee-for-service Medicaid program.[19] Care for children under AHCCCS was in greater conformance with generally accepted pediatric guidelines than was care under New Mexico's program. Compliance with recommended immunization schedules was found to be comparable to the New Mexico program, but the rates were generally below the American Association of Pediatrics national standards in both states. Pregnancy care and pregnancy outcomes were similar in the two states, except that AHCCCS had a higher cesarean section rate, a smaller number of prenatal visits, and a later initiation of prenatal care.

We reported in 1992 that Oregon's Medicaid managed care program met federal requirements for safeguarding the quality of care.[20] Oregon's Health Care Cost Containment Advisory Committee concluded that quality of care for Medicaid beneficiaries differed little from that of the general population, and advocacy group representatives we interviewed were generally satisfied with the quality of services provided under Oregon's program. Lastly, medical record reviews by the Oregon Medical Professional Review Organization identified relatively few quality problems in Oregon's managed care program, except that health screening and preventive services for children needed to be improved.

Finally, Minnesota contracted with the Joint Commission on Accreditation of Healthcare Organizations to conduct a quality assurance review in 1990.[21] The review identified a set of indicators to determine whether health plans were providing a quality of care that met community standards. The Joint Commission found that immunization levels remained low at all three childhood levels reviewed, and prenatal care and women's health care were good but incomplete. The health plans scored well in areas such as home care planning, post-surgical readmissions, and emergency room care.

However, a review of Minnesota's managed care program completed in 1992 by another independent organization, HealthPro, reached a different conclusion.[22] This study reported an overall lower level of compliance by the managed care plans with standards for all major components of care established by a panel of health practitioners. HealthPro's review included an assessment of well-baby, early and late childhood, and women's preventive, prenatal, and chemical dependency care.

Cost-Savings Reported but Still Being Debated

The results of studies on the effect of managed care on Medicaid program costs are unclear. While states report cost-savings, there are questions about how significant these savings are once all factors affecting cost are considered. Whether managed care can save money in the Medicaid program is uncertain. Nevertheless, there is evidence that managed care can result in more predictable program expenditures when capitated programs are used. This is due to the fact that once Medicaid directors know how many people are enrolled in their program, they can compute capitation rates and determine their total costs.

The body of research that has tried to evaluate managed care's effect on cost-savings in the Medicaid program has taken a variety of methodological approaches. Our review of the literature found some studies with designs that contained a control group. Other studies depended more on pre- and post-measurement. Finally, some of the studies are analyses across many independent evaluations. An attempt was made in all of these studies to control for all other factors, in order to assess the effect of managed care alone, but data and methodological limitations in evaluating these programs precluded controlling all factors that might influence cost. Finally, presented here are two types of studies—those measuring cost savings, and those measuring cost-effectiveness, by holding other factors constant.

In its 1992 annual report, the Physician Payment Review commission concluded that although research studies of Medicaid managed care temper the claims of advocates, on balance they demonstrate that managed care can often lower costs.[23] The Commission also noted that an important benefit of capitated managed care is that it makes expenditures more predictable. That is, if a plan contracts to provide all care for $150 per month, the state will never have to pay more than $150.

Testimony by the Congressional Budget Office in 1992 suggested that, of both public and private managed care programs, only staff and group model HMOs have been able to achieve significant reductions in costs per enrollee.[24] On the other hand, a 1991 analysis of previous evaluations of 25 managed care programs in 17 states concluded that managed care programs—including PCCMs—were able to achieve models cost savings.[25] Health researchers at Virginia Commonwealth University and Indiana University based their assertions on a subset of 13 programs that were judged to have the most reliable evaluations. According to their report, approximately 80 percent of the programs reported cost savings ranging from 5 to 15 percent.

The question of cost savings is made even more complex by other factors, such as favorable selection,[26] that could affect program expenditures. In 1992, the Rand Corporation conducted an evaluation of the cost and use of capitated medical services in state programs.[27] Researchers compared Medicaid HMO programs in New York and Florida and found very different results. In analyzing the effect on costs, Rand concluded that HMO-type plans can save money but these savings may be the result of patient mix rather than efficient program management. Florida's program attracted many of the sicker poor and thus saved money with a capitated payment system. New York, on the other hand, had difficulty convincing beneficiaries to enroll in managed care and those who did were healthier than those who remained in the fee-for-service system. New York spent more on these beneficiaries than it would have under fee-for-service because their medical needs were relatively low. The potential for cost savings in the long term may depend on whether the states can anticipate such selection activity and adjust capitation levels accordingly.

Studies we obtained of Medicaid managed care programs and specific plans in the six states generally show them to be cost-effective.[28] However, some health care experts acknowledged that there are data limitations that impair their ability to measure and compare costs. Despite these problems, some Medicaid officials believe their managed care programs have achieved cost-savings compared to fee-for-service programs. The officials generally attributed the savings to effective management of care by providers and, in particular, to reductions in the inappropriate use of emergency rooms and prescription drugs.

In 1991, HCFA reported $227 million is projected two-year cost-savings from states operating Medicaid managed care programs with 1915(b)(1) waivers. In November 1992, a HCFA official provided us with a revised two-year savings projection totaling about $326 million.[29] The six states we visited commissioned independent evaluations of some of their programs, and all reported substantial cost savings.

In Arizona, SRI International reported that the cost of the AHCCCS program (excluding administrative costs) during its first five years averaged 6 percent less than what a fee-for-service Medicaid program would have cost.[30] Evaluations of two Medicaid managed care programs in Erie County, New York, reported that the programs were less costly than an actuarial equivalent fee-for-service program would have been.[31] A cost analysis of both programs concluded that there were substantial savings in the areas of inpatient hospitalization, outpatient clinic care, physician services, pharmaceutical services, and emergency room services.

Two studies in Kentucky also concluded that Medicaid managed care saved money. Estimates of the cost savings differed significantly because the two studies assumed different population estimates and utilization rates when calculating the savings. One study estimated that the program saved $125 to $150 million annually,[32] while the other estimated that the program saved $13 million in 1987 and would save $93 million in 1994.[33]

Evaluations by an independent actuarial firm found Oregon's Medicaid managed care program to be cost-effective.[34] An October 1991 evaluation concluded that from October 1988 through September 1990, the program had saved about $8.7 million, or $8.78 per enrollee per month, when compared with the estimated costs of health care under traditional Medicaid fee-for-service.

An evaluation of one of Michigan's managed care plans—the Physician Sponsor Plan—determined that the combined cost savings for Aid for Families with Dependent Children (AFDC) and SSI recipients in fiscal year 1989-90 was $24.2 million, or 17.5 percent of the combined expected Medicaid fee-for-service expenses.[35] After deducting nonmedical expenses (management fees and administrative costs), the net savings was $20.2 million, or 14.6 percent of the expected fee-for service medical expenses. An evaluation of Michigan's Capitated Clinic Plan calculated medical expense savings of $1.1 million for 1988.[36] After deducting incentive and administrative costs of the plan, the net savings was $767,001, or 15.2 percent of expected costs for the plan's beneficiaries.

Finally, Minnesota examined the cost experience of its Medicaid managed care programs and estimated cost savings.[37] The resulting study estimated that the state's Prepaid Medicaid Demonstration Project saved $13.7 million in the three-year period from 1987 through 1989. Estimated savings for the AFDC Voluntary Program was slightly more than $400,000 in 1989.

1. Timothy Carey and Kathi Weis, "Diagnostic Testing and Return Visits for Acute Problems in Prepaid Case-Managed Medicaid Plans Compared With Fee-for-Service," *Archives of Internal Medicine,* Vol. 150, No. 11, 1990, pp 2369–72.

2. Robert Hurley, Deborah Freund, and Donald Taylor, "Emergency Room Use and Primary Care Case Management: Evidence From Four Medicaid Demonstration Programs," *American Journal of Public Health,* Vol. 79, No. 7, 1989, pp. 843–46.

3. Freund, Rossiter, Fox, Meyer, Hurley, Carye, and Paul, "Evaluation of the Medicaid Competition Demonstrations," *Health Care Financing Review,* Vol. II, No. 2, Winter 1989, pp. 81–97.

4. *Annual Report to the Congress,* Physician Payment Review Commission, 1992.

5. *Evaluation of the Arizona Health Care Cost Containment System: Final Report,* SRI International, January 1989. To assess access to care, SRI International conducted a survey of 897 AHCCCS, AFDC, and SSI

clients in Arizona and 553 Medicaid fee-for-service clients in New Mexico who had been enrolled at least 12 months as of March 1985. The sample in Arizona was selected based on zip code, AHCCCS enrollment age, urbanicity, and race. A comparable sample was selected for New Mexico. Results were weighted based on response rates of the sample groups and the characteristics of those sampled.

6. Bradford Kirkman-Liff and Jennie Kronenfeld, "Access to Cancer Screening Services for Women," *American Journal of Public Health,* Vol. 82, No. 5, 1992, pp. 733–735.

7. Joyce Beaulieu, *Evaluation of KenPAC III: Final Report,* November 29, 1991. To measure quality, a questionnaire was mailed to over 6,000 KenPAC clients, and follow-up questionnaires were sent to assure an acceptable response rate. Of the 6,000 questionnaires mailed out, 44.5 percent were returned and entered into the data base, 3.5 percent were returned not completed, and 52 percent were not returned. Primary care physicians were also surveyed about the quality of care provided through KenPAC, with questionnaires mailed to all 1,530 participating physicians. The response rate was 28 percent, with 428 completed questionnaires received.

8. *An Evaluation of the Cost Effectiveness, Access to Care, and Quality of Care of the Capitated Clinic Plan of the Michigan Medicaid Program,* Health Management Associates, Michigan Peer Review Organization, and Gini Associates, September 1990. This report was prepared for the Medical Services Administration of the Michigan Department of Social Services. Access to care was evaluated in five ways: (1) the plan's utilization rates were compared to available utilization measures for HMOs and for the state's other Medicaid managed care plan—Physician Sponsor Plan; (2) data on the number of physicians and their specialties serving the plan's clients was collected and analyzed; (3) the average waiting times for various types of physician appointments was determined and compared to Medicaid fee-for-service clients; (4) the number of clients leaving the plan but still retaining their Medicaid eligibility was compared to the disenrollment rates for three other groups of Medicaid clients (fee-for-service, HMO, and the Physician Sponsor Plan); and (5) the complaint process and complaint history at each of the plan's clinics was examined.

9. *Medicaid: Oregon's Managed Care Program and Implications for Expansions* (GAO/HRD-92-89, June 19, 1992).

10. An incentive to underserve can occur when providers in capitated programs agree to deliver or arrange for all service needed by enrolled individuals in exchange for the per-capita payments. Providers are liable for the difference when the cost of services to all enrolled recipients is greater than the total payments received. Conversely, providers retain the difference when the cost of services is lower than the amount received as capitation payments.

11. Timothy Carey, Kathi Weis, and Charles Homer, "Prepaid Versus Traditional Medicaid Plans: Lack of Affect on Pregnancy Outcomes and Prenatal Care," *Health Services Research,* Vol. 26, No. 2, 1991, pp. 165–181.

12. James Krieger, Frederick Connell, and James LoGerfo, "Medicaid Prenatal Care: A Comparison of Use and Outcomes in Fee-for-Service and Managed Care," *American Journal of Public Health,* Vol. 82, No. 2, 1992, pp. 185–90.

13. Neil Goldfarb, Alan Hillman, John Eisenberg, Mark Kelley, Arnold Cohen, and Miriam Delheim, "Impact of a Mandatory Medicaid Case Management Program on Prenatal Care on Birth Outcomes," *Medicaid Care,* Vol. 29, No. 1, 1991, pp. 64–71.

14. *Evaluation of the Michigan Medicaid Program's Physician Sponsor Plan, FY 1988-1990,* Health Management Associates, Michigan Peer Review Organization, and Gini Associates, February 1992. This report was prepaid for the Medical Services Administration of the Michigan Department of Social Services. The basic method used to assess quality of care was to choose a set of criteria with which to measure quality and then apply these criteria to care provided to groups of beneficiaries in the Physician Sponsor Plan and fee-for-service program. Thirty physicians were selected per plan. For each selected physician, a random sample of five beneficiaries was drawn. The sampling procedure was performed twice—once for the Physician Sponsor Plan physicians and once for fee-for-service physicians. If a physician had both Physician Sponsor Plan and fee-for-service beneficiaries, the physician could appear in both samples. An

on-site ambulatory care record review was then conducted for each of the 300 beneficiaries (150 Physician Sponsor Plan and 150 fee-for-service beneficiaries).

15. *Evaluation of Michigan Medicaid's Clinic Plan.* A sample of patients who had three or more physician visits during 1988 was selected from both the capitated Clinic Plan and the fee-for-service program. Once the sample was drawn, ambulatory records were reviewed by trained nurse reviewers who applied a generic protocol that can be used to assess ambulatory encounters. The records were reviewed to determine whether the physicians followed appropriate processes in providing care. In addition, for two types of medical encounters—well-baby care and prenatal care—more detailed review criteria were used to assess quality. When an obstetric hospitalization occurred in 1988, the hospital record was also examined. Diagnostic-specific criteria were applied to the entire hospital episode.

16. *Erie County Department of Social Service's Physician Case Management Program I, Compliance Review of the Freedom of Choice Waiver Requirements Issued by the Health Care Financing Administration of the United States Department of Health and Human Services,* New York State Department of Social Services, March 1991. This study analyzed the quality of care for 32 beneficiaries who were in the program at least 6 months and had at least one medical encounter with their primary care physician. Additionally, medical records for 13 of the 32 beneficiaries were reviewed for care they had received before enrollment to establish a quality of care comparison.

17. *Erie County Department of Social Services, Physician Case Management Program I, Compliance Review of the Freedom of Choice Waiver Requirements Issued by the Health Care Financing Administration of the United States Department of Health and Human Services,* New York State Department of Social Services, March 1991. This study analyzed the quality of care for 37 beneficiaries who were in the program at least 6 months and had at least one medical encounter with their primary care physician. Additionally, medical records for 13 of the 37 beneficiaries were reviewed for care they had received before enrollment.

18. Beaulieu, *Evaluation of KenPac III: Final Report,* supra note 7.

19. *Evaluation of the Arizona Health Care Cost Containment System: Final Report,* SRI International, January 1989. To assess the quality of care received through AHCCCS, researchers from SRI evaluated four conditions: (1) prenatal care, (2) pregnancy outcomes, (3) well-child care, and (4) treatment of otitis media. These conditions frequently occur among the study population. Researchers compared outcomes for the AHCCCS population with outcomes for a comparable population in New Mexico that received care through a Medicaid fee-for-service program. Data were collected from outpatient and inpatient medical records for 738 AHCCCS recipients and 730 New Mexico Medicaid clients; 445 children in each state with primary care utilization between July 1986 and April 1987; and 293 women in the AHCCCS program and 285 women in New Mexico's Medicaid program with pregnancy outcomes between November 1985 and April 1987 and with at least 9 months of continuous AHCCCS enrollment or New Mexico Medicaid eligibility.

20. *Medicaid: Oregon's Managed Care Program and Implications for Expansions* (GAO/HRD-92-89, June 19, 1992). As part of the evaluation, we contracted with a group of physicians from the George Washington University to validate Oregon's independent medical record review process performed by the Oregon Medical Professional Review Organization. The consulting physicians used the peer review organization's criteria and process to review a sample of the records the peer review organization reviewed in 1990. A proportional random sample of about 10 percent of the records the peer review organization reviewed was selected.

21. The Minnesota Department of Human Services contracted with the Joint Commission on Accreditation of Healthcare Organizations to conduct a 1989 quality assurance review of its managed care program. The review is discussed in a report issued by the Department of Human Services in March 1991, *Minnesota Medicaid Interim Report.* As part of the review, the Joint Commission conducted a review of medical records to determine if care was being provided by health plans in a manner that met community standards. The conditions of interest reviewed were: prenatal care, well-baby care (birth through 11 months), well-baby care (12 months through 4 years), late childhood care, otitis media, chemical dependency, home care, preventive health care, women's health care, surgical readmission within 30 days of discharge, and use of emergency services. The Joint Commission's 1989 quality assurance review was completed in June 1990.

22. *State of Minnesota Prepaid Health Plans Review of Quality Health Care,* HealthPro, February 15, 1992.

23. *Annual Report to the Congress,* Physician Payment Review Commission, 1992.

24. Statement of Robert D. Reischauer, Director, Congressional Budget Office, before the Committee on Ways and Means, U.S. House of Representatives, March 4, 1992. According to this statement, less structured managed care organizations had little or no effect on health care spending. The Congressional Budget Office concluded that staff model HMOs and fully integrated group model HMOs can reduce hospital use by 15 to 20 percent, which in turn can lower total health spending for their clients by perhaps 10 to 15 percent. Other forms of managed care had been found to have an effect ranging from no impact to 8 percent reduction in hospital use.

25. Robert E. Hurley and Deborah A. Freund, *Primary Care Case Management Evidence From Medicaid: Synthesizing Program Effects by Program Designs,* 1991.

26. Favorable selection means that healthier people who are less expensive to care for enroll in the HMO, while sicker people do not.

27. Joan Buchanan, Arleen Leibowitz, Joan Keesey, Joyce Mann, and Ceryl Damberg, *Cost and Use of Capitated Medical Services: Evaluation of the Program for Prepaid Managed Health Care,* The Rand Corporation, Santa Monica, Calif., 1992.

28. In the context of this discussion cost-effective means that managed care programs spent less money than would have been spent on the same population for the same services under the traditional fee-for-service program.

29. HCFA computed these savings by totaling individual state 2-year projected savings reported for operating 1915(b)(1)-waiver managed care programs as compared against the estimated costs for traditional fee-for-service. However, while each state waiver program covers a 2-year period, the periods vary.

30. *Evaluation of AHCCCS.* Cost-savings were calculated as the difference between the actual incurred costs and the estimated cost of a fee-for-service, Medicaid program in Arizona. The cost of a fee-for-service program was estimated by calculating the per-capita costs of Medicaid programs in several states and adjusting the costs for differences, ineligibility, and geography. The comparison states were chosen based on the quality of cost and eligibility date kept in these states and the similarity of the Medicaid programs in these states to the AHCCCS program in Arizona. Administrative costs were not included in this analysis because the comparison was considered unreliable. The study noted that it may be difficult to compare Arizona to states that have more than 20 years of experience operating Medicaid programs because Arizona had only 5 years of experience with the AHCCCS program and management of the program was changed from a private administrator to a state agency.

31. *Erie County Physician Case Management Compliance Review Program I; Erie County Department of Social Services, Physician Case Management Program II, Compliance Review of the Freedom of Choice Waiver Requirements Issued by the Health Care Financing Administration of the United States Department of Health and Human Services,* New York State Department of Social Services, March 1991. To measure cost-effectiveness, researchers in both studies compared 1 year of medical costs for Physician Case Management Program beneficiaries. For these comparisons 100 participating Program I, 100 participating Program II, 100 nonparticipating Program I, and 50 nonparticipating Program II beneficiaries were randomly selected. Eighteen beneficiaries from the nonparticipating group were eliminated from the Program I evaluation because they were found to have participated in case management.

32. Beaulieu, *Evaluation of KenPac III: Final Report,* supra note 7. Savings were based on projected changes in utilization patterns due to the KenPAC program. Units of service were multiplied by cost per unit of service, adjusted for inflation, and the estimated number of people eligible for KenPAC. Gross savings were adjusted to take into account the administrative costs of running the KenPAC program.

33. *Request for Waiver Extension Under Section 1915(b)(1) of the Social Security Act,* Commonwealth of Kentucky, Kentucky Patient Access and Care System, October 29, 1991. To determine cost-effectiveness, the research considered (1) the growth in client population, (2) the cost per eligible and utilizing client, and (3) the units of service utilized per client. The estimated cost-savings were based on the difference

between the projected number of units of service utilized under KenPAC and the projected number that would have been utilized without KenPAC. Administrative costs and management fees were also considered in determining net savings.

34. Evaluations of cost-effectiveness, necessitated by HCFA requirements for waiver renewal, were performed by Coopers and Lybrand. The most recent evaluation, *Cost-Effectiveness Analysis for the PCO (Physician Care Organizations) Program for the Period October 1988 through September 1990*, is dated October 17, 1991. The cost-effectiveness of Oregon's physician care organizations was measured as the difference between providing services on a fee-for-service basis and the costs of the prepaid program's administration plus capitation and incentive payments for the physician care organizations. The costs of inpatient and outpatient maternity services were excluded from the calculation because pregnant women who are in their third trimester of pregnancy when they become eligible for Medicaid have the option of continuing to receive services on a fee-for-service basis.

35. *Evaluation of the Michigan Medicaid Program's Physician Sponsor Plan.* The basic methodology for the analysis of AFDC cost-effectiveness was to compare the cost experience of a sample of Medicaid clients enrolled in the Physician Sponsor Plan to the cost experience of a sample of Medicaid clients who were enrolled in the traditional fee-for-service program. The study period covered services provided between October 1, 1989 and September 30, 1990. The total actual cost for Physician Sponsor Plan's AFDC beneficiaries was calculated by summing the costs of medical services, administrative costs, and monthly management fees. In the cost-effectiveness analysis of the Physician Sponsor Plan SSI population, a different design was used because the health status differences between the Physician Sponsor Plan and fee-for-service populations were so great. A methodology was employed using a longitudinal sample to measure the effect on medical costs of the Physician Sponsor Plan program. This methodology compared the change in costs over a 2-year period for a sample of Physician sponsor Plan SSI beneficiaries and a sample of fee-for-service SSI beneficiaries. In choosing the AFDC and SSI samples, only persons who were Medicaid eligible and enrolled in either the Physician Sponsor Plan or fee-for-service programs for at least 6 months were selected. In addition, only those persons receiving some medical services during the study period were selected.

36. *Evaluation of the Michigan Medicaid Clinic Plan.* The evaluation of basic cost-effectiveness was performed by comparing the actual costs incurred by the plan's clients in calendar year 1988 with the 1988 expected costs for a similar group of clients in the fee-for-service market. The actual costs for the plan's clients were calculated by summing actual capitation payments, actual inpatient costs, actual inpatient bonus payments, administrative costs, system modification costs, and marketing incentive costs for 1988.

37. *Minnesota Prepaid Medicaid Programs: Analysis of Cost Savings, Calendar Years 1987-1989,* prepared by the Minnesota Department of Human Services, April 1991. A fee-for-service comparison group was used to estimate cost savings. The Minnesota fee-for-service program has some managed care components, but the Minnesota Department of Human Services considers the comparison group to be the most accurate measure of the success of Minnesota's prepaid health plans. It is the Department's goal to compare prepaid programs with the state's current fee-for-service delivery system, and the fee-for-service experience is the standard federal measure of prepaid program savings.

Part 2

MANAGED CARE

6.   Managed Care: The Solution or the Problem?

George W. Rimler   Richard D. Morrison

Managed care is widely touted as a solution to many of the problems of health care access, quality, and cost containment, but less often discussed are the problems associated with it. An emphasis on managed care may help provide medical services to more people, but not without constraining the traditional relationship between patient and provider.

Managed care is a term in common use—but often used imprecisely—to refer to forms of health-benefits coverage and health-service delivery that are alternatives to traditional fee-for-service medicine. These alternatives range from delivery systems, such as health maintenance organizations (HMOs) and preferred provider organizations (PPOs), to utilization review procedures exercised by payers, insurers, or providers, to hybrid forms of insurance, service delivery, and utilization management.

The exact meaning of the term depends largely on the context in which it is used, and frequently on the interests of those who use it; use of the term is seldom value-neutral. Those who coined the concepts of managed care apparently believed that it could be an effective remedy for the feverish rise in health-care costs. Others came to see it as an anathema to the highly prized physician-patient relationship. If a true definition of "managed care" is to emerge, it will likely be found somewhere between these extremes. There is no doubt, however, that managed care dramatically modifies the traditional fee-for-service, free-enterprise approach to medical care.

Some alternative definitions of managed health care can be found in Exhibit 1.

Exhibit 1. Alternative Definitions of Managed Health Care

Managed care is a comprehensive approach to health-care delivery that encompasses planning, education, monitoring, coordinating, and controlling quality, access, and cost, considering the interests of patients, providers, and payors. *(American Managed Care and Review Association)*

Managed care [is defined as] systems or techniques generally used by third-party payers expressly to provide what they consider an appropriate mix of medical and social services at the lowest cost to payors and patients. *(American Medical Association)*

Managed care is a coordinated approach to design, financing, and delivery of health care, which balances price and utilization controls with access to high-quality care. A managed care program combines these essential elements:
- Limited access to providers (physicians and hospitals)
- Utilization controls
- Quality of care controls. *(Blue Cross of Virginia)*

[*Managed care* involves] a variety of interventions of health-care delivery and financing intended to eliminate unnecessary and inappropriate care and to reduce cost. These include reviewing and intervening in decisions about health services to be provided, either prospectively or retrospectively; limiting or influencing patients' choice of providers; and negotiating different payment terms or levels with providers. *(Congressional Budget Office)*

[*Managed care* involves] systems that integrate the financing and delivery of appropriate health-care services to covered individuals through the use of four elements: arrangements with selected providers to furnish a comprehensive set of health-care services to members; explicit standards for choosing providers; formal programs for ongoing quality assurance and utilization review; and significant financial incentives for members to use the plans' providers and procedures. *(Health Insurance Association of America)*

Managed care is a set of techniques used by or on behalf of purchasers of health benefits to manage health-care costs by influencing patient care decision making through case-by-case assessment of the appropriateness of care prior to its provision. *(Institute of Medicine/National Academy of Science)*

Managed health care is a coordinating strategy of a variety of organizational structures and procedures to direct patients to appropriate, effective, and efficient providers of care. *(Virginia Department of Medical Assistance Services)*

Managed health care consists of procedures, processes, and organizational forms that constrain the health-care decisions of patients and health-care providers designed to reduce overall health-care costs while concurrently assuring (1) that the patient has access to quality health care, (2) that the appropriate level of care is available to the patient, and (3) that the patient receives a continuum of care appropriate for his or her medical condition. *(Virginia Hospital Association)*

With great speed and relatively little public awareness, a significant change has occurred in the way some decisions are made about a patient's medical care. Many decisions . . . once the exclusive province of the doctor and patient now may be examined in advance by an external reviewer. *(National Academy of Sciences–Institute of Medicine)*

MANAGED CARE AND COST CONTAINMENT

The increasing emphasis on managed care leads to some significant ethical considerations. In an attempt to increase the availability of a basic and necessary service (medical care), certain constraints are placed on the traditional patient/provider relationship. Does the potential for good (more individuals able to obtain care) outweigh the potential negative consequences?

In the brief time since the emergence of managed care, public policy concerns have simultaneously broadened to include all aspects of managed care and narrowed to focus on the role of government in balancing cost-containment imperatives with consideration of issues related to the protection of the public health, safety, and welfare. These concerns reflect anxiety on the part of the public, health-care professionals, and health-care policy makers as all aspects of health care come increasingly under greater scrutiny, influence, and control by external and often remote "third parties."

House Joint Resolution No. 399 of the 1991 Session of the Virginia General Assembly reflected these concerns in a request for a study of the ethics of managed health care. It asked the Board of Health Professions to conduct the study and to report its findings and policy proposals to the Commission on Health Care for all Virginians for inclusion in the Commission's report to the 1992 session of the General Assembly. The task force held public hearings and received comments from more than 50 advisory groups.

Does managed care add to the efficiency of market utilization by improving the free market allocation process, or is managed care merely another intrusion into market economics? What are the public policy concerns with, and consequences of, the growth of managed care? These questions do not lend themselves to simplistic, black-and-white answers. This article attempts to provide insight into these issues on the basis of literature review, public testimony, and primary and secondary data.

THE REAL NEED FOR COST CONTAINMENT

Expenditures on health care in the United States are approaching 13 percent of gross national product. Health insurance premiums are increasing at a double digit annual rate, and, according to some estimates, employers may well be paying more than $20,000 per employee for health insurance by the decade's end. These are cold numbers based on real, concrete, documented facts. But is this the real cost?

The real cost, in our opinion, is the chilling effect this outrageous expenditure has on initiative as it transfers dollars to the health-care segment of our society. Anybody with a calculator can determine the dollar amount of the cost, and basic unimaginative data compilation reveals that more jobs were created in the health-care industry than were lost in the construction industry during the past three years. These are the hard data that are recognized. Yet the real cost is frequently understated.

Every day people propose well-thought-out, well-researched, well-documented business plans, and are ready to start their own enterprises. The risk is formidable but probably manageable. Self-employment is, after all, the American dream. The data reveal that small firms have provided most (upward of 85 percent) of the private job growth in the United States in the last few years. While large firms were restructuring, cutting, downsizing, and moving overseas, small firms have stabilized the economy. The fact is that the *Fortune 500* keep cutting jobs in the United States while the small firms have taken up the slack.

It is, however, very intimidating for prospective entrepreneurs to venture forth when they are confronted with the mammoth cost of providing medical insurance for themselves and potential employees.

Increasingly large companies have become more sanguine in their views about national health insurance because they realize that the present situation puts them at a major disadvantage in competition with their overseas counterparts. Automobile companies claim that their entire domestic manufacturing cost disadvantage is related to health-insurance costs. The failed efforts to contain costs and the adverse effect of those costs on U.S. industry have resulted in businesses, in the words of Lee Iacocca, "not just whispering, but talking out loud about making health-care financing a government responsibility." But how does one measure the cost of not starting an enterprise because of the fear of exorbitant health-insurance costs? How much investment in people, new products, and machinery is forgone on this basis? How much strife is generated between labor and management, and how much teamwork is negated as individuals in an organization jockey to see who will pay for ever-increasing health costs?

The real cost of the medical cost mess is the stifling of initiative, ingenuity, and risk taking—the very things we need more of. No charts, graphs, or expert opinion can measure what might have been. Can managed care help remedy the situation?

BACKGROUND

The Historic Context of Managed Health Care

At least a part of the anxiety many Americans feel about their health care results from a growing disparity between their expectations and the willingness of government, insurers, and employers to pay for health-care services that they, as payers, believe to be inefficient, unnecessary, overpriced, or inappropriate.

The great majority of those Americans who are fortunate enough to have access to health-care services obtain their benefits from private sources—

primarily from health-insurance benefits paid for wholly or in large part by employers—or from programs funded by federal, state, or local governments. Very few pay for health care out-of-pocket, and as a result, the cost of health care remained "hidden" to the general public until very recent times.

Widespread health-care benefits coverage in the United States first took root in the early 1950s. Before and immediately after World War II, health-benefits coverage was limited to isolated pockets of the population. During this early period, those who could pay for care did so, while those who could not were usually assisted through religious or secular philanthropy, or simply did without.

The supply capacity of the health-care system was substantially expanded following World War II. With the enactment of the Hill Burton Act, Congress provided federal funds to assist hospital construction projects throughout the country. Many federal, state, and local programs directly and indirectly subsidized the educational expenses of health-care practitioners, substantially increasing the size of the health-care workforce.

As dramatic as these developments may have been, the most rapid period of growth in the availability and distribution of health benefits had yet to come. During the 1960s, Medicare, which guaranteed health benefits to the elderly, was passed and unions bargained for, and usually got, employer-sponsored medical benefits. As health-care benefits coverage became more widespread, a new awareness of the gap between the rich entitlement of the employer and the meager or nonexistent benefits available to those who, at no personal fault, were unemployed, underemployed, or in some way disenfranchised, developed. Medicaid, the jointly funded federal and state program to provide medical assistance to the indigent, was the response to that disparity.

The early 1970s witnessed a continuation of governmental initiatives to expand health benefits coverage. Medicare benefits were made available to greater numbers of Americans in 1972 by amendments that extended coverage to individuals with end-stage renal disease and permanent physical disabilities. Along with continued expansion of program benefits and eligibility, however, came the concomitant implementation of various cost-control measures. Following the inflationary economy of the early post-Vietnam period, Congress and the executive branch began to organize serious efforts to contain and control health-care expenditures. By the 1980s, because of the inexorable rise in health-care costs, the earlier social policy objective of expanding access to health-care services was reversed. Shifts in the political climate and the need to remain competitive in a world economy created new constituencies for aggressive public and private efforts to contain costs. Meanwhile the use of appropriate access and care came to be known as "managed health care."

Government health benefits continue to lead the way in cost containment during the 1990s. Medicare is preparing to implement a revolutionary change in the way that physicians' services are compensated. The change in focus from control of hospital costs to control of outpatient service costs results from recognition that many services previously provided in inpatient settings are now provided on an ambulatory basis. A slowing in the rate of increase in the cost of inpatient services was accompanied by rapid increases in payments for outpatient physician services and prescription drugs.

Utilization review (UR) has become a common component of most health-benefit systems, whether public or private. Virtually all payers have incorporated UR activities into the claims payment process. Precertification activities (that is, requirements to obtain approval or authorization from an insurer for admission or initiation of treatment) appear to be the most common form of utilization review. Concurrent and retrospective review, however, have also become increasingly frequent parts of the utilization review effort. A comprehensive overview of the managed care continuum is shown in Exhibit 2.

CONSEQUENCES OF MANAGED CARE

Effects on Cost

The most credible of contemporary assessments of the effects of one set of managed-care techniques—utilization review—is the study of cost control and change in patient care published by the National Academy of Sciences Institute of Medicine in 1989.[1] That review of the empirical and conceptual policy literature found the following relationship between utilization management and the use, and consequent cost, of health care.

- Utilization management has helped to reduce inpatient hospital use, measured by a decrease in hospital inpatient days ranging from 5 percent to 15 percent. This reduction is beyond what could be expected from such other factors as growth in outpatient resources, changes in benefit plan design, and shifts in methods for paying hospitals.
- Employee groups with higher initial levels of hospital use tend to show more change than do groups with lower initial hospital utilization.
- The impact of utilization management on net benefits cost is less clear. Savings on inpatient care have been partially offset by increased spending for outpatient care and program administration. Some of this offset is an expected result of utilization management, and some is an unwanted consequence of moving care to outpatient settings where fewer controls on use and price now operate.
- Although it probably has reduced levels of expenditure for some purchases, utilization management does not appear to have altered the long-term rate of increase in health-care costs. Employers who saw a short-term moderation in benefit expenditures are seeing a return to previous trends.

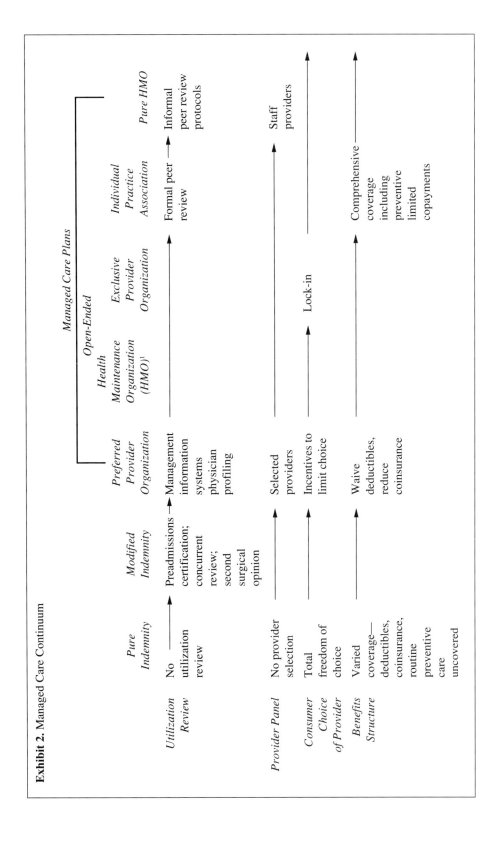

Exhibit 2. Managed Care Continuum

	Pure Indemnity	Modified Indemnity	Preferred Provider Organization	Managed Care Plans Open-Ended Health Maintenance Organization (HMO)[1]	Exclusive Provider Organization	Individual Practice Association	Pure HMO
Utilization Review	No utilization review	Preadmissions certification; concurrent review; second surgical opinion	Management information systems physician profiling			Formal peer review	Informal peer review protocols
Provider Panel	No provider selection		Selected providers				Staff providers
Consumer Choice of Provider	Total freedom of choice		Incentives to limit choice		Lock-in		
Benefits Structure	Varied coverage— deductibles, coinsurance, routine preventive care uncovered		Waive deductibles, reduce coinsurance			Comprehensive coverage including preventive limited copayments	

Exhibit 2. Managed Care Continuum *(continued)*

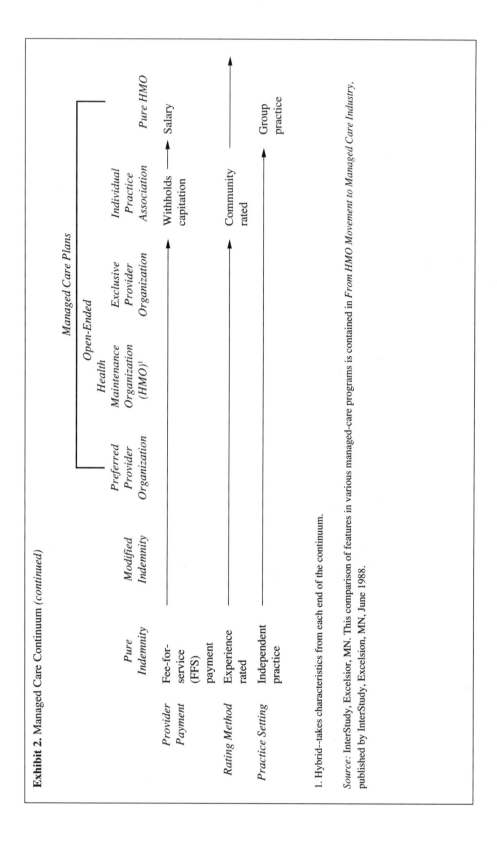

	Pure Indemnity	Modified Indemnity	Preferred Provider Organization	Health Maintenance Organization (HMO)[1]	Exclusive Provider Organization	Individual Practice Association	Pure HMO
				Open-Ended			
				Managed Care Plans			
Provider Payment	Fee-for-service (FFS) payment					Withholds → Salary capitation	
Rating Method	Experience rated					Community rated	
Practice Setting	Independent practice						Group practice

1. Hybrid—takes characteristics from each end of the continuum.

Source: InterStudy, Excelsior, MN. This comparison of features in various managed-care programs is contained in *From HMO Movement to Managed Care Industry,* published by InterStudy, Excelsion, MN, June 1988.

Exhibit 3. Accessibility to Care

Blue Cross and Blue Shield of Virginia Utilization Review Data
January 1—December 31, 1990[1]

Inpatient Admission Requests (109,844)

02.2%	of admission requests denied.
06.5%	of denied admission requests appealed.
00.0%	of denied admission requests overturned on appeal.

Continued Length of Stay Requests (456,651)

00.9%	of continued stay requests denied.
28.0%	of denied continued stay requests appealed.
04.6%	of denied continued stay requests overturned on appeal.

Medicare Precertification Review Data
April 1, 1990–March 31, 1991[2]

Procedure	Authorized	Denied
Carotid endarterectomy	1,004	0
Cataract surgery	22,778	11
Cholecystectomy	2,896	2
Coronary bypass with graft	2,897	0
Hysterectomy	1,247	0
Inguinal hernia repair	2,906	0
Laminectomy	673	0
Major joint replacement	4,235	0
Percutaneous angioplasty	1,888	0
Prostatectomy	4,330	0
	44,854	13 (0.03%)

Champus Precertification Review Data
April 1, 1990–March 31, 1991[3]

Procedure	Authorized	Denied
Bronchitis/Asthma	231	0
Cardiac catheterization	354	1
Carotid endarterectomy	12	0
Cesarean section	797	1
Cholecystectomy	194	0
Coronary bypass with graft	136	0
Hysterectomy	349	1
Gastritis	132	0
Percutaneous angioplasty	143	0
	2,496	3(0.12%)

Medicare Inpatient Review Data
April 1, 1990–March 31, 1991[4]

Cases with Completed Reviews (3,589)

0.3%	of cases found to have confirmed quality problems.
0.3%	of cases denied on the basis of utilization and necessity.

Footnotes:

1. Blue Cross/Blue Shield of Virginia submission to Virginia Board of Health Professions. Summer 1991. Richmond, Virginia.

2. Medical Society of Virginia Review Organization Reports, Vol. 7, No. 3, May 1991, p. 8.

3. Medical Society of Virginia Review Organization. Summer 1991. Richmond, Virginia.

4. Medical Society of Virginia Review Organization. Summer 1991. Richmond, Virginia.

Effects on Quality

The same Institute of Medicine (IOM) study concluded that systematic evidence about the impact of utilization management on the quality of care and on patient and provider costs is virtually nonexistent.

In the current review, the task force sought evidence of either higher or lower quality of care associated with managed-care techniques and systems. As in the IOM review, no evidence was found of a systematic relationship between managed care and quality of care. Nonetheless, the current study robustly confirmed the following observations in the IOM report:

1. The process of utilization management and associated changes in course of treatment cause anxiety among and inconvenience to some patients.
2. Utilization management adds to the administrative burden of practitioners and institutional providers and contributes to resentment about reduced professional autonomy and satisfaction.

Effects on Access

"Patient satisfaction" may not be a completely valid measure of access to health care, but most of the concerns consumers expressed were related to problems of access and choice. (See Exhibit 3.)

With respect to patient satisfaction with access, the task force reviewed convincing but conflicting evidence from both industry studies, and testimony and written comment from providers and enrollees. In addition, the task force considered the possibility that managed care—while it may not jeopardize quality and access for enrollees—may be a contributing force in transferring or shifting risk from the private to the public sector. Without question, managed care has shifted some risks and costs to employers and to patients.

While the preponderant evidence confirms that the average enrollee, with average health-care needs and use, is largely satisfied with managed health-care systems and benefits, the same cannot be said of a substantial group of consumers whose needs or choices lie outside the "average" range.

Two types of complaints occurred frequently in testimony and written comments submitted to the task force. First, enrollees complained of their inability to access specific types of providers, either because contract provisions did not provide for the reimbursement, or because the practice ideologies of primary care "gatekeepers" prevented access. For example, contract provisions often prevent direct access to the services of dental hygienists, physical therapists, or such specialists as dermatologists without referral from a primary care gatekeeper. A more frequent concern was that—although contracts often provide for their use—access to chiropractic care was effectively foreclosed by either the primary care physician gatekeepers or by utilization review agents who discriminated against chiropractic care.

Second, a more prevalent source of consumer and provider concern was the limitation of benefits for the treatment of psychiatric illness, emotional disorder or distress, and substance abuse. Dissatisfied enrollees and providers complained that a "benefits backlash" against the surge of costs that followed the inclusion of mental health and substance abuse service in benefits plans prevented those with legitimate needs for continued treatment from accessing that treatment. (See the sidebar for a discussion of the state of the art in mental health.)

Parallel concerns were expressed for inadequate coverage for extended needs for physical rehabilitative treatment for enrollees with disabilities, or for the special needs of those with catastrophic illnesses.

These and other concerns expressed to the task force call attention to the important distinction between *contractual* and *managed* care issues. Much of the discontent with the completeness or other facets of managed health-care benefits coverage is not directly or solely connected to managed care.

Health benefits are usually provided either through a contractual agreement or through social entitlement. Conflict or disappointment emerges when the terms of the contract or entitlement do not match the perceived or actual need for care.

Among examples of these disparities are the following:

- Denial of reimbursement for *noncovered services* (e.g., eye examinations are reimbursed, but eyeglasses are not; liver or other organ transplantation may be excluded).
- Denial of reimbursement for *exhausted benefits* (e.g., limitations on inpatient hospital stays for mental illness or substance abuse, or limitations on rehabilitative services; in fact, virtually all categories of benefits are capable of being exhausted).
- Denial of reimbursement for *nonparticipating providers* (some mid-level or nonphysician providers may be excluded).
- Denial of reimbursement for *"point of service"* (for example, insistence on the use of outpatient rather than inpatient care).

Additional Concerns Related to Managed Care

These additional concerns are less forcefully supported by empirical investigation, but remain as issues for study and possible action.

- It should not be assumed that the sole objective of managed care, with its focus on increasing cost effectiveness of health care, is the containment of overall health-care costs. Equally viable objectives may include increasing the share of wealth and power of the industry in an ever-increasing cost-escalation environment, and the shifting of costs and risks to employers, enrollees, and the public sector through termination or transfer of the coverage

Mental Health Benefits and Managed Care: The State of the Art

Mark Heitner
Rocky Mountain Regional Director
The American Academy of Psychiatrists in Alcoholism & Addictions

Over the past five years, mental health costs have shown the greatest rate of inflation of any component of the employee benefits package. Corporate benefits managers struggle to provide adequate mental health services to employees while controlling mental health-care costs. In 1988, mental health benefit costs rose three times as fast as those of other benefits. The average annual cost of employer-sponsored medical plans in 1990 was $3,161 per employee (A. Foster Higgins and Co.).

Corporate benefits managers have responded in a number of ways. They have placed an annual and lifetime maximum on mental health and chemical dependency benefits payable for employee mental illnesses. Common annual maximums range from $5,000 to $250,000. Contracting with health maintenance organizations has also proved to be a useful strategy. Many companies have set up employee assistance programs, in part to manage costs, and also to meet requirements of the 1988 Drug-Free Workplace Act.

Many large corporations have hired managed-care firms to reduce the total number of admissions and the average lengths of hospital stays. In addition to avoiding unnecessary hospitalizations, managed-care companies often establish provider networks to render clinical services on a contractual basis. Such companies contract with individual practitioners and programs throughout major cities to provide services for a discounted fee.

Such firms are reshaping the delivery of mental health services nationwide. This process of change has not been without difficulties, however. One study that appeared in the *New England Journal of Medicine* warns that we should not anticipate further reduction in the number of inpatient days for mental health patients. Furthermore, hospital costs for such patients can be expected to rise, the study said, unless other effective measures to contain costs are implemented. A report by the author that appeared in *Medical Interface* focuses on some of the clinical issues that have been an unfortunate side effect of managed care: among them, inconsistency in the quality of the providers in the provider network.

The Managed-Care Challenge

Perhaps the most critical issue facing a managed-care company is that of provider selection. Managed-care companies need to contract with high-quality providers and practice in a cost effective manner. In setting up a provider network, the managed-care company's goal is not simply to find practitioners who are willing to work for a reduced fee, but to find high-quality practitioners. Ideally, a provider panel should be a multidisciplinary panel of providers with a common treatment philosophy and orientation. The provider panel should not be static. Rather, members of the panel should change from year to year depending on the results of performance monitoring.

There have been two significant innovations in constructing provider panels recently. One managed-care company has set up a 100-hour training program, during which all of its therapists are oriented toward a common approach to patients. Another company goes one step further, not only providing therapists with an in-house training program, but also supplying them with medical records, treatment planning formats, written treatment protocols, and lecture materials—in short, an entire treatment program. This program contracts with large corporations directly to provide chemical dependency treatment services "in-house."

Designing Mental Health and Dependency Benefits

Current thinking in the field suggests that, in the long run, it is much less expensive to treat a mental illness in its early states. Therefore, the benefits package should be designed to encourage patients to seek early treatment of their difficulties. Thus benefits covering mental health and chemical dependency should not include deductibles because that might deter an individual from seeking help when symptoms first occur. For the same reason, the ten initial outpatient visits should be paid in full—no co-payments should be required. Annual and lifetime dollar maximums on mental health benefits are also quite helpful in cutting costs.

Since relapse is a common occurrence in the course of a successful treatment for chemical dependence, it is not at all uncommon for an alcohol or drug treatment to require two separate courses of treatment. Therefore, coverage that provides for two courses of treatment would be beneficial in cutting long-term costs.

Finally, intense outpatient and partial hospital treatment programs should be covered at least to the same extent as inpatient treatment programs. A remarkable number of mental health-benefits packages cover only inpatient and limited outpatient treatment—for example, they cover inpatient treatment plus 20-outpatient visits per calendar year. Yet, intense outpatient treatment programs, which may run $2,000 for 100 visits, are as effective as the more expensive inpatient programs. Unfortunately, since intense outpatient treatment programs are not covered by many benefit plans, the more costly inpatient treatment program is the most frequently used.

What Lies Ahead?

Employee assistance programs will have an expanded role in the future. Most large employers will contract with such a program, which may, in fact, be administered in-house. This will make early identification and treatment of impaired employees easier. One analyst predicts that large corporations will contract directly with mental health providers, eliminating the managed-care middleman. Since contracting directly with providers will lead to yet another substantial decrease in costs, this alternate may indeed prove attractive to employers.

Mark Heitner is the Rocky Mountain regional director of the American academy of Psychiatrists in Alcoholism and Addictions. He advises psychiatric hospitals, managed-care companies, and employee benefits managers on alcohol and drug treatment issues. Dr. Heitner was previously the medical director of Charter Hospital of Albuquerque. He completed his medical training and psychiatry residency at Cornell University Medical College. He is a diplomate of the American Board of Quality Assurance and Utilization Review Physicians.

of cost-burdensome risk pools and individuals. (This observation comes from the Medical Society of Virginia Review Organization.)

- The relationship between the spread of managed care and utilization review—which now cover an estimated 95 percent of all those whose health benefits are employment-related—and the growing numbers of uninsured and under-insured people bears further investigation beyond the resources available for the current study. While the relationship may not prove to be causal, the association of these factors over time is notable.[2]

- While the original tenet of the HMO movement was that cost-effective services could be best provided in a system that emphasizes prevention and primary care, it is alleged that the overall managed-care system shares with health insurance in general a bias against primary and preventive care.

- Managed-care systems have not fulfilled their potential to promote and support innovative, cost-effective service delivery. Insurers who rely on licensing systems as a basis for credentialing providers and to delineate systems inhibit innovation in allocation of tasks within the health-care workforce.[3]

- Managed care shares with other health insurance systems the failure to address in adequate fashion the problems of catastrophic illness. In addition, the lack of benefit portability for enrollees with preexisting illnesses or conditions may induce workers to remain in jobs they do not want, to the detriment of their own potential and to organizational productivity.

- A frequently discussed intended consequence of the current situation is the possibility of reimbursement mechanisms creating incentives for withholding care. Managed care often, for example, shifts some financial risk for covering health care to providers through such limitations as capitations or as potential income collected in risk pools. Shifted financial risk is intended to prevent unnecessary care. The same incentives, however, could prevent appropriate care in some cases. There is, however, no documented evidence that this type of unintended consequence occurs with any detectable frequency.

- The deterrent "sentinel" or "Hawthorne" effect of expecting to be monitored (probably an intended effect) is a frequently noted asset of managed care and utilization management. It is likely that this effect could be achieved at least as well through systematic random monitoring as through universal utilization review.

- Patients may become frustrated when primary physicians attempt to treat them instead of referring them to a specialist. In some forms of managed care, primary care providers are negatively impacted by the costs of specialty services since these costs are deducted from the capitation fund or risk pool. In this situation, primary care providers have an interest in avoiding referral of their patients to specialty services.

- Questions arise concerning the makeup of review and appeal panels. Should individuals without medical credentials be allowed to sit on appeal panels?

Also, what professional qualifications and licensing procedures should be required of those individuals employed by insurance companies who have to monitor patient utilization?

- Some providers feel insulted and irritated by challenges to their autonomy and by the monitoring of their clinical decision making. They believe that the influence of utilization reviewers, most of whom have less clinical training, inappropriately challenges the legitimacy of the decisions they reach. In a similar vein, second guessing of provider decisions reduces the confidence patients have in the abilities of their providers.

- A great deal of the concern about "unintended effects" came from providers who are frustrated by the "hassle factor" of managed care and utilization management. Hospitals and large group practices must often deal with scores of payers, each with idiosyncratic review criteria that insurers refuse to disclose. At the most basic level, the intermediaries employed by providers to secure appropriate benefits must cope with hundreds of unique claim forms.

- Patients who know that the details of their injuries and illnesses (particularly mental health issues) will be discussed with third parties may not confide completely in their physicians or other providers.

- Placing the liability for procedural compliance with patients (i.e., for precertification or admission notification) may inappropriately match responsibility and behavioral expectations. Unless they are informed of the requirement by their physicians, patients may not be aware of their responsibility despite education efforts by employers and insurers. Expecting compliance behaviors from emotionally and physically stressed people may be inappropriate.

- By its nature, managed care limits patient choices to a greater or lesser degree. Some managed-care enrollees complained that their access to alterative or mid-level providers (chiropractors, nurse midwives, physical therapists, etc.) was limited either by the terms of their group contract or, when allowed by the contract, by the philosophies or ideologies of utilization managers or primary care gatekeepers.

- Finally, with respect to patients, the complexity and frustration the insured public may come to expect from managed care may deter them from seeking care.

1. National Academy of Sciences Institute of Medicine, *Controlling Costs and Changing Patient Care? The Role of Utilization Management* (National Academy Press, 1989).

2. RG Evans, "Tension, Compression, and Shear: Directions, Stresses, and Outcomes of Health Care Cost Control, "*Journal of Health Politics, Policy, and Law*, Spring 1990.

3. UE Reinhardt, "Breaking American Health Policy Gridlock," *Health Affairs*, Summer 1991.

7.   Choosing Among Managed Care Options: What Elements Work Best?

Lawrence Goelman

The bewildering variety of managed care options available on the market today makes choosing the right vendor and the right program for your company a complicated—but very important—decision. The good news is that with so many options, there's probably a program suited perfectly to your situation. Making the correct choice will mean maximum savings for your company and improved quality of care for employees.

In order for your managed care approach to be successful, you need to have a clear idea of your goals. Choose your managed care option well so that it meets your specific needs, and communicate the objectives of the program as well as the details of compliance to your employees in an easy-to-understand format. With this said, however, there is still an important issue to consider: How do you evaluate which elements of a cost management program would be the most effective in accomplishing your goals? This article is intended to provide some ideas to consider when thinking about what you really need to manage costs for your plan.

The natural first step is to create an outline of your goals, as these will form the basis of your approach to managing care. For example, are you most concerned with the bottom line—are your plans' costs your primary concern? If so, you are not alone. Many companies are first driven to try managed care as a result of spiraling health care costs, and a good managed care program can bring these cost increases under control. A recent Foster Higgins survey found that the average cost of traditional indemnity plans rose by 14.2 percent in 1992, as compared to a 10.5 percent increase for preferred provider organizations and an 8.8 percent increase for HMOs.[1] As these figures indicate, managing your health care costs is smart business.

COST MANAGEMENT

In your own business, you already know that whenever you order goods or services for your company, their total cost is equal to the number of units times the price per unit. Health care is no different. If you want to keep costs down, you need to monitor the utilization of services (number of units) and control the price for those services (price per unit). It makes sense, then, that the most cost-effective managed care plans are those that incorporate effective utilization review (UR) with negotiated rates. These plans address both sides of the cost equation.

So what kind of structure accomplishes this goal of cost management best? It depends upon your unique needs. For many employers, a quality network in the form of an HMO or a PPO is the best option because it manages both price and utilization. Networks can offer an attractive package for employers—both in terms of quality and cost management—but not all networks are equal. There are great variances. For example, it is considered a part of "due diligence" for a network to credential the providers with whom it contracts to ensure that they are licensed to practice medicine. How frequently should they do this? Every 18 to 24 months will ensure the accuracy and effectiveness of the information provided. Also, many networks work to ensure that their providers practice quality medicine.

An effective network will also offer utilization review—defined as the clinical evaluation of the necessity of specific kinds of medical care—in addition to negotiated rates. Employers should be wary of any network that does not offer both, as the network may be adding to the plan's administrative costs without producing the expected savings. For example, if you receive a 20 percent discount on four days of care, that discount would appear to be saving plan dollars. However, if it turns out that two of those days were not medically necessary, your savings will prove to be illusory.

Many networks will also offer some form of "gatekeeping" as another method of managing utilization. As the *New England Journal of Medicine* explains, a gatekeeper fulfills two roles: "that of an advocate who can protect patients from the possible adverse effects of unnecessary care and that of a critical decision maker who can ensure the appropriate use of health care services."[2] Essentially, a gatekeeper controls patient access to specialty care.

How does managing access to specialty care reduce plan costs? To begin with, patients do not always choose the right physician to visit. For example, if a patient is suffering from headaches, the cause could be any one of a number of things: stress, sinus trouble, eye strain, a brain tumor, etc. Without a gatekeeper of some sort, the patient could bounce from specialist to specialist before finding relief. If the headaches were simply the result of a sinus infection, the primary care physician would have been able to treat them. Considering that at least 20 percent of patients will self-refer to a specialist, this ping-ponging from specialist to specialist can generate significant costs.

The traditional approach to gatekeeping is to have a network primary care physician control patient access to specialty care. For example, if a patient has a rash, he or she needs to see a network primary care physician first, who will then determine whether the patient needs to see a dermatologist. The disadvantage of this approach is that it only works in a network setting. If the patient's primary care physician is not under contract in the network, then the patient must choose a new one. Beneficial, long-standing relationships between patients and their primary care physicians may be disrupted. Additionally, in areas where networks are not feasible, it is not possible to offer this kind of gatekeeper.

To determine your own needs, one of the first issues that must be addressed is your plan's experience with managed care. If your plan currently offers an indemnity benefit only, with no cost management features, then you might want to go slowly in introducing a program. Most managed care approaches require employee involvement, and your employees will need time to adjust to their new role in the process.

Secondly, you will need to consider the issue of patient freedom of choice: Will you be able to restrict your employees to using physicians only from a specific list? Most HMOs, for example, are structured so that there is no benefit for patients who see physicians outside of the network. PPOs, on the other hand, will allow your patients greater freedom. Even more freedom of choice is available to patients in managed indemnity plans (such as those that incorporate utilization review with point of service fee negotiation).

A third consideration is your geographic location. A number of managed care approaches are based on coordinating the delivery of care. For example, PPOs and HMOs contract with physicians and hospitals in an area to form a network of providers. Since medicine is practiced almost exclusively on a local basis, these options are tied to specific geographic areas and are not available in every market. If you have a population that is in a particularly rural area, or if it is outside of one of the primary markets for network services, you may be left without many network options.

To overcome this difficulty, a number of employers choose to have networks built specifically for their needs. However, not all employers have this option. Traditional network structures require a volume of patients and providers concentrated in a specific health care market area to work effectively. These structures assume that there is a number of providers to choose from and that these providers are competing with each other for patients. In rural locations, the choice of providers is already limited by distance and provider availability. In these areas, it is often necessary to develop an approach to the total management of care that is not dependent upon contracting.

In the past, there have not been many options outside of networks that offer the possibility of managing both the price and utilization of costs. However, the next generation of managed care is likely to be aimed at providing a 100 percent managed care solution for employers, so that they may control costs in all employee locations.

QUALITY OF CARE

It is possible to use your managed care program to improve the quality of medical care your employees receive. For example, if your plan incorporates clinically based utilization review, it ensures that your employees are not receiving unnecessary medical services. As all medical care carries with it some risk of complications or side effects, unnecessary care is potentially dangerous. By implementing a clinically based utilization review program, you are protecting your employees' health.

The better a utilization review (UR) program is at identifying unnecessary or poor quality care, the better it is at enhancing the quality of care provided to your employees. While it may seem that "utilization review is utilization review," it does make a difference which UR firm you choose. If you choose a managed care vendor that uses a nurse to evaluate proposed treatments against a set of statistical guidelines, it is not likely that your utilization review program will improve the quality of care. Conversely, if you choose a plan that has a physician review all proposed treatments against clinically based medical protocols, then your UR program can impact the quality of care that your employees receive.

A physician "peer review" approach to utilization management can work to improve physician's patterns of practice in your area. The best way to affect a physician's behavior is to have another physician review the proposed care and discuss any issues of medical necessity, appropriateness of setting, and treatment alternatives directly with the attending physician on a peer-to-peer basis. Physicians are the best and most qualified agents in the process of educating other physicians and modifying their behavior.

But quality costs more, right? Not true at all—the value of this approach is that quality care is ultimately the most cost-effective care. If a patient receives the right kind of treatment at the right time, then a number of complications and further treatment can often be avoided. Doing it right the first time may improve the quality of care that your employees receive as well as being the most cost-effective move.

A utilization management program is only one avenue for quality improvement; there are many others. As mentioned above, network options enable you to credential the physicians and facilities your employees visit to ensure that they are quality providers of care. To protect against the risk of liability for poor quality care, most networks will check that their contracted physicians are licensed and have malpractice coverage. Additionally, many will ascertain that the physician provides some form of on-call access 24 hours a day.

Beyond these credentials, a network could actively seek quality, cost-effective providers. For example, the best networks refuse to contract with physicians who have had their hospital privileges suspended or revoked, or who have a long history of legal problems (personal or professional). That the provider's eligibility for participating in Medicare or Medicaid has not been limited, suspended, or terminated should also be checked. In this manner, network credentialing criteria can be used as a tool for ensuring quality.

However, credentialing is often seen as a one-time snapshot of participants, and not as a dynamic process for identifying quality issues. Ongoing, regular evaluation of providers is necessary to ensure that the network offers quality care. You may want to ask your network administrator how often provider credentials are checked; recredentialing every 18 months to 24 months is recommended.

Beyond credentialing, it is possible to evaluate physicians on a more frequent basis by using claims and utilization review data to profile the physician's pattern of practice and to measure treatment outcomes. This is still new and few networks are capable of sophisticated statistical analysis of medical outcomes as yet. However, many are able to track hospital readmission rates, rates of complication, and mortality rates. The next generation of managed care will undoubtedly feature more advanced profiling and outcomes measurement, so that it would be possible to channel patients to only high quality, cost-effective providers.

CONCLUSION

Since managed care was introduced over two decades ago, a profusion of options has proliferated in the market. The staggering amount of variety is largely in response to the many different needs of employers and other group plan purchasers. Each option has its niche market; each approach fulfills a different need. The key to a successful plan is to identify specifically what are your needs and to choose an option based on those needs. Keep in mind that what works for one group will not necessarily work for another. Recognize that there are significant differences in quality and scope of services offered by different managed care vendors. And above all, demand quality—your employees deserve nothing less.

1. *Health Care Benefits Survey*, A. Foster Higgins & Co, Inc (New York: 1992).

2. Peter Franks, Caroly Clancy, and Paul A Nutting, "Gatekeeping Revisited: Protecting Patients from Overtreatment," *New England Journal of Medicine,* 6 Aug 1992.

8. Evaluating Health Care Providers and Networks: An Employer Perspective

William Willson

To be sure they are spending their health care dollars wisely, employers need to be able to evaluate and compare providers and networks on the basis of cost, quality, and access. However, health care is an inherently complicated business and not easily quantified into simple measures or comparisons. While there are a number of systems and methods in existence for evaluating networks and providers, some are better than others, and none are perfect. Nevertheless, understanding the strengths and weaknesses of the different methods and using them appropriately can help employers make the best decisions as to how and where to spend their health care benefit dollars.

One of the most important and challenging responsibilities facing a health benefits manager is the evaluation of specific health care providers and networks. Because there is such wide variation in cost and quality outcomes from provider to provider for particular conditions and procedures, there is a great need for accurate provider evaluation. At the same time, the complexity of health care combined with limited data make accurate provider network evaluation exceedingly difficult. There is, for example, a serious danger of identifying a particular provider as high cost when, in fact, that provider cares for especially sick patients. To compound these difficulties, there is substantial variation in outcomes by condition or procedure even for the same provider. A particular provider, for instance, may produce especially good cost and quality outcomes for knee surgeries, but not for shoulder surgeries.

This article discusses specific measures to evaluate health care networks and providers in terms of three issues: cost, quality, and access. Further, general observations are offered for each area concerning the availability of data and validity of measures. Finally, several conclusions are drawn concerning the role of employers in evaluation of provider networks.

COST

General Approaches and Limitations

Theoretically, an employer should be concerned with its total health care expenditures, including costs for the company-sponsored health benefits program, workers' compensation, and lost productivity due to accident, injury, or illness. However, given the complexity of determining the measure of total health care costs, most employer measures of cost relate only to their health benefits program, which may be more practically determined. For the same reason, this article will focus only on health benefit program costs.

Yet, unless the employer is comparing bids from competing networks on a fully capitated basis, it is difficult to make a precise and comprehensive cost comparison. While capitation bids allow the most accurate cost comparisons (and contain the strongest financial incentive for cost management), self-funded employers have been reluctant to embrace capitation.

Employers, then, are faced with a number of difficulties in making valid cost comparisons between specific providers and networks. In most markets, no organization collects and makes available charge data by service and provider. A single employer rarely accounts for a high enough portion of the health care market to allow meaningful analysis of its own internal health care claims data. An encouraging trend is the merging and sharing of health care utilization and provider charge data among multiple employers, but such cooperative arrangements are not widespread.

Even those employers that have access to a substantial database are not generally able to assess comparative utilization levels. A physician, for example, may charge a comparatively high price for a given service but still be associated with a relatively low total case or episode cost owing to low utilization levels. In the absence of this area-wide information, it is not possible to make valid cost comparisons between providers and networks if reimbursement is made on the basis of a percentage of billed charges. Further, reasonably sophisticated measures of total cost for specific services are only available for inpatient facility services.

A promising means of making informed and valid evaluations of providers even in the face of such constraints, however, is a practice called *prospective payment*. That is, if employers require submission of prospective price bids for a wide range of specific health care services, the employer can make more valid comparisons of total costs between providers and networks. If an employer receives, for example, multiple facility bids for a tonsillectomy, the employer can identify the high cost providers from the low cost providers.

One challenge presented by prospective payment, however, relates to the employer's information system for its health benefits program. Informed negotiations on a prospective price basis require more detailed charges and paid data than many employers possess. Negotiations in the absence of such information provide little assurance that the prospective price will, in fact, be lower than a simple percentage of billed charges.

A final challenge related to evaluation of health care networks from a cost standpoint is that of antiselection—the tendency for higher risk and therefore more expensive patients to select one health care network over another. For instance, if a self-funded employer offers a traditional self-funded plan while also offering a premium-based managed care plan, comparatively healthy individuals might be more likely to select the managed care option, leaving the employer with the more expensive patients. The effect of antiselection in this example is to increase the cost of the self-funded plan while, in effect, subsidizing the managed care plan.

Differences between plans with respect to their provider network or benefit design usually are the prime determinants of antiselection. If the managed care plan's health care network does not include the same proportion of specialty providers as the entire market, those under care from such providers will tend to stay with their traditional indemnity plan. Also, some plans tend to enrich their benefits in areas that tend to attract young, healthy families or reduce benefits of greatest need by a particular type of high cost patient, leaving the self-funded plan with the more expensive employees.

Some employers have begun to assess a "risk surcharge" to offset the financial effects of antiselection. The premium surcharge can be based on the demographics of employees enrolling in the managed care plan. Quantification of the health care needs of the population—called disease density measures— represent a more sophisticated measurement system. Assessment of disease density can be based on the diagnostic information contained on claims forms, or it can be based on a self-reported, functional health status measure.

Inpatient Hospital Facility Services

Employers are better able to obtain comparable bids for inpatient services than for other major health care services. Such effective comparability is made possible by using diagnosis related groups (DRGs) as the definition of almost 500 individual inpatient categories/products. By using the DRG system, a bid or price for a particular DRG can easily be compared with the bids of other providers.

DRGs were first developed and used by the Health Care Financing Administration (HCFA) to pay for inpatient services for Medicare patients, but are increasingly used for payment for the general population as well. While the DRG system does not account for differences in severity between patients assigned to the same category, DRGs can serve as a very useful cost evaluation tool, as well as a prospective payment method for an employer, particularly if certain refinements are made to the HCFA's original DRG system.

DRG weights and base rates should be based on the employed population. HCFA has assigned a weight to each of its 492 DRGs based on the Medicare population. The weight is simply the average cost of a particular DRG divided by the average cost across all DRGS. The DRG weight is then multiplied by a base rate to yield the DRG-specific payment amount. A base rate, then, can be used as a total price level indicator. That is, the hospital with the lowest base rate has the lowest complete price or bid level.

Employers should specify that hospitals submit bids based on an employed, nonelderly population. An employer might also consider using consulting firms or statewide hospital discharge and cost studies as sources of charge data by DRG. Using alternative data allows employers to independently compute weighting factors by DRG and total base rate for comparison. In addition, the employer needs to identify which DRGs account for the highest volume admissions and payments. This employer-specific volume provides a weighting factor so that those services most frequently used are weighted more heavily than those infrequently needed.

Adjustments should be made for outlier cases. To recognize the fact that some patients require an inordinate amount of resources, an outlier provision should be included. Typically, once a case exceeds a specified length of stay or charge amount, the entire case (or that portion of the stay in excess of the outlier cutoff point) is paid on either a per day or percentage of billed charges basis. An outlier cutoff point of two to three standard deviations from the mean charge is often used as the cutoff point. To facilitate more accurate comparison from one facility to another, this cutoff point should be specified by the employer and should apply to all facilities or networks evenly.

Certain services should be excluded from the prospective payment system. A valid criticism of the DRG system is that it does not adequately recognize patient severity within a category. Some services are particularly susceptible to a high degree of variation not explained by DRGs. Rehabilitative and neonatal intensive care services are examples of services that might properly be excluded from a DRG-based evaluation and payment system.

Patient severity should be recognized within a DRG. There are many inpatient severity systems available to improve recognition of patient severity within a particular DRG. Unfortunately, if an employer is evaluating many different hospitals, it is unlikely that the same severity adjustment system, if any, is used by the different facilities. A simplistic approach to further recognizing patient severity beyond the DRG system is to group hospitals into three or four categories and compare the base rate of each hospital group (tertiary, secondary, primary). While the actual grouping of hospitals can be controversial, it can serve as an important refinement.

Sustainability of the bid should be assessed. Is it likely that a particular facility can provide a service near the bid price over a significant period of time? One measure of sustainability might be a particular facility's per case charge inflation over time. A second measure is the effective discount expected to be produced by the fixed price bid or contract. If the discount is high (30 to 50 percent), it will be increasingly difficult for the facility to sustain its contract price as a growing proportion of its revenue comes from fixed price contracts and a decreasing proportion is available onto which costs may be shifted.

Physician Services

Methods for the evaluation of the cost of physician services have only recently become available and are properly used only as crude pointers for further evaluation. Historically, physician cost evaluation has focused entirely on the charge levels of the physician. The problem with such a narrow view is that physician fees account for less than 20 percent of total health care expenditures, while the physician provides or orders 75 to 85 percent of total health expenditures. Another reason that physician fee analysis is of dubious worth is that if a physician is subject to a fee schedule, actual variation in physician charge levels has little effect on total physician expenses by the payer.

Physician profiling systems have been increasingly used to assess physicians' patterns of utilization and cost, and, to a more limited extent, quality. While a variety of profiling methods and products exist, most seek to compute the total cost of patient care for a particular type of condition or episode, assign responsibility for these costs and services to a particular physician, adjust the cost for case mix of the physician, and make a comparison to a peer group or some normative standard.

At present, physician profiling is sufficiently primitive that little confidence is warranted in the determination that a particular physician is truly high or low cost based solely on physician profiling data. Detailed additional analysis including discussion with the particular physician is essential. Following is a listing of some major problems with physician profiling systems:

- *Inadequate adjustment for patient severity.* In that most profiling systems are claims-based, measures of severity within a particular patient category (if severity measures exist at all) are seriously limited by the data contained on a claim form. ICD9 (*International Classification of Diseases*, 9th edition) classification alone is insufficient to account for severity within most conditions.

- *Improper assignment of costs to physicians.* Claims-based profiling systems assess responsibility for specific services to particular physicians in one of four ways. First, all cost may be assigned to a patient primary care physician. Second, costs may be assigned based on that physician accounting for the highest charges to a patient. Third, the physician may be linked to the services simply because his or her date of service most closely preceded the services in question. Finally, the attending or ordering physician may be assigned the cost for such services, although most plans do not keep this type of information. All of these methods for assigning cost responsibility to physicians clearly have serious flaws and limitations. Nevertheless, if applied carefully and in close cooperation with physicians, such systems hold substantial promise of quality improvement and cost reduction.
- *Poor data quality.* Because physician profiling systems typically use claims data, the quality of the data is a strong determinant of the quality of the output; the rule of "garbage in, garbage out" is clearly in effect. Data that are not generally essential to the determination of payment—such as ICD9 codes to the fifth digit—are often either not submitted or not entered with precision. Greater use of claims data will undoubtedly improve its quality and accuracy, but at present, findings based on claims data should be viewed critically.
- *Limited scope.* Most systems omit certain key aspects of the total medical care system, most frequently prescription drug and inpatient facility services. A less than comprehensive scope of services is susceptible to an inaccurate view, particularly if a service not included is a substitute for those included in the evaluation. A physician who, for instance, aggressively uses outpatient services in lieu of inpatient services would be improperly classified as high cost if the profiling system looks only at outpatient services.

In short, while physician profiles provide a very useful pointer for further analysis and evaluation, the serious limitations of profiling systems at present preclude the use of profile reports alone in assessing relative efficiency of physicians. On the other hand, profiling systems do hold substantial promise of providing meaningful feedback to physician network participants. As such, networks that use or are developing profiling systems may show a level of sophistication and commitment to improvement that employers will consider valuable.

Ambulatory Surgery

In contrast to inpatient facility services, there is no generally accepted fixed payment or evaluation methodology for ambulatory surgery. The HCFA is expected to implement an Ambulatory Patient Groups (APG) methodology that may soon become the standard. In the meantime, three major methods exist for evaluation and prospective payment.

1. *Medicare ambulatory surgery center (ASC) groups.* This method classifies most outpatient surgeries into nine groups, based on the Physicians' Current Procedural Terminology (CPT) code of the procedure. A patient with multiple procedures is classified into multiple groups and receives full payment for the highest group and one-half payment for subsequent groups. While ASC does make it easy to make charge comparisons between facilities, such comparisons may be very misleading. There is a high degree of cost variability within each ASC group, making it difficult to distinguish facilities with low cost from those with low case complexity.

2. *CPT codes.* This system classifies outpatient surgeries into over 1,000 categories. A patient with multiple procedures is classified into multiple groups and receives full payment for the highest CPT code, and perhaps one-half payment for subsequent CPT codes. According to one health care system's estimation, approximately 80 percent of all ambulatory surgery volume is accounted for by 228 codes. Evaluation and payment on a CPT basis effectively accounts for most of the variation in resource use and is familiar to payers and providers. On the other hand, the large number of codes makes it cumbersome for use as a payment method. In addition, there are problems in paying or evaluating multiple procedures (which accounts for approximately a third of all ambulatory surgeries).

3. *ICD9 codes.* Under this system, outpatient surgeries are classified into over 900 ICD9 codes. Approximately 80 percent of all surgeries were accounted for by 120 ICD9 codes. The use of ICD9 codes is, perhaps, the most effective evaluation method because it is the system most highly correlated with resource use and because it avoids the problems of multiple procedures. On the other hand, it is not well-suited for prospective payment purposes, since many payers do not capture ICD9 data and many freestanding surgery centers do not submit claims with ICD9 codes on the HCFA 1500 bill (the format typically used for the submission of bills for professional services).

Outpatient Laboratory and Radiology

One of the more straightforward types of services to evaluate with respect to charge or bid price is that of laboratory and radiology. For these services, the CPT coding method is generally well-suited to evaluate cost and is widely used. Several complicating factors related to laboratory and radiology services and one overall consideration related to outpatient ancillary services in general, however, should be recognized.

First, most laboratories assess a handling fee beyond the fee for performing the laboratory test. A handling fee should be included in the total bid to facilitate comprehensive and accurate provider cost comparisons. Further, most laboratories provide a discounted price to physicians, who then bill for the test themselves. In these cases, the payment is dictated by physician fees and payer fee schedules rather than the laboratory price. Finally, the strong preferences many physicians have regarding particular laboratories need to be considered.

In radiology, select invasive procedures have been unbundled into both the diagnostic and surgical components. Since considerable expertise is required in properly coding these procedures, there is a significant potential for error.

A general consideration relates to the potential linkage between inpatient and outpatient facility costs. Simply stated, many inpatient hospital facilities charge significantly more than freestanding ancillary providers. Hospitals may be less generous with their inpatient bids if they expect a significant loss of their lucrative outpatient ancillary volume. Another factor that exacerbates the price differences between hospitals and their freestanding competitors relates to the tendency for hospitals to treat more complex cases.

QUALITY

While there are many limitations related to cost evaluation, a properly structured cost evaluation process is likely to produce valid comparative data. On the other hand, no organization, individual, or process possesses the requisite data or method to make valid health care provider or network comparisons based on quality. Reasons for the lack of data on quality include the complexity of health care and the low demand for such information on the part of employers and other payers.

While a number of specific quality measures are proposed, this discussion is intended to be illustrative rather than definitive. Further, some measures suggested will be unavailable—either on a comparative network basis or by an individual plan. Progress toward relevant quality measures and data will be accelerated as employers begin to demand specific quality indicators and as managed competition becomes more sophisticated.

Employee, Member, and Patient Satisfaction

Customer satisfaction is one of the few areas pertaining to health care quality that lends itself readily to measurement. Due to problems of comparability, however, it is unlikely that an employer will be able to accurately assess relative levels of satisfaction between different networks or providers as part of a network evaluative process. Nonetheless, results of satisfaction measures conducted by specific providers and networks may provide useful information, including insight to the organization's interest in and commitment to customer satisfaction.

The employer is, however, well-positioned to establish some initial baseline measures of plan or network satisfaction. If employees are provided the option of several plan types or networks, measures of employee/network member satisfaction can be developed.

One measure of network or provider preference is already contained in claims data. Employers can identify the providers that employees prefer, simply by tallying up that information from their claim forms.

Illness Prevention Measures

Another measure of quality that may be available from the health plan/network relates to disease prevention. If a plan does not have such information currently available, their interest in and commitment to developing these measures may provide an indication of their interest in this area. Of course, such measures are most useful if covered by the health benefit program—a situation far from common. Following is a sample listing of measures of preventive processes and outcomes:

- Percentage of members under two years of age immunized for DPT (diphtheria, pertussis, and tetanus), polio, MMR (measles, mumps, and rubella), HIB (hemophilus influenza-B), and hepatitis B
- Rate of pregnant women with initiation of prenatal care during first trimester
- Percentage of female members over the age of 50 with annual mammogram
- Percentage of female members over the age of with annual pap smear

Disease Management Measures

Measures of aggressiveness in early intervention or in effective disease management might include:

- Percentage of patients with high blood pressure undergoing medical treatment
- Percentage of diabetic patients with annual eye exam and use of hemoglobin A1C
- Cesarean section rate (lower is better)
- Rate of emergency room visits, hospital admissions, and readmissions for chronic asthma patient
- Postoperative wound infections

Again, most health care networks or plans do not have these data readily available. Their response to your request for these data, however, may provide you with a subjective measure of their long-term interest in truly measuring and managing care.

Quality Process Measures

A number of possible measures of a plan's commitment to monitoring and ensuring its own quality are available, including reports by accrediting organizations that may be reviewed. For instance, plan accreditation by the National Committee for Quality Assurance shows an aggressive stance with regard to the systematization and documentation of quality assurance, provider credentialling, and the organization of the quality improvement function; accredited plans will have a Final Assessment Report that can be reviewed. Health care facility accreditation by the Joint Commission of Accreditation of Healthcare Organizations includes a production of an Accreditation Report, which may be reviewed.

Review of network credentialling criteria and personnel application information verification processes is another way to measure commitment to quality; there is a wide extent of variation in the degree to which information is verified and acted upon. Also important is a review of any plan or provider studies regarding extent and cause of variations in utilization of certain procedures, including laminectomy, hysterectomy, coronary artery bypass graft, coronary angiography, and percutaneous transluminal coronary angioplasty. Such studies indicate a level of sophistication of the health plan or network that may ultimately lead to lower cost and higher quality.

ACCESS

The final evaluative area relates to geographic accessibility, extent of choice of provider, and availability of services. Geographic access is typically most important for services with high frequency of use, such as primary care services and prescription drugs. Geographic access may be less important to employees for less frequently used services such as specialized cardiac services.

While employees certainly prefer more provider choice to less, it may be useful to obtain employee data concerning their willingness to exchange cost for choice. Many employees, for instance, may be unwilling to pay an extra $50 per family per month for traditional indemnity coverage instead of a staff model health maintenance organization (HMO).

Availability refers to capacity and hours of operation. The presence of urgent care centers as part of a health care network, for instance, may boost employee satisfaction as well as reduce the utilization of expensive emergency rooms. Some networks offer a phone consultation services for triage and health information.

Some networks have a serious shortage of primary care capacity. If you have a concern regarding availability, a spot check regarding the time for an appointment may be warranted.

Perhaps the most useful means of assessing employee access preferences is to conduct research on their preferences with several health care networks. To maximize the utility of this research, a brief profile of each network including price (premium and cost sharing) should be presented.

Of critical importance to this research as well as the proper functioning of the health care market is the method in which the employer contributes to employee health care benefits. Simply stated, most employers insulate their employees from the differences in the cost of various health care networks. For instance, if one health care network can provide a set of benefits for $400 per month for a family and another provides the same benefits for $300, the employee is being subsidized for selecting a less efficient network if that employee is not fully responsible for the additional $100 per month network. Such a "level employer contribution," in fact, is a requisite for a price sensitive health care network. Only by providing employees with choices and financial accountability for such choices, can the employer expect its employees to become partners in the search for a higher value health care network.

CONCLUSION

Meaningful evaluation of provider networks is a complex undertaking that is only partially supported with accepted methods and data. Cost comparisons of provider networks are best performed by relying on prospective payment methodologies. Even these generally accepted cost methodologies require substantial sophistication and provider involvement. By contrast, access comparisons tend to be more straightforward.

Assessment of quality is made difficult by both the scarcity of accepted methods and by the paucity of meaningful data. Individual employers are in a position to demand more and better quality measures, and can develop their own employee satisfaction instruments. At this point, however, the employer is best served by assessing a network's quality processes and organizational investment in quality improvement. Specific quality outcome measures are largely beyond the industry's capability.

Finally, an employer should carefully scrutinize its internal resource capability with respect to evaluation of provider networks. Many moderate and large firms do not possess the needed data or methods to properly assess specific providers and networks. Employer coalitions, purchasing cooperatives, health care data organizations, and the like may represent the most promising avenues for future network assessment.

9. HMOs' Gatekeeper System: Imperfect in Practice

Neil J. Waldron

A recent study by Mass Mutual revealed some of the imperfections in the "gatekeeping" features of HMOs. The study included interviews with the doctors charged with gatekeeping duties for HMOs in New York, Chicago, and Washington, D.C., and found that, for a number of different reasons, the financial incentives intended to encourage primary care physicians to limit expensive referrals to specialists often don't work.

The "gatekeeper" is one of the most popular cost-control features of many HMOs. But the gatekeeping system—which in theory reins in costs by controlling patient access to more expensive care—is not always perfect in practice. So say doctors in three major metropolitan areas who work as gatekeepers, and who participated in focus group studies conducted by Mass Mutual Life & Health Benefits Management.

The gatekeeping system relies on a primary care physician (PCP) to act as a "gatekeeper" and decide if patient ills require more costly, specialized treatments. To limit these referrals to specialists, HMOs offer PCPs financial incentives.

However, the incentives alone are not enough, as some patients are still finding their way to unnecessary, costly care, thus thwarting the system's efforts to control costs. An HMO's financial incentives are considered by physicians prior to their joining a managed care network, but they do not often change their practice methods once in. And inefficient habits can limit an HMO's ability to save money.

Reprinted with permission from *National Underwriter,* ©1993, The National Underwriter Company; *National Underwriter, Life & Health/Financial Services Edition,* September 7, 1992.

Some PCPs also note that their role as gatekeepers can strain the trust of the doctor/patient relationship, especially with those patients more aggressive in seeking higher-cost specialty treatment. And the physicians, fearful of heightening tensions, allow the referral, surrendering some of their capabilities to better manage patient care and keep costs down.

The PCPs that Mass Mutual interviewed, work as gatekeepers in independent practice association (IPA) HMOs in New York, Chicago, and Washington, D.C. By far the most popular form of HMO, IPAs serve 41 percent of the nation's entire HMO membership. These doctors raised two points about gatekeeping;

1. Financial incentives alone are not enough to influence their behavior because many doctors limit their number of HMO patients.
2. Patients don't understand the system well, and physicians are reluctant to limit patients who push for more specialized services.

"The gatekeeper concept creates friction between you and the patient," said one doctor. "It is unnatural—an odious concept—and interferes with the doctor/patient relationship."

This was one of the most serious problems physicians saw with the gatekeeper concept. While the focus group participants supported the idea of the PCP as the first and main source of patient care, they also felt their role as gatekeepers hindered their performance as physicians because it eroded the trust between them and their patients.

According to Mass Mutual's studies, a main problem is that the financial incentives, designed to limit unnecessary care by appealing to a physician's financial motivation, in some cases may have little impact once a doctor joins a network.

In fact, the only time a network's financial incentives matter to some physicians is when they consider joining. When reviewing a network, some physicians examine its reimbursement structure and determine whether treating network patients will be profitable. Once they join, they often practice as before.

But the IPA physicians in Mass Mutual's focus groups said they were feeling a loss of independence and control over their practice because of the growing number of managed care networks. To maintain their autonomy, these physicians limit the number of HMO patients they accept, often using them only to fill out their practices.

The result of this is that the HMO financial incentives are a very small portion of their practice incomes. And while the incentives are designed to promote a judicious use of referrals, at such relatively small amounts, they often have little impact on the physicians' methods.

Doctors in this position are far more likely to guide their decision based on training, experience, and the advice of other physicians. Several noted their distaste for financial incentives, as they think it stresses financial concerns over their medical judgment as the basis for care.

To further reduce outside influence on their practices, physicians often join several networks and diversify their limited number of HMO patients among several HMOs.

With their multiple affiliations, doctors can walk away from some HMOs, if they find demand on their services not worth the fees received.

The diluted control of the HMOs and the doctors' disregard for the financial incentives were evidenced by the fact that most of the physicians in the Mass Mutual study couldn't list the specific incentives for networks to which they belong.

And some doctors said they are willing to refer patients to specialists regardless of the incentives. "The HMO lends itself to refer out when you are behind schedule," said one doctor. "It is very easy to sign the referral form and not have to see the patient."

Conversely, PCPs note that gatekeeping systems in IPA HMOs lack proper financial incentives for patients, which can lead to frustrations among doctors and conflicts with their patients.

And the doctors believe it tends to make these HMO patients—a relatively healthy group—prone to overusing medical care because they have no financial concerns to inhibit their use of the system.

"Patients [in HMOs] think . . . their insurance card is like a Visa card with no payment," said one doctor. "I think it's the patient who is badly trained," said another. "HMOs should spend money educating patients. Then you'd have savings."

Some physicians said HMOs should better educate patients and offer them incentives, like required co-payments on all visits. In its current form the inequity of incentive—doctors have them to limit care but patients don't—can place a doctor and patient at odds over care, whether it's a PCP office visit or a referral to a specialist.

A major part of the problem is that patients aren't always fully aware of their benefits, and some at times believe they have a richer benefit package than is actually the case. And when they learn the extent of their plan coverage, the patients sometimes take it out on the PCPs.

"The patient is sold heaven and delivered crap," said a doctor. "When they realize this they get real mad. They think that you are responsible for it."

According to Mass Mutual's studies, a porous gatekeeping system can limit the savings it is intended to provide. Meanwhile, this system can also compromise the needed trust in the doctor/patient relationship, creating unhappy physicians and patients. A viable gatekeeper network needs to address these points if it expects to work properly.

Future approaches to gatekeeper systems may have to incorporate ideas that help patients better understand the system, and encourage them to have more trust and work more closely with their physicians.

The networks must make efforts to improve their selection process and recruit doctors who already have efficient practice habits. They may also need to develop ways of promoting better treatment methods to which the network staff will be receptive.

10. Implementing Point-of-Service Managed Care: Effort Pays Off
Ron Fontanetta

Point-of-service managed care has been proven effective as a method of providing quality health care benefits at a lower cost, but making the change from an indemnity plan to POS represents a dramatic shift for employer and employees alike. The experiences of companies that have made the switch to POS make it clear that implementation takes time and considerable effort on the employer's part, but these investments will pay off in the long run. Understanding the lessons learned by those companies can make the transition to POS considerably smoother, and help ensure a successful first year.

Point-of-service (POS) managed care programs began to attract attention in the late 1980s with such pioneers as Southwestern Bell, May Department Stores, and Allied-Signal reporting success with their programs. Since then, POS has been one of the fastest-growing forms of managed care offered by U.S. employers, and for good reason. Among the features of POS programs that appeal to employers include:

- Flexibility of provider choice each time employees seek medical care (although some restrictions do apply to in-network utilization—e.g., patients must be referred to specialists by a primary care physician);
- Higher benefit levels for in-network services than are typically available under traditional indemnity arrangements;
- Coverage for services not usually included in indemnity plans, such as preventive care;

117

- The ability to attract to network-based arrangements employees who have historically been reluctant to enroll in HMOs;
- Provider accountability for the quality of care employees receive; and
- Very promising financial results.

Nevertheless, the fundamental differences between indemnity programs and POS do pose challenges. Simply put, fee-for-service is a "non-system" of health care delivery. Network-based managed care, on the other hand, is a controlled system that limits access to selected providers and delivers services through primary care physicians. For most employers, the decision to implement this type of program represents a dramatic shift in benefit strategy, and a sizeable staff commitment as well.

The full implementation process—including planning for the change, selecting the network manager, visiting local networks, educating management and employees, and getting through the program launch—may take well over a year. And once the program is in place, an adjustment period naturally follows. For example, a recent Towers Perrin survey of 81 employers with POS programs found most reporting a "shakeout period" of six months to a year.[1] Closer examination of the issues reveals that some are inherent to the nature of network-based programs, while others are rooted in implementation and communication planning and execution. In any case, the results of thorough preparation—or lack thereof—usually show up in first-year POS experience.

Key success factors include the breadth and maturity of the network or networks, the administrative capabilities of the vendor, employer attention to transition issues, the level of communication and training support provided, the degree to which providers and employees understand and accept the program's medical management features, and the environment into which the program is introduced.

THE ROLE OF THE NETWORK MANAGER

To achieve the results they expect from managed care, employers are relying heavily on a new player—the network manager—who takes responsibility for developing, administering, and managing the network and its providers. National and regional insurance carriers typically fill this role, although HMOs and other organizations are becoming more active in this area.

Shared responsibility between employers and network managers—based on actual results—is a hallmark of contemporary managed care programs. In addition to shared financial risk in meeting specific cost targets, arrangements with network managers now also frequently include "performance guarantees." Under these arrangements, network managers guarantee, against penalties and bonuses, the qualitative elements of performance such as service, levels of employee satisfaction, performance relative to clinical standards, and responsiveness to an employer's special needs for network or service customization. Clearly, selecting the "right" network manager is fundamental to a successful POS implementation.

PLAN DESIGN

As long as they use network providers, employees covered under POS plans make only modest copayments and are covered for a wide range of services, usually including preventive care. If they choose to use non-network providers, however, employees pay a larger portion of the costs, usually have to file claims, and generally aren't covered for as many services. Thus, the POS design combines the cost-control potential of an HMO (within the network) with the element of employee choice offered by preferred provider organizations (PPOs). Nevertheless, balancing cost containment objectives and choice is an issue employers must consider when implementing POS. Clearly, the design should steer employees into the network, but at the same time provide a meaningful alternative.

First generation POS plans often placed heavy emphasis on financial steerage, with fairly large differentials between in- and out-of-network benefits (i.e., differences in plan value of up to 30 percent). But as experience with POS has increased and in-network usage has proved more than adequate, employers have learned that steep benefit differentials are less important in attracting employees than two other key factors: simplicity in the design and procedures, and the quality of the network.

NETWORK ACCESS

Most network managers contract with 25 to 30 percent of the providers in a metropolitan area. A key employee concern is adequate access to qualified physicians, hospitals, and other providers. A common criticism leveled at some of the early POS programs—particularly those that involved emerging rather than mature networks—was that some locations (zip codes or counties) lacked sufficient choice of primary care physicians.

In response to this concern, Towers Perrin developed a software tool called Geographic Network Analysis, which can identify geographic areas that lack sufficient access based on guidelines developed with the employer. Using this software for analysis, employers can direct their vendors to enhance provider recruiting in these low-access areas, or to exclude these areas until access improves.

As part of the implementation planning process, some employers also analyze claims data under the indemnity program to identify high-volume hospitals or physician groups. By directing their network managers to target these provider groups for any further recruiting, employers can minimize provider changes for employees willing to use the network. A word of caution, however: Many networks want to add physicians or hospitals only where current access is demonstrably unsatisfactory.

Access to ancillary providers—labs, radiology facilities, pharmacies, home health agencies, durable medical equipment suppliers, and others—is another issue network managers and employers must address early in the POS planning process. While hospital and physician expenses account for approximately 70 percent of most employers' medical expense, services from ancillary providers account for the rest. Accordingly, many managed care vendors have recognized the value of contracting with ancillary providers. However, the breadth and type of ancillary services available in-network vary considerably. Employers must therefore investigate access well before the program launch—and ensure that network physicians and employees receive the information they need about ancillary providers available in the network when the program is introduced.

ADMINISTRATION

Consistency in plan design and administration is a frequently cited objective of multi-state employers, especially those consolidating benefits programs across divisions or properties. While most vendors have taken steps to minimize design and procedural differences in their networks, differences persist for several reasons, including:

- Programs that remain insured (rather than self-insured) are subject to state benefit mandates, resulting in different coverage levels for certain services.
- A POS program that uses an existing HMO as the platform for its network may face design limitations based on how the HMO product was defined in regulatory filings in a given state.
- Many vendors have decentralized their decision making on network design, provider contracting, and administrative procedures so they can react more quickly to local trends.

As a result of these and other factors, many employers have had to train local human resources staff to handle variations in design or delivery. Fortunately, over the past few years, vendors have improved their local and regional coordination to better serve national accounts. Nevertheless, employers should be prepared to handle some variations and provide support to local staff where necessary.

TRANSITION ISSUES

Moving from an indemnity plan to a network-based POS program raises a host of transition issues. Since benefits differ for services received in- vs. out-of-network, employers must consider cases where employees might be better served by continuing treatment out of the network for a specified time.

In launching their POS programs, Southwestern Bell and AT&T, for example, let employees request "continuation of care" by their current (non-network) physicians for certain serious medical conditions. These employees received in-network benefits for this care for a certain period after the launch. Similarly, most employers allow women who are pregnant when the POS program becomes effective to continue with their current obstetricians and receive in-network benefits.

Other transition issues include policies for COBRA participants and students or other dependents away from home for extended periods, as well as for employees who travel extensively on business. Explicitly defining and clearly communicating policies on these transition issues can go a long way toward avoiding misunderstandings after the program takes effect.

Customer Service

Even if the new POS program is described extensively through employee communications and meetings, employees tend to have many questions about the program beginning at the time of enrollment (two to three months before the effective date of the program) and continuing for four to six months after the program takes effect. These questions typically focus on the provider network (e.g., a provider's qualifications), program design or coverage levels, claims procedures, ID cards (e.g., cards showing incorrect information), and the transition issues just described. Support provided by the vendor's customer service unit, which fields many of these inquiries by phone or mail, is critical during this startup phase.

Recognizing the importance of an adequately trained customer service unit, many employers are more actively assessing the training and readiness of this unit to answer their employees' questions. To better control member services, some vendors have centralized this function for clients; other vendors maintain local units but have enhanced their systems to support national clients.

To monitor the questions and concerns raised by their employees, many employers request monthly or quarterly summaries of inquiries, categorized by type of issue. They are then well positioned to act, if required, to amend a policy, add providers to the network, improve vendor responsiveness, or better communicate certain plan provisions.

Communication and Training

Effective communication—for both employee and provider audiences—is essential to a successful POS implementation. Employee communication programs typically aim to meet three general objectives:

1.   Explain managed care concepts and the reasons for adopting a POS program;
2.   Describe procedures and required employee actions; and
3.   Reinforce certain employee behaviors (e.g., contacting the primary care physician).

Employers who have invested significant time and effort in communication in the months preceding the effective date of the program frequently report more efficient enrollment and higher utilization of network providers. Moreover, since many employees use medical care only intermittently, successful programs continue to reinforce key messages—such as the process for changing primary care physicians or appropriate use of the emergency room—throughout the first year of the program. Some employers also have their network managers conduct employee satisfaction surveys, which can serve as valuable communication vehicles as well as information gathering tools.

POS programs represent significant change for providers, particularly primary care physicians, as well as employees. Until recently, almost all communication and training efforts focused on employees, but employers and managed care vendors are committing more resources to ensure that providers also understand their obligations under a POS program. Vendors find provider education particularly important for physicians who are new to POS managed care, or in instances where the network has been expanded to accommodate an individual employer.

Medical Management

Provider accountability is one of the fundamental differences between managed health care delivery systems and fee-for-service medicine. Network managers are responsible not only for ensuring that the program meets the employer's financial objectives, but also for clinical oversight of the care that providers deliver. This oversight takes various forms: provider credentialing, preauthorization of certain procedures, and, in some cases, ongoing evaluation of clinical quality. While these efforts serve to ensure the appropriateness and quality of care delivered by network providers, employees or their physicians may initially resist input from a third-party medical reviewer or appeal the decisions of a local medical director. In addition, some employees might view the primary care physician as an intruder in their relationships with specialists.

Clearly, effective prelaunch communication and ongoing education can help reduce resistance to the program's medical management features once the program is in place. In developing a communication strategy, many employers have found prelaunch employee surveys and focus groups invaluable tools in gauging attitudes toward health care issues, including quality. Not surprisingly, some employees equate quality with unlimited access, and some view cost management as a threat to quality. Nevertheless, research does show that, when offered choices in health coverage, employees are sensitive to value (good coverage at the right price), less concerned about provider choice, and are satisfied with the quality of care they receive under managed care programs.[2]

Armed with insights like these, employers are in a much better position to anticipate and address employee concerns about medical management issues. Successful programs, for example, help employees understand the importance of primary care and the role of the primary care physician in ensuring that they receive effective, appropriate treatment. Innovative programs also aim to show employees how they can take charge of their health care by building more effective relationships with providers.

FINANCIAL RESULTS

POS programs have grown rapidly because they can generate meaningful savings while retaining employee choice of providers. While the financial results of these programs vary, several consistent trends have emerged. First-year costs under a POS program generally result in savings of 12 to 25 percent relative to projected costs under an indemnity program—and frequently do so while providing a higher level of benefits to employees. Many employers report single-digit inflation in the first year of program operation, a substantial improvement over inflation rates under the indemnity plan.

Several factors affect first-year savings, including the actuarial value of the POS plan design relative to the indemnity plan, the demographics of the group, historic utilization patterns, the location of employees, and the vendor administering the program. POS savings are attributable primarily to three factors: the significant pricing advantages that managed care networks enjoy relative to indemnity payors, marked reductions in hospital and specialist utilization (though offset, in part, by higher utilization of primary care physicians), and more selective provider contracting.

OTHER FACTORS

Employers face additional challenges if they introduce POS at the same time that they consolidate benefit programs and vendors across divisions. The issues associated with consolidation—such as different vendor or design preferences, linking multiple payroll or human resource information systems, local vs. centralized decision making—are often as critical to program success as the issues involved in POS design and implementation.

SUMMARY

While employers' experiences in the first year of POS have varied considerably, some themes recur:

- Key issues for early POS programs were geographic gaps in provider networks and inconsistent vendor administration. Today, better tools for assessing networks, improved administrative systems and procedures, and more mature networks are strengthening first-year results.
- The change to POS managed care is significant and often emotional for employees, largely due to initial concerns about loss of provider choice. An established provider network, effective communication, an experienced vendor, and a well-trained customer service unit are therefore critical to successful implementation.
- The chances for first-year success are enhanced by carefully planning an implementation and communication strategy that draws on other employers' experiences, includes employee research, and is detailed enough to address issues that might arise in the critical period following the program launch.
- Ongoing communication and education, highlighting the plan features employees care most about, can help avoid problems encountered by earlier POS programs.
- Utilization of network providers is high—over two thirds of participants in the Towers Perrin employer survey report that 80 percent or more of medical claims are incurred in the managed care network.
- Financial results have been consistently favorable.

These trends suggest that POS programs require effort (before, during, and after implementation), but that the effort pays off—for employers and their employees.

---

1. *Managed Care: Employer Perspectives 1992* (Towers Perrin; 1992).

2. *Supra* note 1.

11. Coalitions and Purchasing Groups:
Pooling Small Businesses to Control Health Care Costs and Improve Access to Health Insurance Products
Michelle R. Maynard

Small businesses are usually at a disadvantage in the health care benefits market because of their size; health insurance is often prohibitively expensive if available at all. Pooling small businesses into large health care purchasing groups can solve these problems by spreading risk and consolidating the market influence of small business. The Good Neighbor Alliance Corporation, based in Rhode Island, is an example of how a successful health care purchasing group functions.

Health care purchasing groups such as The Good Neighbor Alliance Corporation (GNAC) are becoming powerful purchasers of health insurance and are attempting to reshape local health care delivery systems. There are about 150 purchasing groups nationwide that are designed to bring together the private organizations of hospitals, physicians, employees, laborers, and insurers. Sometimes the government is brought in to assemble and exchange data and to discuss the implications for health care financing and delivery. Most of these organizations began in the late 1970s and early 1980s, out of growing concern about health care costs, access, and quality. Most cities with 100,000 people or more seem to have formed this type of organization.

Although there is no universal definition of "health care purchasing group," the American Hospital Association defines a "health care coalition "as a voluntary alliance of discrete interests sharing the principle of improving health care cost within a community while assuring access to quality services. Health care

Michelle R. Maynard is the managing editor of the Business Letter which is published by The Good Neighbor Alliance Corporation, Warwick, Rhode Island.

purchasing groups represent private sector initiatives that address health issues including the rate of increase of health care expenditures, access, utilization, and quality. They are sponsored by one or more integral groups and create programs to improve costs efficiency in the delivery of health care services.

Successful purchasing groups regularly monitor certain health management factors comparing the cost, utilization, and outcome of each plan. Monitoring health plan rates along with renewals of pooled groups is essential to a coalition's effectiveness.

A number of reform proposals have been initiated at the federal level. These health reforms target small groups and guarantee access to insurance, reduce restrictions on preexisting conditions, allow for portability of plans for workers, and set controlled rates within industries. The states will be given increased latitude to develop legislation to further develop these reforms.

Providing universal access to health care services, controlling health care costs, and maintaining and increasing the quality of health care services remain the primary concerns for health care purchasing organizations. In 1982, GNAC began the quest to deliver a system that could satisfy these goals. As a knowledge-able negotiator with health insurers, GNAC replaced the individual consumer and employee benefits manager for small companies. Insurers were placed under contract to review individual applications for predetermined health plans contain-ing limited underwriting requirements.

GNAC, located in Warwick, Rhode Island, is privately owned. Its original mission was to be a referral service that also advertised statewide for small businesses. In its third year, GNAC recognized the growing need for access to health insurance for small business owners. This business sector experienced a great deal of frustration when attempting to obtain health insurance for them-selves and their employees. Some of the barriers encountered were meeting group standard size, participation levels, and premiums requirements. To eliminate these barriers, GNAC formulated a pooling mechanism that includes small business sole-proprietorships, partnerships and companies for up to ten employees. This pooling mechanism allowed for the smallest of companies to participate in group rates and have access to numerous health plans previously unavailable to employers of ten or less. The pooling mechanism also relieved the participation requirements responsible for low enrollment in health plans.

GNAC is also involved in underwriting on individual merit, allowing companies of one to ten employees to have plan choices without having to pay 100 percent of the employee's premium. GNAC offers each employee the flexibility to choose their own plan options. Through the years, GNAC has remained a reliable service for more than 3,000 small businesses in Rhode Island, Connecticut, and southeastern Massachusetts.

GNAC acknowledged the fact that the quality of health care provided to patients corresponds with the patient's insurance status. A patient without in-surance will not be treated and cared for as diligently as a patient with health coverage. Because they lack insurance, these patients may also be excluded from being advised of follow-up appointments. Awareness of this compelled GNAC to offer health care coverage to as many people as possible.

To become a member there is an initial fee of $75, and a $60 fee for each year thereafter. This fee has remained the same since the program began. Itself a small business, GNAC empathizes with the costs associated with managing and owning a small business, and does not intend to increase their membership fees.

GNAC has contracted with HMOs to enroll small companies by pooling the enrolled. They are able to offer the benefits to the employers at group rates. The ten employee minimum does not apply to the pool. Once a company has six or more employees, GNAC offers to transfer the group directly to the carrier. GNAC than becomes the company's broker, handling the clients' paperwork needs, yet transferring the billing responsibilities to the carrier. Also provided are brochures, presentations, and personal services to companies needing individual attention.

GNAC serves as an insurance broker for companies qualifying in the small group market. For these small groups, comparison proposals are provided between the HMOs and the indemnity plans available. This process provides the client with the information necessary to make an informed choice of products available. Once the choice is made, GNAC begins the enrollment process, verifying form completion, group enrollment requirements, and premium payment schedules. An essential part of reducing the cost of doing business is being able to control administrative expenditures. GNAC has decreased the number of times applications are handled and created a network of informed purchasers of health insurance. GNAC also presents the health and welfare benefit packages to the company's employees. This takes the responsibility away from the employer, who may not have the time or the knowledge to explain the program. It also gives the employees a chance to ask questions and to receive direct answers. Small companies require explanations of various health plans, such as the differences between HMOs, PPOs, and indemnity plans with network options. Small business owners also require assistance in completing group application forms, requesting plan changes (such as name, address, dependents' status, and billing adjustments). When a company enrolls in GNAC, the burden of paperwork is considerably reduced.

Another important aspect is negotiating with carriers over rate renewals. GNAC regularly intercedes at renewal time, suggesting that plan changes and experience reviews be examined to effectively reduce renewal rates. This ensures the affordability of plans.

As an example of GNAC's positive effects on intervention and cost containment, in 1989 the average increase for plan renewals in Rhode Island was between 25 to 30 percent. When the first group renewal was due, GNAC feared the industry's normally high rate and began negotiating for plan adjustments to avoid such increases. The result was no increase in rates with only minor adjustments to plans. The copayments for office visits changed from $5 to $10 and the prescription copayment went from $3 to $5. A similar adjustment was applied to the hospital room and board, changing from 100 percent coverage to 80/20 with a limited out-of-pocket expense of $1000. Physician services remained 100 percent covered. This demonstrated that the cost of health insurance can be reduced through increasing copayments and deductibles, yet preserving the basic health maintenance, hospitalization, and immunization coverage. Since this time, the rate increases have remained between 9 and 12 percent. Currently, choices are available allowing copayments and deductibles for managed care as well as indemnity insurance health plans.

GNAC differs from chambers of commerce because they target services relative to cost effective group purchasing of employee benefits. These benefit programs include not only insurance but tax-saving Section 125 premium payment plans and pension plans such as the profit sharing plan. These programs offer pretax benefits for the employer and employees. GNAC also designs policy and procedure handbooks—essential for small employers. As a resource service to small firms, GNAC realizes that it is essential to provide prospective clients with all the information necessary to weigh the facts involved in owning a business. GNAC takes the time to explain their programs in full over the phone and by appointment. GNAC has been singled out as a national model because its programs clearly target small businesses.

Today there is an increasing demand for companies like GNAC. Of the 14.2 million working Americans that are without employer provided health insurance, 74 percent are employed by firms with fewer than 50 employees. The cost of providing health benefits is preventing many companies from offering such benefits.

The Small Employer Health Insurance Availability Act of Rhode Island, in July 1992, restricts a number of insurance company practices that made it difficult for small businesses to obtain and maintain health insurance for their employees. It prevents insurers from dropping groups or imposing sizable rate increases due to high experience for the group during a particular year. This law limits insurers' ability to offer reduced rates in the first year of coverage, only to raise them 30 to 40 percent on renewal. The law applies to businesses with 50 or fewer employees, which accounts for 96 percent of Rhode Island businesses.

The law also states that an insurance company wishing to market health care benefits to small businesses must accept all members of a group with no exceptions. Policies must be renewed at pre-approved industry renewal rates, regardless of the groups experience during the year. This protects small companies form 40 or 50 percent renewal increases. The insurer may cancel only in cases of fraud or failure to pay premiums. There are two low cost plans defined by this law. The law is expected to give access to health benefits to companies previously rejected for health risk reasons.

The business world has become more and more concerned with the rates of increase in health insurance premiums. When a business owner begins to search for employee benefits, the first priority is affordability. Employers are also concerned with the insurer's financial stability. Administrative efficiency is another important factor, because if claims justification is not processed in a timely and equitable fashion, the employer invariably becomes the villain in the eyes of the employee. GNAC agrees it is good business to take steps to see that your employees remain protected by quality health and welfare programs.

GNAC has developed a wide range of health plans to offer to small businesses. For example, the Ocean State Physicians Health Plan (an HMO) has several options available including deductibles, copayments, and major medical out-of-network coverage. The company may choose the plan that best suits their employees' needs. Another HMO, Harvard Community Health Plan of New England, is suitable for persons and families without preselected health providers. The Harvard Plan (a staff model) provides doctors and other professionals within their own facilities. Employees can select the location nearest to them and the rest is simple. The Guardian Health Plan is an indemnity plan offering major medical coverage along with preventative care elements. GNAC favors plans that carry no maximum dollar limit and offers deductible and copayments to help reduce premiums. These deductibles and copayments usually include an out-of-pocket limit. GNAC also offers dental, life, and disability benefits at group rates. A total of 30 companies are represented by GNAC.

To maximize a company's tax savings, allowing more dollars available for benefits, GNAC aggressively markets Section 125 tax-savings payment plans. These plans relieve payroll tax liability for employer and employee, also relieving federal and, in most states, state income taxes paid on the amount of premium dedicated. An integral part of this plan is the expansion of benefit programs. Each employer will find additional monies to be saved or spent on more benefits such as dental, vision, disability, or life insurance.

If a company is thinking of passing some of the high cost of health benefits on to his employees, or if the employees already pay a substantial amount of their benefits, then it may be time for a Section 125 premium payment plan. Section 125 refers to a section of the tax code that provides that, if an employee is given a choice between taking pay or a company-offered benefit, the employee will not be subject to income taxes on the amount paid for the benefit. Thus, Section 125 allows benefits to be paid for with pretax dollars. The employee's contribution is made by reducing his or her salary. For example, if a person makes $1000 per month and contributes $50 toward health insurance, the taxable income would be $950, not $1000. The annual wage base would be figured as $12,000 less $600, or $11,400 of taxable income.

GNAC has an IRS-approved plan ready to be installed. The cost for companies of less than ten employees is $300. For 11 to 20 employees, it is $395 and gradually increases with the number of employees. The company benefits because the cost of benefits can be shifted and the amount of matching payroll taxes is decreased. Each employee is provided a summary plan description which is required by law, and required recordkeeping is accomplished by the document binder provided by GNAC. Employee election forms and enrollment options are explained during the presentation of the plan. GNAC will coordinate dates of renewal for benefits and offers support on completing the IRS Form 5500, with no annual administration fee. Once installed, the plan contains instructions for annual maintenance of employee elections forms and waivers to remain on file in the binder provided.

12. Direct Provider Contracting

Kenneth W. Drummer

To minimize health benefits costs while ensuring quality, employers must cut out the middlemen, accept a fair share of responsibility and risk, and begin working closely with health care providers. Direct provider contracting allows employers to have all of the cost-saving advantages of an HMO without the HMO.

The past decade has seen tremendous changes in employee health benefits. What began as an attractive fringe benefit that allowed employers to use the tax code to cost-effectively deliver a valuable benefit to employees soon became an uncontrollable financial burden that increasingly drained profits and shareholder value as health care costs grew. Companies have been wrestling with health care costs for years with varying degrees of success, but this most recent wrestling match pits a 97-pound weakling against a 450-pound sumo wrestler armed with an Uzi and a hand grenade.

In order to develop a viable strategy for controlling health care costs, it is useful to begin with some historical perspective to today's employer cost containment initiatives. This article will provide such a perspective as a context for a discussion of the basic principles of contracting for health care services, followed by a case study that illustrates how one company developed and implemented a contracting strategy that effectively addressed its needs and concerns.

In 1973, Congress passed the Health Maintenance Organization (HMO) Act, requiring all companies with more than 25 workers to offer their employees the option of joining a health maintenance organization if one was available. This was met with as much employer resistance as it was with public fanfare. At the

Based on an article that appeared in *Managing Employee Health Benefits,* Vol. 1, issue 1, Fall 1992. A Panel Publication, Aspen Publishers, Inc., in Association with Epstein Becker & Green, PC.

time, the driving force for the HMO Act was actually the maintenance of health, not the control of costs; that wouldn't come until much later. These prepaid organizations were required to provide a broad range of services, including well baby care and annual physicals. In addition, they were required to provide an unlimited amount of most hospital and physician services. They were also required to admit anyone without regard to any preexisting condition, and they were required to set their premiums on a community-rated basis. As it turned out, these mandated service and underwriting requirements drove the premiums for many early HMOs above the premiums of most traditional employer plans.

The HMO of the early 1970s was little different from today's HMO in terms of the scope of benefits and the way those benefits are provided to HMO members. What has changed is the employer's desire to implement the features of the classic HMO that work to control cost. An employer has a good shot at controlling costs if it can replicate the HMO infrastructure in its contracts with providers, insurance carriers, or third party administrators (TPAs). Key elements of the HMO infrastructure include a network of providers whose practice patterns are consistent with cost-effective quality care, provider reimbursement that includes a certain amount of risk sharing, and effective utilization review and treatment protocols. In other words, managed care.

The agreement between the employer and the delivery system—whether it's a contract between the employer and one or more providers, or a contract between the employer and an insurance carrier or TPA that, in turn, subcontracts with providers—defines the employer's ability to manage its health care costs.

IMPLICATIONS FOR PROVIDER CONTRACTING

The employer can no longer hope to manage health care costs from the sidelines. In today's health care arena, the employer must put on a uniform and get in the game. One way an employer can do this is to work closely with health care providers (directly, or through its insurance company or TPA) to share financial risk, ensure adequate access, provide acceptable levels of service, and deliver quality health care consistent with recognized standards of treatment.

Risk Sharing

Health economists have long known that providers at financial risk will alter their treatment planning and their patterns of care in order to optimize reimbursement. Positive ramifications of this type of incentive include fewer unnecessary tests and procedures, increased use of paramedical personnel for patient intake and education, greater efficiencies in the office, and expanded scope of primary care practice (e.g., fewer specialty referrals). However, critics of risk sharing argue that the quality of care may suffer in this environment because fewer tests may leave conditions undiagnosed, use of paramedical personnel exposes the patient to staff who are not fully trained, office efficiencies may come at the expense of the doctor-patient relationship, and primary care physicians are encouraged to treat conditions beyond the scope of their training. On balance, the risk sharing arguments should carry the day, provided there are sufficient checks and balances to ensure ongoing quality care (however that term is defined).

Access and Channeling

The underlying principle of all managed care schemes is that care delivered by network providers will be more cost-effective than care delivered outside of the network. This is due primarily to the existence of favorable financial arrangements with network providers coupled with various mechanisms to ensure the delivery of medically necessary care in the most cost-effective setting (e.g., utilization review, treatment protocols for certain conditions, centers of excellence for high cost/high risk procedures, etc.).

Obviously, these economies can only be achieved if employees use network providers. This creates a dilemma for employers. On the one hand, a large network will help ensure that employees will not have to change physicians in order to get the maximum benefits available under the plan. Unfortunately, a large network is more likely to include expensive and inefficient physicians than a small network of carefully selected providers. On the other hand, a small network should be better positioned to control costs. Unfortunately, a small network does not meet the same standards of access as a larger network.

Employers that opt for the smaller network must have effective channeling to encourage network use. Typically this channeling involves the use of economic incentives (for example, no deductible and nominal copayments in the network versus significant deductibles and as much as 30 percent coinsurance outside the network). The principle of channeling has always existed in the HMO environment where the patient who fails to use the HMO provider gets no benefit at all. However, until recently, this type of channeling only existed outside of the employer sponsored plan. The employee was always free to remain in the employer plan where he could enjoy unrestricted choice of physicians. It can be argued that significant financial channeling in the employer plan will hold the employer to a higher standard of network access and quality than existed under the old indemnity fee-for-service environment. I suspect that this standard would be even greater for the employer who contracts directly with providers.

Acceptable Levels of Service

The move from indemnity plans to provider networks has not been an easy one. In the old indemnity environment, patients had unlimited choice of providers and the only other limits they encountered were the occasional reduction in reimbursement due to the application of usual, customary, and reasonable limits (UCR). With the introduction of the provider network, employers must deal with their employees as a "captive audience." In today's network, there are really two types of service that should be addressed. The first concerns how networks and other vendors relate to the employer: Do they provide data in a timely fashion? Do they monitor service and provide feedback? Are the network and vendor representatives accessible to the employer's benefits staff? The second level of service is the employee level: Do employees have to wait for appointments? Are they informed about the treatment they are receiving? At this level, many of the issues revolve around whether the program works as advertised. For example, are there really no claim forms? Is the provider directory up to date? Are referrals to specialists timely? Are medical records transmitted to the specialist office? Is the utilization review procedure transparent to the patient?

Quality Care

As employers move toward managed care arrangements, there is a growing emphasis on quality of care. Quality is a very elusive standard, but it is nevertheless an important consideration in contracting with provider networks as well as with insurance companies and TPAs that offer network services. Perhaps the employer's responsibility vis-à-vis quality is to focus on credentialling and health care delivery procedures. In other words, does the network do a thorough job of credentialling its providers? And does it have an active quality assurance program that measures health outcomes, monitors provider treatment patterns, and provides feedback to providers who practice outside of accepted community norms?

CONTRACT PROVISIONS

The first step in the development of a contracting strategy is to identify the activities where the employer wishes to monitor performance, and to specify where the employer expects the network, insurance carrier, or TPA to accept responsibility. The next step is to identify the expected level of performance, define the process for measuring results, and specify any deliverables and the timing of their delivery. Think of the contracting strategy as a prenuptial agreement. You hope the relationship works out, but just in case you encounter rocks along the way, you want to have the duties and responsibilities of all parties clearly defined in advance. Some of the specific issues you should consider before you sit down at the bargaining table with a provider network, insurance carrier, TPA, or other health care vendor are discussed below.

Due Diligence

Due diligence refers to the employer's responsibility to evaluate and verify provider credentials, methods of operation, and quality standards. Due diligence raises an interesting distinction between the employer who contracts directly with health care providers versus the employer who contracts with a carrier or TPA that, in turn, contracts with physicians and hospitals for health care services. It would appear that an employer who contracts directly with providers would have a greater burden to monitor its network than would the employer who contracts with a third party. On the other hand, an employer that contracts with a third party for the delivery of health services through a contracting provider network must, at a minimum, satisfy itself that the third party maintains an effective provider credentialling and quality assurance program. Furthermore, the employer would be well-advised to maintain an oversight role to ensure the ongoing quality of the network and the care it delivers.

Access to Care

Access extends beyond having a "sufficient" number of physicians in a given geographic area. Employers need to do a better job at determining whether the network has acceptable ratios of physicians in each specialty to serve the covered population. For example, a network with lots of physicians might be deemed to provide inadequate access to a predominately female population if there were only a few OB/GYN specialists. The same holds true for a network that covers areas separated by natural geographic barriers (i.e., lakes, mountains, state parks, etc.) that effectively deny access to its providers. Likewise, an employer should satisfy himself that the network addresses community boundaries as well as language and ethnic considerations.

Liability

The central liability question is this: Does an employer who endeavors to evaluate the quality of care delivered by a provider network certify to that quality? Alternatively, does an employer distance himself from the issue of quality by serving in an oversight capacity in which he satisfies himself that the provider credentialling process and ongoing quality assurance procedures are thorough and well-documented?

When contracting with a third party to manage the network, the employer would be well-advised to include contractual language that holds the third party accountable for maintaining effective provider credentialling procedures, minimum access standards, and ongoing quality assurance programs. Furthermore, the contract should specify that the third party will hold the employer harmless for the medical care delivered by the network.

Antitrust Issues

The purpose of antitrust legislation is to promote competition. An employer concerned about antitrust issues would need to determine whether its contracting strategy promotes either a conspiracy of buyers or is the victim of a conspiracy of sellers of health services. Where an employer coalition accounts for a market share of 35 percent or more and could effectively put a hospital out of business by refusing good faith negotiations on price, utilization controls, and/or quality outcome measures, caution may be justified to avoid allegations of a group purchasing conspiracy with an unreasonable effect on competition. On the other hand, a conspiracy of sellers might exist among a nonfinancially integrated group of physicians that acts to boycott an employer, particularly when the group includes more than, say, 20 percent of all local private practice physicians or has "market power" in one or more physician specialties.

An employer's antitrust exposure can be minimized by planning. Planning activities might include an assessment of the purchasing power represented by the employer or employer coalition in the relevant geographic market. If exclusivity provisions are employed, planning activities should include an analysis of the degree of foreclosure in various sectors of the provider community. "Foreclosure" refers to the extent to which providers are barred by contract from participating in competitors' networks. An excessive degree of foreclosure might justify allowing physicians greater latitude in joining other networks.

Method of Provider Payment and/or Patient Reimbursement

Here the issue is one of adequacy. An employer must be knowledgeable about the provider reimbursement practices used by the program administrator. If the reimbursement schedule is too low, there is a real danger that the provider network will fall apart because the provider's income requirements are not being met. If the reimbursement is overly generous, then plan costs will soon become excessive. Another reimbursement risk that employers need to be aware of deals with market share. If the program administrator cannot deliver meaningful market share to local providers, then it is possible that the effectiveness of utilization controls will be degraded and some of the physicians might elect to resign from the network. An employer must be wary with respect to the promise of short-term savings if they come at the expense of network stability.

Penalties and Disincentives

What constitutes noncompliance? In the early days of cost containment, many employers implemented second surgical opinion programs where an employee could be penalized (i.e., receive reduced reimbursement) for not following the "weight of opinion." In other words, if two consulting surgeons said the surgery was not indicated and the patient went ahead and had the surgery anyway, then payment would be reduced. Today's approach makes the second opinion an administrative requirement for certain procedures. Failure to follow the administrative rules could result in a reduction in reimbursement.

In the case of the precertification of a hospital admission, the typical program involves a nurse's review of the attending physician's diagnosis and proposed treatment plan. If the review organization disagrees with the attending physician, the case is referred to another physician who attempts to reach a consensus with the attending doctor. Generally, this is sufficient to resolve the situation.

There are two types of reviews. The first type involves a review of a physician's recommendation where both the physician and the reviewer are contractually bound to the same organization. In this situation, the contract with the attending physician binds the doctor to the review process. Here, it is almost universally true that an agreement will be reached between the attending physician and the reviewing entity. Furthermore, that agreement will be, in almost all cases, transparent to the patient.

The second type of review involves an attending physician outside of the network. In this case, the attending physician may not be as likely to follow the recommendations of the review organization. Where this occurs, the review organization should only consider reduced patient (or provider) reimbursement where the proposed treatment plan clearly lies outside of accepted local medical patterns of practice. (This situation, more than any other, argues for the employer to distance himself from the actual operation of the network.)

Grievance Mechanism

Managed care programs, like HMOs, have various rules that patients and providers must follow in order to receive benefits or payments from the program administrator. If those rules are not followed, or if they are followed and an undesired outcome ensues, it is likely that a disagreement or dispute will occur.

For this reason, it is imperative that there be a formal grievance mechanism in place. The grievance program should be in writing and it should spell out the rights of the parties, the steps that patients (or providers) must take to preserve their rights, the documentation that is required, the different stages in the grievance process, the time frames of each stage, and the responsibilities of the parties to the dispute.

Administrative Requirements

Administrative considerations relevant to a directly contracted network include:

- Defining the employer's data requirements;
- Establishing eligibility verification procedures to be followed by network providers;
- Documenting billing and payment administration;
- Protecting against business interruption (i.e., strikes by physicians, nurses, or other professional groups if contracting with a clinic or hospital, and providing terminations when contracting with a network of independent contractors); and
- Providing for continuation of coverage in the event of bankruptcy or plan termination.

Additional provisions are called for when contracting with an HMO. For example, the duration of the enrollment period and the methodology used to set community or experience rates would help clarify the employer-HMO relationship.

Remedies

When an employer contracts with a program administrator or directly with providers, there is an expectation that the services contracted for will be provided in accordance with the terms of the contract. However, in the event that services are not provided, the contract should address the question of remedies. For example, the employer may want to ensure that employees will be satisfied with the services provided by the program administrator. The employer might suggest the following contract provision to address this issue:

> [T]he Program Administrator will conduct a survey of employees each year using a written survey instrument acceptable to the Employer. An employee satisfaction rating of less than 70 percent will be deemed unacceptable and will result in financial penalties to the Program Administrator equal to one month's administration charge. In addition, the Program Administrator will be required to furnish a Remedial Plan of Action to the Employer within 45 days of the survey date. This Plan of Action will serve as the basis for

Employer/Program Administrator initiated activities to correct program deficiencies identified in the survey. This proposed language would then be negotiated by the Employer and the Program Administrator and included in the contract that will govern their relationship.

A Case Study in Network Contracting

A 4,000 life multi-site employer in northern California was unhappy with its multiple vendor program. The company had separate contracts with its TPA, a preferred provider organization (PPO) network, and with an independent utilization review firm to monitor patient care. After a review of the situation and consideration of available options, the company elected to market its health benefits program. Our client felt that a single vendor might offer a more coordinated approach along with an expanded provider network, and possibly even better discounts than those available through their TPA/PPO network arrangement.

We prepared detailed bid specifications, sent requests for proposals to a group of vendors, evaluated the responses, and interviewed the three most qualified vendors. Based on the interviews and the objective analysis of the detailed proposals, we were able to select the vendor that promised the best fit with our client. We defined "best fit" in terms of meeting our client's financial and personnel objectives. The successful vendor also demonstrated that its business philosophy was compatible with our client's. Everyone was convinced that the right decision was made, that there was a good fit, and that a long and mutually rewarding relationship lay ahead. Then came the fun part: Negotiating a contract before the honeymoon was over. Here are some of the concerns that helped define our negotiating strategy:

- Our client is in a low margin business, so stable predictable costs were a prime concern.
- The company has a tradition of providing quality benefits, so access to popular network providers was an issue.
- Customer service is a hallmark of the company's operations, so efficient and helpful service was a must from the new vendor.

We began the negotiations prior to the final selection of the vendor by making the selection contingent upon their agreement in principle to negotiate the following:

1. A rolling three-year contract where the financial terms of the fourth year of the contract are negotiated at the end of the first year, the terms of the fifth at the end of the second, etc.;
2. Performance standards on measurable service levels; and
3. Provision of specific deliverables within specified time frames.

The financial contract turned out to be the most straightforward phase of the negotiations. Here we were concerned with both fixed and variable costs. The key to the financial arrangements was to obtain all of the assumptions for all of the projected costs before actually sitting down to bargain. At our request, the vendor provided a detailed breakdown of its fixed administration costs. The vendor proposed that year-to-year increases in these costs be limited to the Bay Area CPI (currently at 3.5 percent) as measured for the period October to October. As this seemed to be a reasonable proposal, we accepted and moved on to the more complex issue of stop-loss insurance.

The vendor initially provided an estimated monthly claims cost per employee, and a monthly charge for stop loss insurance for amounts in excess of the estimated claims. Although this information was necessary, it was not sufficient for purposes of nailing down the economics of the relationship, so we asked for their assumed split between network and non-network usage and the components of trend for network services separate from non-network services. Our goal was to identify which assumptions were reasonable and which were not; with the level of detail this information provided, we could isolate and effectively challenge unreasonable assumptions. For example, the vendor proposed an 18.5 percent overall trend for the 1993-1994 period. Although this might appear to be in line with prevailing practice, upon closer examination, the 18.5 percent was a blend of reasonable non-network trend components and unacceptably high network trend components (6 percent inflation and 10 percent utilization for network physician services). Based on this information, we argued that the carrier should either lower its stop-loss premium to reflect the conservative trend assumption for network usage, or lower the attachment point to reflect their actual risk.

Negotiating performance standards begins with the identification of services that are important to the employer and to its employees. Our client was concerned with, among other things, claims turnaround for out-of-network claims, network access, and timely utilization and financial reports. For each area, we determined a range of acceptable performance and we identified both how the performance was to be measured and the financial penalty for not meeting the standard. In all cases, we specified that the remedy included a business plan to correct any deficiency, a time frame to bring the situation into compliance, and the identity of the individual responsible for the corrective action.

Claims Turnaround

The negotiated standard was 90 percent of claims within ten business days. A penalty of 5 percent of the administration fee would be assessed for each day (or fraction of a day) that the turnaround (as self-reported by the vendor) was in excess of the standard for two consecutive months or three months in any six-month period. The vendor also agreed to an outside audit upon 30 days notice when requested by our client.

Network Access

Here we identified appointment lead time as a measure of accessibility. The vendor is required to monitor the waiting time for routine family care, specialist referrals, surgical consults, and appointments for routine physicals. The measurement consists of a random survey of network providers; the next available appointment for each of the services is recorded and reported on a quarterly basis. For example, two weeks is acceptable for a specialist referral while 30 days is okay for a routine physical. There were no financial penalties associated with this standard. However, we felt that monitoring the appointment lead time would be useful in the early identification and correction of problems with network capacity.

Timely Financial and Utilization Reports

We identified the content of the financial and utilization reports (summary level, detail level, and *ad hoc* reports), the timing for delivery (15 business days following the close of the month or quarter and 30 business days following the year-end close), and the penalty for late reports ($1,000 to $5,000 per week or fraction of a week, depending on the report).

Summary

Contracting with health care providers is not very different from contracting with a vendor to provide a manufacturer with raw materials. In exchange for financial consideration, the vendor agrees to provide specific services or to deliver a quantity of goods in accordance with the terms and conditions of a contract. In contracting for health services, be sure to address the following three issues.

Understand the Risk

The least exposure appears to be the case where an employer doesn't sponsor a health insurance program. An employer who only offers HMOs probably doesn't have much exposure since HMOs are licensed by the state and often by the federal government and must adhere to their regulatory requirements (although for many people this provides very little comfort). Employers who impose financial penalties for employee or provider noncompliance with plan rules may begin to feel the tug of legal exposure since an employee's health care decisions could be influenced by plan economics. Employers who implement point of sale (POS) programs have the greatest exposure for two reasons. First, they have a network of providers that is by definition a subset of the universe of local providers. This situation can result in questions of reasonable access (providers are too distant, not fluent in the employee's native language, etc.). Second, the POS plan includes significant financial penalties that could influence patient behavior. Finally, employers who contract directly with providers probably have a greater exposure than would employers who contract with a third party.

Standards of Performance

The process that an employer goes through to design its benefit program and to select a program administrator is as complex as it is time-consuming. During the process, the program administrator is likely to make all kinds of representations regarding provider credentialling, quality assurance, network operation, claims adjudication, training of physician office staff, claims data availability, etc. The employer would be well-advised to take these representations with a grain of salt. Once a program administrator has been selected, the employer must be prepared to clearly define the performance standards that it will expect from the administrator. The contract should identify the standards of performance, define how performance will be measured, describe how often and by whom the performance will be measured, and provide details regarding the remedy that will be applied in the event the performance standards have not been met. Standards of performance include physician ratios, minimum geographic access, data reporting, employee satisfaction measures, grievance resolution reporting, patient waiting time for appointments and selected procedures, quality assurance program documentation, and claim turnaround time for out-of-area claims.

Fiduciary Responsibility

Even where the employer has negotiated standards of performance to its complete satisfaction, there exists the possibility that an employee will bring a cause of action against the provider, the program administrator, and the employer. The employer should make every effort to have the program administrator accept full fiduciary responsibility for the operation of the network—specifically, provider credentialling and utilization review activities. Whenever there is an undesirable medical outcome there exists the possibility of litigation. Employers must be absolutely satisfied that adequate amounts of malpractice insurance are maintained by the program administrator, and that the program administrator requires that all contracting providers maintain their own policies in amounts acceptable to the employer.

CONCLUSION

Contracting for health services is one of the most difficult activities on the benefits manager's agenda. It requires a clear statement of financial and human resources objectives, a thorough understanding of health care delivery, an awareness of prevailing practices, and a working knowledge of contracting strategy and performance measurement. The good news is that successful implementation of a well-conceived provider contracting strategy will pay significant dividends in terms of satisfied employees and a healthy bottom line for the company.

13.   The Designated Service Plan

Linn J. Baker   Lori Sawyer Jenson

Introducing competition at the premium level has proved effective at controlling health care benefit costs, but as the state of Utah realized, competition at this level alone is not enough. In response, Utah's Public Employees Health Program has developed a bold new plan that brings market forces to bear on all aspects of health care delivery, rewarding providers for efficient and effective care and plan members for intelligent and cost-conscious benefit utilization.

In the 1970s, the state of Utah began experimenting with various programs and plans in an effort to control health care costs, and although it has had some success—the rate of increase of health care costs has been held to 7 percent over the past six years—the need to develop more innovative programs still exists. In 1993, Utah's Public Employee Health Program (PEHP) launched its newest effort, the Designated Service Plan (DSP), in an effort to control rising costs through the use of natural market forces.

UTAH'S SELF-ADMINISTERED HEALTH PROGRAM

In 1977, Utah created its own self-insured health program for public employees, which became the Public Employees Health Program (PEHP). The new self-funded and self-administered program saved money in a number of ways. First, it saved the money normally spent on agent or broker fees and commissions. Second, it eliminated the retention fees that had previously been paid to carriers. Third, the low administrative fees, kept below 4 percent of premiums (currently averaging 2.5 percent), included a variety of services such as premium tax, administrative costs, risk charges, and reinsurance charges, which generally add another 10 to 15 percent to premiums. Finally, interest earnings on reserve accounts offset most of the administrative overhead.

PEHP Uses a Competitive HMO Model

In the early 1980s, PEHP began to understand the importance of offering multiple health maintenance organization (HMO) options to its members. To stimulate competition at the premium level, Utah required potential HMOs to bid on a defined benefit package for a three-year contract period. Plans were required to hold their second and third year premium increases to the medical cost component of the consumer price index, preventing any plans from offering a low first year rate that would "buy" the business and then make profits the second and third years by disproportionately raising prices.

Defining benefits and requiring that all medical specialties be represented in the provider network prevented any carrier from avoiding risk through benefit design or by excluding high-risk specialties. The state's share of the premium was then determined to meet the requirements of law requiring equal contributions toward insurance. As a result, these premiums served to motivate employees to select the most cost-effective carrier (i.e., those who offered the lowest premium). By evening the competitive playing field in this fashion, Utah stimulated competition at the premium level.

PEHP Creates a PPO

In 1985, PEHP organized a statewide preferred provider organization (PPO) as a self-administered, managed care option for its employees. As part of the PPO, PEHP developed a preferred panel of providers, physician global fees, and a draft system that provides immediate payment to hospitals and physicians.

In selecting physicians for its preferred panel, PEHP implemented a profiling system that reviewed high-volume medical procedures to determine which providers were most cost-effective. Physicians with proven records of quality and efficiency were identified as potential candidates for the PPO. PEHP's approach was to select a small panel of efficient providers, representing roughly 25 percent of Utah's providers, who would agree to use the diagnostic related groups (DRG) system and physician global fees to provide services to PEHP's 85,000 members. The small panel allowed PEHP to direct a greater volume of patients to its PPO, which has placed PEHP in a strong position when negotiating fees.

Currently, 50 percent of state employees are members of the preferred care system. Because employees in the traditional plan are encouraged to use preferred providers at the point of service for a lower copayment, 80 percent of PEHP's claim costs are paid to preferred providers.

PEHP physician global fees were designed for high-volume inpatient and outpatient procedures. These fees include the costs of pre- and postoperative care, diagnostic tests, and assistant surgeon's charges when appropriate. Physicians are free to use any PPO facility, as the PPO global surgical fee does not include facilities. This system provides physicians with financial incentive to control unnecessary utilization by providing them with greater profit when they are efficient and keep total charges less than the global fee. Under the traditional system, inefficient physicians make greater profit by providing more services, even when the additional care is unnecessary.

PEHP had an initial concern that physicians might provide poor care to increase profit from physician global fees. In the last eight years, however, PEHP has encountered no complaints from patients about this issue. Physicians take pride in the care they render, and their concern for malpractice issues along with their desire to provide quality care are the most important factors in delivering care.

PEHP developed a draft system similar to a credit card system to pay preferred providers. The draft system pays the provider immediately upon completion of service, limits paper work, and requires low administrative over-head. Providers are issued draft forms as needed, and are required to verify members as eligible before performing a service. Upon completing a service for which physician global fees have been established, participating physicians call PEHP and request an authorization number for their draft. The claim is processed while the physician is on the phone. Once an authorization number from PEHP is received, the draft can then be deposited as a check. Providers then submit an itemized bill to PEHP, which is verified against the draft claim for accuracy. If discrepancies arise upon verification, they are handled through PEHP's audit department.

UTAH SEEKS ADDITIONAL CHANGES

During the past six years, Utah's self-administered plans have experienced claims cost increases averaging an annual rate of only 7 percent. In the role of employer, insurer, and managed care provider, PEHP has come to believe that managed care has done an excellent job of reducing unnecessary utilization and has provided fees that are the lowest in the industry. In spite of these successes, however, managed care has not yet demonstrated the long-term ability to significantly control the rate of premium increases. PEHP believes that competition must be extended beyond the premium level if health care costs are to compare favorably to cost increases in other industries.

Generally, managed care systems continue to insulate members from quality and cost information before an episode of care is provided. Current methods of managing unnecessary utilization, such as contracting with specific facilities for *all* services, as opposed to contracting with specific facilities for specific procedures, is inefficient and far too costly. This method of managing care does not encourage specialization at the hospital level when negotiating for hospital services. Although managed care systems do receive lower charges than their competitors, these systems often lack sufficient influence over the increase in rates. (When a hospital grants a discount of 20 percent, these systems have no way of knowing what kind of discount 20 percent really is because they have no control over the base on which the discount is computed, nor how that base increases over time.)

THE DESIGNATED SERVICE PLAN

During the past year PEHP has created the Designated Service Plan, which is best described as a managed care network making use of market forces to discipline the health care marketplace. These market forces allow competition to function as efficiently as it does in other industries. PEHP believes that competition, although essential at the premium level, must also be present throughout the industry and extend all the way to the point of service.

At the core of the DSP is the concept that health care services must be clearly defined because appropriate patterns of treatment enhance the episode of care and reduce costs. Rather than dictate protocol to providers, PEHP met with groups of local physicians and health care experts and allowed them to define the necessary components of various episodes of care. Practice guidelines were created to maintain quality of care while encouraging effective, consistent patterns of treatment that lead to reduced costs.

Appropriate patterns of treatment not only optimize the episode of care and define the medical product, they allow the DSP to negotiate a price for the care. This price is a true global fee that encompasses the cost of all essential components for each episode, including hospital, physician, diagnostic tests, and anesthesia charges. Several hundred Utah physicians and over a dozen hospitals have agreed to these fees.

Global fees have also been negotiated for outpatient medical care, including chronic conditions such as allergies, asthma, back pain, and chiropractic care. For inpatient mental health, four global fees have been allocated to four case categories depending on patient age and diagnosis.

To understand how the DSP is used by members of PEHP, consider the following example: PEHP member John Smith recently played a game of volleyball in which he tore the anterior cruciate ligament in his knee. He visited his orthopedic surgeon, Dr. Payne, who recommended arthroscopic

surgery. John knows that he can pay 10 percent of the facility charge and have
Dr. Payne perform the surgery in any facility, or he can use a DSP provider
and pay a predetermined copayment that is roughly half the charge under
traditional plans. John looks up the surgery he needs in his *DSP Health
Information Guide,* where he finds the reasons for surgery, expected outcomes,
risks, expected hospital stay, expected disability or time off work, and information about anesthesia and its risks. Then John consults the *DSP Consumer
Guide* for eligible DSP orthopedic surgeons (those who have agreed to global
fees), where he finds that Dr. Payne is a DSP participator at facilities A and
C. He chooses to have Dr. Payne perform the surgery at facility A. John's
copayment under the DSP is $250. Under traditional plans, 10 percent copay-
ments for the same procedure average $538, but are as low as $415 and as
high as $711. (These charges are based on routine procedures without com-
plications. No outliers were included.)

The DSP is Unique

The DSP differs from a PPO or an HMO in three important ways. First, the
DSP contracts for specific, identified services rather than individual facilities.
In an independent practice association (IPA), HMO, or PPO, groups negotiate
with hospitals for reduced rates for every service offered by that hospital.
Typically, the reductions are granted in the form of DRGs, per diems, or
percentage discounts; the larger the group, the greater the discount. Under the
DSP, groups contract with hospitals for only those services the hospital
delivers most efficiently, rather than for all services. This encourages
specialization and, ultimately, cost control.

Second, the DSP allows providers to control utilization. With an IPA, HMO,
or PPO individuals other than those providing service dictate what care is
delivered. The DSP transfers issues of utilization and appropriateness of care back
to the provider community.

Third, the DSP transfers risk back to the provider community. With other
forms of managed care, insurance carriers typically absorb risk, leaving
providers free to benefit from overutilization (i.e., create greater profit by
providing more services, many of which are unnecessary). PEHP found that
providers in the community were interested in changing the current market
and were committed to cutting costs. In turn, the DSP global fees are structured
so that providers are rewarded for efficient treatment and care, and are at
financial risk for overutilization or inefficient treatment of conditions.
Providers are, however, protected from complicated cases; if total charges
exceed the global fee by 40 percent or more, the claim is paid through the
conventional system.

Selecting Participating DSP Providers

PEHP used its PPO selection process to qualify physicians for the DSP. They reviewed high-volume medical procedures to determine which providers were most cost-effective, and identified physicians with proven records of quality and efficiency as potential candidates. PEHP's approach was to select a small panel of providers, allowing it to direct a greater volume of patients to DSP providers.

In selecting hospitals to participate in the DSP, PEHP used a novel approach and contracted with various hospitals for *only* those services they perform most efficiently, rather than contracting with specific hospitals for all services. This approach encourages specialization and discourages hospitals from providing services already available to the community elsewhere at competitive rates and excellent outcomes. This contracting process focuses volume more intensely than a typical managed care system that contracts with several hospitals for all services.

The DSP simplifies billing, payment, and administration by paying the global fee to one entity (the hospital), which then pays each participating provider (surgeon, anesthesiologist, etc.). The process streamlines billing and eliminates many costly utilization review services, resulting in reduced administrative costs. It also allows hospitals and physicians to form partnerships to provide profit incentives for all participants.

Global Fees Benefit Everyone

Global fees work for everyone. They are designed to help insurers, consumers, and health care providers. They allow insurers to offer lower, competitive premiums and control spiraling health care costs. They provide consumers with lower premiums and copayments, encourage them to actively participate in choosing quality, cost-effective care, and provide them with predetermined copayments *before* an episode of service. Global fees encourage providers to specialize and offer competitive rates for similar services, and enable them to understand how their charges compare to others in the community.

Global fees have the following effects on the market:

- Efficient providers whose cost is less than the global fee make a greater profit. Contrast this to the current system of inefficient providers making greater profits by providing more services, even when care is unnecessary.
- The market principle of volume is greatly enhanced by the DSP's global fees. Unlike federal programs such as Medicare and Medicaid, which dictate price and provide no additional patient volume to the more efficient provider, the DSP contracts global fees with specific providers and then funnels patients to them.

- Insured employees become price sensitive because they know the cost of care before it is given. In addition, they are at risk for the additional charges (the amount of which is often unknown until after an episode of care) when they use a plan that does not utilize global fees.

Information For Consumers

Because the DSP negotiates fees in advance, cost and copayment information is available through the *DSP Consumer Guide*. The guide also publishes community charges for high-volume procedures including charges for hospital, surgeon, and anesthesia, and price information on brand-name and generic drugs.

The *DSP Health Information Guide* is a companion volume to the *DSP Consumer Guide* that includes information on preventive care and common medical conditions (see Exhibits 1 and 2). The guides provide consumers with the following information to help them make informed choices when surgery is necessary:

- Reasons the procedure may be necessary
- Description of the procedure
- Complications and risks associated with the procedure
- Expected length of stay for hospitalization
- Recovery time
- Range of cost from local providers
- Which providers have agreed to global fees and are participating designated providers
- Prescription drug information, including the benefits and risks of each drug, side effects, and drug interactions

The changes already taking place are exciting to see as individuals in the health care industry respond to traditional market forces. Provider concern for competitive charges in the community is motivating them to change their behavior and become more aggressive in controlling costs, and efficient providers willing to optimize outcomes by following practice guidelines are rewarded with greater profit. In return for creating and adhering to practice guidelines and accepting responsibility for financial risk, the responsibility of proper utilization and appropriateness of care is being returned to providers. Controlling unnecessary utilization through global fees places the physician, not the carrier, in the appropriate role of managing the patient's care.

Providers Have Responded Favorably to the DSP

The DSP has been overwhelmingly accepted by providers. Physicians are eager to participate, in part because it gives them the opportunity to actively reform the

Exhibit 1. Example of *DSP Health Information Guide* Entry

EAR, NOSE, AND THROAT

THROAT

Tonsillectomy & Adenoidectomy

A T&A is the surgical removal of your tonsil and adenoid tissue. The tonsils are lymphatic tissue located on each side of your throat behind your tongue. They are easily seen, especially if enlarged. Extreme enlargement of the tonsils is occasionally a reason for removal. More often, they are removed because of repeated tonsillitis (infected tonsils). The adenoids are also lymphatic tissue located in the back of the nasal passages and upper throat near the eustachian tube opening. They are hidden from view by the palate. Adenoids are occasionally removed without a tonsillectomy to improve breathing or to decrease the incidence of ear infections.

Reasons for Surgery
- Frequent tonsillitis despite adequate medical therapy
- Enlargement of tonsils and adenoids causing respiratory obstructions
- Chronic strep carrier state, non-responsive to adequate medical therapy
- Chronic ear infection associated with recurrent tonsillitis and/or enlargement of adenoids

Anesthesia
- General anesthesia

Expected Outcome
- Reduction of mouth breathing and snoring
- Stops tonsillitis
- Reduction of incidence of strep infections

Risks of Surgery
- All surgeries have benefits and risks. The risks of outpatient surgery are no different than for inpatient hospital surgeries. Complications for outpatient and inpatient surgeries are rare and most can be avoided if you follow your physician's and anesthesiologist's instructions. The most common complications occur less than 1 percent of the time and include bleeding (risk of transfusion), respiratory complications, injury to surrounding tissue, and infection.

  Many complications depend on the patient's health, not just the type of surgery. Before any surgery, make sure you discuss with your physician in detail all of the possible complications for which you are at risk. It is your physician's responsibility to thoroughly inform you of risks and benefits so you may give an informed consent.

This guide is designed to introduce information allowing you to discuss risks and benefits involved in medical care, including surgery. You and your physician can decide which recommendations are best for your needs and ensure that your surgery experience is safe and successful.

Expected Hospital Stay
- None. This is an ambulatory surgical procedure.

Expected Disability/Time Off Work
- T&A: 10–14 days off work or school
- Adenoidectomy: one to two days before resuming normal activities

Other Procedures Commonly Performed at Time of Surgery
- Tympanostomy (ear tubes)

Range of Cost, Copayments, and Physicians
- Please see the DSP Consumer Guide, Exhibit 2: Example of *DSP Consumer Guide* Entry

inefficient health care system. Because the *DSP Consumer Guide* also publishes community charges for DSP procedures, the DSP allows them to see how they compare with other providers in the community.

Hospitals are also eager to participate and adjust to the competitive marketplace. Several hospitals in the Salt Lake Valley perform open heart surgery with some of the best outcomes rates in the nation. One of those hospitals performed the procedure for $10,000 less than another, with identical or improved outcomes. PEHP agreed to contract for open heart surgery with the more efficient hospital based on outstanding outcomes and efficiency, but declined to contract with the more expensive hospital because of their inefficient pricing. As a result, the more expensive hospital reevaluated their charges to determine the cause for the discrepancy in price. They determined that the difference was not warranted and decreased their charges to compete with local hospitals.

PEHP believes the same market forces that are effective in other industries can be equally effective in the health care market. Americans should not assume that we cannot overcome the absence of real market principles of the health care market of the past. PEHP has shown that market principles can be effectively applied to the American health care market without excessive regulation, and that

Exhibit 2. Example of *DSP Consumer Guide Entry*

Ear, Nose & Throat

Out-Patient

Participating Facilities/Providers
See E.N.T. Providers

Tonsillectomy (under 12) (42825)

Cost Range:	Low	Average	High
Surgeon	$ 300.00	$ 367.00	$ 500.00
Anesthesia	$ 189.00	$ 259.00	$ 350.00
Hospital	$ 713.00	$ 904.00	$1,737.00
Total:	$1,202.00	$1,530.00	$2,587.00
Usual Copay*	**$ 71.00**	**$ 90.00**	**$ 174.00**

DSP Copay: $25.00

Tonsillectomy (over 12) (42826)

Cost Range:	Low	Average	High
Surgeon	$ 328.00	$ 413.00	$ 500.00
Anesthesia	$ 180.00	$ 266.00	$ 340.00
Hospital	$ 545.00	$1,014.00	$2,635.00
Total:	$1,053.00	$1,693.00	$3,475.00
Usual Copay*	**$ 55.00**	**$ 101.00**	**$ 264.00**

DSP Copay: $50.00

Tonsillectomy & Adenoidectomy (under 12) (42820)

Cost Range:	Low	Average	High
Surgeon	$ 250.00	$ 336.00	$ 537.00
Anesthesia	$ 130.00	$ 262.00	$ 465.00
Hospital	$ 457.00	$ 930.00	$2,018.00
Total:	$ 837.00	$1,528.00	$3,020.00
Usual Copay*	**$ 46.00**	**$ 93.00**	**$ 202.00**

DSP Copay: $25.00

Tonsillectomy & Adenoidectomy (over 12) (42821)

Cost Range:	*Low*	*Average*	*High*
Surgeon	$ 340.00	$ 423.00	$ 576.00
Anesthesia	$ 154.00	$ 285.00	$ 403.00
Hospital	$ 650.00	$1,132.00	$2,568.00
Total:	$1,144.00	$1,840.00	$3,547.00
Usual Copay*	**$ 65.00**	**$ 113.00**	**$ 257.00**

DSP Copay: $50.00

by doing so, innovation, new technology, quality, and responsive care are all enhanced. If Americans want a health care system that controls costs with natural market forces, it is up to them to initiate the controls that allow market reform.

14. The Wisconsin and Milwaukee Employee Health Plans: Two Managed Competition Success Stories

David R. Riemer

Although its critics might want you to believe otherwise, managed competition has been proven to work. The governments of Milwaukee and Wisconsin have both implemented managed competition systems and saved themselves a lot of money in the past few years—without diminishing participant choice or benefit levels. While the Wisconsin/Milwaukee model of managed care is not perfect, it has nevertheless been remarkably successful at controlling costs while providing quality health benefits. If built into the national health insurance program, it could easily do the same or better for the nation as a whole.

Managed competition is the method of using carefully structured competition among HMOs and other health care plans to improve quality and hold down health insurance cost increases, and it is all the rage these days. America's health care gurus—Alain Enthoven, Paul Ellwood, Paul Starr, and the members of the "Jackson Hole Group"—preach it. President Bill Clinton believes in it. First Lady Hillary Clinton wants it to be the backbone of the Administration's national health insurance plan.

There are critics, of course. Representative Pete Stark, who chairs the House Committee's Ways and Means Subcommittee on Health, has declared that managed competition is baloney. The critics' main argument is that the theory of managed competition is just a theory; it has never been tried, they say, and therefore there is no way to know whether it will succeed. It would be folly, they conclude, to make such an untested concept the basis for a giant federal program.

Reprinted with permission from *Government Finance Review,* February 1993, published by the Government Finance Officers Association. Excerpted from "Milwaukee's Successful Effort to Control Health Care Costs."

It is not true, however, that managed competition is untried. California's state employee health plan, CALPERS, relies on a form of managed competition for its 880,000 state and local government enrollees, and Minnesota's state employee health plan also uses a version of managed competition for its 57,000 enrollees. Perhaps the longest-running versions of managed competition, however, are the employee health plans of the State of Wisconsin and the City of Milwaukee.

The Wisconsin/Milwaukee model of managed competition proves that managed competition works. Using essentially the same variant of managed competition, the State of Wisconsin for ten years (1984–1993) and the City of Milwaukee for five years (1989–1993) have provided roughly 58,000 and 8,000 active employees, respectively, with an array of high-quality health care plans in a manner that lets patients choose their doctors and keeps costs under control.

The Wisconsin version was developed in 1983 by former State Senator Paul Offner (now an aide to U.S. Senator Daniel P. Moynihan) and former State Senator John O. Norquist (now the Mayor of Milwaukee) in collaboration with the administration of former Governor Anthony Earl. Immediately after Norquist's election as mayor in 1988, he adapted this approach to Milwaukee with the cooperation of the City's Common Council.

HOW THE PLAN WORKS

The model is simple. The employer first sets up tough standards regarding scope of benefits and financial stability for HMOs, and then invites qualifying plans to submit premium bids. Individual employees are entitled to join any qualifying HMO, or may choose to enroll in a traditional fee-for-service plan with managed care features. If an employee enrolls in a plan whose premiums is less than 105 percent of the lowest bidding HMO's premium, the employee pays nothing. Employees that choose to enroll in plans with higher premiums must pay all (or at least a large part of) the difference between the 105 percent benchmark and the higher premium. Both the city's and state's version of the managed competition works very much like the model, though there are some differences between the two in details.

MILWAUKEE'S PLAN

Milwaukee's city employee health plan is administered by the Employee Benefits Administration (EBA), a division of the Department of Employee Relations. EBA invites bids from all HMOs in the area that meet the city's standards for health care benefits, quality control, and financial stability. Each bid must be developed independently and transmitted to the city in a sealed envelope. Each bid also must state the HMO's proposed monthly premiums for single and family coverage.

Simultaneously, the premiums for the city's standard health insurance plan—a traditional indemnity plan that offers enrollees a free choice of physicians and hospitals but that has some managed care features—are also developed and, in effect, sealed. Until the HMO bids are opened, the standard plan premiums are not disclosed to any of the HMOs or anyone else except the staff of EBA. The standard plan covers fewer services and imposes a deductible. It is administered by a third-party administrator, but the city accepts the morbidity risk through self-insurance.

On a predetermined date each fall, the HMOs' sealed bids are opened and the standard plan bid is disclosed. The lowest single coverage premium and the lowest family coverage premium are identified.

City employees are offered the opportunity to enroll in any HMO that meets the city's standards, or they may enroll in the standard plan. The city covers the entire cost of the lowest-bidding HMO and any of the other HMOs whose premiums are within 105 percent of the lowest bid. Those employees who select plans—whether an HMO or the standard plan—that cost more than 105 percent of the lowest-bidding HMO must pay all or part of the additional cost. The employee contribution for enrollment in the expensive standard plan is capped at $7.50 per month for single coverage and $15 per month for family coverage. (The state plan does not impose such a cap. In its first year, the city plan also did not impose a cap; it was added to win union support of the overall approach.) Employees' contributions are deducted from their biweekly paychecks.

The Old Way

It is necessary to know how the previous state and city employee health model worked and to grasp the old model's basic flaw in order to understand the advantage offered by the new approach. The old method of buying health insurance for state and city employees was to pick a small number of HMOs, try to bargain down their premiums, and then pay 100 percent of the premium costs, as well as 90 percent to 100 percent of the standard plan premium.

This approach presented the HMOs with two fundamentally conflicting incentives: to lower their premium increases *and* not to lower their premium increases. The HMOs had an incentive to hold their premiums down somewhat; otherwise, they might not be among the HMOs selected to be made available to employees. However, the HMOs had an equally powerful incentive *not* to lower their premiums. Once selected, lower premiums would reduce their income without giving them a competitive advantage in persuading employees to enroll with them instead of with one of the other selected HMOs or the standard plan. Since all available HMO plans were free to employees, and since an employee's

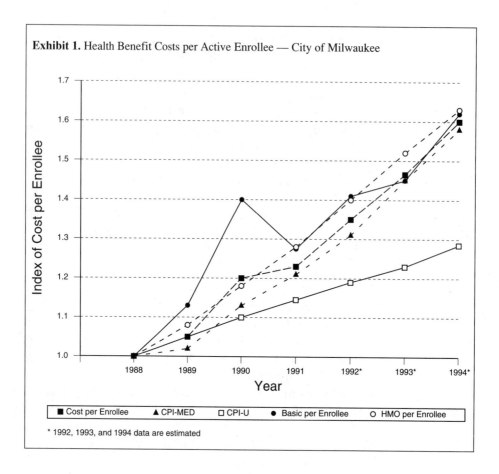

Exhibit 1. Health Benefit Costs per Active Enrollee — City of Milwaukee

* 1992, 1993, and 1994 data are estimated

cost to join the standard plan was based solely on the standard plan's premium, lower prices failed to give the HMOs the one thing a lower price is supposed to afford a competitor: a better shot at getting more customers. In short, except in order to get in the door, HMOs had no incentive to offer lower premium increases.

The new approach used by the state and city greatly reduces this disincentive. The new model rewards those HMOs that come in with relatively low premiums by allowing employees to enroll in such plans at no or little cost. Conversely, it penalizes those HMOs that come in with relatively high premiums by requiring employees to incur an out-of-pocket enrollment cost. The basic rule of the marketplace is restored; a lower price now gives a competitor an important edge in recruiting customers.

The results of both the city's and state's version of managed competition have been positive on every count. Employees are protected from bad plans—for example, plans that exclude individuals, fail to cover preexisting conditions, offer meager benefits, or have weak financing—because the employer refuses to offer them. Employee satisfaction, as measured by surveys, has been very favorable. Employees also get extensive provider choice. Virtually every doctor and hospital is available. This happens because, first, all or most HMOs are offered, and second, a fee-for-service option offering every doctor and hospital also remains available (though at a price).

Finally, the model constrains health care costs. From 1983 through 1988, the state version held the employer's per-employee cost increases to an average of 5.9 percent per year, less than the average growth of the CPI's medical component. Subsequent benefit changes and regulatory requirements have increased the state plan's cost in recent years, but nonetheless, the state plan has averaged less than a 10 percent annual growth rate for the past decade. The city version, since 1988, has kept per-employee cost increases to 10 percent per year, again less than the growth in the CPI's Medical Sub-Index. (See Exhibit 1.) More meaningfully, the city plan's per-employee cost has grown far more slowly than that experienced by other large and midsize corporations. A study prepared by Foster Higgins of 2,448 large and midsize corporations shows that while the city's per-employee cost rose from $2,533 to $3,406, or 35 percent, from 1988 to 1992, the average increase for the corporations surveyed was from a lower starting point of $2,354 per employee to a much higher ending point of $3,968 per employee over the same period, a 69 percent increase. In short, the city plan, relying on managed competition, curbed the growth of per-employee health costs far greater than the corporate average. (See Exhibit 2.)

The results are clear: Managed competition works.

The Plan's Flaws

The specific version of managed competition used by the Wisconsin and Milwaukee is of course not perfect. There are two significant flaws in the formula that both the state and city use.

First, neither purchaser has established a uniform benefit package that all qualifying bidders must meet without variation. The competing health care plans must meet minimum benefit requirements, but they are allowed to offer different benefit packages and thus compete on the basis of benefits. Because of this, the differences in their quality and cost are diminished in importance, and there is less than optimal price competition. Requiring a uniform benefit package would, without doing any harm to enrollees, increase the emphasis on price competition; this would lower the growth in the low bid from year to year and the resulting growth in per-enrollee costs.

Second, neither the state nor the city sets the per-enrollee contribution at exactly 100 percent of the low bid submitted by the qualifying bidders. They instead use a benchmark of 105 percent of the low bid. Setting the maximum per-enrollee contribution at no more than the cost of the lowest priced plan, however, is essential to achieving the maximum benefit from managed competition. Even minor variations in this contribution rate can begin to erode the effectiveness of the system.

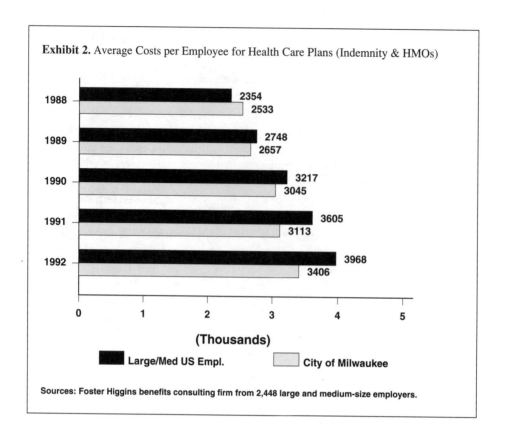

Exhibit 2. Average Costs per Employee for Health Care Plans (Indemnity & HMOs)

Sources: Foster Higgins benefits consulting firm from 2,448 large and medium-size employers.

The extra 5 percent is the result of collective bargaining concessions. While that small of a variance in employer contribution over the low bid may seem inconsequential, it in fact plays a significant role in encouraging bids that are higher than necessary. The 105 percent benchmark is not a financial incentive to be the lowest bidder, as it should be. Rather, it acts as an incentive to be the HMO that bids 5 percent over the cost of the low cost plan, since this price will maximize premium income with no disincentive to prospective enrollees. The low cost plan, by contrast, has given away 5 percent and in return gained no competitive advantage in attracting prospective enrollees. In short, if the per-enrollee contribution is set at 105 percent (or any percentage above 100 percent) of the low bid, the message that goes out to HMOs is to be slightly higher than the low bidder.

Setting the employer's contribution at exactly 100 percent of the low bid eliminates this significant distortion. It sends an unequivocal signal to all bidders that the low bidder—and only the low bidder—is the winner. Had the state and city plans used a uniform benefit package and fixed the employer contribution at exactly 100 percent of the low bid, they might have experienced average per-enrollee growth rates in the range of 5 to 8 percent per year rather than the 10 percent average (still far better than the national average) that they actually experienced.

CONCLUSION

Managed competition works. What managed competition has done for the State of Wisconsin and the City of Milwaukee, it can do for the nation as a whole. In fact, it can do an even better job for the nation as a whole. The form of managed competition described here, if used only by a few purchasers that constitute a fraction of the market, will of course permit the HMOs, other competing plans, and their participating providers to shift costs to all the other purchasers who buy from them. But if all or most purchasers—i.e., if the entire or nearly the entire country—used such a model of managed competition, then providers would have no place onto which to shift costs. Their only options would be to justify their low prices by becoming more efficient, or to go out of business.

Isn't this exactly what we want? A system that, on top of providing universal coverage, offering extensive benefits, disqualifying inadequate plans, and offering a broad choice of both plans and providers, also has powerful built-in incentives to reward cost-effective health care services and drive the excessively costly or low-quality plans and providers out of the market?

With careful planning, this model could be quickly put into effect for the entire country. It need not take long to implement. One or two years should suffice. Wisconsin's version was implemented between July and November of 1983, and became effective in January of 1984. Milwaukee's version was implemented between July and November of 1988, and became effective in January of 1989. If the federal government were to enact a national health insurance program based on this form of managed competition during the course of 1994, it should be possible to enroll Americans in the fall of 1995 for coverage starting January 1, 1996.

The author wishes to thank John O. Norquist, Mayor of the City of Milwaukee; Thomas C. Korpady, Director of Health and Disability Benefits, Department of Employee Trust Funds, State of Wisconsin; Florence Dukes, Manager of Employee Benefits, Department of Employee Relations, City of Milwaukee; and staff of the Employee Benefits Division of the City of Milwaukee, for the insights and information they provided in connection with the writing of this article.

Part 3

FLEXIBLE BENEFITS

15. AT&T's Flex Benefits Program Communications
Carol Kitchell

The transition to a flexible benefits plan is never simple, but the long-term advantages of a successful flex plan can be enormous. When AT&T decided to implement a flex plan for its 110,000 employees, it knew it was faced with a formidable communications challenge. By basing its communications strategy on careful planning, attention to employee needs and opinions, and a carefully designed communications strategy, however, the company made the transition painless and efficient, which in turn has been crucial in the flex plan's ulitmate success.

In the fall of 1990, AT&T implemented a flexible benefits program for 110,000 full-time management employees across the U.S. and around the world. The reasons for introducing flex? The company needed both short- and long-term health care cost containment strategies for the 1990s to manage its steadily rising expenses—a situation that many employers face today. At the time, AT&T, which is self-insured, was spending in excess of $1.3 billion per year on claims reimbursement, 60 percent of which was for dependents. After conducting a feasibility study in 1988, the company determined that introducing a flex program was a viable cost-control option. AT&T had also discovered, as many companies have, that a one-size-fits-all approach to delivering benefits doesn't meet the needs of today's diverse work force. Flex would give employees the opportunity to make benefit choices that would better meet their specific needs. By introducing flex as well as a managed care program, AT&T began to meet the challenge of maintaining its competitiveness through cost management and by offering benefit programs that were more in line with the programs offered by its competitors.

AT&T'S FLEX PROGRAM

AT&T's program, which became effective in July 1991, includes medical and dental coverage; long-term disability coverage; health care and child/elder care reimbursement accounts; and life, dependent life, and accidental loss insurances. Among the new plans offered were long-term care, dependent accidental loss insurance, and a vacation buy option. Within each plan, employees were offered a number of options, including, in some cases, the option of no coverage.

AT&T allocated enough benefit dollars to cover the costs of the benefits the employees had prior to flex: basic/major medical coverage for employees only, standard option dental coverage, one-times-pay life insurance, one-times-pay accidental loss insurance, and 50-percent-of-pay long-term disability coverage. As a part of the new flex plan, the company required employees to choose a minimum level of medical, life insurance, accidental loss insurance, and long-term disability coverage, beyond which the choice was theirs.

A STRATEGIC MODEL FOR DEVELOPING A COMMUNICATION PLAN

The success of this ambitious effort was due, in large part, to the thoughtful process the company followed when designing its implementation strategy. Comprehensive planning, a communication strategy adaptable enough to respond to changes as the needs arose, and an independent evaluation of the implementation process ensured that the project's goals were met.

AT&T enlisted the assistance of the Wyatt Company for its expertise in the areas of flexible benefits plan design, communications, training, and environmental analysis. Together, they comanaged the development of the flex program. AT&T assembled an internal task force of specialists who were experienced in systems development, benefits administration, communications, plan design, and training. The AT&T team members were dedicated solely to the implementation, a factor that greatly facilitated the formidable undertaking.

The strategic model employed to develop the communications plan consisted of four steps:

1. Defining the company's goals and determining its stance in communicating to its employees;
2. Conducting an organizational assessment to analyze the environment;
3. Defining the communications objectives, and

4. Developing a program strategy that would incorporate the first three steps, as well as address unique issues or challenges.

AT&T's Communication Goals

AT&T believed its employees would rise to the challenge flex presented, and accept the program after a period of adaptation. Then, as the company saw it, benefits selection and cost sharing would become business as usual. Conceptually, the company wanted employees to understand the importance of managing rising health care costs and view the flex program as a solution that would be in everyone's best interest. By making employees aware of the company's actual medical expenditures and its position in the global marketplace, it hoped to emphasize AT&T's need to remain competitive.

The company also wanted employees to know that although the way in which they had been provided benefits in the past was changing, the benefits themselves were not being cut. They would still have a comprehensive, very rich benefits package from a company committed to ensuring employees' access to high-quality, affordable health care. The company also recognized that employees would need to be prepared to make behavioral changes, such as reading communications materials to become better informed consumers, making benefit decisions themselves, and taking specific actions to enroll. Employees' only previous experience had been in electing reimbursement account coverage the year before.

Finally, the company wanted a low-stress enrollment process with minimal back-end administrative problems, the success of which would be measured both in terms of actual enrollment numbers and by employee satisfaction with their benefit selections and the enrollment information they received.

Organizational Assessment

At the outset of the implementation, Wyatt conducted an environmental analysis with three goals:

1. Assess the existing level of employee benefit knowledge, understanding, and appreciation;
2. Identify the level of employee understanding of flexible benefits and determine the degree of potential resistance to or acceptance of the program; and
3. Identify what employees viewed as effective communication vehicles.

A questionnaire was sent to a random, representative sample of 18,000 management employees nationwide. This survey solicited quantitative data through 21 multiple-choice questions in the topic areas of general AT&T benefits, communications, and flexible benefits. Wyatt also conducted national focus groups with AT&T (again using randomly selected, representative participants) to obtain subjective, qualitative data to enhance the questionnaire data.

The environmental analysis revealed that employees who received sufficient information understood their benefits better, and those who understood better were more satisfied. However, most had little or no knowledge of flex. Those who had knowledge understood flex as a cost-saving strategy that could meet diverse work force needs, but still saw it as a loss of benefits. Many thought flex was a choice among benefits, not among options within benefit areas, and many expressed anxiety about making wrong choices. Although employees had a general understanding that health care costs were escalating, they didn't necessarily associate this with AT&T's ability to remain competitive. And they were skeptical about the company's motives, fearing dramatic cost shifting. Above all, they didn't want cost-sharing messages to be hidden behind the advertised advantages of the program.

The analysis showed that employees like customized, benefit-specific materials because such vehicles are perceived to have more credibility in the subject area than general, in-house publications. They wanted items sent to them to be identified as important benefit information, and they wanted communications to be clearly written, user-friendly, and inexpensive. Although printed materials were viewed as the most useful source of information, with hotlines a close second, employees encouraged the use of all types of media available.

Communication Issues/Challenges

The challenges the flex communication team had to face included meeting the company's goals and addressing the issues identified in the environmental analysis, as well as considering both the general needs that change creates and the specific needs of a company like AT&T.

The team recognized that employee perceptions were critical. The communications had to respond to those perceptions, even if the perceptions were not accurate or realistic. They also had to imagine what employee reaction to the change might be in order to address potential problems. Culture change can be very threatening. A workplace mythology exists in every company. With the introduction of a new benefits program like flex, the "stories" about the company's values and what constitutes a safe and comfortable environment have to be modified. The job of the communication team is to help effect that transition by planting the seeds of new ideas and providing ways for employees to regain their prechange comfort level.

Benefits are an especially sensitive area because they affect employees' personal lives and the lives of family members. Upsetting the status quo can produce discomfort, anger, and apprehensiveness, even when people understand on some level that the change is necessary for well-founded reasons and may ultimately be for the best. Because of the full entitlement employees had prior to flex, they didn't have to make choices about benefits. This emphasized the need to establish clear, focused objectives for communicating changes that required employees to make decisions about their benefits.

The AT&T corporate culture was historically characterized as paternalistic. Many employees had been with AT&T from its less competitive pre-divestiture days and believed in a mutually beneficial work relationship in which the company "takes care of" employees who invest their energy into doing a good job. In recent years, more and more policy changes and work force downsizing suggested to them that traditional value systems were also changing. If not implemented appropriately, the flex program could have been seen as one more of those changes, and been met with the disillusionment and disappointment that can be associated with corporate culture evolution.

Another challenge was communicating employee cost sharing. Although the contributions for dependent coverage were not really tied to the flex program, they were implemented at the same time. This presented a challenge because employees who feared hidden take-aways might see the request for contributions as being disguised by the promotional message that they could keep pace with their changing life situations by choosing a specific package of benefits from the flex menu. Employees would need to understand the cost-control goals of the company, and be shown that the actual cost increases associated with flex occurred only if the benefits they wanted cost more than the benefit dollars the company provided.

Finally, in an environment in which employees identified with both their specific business unit and the larger collective corporation, the communication team needed to elicit the buy-in of the business units' senior personnel first so they would actively demonstrate their support and encourage employees to enroll.

A graphic symbol representing the flex program had to be developed so employees would be able to easily recognize flex materials and promotional pieces. When designing the actual materials, the team had to identify parameters suitable for the AT&T culture. General, informal corporate criteria existed that discouraged the use of very unconventional themes, and the overall look had to be acceptable to a wide range of employee types (single/family members, technical/non-technical, urban/rural, men/women, etc.). Many approaches were examined and rejected. For example, comedic approaches were deemed to be incompatible with the gravity of the benefits change. The final design utilized photographic collages of objects associated with specific benefit areas, and bright, clear colors (one for each benefit plan offered under flex). Communication surveys distributed routinely by the company showed that employees disap-proved of papers and packaging that they perceived to be expensive. Expensive looking materials were thought to be especially inappropriate when the company was sending cost-cutting messages. The AT&T population is also very environ-mentally conscious, so recycled papers were used.

Communication Plan Objectives

To meet the needs of a diverse work force, the communication team planned to use a multimedia approach involving written communications sent to the home, articles in nationally distributed AT&T publications and business unit magazines, an enrollment center hotline, advertising posters and tent cards, reminder letters and phone calls, and a videotape for use in voluntary employee information meetings. Most of the communications items were developed to fall into one of two categories: "need-to-know" information, which was sent to the home, and "nice-to-know" information, which was distributed at work.

By delivering the critical messages about the program at the beginning of the communications campaign, the team hoped to diffuse potential buildup of negative response and help employees to move on to concentrating on the benefit election information. By designing materials that stimulated interest and clearly explained all aspects of the program in sufficient detail to support informed decision making, and by providing user-friendly, use-tested enrollment instructions and tools to facilitate the enrollment process, the team aimed to elicit the employee response: "This is not so bad."

Communication Plan Strategy

Initially, a pre-announcement article in the official AT&T benefits magazine described flex and explained why it was being implemented. Earlier articles had positioned health care cost issues from a national perspective. This was followed by a program announcement letter from the human resources vice president. An introductory brochure provided a brief overview of how the program worked and what type of information employees should anticipate receiving, reasons for the implementation, and a summary of benefit coverages. This was followed by a series of four biweekly employee newsletters that built momentum, interest, and awareness about the program. Each of these newsletters covered a specific set of benefits issues (medical/dental, long-term care, insurance/long-term disability/vacation buy, and enrollment/default), and provided the information employees needed to make their choices, including important restrictions or guidelines that affected coverage and suggestions employees might consider when making their elections (for example, the types of medical expenses are expected in the coming year). At the same time that each piece was mailed to the home, a related poster and tent card was exhibited in work locations such as cafeterias and building lobbies. With the first newsletter, employees also received an employee meeting schedule and a file folder in which to store their materials. During the pre-enrollment and enrollment periods, ongoing informational articles appeared in internal AT&T publications, including business unit magazines.

The company worked closely with its subsidiary, AT&T American Trans-tech, Inc., to further establish the Benefit Directions Enrollment Center (BDEC), Transtech's enrollment processing facility and employee information center. The BDEC used AT&T's Conversant system, an automated enrollment transaction phone line. Enrollment representatives were also available to process enroll-ments. BDEC's information hotline was open from the program announcement through the beginning of the enrollment period, at which time it became the enrollment phone number. Detailed scripts were written for telephone repre-sentatives, and the Conversant system script was tested for accuracy and ease of use. Presentations were prepared for AT&T executives, and an employment recruiter kit and training program were developed. Training programs were also developed for hotline operators, enrollment representatives, benefit administra-tors, and employee meeting leaders. The meeting leader training was twofold: a three-day class offered benefit training, followed by a segment on presentation skills.

The program name, "Flex Benefits '91," was chosen to engender a sense of straightforwardness and to respond to employee requests to "call it what it is." The tag line, "Solutions for Our Changing World," helped emphasize that the program was a balanced cost-control approach for both the company and its employees, and a way to obtain a benefits package that would better meet personal needs.

The enrollment kit contained personalized benefits information in each benefit area, including benefit dollars allocations and price tags for each option. A computer modeling program, included on a diskette contained in a pocket on the inside front cover, enabled employees to experiment with a variety of benefit elections by adding up price tags, comparing them to benefit dollar allocations, and estimating the effects of different scenarios on their pay and taxes. A worksheet included as a foldout panel on the back cover of the booklet provided another way to add up price tags and benefit dollars.

After enrollment, employees received a confirmation statement listing their elections. Toward the end of the enrollment period, reminder letters were sent to those employees who had not yet enrolled. After the enrollment period ended, default letters were sent to those who still hadn't enrolled. All pieces sent to the home were clearly designed to indicate that important enrollment material was enclosed.

The company chose to introduce flex with a spring enrollment period for an initial 18-month "plan year." Then, during the regular fall enrollment period that same year, employees could keep their initial elections by not enrolling except in those benefits that require an annual re-enrollment (reimbursement accounts, for example), or they could change their elections by re-enrolling. The fall enrollment was characterized as an opportunity to review spring elections in light of their experiences and information presented in a wrap-up newsletter and in-house magazine articles following the spring enrollment. This helped employees feel that making elections in the spring wouldn't be too traumatic or final, because in most cases they could change several months later. The fall enrollment kit was a streamlined booklet with three tabs: enrollment instructions, plan highlights, and an insurance forms pocket. A personalized benefit information fact sheet, on which employees circled chosen options, was included. The updated diskette was sent on request in a special mailer. As before, confirmation statements were issued after enrollment.

ASSESSING THE RESULTS: WHAT WORKED AND WHAT WAS LEARNED

AT&T enlisted the services of Maritz, Inc. to conduct extensive telephone surveys during and after the enrollment period to determine employee response to the program rollout and to identify problems that could be addressed immediately or in preparation for the fall enrollment. Maritz also tracked a control group of 600 employees before, during, and after the enrollment period to determine their reactions to each stage of the implementation. The post-enrollment results were very favorable, particularly because they represented technical, headquarters, sales, and manufacturing employees. Nine of every ten surveyed employees thought flex met their needs; 92 percent felt confident in their ability to make the right choices; 95 percent felt the information was clear and understandable; the enrollment kit was seen as the most useful piece, and the worksheet and modeling diskette were thought to be helpful by nearly all respondents; 91 percent felt the enrollment process was easy; and nine of every ten used the Conversant system to enroll and thought it was simple and convenient. The greatest number of complaints were related to the required contributions for dependent coverage, and most respondents wanted the cost information supplied at the beginning of the communication campaign.

Lessons Learned

The communication team had to be able to remain responsive and reactive. They needed to have damage control strategies ready to address situations as they arose during the implementation, and they needed to be prepared to change the communication products or the way in which information or concepts were being presented, if necessary. Within the parameters of the production schedule, the communication strategy model had to be flexible enough to accommodate change and be responsive to employee needs as they were identified.

But not all issues can be identified, even with preliminary research; the "hot buttons" can't always be known ahead of time. For example, AT&T's benefit plan policies didn't change with the implementation of flex, but employees' awareness of them did. In some cases, publishing benefits information called attention to policies with which employees had problems, and then those problems had to be officially addressed. AT&T also found, in some cases, that employees' confusion resulted from not reading the materials. However, where interpretation appeared to be the issue, the team rewrote future communications to improve their comprehensibility.

The success of AT&T's flex program implementation was demonstrated by a 97 percent enrollment rate, a much higher statistic than Wyatt had predicted, given the size of AT&T and the absence of mandatory employee meetings. This enrollment rate and the favorable post-enrollment feedback suggested that the communication strategy and the materials themselves met the goal of the company: to have as many employees as possible enroll and choose the benefits they needed and wanted without major administrative problems.

Of course, not every company needs as complex an implementation strategy as AT&T's, but the key components of AT&T's communication plan can be applied to any company's program introduction:

1. Determine the project's goals and analyze the environment;
2. Develop a clearly defined plan that incorporates the goals and the analysis results;
3. Ensure that employees receive the information they need to make the transition; and
4. Respond to needs as they're identified throughout the process.

AT&T's plan had each of these components. The strategy was adaptable to ensure that modifications could be made, if required. The communications moved people from feeling apprehensive, skeptical, or angry about changes to their benefits to feeling capable of making good decisions, taking action, and accepting change. Today, due to the groundwork established by the flex communications, employees are accustomed to messages of change, and often make suggestions about what they'd like the flex program to include in the future. AT&T, in turn, is continually looking for ways to improve its enrollment packages, keeping in mind when creating them that the "customer" is the reader—the employee who must make decisions and take action.

16.   Equitable Pricing Reflects the Real Value of Benefits
Michael W. Schionning   Coleen W. Young

Changing prices and enrollments can make flexible benefits confusing, and can worsen the problems of non-uniform risk distribution. Equitable pricing alleviates these problems by changing the basis for medical benefits pricing; rather than basing prices on the option's previous claim-cost experience, equitable pricing sets each option's price to reflect the amount of coverage provided.

Today's increasingly expensive health care forces employers to share costs with employees and to use creative means to soften the blows. One way has been to offer a choice of benefit options, allowing employees to get the most for their money by selecting the benefits most valuable to them.

Offering choice heightens employee awareness of benefits and responsibility for them, but it can result in chaos; many benefit managers who have multiple-option programs find themselves juggling fluctuating prices and enrollments among and within coverage options from year to year. They must explain the changes and still maintain their credibility.

HR managers also face a widening cost gap between options, threatening affordability of the higher-cost options. Most firms want a comprehensive indemnity plan, but the cost increases are simply too steep for the employers—or employees—to justify the expense.

A solution to these problems is equitable pricing, a method for setting medical benefit prices, while still offering choice. Equitable pricing can relieve the erratic confusion of changing prices and enrollments for both employers and employees. The basic premises include:

174

- Each option's price should reflect the amount of coverage it provides, not its previous claim-cost experience.
- The sum of all the options' prices multiplied by the enrollment in the option should equal the total possible medical program cost. This means that, although pricing covers an employer's expected costs, each option's price reflects only the relative value of is coverage, not the risk characteristics (and ultimately claims) of the people enrolled in it.

Using equitable pricing alleviates the difficulties that cause the instability in traditional group insurance planning. Instability occurs when employers price each benefit option based on the claim experience of the previous year. The problem of instability is worsened by risk segmentation, which occurs when each option has an unbalanced proportion of high- or low-risk employees. What happens with traditional group insurance pricing is that an employer sets each options' price based on the option's premium or claim experience. Carrier and provider rates may rise sharply in any given year because of bad claim experience during the previous year, low enrollment, a few catastrophic claims, or heavy capital investment—all of which create price inconsistency. Rates also can decrease because of market competition or lower-than-expected claim experience of a particular option.

To compound the problem, these options are priced based on an assumption that the group has a uniform distribution of risk. In other words, each group is expected to contain a mix of low- and high-risk employees, so that the low claims of low-risk individuals offset the high claims of high-risk individuals.

When no choice is involved, an employer has a single plan with a uniform distribution of risk. The annual option pricing is simply a matter of the increasing cost of medical care. Given a choice among options, however, employees select according to their own financial and health-related needs, basing their decisions on the probability (or risk) of their need for medical services during the coming year. High-risk individuals choose comprehensive options; those having a low risk choose low-coverage (usually less expensive) options.

This self-selection prevents each option from having a uniform distribution of risk. Instead, a high-coverage option has fewer low-risk individuals to offset the employees who have a high risk and to level out the cost per employee. The high-coverage option becomes less affordable to employers and employees. If priced to recover its own costs, the higher-priced option plan will be priced out of existence.

Below is an example using a sample cafeteria plan to illustrate what happens throughout a period of a few years while using the **traditional health coverage** options. Although this is an oversimplification, it shows a common course of events that can make a comprehensive option no longer affordable.

Example. The program has two medical indemnity choices. Prices are set according to the previous year's claims for each option. Option A's price is higher and has a $100 deductible; option B's price is lower and has a $600 deductible. Employees pay for their own benefits.

The company gives employees an annual dollar allotment to spend on benefits—enough to purchase option A. Employees electing option B may use the rest of their benefit dollars to purchase higher benefit levels. This is the result:

Year one. More of the high-risk employees choose option A and more of the low-risk employees choose option B. During the year, option A claims are higher than expected, and those for option B are lower than expected. As a result, for year two, the company raises the price more for option A than for option B.

Year two. Employees whose claims exceed the price of option A remain in option A; the others move to option B. Because of the greater concentration of high-risk individuals in option A, claims for this option are again higher than expected. The company raises the price for A for year three more than it does for B.

Year three. Employees in option A no longer can justify paying the extra out-of-pocket money for such an expensive choice, so all but the employees who have the highest risk remain. Option A now costs more than most employees want to pay for it. It's no longer practical.

Year four of this example shows what happens with **equitable pricing:**

Year four. The company institutes equitable pricing. Benefits in options A and B are assessed for their relative value. Next, to determine the price, the total anticipated claim and administrative costs are allocated to each opinion, based on this relative value and the expected enrollment. (The sum of the prices for all of the options, multiplied by the enrollment, equals the company's total expected costs for year four.) As a result, option A's price is lower than it was for year three, prompting more lower-risk employees to enroll. Claims per employee are reduced for option A, enabling the company to keep the option and increase its price at the same rate as option B for year five.

Year five and beyond. The company avoids dramatic premiums and enrollment fluctuations from year to year and can forecast a health care budget with greater accuracy. Risk segmentation is managed effectively. Equitable pricing spreads the high cost of high-risk employees' claims and the low cost of low-risk employees' claims across all options. This fosters stability in option prices and enrollments.

As well as offering stability, equitable pricing promotes partnership between employers and providers and reduces overall cost. Employers can avoid excessive premiums for low-risk employees by encouraging them to choose the most appropriate options, and by negotiating with providers to base the rates on actual claim experience. First-year savings can reach 15 percent. Management also can predict premium costs more accurately and encourage competition among providers to ensure cost-effective, quality care.

Equitable pricing has benefits for employees as well that include:

- A full range of fairly priced, stable options;
- Prices that reflect the value of each options' coverage;
- A relationship between respective price and coverage that encourages employees to elect the options that suit their needs best—not necessarily the option that costs the least; and
- Stability of prices from year to year that reduces employee jumping between options because of price fluctuations.

Another advantage is that the principles of equitable pricing aren't restricted to traditional indemnity or preferred-provider organization (PPO) plans. They're just as applicable to health maintenance organizations (HMOs). Most employers that have multiple-option programs offer HMOs, generally setting their prices the same as HMO premiums. The premiums, however, may not be based on an employer's actual claims and may be different from prices for other options.

There's nothing to preclude pricing HMOs the same way as any other option, however. Employers can set employee prices independently of HMO premiums and reduce the price variation among options—just as it does for indemnity or PPO plans—while ensuring that total costs equal total option prices.

Equitable pricing and negotiating with HMOs can yield an additional benefit. Amendments to the federal HMO Act allow them to contract individually with these organizations so that costs more closely mach those incurred by employees in the HMO. An employer can discuss equitable pricing with the HMO during contracting and agree on how it may be compensated fairly. The employer may reimburse the HMO for costs incurred by employees, including a reasonable profit.

It's time for employers to gain more and be able to pay the true cost of the benefits that employees use. Equitable pricing offers that control.

17. Implementing Flexible Benefits

Thomas K. Langston

A critical step in avoiding the pitfalls that have plagued flexible benefits programs is communication. All of the elements for a successful flex program—involving the human resources, payroll, and administrative departments—are outlined in the following article.

Much has been written and countless meetings have been conducted describing the formula for the absolute failure for flexible benefits implementation. Many of these articles and meetings have stressed that the key to a successful flex plan is employee communication. While written and other forms of communication directed at plan participants is crucial, in the planning stages of the flexible benefits program communication among the departments of a company that are responsible for the administration of employee benefits is even more important.

Interdepartmental communication ensures that the "systems" necessary to administer an employee benefits program are developed properly, and that the administration procedures are established to ensure successful implementation and the successful ongoing operation of the plan. Those responsible for the development of these systems must be aware of some of the more important issues that no amount of employee communications will address.

Long before the participant newsletters have been written or the video for employee meetings has been produced, human resource, payroll, and MIS staff must work together to develop a strategy for data collection and system coordination. This system coordination will involve assurance that the human resource

Reprinted from *Compensation & Benefits Management*, Vol. 8, No. 4, Winter 1992. A Panel Publication, Aspen Publishers, Inc.

information system (if one exists), the payroll system, and the flexible benefits system are compatible and will communicate with one another.

THE FLEXIBLE BENEFITS SYSTEM

Whether developed in-house or purchased, the flex system must perform basic functions that are critical to the success of the plan. These basic functions include: data collection, financial issues, benefit eligibility determination, personal information, and payroll deduction amounts.

Data Collection

The system should have the capability of accepting data from multiple sources. Most common sources will be the human resource information system or the payroll system. It will also be important for the system to have flexibility to accept data from a mainframe or personal computer. In situations where mainframes or personal computers do not exist, the system must be able to accommodate manual entry of pertinent data.

Outside payroll services should not be overlooked. If outside services are used, it is important to ensure that the flex system and outside payroll system are compatible and that data can be transferred easily from one system to the other.

While the preferred method of data collection, regardless of the source, should be electronic, where data is transferred within an integrated system on the mainframe, or the mainframe to a personal computer, manual intervention remains an important feature. Human resource staff should have the capability of manually adding a new participant to the plan or of making changes to a current participant's file.

Another important feature that should be considered is the collection of plan election data directly from the participants. Interactive systems are becoming more common and are an efficient way of entering employee selections under a flexible benefits plan. For example, a telephone enrollment system significantly reduces the errors inherent with a paper enrollment system because the system will not accept incorrect elections from participants. Since the participant is literally making the entry into the computer, the possibility of key punch errors on the part of human resource or payroll staff is significantly reduced.

Whatever the method of data collection, the system must include an edit function to ensure that the data in the system are correct. Everything from eligibility determination to credit and price tag development may be dependent upon the data collected by the system. The system should be written so that edit reports are produced on a regular basis identifying incorrect data in the system.

Financial Issues

Establishing the pricing structure of a flexible benefits program is an extreme-ly important step in the development of the flex system. The system must have the capability of calculating benefits credits and price tags for each of the benefits available to participants under the plan, utilizing the cost information prepared by the insurance company or the plan's actuary. This pricing system is a key consideration in the development, implementation, and operation of the plan.

Benefit Eligibility Determination

For employers without human resource information systems that calculate benefit eligibility, the flex system should have the capability of determining eligibility for each benefit. The system should be able to accommodate different waiting periods for each benefit under the plan for those situations; for example, employees may be required to wait a longer period of time to receive life insurance than to receive medical insurance.

Personal Information

Personal "fact sheets," which include all the necessary information needed for each participant to enroll in the plan, must be produced by the system. The system should give the user the flexibility of customizing the fact sheet so that the presentation of credits and price tags can be altered to meet the company's needs.

The system should also produce an individual "confirmation statement," confirming the applicable information for a benefit determination for each employee, as well as the benefits elected by the participant during the enroll-ment period. These statements should be produced for all participants after the annual enrollment period, and individually after a new hire makes benefit selections or after eligible benefit changes are made by active plan par-ticipants.

Payroll Deduction Amounts

The communication between the flex system and the payroll system may be the most important link. Employees are very intolerant of incorrect deductions from their paychecks, and even more intolerant of deductions in subsequent paychecks to correct prior deduction problems.

A critical decision is whether the system should calculate the actual payroll deduction amounts or simply send both credits and price tags to the payroll systems so that the payroll system can determine the actual deduction amount.

ADMINISTRATIVE TASKS

When planning for implementation, the following administrative tasks should certainly be considered and incorporated into the flex software: monthly premium billings, flexible spending account (FSA) interface, COBRA administration interface, user definable tables, ad hoc reporting, and import/export of data.

Monthly Premium Billings

Non-flex premium statements for medical and dental plans are relatively easy to prepare, since, in many cases, when plans are insured, the statements are generated by the insurance carrier and sent to the employer for editing. Usually single or family coverage is available, resulting in only two amounts that will show on the statement. Flexible benefit loans, on the other hand, may have multiple options and at least three coverage levels available, resulting in may possible premium amounts. Flex systems should have the capability of producing a monthly premium statement to be used for remittance of premiums to carriers, or in the case of self-funded plans, to a trust. If the human resource system currently produces these statements, adjustments to that system will likely be required and should be considered very early in the flex planning process.

For self-funded plans, the monthly premium statements are most likely used to provide information for the contributions to a trust. Separate reports may be necessary for the third party administrator (TPA) indicating new participants, terminations, and changes in coverage.

The flex system should have the capability of producing these reports, or preferably, simply producing a file that can be transferred on disk or tape to the TPA. Discussions with the TPA should begin early so that systems compatibility can be established and file layout can be determined. A breakdown here, after flex implementation, may mean serious problems with eligibility verification on the part of the provider, and very serious employee relations issues.

Careful coordination with the carriers involved with other insured benefits under the flex plan, such as life insurance and long-term disability, is also critical.

If the system is being designed to prepare the premium statements for these coverages, it is necessary to verify that the carrier is willing to accept the statements in the form produced by the system.

Flexible Spending Account (FSA) Interface

If the FSA administration is a stand-alone system, or an outside administrator is handling this function, the flex system should interface with the FSA system or outside vendor. Participant election should be transferred to the system or vendor on tape or disk, rather than simply printing reports to be used for data entry.

COBRA Administration Interface

Stand-alone administration systems of the Consolidated Omnibus Budget Reconciliation Act of 1985 (COBRA) as well as outside COBRA administrators will require information on participant qualifying events. Communication among the payroll, human resource, flex and COBRA systems is another key consideration in the development of the flex program, since each is affected by COBRA qualifying events.

User Definable Tables

The flexible benefit system should include tables that specify information such as waiting periods, hour requirements for each benefit, employer location, and possibly benefit cost information. Employers should have access to these tables through a menu item, so that changes in waiting periods, new locations, and so on, can be entered without the need for additional programming and the accompanying costs. Proper security measures should be taken for access to these table.

Ad Hoc Reporting

While the standard reports relating to premium, participation, and elections will most likely be part of any flex software package, the system should also give the user the capability of producing ad hoc reports. The system should provide a reasonably simple approach to develop reports utilizing any of the fields that exist within the flex data base. Once created, the system should also allow the report format to be saved as a template for future use.

Import/Export of Data

The system should allow the user to download data in standard ASCII format to files that can be transferred to other software packages. The ability to transfer raw data into a graphics or spreadsheet software package may prove very beneficial in the overall management of the benefits program.

HUMAN RESOURCES

The number of decisions that the human resource department must make during the planning stages of a flexible benefits implementation is considerable. The programmers charged with developing the flex system or modifying the human resource or payroll systems must have clear direction from the human resource department about plan design and the administrative issues. Many decisions will require coordination with the human resource and payroll department, since both departments will be affected by the flexible benefits program.

While many issues need to be addressed in the development of any benefits package, the items in the following list relate particularly to the flexible benefits arrangement and require special attention:

1. *Plans included.* The plans to be included within the flex program as well as the number of options to be offered within each plan must be established. Careful consideration should be given to whether the plan will include only the traditional "insured" benefits or if the inclusion of vacation within the flexible benefits program is desirable.

2. *Eligibility requirements.* Many issues related to eligibility must be addressed. Should the requirements be the same for all benefits within the flex program, or will some waiting periods be longer than others, depending upon the benefit? Will only full-time employees be eligible for the benefit package, or will part-time employees also be included, and if so, at what number of hours per week does participation become available? Does this regulation apply across all benefits, or will the hour requirement be different depending upon the benefit?

3. *Coverage effective date.* Once an employee satisfies the eligibility requirements, when will coverage actually begin? Will it be immediately upon satisfaction of the requirements, the first of the month following, or the next open enrollment?

4. *Opt-outs.* Will the flexible benefits plan allow an employee to opt out of any of the coverages offered? If so, in the case of medical insurance, will evidence of coverage under another plan be required? Additionally, will the plan reimburse the employee the full credits available for that option or only some portion of that amount?

5. *Core/Default coverage.* What will the core levels of coverage be for each benefit, and what options will the employee receive in the event that the employee makes no election?

6. *Credit adjustments.* With respect to those benefits that are salary driven, should the flex system reallocate credits upon salary adjustments during a plan year, or should the adjustments be made with the next open enrollment?

7. *Flexible spending accounts.* If the plan is to include flexible spending accounts, what range of deposits will be allowed? What will be the frequency of the reimbursement, and how long after the close of a plan year may claims be submitted?

8. *Enrollment.* How employees enroll in the flexible benefits program is also an issue that will require attention. Large employers may consider the use of an interactive system, which will allow employees to make their elections with the use of a telephone or a personal computer. If the interactive system is to be used, will it be used only during the annual open enrollments, or as individuals are hired or make changes in their coverages? Multiple location employers will possibly have to consider the cost of maintaining an interactive system for anything other than the annual open enrollment.

    Once the method of enrollment has been determined, decisions relating to the time frame to be used for annual open enrollments must be made. Whether a manual system or an interactive system, a sufficient amount of time after the enrollment window closes must be allowed for employees to review the personal confirmation statements and confirm that their elections have been properly recorded. This time frame should be sufficient to allow employees to change incorrect entries before the transfer of deduction information to the payroll system.

9. *Change in status.* Changes in coverages due to changes in family status will require additional effort due to the very specific requirements of Internal Revenue Code Section 125. Procedures should be developed and time frames established for individuals to notify the human resources department of legitimate changes in family status.

10. *Administrative forms.* In developing the flexible benefits program and working with the programmers to write the software package, the day-to-day administrative tasks should not be overlooked. It should be established early whether the developers of the system will also provide the administrative forms necessary to administer the plan. Since non-flex administrative forms may not accomplish all that is necessary, these forms will be developed in-house or by the developers of the software. The following types of forms should be considered:

    *   Enrollment
    *   Change in Family Status
    *   Dependent Information
    *   Beneficiary Designation

- Termination of Employment
- Flexible Spending Claim
- Payroll Adjustment

PAYROLL

The importance of the link between the flex system and payroll system cannot be overemphasized. Complete and accurate payroll data are absolutely essential and should not be jeopardized by the implementation of a flexible benefits program. If the flex system is incorrectly calculating payroll deductions, obvious employee relations and general ledger issues will exist. Therefore, the involvement of the payroll staff in the planning of the flexible benefits program is critical. Numerous questions will have to be answered, about the development of the flexible benefits software and about the changes necessary in the employer's payroll system to accommodate flex.

Issues that should be considered by the payroll department in the development and coordination of systems are discussed below.

How Easy Are Changes?

Whether using an internal system or an outside vendor, the ease of changing the payroll system to accommodate flex must be determined early in the planning process.

Number of Payrolls

If the employer has multiple locations, are all of the payrolls on a single system, or are they individual payroll systems? Are there any "confidential" payrolls that need to be identified? Do the payrolls run on computers, or are they manually prepared?

What Is a Pay Period?

In order for the flex system to properly determine the payroll deductions it's important that the system know whether employees are paid on a weekly, bi-weekly, or monthly basis and whether the system will have to accommodate more than one pay cycle.

When pay-period deductions should be taken for employee benefits has to be decided. If the normal payroll frequency is 26 pay periods, it may be beneficial to make payroll deductions for the flex plan over 24 of these pay periods, leaving the first and last pay periods without the deduction amounts. This may give additional time during a critical period to ensure that the transition from one year to the next goes smoothly. A 24-deduction arrangement will also make it easier to reconcile monthly premium statements, since two deductions should equal the total employee portion of the monthly premium amount.

Actual Pay Dates

Due to the before-tax nature of the deductions under a flexible benefits program, it is important to determine when the pay checks are actually received by employees, and whether it is within the same taxable year for which the payroll deduction has been made. For example, if the actual pay date for the last pay period in the calendar year occurs in the subsequent calendar year, and a person has elected the maximum payroll deduction for a dependent care spending account, it is possible that the deductions in the subsequent calendar year will exceed the statutory limit.

Before-Tax Vs. After-Tax Deductions

Certainly one of the advantages of a Section 125 program is that the deductions for benefits can be made on a before-tax basis. However, there may be situations when employees are concerned about the impact on their Social Security benefits and would prefer to make their contributions on an after-tax basis. The employer must decide whether the after-tax contribution will continue to be an option after the flexible benefits program has been implemented.

Deduction Capacity

Depending upon the system, it will be necessary to ensure that there are a sufficient number of fields left within the payroll system to accommodate a flexible benefits program. The timing and cost of adding additional capacity should be considered in the development process.

Check Stub Issues

The limitations of the employer's current check stock should be identified. Is there sufficient space on the check stub to reflect the individual deductions by benefit, or will the use of a single deduction for all benefits be necessary? The cost of purchasing additional check stock and the programming to redesign the layout of the check to accommodate the flex deductions are factors to be considered.

The handling of excess income generated from opt-out credits is also an important point to discuss with the payroll staff. Employees generally like to see the excess income resulting from opt-out credits shown as a separate item on the check stub.

Deduction Timing

Depending upon the decision on coverage effective date, the timing of the payroll deductions for coverage must be established. Will the payroll system be required to prorate premium deductions during a pay period if an individual's coverage effective date occurs within that pay period? It may be easier administratively to simply wait to take the deduction until after the first pay period following the coverage effective date. This decision may be influenced by the policy of the insurance carrier, which may require the prorating of monthly premiums.

Payroll Adjustment

Inevitably, the implementation of the new benefits program will result in errors that may affect a participant's payroll deduction and impact take-home pay. The importance of establishing a procedure to make fair and timely adjustments for incorrect payroll deductions should not be overlooked in the planning process. Even the most comprehensive employee communication program cannot help if a way to correct the paycheck has not been established.

COMMUNICATION AND TRAINING

Communicating directly to participants is a very important part of any flexible benefits implementation. After the internal communications among the human resource, payroll, and MIS staff have been firmly established, and decisions have been made about the systems to be used and how the enrollment process will be handled, the challenge of communicating the flexible benefits program to employees can be addressed.

In addition, the administrative requirements of the flexible benefits plan may be very different from the procedures established under a nonflexible benefits arrangement. Therefore, all staff involved in the administration of benefits and payroll should be properly trained once the systems have been developed.

Communication

Although becoming more common, a flexible benefits plan is a more complicated program than employees may be accustomed to. The best approach to communicating flexible benefits is to provide a clear description of the operation of the plan, over time and in several different formats. A communications plan should be established, and might include the following:

1. *Announcement letter.* The announcement letter should be signed by a senior management person and explain that the rationale for developing a flexible benefits program is to give employees the opportunity to develop their own benefits package.
2. *Newsletters.* Several newsletters may be appropriate, strategically timed over the months preceding the implementation of the program. That is a critical time to explain the operation of a flexible benefits program and the options available under the plan.
3. *Videotape or sound/slide presentations.* These presentations should summarize the key messages, explain the main features of each plan, and review the enrollment process. This ensures that employees will have an understanding of what to expect during the enrollment process and, if multiple locations are a factor, that consistent information is presented to all employees.
4. *Employee meetings.* At these meetings, the employees review the presentation (videotape or slides) and are allowed to question of human resource staff regarding the plan options and the enrollment process.
5. *Flexible benefits hotline.* It may be advisable to establish a phone number for employees to call during the communication and enrollment process in order to respond to questions about the program. This may not be feasible with multi-location employers, unless the employer is willing to establish a toll free number.

In addition, other forms of communication such as special flex bulletins, payroll stuffers, and posters could be distributed or posted throughout the year to keep employees' awareness of the program fresh. The legally required disclosure, the Summary Plan Description, is also an effective communication piece.

Training

The training of those individuals who will be required to administer the flexible benefit program on a day-to-day basis should not be overlooked. Employees actually involved in the process should be trained early on in the project. It is likely that staff from the human resources, payroll, finance, and accounting departments will be affected by a change to a flexible benefits arrangement.

Communicating the changes in the administrative effort through training sessions with these individuals will minimize the post-implementation problems.

It will also be beneficial to identify a group of people to lead the employee meetings, and train these individuals for this task. Trained meeting leaders provide information to employees and help to illustrate the advantages of a flexible benefits program.

CONCLUSION

Over the last decade, flexible benefits plans have been adopted by more and more employers in order to achieve goals such as cost control and enhancing employee appreciation of benefits, and this trend is expected to continue. Successful implementation and operation of the program requires an understanding very early in the planning stages of the functions of flexible benefits systems, the administrative tasks involved, the changes for the human resources and payroll departments, and most importantly, the elements of effective communication and training.

Part 4

SELF-INSURANCE

18.   Self-Funding and the Small to Medium-Sized Company: Chart Your Own Map by Asking the Right Questions

William J. Danish

Self-funding is an increasingly popular option for small to medium-sized companies, but successfully implementing a self-funded plan requires asking the right questions of both your company and potential vendors. Understanding all the issues involved in self-funding is the only way to ensure that the full potential for cost savings, at the minimum risk, is realized for your company's unique needs.

Imagine a company that has just made the decision to leave the insured environment and self-fund its company's health insurance program; all that is left is implementation. Our imaginary company fits the general description of most companies that are making this decision today—it's a small to medium-sized employer (25 to 1,000 employees), with a history of annual rate increases ranging from 15 to 50 percent or more. Included in our company's health plan design are numerous features to bring the company into compliance with state regulations as well as some utilization reviews to control costs. The basis for our decision to move to a self-funded program was to control costs and possibly improve design flexibility. However, the decision to self-insure health benefits does not mean that we've decided to take on an unlimited liability, so some form of stop-loss insurance will be purchased. In implementing the new plan, we do not want to adversely affect the delivery of benefits to the employees, so we will be looking to maintain a high level of administrative services from the claims payor—but we are interested in saving money on administrative charges. Our goal is to maintain the same plan design that we had prior to changing the funding vehicle.

The good news is that we can accomplish all of this. To do so, however, we must recognize that, as in all things, we cannot assume too much. The thrust of this article, which will use our imagined company for illustration, is twofold:

1. To raise those issues that may warrant a rethinking of the initial decision to self-fund; and
2. To probe more deeply into the issues that hold the potential for "problems" in the future.

WHAT IS OUR PLAN?

Let's start with the easy part and duplicate our current plan. This gives rise to all kinds of questions, the first and most notable of which is determining what, exactly, our current plan is.

Our current plan is like the typical plan. It provides reimbursement for all eligible charges subject to annual deductible and coinsurance provisions. Some benefits, such as mental health care and substance abuse treatment, might be covered with annual maximums, coinsurance provisions, and lifetime maximums different than those of the balance of the program. Most other health care claims are subject to a combined lifetime limit.

The benefits are neatly summarized in a booklet provided by the insurance carrier, but this summary does not fully describe what the plan covers; certain provisions and definitions are covered in the insurance contract itself. However, even both of these documents together may not answer all the questions that will be raised when we attempt to duplicate coverage. There are the less tangible things—employee perceptions, for example—to consider as well.

For employees, the real definition of the coverage of the plan is the paid benefits. The issue is how the administrators determine reasonable and customary (R&C) charges (alternatively described as usual and customary, or prevailing charges). The majority of third party administrators (TPAs) subscribe to the Health Insurance Association of America (HIAA) database to determine R&C charges. But even two administrators using the same table may reimburse at different levels. Some may describe R&C as the 90th percentile charge for a given procedure in a given location. This means that 90 percent of the providers charge at that level or less. Other TPAs may reimburse at the 80th percentile. Even two administrators using the same percentile ranking may reimburse a claim different-ly, depending on when they update their data (annually or semi-annually).

Although this may not seem like much of a difference, if the goal is to duplicate current coverage levels, it is incumbent upon us to determine if the same definitions and databases will be used under the new plan. We must decide if we will allow some coverage levels to change, and if so, we must decide how to communicate this to the employee population.

One item often overlooked is the application of lifetime maximums. Many programs restart all maximums at the time of a change in carrier or funding technique. In general, the cost of such unintentional benefit improvements may be slight, however, the issue should be addressed.

WHO DECIDES WHAT TO PAY?

We expect to hire a TPA to pay our claims in accordance with our plan (refined to address the points covered above). One might presume that, once hired, the TPA decides what claims to pay, but one very significant difference between insured and self-funded plans is that the employer assumes the fiduciary role in determining how (or what) claims are paid. What is a medically necessary claim? What is an experimental treatment? What type of exceptions will we make on a claim payment? For most issues, the company can and should look to the TPA for guidance, but fiduciary responsibility for the claim payments will now rest with the employer.

This latter responsibility has become clearer in a recent court decision (U.S. Court of Appeals, 3rd Cir.) concerning an employer's ability to sue its TPA as a plan fiduciary under the Employee Retirement Income Security Act (ERISA). The court held the TPA did not have discretion in paying claims and its duties were ministerial.

WHAT CLAIMS ARE WE PAYING?

The standard insurance contract provides for payment of all claims "incurred" within a given period of time. The insurance company has established a claim reserve to use for the payment of claims incurred but not yet reported. Unless the company had made other arrangements—such as to take back that liability from the carrier—all claims incurred before the date the program becomes self-funded are the responsibility of the prior carrier.

This issue is not as clear as it first appears. Questions that should be resolved before implementing the self-funded plan include:

- Who will pay for maternity claims? It is not unusual to have open maternity claims upon transfer of coverage. The important issue is to determine which administrator will pay for the claim at delivery.
- Who will pay claims for currently disabled employees, and for how long? Will all claims on the disabled employee be paid, or only those associated with the disability?

- How long will the current insurer allow for submission of incurred but unreported claims?

These and other related questions should be resolved before the effective date of the self-funded plan.

WHO IS COVERED?

The general intention of most plans is to cover employees and their dependents. To avoid the potential additional administration of individual billing and collection, some employers contract with their health insurer to administer COBRA participants for their corporate plan. (The Consolidated Omnibus Budget Reconciliation Act permits participants to continue health care coverage at their own expense for up to 36 months after it would otherwise terminate.) Moving into a self-funded plan, it is incumbent upon the employer to review the records associated with each COBRA participant to determine the length of eligibility that remains.

Under an insured plan, those employees not actively at work on the effective date are excluded from the program (to be eligible when they return to active employment status). Excluded dependents are those who are either home or confined to a hospital on the effective date. Arrangements can and should be made to include such employees and dependents under a health plan, either with the prior insurer or under the new self-funded plan. Fundamentally, the issue is determining who will pay for what.

ASSESSING RISK AND CASH FLOW

The decision to self-fund is made for a variety of reasons, with cost generally being the central issue. In implementing a self-funded plan, all parties should understand the level of risk (and potential cost) being taken on, both in terms of short-term cash flow fluctuation and maximum annual exposure.

One significant advantage of an insured program is the certainty of cost over a limited time. Monthly rates set at renewal are, by practice, generally good for one year. Monthly and annual premium cost to the employer is a function of covered lives times the applicable rate. Under a self-funded plan, the costs of the program are a direct function of the claims paid. If monthly claims exceed expectations, it is the company's responsibility to pay them, and this can hurt the company's cash flow. While the monthly exposure can be limited by individual and aggregate stop-loss coverage, cash flow management may be an important consideration for some employers.

One gain generally achieved in the first year of a self-funded program is improved cash flow. This statement is not at odds with the above paragraph.

Because of claim lag, most self-funded plans will incur little expense in the first three months of the new program. Usually, most claims that would have been paid during the first three months are the responsibility of the prior insurance carrier and are paid out of existing (pre-paid) reserves. This advantage is limited to cash flow, as the company will have the liability associated with "run-out" of the incurred but not reported claims at the end of the self-funded arrangement. The payment is simply deferred. Employers have the option either of setting up book reserves reflecting the liability, or of actually funding the potential liability. If funded, a trust should be established.

While short-term cash fluctuations usually do not make employers reconsider the decision to self-fund health plans, the maximum exposure to risk may. The most common method of avoiding the unlimited risk associated with a health plan is through the purchase of specific (individual) or aggregate stop-loss insurance coverage. Specific coverage limits the annual exposure on an individual to a predetermined dollar amount. Aggregate coverage limits the risk exposure on the entire group to a percentage above the expected claim level (typically 120 or 125 percent of projected claims). While limiting risk, purchasing this coverage increases the total cost of the program.

When deciding how much protection is required, the basic issue is determining how much risk the company can afford to take. On an aggregate basis, can we afford a fluctuation above 125 percent of expected claims? Above 150 percent? 200 percent? Once we have determined whether we can afford a level of fluctuation, we must decide whether we want to. When assessing aggregate loss protection, will we be comfortable explaining why we purchased a level of coverage that we didn't use? Or alternatively, will we be able to explain to corporate management why we didn't purchase the coverage for an amount considerably less than the amount of additional claims we had to pay? Similar questions should be asked in assessing individual stop-loss protection. Will one claim cause us to hit our aggregate level?

Risk tolerance is an individual issue. In theory, over time, the premium expended will equal the claims avoided. In a perfect world, this would occur annually. Of course, we don't live in a perfect world.

CHOOSING THE CLAIMS ADMINISTRATOR

The choice of the TPA to pay the health claims may be the most costly decision of all. Part of the reason to move to a self-funded plan was to lower the cost of administration, to do away with some of the overhead of the insurance carrier by paying only for needed services.

A number of organizations exist solely to pay claims. Some are national, others are regional or local. Additionally, using the current insurer as a TPA is usually an option warranting consideration. The first pass at selecting a claims administrator involves determining the costs associated with paying claims. Care must be taken to ensure a full understanding of how fees for the claim administration services are determined. Important questions to be answered include the following:

- Are the fees determined based on the number of claims processed, checks issued, percentage of claim dollars spent, or number of covered employees?
- What is a claim? Is everything that comes in one envelope considered one claim? Who determines this?
- What is a claim transaction? Is it a rejection of a claim? Does it include claims that do not produce a check, such as claims applied to the deductible?
- What about a "percentage of claims" fee arrangement? Is it based on a targeted amount of claims? What if claims exceed the target? Both percentages of claims and flat dollar charges per covered employee need to reflect underlying assumptions about the number of claims or transactions expected over the course of the year, to be a reasonable attempt to pay for the actual services rendered.

Once we have identified a common basis for measuring costs among various TPAs, we need to decide what criteria we will use to select our new administrator. In selecting a new claim administrator, we must avoid choosing one who will make our costs go up. Selecting the lowest cost administrator will not save the company money if the administrator pays every claim that comes in without review.

A good test of all the finalists in our review will be to have each of them pay a variety of actual claims. In theory, all will achieve the same cost result. In practice, this exercise will enable us to review how each system tracks, adjudicates, and measures the components (including R&C charge profiles) for our plan. For instance, how are the profiles determined and how often are they updated?

It is expected that the TPA will audit all claims over a certain dollar threshold, but what about routine claims? Are these audited? A quality TPA will have stated review procedures in place, monitoring claims to ensure accuracy in payment.

A number of other issues need to be considered as well. How is eligibility for benefits determined and how is this tracked on an ongoing basis? What is required of the employer and the TPA? How is a coordination of benefit (COB) provision handled? What level of COB savings can be expected? Is the claim system able to "rebundle" claims?

The organization selected to administer the program can and should be held accountable to the company for mutually agreed upon accuracy and timeliness. These can take the form of financial performance guarantees, or other acceptable alternatives. The goal in selecting an administrator is to build a long-term relationship, not just to get a low price.

If possible, a site visit for the finalists is recommended. A site visit will enable the purchaser to actually view the claims operation, to verify the systems and methodology used in processing claims, and to meet with the individuals who will be processing the claims. In reviewing the processing of claims, the system itself should perform a level of audit, eliminating impossible claims (e.g., maternity charges for males), and flagging suspect items. The system will be supported by material relevant to the processing of claims for the company's plan design. The degree of integration, systematization, and auditing are all important in determining which administrator will do the best job for the plan.

In defining a long-term relationship with a TPA, we need to look down the road at future needs. Does the TPA have arrangements with managed care networks or discounted providers? Can they work with pre-established networks? Are there arrangements in place to utilize specialized centers for transplants and other major care items?

Utilization review (UR) is another area that needs to be examined. What type of UR is performed and by whom? How does the UR interact with the claims administration? What notification and screening is done to get early intervention and alternative treatment modes in place for catastrophic claims? Does the employer have the ability to use any UR firm of its choosing, or is it locked in to the TPA's choice? Can the TPA administer "carve-out" programs? Can they work concurrently with a variety of UR firms for one employer?

Another important TPA function that deserves attention is data collection and reporting. What kind of reporting will be available for the program? Can claims be tracked by diagnosis, outcome, or other criteria? What type of "normative" information is available for comparison with the company's utilization? Will the new TPA be able to accept historical information about claim maximums from the prior administrator?

Having ascertained the answers to these questions, we should revisit an underlying theme in the selection process: *Does the new administrator pay claims the same as the prior administrator?* It may be that we no longer want the plan to be administered in the same fashion.

OTHER ADMINISTRATIVE SERVICES

In addition to providing claim administration services, the TPA may be in a position to provide other services for additional fees. In selecting a TPA, the company must be clear on what additional services may be needed and who will provide them.

Though the cost of the self-funded plan will now be decided by the actual claims submitted and paid, the company will still need a monthly premium "rate" for purposes of determining HMO contribution levels and for COBRA. On an ongoing basis, actuarial rate-setting skills will be required to measure the impact of potential plan changes. These services are available from a number of sources, including the TPA.

COBRA administration will also remain an issue for most employers. Does the TPA provide COBRA administration services? Will they provide these services for coverages on which they do not pay claims? Beyond COBRA, the company policy may be to provide conversions to individual policies for employees. What arrangements does the TPA have to provide conversion coverage, and at what cost level?

Good communication with employees is the key to a successful benefits plan. Does the TPA offer services in this area? If so, to what extent? Since the summary plan description (SPD) will provide a basis for the employees' understanding of the plan, can the TPA prepare an SPD? If we would prefer to do our own communication and SPD preparation, will the TPA be willing to review our material for accuracy?

The plan may include provisions for late entrants to come into the program contingent upon providing satisfactory medical evidence of insurability. What are the TPA's capabilities in the medical underwriting area?

As we have seen, the employer has fiduciary responsibility for the payment of claims under a self-funded program. It may be that the TPA is willing to take back (insure) this exposure, and this option should be explored. Absent acceptance of this responsibility, what source of guidance will the TPA provide in terms of payment on "questionable" claims? The questionable claim may have arisen because of a concern on the medical necessity or the experimental nature of the procedure. In both of these areas, the company will need to rely on the experience and expertise of the administrator.

There are also the requirements and obligations of law, many of which are still evolving. For instance, adopting a self-funded plan may have the advantage of eliminating state insurance provisions, but it does not relieve ERISA requirements. Will the TPA provide assistance in completing the Form 5500 or the attachments? What about the Summary Annual Report? Will the TPA provide updates on changes to state and federal law? Although the plan may not have to comply with state guidelines, the company may choose to do so, and will need to be aware of any changes. Federal requirements must be followed. Many of the changes affecting the plan will arise from emerging case law. Does the TPA provide information and guidance with respect to legal changes affecting the program?

Will the TPA arrange for the purchase of stop-loss coverage? If so, what markets do they use and what relationships do they have with the selected carrier? Can the company elect to use its own stop-loss carrier? How many stop-loss carriers recognize and will approve the TPA as a claims administrator and issue stop-loss coverage?

The TPA is not expected to provide all of the services required in administering an employer's health plan. A multitude of other sources exist to service these needs. However, in many cases, the insurer for a number of employers has provided these services as a one-stop plan administrator. In moving to a self-funded plan, these services may not be provided as part of the "deal" and should be addressed.

SIGNING THE CONTRACT

Now that the best TPA has been identified, the company must enter into a contractual arrangement. Although it should be obvious to the buyer, what is being agreed to is not an insurance arrangement. The TPA contract is for the administration and payment of claims in connection with a plan of benefits offered by the employer. The contract between the employer and the TPA defines the services to be provided by the TPA and outlines the responsibilities and liabilities of both parties.

In reviewing the contract, a clear understanding of the fiduciary responsibilities and obligations of each party should be determined. The TPA may wish to act as an extension of the employer and seek to be indemnified and protected from any legal action or losses that may arise, even if they occurred because of errors or wrongdoing on its part. However, the TPA should have errors and omissions insurance to protect the employer from willful misconduct, negligence, or mistakes made by the TPA in the course of discharging its duties.

Although the responsibilities of all parties will be spelled out in the contract, employers should assume that they, not the TPA, are ultimately responsible for the accurate payment of claims and compliance with local, state, and federal guidelines. Accepting this level of responsibility will help guide the TPA in fully discharging its contractual obligations.

The contract between the TPA and the employer is an important document. It is highly advisable to seek review of the document by legal counsel.

At the outset of the TPA agreement, it should be the intent of both parties to become partners for the long term. To facilitate the continuation of the arrangement, it is necessary to understand how the TPA will price its services in future years. Minimizing surprises will help build a healthy relationship. Although one may expect to continue to retain the same TPA over the long run, nothing is forever. It is critical for the employer to understand what will happen at the dissolution of the contract. What notice period is required by each party of the intent of the other party to terminate the contract? What happens to claims that are filed and not processed as of the termination date? Will the TPA continue to accept and pay claims submitted after the termination date? Is this desirable?

Changing administrators is a time-consuming and costly endeavor. Time is better spent building a strong working relationship with the claims administrator. Annual audits of the TPA would serve toward that end. The purpose of the audit should not be to focus solely on mistakes, but to work on process. The successful audit will tell the employer what is going right and what can be done to improve the process. Where errors have occurred, the audit should address corrective measures needed to avoid future problems. Dealing with the claim administrator should not be adversarial in nature.

PURCHASING STOP-LOSS COVERAGE

A separate but related issue in moving to self-funding is the management of excess risk. As discussed above, this is usually done through the purchase of stop-loss insurance. Some key areas to review relate to the type of coverage being purchased and how it fits with the company's understanding of risk transfer. Included in the review should be a mutual understanding between the TPA and the reinsurer in terms of "covered claims" and procedures. For example, both parties should have a common definition of experimental treatment so that no coverage gaps exist, now or in the future.

The stop-loss carrier needs to understand how claim run-in and claim run-out will be handled and how each applies to the coverage limits. Any information on disabled employees should be prepared and submitted to the reinsurer in advance of the quotation and again as the effective date approaches.

Stop-loss markets are becoming increasingly focused on the risk that is insured. Care must be taken to present, on an "apples to apples" basis, competing quotes from the insurance carrier. Further, the company must understand all provisions of competing quotations to ensure that the product purchased is consistent with the perception of the risk being shifted.

Selectively excluding certain coverages or individuals—a technique called "lasering"—is an emerging tool employed by reinsurers (sometimes at the request of the employer). If a procedure, such as organ transplants, or certain individuals are being excluded, the company must know of this before contracts are signed.

Financially, the company is expecting the stop-loss carrier to step in a pick up claims in excess of certain predetermined limits. The financial stability of the carrier is very important and the company should obtain as much financial information about the carrier as is available. The readily available sources of financial information, in addition to the carrier's annual report, would be an A.M. Best's insurers rating as well as the SEC-required 10-K or 10-Q.

As with the TPA, the goal will be to establish a long-term, mutually rewarding relationship with the stop-loss insurer. Towards that goal, the renewal process should be discussed and understood at the inception of the program. Will the policy be renewed based on the company claims, its demographics, or other factors? How will plan design changes affect the rating of the plan? What about changes in the demographics of the group—for example, additions to or termina- tions of current staff? Are there minimum premium or lives requirements? Must other coverage, such as life insurance, be placed with the reinsurer to obtain a policy? Can multiyear rate guarantees be negotiated? Finally, what are the termination and cancellation requirements between the company and the reinsurer, and between the reinsurer and the TPA?

The stop-loss carrier and the TPA should work in concert for the protection of the company. Information should flow smoothly from one party to the other, and the company should always be informed.

WHAT ELSE?

Communication of the benefit program has been mentioned and should be mentioned again. A health benefit plan offers protection for the employees and their dependents from catastrophic loss. To the employee, this protection is often assumed to come not from the employer, but from the insurance carrier. This misperception should be addressed, and the employees should understand how the new self-funded plan will work for them.

Up to this point, we have reviewed the mechanics and the issues that arise in implementing and selecting stop-loss carriers and claims payers. We also have a financial obligation and will need to establish the appropriate banking arrangement to ensure the smooth flow of dollars from the company to the TPA and on to the providers or participants. The latter is the responsibility of the TPA, but the former is the company's and the TPA's joint undertaking. Typically, the employer will establish a bank account to which the TPA will be provided access to pay claims. This is not an unlimited account, and the TPA will need to instruct the employer how much to put into the account and on the timing of the deposit. This can be done through wire transfers. The employer should verify the amounts of the wire with the claims paid and maintain a vigilant audit process. The expectation is that the TPA will do this, and most do, but it doesn't hurt to be sure.

The company may wish to establish a trust to hold reserves and any employee money that is received in the form of contributions. Trusts established under Internal Revenue Code section 501(c)(9) may offer certain financial and tax opportunities for an employer. These should be reviewed. Any established trust will require a formal filing and ongoing audits.

LOOKING FORWARD

Health care reform may dramatically reshape benefit plans and funding alternatives. However, it is not likely that the action of any one company will hasten or delay reform. Furthermore, it is unclear what shape reform will take, and how long it may be before any reform is implemented. Therefore, we must focus on resolving current issues based on current facts.

Emerging case law and state and federal legislation will need to be monitored on a continuous basis. Recent guidance released by the Equal Employment

Opportunities Commission on the application of the Americans with Disabilities Act of 1990 may impact self-insured plans more dramatically than insured plans. There are also proposals to grant certain states ERISA preemption waivers, including allowing state taxation of self-funded health plans.

CONCLUSION

By remaining informed on the issues, and understanding the initial reasons for the decision to self-fund health benefits, we can continue to benefit from our decisions. Most items that will impact on the financial conditions of our plan are under the employer's control. By asking the right questions and structuring arrangements to fit the company's unique needs, self-funding can be an effective health plan cost management tool.

Finally, although self-funding is an effective cost-management tool, it is only one of the control mechanisms available to companies sponsoring employee medical coverage. Self-funding is not a panacea. To control costs over the long haul, we will need to understand the real drivers of health care inflation and continue to monitor and manage these.

19. Stop-Loss Insurance for Self-Funded Plans
John C. Garner

Employers that self-fund their employee health benefit plans have the advantages of greater plan flexibility and greater control over costs than other funding methods—advantages that usually translate to a substantial savings—but at the cost of assuming the risk for health claims. Stop-loss insurance represents a way to limit that risk by insuring against excessive claims costs, but choosing the proper stop-loss policy is not always as simple as it sounds, and there are a number of pitfalls along the way for the unwary.

Self-funding health care benefits can generally reduce costs in the short term, and can almost always reduce costs over a long period of time. But self-funding means assuming risks that an insurance company normally takes, and except for very large groups, most plan sponsors are unwilling or unable to assume complete risk. Therefore, most plans purchase reinsurance, also known as stop-loss insurance, to cover some of this risk. Even with stop-loss insurance, however, there are risks and pitfalls. Buyers who are not aware of potential problems can spend more than necessary, have gaps in their coverage, or both.

Stop-loss insurance takes two forms, specific and aggregate. Specific stop-loss insurance protects plans against the risk that any one claim will exceed a specific dollar amount, known as the attachment point. Aggregate stop-loss insurance protects plans against the risk that the overall level of claims will exceed what is expected by more than a specified percentage (also known as the attachment point). Many plans purchase both types of reinsurance.

Specific stop-loss insurance can be purchased for any amount agreed upon by the plan and the carrier. Typical amounts range from $5,000 for small employers to $150,000 or more for large employers. At the lower end of the scale, employers might choose a high-deductible plan rather than specific stop-loss insurance, although these plans are not fully self-funded. Under a high-deductible plan, the employer purchases a traditional group insurance policy with a high deductible, such as $1,000. In this case, the employer would tell the employees they have a lower deductible, such as $250, and that the difference between $250 and $1,000 is self-funded. With a specific stop-loss policy, the deductible might be the same, but the whole plan is self-funded. The key difference is that with the high-deductible plan there is a group insurance policy; each employee is covered and entitled to a certificate of insurance. With a specific stop-loss policy, it is the employer who is insured—against the risk of an employee or dependent incurring a claim in excess of the stop-loss amount.

With aggregate stop-loss insurance, the attachment point is most commonly set at 125 percent of the expected claims. The most common variation is 120 percent, and some insurers have offered 115 percent. An underwriter establishes the level of expected claims using traditional underwriting practices. The expected claims are typically calculated based on the group's experience over the past 12 months, plus anticipated increases in costs (trend). The expected claims are usually expressed as an amount per employee per month. Sometimes this amount is set based on one amount for single employees and another amount for employees with dependents. If there is a change in the size of the group, the expected claim level will be adjusted automatically by multiplying the number of employees in each category by the expected claims for that category. Many contracts reserve the right to recalculate the expected claims if there is a significant change in the size of the group. This is appropriate because a large change in the size of the group can mean the nature of the risk has changed. For example, the average age of a group is typically higher after a layoff than before the layoff. Some contracts set a floor by establishing a minimum level of expected claims based on the enrollment as of the date of the census provided for the quotation, but will increase the level of expected claims if the population increases (but will not decrease it).

Although many plans choose to purchase only specific stop-loss insurance, aggregate stop-loss insurance is the more important because what really matters to a plan sponsor is whether it can afford to pay the benefits it has promised to pay. It is possible that although there is a large claim, claims in total are still within the budget. The reason many employers purchase specific over aggregate stop-loss insurance is that the chances of collecting under the latter are generally remote. If, for example, expected claims for a group are $2.5 million, actual claims must exceed that amount by $625,000 (with an attachment point of 125 percent) before the plan sponsor can collect anything. Plan sponsors purchase specific stop-loss insurance to minimize the damage of underestimating claims, because it is unusual to have a bad year of experience without also having large claims. Specific stop-loss insurance may not be as necessary, and is much more expensive, but many employers feel that the higher probability of collecting under the specific stop-loss insurance makes it a good value. Many refer to aggregate stop-loss insurance as "sleep insurance"—purchasing it allows the risk manager or benefit manager to sleep at night knowing that if things go really wrong, there is insurance to pay the bills.

Because it is unusual to collect under an aggregate policy, the premiums are typically very low, such as $2,000 to $7,500 annually. Some insurance companies charge the same premium for aggregate policies regardless of the size of the group, but the law of large numbers says that claims are more predictable for large groups. Since claims are less predictable for a small group, the premium is sometimes higher and the insurance company may insist upon a specific stop-loss policy in conjunction with the aggregate stop-loss policy. The higher the specific stop-loss attachment point, the more expensive the aggregate policy is, and vice versa (amounts collected under the specific policy do not apply to the aggregate attachment point).

Specific stop-loss premiums have been rising even more rapidly than the general level of increases for health insurance because of the leveraging phenomenon. For example, if a plan has a $50,000 specific attachment point and a claim of $55,000, the stop-loss policy pays $5,000. If medical inflation pushes that claim up to $60,000 the next year, the stop-loss policy pays $10,000. In other words, a 9 percent increase in total claims can lead to a 100 percent increase of stop-loss claims. Therefore, plans are typically faced with a choice each year of increasing their attachment point, which means taking on more risk, or paying sharply higher premiums.

Because of rising costs, co-insurance appears to be a growing trend in the stop-loss field. Traditionally, stop-loss policies have reimbursed 100 percent of claims in excess of the attachment point. Now, more policies are being issued with an element of co-insurance, where the carrier will pay a percentage (for example 90 percent) of claims in excess of the attachment point.

Another factor that affects costs is market cycles. Stop-loss insurance is more typical of property/casualty insurance than life/health insurance. This means that the underwriting cycles are more pronounced, which leads to greater volatility in the number of insurance companies and the rates they charge. In a "hard" market, an employer might find it difficult or impossible to purchase stop-loss insurance at an affordable price, particularly if the incumbent stop-loss carrier decides to leave the stop-loss market.

TIMING OF CLAIMS AND PAYMENTS

A major consideration in evaluating stop-loss policies is the period of time during which claims are paid. Specific stop-loss insurance is often issued on a "12/12" basis, meaning that the claims insured by the policy must be both incurred and paid by the plan during the same specified 12-month period. This is a problem when a large claim is incurred at the end of the period. If someone has a major hospitalization and surgery a couple of weeks before the end of the period, there is virtually no chance that the claim will be paid by the end of the period. Obviously, plan sponsors should try to obtain more liberal policy terms.

Some insurers offer pure incurred contracts, meaning they will insure any claims incurred during the period of coverage, but a more common provision is "12/15," which means that claims incurred in the 12-month period must also be paid during that period or within the following three months. There is still a danger that a large claim will be incurred late in the period and not paid within three months, but the exposure is much less than with a 12/12 contract. Often the plan sponsor knows of the large claims before the claim is paid and has an opportunity to get it through the system in time to be covered by the stop-loss policy.

Trying to get a claim paid on a timely basis is legitimate, but because the timing of claims is so important, there is a temptation for some employers to manipulate the dates on which claims are filed. Aggregate policies are usually written on a "paid in 12" basis, and "incurred and paid in 12" is typical for the first year of a policy. These policies, however, present a temptation for a self-administered plan to bunch claims into certain years. For example, in year one, claims are delayed at the end of the year and not paid until year two. At the end of year two, claims are rushed through in order to be paid before the end of the year. It may be possible to pay 15 or more months worth of claims during a 12-month period by doing so, which would make it very likely to collect under a stop-loss policy without really having bad experience. Many insurance companies will not insure plans that self-administer their claims because of the potential for abuse.

On the other hand, if a third party administrator (TPA) and the stop-loss carrier are the same or related companies, there is a danger that they will play the game in reverse in order to avoid paying legitimate claims under the stop-loss policy. One large TPA was sued recently for allegedly engaging in such practices. Employers should be wary of the potential for these type of abuses.

Upon renewal of a policy, many reinsurers will be more liberal, often underwriting aggregate policies on a purely paid basis and specific policies on a 24/12 basis. This means that all claims incurred during the two years the policy has been in force and paid during the current year will be covered under the stop-loss policy. This is a good feature for long-term relationships, though it does lock the employer in with the carrier, which reduces flexibility.

Timing of payments is also an important issue to consider when evaluating stop-loss policies. The typical specific stop-loss policy requires the plan to pay the claim and then be reimbursed by the stop-loss carrier. To alleviate the cash-flow difficulties this can cause, some insurers will assume the responsibility for paying claims once the attachment point has been reached and the claim has been approved by the stop-loss carrier. Other carriers will make an exception and pay a large claim if a small employer is simply not capable of paying the claim and waiting for reimbursement.

Generally, aggregate policies reimburse plans for amounts in excess of the attachment point after the end of the policy year. If the aggregate attachment point has been penetrated, this can mean a substantial cash outlay and a long wait for reimbursement. Therefore, a few stop-loss carriers treat their aggregate policies more like minimum premium plans and set the attachment point on a monthly basis. For example, if the expected monthly claims are $100,000, the attachment point is $125,000, and the first month's claims are $130,000, these carriers would reimburse the plan $5,000. But, if the second month's claims are $115,000, the total claims for the two months would be $245,000, which is less than the cumulative two-month attachment point of $250,000, and the plan would have to refund the $5,000. These types of arrangements are very beneficial, obviously, but unfortunately they are also hard to obtain.

LASER UNDERWRITING

Another potential problem for the purchaser of stop-loss insurance is "laser underwriting." With a traditional group insurance policy, a large claim may lead to higher rates, but continued coverage is not usually a problem. Some stop-loss carriers will refuse to cover known claims. If a group has a $15,000 stop-loss limit and a $40,000 cancer claim, the stop-loss carrier may agree to renew the policy, but only if the cancer patient is excluded, or only if that person has a higher attachment point, such as $100,000. Laser underwriting is most common with specific stop-loss, but is sometimes done with aggregate as well. A milder form of laser underwriting applies to retirees. Some carriers will not cover retirees under specific stop-loss policies, but they will usually cover them under aggregate stop-loss policies. These practices add significantly to the risks associated with self-funding.

There is another limitation employers should be wary of. Some stop-loss policies terminate immediately if the employer becomes insolvent or files for bankruptcy, although this is the point at which the employer needs the insurance protection the most. Even though the employees are not themselves insured by a stop-loss policy, without the policy their claims may not by paid.

Many stop-loss carriers insist on having the plan use the carrier's own utilization review (UR) organization and/or case managers, or a UR organization approved by the carrier. This eliminates the possibility that a case manager might unknowingly approve a service the carrier would deny, leaving the plan to pay the entire bill.

Stop-loss carriers also often have certain TPAs with which they deal. Even if claims are paid by an approved TPA, most reinsurers will audit the claims. Typically, all specific stop-loss claims are sent to the reinsurer's office for review and approval. Aggregate stop-loss generally involves too many claims for the carrier to approve each one, but the reinsurer will often audit a sample of claims paid under an aggregate insurance policy if the attachment point is reached.

When a specific claim is submitted for payment under the stop-loss policy or when an audit is done of aggregate claims, one of the issues that can arise is whether claims have been paid in accordance with the terms of the plan document. Stop-loss carriers usually review the plan document very carefully before issuing a contract; if the plan is not being administered the way the underwriter expected it to be, the carrier may refuse to pay all or part of the claims.

Most TPAs are set up to track administrative exceptions separately from the amounts to be claimed under the reinsurance. As long as a self-funded plan is not discriminating in favor of highly compensated employees, the plan has great latitude in determining whether to pay a particular claim. However, if the claim is clearly not payable under the terms of the plan document approved by the stop-loss carrier, the TPA should pay the claim but not count it toward the attachment point. If this is a common occurrence, the plan sponsors should keep in mind that, as a general rule, it is better to amend the plan rather than make frequent exceptions. However, the stop-loss carrier usually reserves the right to approve plan changes before accepting liability under the new provision.

Because stop-loss carriers and TPAs have established relationships, arrangements for stop-loss insurance are frequently made by the TPA. Bids for TPA services often include stop-loss quotations; employers should evaluate the combination of TPA capabilities and stop-loss insurance in selecting a TPA. Brokers and consultants may also help employers obtain and negotiate stop-loss insurance.

HOW MUCH IS ENOUGH?

How much reinsurance should a plan purchase? Options are limited with regard to aggregate insurance, but there are many choices with specific. One theory is that an employer should purchase an attachment point equal to 100 times the number of employees to be covered. This works fairly well for many employers, with a group of 50 employees purchasing a $5,000 specific policy and a group of 1000 employees purchasing $100,000. But the answer depends on how "risk averse" an organization is and upon its resources. A group of 250 employees that is the parent company of a group of 10,000 employees may have sufficient resources to pay any claims that come along. However, if the group uses strict cost accounting by unit it may still want reinsurance.

Self-funding is a viable way to reduce health care costs and stop-loss insurance is vital to most self-funded plans. Despite the difficulties with stop-loss insurance described here, if plan sponsors are careful and informed in choosing a policy they can enjoy the reduced costs and other advantages of self-insurance while protecting themselves from its risks.

20. Risk Management and Health Benefits
Richard S. Betterley

In their efforts to slow rising benefits costs, employers are getting more involved in their employees' health care decisions, and this increased involvement means increased exposure to risk. For their own protection, employers must understand and learn to manage the various risks involved in implementing self-insurance, managed care, wellness programs, and other cost containment strategies. The techniques of risk management can contain liability so that these strategies can do what they're designed to do—save health care dollars.

In the struggle to contain health care cost increases, a key strategy has been for employers to become more involved in the management and insuring of health care services. While this strategy has been successful at controlling costs, it brings with it increased employer exposure to liability. Fortunately, these liabilities can be managed using the familiar techniques of risk management.

To assess accurately the value of such strategies, employers and benefits managers need to understand the liability risks that may arise and how to manage them. Potential liability should not deter benefits managers from developing and installing vitally needed cost containment strategies.

WHAT IS RISK MANAGEMENT?

Risk management is usually thought of in terms of so-called "pure" risk, as opposed to "speculative" risk. A pure risk is one in which there is no chance of gain but only of loss. A good example is an automobile accident. There is a risk as you drive down the road that you may be in a car accident, but there is certainly no profit if you avoid the accident—there is only the avoidance of loss. Speculative risk, on the other hand, is business risk. Deciding whether to develop a new product line, for example, in which there is a chance of profit or of loss, is a good example of speculative risk.

Pure risk is sometimes thought of as insurance risk, but that thinking is generally too narrow. Insurance risk would imply that the risk is one that can be covered by insurance, but not all pure risk is insurable. For our purposes, though, pure risk can be thought of in the context of insurable risks.

Classically, there are several steps to proper risk management: identify and analyze the risk, eliminate it wherever practical, and then either control the risk or transfer (fund) it.

RISKS OF HEALTH CARE COST CONTAINMENT

How does risk management apply to the self-insured employee benefit plan? All business activities seem to generate some form of pure risk. For example, benefits managers necessarily influence people and corporate activities, and some of these activities may result in a liability suit. Another risk is that the plan may not have enough protection against the possibility of catastrophic loss, such as a multiple organ transplant.

Risk management can help minimize risks like these. Some of the specific risks associated with health care cost containment strategies, and how to manage those risks, are discussed below.

Managed Care Strategies

The exposure created by managed care strategies is by far the biggest risk to employers, and it is still evolving. In the past, employees and their families made their own health care decisions, in consultation with the family doctor. Employers were not involved in employees' decisions concerning which health care provider to go to, when and how often to seek care, and how long to remain in the hospital. The health insurance (or self-insurance) program was neutral on these decisions and paid the cost of these services when they were covered under the benefits plan. Judgments were not made as to whether the service should be utilized, only whether it was covered.

Now, of course, employers have a major involvement in health care purchasing decisions, either directly by managing access to care, or indirectly by negotiating and contracting for services with managed care companies and providers, including HMOs, hospitals, and large group practices. Employers now influence which doctor you will go to, how long you will stay in the hospital, whether you will have access to home care, whether you can use certain prescription drugs, and many other health care decisions that used to be left to employees and their doctors.

Until managed care became pervasive, a suboptimal medical outcome—often resulting in a medical malpractice suit—had no direct impact on the employer. Since the employer was not involved in the health care process but was only a source of funds to pay for it, the employer was outside of the risk.

Managed care has made things quite different; a suboptimal medical outcome leading to an injured or dissatisfied employee can result in a lawsuit involving the employer. If the employer was involved in the health care decision making process—and this does happen—the employer is subject to a lawsuit, just as are the hospital and the doctor. Even an employer that has contracted managed care services to another party is not immune from a lawsuit. Any employer involved in the decision to install managed care, the selection of managed care, or consultation on individual questions is exposed to allegations of influencing the delivery of medical services, with its attendant risks.

Injured patients do not want to believe that they were just victims of unfortunate or unexplainable circumstances; they want to find someone to blame. With managed care, the employer gets to be among those who might be blamed.

There are some protections for the employer, principally from the Employee Retirement Income Security Act (ERISA). Recently, in cases concerning the liability of employers involved in managed care, courts have found for the employer on the basis that ERISA preempted such liability suits. However, employers would do well to not depend solely on this ERISA interpretation.

How do you manage the risk of a lawsuit alleging improper medical care for an employee? First, and certainly most important, try to avoid the risk. It is always much better to avoid lawsuits whenever possible. This comes about from full and open communications with your employees and, more importantly, the selection of capable, reputable vendors for provision of health care and case management services. As you are negotiating with managed care firms, picture yourself on the witness stand defending your decision to utilize this company. Could you do it with pride, such that a reasonable person would agree with your decision? Or is the vendor you're considering some low-cost, upstart company that may cut corners, to the detriment of your employee? Certainly, you would rather defend the selection of a well-established managed care vendor than the choice of a low-cost vendor for which you have to apologize.

Plans that self-manage care should perform the same test on themselves, evaluating whether they have capable people, systems, and support that are as good or better than that available in the commercial marketplace. It is harder to self-examine one's capabilities, so you might want to have an outside expert take a look at your managed care services and compare them with those available from vendors.

Transfer risk to the vendor, whenever possible, through appropriate contract language. Require that the vendors provide you with airtight hold-harmless agreements, in which they bear the risk of suboptimal medical outcomes that are a result of the managed care services they provide. Of course, you can't hold them responsible for the medical malpractice of the care providers, but you can hold them responsible for allegations and findings that their services harmed your employee.

In addition, make sure that your corporate insurance program properly protects you against these risks. Your company's liability insurance program is probably not clear as to whether it covers liabilities arising from managed care situations. It is not clear whether an insurance company would have a very hard time denying coverage, given the ambiguities of the insurance policy. However, it would be best if you could work with your risk manager, consultant, and insurance broker to develop specific coverage wording for your company's general liability and umbrella liability policies.

Finally, make sure your employees never get so angry that they want to sue you. Most lawsuits against employers come out of frustration, when the employee thinks they have a legitimate complaint and the employer doesn't seem to be sensitive. Have a process whereby employees can appeal managed care decisions, and be generous in allowing exceptions to the rules of managed care. While it might be slightly more expensive, managed care services need to be provided in a human, caring way. The advantage that this will reduce lawsuits is a secondary benefit.

Wellness Programs

Attempting to make the employees and their families healthier and thereby reducing the demand for health care services are laudable goals. Offering exercise classes at work, providing educational programs and materials, and even subsidizing health club memberships, are good ways to encourage wellness. However, these activities create pure risk for employers, although these risks can be controlled through risk management.

The liabilities created by wellness activities are less severe than managed care, but are nevertheless important. For example, workers injured in exercise class sponsored at their worksite would probably claim that such injuries fall under state-mandated workers' compensation coverage instead of regular health insurance. That means that medical costs arising out of the injury would be paid through your workers' compensation insurance program and that you would even owe them lost wages if they missed work for an extended period of time. There are cases reported in which employees are injured at home on the weekend, but blame it on exercise class or the softball game sponsored by their employer. This shifts the cost from your health insurance program to your workers' compensation insurance program. Unfortunately, workers' compensation administrative costs are substantially higher than health insurance administrative costs, thus making the same injury more expensive to settle under workers' compensation than under health insurance.

Incidentally, not all states would permit a sports-related injury, even at a company-sponsored event, to be claimed as a workers' compensation compensable benefit, so you should check on how your state interprets this exposure.

The classic processes of risk management can help protect against such risks. First, try to eliminate the possibilities for injury. Use only appropriate exercise machines and make sure that the exercise site is well-protected with floor mats and other safety equipment. Be sure to use qualified instructors and have them trained in first aid.

It's not all that likely that you're going to have outside vendors providing these services, so there isn't much contractual risk transfer to do. Since most of the insurance risk is workers' compensation, and all employers either have workers' compensation insurance or qualified self-insurance plans (or some related protection), there isn't much that you need to do on the insurance side, either. The main thing is to make sure that the wellness programs don't create injured workers, who then end up creating insurance claims.

Catastrophic Insurance

Most self-insured health plans utilize stop loss insurance, sometimes called reinsurance, to protect against either individual large claims or an accumulation of claims. This insurance protects against the financial consequences of a dramatic increase in losses in any given year. For example, if a member of your group gives birth to a premature baby, medical expenses could total $250,000. If you purchase stop loss insurance protection, for example, with an attachment point of $50,000, the insurance company would pay $200,000 to the self-insured fund. The actual loss to the fund, therefore, would only be $50,000.

Most self-insured programs purchase such specific catastrophic protection, but some plans purchase aggregate protection, which protects against the total amount of losses exceeding the predicted level. Common attachment points are 110 percent and 125 percent of expected losses. For example, for an employer with stop loss insurance with a 110 percent attachment point and expected losses of $1 million but actual losses of $1.3 million, the aggregate insurer would pay $200,000.

It is important when purchasing such insurance to use a reputable insurer, one that will be able to cover the substantial financial loss that you may incur. It is also important that they be committed to the marketplace, so that they are your insurer for not only the good years in which you don't have any catastrophic claims but the bad years in which you do. The only way to tell if they'll be with you for the long term is to interview the insurance company's representative, as well as the broker, and ask them:

1. How long have you been offering this type of insurance?
2. What share of the market do you have?
3. Is your line of insurance profitable?

The answers to these three questions will usually tell you if they are a committed participant in the catastrophic stop loss insurance market.

CONCLUSION

Risk management plays an important role in protecting employers against possible losses arising out of managed care arrangements and self-insured health benefit plans. Both managed care and self-insurance programs, properly run, can dramatically decrease the expense of health benefits for employees, but also generate additional liabilities for employers. Using the proven techniques of risk management, you can control these liabilities and make sure that the savings from these programs aren't lost.

Part 5

COST-EFFECTIVE
PLAN DESIGN

21. Controlling Prescription Drug Costs
Dennis J. Nirtaut

Prescription drug costs have outpaced general medical care costs in recent years, and today prescription drug benefits can account for more than 25 percent of an employer's health plan spending. A number of options to the traditional indemnity plan coverage of drug costs are available, each with its advantages and disadvantages, but the best solution for controlling costs may be a hybrid plan combining different approaches. They've implemented such a plan at Continental Bank in Chicago, and the early results have been impressive.

The sharply increasing costs of prescription drugs has become a matter of serious concern and discussion, especially to those footing the bill. Employers are now taking steps to control the rising costs of providing prescription drug benefits. During the period 1975 through 1980, the medical care component of the consumer price index increased by 76 percent, compared to 50 percent for prescription drugs. This trend reversed for the period 1981 through 1988, when the medical care component increased 85 percent and prescription drugs increased 109 percent. According to the Health Care Financing Review, the national aggregate drug expenditure for 1990 was $48.5 billion; in 1995, it is projected to be $67.7 billion, and in the year 2000, $91.0 billion—an increase of 87 percent from ten years earlier. In employer plans generally, prescription drugs may account for as much as 25 percent of total health care costs, and in employer plans that provide coverage for retirees age 65 and above, prescription drugs may account for 40 to 50 percent of the plan's total cost (this is because retirees that age are covered by Medicare, which covers the majority of medical expense but none of the prescription drug expense).

Another element of prescription drug cost for retirees is that retirees consume more prescription drugs. Data reported by PCS, Inc. indicates the following:

- Retiree drug utilization is nearly three times greater than that of active employees (12.95 prescriptions per member per year vs. 4.44 for active employees).
- Retiree cost is 14 percent greater per prescription ($28.38 vs. $24.63).
- Retiree average annual cost is almost two and a half times greater than employees ($267 vs. $110).

The rising cost of prescription drugs for retirees is also a significant issue in light of Statement of Financial Accounting Standards No. 106 (SFAS 106), "Accounting for Post Retirement Benefits Other Than Pensions." This accounting rule requires employers to recognize on their financial statements the liability of retiree benefits. The impact on corporate income of implementing SFAS 106 has been estimated to be $1 trillion. General Motors, for example, took a one-time charge to earnings of $22 billion in implementing SFAS 106.

WHY DRUG COSTS ARE INCREASING

Everyone is asking why there is this significant increase in the cost of providing prescription drug benefits. Although there is no single answer to this question, a number of the factors involved can be identified. Some of these are discussed below.

High Cost of Research and Development

According to a study conducted by Tufts University Center for the Study of Drug Development, it takes on average 12 years of research and development and $231 million to bring a new prescription drug to market. Most new drugs are patented immediately upon discovery and are then further refined and tested. Since a patent on a drug is for 17 years, once the average drug is approved, the drug manufacturer has just five years remaining to recoup its research and development costs. Another element is that the average Food and Drug Administration (FDA) approval rate is only 25 percent; drug manufacturers needs to recoup the expenses of the 75 percent of their products that failed to make it to the marketplace.

One positive step taken by the FDA was to increase staff in an effort to cut product review time in half by October, 1997. Review time is expected to drop to between 6 to 12 months, from as much as 20 months. The FDA will add as many as 600 staffers, to be financed by application fees from the drug companies. Since time is money for drug companies, this should help reduce prescription drug costs.

Aging Population

As the "baby boomers" continue to age and begin to retire, this large group will consume an increasing amount of increasingly costly prescription drugs. This aging demographic bulge will serve to increase per capita prescription drug costs.

Increased Consumer Knowledge and Expectations

Consumers are much more knowledgeable today about prescription drugs and expect doctors to prescribe medication. If you're sick, you go to the doctor and you expect medication to make you feel better so that you can be fully functional. Part of this expectation level may be due to advertising by the drug companies. According to a 1992 survey, 54 percent of 3,600 physicians reported that patients initiated discussions of drug treatment based on advertising.

Creep Mix and "Me Too" Drugs

Creep mix is the displacement of older, lower cost drugs by new higher priced drugs with no therapeutic improvement. These new drugs are often referred to as "me too" drugs. According to one study, of the 348 new drugs introduced between 1981 and 1988, only 12 (3.4 percent) were rated as having important therapeutic potential, and 44 (12.6 percent) were rated as having modest therapeutic potential. The bottom line is that we are paying more for new drugs that are not providing improved results.

New and Expensive "Wonder Drugs"

Two specific treatment areas where high-priced "wonder drugs" have been introduced are AIDS and infertility, and these two areas are projected to continue to grow. The spread of AIDS continues, and couples today are trying to start families at older ages (there appears to be a direct correlation between age and fertility problems).

Omnibus Budget Reconciliation Act (OBRA) of 1990

OBRA '90 requires granting the federal government a best discount price for state Medicaid programs. Since Medicaid accounts for approximately 12 percent of drug sales, the expectation is that drug manufacturers are cost shifting to employer plans, managed care plans and volume purchasers.

TYPES OF PRESCRIPTION DRUG COVERAGE

The options available for prescription drug coverage include major medical plans, retail prescription card programs, mail-order prescription programs, and a combination of a retail card and mail-order program. Each has its advantages and disadvantages in terms of cost and quality.

Major Medical Plan

Under a major medical plan, reimbursement for prescription drugs is generally subject to an individual and family deductible, and employees must make a copayment, generally around 20 percent.

The major disadvantage of covering prescription drugs under a medical plan is that the plan pays benefits based on full retail prices, and these often exceed wholesale prices by 20 percent or more. From a pricing perspective, buying prescription drugs through a medical plan is the least attractive method. Also, drug reimbursement through a medical plan generally is not effective for monitoring utilization or encouraging the use of generic drugs.

The major advantage of medical plan drug coverage is that a deductible must be paid, and payment of a deductible appears to control utilization.

Prescription Card Program

Under a card program, eligible employees present an identification card at a participating pharmacy and make a copayment. The program administrator is paid by the employer based on a negotiated rate, which includes a discount from retail prices. Most programs provide utilization data. Also, the company must pay administrative fees to the card program administrator.

With this type of plan, there is sometimes a problem concerning control over the cards. Unless the program administrator has a computer system that confirms eligibility at participating pharmacies, former employees can continue to use the cards. However, most administrators do have computerized operations that can not only verify eligibility but also allow the pharmacist to apply deductibles and copayments, perform drug utilization review, and monitor potential drug interaction, abuse, and waste.

Mail-Order Program

Mail-order prescription programs provide employees and retirees the convenience of obtaining maintenance medication through the mail. Such programs provide a 60- or 90-day supply of drugs and require employees to make a copayment. According to survey data, the most common copayment for a mail-order program is approximately $10 for a 60- to 90-day supply. However, as prescription drug costs increase, these copayments are increasing to $15 and more. (Mail-order plans often provide for a smaller copayment if the patient opts for a generic drug.)

The major advantage of a mail-order program is the discount. Due to the higher volume (compared to retail), discounts are larger in mail-order programs. Also, a properly designed copayment will encourage use of generic drugs. Disadvantages include the lack of a deductible and loss of what is called the shoebox effect. The shoebox effect occurs in any plan where the employee must file a claim; in any given covered group, a certain number of individuals will fill prescriptions, place the receipt aside somewhere (like a shoebox), and then never file the claim. The loss of the shoebox effect can cost a plan as much as 10 percent of plan costs.

Combination Retail/Mail-Order Program

Combining a retail and mail-order program can have a synergistic effect on savings. With a mail-order program alone, large savings on maintenance drugs are realized, but opportunities for discounts for acute care drugs at the retail level are missed. By combining a mail-order program with a retail program, this problem can be solved. The challenge is to design the plan to encourage the use of the retail program for only acute care drugs, and the use of the mail-order program for the filling of long-term or maintenance drug prescriptions. To accomplish this, there should be a limit on the supply and refill availability at the retail level. For example, a retail program might allow for up to a 30-day supply of a prescription drug, with only one refill. Ideally, the plan will be able to collect from both the retail and mail-order programs the data necessary for effective plan administration. Also, a shared database is beneficial so both the retail and mail-order pharmacists can review the individual's drug history at the time a prescription is being filled in order to check its appropriateness.

PLAN DESIGN ISSUES

Utilization

Utilization refers to the number of prescriptions filled, the prescription size (number of days filled and refill rate), and the number of refills allowed under the plan. In order to control utilization, many drug plans exclude certain types of drugs. Some types of drugs that are commonly excluded include infertility drugs, nicotine patches and gum, injectibles (except insulin), cosmetic items and in some cases birth control pills.

Deductibles can have an important effect on utilization. For example, if an employer moves from having prescription drugs filled under a comprehensive medical plan to a plan that does not require a deductible, factors such as the shoebox effect (described above) and the "hesitation effect"—where because of the deductible the employee hesitates for a day or two to fill or renew a prescription, hoping the condition might resolve itself—come into play. Eliminating a deductible in a drug plan is estimated to cost approximately 5 percent due to losing the "hesitation effect;" losing the shoebox effect may cost as much as 10 percent.

Price

The price paid for drugs is going to impact your plan's overall cost. If prescription drugs are provided through your medical plan, you are paying full retail price. Moving to a retail card program or a mail-order program will result in a discount in the price plus the dispensing fee. Mail-order programs offer the largest discounts (5 to 15 percent for brand names, and 20 to 40 percent for generics), while retail programs offer a discount of 5 to 15 percent. Also, mail-order or retail programs should offer a more competitive dispensing fee, in the range of $2.00 to $3.50.

There is a tremendous opportunity for cost savings through increased generic usage. After a patent expires on a drug, other drug companies may manufacture an exact chemical duplicate and market it under the drug's generic or chemical name. Since these generic drug companies do not need to amortize the huge front-end costs of drug development, generic equivalents are substantially less expensive. On average, the cost savings in a generic version of a drug is approximately 50 percent, but is often significantly higher. Today, generic drugs account for approximately one third of all new prescriptions filled. If your plan's generic substitution rate is less than this, you are missing a real opportunity for cost saving.

From a design perspective, there are several options to encourage generic usage. In mail-order programs, which most commonly require a specific dollar copayment, the usual approach is to require a lower dollar copayment for the generic drug. At the retail level, where the copayment is more commonly a percentage, a plan will usually require a larger copayment percentage for the brand name drug where there is a generic equivalent. For example, at Continental Bank, the plan provides for the employee to pay a 50 percent copayment if the employee opts for a brand name when a generic equivalent is available; the normal copayment is 20 percent. Another approach is to base the reimbursement on the cost of the generic equivalent. For example, if a plan normally would pay

80 percent and an employee opts for the brand name drug where a generic equivalent is available, the plan could base its reimbursement on the price of the generic rather than the brand name drug. If the generic costs $10 and the brand name costs $50, the plan would pay $8 and the employee would pay the balance—$2 if the employee chose the generic, $42 dollars if the brand name. This approach provides the employee or retiree with a significant motivation to change to a generic drug.

Cost Sharing

The amount of cost sharing between the employer plan and the employee through the plan design will also have a significant impact on plan costs.

As discussed above, it is important to design the plan to encourage generic usage. Also, the level of the copayment amount will also impact cost. The more effective approach to copayment is through use of a percentage rather than a specified dollar amount. The reason for this is that the percentage copayment automatically adjusts to the increasing price of drugs, whereas with a dollar copayment, the amount needs to be adjusted regularly to reflect the increasing prices. A percentage copay is generally easy for retail networks, but is more complicated with mail-order plans since the plan participant may not know the price of the drug upon which to base the copayment percentage. The use of a charge card eliminates this problem.

Another means of cost sharing is through plan deductibles. Plan deductibles increase the complexity of administration with either a retail or mail-order program, but they help control cost and utilization.

CONTINENTAL BANK'S PRESCRIPTION DRUG PROGRAM

Effective July 1, 1991, Continental Bank moved to a combination retail network/mail-order program by implementing the following design elements:

- Outpatient prescription drug coverage was removed from the medical plan.
- A mail-order prescription drug program was set up with Caremark, using a $10 copayment for up to 90-day supply of drugs.
- A retail arrangement was set up with American Drugs. This retail program provides for up to a 28-day supply with one refill. Employees pay 20 percent of the discounted price at the time of purchase, and Continental is billed for the balance. To encourage generic drug use, the copayment for brand name drugs when a generic equivalent is available is set at 50 percent of cost.
- Use of non-network pharmacies was allowed, however, employees/retirees must pay the full cost and then seek reimbursement from Caremark.

A very important element of this program is the drug utilization review that it offers. All of the prescription drug information is being gathered from all sources (retail network, retail non-network, and mail order) by Caremark, creating a very valuable database that the Caremark pharmacist can access when filling a prescription. This database can be used to check for drug interaction, drug abuse, and too early refills.

One program that has been more successful than anticipated is the DAW call program. In this program, when a prescription is written DAW (Dispensed As Written)—meaning that a generic cannot be substituted—the Caremark pharmacist calls the doctor to request that the generic be substituted. Our latest statistics show that doctors have approved the generic substitution 55 percent at the time.

This new program has saved money for Continental Bank by providing for discounts at both the retail and mail-order environments, shifting much of the volume from retail to the mail-order program where the larger discounts are available, increasing generic drug utilization through both plan design and the DAW call program, and finally, improving management of the program through data collection. Since all drug data is received by Caremark, we now have a database of all Continental Bank prescription drug usage. This allows us to closely monitor our drug costs and usage and helps us in making plan design decisions.

Some of the results from the first full year of the program include the following:

- Per capita cost increased only 2.4 percent.
- The average monthly number of prescriptions in the mail-order program increased 60 percent. This was by design since the larger discount is received through mail order.
- The average cost of a prescription decreased 14 percent.
- Usage of the retail network was 71 percent.
- The generic substitution rate when a generic product was available was 68 percent (the overall generic rate was 30 percent).

Overall, we are very pleased with the first year results from the prescription drug program, but have continued to make minor adjustments in plan features. Based on the review of the data now available through the program, we changed the mail-order copayment in 1992 from a flat $10 for a 90-day supply to $15 for a brand name and $7.50 for a generic. Effective July, 1993, we have extended our prescription drug program to our employees who receive their health care through HMOs. Since prescription drugs are no longer offered through the HMOs, the HMOs reduced their fees and larger discounts were offered by both Caremark and American Drugs since there will now be a larger volume of prescription drugs through their programs. With prescription drugs being provided to our employees and retirees through a single program, we hope to gain efficiencies that will help control our costs. By continually monitoring results, we will be able to make further adjustments where necessary.

22. Two Dental Plans Show Cost Savings at Hewlett-Packard

Joyce E. Santora

Applying the principles of managed care, Hewlett-Packard's new prepaid dental plan saves the company an average of 20 percent per employee compared to its regular fee-for-service plan, and it offers increased preventative service.

At Palo Alto California-based Hewlett-Packard Co., a self-insured, fee-for-service plan had been the mainstay of its dental coverage since the mid-1970s. But when the cost of that approach rose 14 percent in both 1985 and 1986, executives at this computer and electronics company began to look at alternatives.

Although human resources executives there chose to continue using self-insurance as the foundation of a new dental benefits plan, they added the option to exchange the fee-for-service method of reimbursement for the attractive features of managed care.

In 1987, Hewlett-Packard made a prepaid dental plan available to employees in select areas. To employees choosing the new option, named Dental Plan II (DPII), the main difference was that, in exchange for receiving improved dental coverage, they had to give up their unlimited choice of dentists. After a pilot program in three geographic locations proved successful, the company has expanded this option to locations employing roughly half its U.S. employees. Today, based on four years of experience in operating two plans, Hewlett-Packard finds the newer, prepaid plan costs the company an average of 20 percent less per employee than its regular fee-for-service plan.

Simply stated, with a prepaid plan, participating dentists or dental groups are paid a fixed monthly fee for each employee and dependent enrolled, as opposed to providing care on a fee-for-service basis. Following the same concept used with health maintenance organizations (HMOs) for medical benefits, employees select their dentists from a list of participating providers.

"Our primary goal was to provide 100 percent preventative coverage, to encourage our employees to get in, have the care, and improve their overall dental health," explains Jean Puetz, the program manager for DPII at Hewlett-Packard. "Another goal was to provide the employees with a higher benefit without a higher cost to them. A final benefit was to help Hewlett-Packard manage its overall dental plan cost."

In six geographic locations, Hewlett-Packard now offers employees a choice of two different dental plans. The first, a fee-for-service plan called the Regular Dental Plan (RDP), offers employees freedom of choice in selecting a dentist, and provides coverages and limits typical to many dental plans today.

With RDP, the overall maximum benefit per year is $1,500 per employee or dependent. Preventative and restorative care is reimbursed at 80 percent, after employees have paid deductibles of $50 per individual or $150 family. Endodontic and periodontic care is reimbursed at 50 percent and payment for orthodontics carries a $1,000 lifetime maximum per individual.

Hewlett-Packard pays for RDP coverage on a fee-for-service basis, and the plan is administered by ALTA Health Strategies of Salt Lake City, Utah, which also receives a fee for this service. For reimbursement, employees either complete a claim form and submit it along with a copy of their paid dental bill, or have the dentist bill ALTA directly.

Under the DPII plan, the annual maximum benefit paid is higher, set at $2,500 per individual. Preventative care is covered at 100 percent with no deductible. Restorative care also is paid at 100 percent but carries a $25 per individual or $75 per family deductible. Reimbursement for endodontic and periodontic work is 0 percent. For orthodontic care, Hewlett-Packard still pays a $1,000 lifetime maximum. However, the company has contracted with several orthodontists to provide a full course of treatment at a set cost of $2,075. Therefore, the cost to employee or dependent is a known $1,075. ALTA Health Strategies administers this program as well.

Initially, Hewlett-Packard made this choice of plans available to employees in three locations: the San Francisco Bay area, which has 17,000 employees; Boise, Idaho, having 2,500 workers; and Colorado Springs, Colorado, having 2,000 employees. According to Puetz, these areas were selected because of their large concentrations of employees. At Hewlett-Packard, 60 operating divisions are spread throughout 20 geographic locations, and 150 sales offices are located throughout the United States.

In setting up the new program, Hewlett-Packard first did a computer run of dental claims paid the previous year, to ascertain where employees in these locations received their dental treatment: "Dentists and dental groups, that served significant numbers of employees were targeted for DPII participation."

Selling points that were used to persuade dentists to join the program included the opportunity to attract additional patients and receive a guaranteed income based on those patients. Although the goal is to have as many dentists as possible on the designated list, says Puetz, the DPII or any prepaid plan can be offered in a location having as few as one dentist or dental office participating, as was the case initially in Colorado Springs.

"In some areas, it's difficult to get dentists to agree to such a plan," says Puetz, explaining that prepaid plans carry much of the same risks and advantages to participating dentists as are found in HMOs. Although a primary advantage may be the guaranteed flow of income, the main disadvantage is that the cost of treatment could exceed those monthly payments.

Usually, says Puetz, 50 employees choosing a particular dentist translates into 100 patients. After a few years, that patient population can grow exponentially, as more employees join the program. Hewlett-Packard doesn't set any limitations on the number of patients a dentist must accept in order to participate in the program, but some dentists do set their own maximums.

Although Puetz declines to discuss the actual dollar amount of fees paid to the participating dentists, she stresses that every office in a given area receives the same amount based on the number of enrollees for that office. In addition, fees are reviewed annually and have increased over the years for all dentists.

The company presented this second dental option to employees during its annual open enrollment period, when employees are allowed to make changes in their medical and dental coverages. Initially, enrollment in DPII ranged from 10 to 20 percent—a high percentage for a new program, according to Puetz.

In 1989, the prepaid program expanded to two more geographic locations: Corvallis, Oregon, having 2,200 employees, and northern Colorado, having 4,600 employees in Loveland, Ft. Collins, and Greeley. In 1990, Roseville, California, having 2,500 employees, was added as well.

To date, based on all six locations, enrollment in DPII has increased steadily to as much as 12 to 25 percent, says Susan Moriconi, health benefits manager at Hewlett-Packard. Enrollment in the plan varies from location to location, she adds, depending upon such factors as the number of dentists involved and employee demographics.

"Enrollment may be limited in some areas because of the distance between employee's homes and the dental offices, such as is the case in the San Francisco Bay area," Moriconi elaborates. "In other instances, it's a mater of personal choice. Some prefer to keep their selection of a dental office open, and others already have an established relationship with a dentist not on the plan."

In 1991, 11 dental offices were participating in the DPII in the San Francisco Bay area. There were six dentists in Boise, five in northern Colorado, four in Roseville and three in Colorado Springs. Corvallis had only two.

These six locations already represent about half of Hewlett-Packard's U.S. employees, but Moriconi says the company will continue to evaluate further expansion of the program. "We're trying to roll this out in an orderly fashion," she says, "so when we've targeted an area, we've been successful. This program will work only in areas that have a large number employees and a dental community that's interested in becoming a part of it."

Moriconi says that one of the risks prepaid plans present for employees is the potential for undertreatment. Therefore, she cautions, it's important that an outside dental auditor be retained to monitor the care given by the participating dental groups.

At Hewlett-Packard, these audits run the gamut from actual on-site visits to comparative analyses of care received. In an on-site audit, a dental auditor will pull patient charts, review the treatments received, and determine whether it was appropriate and adequate, and whether referrals, if necessary, were made in a timely manner. Comparative analyses are conducted in the offices of the program administrators, using data submitted by the different dental offices.

"They'll review what proportion of preventative care is given by dental office A, as opposed to C, D and E," Moriconi explains. "They'll break the care down by individual services performed and compare care given in each office to norms. In addition to on-site audits, they also do customer satisfaction surveys with our employees."

Moriconi stresses that this prepaid plan follows Hewlett-Packard's general philosophy regarding providing employee health care benefits. "Our general direction is to introduce more managed care, continue to design features into our program to encourage preventative care in a timely manner, and offer choice, where possible," she states.

Although dental coverage isn't typically considered a big ticket item when it comes to providing employee benefits, Hewlett-Packard considers it "important in providing a well-balanced package," according to Moriconi. In 1990, the cost of providing dental coverage to the company's 56,000 U.S. employees and their dependents was $15 million, compared with $150 million for medical benefits.

"Typically, dental benefits aren't as important to most employees as medical benefits," she says, "but we have a package approach at Hewlett-Packard, and in order to offer employees a comprehensive, competitive package, we feel that dental plans should be included."

23. Evaluating Health Plan Efficiency
Douglas G. Cave

Claims data evaluation has evolved from the first-generation systems of the 1970s, which concentrated on analyzing excesses in the hospital setting. Second-generation systems, currently in widespread use, focus on ambulatory care. Now a new claims data system—episodes of care—offers precision decoding of a health care plan's cost performance. It studies all the elements involved in treating an individual's medical condition within a specific time period.

In the late 1970s, a precipitous increase in medical care costs prompted many employers to evaluate the reasons behind this upsurge. These first-generation claims data evaluations generally concentrated on analyzing charge and utilization excesses in the hospital inpatient setting. As a result of the evaluations, employers often implemented precertification utilization review (UR) programs—to control unnecessary inpatient admissions and days—and preferred provider organizations (PPOs)—to manage per-day charge increases.

However, first-generation data claims analysis was short lived. After Medicare implemented the prospective payment system (PPS) in 1983, the number of hospital inpatient days significantly decreased for both the Medicare and non-Medicare populations. The PPS provided physicians with financial incentive to treat certain patients in the ambulatory setting.

As more health care dollars were spent on ambulatory services, employers realized that both hospital and ambulatory experience had to be evaluated to determine the principal reasons for benefit cost increases. Thus, insurance carriers and consultants developed second-generation data analysis systems focusing on ambulatory utilization and charges.

Reprinted from *Compensation & Benefits Management,* Vol. 9, No. 3, Summer 1993. A Panel Publication, Aspen Publishers, Inc.

Exhibit 1. Variables Comprising an Episode of Care

VARIABLE	DEFINITION
Total eligible charges	All reasonable and customary (R&C) charges for services covered under a health plan minus all duplicate billings minus all PPO discounts (if applicable).
Hospital inpatient facility eligible charges	All benefit eligible charges minus any PPO discounts for hospital inpatient room and board services and ancillary service. No physician charges are included here.
Number of hospital admissions	Number of inpatient admissions to a hospital facility
Number of hospital inpatient days	Number of inpatient days corresponding to the hospital admissions.
Other inpatient eligible charges	All benefit eligible charges minus PPO discounts for inpatient services other than hospital inpatient room and board and ancillary services. Other inpatient services include birthing centers, skilled nursing and custodial care facilities, surgical centers, and residential mental health facilities.
Number of other inpatient days	Number of inpatient days corresponding to the other inpatient facility admissions.
Hospital outpatient facility eligible charges	All benefit eligible charges minus any PPO discounts for hospital outpatient visits. No physician charges are included here.
Number of hospital outpatient facility visits	Number of outpatient visits at a hospital facility.
Physician eligible charges	R&C charges minus any PPO discounts for all medical doctors and osteopaths.
Number of physician visits	Number of visits made to medical doctors and osteopaths, including both inpatient and ambulatory care.
Other provider eligible charges	R&C charges minus any PPO discounts for health care providers other than medical doctors and osteopaths. These providers include chiropractors, podiatrists, nursing services, psychologists, and home health care.
Number of other provider visits	Number of visits made to other providers, including both inpatient and ambulatory care.
X-ray/laboratory/diagnostic testing eligible charges	R&C charges minus any PPO discounts for all ambulatory X-rays laboratory, diagnostic and therapeutic diagnosis testing, and imaging services.
Number of X-ray/laboratory/diagnostic testing services	Number of X-ray, laboratory, diagnostic testing, and imaging services provided to treat an episode of care.
Prescription drug eligible charges	All benefit eligible charges minus any PPO discounts for prescription drugs.
Number of prescription drugs	Number of drugs prescribed to treat an episode of care.

VARIABLE	DEFINITION
All miscellaneous eligible charges	R&C charges minus PPO discounts for all other benefit eligible services. These services include transportation, durable medical supplies, speech therapy, rehabilitation, physiotherapy, psychotherapy, and audiology.
Number of miscellaneous service	Number of services provided for all other benefit eligible services.

Most second-generation data claims analysis systems currently evaluate utilization experience per 1,000 covered individuals (i.e., employees and their dependents), and charges on a per-service basis. For example, common utilization rates include the number of hospital admissions, physician office visits, and prescription drug fills per 1,000 individuals. Charge rates consist of charges per hospital day, per X-ray/diagnostic testing service, and per physician office visit.

Using second-generation systems, gross overutilization and significant excess charge patterns can be identified in hospital and ambulatory care settings. For instance, if the number of pharmaceutical drugs prescribed per 1,000 covered individuals is 50 percent greater than an expected value, the employer can be reasonably sure the company has a problem with prescription drug utilization.

For various reasons, however, these second-generation systems are not very accurate at assessing a health plan's overall cost efficiency. Cost efficiency means that a plan's providers treat medical conditions with the least expensive level of medical care possible and still achieve the desired health outcome for the patient.

Consequently, over the past year or so, Hewitt Associates developed a third-generation claims data system that provides a more accurate evaluation of health plan cost efficiency. This article discusses how the system works and provides results from a recent analysis Hewitt Associates performed for a large employer.

SECOND-GENERATION SYSTEMS

Employers recognize that their current claims data systems do not provide sufficient information to make informed cost-containment strategy decisions. There significant employer concerns deserve discussion.

Piecemeal Solutions

Second-generation systems generally do not combine and evaluate all hospital and ambulatory services incurred for treating an individual's medical condition. Instead, these systems divide individual's claims into 20 to 25 different utilization and charge categories. Each category is then analyzed separately to determine whether there is a problem with utilization per 1,000 individuals, charges per service, or both. If problem areas are identified, employers develop specific cost-control strategies to contain future benefit increases.

This process, however, is a piecemeal approach for evaluating the cost efficiency of a health plan. And employers may draw wrong conclusions from such an analysis. For example, assume an employer determines that the number of physician office visits per 1,000 individuals is 30 percent higher than an expected value. A logical conclusion is that the health plan's physicians are not practicing cost-efficient medicine.

Yet if the employer observes that the number of hospital admissions is 20 percent lower than expected, a different conclusion may be reached: perhaps, for example, physicians are practicing cost-efficient medicine.

Yet if the employer observes that the number of hospital admissions is 20 percent lower than expected, a different conclusion may be reached: perhaps, for example, physicians are practicing cost-efficient medicine by treating patients in the ambulatory setting whenever possible. The employer must then make a subjective assessment as to whether a 30 percent higher-than-expected physician office visit rate is acceptable or too high given the low hospital admission rate.

Reliable Employee Data

As previously stated, second-generation systems evaluate utilization experience on a per-1,000-members basis. Thus, these systems require accurate counts of total employees and all dependents for valid utilization rates. Most employers, however, have no internal system for tracking total health plan membership. Employers generally track only their employees' health plan participation (i.e., employee-only coverage, employee-plus-spouse, employee-plus-child(ren), and employee-plus-family). Actuarial assumptions then are used to derive the total number of health plan members.

However, these assumptions can result in significant utilization rate errors. For instance, depending on the average dependent number applied, we found that one employer's hospital admission rate varied from 80 admissions per 1,000 members to 105 admissions per 1,000 members—a difference of over 20 percent. This error rate can be significantly higher if an employer does not have accurate employee participation numbers.

Incomplete Adjustments for Health Status

Some employers now have 50 to 60 percent of their employees enrolled in health maintenance organizations (HMOs). Typically, per-member medical costs for individuals remaining in the indemnity plan are very high compared to employers with only 10 percent or 20 percent HMO enrollment. High indemnity costs may be the result of many rounds of favorable selection (healthier-than-average individuals) into HMOs, leaving the indemnity plan to serve an increasingly adverse population (sicker-than-average individuals).

We found several instances where adverse selection against an employer's indemnity health plan resulted in employers paying indemnity plan claims of $2,500 or more per covered individual. (On average, in indemnity plans not significantly affected by adverse selection, employers paid about $1,250 per covered indemnity individual.)

After age, sex, and case-mix adjustment, these employer's per-individual costs dropped from $2,500 to only about $1,900 (almost 50 percent higher than the expected $1,250 value). Our studies, like many others, demonstrate that age/sex and case-mix adjustments control only for a certain percentage of population health status differences.

Therefore, when an employer compares adjusted utilization and charge rates to expected rates, the results should be interpreted with cation. Higher-than-expected employer indemnity rates may be the result of inefficient provider care, adverse population differences that were not controlled by age/sex and case-mix adjustments, or both. Thus, second-generation claim systems often do not provide a definitive answer on health plan cost efficiency.

THIRD-GENERATION SYSTEMS

Third-generation claims systems provide study results that more accurately assess a health plan's true cost efficiency than do second-generation systems. The accuracy difference is a result of the unit of analysis used under each system. While second-generation systems use 1,000 individuals as the unit of analysis, third-generation systems use episodes of care.

An episode of care is defined as all hospital inpatient and ambulatory care services incurred for treating an individual's medical condition within a specific period. This period is based on the maximum number of days between contact with a provider (or the window period). If the date of service for an individual's specific medical condition is separated by a longer period than the window period, this date of service is considered the start date for a new episode of care.

For example, assume the window period for acute upper respiratory infections is 30 days. Also, assume that in 1991 an individual incurred medical services for a respiratory infection on January 5, January 17, January 28, August 14, and August 23. Using the definition provided previously, this individual had two episodes of care: one started on January 5 and ended on January 28; episode two started on August 14 and ended on August 23. The January 28 and August 14 dates were separated by more than the window period (30 days), resulting in two episodes of care.

In using the episode-of-care approach, we examine all services used to treat a patient's condition. Therefore, we no longer evaluate an individual's utilization experience in a piecemeal fashion. Moreover, we do no require reliable counts of an employer's employees and dependents because utilization experience is analyzed on a per-episode-of-care basis, not on a per-1,000-individuals basis. Finally, because we use the same exact episode-of-care mix—or market basket of episodes of care—when comparing employer's health plans to one another or to expected results, we are able to adjust accurately for health status differences between employers' populations.

For these reasons, we can determine more accurately whether an employer's health plan is performing as efficiently as possible. The process for performing an episode-of-care evaluation is discussed in the following paragraphs.

Preparing the Claims Data

Episodes of care are derived from diagnosis codes taken from submitted medical claims. However, carriers and third-party administrators (TPAs) do not always capture this information on ambulatory claims. For instance, some claim tapes are missing diagnosis codes on over 50 percent of ambulatory claims submitted for payment.

Because episodes of care are diagnosis-code driven, ambulatory claims without a diagnosis code will not appear in any episode of care. Consequently, unless a valid diagnosis code can be assigned to claims with missing values, some episodes of care will have underrepresented ambulatory care experience.

To address this problem, we developed an algorithm that assigns a diagnosis code to each claim with a missing value. Although detailed description of the algorithm is beyond the scope of this article, we can state that our algorithm validity assigns diagnosis codes to over 90 percent of all claims.

Defining The Components

Each episode of care is composed of up to 18 different components. These components are defined in Exhibit 1.

Developing Market Baskets

We developed episodes of care for 85 of the most prevalent medical conditions. Our evaluations show that these 85 conditions comprise about 75 percent of all medical services delivered to an employers' employees and dependents annually.

Exhibit 2. Average Total Eligible Charges (Per Episode of Care)

Medical Condition Category	Employer's Indemnity Plan	Well-Managed Plan
Least-complex conditions	$ 195	$ 110
Complex conditions	560	400
Most-complex conditions	1,580	1,375
All conditions	$ 720	$ 580

Exhibit 3. Average Number of Hospital Admissions (Per 100 Episodes of Care)

Medical Condition Category	Employer's Indemnity Plan	Well-Managed Plan
Least-complex conditions	0.3	0.1
Complex conditions	3.1	1.1
Most-complex conditions	10.7	9.5
All conditions	4.2	3.3

Exhibit 4. Average Number of Physician Visits (Per Episode of Care)

Medical Condition Category	Employer's Indemnity Plan	Well-Managed Plan
Least-complex conditions	2.5	1.3
Complex conditions	2.4	1.6
Most-complex conditions	3.5	2.7
All conditions	2.8	1.8

We then divide these episodes of care into three categories based on the medical resources generally needed to treat the conditions:

1. *Least complex medical conditions.* About one-third of the medical conditions are easy-to treat conditions (i.e., low case-mix complexity). Examples include acute upper respiratory infections, sprains, and strains, dermatitis, gastroenteritis, sinusitis, and urinary tract infections.

2. *Complex medical conditions.* Another third are of moderate case-mix complexity, such as asthma, bursitis, hypertension, low back pain, peptic diseases, and thyroid conditions.

3. *Most complex medical conditions.* The remainder of the medical conditions are of high case-mix complexity. Conditions include cancer, cerebrovascular disease, congestive heart failure, diabetes, ischemic heart disease, and psychotic conditions.

For each medical condition category, we use a consistent market basket of episodes of care. These episode-of-care market baskets remain the same for every employer health plan we compare against our expected episode-of-care values. This market basket approach allows us to control for differences in populations' medical conditions and severity of illnesses.

The end result is an apples-to-apples comparison of an employer's health plan performance and the plan's expected performance. For the expected plan, we could use episodes of care obtained from employers with an indemnity plan and no cost management features (i.e., non-managed plan), an indemnity plan with integrated PPO and hospital precertification UR (i.e., average performing managed care plan), or an indemnity plan with integrated PPO, hospital precertification and concurrent and ambulatory UR programs (i.e., well-managed plan).

Third-Generation Analysis Results

As an illustration of the episode-of-care approach, we compare episode-of-care results from a large employer's non-managed indemnity plan to our internal database of employers with well-managed plans. Exhibits 2 through 4 show results of this employer's episode-of-care evaluation.

Exhibit 2 analyzes average total eligible charges per episode of care. Charges for treating all medical conditions were 24 percent higher for the employer than for a well-managed plan (i.e., $720 versus $580). However, charges for treating the least complex conditions were over 75 percent higher than for a well-managed plan (i.e., $195 versus $110).

Exhibit 3 compares the average number of hospital admissions per 100 episodes of care. Hospital admissions for treating all medical conditions were 27 percent higher than for a well-managed plan (i.e., 4.2 admissions versus 3.3 admissions). Treatment of complex medical conditions was responsible for a large percentage of the employer's higher-than-expected indemnity plan rate; hospital admissions for treating complex conditions were over 175 percent higher than for a well-managed plan (i.e., 3.1 admissions versus 1.1 admissions).

Exhibit 4 analyzes the average number of physician visits per episode of care. Physician visits for treating all medical conditions were over 50 percent higher than for a well-managed plan (i.e., 2.8 versus 1.8). Treatment of the least complex conditions was responsible for much of the employer's higher-than-expected indemnity plan rate; physician visits for treating the least complex conditions were 90 percent higher than for a well-managed plan (i.e., 2.5 visits versus 1.3 visits).

Future Approaches

The previous results illustrate how third-generation data claims systems can be used to evaluate the overall performance of a health plan. Our episode-of-care evaluation showed that the employer's indemnity plan performed about 24 percent less efficiently than a well-managed plan. Additionally, we showed that excess hospital admissions and physician office visits were primary reasons for the employer's poor indemnity plan performance.

Based on these results, the employer developed a strategy to contain future indemnity plan cost increases. The employer's main goal was to gain better control over excess physician office visits and the services ordered during these visits. To help achieve this goal, the employer decided to implement a point-of-service (POS) plan (commonly referred to as an open-ended HMO). The POS network emphasizes the "gatekeeper" approach, where primary care physicians direct patient care and are placed at some financial risk for medical services delivered.

As more employers realize the advantages of third-generation claims analysis systems, second-generation systems will go by the wayside, much like first-generation systems. The 1990s will prove to be a decade of new and innovative medical claims analysis.

24.   Second Opinion Programs: Continued Savings from Nonconfirmed Surgeries

Amelia Chu   Victoria Lavoie   Eugene G. McCarthy

Mandatory second surgical opinion programs have been criticized as producing very little savings for very high costs, and some major companies have discontinued second surgical opinion requirements from their benefits programs. Several studies, however, reveal that these programs effectively screen out inappropriate surgery, and, despite their cost, result in net savings of millions of dollars in heatlh care costs.

Health care cost containment has become a major concern of health insurers. Many strategies have been proposed in an attempt to control medical care costs that have reached 12 percent of the nation's gross national product and are rising. According to Uwe Reinhard, professor of political economy at Princeton University, national health expenditures, now growing at an annual rate of 10 to 11 percent, will reach an unprecendented 15 percent of GNP (about $1.5 trillion) by the year 2000.

The mandatory second surgical opinion (SSO) program is an early form of cost saving, designed to eliminate surgery that could be avoided by alternative medical treatment. The second surgical opinion requirement, initiated in the early 1970s, is now an established component of managed care implemented by many health insurers. Approximately 50 to 75 percent of employees nationwide are

"Second Opinion Programs: Continued Savings from Nonconfirmed Surgeries," which appeared in the September 1992 issue, was reprinted with permission from the *Employee Benefits Journal,* published by the International Foundation of Employee Benefit Plans, Brookfield, WI. Statements or opinions expressed in this article are those of the author and do not necessarily represent the views or positions of the International Foundation, its officers, directors, or staff.

bound by this policy whenever surgery is recommended. A number of employers, however, have recently complained that mandatory SSO programs save very little and that, in fact, the rising costs of managing the program could exceed the net savings. Recent articles in *Business and Health* reported that General Electric, Alcoa, Borden, PepsiCo and GTE, among others, have decided to discontinue their mandatory second surgical opinion requirements because of potentially high operating costs.[1]

Other experts in health care management, however, think otherwise. In their study on New York City's 165,000 non-Medicare municipal employees. Rosenberg *et al.* showed that mandatory SSO requirements helped the city save a total of $1.8 million in fiscal year 1990.[2] In addition, patients receive valuable information and reassurance through the SSO program while they decide whether to proceed with surgery.

According to a two-year follow-up evaluation study carried out by Dr. Eugene G. McCarthy at the Cornell University Medical College–New York Hospital and published in 1978, the majority of those who were not confirmed for surgery had not had the surgery nor reported receiving medical treatment one year after the consultation. Among the many noncomfirmed cases, the decision against the surgery was made on the basis of the second opinion consultant's recommendation.[3] This shows the ability of the second opinion program to screen potential surplus surgery. Savings from the avoidance of inappropriate surgery are estimated to be in millions of dollars.

In a study comparing the surgical rates of hysterectomy across different regions of the United States, Finkel and Finkel found that out of 1,698 women who were recommended for hysterectomy initially, 135 (8 percent) were not confirmed for the surgery after a second opinion consultation. Among these 135 nonconfirmed cases, 70 did not have the operation. Assuming that the average cost of hysterectomy is $5,000, at least $350,000 (excluding indirect costs such as time off from work for susrgery) was saved.[4]

Data from several union health funds have supported the same trend. District Council 37 (the American Federation of State, County, and Municipal Workers Union, with 250,000 insured), for example, reported savings of $1,650 for each operation canceled as a result of the second opinion consultant's nonconfirmed recommendation. The total returns for surgery avoided were estimated to be more than $2 million.[5]

The mandatory program of the Building Service Local 32B-J Health Fund (120,000 insured) reported a 14.3 percent reduction of inpatient surgical claims from October 1, 1975 through September 30, 1976, resutling in $1 million savings.[6] The fund also found in a followup study that the not-confirmed-for-surgery patients spent less on medical care and had fewer work loss and restricted activity days than the confirmed-for-surgery group. A total of $534,649 was saved from reduced medical care utilization and increased productivity for the non-confirmed group between 1977 and 1978. When gross savings were compared to costs (i.e., the expenditures for consultations, ancillary services, programs operation and out-of-pocket costs borne by program participants), the program exhibited a benefit/cost ratio of $2.63—that is, for every $1 cost incurred, the program yielded $2.63 of benefits.[7] The cost/benefit ratio was even higher ($3.18 for every dollar expended) when considering only those who followed exclusively the recommendation of second opinion consultants.[8]

TRANSIT WORKERS UNION (LOCAL 100) SSO PROGRAM

The Transit Workers Union serves 50,000[9] members working for the Manhattan and Bronx Surface Transit Operating Authority (MABSTOA) and for the New York City Transit Authority. The categories of employment are as varied as bus drivers, subway motormen, conductors, mechanics and token clerks, among others.

A welfare trust fund, established jointly by these agencies and New York Transit Workers Union, provides members and their dependents with health care benefits. The trust's medical benefits for the combined 150,000 insured population are administered by Group Health Incorporated (GHI). Under the GHI plan, union members can choose to see a participating physician at no cost to them. If a nonparticipating physician renders care, the portion remaining unpaid by GHI is the responsibility of the patient/member.

In April 1988, the Transit Workers Union contracted with Health Benefits Reasearch and Services (HBRS), a private health research firm, to implement a mandatory SSO program for 13 surgical procedures (Table 1). An intensive campaign was undertaken to educate members about this new benefit. Brochures, letters and posters clearly defined the presurgical requirement. During the SSO implementation process, members who failed to obtain SSO were allowed to be reimbursed for surgery-related expenses under a forgiveness policy. As part of the continuing benefit education, reminder letters were sent to these members advising that a further infraction of the mandatory SSO requirement would result in rejection of the claim. After a full year of operation, the forgiveness policy was terminated and members were required to seek second opinion consultations for the same 13 surgical procedures or else pay all sugery-related costs out of their own pockets. (See Table 1.)

Since implementation of the SSO program, there have been 3,877 second opinion consultations on these 13 elective surgical procedures. In 418 (11 percent of the cases) the initial recommendation was not confirmed. There was no statistically significant difference in the nonconfirmation rate after the SSO program became mandatory, although the rate in 1984 (while the forgiveness policy was in effect) was slightly higher (15 percent) than the rates (ranging from 8 to 13 percent) in the years following the termination of the forgiveness policy. (See Table 2.)

Table 1. Procedures Requiring Second Surgical Opinion Consultations

1. Breast surgery
2. Bunionectomy
3. Cataracts
4. Cholecystectomy
5. Dilation and curettage (D&C)
6. Herniorrhaphy
7. Hysterectomy
8. Knee surgery
9. Laminectomy
10. Nasal surgery/submucous resection of deviated septum (SMR)
11. Prostatectomy
12. Tonsillectomy/adenoidectomy (T&A)
13. Varicose veins

Table 2. Second Surgical Opinions by Calendar Year

(April 1, 1988 to July 31, 1991)

Year	Total Second Opinions	Number Confirmed	Number Nonconfirmed	Percent Nonconfirmed
1984 (9 months)	298	254	44	15
1985	421	368	53	13
1986	543	474	69	13
1987	530	483	47	9
1988	490	443	47	10
1989	576	532	47	8
1990	567	511	56	10
1991 (7 months)	452	397	55	12
Total	3,877	3,462	418	11

It was evident that the Transit Workers Union's mandatory second surgical opinion (SSO) program could eliminate an average of 11 percent of recommended surgeries each year. The number of nonconfirmed surgical procedures could be directly translated into savings, but a study of the actual impact of the Transit Workers Union's mandatory SSO program was warranted.

An analysis of the Transit Workers Union's mandatory second opinion program studied a cohort of nonconfirmed cases where surgery was eliminated— i.e., patients who opted to follow the recommendations of the second opinion consultant. The findings support the continued cost savings of a second opinion program.

The claims history of patients who were not confirmed for surgery during the period July 1, 1988 to June 30, 1990 were followed for a period of 12 months after their second opinion was rendered. During this time, those patients who decided to have surgery were scheduled for inpatient operation within 180 days following the second opinion consultation. The group that emerged and became the focus of this study did not file any claims for surgery, thus indicating that surgery had not taken place.

The analysis involved two steps:

- Estimating the medical costs avoided by patients whose surgery was not confirmed and who did not proceed with surgery; and
- Calculating the actual costs for all patients who obtained a second opinion.

Calculating the SSO Program's New Savings

The savings of the mandatory SSO program were calculated from the actual and projected expenses of nonconfirmed surgeries. The formula includes several factors:

- The number of second opinions.
- The number of surgical procedures that were not confirmed by second opinion consultants.
- Program costs, including payments for second opinion consulting and ancillary services (e.g., diagnostic tests).
- The savings from surgery actually eliminated as a result of nonconfirmed recommendations by second opinion consultants. Savings were estimated by taking into account the probable payments for hospital, surgery and other surgery-related services had the surgery occurred. (See Figure 1 for the formula.)

Figure 1 shows the formula for calculating the net savings attributable to the mandatory SSO program. *Gross savings* are defined as all surgical and hospital costs not incurred when patients chose not to proceed with surgery after a nonconfirming second opinion. Subtracted from gross savings are total SSO program costs, including payments to consultants for confirmed and nonconfirmed cases.

Data Sources

The number of second opinion consultations for each type of procedure were obtained from the presurgical screening intake forms where the patients' demographic information and the initially recommended surgery were documented. The confirmed and nonconfirmed rates by surgical procedure were

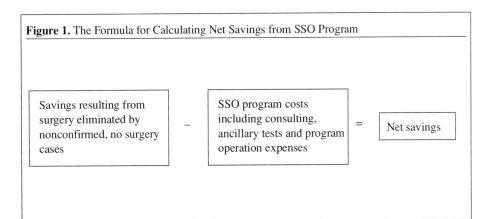

Figure 1. The Formula for Calculating Net Savings from SSO Program

| Savings resulting from surgery eliminated by nonconfirmed, no surgery cases | − | SSO program costs including consulting, ancillary tests and program operation expenses | = | Net savings |

Table 3. Composite of Teaching Hospital and Community Hospital DRG

Procedures	DRG Number	DRG Rate
Breast surgery	262	$3,548
Bunionectomy	225	6,542
Cataracts	039	4,493
Cholecystectomy	196	9,590
Dilation and curettage (D&C)	364	3,164
Herniorrhaphy	162	3,699
Hysterectomy	355	7,156
Knee surgery	222	7,512
Laminectomy	758	7,397
Nasal surgery/ submucous resection of deviated septum	337	5,811
Prostatectomy	055	3,409
Tonsillectomy/ adenoidectomy (T&A)	059	2,607
Varicose veins	119	4,501

extracted from the presurgical screening consultant forms. The costs of second opinion services were obtained from Health Benefits Research and Services.

The costs of the 13 elective surgical procedures were estimated using GHI reimbursement rates, and the hospital costs for each procedure were estimated based on a composite of community and teaching hospitals' DRG rates in New York City. (See Table 3 for the DRG rates.)

Results

Gross Savings from Nonconfirmed, No Surgery Cases
In the 24-month period, July 1, 1988 to June 30, 1990, 61 second opinion cases resulting in nonconfirming recommendations did not have surgery. The cost of

Table 4. Second Opinion Program Nonconfirmed/No Surgery Cohort—July 1988-June 1990 (24 months)

| | SSO Program Expenditures | | | Savings (at GHI rates) | | |
| | Number of Second Opinions | Consulting and Ancillary Fees | Surgical Fees | Assistant[1] Surgeon Fees | Anesthesia[2] | Hospital[3] Costs |
Procedures						
Breast surgery	4	$ 1,095	$ 2,180	$ 0	$ 763	$ 14,192
Bunionectomy	16	3,204	9,240	2,180	3,234	104,674
Cataracts	1	185	1,400	280	490	4,493
Cholecystectomy	3	550	4,200	840	1,470	28,769
Dilation and curettage	4	801	1,680	0	588	12,655
Herniorrhaphy	2	370	1,680	336	588	7,398
Hysterectomy	8	1,572	11,520	2,304	4,032	52,249
Knee surgery	10	2,176	9,350	1,870	3,273	75,120
Laminectomy	5	1,191	9,800	1,960	3,430	36,985
Prostatectomy	3	616	3,750	750	1,313	17,432
Nasal surgery/submucous resection of deviated septum	1	175	1,080	0	378	3,490
Tonsillectomy/adenoidectomy (T&A)	3	585	1,350	0	478	7,821
Varicose veins	1	216	500	0	175	4,501
Total	61	$12,736	$57,730	$10,188	$20,207	$396,698

RECAP: Total Surgical Fees $ 57,730
            Total Asst. Fees   10,188
            Total Anesthesia Fees   20,207
            Total Hospital Costs   396,698
            Savings $484,823

[1] At 20% of surgical fees.
[2] At 35% of surgical fees.
[3] Based on a composite of teaching and community hospitals' DRG rates.

second opinion services for these 61 patients was $12,736. However, had these same patients decided to proceed with surgery as initially suggested, their estimated surgical and hospital fees could amount to $484,823. Table 4 compares the program costs and estimated savings for the nonconfirmed, no surgery cases.

Program Costs

The total SSO program costs in the 24-month period were $217,837 for 1,067 cases that had a second opinion, including cases with confirmed and nonconfirmed recommendations.

Net Savings From Nonconfirmed, No Surgery Cases

New savings for nonconfirmed, no surgery cases were calculated by subtracting the SSO program costs from the savings attributed to those who had nonconfirmed recommendations and no surgery. The net savings were $266,986 (Figure 2).

Cost/Benefit Ratio

In terms of cost/benefit ratio, for every dollar spent on second opinion services, $2.23 can be saved by eliminating the surgeries of some nonconfirmed cases. (See Figure 3.)

DISCUSSION

A 24-month cost analysis of a cohort of cases with nonconfirmed surgical procedures indicated that the mandatory SSO program saved significant amounts of money. The savings were calculated not on the basis of the number of nonconfirmed cases but, rather, based on the net savings that resulted from eliminating surgeries that were either inappropriate or unnecessary.

The benefts of eliminating nonconfirmed surgery continue to exceed the costs of paying for surgery that was not confirmed; the benefit margin was $266,986.

Second opinion programs (voluntary and mandatory) are designed to reduce the incidence of unnecessary surgery, thereby stemming costs. Statistics accumulated in the past two decades have clearly indicated that the receipt of a second opinion consultation is cost effective and beneficial to the quality of patient care. The ability of second surgical opinion programs to screen potential surplus surgery has been demonstrated in study after study.[10]

In addition, mandatory second opinion programs can be a viable mechanism to educate patients about their health conditions. A majority of patients in Rosenberg's study indicated that the consultations not only provided them with reassurance, but also helped them make more informed decisions regarding their surgery. As a result, Rosenberg and his associates asserted that a mandatory

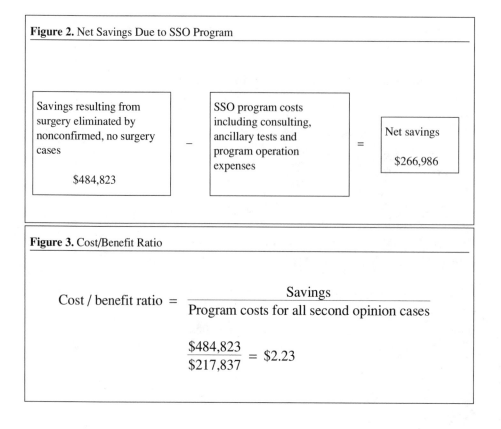

Figure 2. Net Savings Due to SSO Program

Figure 3. Cost/Benefit Ratio

program can be helpful to employees while effecting significant savings for the employer.[11]

Finally, the "sentinel effect" of second opinion programs has been effective in making doctors become more aware that their decision to operate will come under scrutiny by their peers. For some costly procedures, doctors are more willing to try alternative medical treatments or new technologies and/or outpatient surgery.[12]

CONCLUSION

The savings of $266,986 (or $2.23 cost/benefit ratio) produced by nonconfirmed, no surgery cases in the present study support and strengthen the continuation of mandatory second opinion programs. As discussed, statistical evidence collected from the past two decades has consistently shown the value of second surgical opinion programs to employees. Second surgical opinion programs were and are significantly effective in reducing inappropriate surgery, which, in turn, reduces health care costs.

1. "Data Watch: The Human Resource Manager's View," *Business and Health,* September 1990; Sarah Laditka, Philip Caper, Charles R Buck Jr, and Melanie Mastanduno, "GE Goes After High Medical Costs," *Business and Health,* January 1990; Stephen N Rosenberg, Harold Perlis, Donna Lynne, and Leonard Leto, "A Second Look at Second Surgical Opinions," *Business and Health,* February 1991.

2. SN Rosenberg, SA Gorman, S Snitzer, EV Herbst, and D Lynee, "Patients' Reactions and Physician-Patient Communication in a Mandatory Surgical Second-Opinion Program," 27 *Medical Care* 5 (May 1989).

3. The finding was based on an intensive two-year study on inpatient surgical claims from October 1, 1975 through September 1976. EG McCarthy and ML Finkel, "Second Opinion Elective Surgery Programs: Outcome Status Over Time," 16 *Medical Care* 12 (December 1978).

4. Madelon Lubin Finkel and David J Finkel, "The Effect of a Second Opinion Program on Hysterectomy Performance, " 28 *Medical Care* 9 (September 1990).

5. The New York City Employees District Council 37 of the American Federation of State, County, and Municipal Workers was one of the first welfare plans to offer a voluntary second opinion program to its members and their dependents. They approached the Cornell University Medical College—New York Hospital in the early 1970s for assistance. EG McCarthy and ML Finkel, "Second Opinion Elective Surgery Programs: Outcome Status Over Time," 16 *Medical Care* 12 (December 1978).

6. The costs for consultations and associated ancillary procedures were $101,520; administrative costs were $78,700; and program participants' out-of-pocket costs were $23,080. All together, the total costs incurred by the Building Service Local 32B-J's mandatory second opinion program were $203,300 during the two-year period (1977-1978).

7. The benefit/cost ratio equals $534,649/$203,300. EG McCarthy, ML Finkel and HS Ruchlin, *Second Opinion Elective Surgery* (Westport, CT: Auburn House Publishing Co., 1981).

8. Id.

9. The 50,000 members include approximately 31,783 working members and 18,217 retirees who are currently on Medicare.

10. Supra notes 3, 4, 5, 6, and 7.

11. Supra notes 1 and 2.

12. David Holzman, "Interactive Video Promotes Patient-Doctor Partnership," *Business and Health,* March 1992; Madeline Nash, "The Kindest Cut of All," *Time,* March 23, 1992; Raynauld Pineault and Assocites, "Randomized Clinical Trial of One-Day Surgery: Patient Satisfaction, Clinical Outcomes, and Cost," 23 *Medical Care* 2 (February 1985); James B Kenney and Robert L Parrish, "Getting a Fix on Outpatient Surgery Costs" in "Detroit Wants Coalitions in the Driver's Seat," *Business and Health,* September 1991; David Sussman, "Medical Boulevard: The New Walk of Fame," in "Outlook: Hospital Ourpatient Services," *Healthweek,* July 30, 1990.

25. AIDS in the Workplace: One Company's Response

Paul A. Ross, EdD

Digital Equipment Corporation was one of the first American companies to recognize that AIDS is a business issue that has bottom-line effects on productivity, morale, and health care costs. In response, it set up the first full-time corporate office devoted to HIV/AIDS workplace issues.

Human immunodeficiency virus (HIV) infection is now more than an epidemic; it's a pandemic, reaching every continent in the world and infecting an estimated 20 million people by the year 2000. Today, in the United States alone, 1.5 million people are infected with HIV, more than 250,000 have AIDS, and more than 160,000 have died of AIDS-related complications. More Americans have died of AIDS than died in the Korean, Vietnam, and Persian Gulf wars combined.

Since HIV/AIDS disproportionately affects people aged 25 to 44, the working population in the United States is quickly being impacted. The Centers for Disease Control estimates that one in every 100 adult men and one in every 800 adult women are infected with HIV. The toll this will take on corporate America—in both health care costs and in lost productivity—has yet to be measured.

Despite the staggering statistics, most major corporations in the United States, let alone small businesses, have yet to address the issue of HIV/AIDS in the workplace. The reasons for this may include:

- Ignorance of the ramifications of HIV/AIDS on business;
- Discomfort with the subject matter;

- Prejudice against most widely affected communities and behaviors (promiscuity, homosexuality, IV drug use); and
- Uncertainties about where to begin.

Regardless of the reasons, however, American business is not yet equipped to handle the imminent and inevitable impact of AIDS on its work force.

In health care costs alone, this impact will be enormous. People living with AIDS are treated by as many as 15 different medications a day. Many of these drugs are experimental and very expensive, costing as much as $2500 per month. Estimates today suggest that the cost of treatment for one person living with AIDS—from diagnosis to the end stage of the disease—can range from $80,000 to $150,000. Compounding these costs are the lack of community-based support systems in many parts of the country. The economic impact can range dramatically from one area to another, depending on a community's ability to respond to the crisis.

Regardless of geography or chosen therapy, much of the financial burden of HIV/AIDS will be borne by businesses.

MORE THAN THE RIGHT THING TO DO

Without a formal AIDS awareness and/or education program in place, corporations are leaving the difficult business and personal issues of this disease to individual employees, managers, benefits coordinators, and human resource professionals to sort out. Treating people who are sick with compassion and support, dignity and respect, is the right thing to do. Most corporations have policies and practices that ensure fair and sensitive treatment of disabled people or people with other life-threatening or debilitating illnesses, and that same sensitivity must be shown toward people living with AIDS or HIV infection.

But dealing with AIDS in the workplace is more than "the right thing to do." There are legal and economic factors that make setting up an AIDS program a compelling business endeavor. For instance, with passage of the Americans with Disabilities Act, the federal government has clearly defined what constitutes a disability and mandated that, as of July 1992, employers with more than 25 employees must offer reasonable work accommodation for those suffering from disabling conditions, including HIV/AIDS.

Studies have shown that early diagnosis and treatment of HIV infection can lengthen a person's life dramatically and, perhaps more importantly, can greatly improve the quality of that life. Early intervention is also the key for businesses facing the future with a threatened work force. The earlier employees are treated medically, the longer they are likely to stay working. Likewise, if employees infected with HIV understand that their workplace is a safe environment, they are more likely to disclose their condition and therefore are more likely to remain productive and enthusiastic in their jobs. And, as with any disease, getting people into the health care system early, with appropriate treatments, will drive down the per case cost.

Setting up an HIV/AIDS program before there is a crisis will prepare corporations and individuals to be more proactive and productive in dealing with the effects of the disease on the workplace as they emerge.

DIGITAL'S HIV/AIDS PROGRAM OFFICE

In 1988, Digital Equipment Corporation, a multinational corporation employing 100,000 employees worldwide, recognized that HIV infection and AIDS are business problems that must be addressed in the workplace. AIDS and HIV affect productivity and morale, and have significant impact on medical and disability insurance costs.

As a response to this situation, Digital established the HIV/AIDS Program Office, the only full-time corporate office of its kind in the United States, citing three distinct but related reasons for its establishment:

1. Digital believes that "education is the best vaccine" for all employees;
2. Digital recognizes that an individual with HIV infection has the same rights, responsibilities, and opportunities as any other employee with a serious illness or disability; and
3. Digital strives to offer all employees a safe and supportive work environment.

The HIV/AIDS Program Office is part of Digital's Worldwide Employee Relations organization because the corporation views AIDS in the workplace as an employee relations issue, rather than a medical issue. The HIV/AIDS Program Office, is responsible for the development and implementation of a company-wide AIDS education program. This program is designed to help employees understand the AIDS pandemic and protect themselves from infection while creating a supportive environment for those affected by the disease. By including interaction with HIV-positive individuals as part of employee seminars, Digital has been able to "put a face on the disease" to help eliminate stereotypes. At the same time, the HIV/AIDS Program Office works with Digital managers to protect the confidentiality of persons living with AIDS while striving to create a supportive work environment so infected employees may feel free to disclose their condition.

The HIV/AIDS Program Office also works with Digital's Corporate Contributions and Community Relations departments to support AIDS-related programs, services, and research through equipment, support, and program grants totaling more than $15 million in the past five years.

The success of the program office has been based on a number of factors:

•   *Strong philosophy based on the core values of the company.* Digital has a strongly worded policy statement regarding employees with serious or disabling illnesses or conditions. It simply says, "Digital recognizes that employees with serious illnesses including, but not limited to, cancer, heart disease, and AIDS, may wish to continue to engage in as many of their normal pursuits as their condition allows, including work. These employees must be able to meet acceptable performance standards, and submit medical evidence indicating that their conditions are not a deterrent to them or others in doing their jobs. Managers should be sensitive to their conditions and ensure that they are treated consistently with other employees, and that their rights to confidentiality are observed."

- *Managing business from a state of preparedness.* Getting an early start in 1988, when Digital was seeing its very first cases of AIDS, helped the corporation make long-term decisions about how it would treat this disease in the workplace. At Digital, dealing with AIDS in the workplace is a lesson in compromises and balances. Meeting the needs of the individual living with HIV as well as meeting the revenue and productivity goals of a commercial enterprise requires a delicate set of tradeoffs. Managing the business from a state of preparedness has made these goals mutually achievable.

- *High-level support.* From its inception, the Digital HIV/AIDS Program Office has had the support of the highest levels of management in the corporation. Even today, the HIV/AIDS Program Office continues to act as a consultant to executives and senior management on the trends of the pandemic that will ultimately affect Digital, its employees and their families, its customers, and its communities worldwide.

- *Clear communications strategy.* Digital's HIV/AIDS Program Office set reasonable and clear goals that were communicated to managers and employees. With these goals in mind, the establishment of educational seminars, corporate contributions, and employee involvement has proceeded in a planned and strategic manner.

MANAGING THE BENEFITS

Digital believes in offering its employees choices in health care. The challenge is to ensure necessary, cost-effective, high-quality, and equitable health care for employees, regardless of their choices.

For several years, through its indemnity insurance plans, Digital has employed an HIV-specific case management company that has encouraged early intervention for people living with HIV infection. This company—Clinical Partners (Boston and Los Angeles)—offers employees a consistent and reliable health care plan from the early stages of infection through end-stage AIDS. Using the same model, Digital is working in partnership with its HMOs to manage HIV/AIDS as a continuum of individual needs. Beginning in the early asymptomatic phase and continuing through the course of the disease, Digital's objective is to provide access—through individual case management—to high-quality, sensitive care.

ESTABLISHING A CORPORATE RESPONSE

Designing a corporate response to HIV/AIDS in the workplace will be an individual exercise for each company, based on the size of the organization, its geographic distribution, and its core values. Nevertheless, a number of resources are available to assist corporations.

There are many professional groups ready to help corporations establish AIDS education programs. These include the American Red Cross and the Centers for Disease Control, which, in 1992, launched a program called "Business Responds to AIDS," a workplace education campaign aimed at business and labor leaders and public health officials.

The National Leadership Coalition on AIDS (Washington, DC) was founded in 1987 to address HIV and AIDS as a workplace issue. The Coalition addresses the impact of AIDS on business and labor, on employers and employees. It works to prevent the spread of HIV disease by developing effective AIDS policies, practices, and workplace education programs.

There are also regional organizations; Digital is a charter member of the New England Corporate Consortium for AIDS Education, a multi-industry group striving to manage, and help others manage, the issues of AIDS in the workplace through education. It has developed a workplace education program that includes a corporate planning guide, a supervisor's manual, employee brochures, and an award-winning video entitled "Living and Working with AIDS." It also sponsors leadership forums and engages in specific projects such as the New England Workplace Response to AIDS.

Members of the New England Corporate Consortium put together ten principles for corporations grappling with the HIV/AIDS experience in the workplace (see Exhibit 1). The principles, modeled on similar work by the New York/New Jersey Citizens' Commission on AIDS, were adopted through collaboration with the AIDS Action Committee of Massachusetts. Since their adoption, approximately 150 companies have signed the principles.

Exhibit 1. Responding to AIDS: Ten Principles for the Workplace

1. Persons with HIV infection, including AIDS, in our company have the same rights, responsibilities, and opportunities as others with serious illnesses or disabilities.
2. Our employment policies comply with federal, state, and local laws.
3. Our employment policies are based on the scientific facts that persons with HIV infection, including AIDS, do not cause risk to others in the workplace through ordinary workplace contact.
4. Our management and employee leaders endorse a nondiscrimination policy.
5. Special training and equipment will be used when necessary, such as in health care settings, to minimize risks to employees.
6. We will ensure that AIDS education is provided to all of our employees.
7. We will endeavor to ensure that education takes place before AIDS related incidents occur in our workplace.
8. Confidentiality of persons with HIV infection and AIDS will be protected.
9. We will not screen for HIV as part of pre-employment or workplace physical examinations.
10. We will support these policies through clear communication to all current and prospective employees.

26. Utilization Review National Accreditation Program

Allen D. Feezor   Elizabeth E. Friberg

The utilization review, health care, and health benefits industries have recognized the need to set standards and guidelines for the growing number of utilization review organizations. In response, they formed the Utilization Review Accreditation Committee, and now a set of standards and an accreditation process are in place, ensuring quality and consistency in accredited UR organizations nationwide.

In December 1989, the American Managed Care and Review Association (AMCRA) sponsored a meeting in Washington, D.C. of industry representatives from over 80 utilization review (UR) organizations. These representatives sought to address the concerns and frustrations of consumers, purchasers, and providers with the diversity of UR procedures, as well as the growing impact of managed care on physicians and hospitals. At this and a subsequent meeting in March, 1990, there was general agreement that the relatively new and expanding UR industry needed to achieve greater consistency and uniformity in its policies and procedures. Strong support was given to the development of national standards for the UR industry and for the formation of an independent accreditation organization.

Other efforts at standardizing the UR process had been made, with limited success. For example, the American Medical Association (AMA), the Health Insurance Association of America (HIAA), and the Blue Cross and Blue Shield Association (BCBSA) worked together and developed guidelines for prior authorization programs. Similarly, the AMA, HIAA, BCBSA, American Hospital Association (AHA), and AMCRA developed guidelines for concurrent review processes. AMCRA had also worked with the Council of Medical Specialty Societies (CMSS) in developing a standard data set for conducting utilization review. Regional efforts of providers and hospitals to address UR activities—for example, the Tennessee Health Relations Group, which served as a model—reinforced consensus among concerned parties that an effective tool to resolve valid grievances and improve interactions should be developed.

Although leaders of the health industry supported these earlier efforts, it had become clear over time that a more broadly based and credible approach was needed to achieve greater consistency and uniformity in UR policies and procedures.

FORMATION OF URAC

The Utilization Review Accreditation Commission (URAC) was organized on February 14, 1990, as a nonprofit corporation under the laws of the District of Columbia, with recognition as a Section 501(c)(3) charitable organization by the Internal Revenue Service. During its initial year, URAC and other interested organizations strove to develop comprehensive standards for UR organizations.

Effective May 1, 1991, the members of URAC's interim board adopted new bylaws designating the member organizations of URAC. The interim board resigned and a new board of directors, comprised of representatives from each of twelve separate member organizations, took control. The current board contains individuals of widely differing backgrounds and perspectives including providers, government regulators, consumers, business people, third party payers, and UR organizations. The URAC member organizations include the AMA, AHA, BCBSA, HIAA, American Nurses Association (ANA), American Psychiatric Association (APA), Washington Business Group on Health (WBGH), National Association of Insurance Commissioners (NAIC), National Association of Manufacturers (NAM), International United Auto Workers, Managed Care and Review Association (AMCRA), and American Peer Review Association (AMPRA).

THE STANDARDS

In 1992, the board formally adopted the National Utilization Review Standards and the general procedures to be utilized by URAC in its voluntary accreditation program.[1] These standards were developed by a URAC workgroup in a collaborative effort of representatives of the provider, UR, and payor communities. URAC implemented its accreditation program in July 1991, upon the adoption of the standards and the accreditation process by the board.

The standards are designed to:

1. Encourage consistency in the procedures for interaction among utilization review organizations (UROs), providers, payors, and consumers of health care;

2. Establish UR processes that cause minimal disruption to the health care delivery system;

3. Standardize the procedures used to certify medical services and to process appeals;

4. Provide the basis for an efficient process of credentialing and accrediting UR companies; and

5. Provide a credible national alternative accreditation mechanism that can be applied in jurisdictions that choose to regulate UR companies or by purchasers seeking vendors that meet recognized and accepted performance standards.

The URAC standards currently address UROs that perform prospective and concurrent utilization review for all inpatient services, as well as precertification review of outpatient surgical facilities. This utilization review function can be conducted in a variety of health care models that provide external performance monitoring programs.

URAC defines "utilization review" as an evaluation of the necessity, appropriateness, and/or efficiency of health care services, procedures, and facilities. A "utilization review organization" is defined as an entity that conducts utilization review.

The current standards address key operational processes that affect the quality and efficiency of the interaction among the providers, facilities, employees/patients, URO, and payors. The issues include accessibility, availability, date requirements, procedures and timeframes for conducting reviews, notification processes, appeal processes (both expedited and standard appeal), confidentiality, staff qualifications, criteria for review determinations, and quality assurance programs. They are intended to encourage the availability of effective, efficient, and consistent utilization review of health care services, thereby improving the quality of the interaction between the parties involved and minimizing the disruption to the health care delivery system.

For example, URAC's standards require that all inpatient review determinations be completed within two days of receipt of sufficient information to conduct the review. All clinical reviews must be conducted by licensed health professionals, and noncertification review determinations must be rendered by a physician. Appeal reviews must be conducted by a physician who did not render the original decision not to certify, and the appeal physician should be of a similar general specialty as typically manages the medical condition under review.

ACCREDITATION PROGRAM

There are two types of URAC standards: those required, called the "shalls"; and those encouraged, called the "shoulds." To be accredited under the URAC standards, a UR organization must meet all standards designated as "shalls" and at least 60 percent of the standards designated as "shoulds." Variances from particular standards may be permitted only in two circumstances:

1. If a state statute or regulation would make compliance impossible or illegal; or
2. If the UR organization has entered into contractual agreements with providers that vary from the standards but meet their desired outcome.

Both the URAC Accreditation Committee and the URAC Executive Committee must approve the specific variance; it is not automatic. In the case of the second exception, the contractual agreements must be verified by URAC and the nature of the variance must be clearly stated in all benefit plan descriptions. As an example, a preferred provider organization may have contractual agreements with its provider network about notification and rights to appeal. Here, URAC would investigate the provider contract language and the employee benefit plan language to ensure that all parties are informed of their rights and that subscribers will avoid financial liability for the cost of incurred care.

The accreditation application process scrutinizes a wide variety of operational information about the UR company applicant, including:

- Demographic data
- Availability and accessibility of reviewers
- Data collection
- UR procedures
- Appeals procedures
- Confidentiality requirements and protections
- Staffing and staff qualifications
- Program qualifications

The application also requires that certain declarations and assurances be given by the UR organization regarding, among other things, continued compliance with the URAC standards.

The average time required to review and make an accreditation decision from the date of receipt of a complete uncomplicated application to the rendering of a decision, is four months.

When an application is received by URAC, the staff reviews the application for completeness. If the application is not complete or the incorrect fee is paid, the UR company is given 30 days to complete the application. Once complete, a URAC review professional—a registered nurse with experience in utilization review or quality assurance—is assigned to review the application information. The staff member verifies the applicants' responses by telephone, and then makes an initial determination if the URO has met the standards for accreditation. If URAC's staff member finds that he or she cannot interpret the information over the telephone, URAC may either require an on-site inspection of the applying UR company or deny accreditation because the application is not verifiable.

If the URO is determined not to satisfy the accreditation standards, URAC notifies the URO, stating the reasons it failed to meet the standards. The applicant is then given a 90-day correction phase to correct the noncompliance.

Once the URO is determined to be in compliance with the standards, the application is forwarded to URAC's Accreditation Committee. The members of URAC's Accreditation Committee meet twice a month to review applications and the staff's work. The Accreditation Committee's recommendation (for or against accreditation) is presented to URAC's Executive Committee, which makes the final determination. Upon Executive Committee approval, URAC sends a notice and a certificate of accreditation to the UR company.

In the event that the Executive Committee decides against accreditation, the applicant may appeal the decision. The appeal will be reviewed at the next meeting of the full Board of Directors, which has sole authority to adjudicate the appeal. The decision of the full board is final.

Applications submitted to the Accreditation and Executive Committees are "blinded"—all references to the identity of the applying UR organization are deleted. At any time during the accreditation process, either the Accreditation Committee or the Executive Committee can request additional information or require an on-site examination. Action taken by the Executive Committee must be unanimous.

URAC accreditation is for a two-year period, though it may be revoked should the program fail to remain in compliance with the standards. A UR organization may seek renewal of its accreditation at the end of the two years. At that time, the UR organization will undergo a renewal process similar to the application process.

Focus Outcomes

During accreditation, URAC views utilization review as a process. It requires UROs to compare their operations to the standards, provide supporting corporate policies and procedures, and provide sample notification letters, contractual language, etc., in order to achieve a full evaluation of the consistency of the UR program, its formal policies and procedures, and its external communications.

As of May, 1993, URAC has accredited 69 UR organizations. Over three-fourths (77 percent) of these applicants were required to make some change in their operations, formal policies and procedures, and/or notification processes to achieve compliance with the URAC standards. These constructive changes were voluntarily adopted by the UROs to achieve accreditation and the higher, more uniform standard of performance it signifies. Twenty-seven percent of accredited companies improved the notification procedures for UR decisions. They altered noncertification letters to clarify the patient's right to appeal, and rewrote appeal outcome letters to providers to include the clinical rationale for decisions. Thirteen percent improved operations, mainly extending the hours within every time zone that accounts for at least two percent of their business. Nine percent improved staff or program qualifications.

Despite their broad, diverse, and frequently conflicting perspectives, URAC member organization have been able to discuss issues and concerns, and use a consensus development process to set achievable standards that reflect mutual respect and responsiveness to all parties concerned. As URAC approaches the release of revisions to the National Utilization Review Standards for comment, the value of the interaction and commitment involved in URAC processes becomes evident. While in operation for less than two years, the projected revisions will significantly expand the scope of the standards to address specialty, outpatient, and retrospective review. Further refinement in such areas as hours of operation, after hours coverage, parameters of the appeals process, the development of review criteria, quality management programs, and other factors will continually improve the quality and efficiency of the interactions among all parties in utilization review. The 69 currently accredited programs represent more than 80 million covered lives.

State regulators continue to view URAC's processes as a helpful guide to their own evaluation and/or a viable alternative to individual state monitoring programs. Six states now recognize URAC-accredited UROs as meeting state licensure requirements. Two states and the District of Columbia (for workers' compensation review programs) require URAC accreditation. It is anticipated that several additional states will be added to the list at the end of the spring 1993 legislative session.

As the scope of the URAC's standards and the Accreditation Program continue to expand, the effectiveness of a national accreditation program can be fully assessed. URAC has taken a leadership role in developing and providing a cost-effective, efficient, and results-oriented accreditation program that enhances the operational quality of review programs across multiple models. It reinforces the UR organizations' accountability for maintaining and monitoring the integrity of their programs according to the nationally accepted standards developed with the involvement of providers, consumers, and payors. Assisting UR organizations in achieving accreditation improves the quality of the programs available. It provides greater uniformity and efficiencies. It increases the degree of compliance and participation by other parties in efforts to conduct cost containment and quality intervention programs, and produces a corporate sensitivity to the input and concerns of all parties involved. These are the ingredients to continuous quality improvement in health utilization management.

More and more, employer groups are adopting the concept of URAC accreditation as a criteria for vendor selection and bidding qualifications. Facilities are using the URAC standards as a guideline for negotiating relationships with UR vendors. This trend will continue, producing a market influence that will effect change more rapidly.

The utilization review industry of the early 1980s looked at the health care delivery site, the appropriateness of care, and the management of resources. The utilization review industry of the 1990s is now addressing the management of resources in a more sophisticated fashion, as well as the management of the patients. In addition, it is looking at the cost efficiency of utilization management and the quality of care provided.

THE FUTURE

As utilization review and utilization management become even more sophisticated, so will utilization review organizations. URAC recognizes that it must increase its sophistication and continuously strive to ensure that its services are valued and consistent with the needs of an ever-changing health care market.

Changes in the URAC standards must reflect the changes in UR organizations. As the organization that accredits UR organizations, URAC will provide leadership to the industry so that the improvement of utilization review and utilization management can become a constantly evolving standard. URAC is one of the logical platforms for the development of responses and, where possible, for the purchasers of UR services to address expectations.

Payors, patients, providers, and legislators have asked or demanded some changes in the utilization management process. They are concerned about the rationale and professional credibility behind utilization review decisions, and raise three basic issues:

1. How are review criteria developed? What involvement has the medical profession had and how consistent are the criteria that are utilized?
2. Why have the review criteria not been provided to physicians and, now, to state regulatory bodies? Should review criteria be released to physicians?
3. When adverse review determinations are made, have providers and patients received the reasons for the adverse review determinations?

These issues are the focus of URAC's 1993-1994 agenda. URAC anticipates that the process will provide frank and open discussions by all parties represented to clarify questions and to better understand each other. This process can ultimately promote change and increase incentives for individual organizations to achieve viable solutions.

On The Table

As early as August 1992, URAC received from member organizations, other groups, and government officials requests to evaluate overlapping accreditation programs. In a climate of health care reform, critical evaluation of every health care dollar is essential. There is increased pressure to reduce all nonessential administrative costs, including the cost of multiple accreditation processes. URAC recognizes that a private-sector initiative toward possible integration of accreditation efforts is more preferable to governmental approach, and has taken a bold step in stating its intention to address such concerns; it looks forward to being an integral part of such discussion among accrediting bodies to create viable solutions.

1.   The National Utilization Review Standards are copyrighted by URAC.

27.   Retirees and HMOs: A Cost Saving Tactic

Robert P. Power, CEBS

With accounting rules that require companies to project the long-term costs of their retiree medical plans on their financial statements, employers need to find ways to lower the pay-as-you-go costs of their plans. Voluntary enrollment of retirees in HMOs is one tactic that businesses can use to lower their obligations for retiree medical expenses.

The Statement of Financial Accounting Standards No. 106 (SFAS 106) requires companies to project the long-term costs of their current retiree medical plans. The employer's pay-as-you-go costs act as the foundation for most of the required analyses. Any tactic that lowers the current pay-as-you-go cost has the potential to reduce the SFAS 106 liability in approximately the same proportion.

The employer's liability is influenced by a variety of facts and assumptions. The Statement stipulates that today's Medicare benefit package and payment rates must be the basis for projections.[1] The financial interactions between Medicare and the employer's retiree medical plans are usually the most powerful single determinant. The next critical element is the "spread" between the assumed trend in health care costs and the assumed discount rate. The tactic proposed here can have beneficial effects on both of these determinants of the liability.

"Retirees and HMOs: A Cost Saving Tactic," which appeared in the September 1992 issue, was reprinted with permission from the *Benefits Quarterly,* published by the International Foundation of Employee Benefit Plans, Brookfield, WI. Statements or opinions expressed in this article are those of the author and do not necessarily represent the views or positions of the International Foundation, its officers, or staff.

TACTICS AVAILABLE TO EMPLOYERS

Recent surveys indicate that CFO's of medium-sized and large employers will recommend significant changes to their retiree plans if SFAS 106 reduces earnings by as little as 5 percent or 7 percent.[2] Earnings reductions of this magnitude will be the rule rather than the exception.

Most of the current articles and publications contain descriptions of things employers can do to lower the impact of SFAS 106. However, almost all of the suggestions (such as disproportionate increases in monthly retiree contributions, benefit reductions, or a change in the Medicare integration technique) have negative implications for company shareholders. They may affect the employer's public image, sour the employer's relationship with active employees, create pressure for commensurate pension plan increases, or even spark a lawsuit.

A Voluntary Program of HMO Enrollment

Employers should consider a different tactic. If their Medicare-eligible retirees live in or near large metropolitan areas, the employer may be able to work with certain HMOs and similar health plans that have signed special contracts with Medicare. These contracts have unique advantages to retirees and to SFAS 106–affected employers.

The program is called *risk contracting,* and its basic elements are simple. Medicare calculates what it expects to pay under normal Medicare rules for the coming year, by age and sex. It then transfers that per capita amount to an HMO after subtracting a small percentage savings for itself. In return, the HMO promises to provide the normal package of Medicare benefits, although most promise far more comprehensive benefits. This arrangement places a strong incentive on the risk-contracting HMO that the employer can use to its advantage. Most HMOs survive by being frugal with inpatient hospital resources. A larger-than-average percentage of retirees' health care spending occurs in the hospital, so the HMO's proven ability to control these costs creates an opportunity.

Unfortunately, the typical retiree medical plan does not benefit from such frugality. In fact, the smart employer turns off its inpatient utilization review mechanisms for Medicare-eligible retirees and dependents. That makes good economic sense, because the employer's entire risk is merely the cost of Part A deductibles. Ironically, the zealous employer that aggressively manages inpatient care for Medicare-eligibles may do itself a disservice by transferring care from Medicare Part A to Part B, where its ultimate liability may be far greater.

The risk-contracting program eliminates that perverse set of incentives, by combining Part A and Part B into one undifferentiated payment stream. Thus, utilization savings in inpatient hospitalization are available to cross-subsidize other types of care that receive leaner Medicare benefits. Also, risk contracting HMOs are granted the authority either to bargain their own rates with hospitals or to use Medicare DRG-based rates, so their per admission costs are likely to be quite comparable to Medicare's payments.

COMPONENTS OF THE FASB LIABILITY

There are three major types of claims that add to the pay-as-you-go costs but are not Medicare deductibles and copayments. Together, they are often more important than the Medicare deductibles and copayments. If the retiree medical plan covers any of these expenses, the risk-contracting HMO tactic will probably work.

Prescription Drugs

Medicare totally excludes most prescription drugs. Thus, drug costs are likely to generate a disproportionate share of pay-as-you-go costs. Better management of the expense can sharply reduce the accounting liability.

Well-established HMOs have mature pharmacy systems in place to serve their younger populations. These systems can be easily extended to retirees. In addition to bulk purchasing, the systems usually include generic drug substitution, quantity control, computerized drug interaction detection, and more.

Other Services Excluded From Medicare

Some types of care are not covered by Medicare but are covered by the employer's plan. For example, preventive care is totally excluded, with the exception of limited mammography coverage. Most nursing home care is excluded, even when the care is noncustodial and is provided in lieu of inpatient hospitalization. Medicare's coverage of durable medical equipment can be so rigid that the patient often bypasses Medicare altogether and submits the entire bill to the retiree medical plan as a non-Medicare-eligible expense.

Risk-contracting HMOs are not constrained by Medicare payment rules. They can use a broad spectrum of services when those services are beneficial and cost effective, regardless of their status as covered benefits under Medicare. This flexibility saves money.

Balance Billing

Historically, Medicare exercised only loose control over physicians who billed patients for charges in excess of Medicare-allowable charges. These "balance billings" are normally an eligible expense under employer retiree medical plans, so they become a large component of pay-as-you-go costs. The importance of balance billing varies widely by geographic area and by medical specialty. Recent physician payment reforms will further limit balance billing, but by no means eliminate it. In fact, physician dissatisfaction with the new payment methods will probably increase balance billing in some segments of the physician community.

Risk-contracting HMOs remove balance billing as an issue. They are unrestricted by Medicare in their payment levels to physicians. Thus, it is common for risk-contracting HMOs to pay more than Medicare for some services, and the same or less than Medicare for others. In tightly structured HMOs, the payment takes an entirely new form, such as capitation.

THE EMPLOYER'S NEW TACTIC

The employer's tactic is straightforward: In each metropolitan area containing a reasonable number of the firm's Medicare-eligible retirees and dependents, locate the risk-contracting HMOs. Table I lists the largest metropolitan areas with risk-contracting HMOs. Contact the HMO and explain that you wish to do a special enrollment of your retirees who live in its area. If the HMO's benefit package needs to be enhanced to resemble the employer's plan, discuss a small wraparound product with the HMO. Using the net price of the HMO's coverage, simply compare it to the employer's projected average pay-as-you-go costs for Medicare-eligible retirees and dependents in the same period.

If the employer's plan contains any coverage of drugs or balance billings, or if it uses coordination of benefits (COB) as the integration method, the HMO's monthly rate is likely to handily beat the current pay-as-you-go costs. Thus, every enrollment into the risk-contracting HMO represents a proportionate shrinking of the FASB liability.

UNDERWRITING AND ADMINISTRATION ISSUES

Most risk-contracting HMOs are continuously open for new enrollment. All are required to accept new enrollees at least once per year, unless they lack capacity. The employer's promotion can be timed to match the HMO's open enrollment month, if necessary.

By law, risk-contracting HMOs cannot subject new enrollees to underwriting restrictions or preexisting-condition clauses. Thus, in most cases the employer is free to promote the HMO option as a voluntary adjunct to its own program, knowing that the Medicare-eligible retiree or dependent will be assured of full coverage. The employer must assure the retiree/dependent that he or she may reenter the employer's plan at the end of any month. Fears of HMO-generated adverse selection are mitigated by the informality of the arrangement. Normally, the employer will be able to withdraw its administrative "sponsorship" of the

Table 1. Large Metropolitan Areas with Risk Contracting HMOs

Albuquerque	Minneapolis–St. Paul
Boston	New York
Buffalo	Orlando
Chicago	Philadelphia
Cleveland	Phoenix
Daytona Beach	Portland–Vancouver
Denver	Rochester, NY
Detroit	San Antonio
Honolulu	San Diego
Indianapolis	San Francisco
Las Vegas	Seattle
Los Angeles	Tampa–St. Petersburg
Miami–Fort Lauderdale	Tucson

Source: Health Care Financing Administration, "Comparison for Top 50 Counties (in Risk Enrollment)," Office of Financial Management, Office of Prepaid Health Care, September 1993.

risk-contracting HMO at will. If a retiree or dependent were to reject the employer plan to stay with the HMO thereafter, the FASB liability would presumably drop to zero for that person.

Obviously, it costs money to establish links to one or more HMOs. However, these expenses may be immediately recovered via reduction in claim adjudication expenses. Retiree claims tend to be complex, and the payout per claim tends to be very small. These expenses are totally eliminated for HMO members.

TREND ASSUMPTIONS: POWERFUL EFFECT

There are reasons to believe that different (lower) trend assumption can be used for retirees and dependents who are enrolled in HMOs than for other members of the retiree medical plan. The spread between the assumed health cost trend and the discount rate is such a key determinant of the SFAS 106 accrual that the final rule requires a "sensitivity analysis" showing the impact of a 1 percent reduction in the assumed health care cost inflation rate. As part of the process of developing SFAS 106, a field test of 25 companies was performed. Studies were also done of hypothetical companies' plans.

The field test found that a 1 percentage point reduction in the trend assumption yielded a 12 to 16 percent reduction in the expensed amount. The field test documentation states, "HMO costs may be assumed to rise at a rate, in the aggregate, that differs from costs under an indemnity arrangement."[3] The final rule is silent on this issue.

Recent evidence is clear: HMOs' rate trends are five to ten percentage points lower than indemnity plan trends.[4] This is often due to reasons other than efficiency (such as cost shifting), but the spread in trends is real. The Group Health Association of America reports that HMO premiums increased approximately 9 percent for 1993, while indemnity insurers' trends may remain in the 14 to 16 percent range, net of year-end adjustments. A positive spread has occurred in each of the last seven years, despite the health cycle.[5] The HMOs' underlying cost structures are fundamentally similar to those affecting indemnity carriers, so the spread in trends will narrow in the long term.

Based on the field test, the impact of a lower trend of only two percentage points would be to lower the expensed amount by one-quarter to one-third for each HMO enrollee.

HYPOTHETICAL SCENARIO FOR SAVINGS

Excellence Incorporated is a light manufacturing employer with 5,000 active employees/dependents. It remains committed (for now) to its longstanding retiree medical plan. Coverage includes drugs, and most balance billings are eligible under its "usual and customary" charges. Normal active employee deductibles and coinsurances apply to retirees, but the plan used COB as its integration technique with Medicare.

Approximately 60 percent of its $2.4 million pay-as-you-go costs are associated with Medicare-eligible retirees/dependents. Total claim costs are, on average, $160 per person per month for the Medicare-eligibles. Retirees currently contribute a flat $40 per person per month via pension check deduction.

As suggested above, Excellence looks for a risk-contracting HMO with a good reputation in several metropolitan areas in which most retirees reside. The HMOs are open for enrollment and eager to reduce their normal marketing expenses by working with employer sponsors. Their benefit packages cover roughly the same services as the Excellence plan, and they offer 100 percent benefits for almost all physician and hospital services. The HMOs compete vigorously with other local HMOs, so their rates reflect most of their efficiencies. The average HMO premium for Excellence is $80 per person per month,[6] including a drug rider. Medicare kicks in approximately $300 per month.

Few Excellence retirees have voluntarily enrolled in local HMOs because their current cost ($40) is lower than the HMOs' unsubsidized rate. Also, the retiree medical plan is backed by the employer's money and good will and the convenience of pension check deduction. However, the retirees hate the paperwork hassles of dealing with both Excellence and Medicare.

The Excellence benefits manager decides to sponsor special HMO enrollment activities. She decides to encourage voluntary enrollment by lowering the HMO retirees' contribution to $30. After two mailings containing an endorsement of the program, 300 of the Medicare-eligible retirees/dependents enroll in the chosen HMOs. The consulting actuary working on the Excellence liability estimation expresses a willingness to use an HMO health care cost trend that is two percentage points lower than the chosen trend for the regular plan.

RISKS AND REWARDS

Based on the facts above, the tactic will save $140,000 per year on only 300 retirees or dependents. Also, using a lower trend assumption for the HMO members' expenditures will reduce the remaining liability by 30 percent on the HMO enrollees' costs. Together, these changes would yield a total reduction of 10 to 12 percent in the company's SFAS 106 liability.

If this arrangement is so fruitful, why have few employers exploited it? The primary reason is that most employers are still grappling with basic issues, such as refining the promise made to retirees. Second, employers hoped that HMOs would be a panacea for active employees. That expectation is not being met. Third, employers may not understand that these arrangements *replace* Medicare rather than act as a supplement to it.

From the HMOs' side, there have been problems too. First and foremost, HMOs have geared their marketing efforts to nongroup enrollees, who make up the bulk of the Medicare market. Also, risk contracting works best in large HMOs that build specialized geriatric care delivery models. Many smaller players have come and gone. Finally, the Health Care Financing Administration's capitation payments are constrained by the same forces that create Medicare cost shifting. Risk-contracting HMOs are still learning the art of graceful benefit reductions for nongroup enrollees.

In some locales, the employer/HMO retiree linkage is already strong. Hundreds of Minnesota employers offer risk-contracting HMOs to their Medicare-eligible retirees. Only now are the HMOs and their customers learning that these actions also lower the postretirement liabilities.

This is not a high-risk tactic. Financially, the employer's risks are reduced, because the arrangement provides a guaranteed monthly cost for the HMO enrollees. Administrative risks are mitigated by Medicare's recent efforts to streamline the enrollment process. Over one million Medicare-eligible persons (including group retirees) are already enrolled through about 80 different HMOs.

A final advantage of the tactic is that it does not limit an employer's future options. It fits perfectly in a retiree flex design or in a switch to dollar-denominated benefits for future retirees.

1. Financial Accounting Standards Board, "Statement of Financial Accounting Standards No. 106" (Norwalk, CT: FASB 1990): ¶ 40.

2. Towers Perrin, "FAS 106: The View from the CFO's Office" (Towers Perrin: May 1991): 3.

3. Harold Dankner et al., *Retiree Health Benefits: Field Test of the FASB Proposal* (Morristown, NJ: Financial Executives Research Foundation, 1989)

4. "HMO Savings Confirmed," *Business Insurance,* Aug 12 1991, p. 1, referring to *1990 Managed Care Survey* and *Indemnity Plans: Cost, Design, and Funding* (A. Foster Higgins & Co., Inc.: 1991).

5. Group Health Association of America, *HMO Market Position Report: Results From a Fall 1991 Member Plan Survey* (GHAA, Dec 1991): 1 and 3.

6. Health Care Financing Administration, *Expanding Medicare Coordinated Choices for Group Retirees: The Report of the Employer Group Task Force* (HCFA 1991). The national average premium for 1991 was 41.95 per person (page 24); a $10 copayment drug program would add approximately $15.

28. Managing Care, Costs, and the Demand Factor

Michael E. Mihlbauer

Inappropriate health benefits utilization by consumers adds a great deal to the cost of health care, but this demand-side area has been largely ignored by cost management strategists brought up on the managed care techniques of the HMO movement. Providing employees with the training, information, and support necessary to make them better health care consumers can result in considerable cost savings with no real loss in quality of care provided. The modification of consumer demand is the next big challenge for health care cost management.

Cost management efforts have been levied against both the supply side and demand side of the health care purchasing equation. Current managed care technology addresses the supply of medical care services, and protects the purchaser from the cost of inappropriate services or excessive billing by providers. Wellness, lifestyle modification, and health improvement programs address the demand for health care services by focusing on improvement of individual health status. A substantial amount of health care utilization, however, is neither driven by greedy providers nor raging illnesses. It is driven by consumer expectations; experts estimate that at least 25 percent of medical care consumption, and perhaps much more, is driven by needs other than those for medical care. Employers and benefits managers need an additional option in the health care cost management battle: the modification of consumer demand.

MANAGED CARE BACKGROUND

The Health Maintenance Organization Act of 1973 created a federal funding vehicle for the development of community based, not-for-profit health maintenance organizations (HMOs). This act set in motion a competitive market dynamic—"the HMO movement"—that has led to the creation of the managed care business as we know it today. Since this Nixon-era legislation, HMOs have changed from a social experiment to business as usual in most major metropolitan areas.

Furthermore, the export of managed care technology from HMOs to insurers and other purchasers of care has solidified the business-as-usual status of managed care. Managed care products such as preferred provider organizations (PPOs), exclusive provider organizations (EPOs), point of service (POS) plans, and other hybrids all owe their origins to the logical premises upon which the HMO Act was based. This logic is focused on controlling the supply of medical and health care services to enrollees. Historically, this supply-side control has been pursued with virtually no attention to the demand for services.

The basic premises of HMO theory, as advanced by the HMO Act, included first dollar coverage, and placing providers at financial risk for the cost of medical care. The elimination of economic disincentives to patients seeking care, such as deductibles and copayments, was intended to save money; early intervention would lower treatment costs, it was reasoned, because disease states would not have advanced and become more expensive to treat.

The logic in the HMO Act governed the providers of medical care as well. This theory placed the providers at financial risk for the utilization of medical services by enrollees. Placing doctors on a fixed and common budget, it was reasoned, would create peer pressure for cost control. Provider risk was also initiated to limit any financial incentives that could encourage providers to deliver more services than medically necessary. This peer review process, in turn, drove the development of the utilization management tools that are now the hallmark of managed care. These management tools include:

- Pre-procedure or pre-admission certification;
- Documented primary care referrals to specialists or specialty care services;
- Concurrent reviews of hospital stays; and
- Retrospective audits for quality assurance.

Practice pattern analysis, which rank orders physicians by cost performance, is also an outgrowth of the original HMO peer review process.

The HMO model addresses provider control of the utilization of health care resources, but not consumer control. In essence, the entire managed care model is based on eliminating provider abuses.

Managed Care and the Demand Factor

As HMOs eliminated or reduced the economic disincentives for patients to seek care, a cultural value was reinforced. This value holds that medical care should be available for little or no cost to every American—that access to health care is a right. Titles XVIII and XIX of the Social Security Act, the Medicare and Medicaid entitlement programs respectively, had opened this door of perception for other population segments a decade before the HMO Act was passed.

Traditional managed care technology, as taken from the HMO movement, can limit expenses for inappropriately or unnecessarily rendered care. However, with benefit plans that encourage early intervention, managed care has not been able to fully address inappropriate or unnecessary visits to the doctor.

Managed Care and Insurance

Neither indemnifiers nor HMOs insure health, they fund the consumption of medical care. Health status or episodes of sickness are not covered events; rather, they may contribute to or in some cases cause the consumption of medical care, which is the covered event.

Risk management is a strategy of minimizing the occurrence of covered events, and the first step in risk management is effective medical underwriting. In writing group health insurance, particularly for small groups, risk management is not just a way of saving money, it is a means of survival. Because their financial interests are similar, both HMOs and indemnity health insurers historically have had a financial stake in covering only those groups likely to require less medical care to start with—lower risk groups.

In response to this situation, first the HMO business and then the managed care and insurance businesses have managed risk by focusing on controlling the supply of medical care through utilization management tools applied to the providers of care. With new health care reforms, medical underwriting is becoming more and more regulated; several states have already eliminated it completely, others only partially. Most universal access plans will eliminate it all together. The first step in risk management for the traditional health insurance business may soon become a thing of the past, putting even more pressure on utilization management models to produce savings and control costs.

MANAGING RISKS

The cost of medical care is driven, at least in part, by the demand factor. The demand factor has two components:

1. Medical need, as expressed by medical indications or deficits in health status; and
2. Individual (personal) expectations.

Medical need or health status can be impacted by health education, wellness, lifestyle modification, and public health programs. A significant part of the spending on medical services is for maladies caused by lifestyle or behavioral variables, including factors such as diet, exercise, stress, rest, and consumption of alcohol. There is a substantial body of knowledge on wellness and lifestyle programs; these programs can be effective, and can produce measurable long-term results.

Consumer expectation, however, has yet to be fully addressed as a risk factor. Experts often estimate that between 25 percent and 85 percent of ambulatory care visits, for example, are assurance visits. In other words, a substantial amount, if not a majority, of routine care, and probably some related specialty care, is for self-limiting maladies (most of which cure themselves), or the need for information.

For example, viral upper respiratory infections (URIs)—i.e., common colds—are self-limiting maladies, during the course of which most people can function normally. Methods to alleviate symptoms, such as eating hot chicken soup, do not require a doctor's advice. A managed care industry standard for HMO enrollees is that 25 percent of a given population is made up of the "worried well"—well people who nonetheless consume medical care. Moreover, managed care research data frequently shows that the majority of first visits to internists are for symptoms with substantially psychosocial causes.

Medical care that involves the diagnosis and successful treatment of an illness represents much less of the health care picture than most people assume. According to Lowell S. Levin, professor of public health at the Yale School of Medicine, "Less than 10 percent of the health status of a population is related to medical care; 90 percent of it is related to education, nutrition, accident awareness, pollution, smoking, sanitation, clean water, etc. . . .the contribution of medicine is minuscule."[1]

By the same token, a physician cannot be expected not to bill for services just because the patient has inappropriately sought help or assurance. Physicians are trained in the scientific method and, presented with a patient's complaints, this is what they will try to apply. This raises the following question: How much unnecessary care would have been delivered if the patient had not presented for treatment in the first place?

To sum up, health care cost risks fit three basic categories:

1. Costs caused by provider behavior;
2. Costs caused by medical indications or deficits in health; and
3. Costs caused by consumer behavior or expectations.

MANAGING THE DEMAND FACTOR

Benefits managers traditionally have not been equipped or empowered to manage employee health care expectations. Patients seeking advice regarding pain, function, well-being, health education, or even mental health issues historically have been referred to the family doctor; if the company had a health department, medical director, or employee assistance plan, these may also have been referral sources for the benefits manager. But more frequently, the benefits manager's role is to "sell" the positive attributes of the system, and in some cases, to encourage its use. In terms of employee expectations, however, what benefits managers can and do implement—or purchase on a service specific basis—includes:

- Administrative or management systems (including eligibility, coverage, claims payment, and reporting);
- Medical services delivery systems (including any managed care features, as well as preferred networks);
- Funding vehicles (indemnified, prepaid, or self-funded); and
- Communications programs for enrollees.

Of the above, the communications program is potentially the most powerful risk management tool when it comes to the demand for medical care services. While it may be the last part of the benefit plan a benefits manager concentrates on, it is the first part that an employee sees. The communications plan should be considered both the beginning and the end product of a benefits redesign and risk management effort.

Risk management of the demand factor (making consumer expectations rational) starts with enrollment. This should be more than a process of signing up for an entitlement program; employees need training and support in the health care purchasing process. There is probably no other area in business that grants employees more untrained and unrestricted spending power than the area of health benefits. No other budget line authority of the same size is given to an employee without specific training, background, and management guidelines.

In order to make consumers (employees and dependents) part of the demand management equation, each requires the following:

1. An understanding and working knowledge of:
   a. Their benefits plan (or access to it), and
   b. The health services business;
2. An awareness of costs;
3. An incentive and motivation for wellness; and
4. A strong consumerism ethic.

Starting with a Communications Plan

The communication plan is where it begins. Appropriate copayments, deductibles, and rational benefits are important variables, and how these items are designed and communicated will impact employee expectations. This communication, to be most effective, should be considered comprehensive training in the above four variables.

Communication of the benefit plan must impart a sense of responsibility on behalf of the insured to use it appropriately. To the extent employees understand that benefits are paid in lieu of direct compensation, they will have an incentive to pay attention.

In addition to training about benefits, training about how to access the medical delivery system is important. Education regarding the use of elective services and supportive information regarding care options can substantially affect both consumer behavior and demand for medical services. If assurance visits to physician's offices are driven by the need for information, then convenient, economical access to health information will lessen the amount of physician visits. Health information can certainly be delivered less expensively and much more quickly than through physician visits, and through a variety of communication and training methods as well.

Appropriate vehicles for these communications include:

- *Publications and written communications.* Materials such as handbooks, resource guides, and newsletters can be effective.
- *On-line telephonic coaching.* Telephone consultations or automatic systems can provide information on options in medical treatment, redirection to most appropriate level of care, general information, and reassurance.
- *Training.* In person or video training can be effective for new employee orientation, case specific reviews, and safety training—especially off-site safety.
- *Incentive design (benefit plan structure).* Utilization is shaped by what is covered as well as out-of-pocket expenses, to the extent that these have meaning for insureds. Cost awareness can be substantially impacted by service-specific copayments. For example, $10 per doctor visit will involve employees in their own health care purchasing more than will a copayment based on percentage of billed amounts. A $10 fee is real, immediate, and meaningful, even if it is less than a standard deductible arrangement.
- *On-site counselors or advisors.* In-person interaction or intervention at the onset of illness, injury, drop in productivity, or major change in job status can answer questions and provide information at the time it is most needed, leading to efficient benefit utilization.

In summary, education, coaching, training, incentives, and easily accessible supportive information are interventions that can serve to modify or manage demand and expectations. In addition, a corporate culture that supports consumerism and active participation in health care purchasing will have a far better chance of managing health care costs than would be the case without such a culture.

DEVELOPING A DEMAND FACTOR STRATEGY

The first decision in the development of a strategy to impact the demand factor is whether to buy a program, rent program services, or build your own program.

A number of companies offer services to employers and employees that provide support to enrollees and save on the bottom line. Before building a program, it may be wise to review what options are available from existing vendors. A limited list of vendors follows, as well as their own reports as to their outcomes:

Access Health Marketing (Rancho Cordova, CA). Originally founded as Ask a Nurse, Access Health provides a series of products based on a telephonic support program for insureds. Nurse advisors access current medical databases and assist insured individuals with decisions regarding care. Access Health reports that for symptom driven phone calls from insureds, 73 percent of patients accessed care at a lower level of expense and intensity than they would have before the call. Of that amount, 24 percent decided not to seek care at all. This information comes from the nine-month period ending May 1, 1993 for 150,000 insureds around the country.

Employee Managed Care Corporation (Bellevue, WA). Employee Managed Care Corporation (E=MC2) offers a product called CareWise, which combines a self-care handbook and newsletters with a toll-free number telephone counseling service. E=MC2 claims savings of $2.50 to $4.92 for every dollar spent on their product, the savings growing over time as more and more employees access their program. At Montana Power Company, a CareWise subscriber, health insurance premiums increased an average of 13.5 percent per annum from 1985 through 1992, while the norm group (Blue Shield) averaged 22 percent for the same period. In addition, comparing claims costs for selective producers for the same norm group in 1985 and CareWise groups in 1986 yields substantially lower claims costs as measured by numbers of office visits, hysterectomy, and back problems.

Options & Choices (Cheyenne, WY). Options and Choices provides an on-site support counseling and interactive case management service for all health related benefits. Counselors work with employees on disability, workers compensation, or health benefit occurrences. While Options and Choices does not provide direct treatment or therapy (other than drug testing), they do help insureds interact with their respective health care professionals and help keep employees in production and out of a disability mind set. Options and Choices declined to provide any cost savings or case data, citing competitive fears.

The Center for Corporate Health (St. Louis Park, MN). The Center for Corporate Health has been owned but independently marketed by The Traveler's insurance company since 1984. It offers a number of products and services that directly support and influence employee decision making concerning the management of their health. In addition to several communication materials options (risk appraisals, reference books, newsletters), the Center for Corporate Health offers Informed Care, a telephone-based health decision counseling service; Bright Futures, a comprehensive maternity management program; and an integrated service, the Informed Care/Employee Assistance Program. The Center reports that General Electric Capitol Corporation achieved a savings/cost ratio of 7 to 1 in 1992, saving a total of $62,001 in avoided medical procedures and absentee days for a cost of only $8,840. For 1992, Wells Fargo Bank achieved a savings-to-cost ration of 1.6 to 1, based on the same survey results, with a net savings of $272,994 on a cost investment of $171,000.

Safetyline Consultants (Chesterfield, MO). Safetyline provides an employee newsletter that focuses on off-site safety. According to the 1992 Accident Facts booklet published by the National Safety Council, employers pay an average of $327 per active employee per year for accidents by employees and dependents that are not job related. Of this $327, 91 percent comes from the price of medical care.

Accident rates vary substantially from company to company and industry to industry; however, certain companies have impacted their costs substantially by concentrating on safety. DuPont saves an estimated $150 to $200 million annually from its safety programming, which emphasizes both off-site and on-site safety.

CONCLUSION

Health benefits and direct compensation are both investments in the same resource: the company's work force. The return on investment in health related spending should be as measurable and accountable as the return on investment for other work force allocations such as training and education. Developing a strategy for measuring the impact of health care cost management interventions requires a risk management approach. The risk factors within the universe of health care costs fit three separate categories, each of which has its own specific management intervention. These risk factors are:

1. Excessive or inappropriate provider billing or services;
2. Health status deficits or medical indications for care; and
3. Employee expectations.

Managed care focuses on managing provider behavior and limiting the risk of costs from provider excesses or inappropriate service. Health improvement, wellness, or lifestyle modification programs focus on individual health status improvement. The effectiveness of programs addressing these first two factors, and the rate of return on them, may be measured using any of the many databases available for such purposes.

The last area, demand for care as driven by consumer expectations, has been the focus of this article. If over half of doctor visits are for assurance purposes, managed care solutions and wellness programs will be missing the mark at least half of the time. Consumers need information, training, and support in the health care purchasing transaction. Such programming has been shown to bring a return on investment ranging from 2:1 to 10:1.

It is clear that a complete health care cost management effort requires attention to the demand factor, and that there are already solutions that work—solutions that don't require taking anything away. Buying or building a demand factor management strategy, then, is really a matter of corporate resources and priorities.

1. *The Milwaukee Journal*, "Society should try to get rid of doctors, he says, not coddle them," May 17, 1993, Page D1.

29. Installing Group Long-Term-Care Insurance

Scott J. Macey   Peter A. Hinrichs   Thomas W. Meagher

Employers considering providing long-term-care insurance as an employee benefit must grapple with a number of complex issues concerning plan design, carrier selection, and plan implementation. This article discusses and analyzes the relevant issues, including the current legislative environment concerning long-term-care benefit plans. It also presents a case study of an employer that successfully installed such a plan.

INSTALLING GROUP LONG-TERM-CARE INSURANCE

In the past few years there has been an extraordinary amount of attention given to the growing long-term-care needs of the expanding elderly population of the United States. In the process, the understanding of long-term care has become clearer, and the gaps in insurance coverage with respect to long-term-care expenses have become well known within the human resource departments of more corporations and among the elderly. As the ranks of our elderly have increased, a group insurance marketplace has gradually evolved, and such evolution continues today. Insurers have now begun to devote substantial resources toward the development and marketing of group long-term-care insurance products that permit employers to offer their employees the opportunity to obtain long-term-care insurance protection as part of their employee benefits package. Despite the proliferation of new long-term-care products and recent actions on the part of federal and state regulators, there may still be substantial risks for the unwary.

This article attempts to reflect the experiences of a large employer that recently offered a group long-term-care insurance program to its employees. The article also addresses tax and legal considerations applicable to long-term-care programs offered by employers of all sizes. The issues faced by the employer in our case study are typical of those that will be faced by other employers that are considering a group long-term-care insurance program for their employees. In presenting this case study, we attempt to alert the reader to the concerns of the employer as well as the factors that enter into the final decision-making process.

CASE STUDY

It is estimated that today 150 insurance companies are selling long-term-care insurance products. Although most of these companies offer only individual policies, 15 to 20 percent offer employer-sponsored or group association plans. The companies offering group policies tend to be the larger insurers. In addition, in some areas, group long-term-care policies may also be sold by local Blue Cross/Blue Shield organizations.

The number of Americans covered by long-term-care insurance policies is approaching two million. Although only about 5 percent of this number are covered under employer-sponsored plans, these plans are the most rapidly expanding portion of the marketplace. It is expected that by the end of 1992 over two hundred employers will offer long-term-care coverage to their employees. The above figures are exclusive of accelerated death-benefit riders, which have been recently introduced by the life insurance industry as amendments to existing life insurance contracts to permit limited death benefits to be paid to certain terminally ill insureds.

Why Consider Group Long-Term-Care Insurance?

As the publicity surrounding the long-term-care needs of our elderly population increases, the benefits planning division for our case-study employer began to research the issues involved. After a thorough analysis, they found that indeed their group medical plans did not cover the custodial care required to support individuals with chronic physical and mental disabilities who would find it difficult to take care of themselves over an extended period. They also found that less than 2 percent of these uncovered expenses were paid by Medicare, and that Medicaid imposed onerous "spend-down" requirements before providing coverage. Clearly, employees had a significant gap in insurance protection as active employees and even more so as they moved into retirement.

Not surprisingly, at both the employer and employee levels misconceptions exist as to the coverage provided by existing medical plans. Moreover, the gaps take on an added seriousness when employees themselves are not aware of the serious financial risks they face because of this gap in coverage. Due to employees' lack of awareness—or worse, expectation that all of their health needs are covered by the employers' existing benefit package—few employees have purchased an individual long-term-care policy to cover this risk. With respect to our case study, once the gap in coverage was recognized by the employers' benefit planners, a possible solution became apparent: If a cost-effective long-term-care program could be provided to employees, the gaps could be bridged in what was otherwise thought to be a comprehensive benefit program.

From the employee's perspective, there would be certain advantages to the implementation of a group long-term-care plan by the employer: group insurance is inherently less expensive than individual insurance; the employee would have the convenience of payroll deductions; the evidence of insurability required under a group plan would be less stringent than that required for an individual policy; and the employee could rely on the employer to select an insurance carrier that was financially sound and that offered appropriate coverage and value.

From the employers' perspective, there were also certain advantages to offering group long-term-care insurance coverage to its employees: the employees would appreciate the convenience and the value of a group long-term-care plan; the employer would incur little expense if the plan were offered on an employee-pay-all basis (as most group long-term-care plans are structured); and finally, the employer's employee benefit program would be comprehensive and would continue to remain highly competitive.

There were also some perceived disadvantages, from the employer's perspective, to offering group long-term-care insurance coverage to its employees, such as the difficulty of selecting both a suitable insurance carrier and assuring an appropriate level of benefit coverage that was fairly priced. There was also the possibility that the government might eventually preempt the long-term-care field by expanding Medicare coverage to include long-term-care services. Because federal budgetary constraints have kept the possibility of a significant expansion of Medicare benefits to a minimum, and because actuarial and benefit consultants were available to assist in the design of a comprehensive long-term-care insurance program, the employer decided to begin the process of designing a group long-term-care insurance program for its employees. The first step in the process was for the employer to meet with its benefit planners and advisors to discuss the perceived gaps in existing coverage, possible features of a long-term-care program, and the need to obtain group long-term-care insurance bids from several insurance companies.

Issues Involved in Program Design

Before sending a request for proposal to a selected group of insurance companies, the employer worked closely with its benefit planners and advisors to determine the objective of its long-term-care insurance program. From this process certain objectives emerged:

- A favorable long-term-care plan must offer attractive initial premium rates to a broad spectrum of potential participants who were located in widely varying cost areas across the country.
- The long-term-care plan would be offered on an employee-pay-all basis. This decision was reached for economic reasons and because of the certain tax consequences for the employee if employer contributions were involved.
- The long-term-care premium rates should be based on a participant's entry age and should be designed to be level throughout a participant's lifetime. Premium rates could be increased on a class basis, however, should experience be worse than expected.
- Coverage should be guaranteed renewable (i.e., as long as premiums were paid the insurance could not be cancelled). Thus, it was important that the plan be well-designed, carefully underwritten, and the initial premium rates set at a sufficient level so as to keep the risk of future increases to a minimum without discouraging enrollment.
- The coverage provided must cover the catastrophic costs of long-term care (a minimum of five years of lifetime benefits would be considered), and it must avoid the pitfalls and criticisms that were being voiced by various consumer groups about long-term-care products, such as renewability and misleading advertisements.
- The coverage must keep pace with increasing costs in health care.
- The underwriting must be simple and up-front; post-claim underwriting would not be permitted. (Post-claim underwriting occurs in situations in which insurance carriers accept premiums for coverage but then attempt to avoid paying claims by arguing that the insured did not satisfy coverage criteria at the time the policy was originally issued.)
- The coverage should also provide for a grace period and reinstatement in the event the individual's coverage lapses.

From the employers' perspective, a request for proposal would obviously be sent only to those insurance carriers with the highest-rated financial and claims-paying records and whose products were likely to meet all or most of the above criteria.

As the responses to the request for proposals were reviewed, the plan design evolved. Presented below are the features of that plan design and some commentary as to why those features were considered desirable.

Coverage Options

Employees would be offered two coverage options:

1. *Nursing-home-only coverage.* A plan that offers protection against the high cost of nursing home care. All levels of care that are provided in a licensed nursing home would be covered (skilled, intermediate, and custodial care). In addition, as a free, optional service, professional advisors would be available to meet with the insureds once they became eligible for benefits to provide assistance in making decisions about long-term care.

2. *Comprehensive coverage.* A comprehensive plan that provides the nursing-home benefits described above as well as the following additional services:
   - Hospital care—Health care and support services that are provided either at home or in a licensed hospice facility to assist individuals who are terminally ill.
   - Respite care—Temporary care that is provided to allow a care provider (usually a family member or a friend) a chance to take time off.
   - Home health care—Care that is received at home from a nurse, a physical therapist, an occupational therapist, a speech therapist, or a home health aide from a licensed home care agency.
   - Adult day care—Health support and rehabilitative services outside of the home provided to people who are unable to care for themselves independently during the day but are able to live at home at night.
   - Ongoing advisory services—Care advisory services provided by a specialist who will coordinate various types of care, arrange for appropriate services, monitor the care received, and assist with altering the care plan as needs change.

Ideally, in any such program all employees should be covered under the comprehensive plan. Unfortunately, not all employees can afford this level of coverage. On the other hand, some employees might be able to afford the more comprehensive coverage but would prefer the nursing-home-only option in the expectation that, should the need arise, members of their family would be available to provide care in the home. Thus, the employer would want a long-term-care program that would permit employees to choose between comprehensive coverage and nursing-home-only coverage, based on the employees' perceived needs and expectations.

Daily Benefit Options

Under each of the coverage options, three daily benefit options would be available: $60, $100, and $140. The daily benefit amount is the maximum amount that would be paid for each day that the patient is confined in a nursing home. Services such as home care, in-home hospice care, and adult day care would be paid at half this amount.

If employees are located nationwide in a wide range of nursing-home cost areas, or if they can be expected to relocate after retirement to a wide range of cost areas, an employer may decide to offer a range of daily benefit amounts to its employees. This approach would give the employees the opportunity to choose a benefit level that best fits their needs as well as their pocketbooks. Nursing-home coverage today in some metropolitan areas can be as much as $150 or more a day. With ever-increasing nursing home costs, inflation protection is also a necessary ingredient of a long-term-care program. Additionally, some employers have designed long-term-care programs to provide reimbursement for custodial and intermediate care at half the skilled nursing-care daily rate. In order to avoid disputes by employees seeking the full daily benefit amount (when, for example, the cost of custodial care is in excess of half the skilled nursing care daily rate), the better practice may be to provide the full daily benefit amount for skilled, intermediate, and custodial care.

Maximum Lifetime Benefit

For each choice of coverage (i.e., comprehensive or nursing-home-only), a maximum lifetime benefit (in dollars) would correspond to each daily benefit option. The maximum lifetime benefit is the total benefit dollars available to an insured during his or her lifetime. The nursing-home-only coverage provides a minimum of five years of coverage ($109,500, $182,500, and $255,500 for the $60, $100, and $140 daily benefits, respectively), whereas the comprehensive coverage provides a minimum of seven years of coverage ($153,300, $255,500, and $357,700 for the $60, $100, and $140 daily benefits, respectively). The lifetime maximums are arrived at by multiplying the daily benefit amount (e.g., $60 a day coverage) by the minimum number of years of benefits under the plan (e.g., five years).

A very high proportion (80 to 97 percent depending on age and sex) of all nursing home confinements are expected to terminate in less than five years. An even higher proportion will terminate in less than seven years. It should be noted that in some cases, a lifetime maximum benefit expressed as a maximum dollar amount can last longer than one expressed as a maximum number of days. For example, if an insured chooses a $100 daily benefit and the nursing home actually costs $50 a day, the benefit will last twice as long due to the maximum benefit being expressed as a dollar amount as opposed to days of whole or partial benefits.

Eligibility for Benefits

Eligibility for benefits under either the comprehensive or nursing-home-only option is based on the inability to perform certain activities of daily living (ADLs). The ADLs that will normally be considered are eating, dressing, bathing, mobility, transferring (e.g., from bed to chair), toileting, and continence. Benefits may be authorized when an insured is unable to perform three or more ADLs without human assistance, as determined by the insurance carrier. The need for assistance may be due to physical disabilities, cognitive impairments (such as memory loss or need for supervision due to brain disease such as Alzheimer's), or both.

Decisions by the insurance carrier with respect to coverage may be made by a nurse based on information provided by the insured's doctor.

Once approved for a long-term-care benefits, an insured will begin to receive payments after an initial waiting period. The waiting period for nursing-home benefits was designed to be 60 days. The waiting period for home care and respite benefits was designed to be 30 days. Only days of care for which the insured is required to pay for services received are counted toward satisfying the waiting period. Thus, for example, if the insured is incapacitated and cared for at home by a family member, such days will not likely be counted toward any waiting period.

The definition of ADLs varies from insurance carrier to insurance carrier. Also, some insurance carriers will pay benefits when an insured is unable to perform two or more ADLs (rather than three or more ADLs). Almost all insurance carriers recognize cognitive impairments as well as physical disabilities. The use of a waiting period before benefits are payable serves the same function as a deductible does in a major medical plan: It keeps the cost of the insurance plan down by eliminating those short-term claims that an insured can be expected to pay for from his or her own resources without causing financial distress, thus enabling the plan to provide coverage for the long-term-care claims that would otherwise prove to be financially catastrophic to the insured. Waiting periods of 30, 60, 90, and 120 days are common. The employer in our case study chose the 30/60 day combination as a good balance between cost and coverage. In addition, any analysis of a long-term-care product must carefully examine the insurance carrier's claims-paying history and should determine what percentage of claims result in long-term-care benefits being paid. Many times simply identifying the ADLs is not enough to determine the insurance carrier's criteria for claims payments. Prospective purchasers of long-term-care coverage should insist on knowing the full criteria applied by the insurance carrier to determine if an insured is unable to perform an ADL.

Inflation Protection

An insured should be offered the opportunity to increase the daily benefit to an amount that reflects the inflationary increases that have occurred in long-term care since the last inflation protection offer was made. Insureds can do this without proof of insurability as long as they are less than age 85 and have not been eligible for benefits (i.e., in a waiting period or actually receiving long-term-care benefits) during 12 months prior to the offering. An increase in the daily benefit amount also increases the maximum lifetime benefit. The cost of the incremental increase is based on the insured's age at the time the increase is made.

An inflation protection provision is necessary if an insured's benefit amount is to provide adequate coverage at the time of a claim. Insurance carriers offer a variety of inflation protection options. The option described above offers the lowest initial premium rates and allows benefit amounts to be tailored to emerging inflation levels. An alternative approach is to provide automatic increases in benefit amounts (e.g., 5 percent a year) and include the cost of the increases in the initial premium rates. This approach is more costly initially (but not necessarily in the long run) and is less flexible in terms of benefits and costs than other approaches that may be considered by an employer. Other alternatives are available, such as permitting employees to purchase added coverage every few years or permitting employees to purchase incremental amounts periodically without evidence of insurability.

Premium Waiver

Premiums are waived while an insured is receiving nursing-home benefits. However, they are not waived if the insured is receiving home-care benefits.

This is the typical waiver-of-premium provision offered by insurance carriers that use the ADL approach to defining eligibility for benefits. It is significantly less costly than a plan that also provides waiver of premium while a person is receiving home health-care benefits.

Return of Premium

The comprehensive form of coverage may have a feature that returns long-term-care premiums in the event of the insured's death. The insured's estate may receive a percentage of the premium the insured had paid up to age 65, minus any claims paid, once the insured had participated in the long-term-care plan for at least four years. The percentage returned ranges from 20 percent after four years to 100 percent after 20 years.

The return of premium upon death is the least expensive nonforfeiture benefit that can be offered. Other nonforfeiture options that can be offered include return of premium after the policy has been in effect for a predetermined number of years, extended term insurance, and reduced paid-up insurance in the event of lapse of coverage. In our case study, the employer chose the return of premium on death option (and then only under the comprehensive coverage) in order to keep the cost of coverage as affordable to its employees as possible.

Portability

An employee and other participating family members have the opportunity to continue coverage even if the employee leaves the employer or retires. Because of the lifetime nature of this insurance plan, it is essential that an insured be permitted to continue coverage and avoid the need to provide new evidence as to insurability after he or she terminates employment with the employer.

Guaranteed Renewable Coverage

An employee's coverage under the long-term-care program is guaranteed renewable. Thus, as long as the employee continues paying for long-term-care coverage, the coverage will not be cancelled. The guaranteed renewable coverage is obviously a very important guaranteed renewable. It assures the employee that even if his or her health deteriorates, the insurance company cannot cancel the coverage.

Financial Considerations

A very important aspect of the bidding process was the analysis of the cost of the long-term-care insurance plans that were being offered by the insurance carriers. The employer in our case study wanted to understand the actuarial assumptions that were used to determine the premium rates and the formulas that would be used to change these rates in the future. Also, because long-term-care plans generate a high level of policy reserves over time, the employer wanted a portion of these plan assets invested in equities, and, should it find it necessary to change insurance carriers in the future, it wanted a provision in the group long-term-care insurance contract that would permit the transfer of these policy reserves to a succeeding insurance carrier.

Long-term-care reserves are particularly important to an employer purchasing long-term-care insurance. The premiums charged to insureds depend in part on the rate of return on the insurance company assets underlying the reserves. For large employers, the opportunity may exist to have input in the mix of assets used to achieve this rate of return. Obviously, the greater the rate of return, the greater the likelihood that premiums may be held at reasonable levels. The financial considerations associated with purchasing long-term care are discussed in more detail below.

Premium Rates

The premium rates of all insurance carriers were determined on an entry-age-level basis. This means the rates would not increase as an insured got older, nor would they increase should an insured receive benefits under the plan. The rates could, however, be adjusted for an insured's age group if plan costs turn out to be higher than expected. Typically, insurance carriers will charge less for younger insureds in anticipation of having a longer period during which to obtain premiums.

Each carrier submitted the actuarial assumptions that were used to develop its premium rates. This enabled the employer, together with its advisors, to judge the reasonableness of the proposed premium rates and to compare rates among other insurance carriers and among different levels of coverage.

The premium rates of a few insurance carriers were considerably higher than those of their competitors and were deemed excessive. Typically, such high rates may be due in part to the lack of mature data for the long-term-care insurance market, including claims experience. Thus, many insurers are proceeding very cautiously in this area, although we expect the disparity in rates to lessen as the data become more developed. On the other hand, the premium rates of a few insurance carriers appeared so low that the employer became concerned that there was a high likelihood that they would have to be significantly increased in the future.

Premium Rate Guarantees

The employer asked for and received a guarantee from most of the insurance carriers that the initial premium rates would not be increased during a predetermined length of time (e.g., five years).

Expense Loadings

Each insurance carrier submitted the expense-loading formulas used to develop its premium rates. This was an important consideration to the employer because each premium dollar used by an insurance carrier for its administrative expenses would not be available to pay long-term-care benefits.

Renewal Formula

Because each insurance carrier reserved the right to change premium rates after the initial guarantee period ended, it was important that the employer understand the basis on which the renewal rates would be determined. This feature was discussed thoroughly with the finalists in the bidding process. In general, it can be said that each insurance carrier's renewal formula would give some degree of recognition to the employer's actual experience in forecasting future experience, with the amount of recognition depending on the number of employees participating in the plan and the length of time the plan had been in effect. The insurance carriers took varying positions on how past profits or losses in the experience account maintained by the insurance carrier for the employer would be reflected in future premium rates. Each of the insurance carriers reserved the right to change its expense-loading formula and the discount rate used to obtain present values.

Having this renewal information from the insurance company and understanding the actuarial assumptions that went into the initial premium rates, the employer was in a much better position to judge the reasonableness of any rate changes proposed by the insurance carrier in the future. It is important to recognize that these potential future rate changes can go either way: Premium rates can be expected to decrease if claims experience turns out better than expected, and to increase if claims experience turns out worse than expected.

Insurance Company Reserves

Because premium rates are determined on an entry-age-level basis and the benefits provided by the insurance plan increase dramatically with increasing age, very substantial policy reserves are accumulated over the life of the group policy. Therefore, the employer felt that costs under the plan could be reduced substantially if a portion of the plan assets supporting the reserves were invested in equities rather than in fixed-income securities. A considerable amount of time was spent negotiating this aspect of the long-term-care policy with the insurance carriers. A primary objective of both the employer and the insurance carriers was to assure the safety and adequacy of the assets backing up the plan's benefit obligations at all times. In addition, the insurance carriers had to be content with various insurance laws and regulations and with accounting requirements regarding the investment of policy reserves.

In the end, a satisfactory solution was arrived at: A portion of plan assets would be invested in equities commensurate with the degree of safety needed to assure that all future benefit obligations could be provided from plan assets and future scheduled premiums.

Transfer of Reserves

It was hoped that the business relationship between the employer and the insurance carrier selected to underwrite the group long-term-care plan would be an ongoing relationship. However, in the event the employer found it necessary to terminate this relationship, the employer wanted to be able to transfer the assets accumulated under the plan to a succeeding insurance carrier. To this end, the employer sought and eventually obtained a provision in the group policy that permitted this transfer.

Notionally, the assets in the plan represent active life policy reserves (those reserves resulting from the level premium rate basis), disabled life reserves (those reserves resulting from submitted claims), and unreported claim reserves and any plan surplus (or deficit). The insurance carriers took varying positions with regard to releasing these reserves, with some carriers being reluctant to release reserves associated with submitted and unreported claims. Some insurance carriers would give an employee the option of remaining with the original insurance carrier while others would not offer such option. Most insurance carriers required that the succeeding carrier provide a participant with benefits equal to or greater than the original benefits so that there would be no loss of coverage upon transfer.

The employer felt that it was very important that this reserve transfer provision be in the group policy. Such a provision gives the employer greater assurance that renewal premium rates will be determined in an equitable fashion, and gives the employer the opportunity, without loss to its employees, to change insurance carriers should the employer be dissatisfied with the services provided by the original carrier.

Implementation Issues

Despite the best possible design of a long-term-care plan, employee response will be lukewarm at best unless the program is effectively communicated.

Keeping enrollment at a maximum requires that the employer begin the communication effort as early in the process as possible. The communication process, which in many cases must begin as an education program, can begin even before a decision as to the final plan design is made. As with any new program, employees must first feel comfortable that they understand the general intent of long-term-care benefits. In many cases, employers begin the process by meeting with small groups of employees to get their thoughts on possible benefit designs.

In implementing a long-term-care plan, best results are obviously attained if the program is introduced separately as a stand-alone program. From the perspective of the employer in our case study, a separate program offering was not practical. Because the program was to be offered during the employer's regular annual open enrollment period, a number of steps were taken to ensure optimal results.

- *Management and benefits personnel were informed.* Before beginning the employee communication process, it is advisable to inform management and benefits personnel about the nature of the long-term-care program and its intended benefits. Before the program was rolled out to employees, the employer wanted to be certain that the individuals who would be responsible for communicating the information fully understood the program's intent. Employees seemed to feel a greater degree of comfort when the program, particularly an employee-pay-all program, was effectively endorsed by their managers and benefit personnel.
- *Employee information, announcing the future offering of the plan, was distributed.* The employer began the education process by including a description of long-term care in its general benefit newsletters and included some common questions and answers that would be of interest to employees.
- *A separate information packet was mailed.* As the long-term-care program was to be introduced in conjunction with a flexible benefits programs, a separate booklet describing long-term-care benefits was included. We believe mailing this material to the employees' residences resulted in a greater percentage of family members reading the material and ultimately enrolling themselves, their parents, or parents-in-law in the program.
- *Insurance company assistance was requested.* Because long-term care is typically an insured arrangement, the employer was advised to draw on the extensive resources of the insurance company. These resources may include pamphlets on long-term-care, videos, and toll-free telephone numbers to ask questions, as well as statistics on long-term care.
- *Employee meetings were held.* Despite the most well-prepared written materials, employees will inevitably have additional questions. Though this can often be handled by means of a toll-free telephone number to a benefits office, employees appeared to appreciate the value of being able to listen to the answers to other employees' questions in a group setting.

TAX AND LEGAL ANALYSIS

In considering such a program, current legal concerns and requirements as well as proposed state and federal legislation, must be taken into account.

Tax and Legal Considerations

In establishing a long-term-care plan, an employer should be comfortable that the program will be accorded favorable tax and regulatory treatment under current law.

From an employer's perspective, the Internal Revenue Code should ideally provide that an employee may receive long-term-care benefits without being required to include the value of the benefits in his or her gross income. Moreover, the Code should optimally provide that an employee may pay long-term-care premiums on a before-tax basis, or the employer-paid long-term-care premiums should not result in income begin imputed to an employee. Unfortunately, the law with respect to long-term-care benefit is far from clear. Nonetheless, a review of the current provisions of federal tax law provides some guidance regarding the tax treatment of premium payments and provides support for concluding that an employee's receipt of long-term-care benefits should not be taxable to the employee.

The definition of long-term care is of critical importance to a determination of the federal tax treatment to be accorded long-term-care benefits. Although the definition of long-term care may vary among insurers, it may be defined generally as coverage for certain health-related and personal-care services for individuals who may require assistance with ADLs. Long-term care provides benefits that assist individuals with chronic physical or mental disabilities that make it difficult for them to care for themselves over an extended period of time. Long-term care often also involves custodial skills (i.e., skills that many adults can provide, such as assistance with bathing, cooking, and mobility) rather than medical skills.

In analyzing the appropriate tax treatment applicable to a long-term-care program, the employer in our case study examined several possible interpretations of existing law and existing technical pronouncements. Such tax treatment includes treatment of premiums paid by employers and employees, benefits received by employees, employer and employee deductions, use of long-term care in cafeteria plans, and related issues.

One of the most important sections of the Code that has an impact on the federal tax treatment of long-term care is the section defining *medical care*. If a long-term-care plan can be treated as medical care, at least in part, it permits both employers and employees to benefit from its tax-favored status.

Section 213(d) of the Code defines expenses paid for medical care as amounts paid for the diagnosis, cure, mitigation, treatment, or prevention of disease, or for the purpose of affecting any structure or prevention of disease, or for the purpose of affecting any structure or function of the body. It includes amounts paid for transportation primarily for and essential to medical care, or for insurance (including amounts paid as premiums under Part B of Title XVIII of the Social Security Act, relating to supplementary medical insurance for the aged—i.e., Medicare) covering medical care described under the Code.

In determining whether a particular form of benefit constitutes an expense for medical care, the case of *Estate of Myrtle P. Dodge*[1] is particularly instructive. In *Dodge*, the court held that it is the nature of the services rendered and not the qualifications of the provider that determine whether a service is properly a medical expense. Thus, from an employer's perspective, any analysis of long-term-care coverages requires a careful review of the types of services being provided under the long-term-care program, regardless of whether the provider is considered a medical professional.

Premium Payments by Employer

In analyzing long-term-care benefits under the medical care provisions of Section 213(d) of the Code, many employers have taken the position that employees should not be taxed on the value of any employer-paid premiums. These employers may have relied on Section 105(b) of the Code, which states that an employees' gross income does not include amounts paid by the employer directly or indirectly toward medical care for the employee, or his or her spouse and dependents. In examining long-term-care benefits that are provided to an individual in a nursing home, the types of care provided (e.g., dressing, bathing, and feeding) may appear to go beyond what is traditionally known and considered as medical care.

Existing Internal Revenue Service guidance indicates that in order for medical and nonmedical nursing-home expenses to be properly treated as medical care, it is necessary to examine the principal reason for the individual's placement in the nursing home. In the now familiar case of *W.B. Counts v. Commissioner*,[2] the Tax Court concluded that if the need for medical care is primary, incidental meals and lodging will likely be included as medical care. Under Revenue ruling 76-106, however, the IRS concluded that if medical care is not primary, then only medical care expenses would be recognized; incidental, nonmedical expenses would not be included as medical care. Thus, an allocation of expenses between medical and nonmedical services would be necessary.

Due to the nature of long-term-care coverage, however, a more conservative alternative to excluding the entire amount of long-term-care premiums would be to treat only a portion of the employer-paid premiums for long-term-care coverage as medical care expenses. That portion of the premium would then be excludable from an employees' gross income. For employers who pay all or part of long-term-care coverage for their employees, it may be advisable to separately state the amounts payable toward traditional medical-care coverage from that portion payable toward the custodial aspects of long-term-care coverage. At a minimum, such an allocation would provide strong support for excluding at least a portion of the employer-paid premium from an employee's gross income.

From the perspective of the employer in our case study, this issue did not have to be addressed directly, for the intent from the outset had been to introduce a comprehensive, employee-pay-all program without increasing employer costs.

Premium Payments by Employee

To the extent an employee purchases long-term-care insurance with after-tax contributions, existing tax law provisions appear to be favorable to permit the long-term-care benefits to be excluded from the recipient's gross income. Section 104(a)(3) of the Code exempts from income any benefits received for personal injuries or sickness under individually purchased accident or health insurance plans. Because the definitions of "personal injury" and "sickness," as defined in Section 1.105-4(g) of the Treasury Regulations, may both be read to generally include long-term-care benefits as accident or health coverage, the employee should not be taxed upon receipt of long-term-care benefits.

Although the IRS has not yet ruled definitively on the issue, employers may draw an analogy to a prior ruling issued by the IRS in connection with the calculation of reserves maintained by life insurance companies. In Private Letter Ruling 8744057, the IRS determined that group long-term care should constitute accident and health insurance in computing life insurance company reserves. In that private letter ruling, the IRS concluded that reserves held under a long-term-care product were computed on the basis of life, health, and accident contingencies, and the policy thus qualified as a guaranteed renewable accident and health insurance policy under Section 816(e) of the Code. Although not free from doubt, the benefits provided by long-term care seem to fall squarely within the ambit of accident or health insurance coverage.

Thus, long-term-care benefits may be received by the employee without being included in the employee's gross income.

Long-Term-Care Benefits Received by Employee

Section 105(c) of the Code provides that: an employee's gross income does not include amounts paid by an employer or attributable to contributions by an employer to the extent that such amounts constitute payment for the permanent loss or loss of use of a member or function of the body, that are computed in relation to the nature of the injury, without regard to the duration of the employee's absence from work. This means that in reviewing the types of coverage provided by long-term-care policies (e.g., coverage for Alzheimer's disease or the inability to walk or clothe oneself), employers have a reasonable argument for concluding that long-term-care benefits are entirely excludable from an employees' gross income, particularly to the extent the inability to perform ADLs "[affect] *any* structure or function of the body" or "constitute payment for the permanent loss or loss of use of a member or function of the body" [emphasis added]. Moreover, Section 105(b) of the Code further excludes from an employee's gross income amounts paid to reimburse the employee for expenses incurred for medical care notwithstanding the fact that the employer has contributed to the cost of such coverage.

Section 104 of the Code provides that an employees' gross income does not generally include amounts received through accident or health insurance when the insurance is attributable to contributions by the employee for personal injuries or sickness. In examining the possible tax treatment of long-term care, the employer in our case study closely examined what type of benefits would fit within the definitions of "personal injury" and "sickness." The results of such an examination were generally favorable for concluding that long-term-care benefits should not be includable in an employee's gross income. Section 1.105-4(g) of the Treasury Regulations defines "personal injury" as externally caused sudden hurt or damage to the body brought about by an identifiable event, and defines "sickness" as mental illnesses and all bodily infirmities and disorders other than personal injuries. After reviewing the issue with its legal counsel, and in the absence o any conflicting Internal Revenue Service guidance, the employer was in a position to conclude that is employees would not be taxed on the receipt of long-term-care benefits.

Employer Deductions

To the extent an employer considers contributing toward the cost of long-term-care coverage, it wants to be certain that its contributions are currently deductible. Before concluding that a deduction for amounts paid toward long-term-care premiums is available to an employer, the employer must first consider the design of the long-term-care program. Assuming an acceptable design, premiums paid by an employer should be deductible when paid.

A word of caution to employers on the issue of deductibility. Section 162 of the Code, which addresses ordinary and necessary expenses of a trade or business, restricts an employer's deductions for contributions to any arrangement that has the effect of deferring the receipt of compensation. Section 1.162-10 of the Treasury Regulations indicates that, with respect to any program that may defer the receipt of compensation, amounts deductible will be governed by Section 404 of the Code. Unfortunately the regulations under Code Section 404 do not provide any clear guidance on whether programs of a nature similar to long-term care constitute arrangements for the deferral of compensation. Although long-term-care coverage is not normally thought to result in the deferral of compensation, certain features of a plan could raise this issue if employer contributions are involved.

Two features of a long-term-care program that may affect the deductibility of employer contributions are when the long-term-care plan provides *nonforfeiture values* and when *level premiums* are involved. Nonforfeiture value with respect to a long-term-care program means, among other things, a program that provides for the return of premiums after a particular number of years. In the context of long-term care, level premiums are those premiums paid for long-term-care coverage that are equal, or level as to amount, each year. A level premium arrangement is typically designed to require premiums greater than costs in the earlier years so that the premiums in the later years (when premiums might otherwise be prohibitively expensive) will be less than the costs in the later years.

Although there may be arguments to the contrary, if a long-term-care plan is designed with either of these two features (i.e., nonforfeiture values or level premiums), the IRS could attempt to argue that at least in part, the program results in the deferral of compensation and should not currently be deductible. In our case study, the employer considered these issues and was able to address them to its satisfaction. Because the employer wanted a level premium arrangement, it added a simple design feature to alleviate much of the concern over whether level premiums result in the deferral of compensation. This design feature provided that the employee must contribute premiums each year in order for coverage to continue in force for that year; coverage would be discontinued if a premium was missed. Thus, the employer was in a position to argue that premiums paid in one year were not being used to purchase a benefit in a subsequent year.

Although it is not clear that this argument alone will be sufficient to counter any deferral of compensation objections asserted by the IRS, the employer's position on the issue should be strengthened if premiums are required to be paid each year. As to the issue of nonforfeiture values, because the employer in our case study did not contribute to the cost of the long-term-care coverage, the issue of its impact on the employer's deduction did not arise.

Employee Deductions

For employees paying long-term-care premiums with after-tax dollars, the issue of whether these premiums are deductible as a medical care expense (subject to the 7½ percent threshold amount under Section 213(a) of the Code) should be addressed.

From an employer's perspective, the employer should not position itself as providing legal or tax advice to its employees. Moreover, based on existing law, it is difficult if not impossible for the employer to know with any degree of certainty what portion of an employee's long-term-care bills are for medical care as compared to custodial services. Any conclusions to be drawn with respect to the issue of deductibility of after-tax employee premiums will involve an analysis of all the relevant facts and circumstances.

Although we are not aware of the issue of long-term care being reviewed in the Tax Court or in the context of private letter rulings issued by the IRS, our review of analogous decisions suggests that in order for an employee's expense to be properly treated as a medical care expense, it must have a relatively close relationship to the employee's mental or physical condition. Thus, for example, if the custodial expense is incidental to medical care expenses incurred on behalf of the insured it should be deductible as a medical care expense. Employees intending to deduct long-term-care premiums, particularly with respect to programs having nonforfeiture values, should be cautioned that any such deduction should be carefully reviewed with the employee's tax advisors in view of the absence of any definitive guidance from the IRS and its restrictive view of payments toward custodial-only services.

Cafeteria Plans

Employers considering long-term-care benefits often intend that such programs be included as part of a cafeteria plan as an optional benefit. For employers considering this benefit, it may be difficult, if not impossible absent rather severe design changes, to include long-term care in a cafeteria plan. The primary difficulty with including long-term-care benefits in a cafeteria plan lies, once again, with the design of the program and current limitations under the Code.

In order for long-term care to be included in a cafeteria plan on a pretax basis, it must be identified as a form of nontaxable benefits permitted under Section 125 of the Code. The nontaxable benefits recognized under the cafeteria plan rules include group term life insurance under Section 79 of the Code and accident and health insurance under Section 106 of the Code. Although as discussed earlier, long-term care may arguably be treated as accident and health insurance and thus be one of the nontaxable benefits recognized under the cafeteria plan rules, the design of the long-term-care plan could still be of concern.

Potential problems may arise if, for example, the long-term-care plan is designed to provide nonforfeiture values or is structured, as is most common, to provide for level premiums. As discussed earlier with respect to the deduction of employer contributions, the use of nonforfeiture values and, arguably, level premiums, may be viewed by the IRS as deferring the receipt of compensation beyond the period of coverage, which is prohibited under Section 1.125-2, Question and Answer 5(a) of the proposed Treasury Regulations. Essentially, Section 1.125-2 states that amounts contributed in one year may not be used to purchase benefits in a subsequent year. The proposed Treasury Regulations further provide that unused benefits may not be carried over from year to year.

The problem arises when nonforfeiture values are included and appear to result in benefits (e.g., premiums refunds) being purchased in early years to be received in later years. Although a long-term-care plan may be designed so as not to provide nonforfeiture values, subject to any state regulatory requirements, the inclusion of nonforfeiture provisions appears to create a "deferred compensation" program that is prohibited from being included in a cafeteria plan. Similarly, although arguments to the contrary may be made, level premiums could likewise be considered as a possible deferral of compensation unless, among other things, the plan provides for termination of coverage upon cessation of level premium payments.

Other forms of long-term-care designs such as cash values, reduced paid-up coverage, and return-of-premium features may likewise raise deferral-of-compensation concerns with respect to their inclusion in a long-term-care plan that is intended to be part of a cafeteria plan. Generally, to the extent a long-term-care product design avoids cash values or savings and investment features, it may be possible to include it in a cafeteria plan, although there is no definitive authority yet to support such treatment.

In addition, although cafeteria plans permit participation by employees, spouses, and dependents, many long-term-care programs are offered to cover retirees, parents, and parents-in-law of employees. Although retirees may participate in cafeteria plans under appropriate circumstances, unless the parents or parents-in-law are dependents of the employee for federal tax purposes, they wold not be able to participate in a long-term-care plan that is part of a cafeteria plan. Employers may solve this problem by simply establishing a second long-term-care plan outside of the cafeteria plan for nondependents of the employee.

Other Accident and Health Plan Issues

Because the long-term-care plan is treated as an accident and health plan, additional issues under ERISA and COBRA must be addressed.

ERISA. The Employee Retirement Income Security Act of 1974 establishes rules and regulations with respect to employee welfare benefit plans sponsored by employers. Section 3(1) of ERISA defines an "employe welfare plan" as any plan maintained by an employer to provide for its employees medical, surgical, or hospital-care benefits or benefits in the event of sickness, accident, or disability. Based on our earlier analysis, it would appear that long-term care should fit within the definition of an employee welfare plan under ERISA. ERISA does, however, exclude certain group insurance arrangements from the definition of an employee welfare plan when the employer's involvement is minimal (i.e., no employer contributions, voluntary employee participation, no employer endorsement of the program other than to collect premiums through payroll deductions, and no consideration received by the employer in connection with the program).

If the long-term-care plan is determined to be an employee welfare plan, ERISA requires that the employer have a plan document, distribute summary plan descriptions to participants, file annual reports, and be subject to fiduciary requirements.

COBRA. An ancillary issue to treatment of long-term-care insurance as an accident or health plan is that it may also be considered as a group health plan under Section 4980B of the Code, thus subjecting it to the continuation-of-health-coverage provisions under the Consolidated Omnibus Budget Reconciliation Act of 1985. Although it is unlikely that Congress would have intended to require employers to permit employees to continue long-term-care coverage following the occurrence of a qualifying event (e.g., termination of employment), employers must wrestle with the issue of whether it is appropriate to treat long-term care as an accident and health plan for one purpose while excluding it as an accident and health plan for other purposes.

The issue arises under Section 4980B of the Code, which addresses the continuation-of-coverage requirements under COBRA. Section 4980(f)(1) of the Code states that a group health plan will meet the requirement of COBRA only if each qualified beneficiary who would lose coverage under the plan as a result of qualifying event is entitled to elect to continue coverage under the plan. Section 5000(b)(1) of the Code defines a "group health plan" as any plan of an employer to provide "health care (directly or otherwise) to the employer's employees, former employees, or the families of such employees or former employees."

The issues is further muddied under the proposed regulations under COBRA. Section 1.162-26, Question and Answer 7, of the proposed Treasury Regulations under COBRA defines a "group health plan" as any plan maintained by an employer to provide medical care (as defined in Section 213(d) of the Code) to the employer's employees, whether directly or through insurance, reimbursement, or otherwise, and whether or not provided through an on-site facility, or through a cafeteria plan or other flexible benefit arrangement. At present, the IRS has not addressed the issue of COBRA coverage being extended to long-term-care insurance. Unfortunately, a review of the legislative history to COBRA was not particularly enlightening.

Although we do no believe COBRA requirements should apply to long-term-care programs, the COBRA issue underscores the need for legislative relief reflecting the existence of long-term care as a distinct form of health coverage.

Proposed Federal Legislation

Although employers have strong arguments for treating long-term-care coverage as a form of accident and health insurance, favorable legislation addressing ambiguous statutory provisions would be welcomed by employers. Proposed legislation attempting to address long-term-care benefits has time and again recognized the confusion that exists over the tax treatment of expenditures and benefits in connection with long-term-care coverage. Though we believe employers have ample support under the tax law for proceeding to offer long-term-care coverage to employees, it is helpful for employers to be aware of ongoing efforts to clarify existing tax laws in this area.

The U.S. Bipartisan Commission on Comprehensive Health Care (the Pepper Commission) in its report of March 2, 1990, recommended that long-term-care insurance be treated as health insurance under federal tax law. Since then, several bills have been proposed that would, among the other things, treat the expenses of long-term care as medical expenses under Section 213 of the Code, including personal care services for chronically ill persons. The proposed legislation would also expressly provide that long-term-care benefits constitute eligible cafeteria plan benefits and would provide a tax credit for the purchase of long-term-care insurance.

One of the earliest pieces of long-term-care legislation was introduced by Senator Robert Packwood (R-Ore.). This proposed legislation was particularly instructive in that it provided a road map to employers as to the possible federal tax law changes that may be necessary for long-term care to be recognized as a separate and distinct form of coverage under the tax law. In Senator Packwood's legislation, for example, long-term care would be treated like any other form of medical care. Thus, individuals would be able to deduct long-term-care expenses as an itemized deduction on their federal income tax return. Long-term-care benefits received by individuals would also not be subject to federal income tax. Additionally, employers would be permitted to offer long-term care as one of the nontaxable benefits that may be selected under a cafeteria plan. For purposes of the Packwood bill, long-term care would be defined as the care of an individual who requires assistance with daily living for a period of at least 90 days.

Subsequently long-term-care legislation was introduced proposing to establish federal standards for the sale of long-term-care insurance and addressing life insurance policies sold with long-term-care riders. The proposed legislation would establish a Long-Term-Care Insurance Standards Commission that would include state insurance commissioners, consumers, insurance agents, actuaries, long-term-care providers, and representatives from the insurance industry. The Commission would be responsible for setting standards required under the bill that each state would then have to adopt in connection with long-term-care policies issued and delivered in the particular state.

On April 9, 1992, the Long-Term-Care Family Security Act of 1992 was introduced in both the House and Senate (S.2571). The bill is intended to provide long-term health care coverage to all eligible Americans regardless of age. The Senate bill, which is estimated to cost $45 billion a year, did not disclose how revenues would be raised to fund the legislation. The House measure indicates that a payroll tax, an unearned income tax, and a reduction in the amount of untaxed inheritances would be used to fund the program. Although the federal government would be the payer of long-term-care benefits, it is expected that private insurance would continue to be needed to provide greater asset protection and enhanced coverage.

Due to the present state of the economy and existing budget constraints, the prospects for the bill's passage are unclear.

State Regulation

The design of a long-term-care program must also give careful consideration to the state in which the insurance policy will be issued and delivered. Whereas employers located in only a single state will be limited in their selection of favorable state laws, employers with multiple state operations may have additional planning opportunities.

One of the major problems facing state regulators is the need to create a sufficient balance between encouraging insurers to enter the long-term-care marketplace while at the same time establishing a regulatory environment designed to protect insureds. Regulators recognize that imposing too great an administrative burden may discourage insurance companies from entering the marketplace or developing new and innovative long-term-care products.

Just as Congress has not finally developed its position with regard to long-term-care benefits, state regulators are in various stages of development in the regulation of long-term-care policies. Because employers purchasing long-term-care insurance will be subject to state insurance regulation, the design and analysis of any long-term-care program must carefully consider the laws and regulations addressing long-term care at the state level. Although the National Association of Insurance Commissioners has promulgated model rules for the design and regulation of long-term-care insurance policies, at the state level the regulation of this area is still in flux.

Of particular concern to state regulators is the need to protect potential insureds from unfair claims practices, inadequate coverage, misleading policy language, and abusive marketing techniques. Thus, proposed regulations attempt to require strict disclosure requirements, graphic comparisons of benefit levels, inflation requirements, mandatory coverages, waiver-of-premium requirements, and definitions of what constitutes long-term care. In addition, state regulators have attempted to regulate minimum periods of coverage, exclusions for preexisting conditions, and exclusions for certain disorders. In addition, some state regulators, such as those in New York, have sought to require guaranteed renewable long-term-care coverage and to require that long-term-care insurers do not have the right to unilaterally terminate coverage for reasons other than nonpayment of premiums.

CONCLUSION

The effort to introduce a long-term-care program involves a number of issues and requires an employer to make a number of important decisions. If a long-term-care program is carefully analyzed and planned with the assistance of an employer's benefit planners, advisors and insurance company personnel, it can result in a well-designed and cost-efficient program. Most importantly, a carefully planned program can put employees in a position to withstand the otherwise catastrophic effect, both emotionally and financially, of having a family member face expensive nursing home or in-home care and assistance.

1.   20 TCM 1811 (1961).

2.   42 TC 755 (1964), *acq* 1964-2 CB 4.

30. Sole Source Integrated Health Care Programs: An Innovative Way to Manage Costs

Richard Johnson

The two key objectives in implementing a flexible benefits program are effectively and efficiently managing costs and providing meaningful choices to employees. An innovative way to accomplish these goals is the use of a sole source integrated health care program, a new approach to flexible benefits.

Sole source integrated health care programs can improve the overall efficiency and effectiveness of standard flexible benefits plans. Under this innovative new approach to flexible benefits, all health care issues are managed before, during, and after a medical occurrence for a considerable advantage in managing plan costs. In fact, combined with an effective communication and education effort, a sole source integrated health care program may provide as much as a 12 to 7 return on investment. By tying vendors to specific performance standards—they are paid their administrative fees only if they perform up to certain standards—it controls costs and ensures quality.

Efficient plan design is another important cost-saving factor. The core design component of sole source integrated health care is health promotion/disease prevention benefits. This design provides the same quality health care management for urban and rural areas. The program also provides free choice of providers and offers various networks, which may include centers of excellence (for transplants, etc.), mental health/substance abuse facilities, and prescription drug vendors.

SOLE SOURCE INTEGRATED HEALTH CARE PROGRAM

There are four primary factors that contribute to health care cost increases: plan design, technology, health care providers, and patient life style. Of these, life style contributes a substantial portion to the increases, yet has not been properly addressed in the United States. To do so requires focus on four major objectives:

1. Ensure that the benefit program covers the appropriate services for health promotion/disease prevention (HP/DP) from a clinical/design perspective.
2. Create a program that supports a healthy lifestyle.
3. Promote cost-effective utilization of health care resources and services through:
   a. Employee empowerment, to help employees and retirees take greater responsibility for their health through improved access, education, choice, and incentives;
   b. Environmental enhancement, to create a workplace consistent with a program that has a prominent health promotion/disease prevention orientation; and
   c. Effective health care resource management.
4. Make informed decisions using a data analysis system.

A key to the overall success of the program is to manage the "middle people" syndrome by eliminating as many health care vendors as possible. Thus, all claims administration, UR services, patient advocacy services, managed care networks, centers of excellence, and workers' compensation can be provided effectively by one vendor. Though a combination of many elements, a program of this type may be categorized by two major components: medical and disability.

The Medical Component

Sole source integrated health care programs are new to the United States. These programs include an array of services coupled with early intervention, and offer an ideal combination of managed care services, resulting in an elevated level of responsibility for all involved parties, including employers, patients, providers, and payers. These programs reduce redundancy and administration costs, provide managed care and many of the control technologies found in effective HMOs, and do not limit physician choice.

This type of program provides a comprehensive management system using a primary care nurse (PCN). The PCN assists members in assessing their medical care needs, choosing appropriate providers, and deciding among treatment alternatives. It requires commitment before the time an employee, dependent, or retiree accesses the health care system.

Here's how a sole source integrated health care program works. At the introduction of the program, each employee and his or her family are assigned a

PCN, who may be accessed through a toll-free 800 telephone number. Each PCN is fully trained in the employer's benefits and has immediate access to the patient's claims files. The member uses one phone number to access all plan requirements and claims or benefit information. A members can talk to a PCN about any health-related issue or question 24 hours a day, 7 days a week.

PCNs are licensed registered nurses with a minimum of five years training, and they are supported by on-site physician advisors, psychologists, and other licensed professionals. PCNs view the employee or dependent as their client and are committed to:

- Being full-time advocates to patients, serving a comprehensive support role
- Providing general health care information
- Providing clinical advice and counsel, empowering patients to be critical decision makers about treatment choices
- Supporting and facilitating referral to appropriate resources
- Reviewing services objectively for maximum benefit qualification
- Interpreting benefits and resolving problems related to claims and eligibility
- Meeting the general clinical and administrative information and support needs of the patient

The telephone access and ongoing relationship between PCNs and their client patients provides an opportunity for early involvement and intervention. This allows PCNs to:

- Educate the patients
- Advise patients on how to efficiently access care
- Recommend progressive systems and when they should seek care
- Advise patients as to the appropriate provider
- Counsel patients about what to expect in the way of diagnostic work and treatment

The PCNs also serve as clinical resources and patient advocates, coaching patients about alternative treatments they should review with their providers, assisting them in obtaining objective second opinions when appropriate, and intervening directly with their physicians if their needs are not being met.

Finally, it is the PCN's role to help the patient secure maximum plan coverage and minimize out-of-pocket expenses by making sure services proposed are necessary and efficiently provided. For a patient to receive maximum benefit coverage, the PCN must review and certify the treatment received, and must determine that it was medically necessary and efficiently delivered. The PCN also maintains a direct link to the claims system and regularly updates the patient's file about treatment plans approved for maximum coverage. This idea incorporates the concept of single-source funding or 24-hour coverage, which means regardless of the funding source—whether workers' compensation or benefit program—the proposed medical management systems are applicable. Although different vendor networks may be used, the PCNs act as the clearinghouse.

Under the employer medical plan, patients could bypass the PCN and still obtain reasonable coverage. To obtain maximum coverage, however, certification that services meet the tests of necessity and efficiency must be obtained by a PCN. If the care in question was determined to be grossly inappropriate, coverage may be entirely withheld.

This approach allows patients to have complete freedom of choice to seek professional services from any provider. Patients remain subject to standard plan copayments and liable for charges that exceed usual and customary fee schedules. The PCN would be able to assist patients in avoiding balance billing by recommending physicians whose charges are within usual and customary standards.

To ensure compliance with the program, a maximum benefit incentive is necessary. For example, the standard benefit could be set at 70/30 percent, with maximum coverage of 85/15 percent when services have been certified by the PCN. The out-of-pocket maximum concept is replaced by a provision to provide coverage at 90 percent when a patient's condition is determined to be catastrophic and is managed under case management. It could even go to 100 percent under certain circumstances. The PCN, acting as case manager, would determine whether a case is catastrophic using criteria and cost projection methodologies.

Selected hospitals and specialty networks would be contracted with and considered preferred based on their geographic proximity, current referral patterns, adherence to the standards of excellence, and willingness to provide favorable pricing to the plan. Select pharmacies would also be under contract. The new plan design could motivate selection of generics and more efficient, therapeutically equivalent brands.

Combining Resources

The administrative systems that support sole source integrated health care programs are seamlessly integrated into the whole. Exhibit 1 outlines the medical process. They may include:

- Patient advocacy services
- Medical management
  - Medical and surgical review
  - Case management
  - Mental health and substance abuse review
  - Transplant network
  - Disability management services
  - Workers' compensation
  - Centers of excellence
- EAP services (linked to MH/SA)
- Pharmaceutical services
- Claims adjudication and service systems

Exhibit 1. Medical Managment Flow Chart

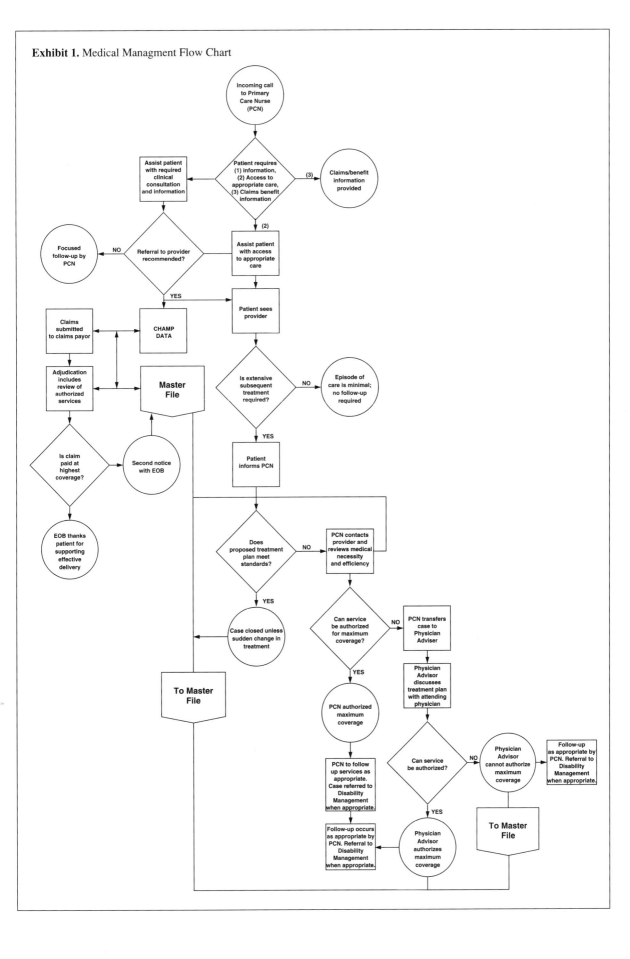

Disability Management

This program provides comprehensive medical and disability management and return-to-work services as close to the point of the employee's injury or illness as possible. In addition to evaluating the appropriateness, necessity, and efficiency of the health care services that are provided, the PCN works with the disabled employee, the provider, and the employer to encourage a safe and early return to work.

Studies show that when an employee has been off work for six months following a disabling injury or illness, it is unlikely that employee will ever return to work. Getting employees back to the workplace is imperative for managing disability costs. Furthermore, an early return to appropriate activity within the work environment can speed the employee's recovery.

Although the health care costs of a disabling injury or illness are often managed by progressive employer programs, the costs of wage replacement benefits and lost productivity undergo much less scrutiny. The emotional, psychological, and economic implications of a disability can take a greater toll on an employee's life then the physical aspects of the condition itself. Unlike a physical impairment, disability is often a learned behavior. Early intervention with education and support can speed recovery and the return to work while minimizing the development of adversarial relationships, addictive behaviors, and additional functional impairment.

Under a sole source integrated health care program, when an employee has a condition that will result in more than five days of consecutive absence, the case is referred to the program for disability screening. If the case qualifies for disability management, a PCN will contact the employee to explain the PCN's role and to obtain information regarding the employee's medical history and current condition. The PCN reviews the physical requirements of the employee's regular job and discusses potential transitional work assignments with the employer, if appropriate.

The PCN then contacts the treating physician to discuss the patient's medical status, activity restrictions, and treatment plan. The information is compared with the program's clinical practice and disability management guidelines for the employee's specific condition. If the treatment plan or activity restrictions fall outside the guidelines, a physician advisor assesses the information and, if necessary, contacts the provider to discuss alternative treatments and/or appropriate activity restrictions. The outcome of these discussions with the provider is communicated to the employer and the claims payor.

If the employee is temporarily restricted from returning to his or her regular job, the PCN works with the employer to identify appropriate transitional work. The PCN stays in close contact with the employee to educate, to provide support in making decisions regarding medical treatment choices and return-to-work

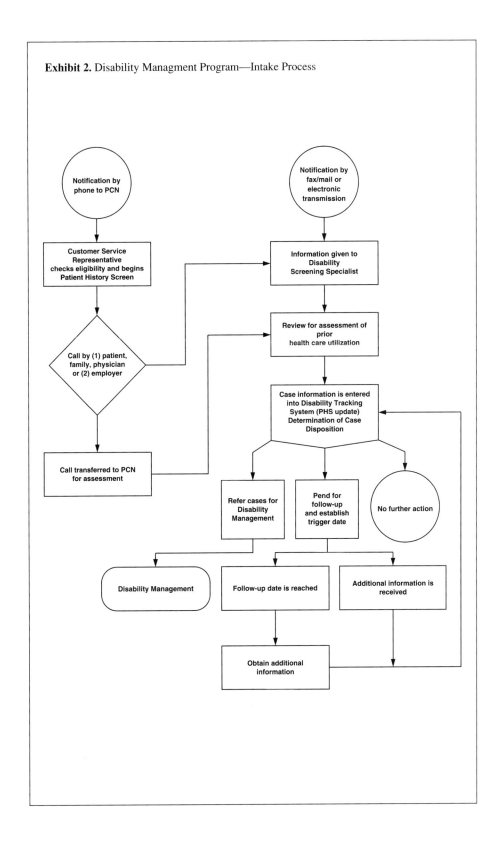

Exhibit 2. Disability Managment Program—Intake Process

options, and to assist the employee in understanding the consequences of the choices that he or she makes.

As the employee continues on the path toward recovery, his or her progress is compared to the program's clinical practice and disability management guidelines. Updated activity restrictions are obtained from the physician at appropriate intervals, and transitional work assignments are modified to facilitate the employee's physical reconditioning and eventual return to regular work assignments. If return to the employee's previous level of function is not a possibility, the PCN works with the employer and the claims payor to develop an appropriate strategy for patient-supportive resolution to the LTD/STD (long-term disability/short-term disability) or workers' compensation claim. Exhibit 2 illustrates how the program works.

CONCLUSION

Sole source integrated health care combines the best cost-saving features of various health benefit plans into a cogent and efficient program. Integration eliminates the costs of unneeded middlemen, streamlines administration, and improves the overall quality of health care provided to employees and their dependents. The use of PCNs is a cost-effective way of managing and reviewing treatment plans and practices, and serves to educate patients along the way. Maybe the most important aspect of this program is that it helps the consumer become a more prudent health care consumer by empowering them and promoting their accountability for their health. This change in attitude goes right to the bottom line.

Part 6

NEW OUTLOOK ON MENTAL HEALTH CARE

31. The Value of Mental Health and Chemical Dependency Benefits: Much More Than Meets the Eye

Jeffrey Berlant   Tom Trabin   Donald F. Anderson

Many employers have unwisely cut their mental health care and chemical dependency treatment (MH/CD) benefits because of rising costs and a poor understanding of the value of such coverage. However, many treatable mental disorders and chemical dependencies have been correlated with physical illnesses and disabilities, absenteeism, and lowered productivity; cutting MH/CD benefits will only serve to increase medical plan, workers' compensation, and other costs in the long term. If appropriately designed and managed, MH/CD benefits are clearly cost-effective at controlling overall health care costs.

The rising costs of mental health and chemical dependency benefits during the 1980s and early 1990s have caused major concern among employers responsible for paying for these benefits. The response to this problem has been varied, leading to a variety of intended and unintended results. In this chapter we will review the recent history of the problem, consider the implications of some common approaches to dealing with it, and propose some guidelines for future action.

RISING MENTAL HEALTH CARE COSTS

Anecdotal reports of escalating mental health costs during the late 1980s drew attention to this sector of benefits. For example, Procter & Gamble in Oxnard,

315

California, reported seeing expenses for inpatient mental health and chemical dependency (MH/CD) care rise from an average cost per case of $3,963 to $29,463 between 1986 and 1988.[1] Nationally, 15 percent of the more than $600 billion spent in the United States on health care in 1990 has gone for direct costs of alcohol, drug abuse, and mental health care.[2] Although the proportion of public health care dollars spent on mental health treatment has not increased appreciably over time, private sector expenditures have risen rapidly due to a number of factors, including:

- Cost shifting from public sector mental health services to private sector services through decreasing grants for community mental health services, severe caps on Medicare expenditures, and long-term freezes on Medicaid benefits, which have led to the growth of private sector ventures in mental health treatment to compensate for provider losses from public sources.

- Greater public education and diminishing stigma about emotional disorders, which have led to enhanced demand for treatment of conditions for which people previously shunned treatment.

- Substantial advances in biological and psychotherapeutic techniques, which have made many conditions more amenable to treatment than ever in history. Some of the increased demand is related to legitimate desires for access to the benefits of new technological advances.

- The increasing prevalence of depression and middle-class substance abuse problems since the end of World War II, which has also represented a legitimate increase in widespread clinical need. The National Institute of Mental Health's ECA (Epidemiological Catchment Area) Program study, conducted between 1980 and 1984, found that over a lifetime, 22.5 percent of adults in the general population had diagnosable non-substance abusing mental disorders, 13.5 percent had alcohol dependence, and 6 percent had other drug dependence or abuse.[3]

- Interest in mental health treatment facilities as substitutes for failures in schools, families, and communities.

- The proliferation of private, freestanding, for-profit psychiatric hospitals in the 1980s, which targeted the markets for chemical dependency treatment and control of adolescent disruptive behavior. Since 1955, there has been at least a 300 percent increase in such facilities, with 80 percent under the ownership of hospital management companies with well-structured public relations departments.[4] Between 1980 and 1984, adolescent admissions to private psychiatric hospitals increased 450 percent.[5] Some of this increase can be attributed to the lifting of certificate of need programs, allowing free market access to highly competitive firms.

- The tendency of many benefit packages to favor richer inpatient than out-patient MH/CD benefits (a practice rarely seen in any other health area), and to provide incentives for providing treatment at the most expensive and restrictive level of care, which also facilitated the growth of the private hospital sector.

- The introduction of well-intentioned, mandated MH/CD benefits in many states, which has also contributed to a rise in costs.[6]

Employer Concerns About the Value of MH/CD Treatment

Employers have become increasingly skeptical about the value of MH/CD treatment services, particularly as the need to contain all health costs has risen, and as the perception has grown that MH/CD benefits have been abused by many elements of the provider community. Given a fixed "pie" for health care expenditures, MH/CD services have come under intense scrutiny as a piece to be sliced thinner.

Traditional stigma concerning emotional disorders remains, resulting in some employers seeing these problems as moral rather than health issues. The occurrence of systematic abuses, employee complaints of ineffective—and at times inappropriate—treatment, and unnecessarily expensive treatment, has fueled cynicism and resentment about behavioral services.

Some employers are unaware of the massive mortality and morbidity caused by mental and substance abuse disorders. Suicide ranks among the top two to three causes of death among young adults, within the top five for middle age adults, and within the top ten for all ages. The vast majority of suicides is attributable to potentially treatable mood disorders and substance abuse.[7] More recent research into the causes of health-related disability has found that disability is more closely associated with mental disorders than with "purely medical" disorders, and more common among those with medical disorders who carry high levels of psychological distress.[8] Studies of worker productivity have uncovered mental disorders as a major source of absenteeism, low productivity, accidents, turnover, job dissatisfaction, and interpersonal conflict.[9] Finally, the costs of care for automobile accidents—approximately 50 percent of motor vehicle fatalities are associated with intoxication[10]—and other unnecessary physical trauma, as well as the indirect social and financial costs, are substantial.

Some employers doubt that MH/CD services are helpful, and are unaware of recent significant advances in the efficacy of psychopharmacological and psychotherapeutic treatments. There is a substantial scientific outcome literature for both that demonstrates evidence of efficacy for both types of approaches.

Some employers are unaware of the effectiveness of specialized utilization control systems for MH/CD services, which are based on the use of generally accepted standards and protocols for allocation of patients to specific levels of care. Some are also unaware of the availability of effective alternatives to inpatient care, or fail to realize that effective utilization control systems can ensure that benefit coverage of these intermediate levels of care will result in substitutions for unnecessarily expensive care, rather than additional costs.

Finally, some employers are rightfully concerned regarding the lack of quality controls on care and the lack of available evidence demonstrating summary clinical outcome data on employees and their dependents who receive MH/CD treatment. Doubts about the possibility of objectively measuring and reporting non-physiological outcomes are raised among those who are unaware of the extensive treatment outcome measurement literature in the behavioral sciences.

EMPLOYER RESPONSES

Over the past three to five years, benefit managers have attempted to rein in MH/CD treatment costs by a variety of strategies. Some employers, particularly those in non-unionized states, have slashed MH/CD benefits, in some cases to as low as a $1500 lifetime maximum, with benefit coverage only for inpatient mental health.[11] Although savings in direct MH/CD costs have definitely resulted, health care costs have continued to rise. Some employers in these states have turned to employee assistance programs (EAPs) as their primary intervention, in order to preserve some counseling services benefit without underwriting expensive care for more seriously ill employees or their dependents. In these instances, MH/CD care often becomes inaccessible to most employees and their dependents due to barriers to access of public sector services and the high out-of-pocket costs of paying for care.

Most employers have implemented MH/CD benefits which are equal to medical-surgical benefits. Many benefit packages have stringent ceilings on inpatient "nervous" benefits, and high copayments with very limited numbers of sessions covered for outpatient care.

Many employers have turned to managed care techniques to establish independent, clinically informed controls on utilization. These employers have endeavored to balance cost containment against the need to offer assistance to employees needing help with emotional problems.

Implications of National Health Care Reform

Prominent proponents of national health care reform have favored placing a high value on mental health/substance abuse services as an important component of a universal health insurance plan. The problem of funding these services remains a substantial obstacle, and there is a strong possibility that MH/CD benefits will remain relatively modest under a favorable proposal. Even in the event of the passage of some type of universal national health insurance, employers will need to consider the costs and benefits of supplementing MH/CD services.

PRESERVATION OF MH/CD BENEFITS THROUGH CAREFUL MANAGEMENT

We believe that MH/CD benefits should occupy a prominent place in a health care benefit package because of the high prevalence of these disorders, their high levels of mortality and morbidity, and the high level of indirect social and workplace costs of not providing effective treatment. The key challenge is to provide adequate support for effective services, minimizing unnecessary treatments and expenditures and avoiding ineffective or inappropriate care. Inevitably, this requires the introduction of managed care techniques for utilization control and the retention of an adequate benefit level. It also requires stimulating the growth of an alternative, non-inpatient MH/CD treatment system that can provide intensive services at a more reasonable cost.

Addressing the problem of the quality of services is particularly important for MH/CD. Seriously ill people can be kept at highly restrictive, expensive levels of care for extensive periods of time without marked improvement when available effective treatments are not provided to them. Several governmental and private studies have documented high levels of poor or unacceptable treatment given in many inpatient settings.[12] Finding mechanisms that manage care by placing patients in the hands of *effective* providers, including providing incentives to increase effectiveness, is a strategy which we believe benefits everyone.

THE VALUE OF MH/CD BENEFITS

There is a large scientific literature documenting the efficacy of psychopharmacological and psychotherapeutic techniques for a wide variety of emotional disorders.[13] Depression, schizophrenia, obsessive compulsive disorder, bipolar disorder, anxiety disorders, and chemical dependency have been rigorously examined using scientifically sophisticated methodological designs, and effective treatments have been identified and specified for each. The efficacy of treatment for these disorders ranks on a par with that for many medical disorders.

The creation of reliable, validated diagnostic categories for mental disorders, as exemplified by the *Diagnostic and Statistical Manual III* (Revised) of the American Psychiatric Association, represents an example of the operationalization diagnostic criteria that has been matched by few medical specialties. More recently, the application of extensive, scientifically validated behavioral outcome measurement tools such as the Global Assessment of Functioning Scale, the Brief Symptom Inventory, the Beck Depression Inventory, the Hamilton Depression

Rating Scale, and the Addiction Severity Index, as well as the development of clinical stratification methods for adjusting for the severity of illness and diagnostic differences, have started to bring powerful descriptive tools out of the research field and into the clinic for everyday use. The wider use of these methods will definitely allow the objective quantification of the impact of MH/CD treatment.

Medical Offset

In the late 1960s, research in health maintenance organization (HMO) settings found that the use of brief outpatient psychotherapeutic contacts substantially reduced medical utilization among high utilizers of medical-surgical services.[14] Subsequent studies (by some counts, there have been at least 78) in indemnity insurance, Medicaid, and HMO environments have in general supported these "medical offset" effects on medical utilization and costs of MH/CD treatment. Few studies, however, have identified either the specific types of MH/CD treatment that have had this effect or the types of medical utilization savings that have accrued.

The best current evidence, based on a carefully conducted study over 14 years of almost 4,000 patients with alcoholism, found that the average monthly medical care costs (including alcohol treatment) of treated alcoholics are about 24 percent lower than for untreated alcoholics during the four years following alcohol treatment.[15] These savings typically do not appear until the costs of alcohol treatment have passed, at least for one year. There is a characteristic "ramp effect," involving a transient rise in costs for the first six months after initiation of treatment; these data are perhaps exaggerated due to the common use of inpatient alcohol treatment programs as the standard method of treatment during the study period. By the seventh month after treatment initiation, total medical costs were approximately 55 percent below treatment costs before treatment. In marked contrast, a control group of *untreated* alcohol patients displayed an almost 84 percent increase in costs above those at the immediate time before identification of an alcohol problem. This particular study was notable for studying the medical cost offset effect in blue-collar as well as white-collar workers, employees and dependents, and HMO members as well as enrollees in fee-for-service plans. These differences did not seem to diminish the observed offset effect.

A recent study in Hawaii of effects of "targeted, focused psychotherapy" on medical expenditures for Medicaid beneficiaries found a particularly strong savings when the therapy was provided to patients with chronic medical conditions such as diabetes, hypertension, and chronic obstructive lung disease.[16] Interestingly, the medical offset was substantially greater with these techniques than with traditional mental health techniques (which were left undefined). It is unclear to what extent the patients who were being treated had conventionally defined mental disorders as opposed to other forms of psychological distress due to a whole host of potential factors. Nonetheless, it is an important study in that it did demonstrate a positive medical offset effect that was most pronounced for certain types of medical conditions and in response to a specified set of psychotherapeutic interventions. More research of this type is clearly needed to optimize the medical offset effects of mental health treatments.

An EAP demonstration project in the Orange County, Florida public school system found that participants in a four-year EAP program demonstrated marked reduction of employee health claim costs, despite having a higher-than-average annual health insurance cost in the year prior to introduction of the EAP, actually falling below the medical expenditures for non-users of EAP services—from $3,173 per capita before the project to $983 per capita in the fourth year.[17]

Effects on Workers' Compensation or Disability Claims

The Orange County study also tracked sick-leave payments to determine the effect of EAP intervention on lost days. Compared to non-EAP employees, the sick-leave utilization rate fell from an average of 6.35 hours *more* sick leave than the average to 13.95 *fewer* sick leave hours than the average after six years of EAP experience, a reduction of over 20 days. The City of Los Angeles Department of Water & Power found that the use of mandatory EAP referrals for alcohol problems resulted in a 33 percent decrease in sickness absenteeism, according to 1985–86 data.[18] The Campbell Soup Company found that use of an EAP resulted in a nearly 20 percent reduction in the incidence of workers' compensation claims for accidents for employees using the EAP, compared to a small increase in reportable accidents for employees who did not use the EAP.[19]

Recent research has found that the highest rates of disability for persons with chronic medical illness occur among those with concomitant mental disorders.[20] In particular, depression, which some studies find occurs at a significant level in a third of white-collar professional groups, is associated with higher levels of disability than most chronic physical disorders.

CONCLUSION

We have seen some of the reasons why private sector MH/CD expenditures have risen sharply during the past decade, we have considered employer attitudes toward these benefits, and we have reviewed some prevalent employer responses as attempts have been made to stem the tide. To some employers, it has seemed logical simply to cut or even eliminate MH/CD benefits as a direct way to control claims costs. As we have seen, however, reducing or eliminating MH/CD benefits is a recipe for increasing medical plan and workers' compensation claims costs, as well as increasing indirect costs such as employee absenteeism. How, then can an employer provide for adequate employee/dependent access to MH/CD care without breaking the bank?

More Effective MH/CD Benefit Design to Contain Costs

The cornerstone elements of proven benefits programs which allow access to appropriate MH/CD care while containing costs are as follows:

1. A benefit plan that covers intermediate MH/CD care levels;
2. A good system for managing utilization so that care is delivered at the level most appropriate for a patient's problems;
3. Availability and accessibility of intermediate level programs and services; and
4. Access to networks of selected providers who demonstrate competence at achieving effective care in a cost-effective manner.

Intermediate levels of care may include a variety of types of treatment programs. Health services research has found that effective mental health and substance abuse services can be delivered in various outpatient settings. For mental health treatment, these have included such developments as partial hospitalization, residential treatment, brief crisis psychiatric observation, community support programs, mobile emergency crisis services, halfway house programs, and a range of individualized, flexible services for patients with unusually complex care needs. For chemical dependency treatment, the use of structured outpatient treatment programs, halfway houses, outpatient detoxification programs, and specialized relapse prevention programs has generated powerful new options. The key element is that *active* treatment should be delivered, in contrast to custodial care or provision of housing, in an environment of strict utilization controls to ensure that all the care provided is necessary.

The employer that takes this approach to MH/CD benefits can enjoy the advantages of supporting the mental and physical health of its work force, while avoiding both the high costs associated with traditional MH/CD benefits and the unacceptable costs of doing without them.

1. RM Yandrick, "Taking inventory," *EAPA Exchange*, 1992: 22–29.

2. Dorwart, Chartock, and Epstein, "Financing of services," in Talbot, Hales, and Keill (eds.), *Textbook of Administrative Psychiatry* (Washington, DC: American Psychiatric Press, 1992).

3. Reiger, "Comorbidity of mental disorders with alcohol and other drug abuse: Results from the Epidemiological Catchment Area (ECA) study," 264 *JAMA* (1990): 2511–2518.

4. Supra note 2.

5.   Supra note 2.

6.   *The Hay/Huggins Behavioral Health Benefits Study,* 1991.

7.   Henricksson, Aro, Marttunen, *et al.,* "Mental disorders and comorbidity in suicide," 150 *American Journal of Psychiatry* (1993): 935–940.

8.   Wells, Stewart, Hayes, *et al.,* "The functioning and well-being of depressed patients: Results from the Medical Outcomes Study," 262 *JAMA* (1989): 914–919; Lyness, Caine, Conwell, et al., "Depressive symptoms, medical illness, and functional status in depressed psychiatric inpatients," 150 *American Journal of Psychiatry* (1993): 910–915.

9.   Mintz, Mintz, Arruda, *et al.,* "Treatments of depression and the functional capacity to work," 49 *Archives of General Psychiatry* (1992): 761–768.

10. US Federal Highway Administration, *Selected Highway Statistics and Charts,* annual; except as noted, US National Highway Traffic Safety Administration, unpublished data from the Fatal Accident Reporting System.

11. Simplot, Incorporated, Boise, ID, 1989.

12. *The SysteMetrics Quality Monitoring Project of the Tidewater Virginia CHAMPUS Mental Health HMO Demonstration Project.*

13. PH Wender and DF Klein, *Mind, Mood & Medicine: A guide to New Biopsychiatry* (Nal-Dutton Publishing, 1982); JK Krupnik and HA Pincus, "The cost-effectiveness of psychotherapy: a plan for research," 149 *American Journal of Psychiatry,* 10 (Oct 1992): 1295–1305; *Psychotherapy in HMOs: The Practice of Mental Health in Managed Health Care* (American Psychological Association, 1991).

14. Cummings, "Prolonged (ideal) verses short-term (realistic) psychotherapy," *Professional Psychology,* 491–501, 1997.

15. HD Holder and JO Blose, "The reduction of health care costs associated with alcoholism treatment: A 14-year longitudinal study," 53 *Journal of Studies on Alcohol* (1992): 293–302.

16. Cummings, Dorken, Pallack, *et al., The Impact of Psychological Intervention on Healthcare Utilization and Costs: The Hawaii Medicaid Project,* NO 11-C-98344/9, Apr 1990.

17. Supra note 1.

18. Supra note 1.

19. Supra note 1.

20. J Lewis, MD, "Subsyndromal symptomatic depression: A new disorder?" American Psychiatric Association Annual Meeting, May 23, 1993 (San Francisco, CA).

32. Impact of Managed Care on Mental Heath Services

Barbara Dickey   Hocine Azeni

Managed care strategies are being used as methods of containing the increasingly expensive provisions of mental health care, but their effectiveness in this benefit area is unclear. This article presents the findings of a study on the effects of applying two managed care techniques—concurrent review and prior approval review—to mental health care.

The cost of mental health care continues to rise at a rate greater than that of the rest of the health care sector.[1] Efforts to contain the rising costs of psychiatric and substance abuse care have spawned different strategies for reducing use of expensive hospital resources. Strategies that focus on the management of hospital episodes case by case fall under the rubric of managed care.

In this article we focus on managed care as it pertains to use of mental health services. We compare the use of inpatient services before and after the introduction of two specific types of managed mental health care programs designed to reduce "inappropriate" use of hospital services.[2] The purpose of these programs is to contain the costs of reimbursed mental health care provided to employees and their dependents who have chosen an indemnity plan for their health care coverage.

MENTAL HEALTH AND MANAGED CARE

One managed care tool, utilization management, has grown in popularity in direct proportion to the increase in the costs of mental health care.[3] To stem the tide of

Reprinted with permission from *Health Affairs,* Fall 1992, pages 197–204.

increasing costs, corporate purchasers have turned to "fourth-party" utilization management firms, which have promised to manage care by reducing hospital use and, implicitly, reducing spending for psychiatric and substance abuse care. Although many mental health professional regard managed care strategies as unwelcome intrusions into clinical affairs, from the point of view of corporations (the payers in most cases) these strategies are alternatives to financially based strategies to reduce costs, such as demand-side cost sharing in the form of day limits on covered services or supply-side cost sharing in the form of prospective payment.[4] Utilization review programs that focus on determination of medical necessity have been around for almost three decades, but specialized programs have been developed only within the past decade or so. It is estimated that virtually all third-party payers conduct or sponsor some type of utilization review.[5] Blue Cross has had several different forms of utilization review programs in place in more than 85 percent of their plans since 1985.[6]

Impact of Managed Care on Use and Costs

Almost no empirical work has been published that describes the effects of managed care on patterns of use of mental health care for members of indemnity plans. Studies of utilization management in acute care hospitals have just begun. Thomas Wickizer has noted that private programs of the type we are examining here have not been rigorously evaluated, and most information about them is anecdotal in nature.[7] He summarizes the studies published to date as reporting reductions in both use and costs but notes that the data supporting these claims are not convincing. In the most analytically sophisticated research to date, two studies tested the effect of managed care programs on measures of utilization and on expenditures.[8] They found that the programs reduced hospital use and expenditures by 8 percent. For mental health, early reports of peer review (that is, retrospective chart reviews) in the Civilian Health and Medical Program of the Uniformed Services (CHAMPUS) suggested that the rate of rising costs had been slowed, but the research was descriptive of that program only, without comparisons to nonreviewed plans.[9] Richard Frank and colleagues used data from Maryland and Washington State to demonstrate that substantial increases in adolescent admissions and admissions for drug and alcohol abuse have been the major contributors to rising mental health costs.[10]

DESCRIPTION OF THE MANAGED CARE PROGRAMS

The two interventions we examine here are representative of two types of utilization review programs:

1. A mandatory prior approval program that certifies all admissions as medically necessary prior to or within twenty-four hours after admission, authorizing a certain number of days to be reimbursed; and
2. A mandatory concurrent review program that subjects all psychiatric and substance abuse admissions to the scrutiny of concurrent review, specific to treatment and discharge planning.

Review occurs after the patient is admitted, and determination of medical necessity by the reviewers is linked directly to reimbursement.

Both interventions studied here were purchased from a commercial insurance carrier by corporations that also purchase their health care insurance form that same carrier. The programs under study are alike in many ways. Both are mandatory; that is, all admissions must be reviewed, and documentation specific to the review is stored within an internal computer network linked to the claims payment department. No claim is reimbursed without determination of medical necessity through the review process. Also, in both programs the claims payment department is notified at the time of review of the expected length-of-stay (and extensions of length-of-stay, as determined medically necessary). A claim is reimbursed at the rate specified in the benefit plan only if the admission has been approved and is so noted in the computerized interactive claims file. The benefit plan contract states that the patient is at risk for all charges incurred for care not authorized by designated review programs. When denials occur, penalties of reduced reimbursement are enforced at the discretion of the corporation. In both review programs, denials are subject to appeal and external review.

The programs are different, however, in their assumptions (and thus their activities) about how best to reduce hospital use. The prior approval program assumes that careful screening of admissions and assigned length-of-stay are adequate management for psychiatric admissions. Once an admission is approved, treatment and discharge planning are solely within the discretion of the attending physician. The concurrent review program, however, was designed by mental health specialists to reflect the probability that these admissions are far more likely to be emergency (rather than planned) admissions and thus to escape the usual preadmission screening process. Rather than denying admission to achieve reduction, focus is on discharge planning after the admission has occurred, requiring attending physicians to provide details of treatment as it relates to discharge. The vendor of the concurrent review program argues that the program "shortens" length-of-stay by encouraging efficiency on the part of the clinical treatment team, rather than by limiting or truncating treatment goals arbitrarily. In special cases, when the reviewer considers it cost-effective, he or she may recommend that the carrier and the corporate benefit manager consider making a benefit "exception" and extend coverage to services not usually available to facilitate a discharge that otherwise might be delayed.

If a managed care program is successful, then fewer individuals are admitted (reducing the total number of bed days reimbursed by the company), but those who are admitted are expected to stay, on average, at least as long as, if not longer than, individuals covered in indemnity plans without similar managed care programs, because of the relative severity of their illness. We could also expect to see an increase in the amount of outpatient services used to substitute for the reduced hospital care. Although insurance claims are inadequate to fully explore these questions, the work we report here improves on earlier studies in several ways. First, the data are comprehensive, including both outpatient and inpatient mental health claims. Second, a number of potentially confounding factors have been controlled, such as the extent of health maintenance organization (HMO) enrollment, benefit plan design, and work-force characteristics. Third, multivariate analyses were used to control for case-mix and different hospital characteristics that might also obscure effects of the review programs.

TESTING THE EFFECTS OF MANAGED CARE STRATEGIES

The Sample

Employees of two large companies and their dependents covered by indemnity health care plans administered by the same commercial carrier in 1985 and 1987 were the sample used to test the effect of two different managed care strategies. The companies were chosen for their similarities: the same benefit design (no day or dollar limits on psychiatric or substance abuse admissions), the same work-force size (20,000 or more employees and their dependents), the same geographic distribution (national companies with headquarters in the East), and similar HMO penetration (about 30 percent).

The study years were chosen to capture data before and after the introduction of managed care in 1986. Individuals who made at least one inpatient or outpatient claim for the treatment of mental health disorders (including substance abuse) were identified. Once these individuals (claimants) were identified as users of mental health services, all of their inpatient and outpatient claims for mental health and medical care were organized into longitudinal claimant-level files (N = 6,534). Exhibit 1 describes the characteristics of the claimants.

Findings

Company A purchased a concurrent review package in 1987; Company B, a prior approval package. Comparing rates of use per 1,000 covered lives, the two companies were markedly different in 1985 and were still different but less so in 1987. Rates of admission in Company A dropped from 9.4 per thousand covered lives in 1985 to 9.0 in 197. Admission rates in Company B rose from 4.2 per thousand in 1985 to 5.6 in 1987. In company A bed days rose from 216.8 to 290.5

Exhibit 1
Personal And Clinical Characteristics Of Claimants, Mental Health Managed Care Sample, 1985 And 1987

Characteristic	Company A		Company B	
	1985 (N = 1,826)	1987 (N = 1,937)	1985 (N = 1,310)	1987 (N = 1,461)
Employee	52%	55%	62%	63%
Male	45	45	39	38
Age				
0–17	16	13	13	11
18–39	42	38	52	50
40–64	38	41	33	35
65 and older	4	7	2	4
Mean age	37 years	39 years	35 years	37 years
Diagnosis				
Psychosis	7%	12%	2%	5%
Alcohol/ drug	<1	<1	<1	<1
Other	93	85	93	92
Inpatient	8	8	5	6

Source: Paid claims data from a commercial insurance carrier, 1985 and 1987.

per thousand; in Company B they rose from 80.1 to 175.0 per thousand. Expenditures on mental health claims rose dramatically in 1987 for both companies, as the increases in bed days suggest. Comparing inflation-adjusted dollars, Company A paid inpatient and outpatient claims of $4,250,785 in 1985 and $4,813,385 in 1987; Company B paid $2,805,156 in 1985 and $3,903,708 in 1987.

These increases are consistent with the expanding health care environment at that time.[11] Two separate trends in mental health care in the 1980s converged to provide a powerful force in raising costs and length-of-stay. First, dedicated psychiatric and substance abuse beds in general hospitals had increased substantially in the 1970s and early 1980s and then leveled off, while beds in private freestanding facilities continued to increase unchecked during the period under study.[12] Pressures by insurers and corporations to limit length-of-stay were offset by pressures to fill beds and cover the cost of rising capital debt. Second, the growth of specialized programs to fill these beds increased the demand for treatment of eating disorders and of alcohol and substance abuse disorders, and especially the treatment of troubled adolescents.[13] The combined effect of these two trends, along with the rising costs of the period, makes it nearly impossible to judge the effectiveness of the two managed care programs in terms of cost alone. Instead, we must ask whether they had any discernible effect at all. Did either of the programs slow the rate of increase, or did the expansion of the mental health market overwhelm everything in its path?

Adjusted Comparison

Exhibit 2 summarizes the results of the multivariate analyses when the data are adjusted for case-mix and hospital characteristics. Unadjusted comparisons of concurrent review and prior approval revealed no discernible effect, but adjusted data suggest that concurrent review contained annual mean claimant costs. The case-mix and hospital adjustments controlled for increases in the number of children and adolescents admitted and the increase in admissions to for-profit hospitals, both of which made significant contributions to the variance in paid claims. We estimated the probability of a client's being admitted if treated for a psychiatric or substance abuse disorder in 1985 and 1987, controlling for the same patient characteristics used in the model presented in Exhibit 2. The likelihood of admission if treated dropped in 1987 in Company A but stayed about the same in Company B, suggesting that the concurrent review program does have a weak effect on admissions.

Other Effects of Managed Care

If inpatient admissions are diverted or shortened, then we might expect changes in other aspects of care as well. At the time that Medicare implemented diagnosis-related groups (DRGs) as a cost containment mechanism, concern was expressed

Exhibit 2
Mean Hospital Use And Paid Claims, Adjusted For Hospital Characteristics And Case-Mix, Mental Health Managed Care Sample, 1985 And 1987

	1985	1987
Length-of-stay per episode		
Concurrent review	17.3 days	24.17 days[a]
Prior approval	10.2 days	23.27 days[b]
Paid claims per episode		
Concurrent review	$ 7,298	$ 8,888
Prior approval	4,751	11,123[b]
Annual bed days		
Concurrent review	25.04 days	29.43 days
Prior approval	12.05 days	26.63 days[b]
Annual paid claims		
Concurrent review	$10,701	$10,155
Prior approval	4,321	11,725[b]

Source: Paid claims data from a commercial insurance carrier, 1985 and 1987.

Note: Estimation model used to adjust data included case-mix variables (age, sex, employment status, and diagnosis), hospital characteristics (teaching hospital status and tax status), and the presence of a managed care program. All cost data were inflation adjusted and logged.

[a] $p \leq .05$.
[b] $p \leq .01$.

that shortened stays would compromise care and lead to rapid readmission of patients. The possibility also existed that these managed care programs would compromise care. Although we did not measure clinical outcomes, we did not find any evidence in these data that care was compromised; readmissions within 30 days fell in both companies.

If the review programs are successful, then we might expect that the individuals hospitalized are more seriously ill, as evidenced by increasing lengths of stay, an increase in admissions with major mental illness, or an increase in comorbidity, defined as psychiatric and substance abuse secondary diagnoses. Our data support these hypotheses. In 1987 there were substantial increases in both the number of admissions for major mental illness (while other types of admissions decreased) and in the level of comorbidity. It is possible, however, that this shift represents physicians' responses to pressure to demonstrate the need for inpatient care. The actual level of severity may not have changed since 1985, but simply the documentation of severity.

DISCUSSION

This study has documented limited support for the effectiveness of the psychiatric concurrent review program and no support for the effectiveness of the prior approval review program. From benefit managers' point of view, there appears to have been no effect at all, as mental health spending rose dramatically in both companies. It is not possible to provide direct empirical support for the casual link between the concurrent review program and the lower rate of increase in expenditures, even though case-mix and hospital characteristics have been accounted for in the estimation models used to adjust costs of hospital care.

Why do we find so little impact from managed care programs when so much has been promised? The health care environment is unstable, with increasing pressures driving up both the supply of and the demand for mental health services. Another factor may be in play: The changing patient case-mix reported here may be a partial response to the interaction of the growth of new types of psychiatric inpatient programs (such as adolescent treatment programs) and physicians' desire to avoid review. New programs provide an opportunity for physicians and facilities to establish new admission criteria and new norms for length of treatment. The data reveal the tendency for the system to expand in new directions when traditional practice patterns are challenged. As conventional patterns of care were challenged in the 1980s, new patterns emerged, changing admissions by age distributions and site of care.

This study is limited in a number of important ways and the findings can only suggest paths for future research. Claims data are notoriously limited in clinical information, and working with paid claims may obscure costs incurred but paid out of pocket by patients. Only two companies were studied, companies that may not be representative of mental health patterns of care. The study investigated only short-term effects on costs and did not include ether clinical outcomes or long-term effects on claimant-level costs. Of particular interest in the future will be investigations of changing case-mix patterns.

This study has been supported by Grant no. R01 MH45089-01A1 from the National Institute of Mental Health (NIMH). The authors acknowledge the contributions of Agnes Rupp, Thomas McGuire, and Carl Morris.

1. RG Frank, DS Salkever, and SS Sharfstein, "Growth in Expenditure for Mental Health Services under Private Insurance, 1986-1989" (Unpublished paper, The Johns Hopkins University, Baltimore, Maryland, 1991); M Bryant, "Are Rising Mental Health Costs Driving You Crazy?" *Business and Health* (January 1991): 36-43; D Hodgkin, "The Impact of Private Utilization Management on Psychiatric Care: A Review of the Literature," *Journal of Mental Health Administration* (forthcoming); and American Psychiatric Association, *Status Report on Developments in the Health Care Industry and the Impact on Psychiatry* (Washington: APA, Office of Economic Affairs, 1990).

2. JD Restuccia *et al.,* "A Comparative Analysis of Appropriateness of Hospital Use," *Health Affairs* (Summer 1984): 130–38.

3. RA Dorwart, "Managed Mental Health Care: Myths and Realities in the 1990s," 41 *Hospital and Community Psychiatry* 10 (1990): 1087–91.

4. SS Sharfstein, "Utilization Management: Managed or Mangled Psychiatric Care?" 147, *American Journal of Psychiatry* 8 (1990): 965–66; and GL Tischler, "Utilization Management of Mental Health Services by Private Third Parties," 147 *American Journal of Psychiatry* 8 (1990): 967–73.

5. D Ermann, "Hospital Utilization Review: Past Experience, Future Directions," *Journal of Health Politics, Policy and Law* 13 (1988): 683–704.

6. RM Scheffler, JO Gibbs, and DA Gurnick, *The Impact of Medicare's Prospective Payment System and Private Sector Initiatives: Blue Cross Experience, 1980–1986* (Report to the Health Care Financing Administration, HCFA Grant 15-C-98757/5-01, July 1988).

7. TM Wickizer, "The Effect of Utilization Review on Hospital Use and Expenditures: A Review of the Literature and an Update on Recent Findings," 27 *Medical Care* 6 (1988): 632–47.

8. PJ Feldstein, TM Wickizer, and JRC Wheeler, "The Effects of Utilization Review Programs on Health Care Use and Expenditures," 318, *The New England Journal of Medicine* 20 (1988): 1310–14; and TM Wickizer, JRC Wheeler, and PJ Feldstein "Does Utilization Review Reduce Unnecessary Hospital Care and Contain Costs?" 47 *Medical Care Review* (1990): 327–63.

9. AR Rodriguez, "The CHAMPUS Psychiatric and Psychological Review Project," in *Psychiatric Peer Review: Prelude and Promise*, ed JM Hamilton (Washington: American Psychiatric Press, 1985).

10. Frank *et al.,* "Growth in Expenditure for Mental Health Services" (supra note 1).

11. Id.

12. RA Dorwart *et al.,* "The Privatization of Mental Health Care," in *The Future of Mental Health Services Research,* ed CA Taube, D Mechanic, and AA Hohmann, DHHS Pub (ADM)89-1600 (Washington: DHHS, 1989); and RW Redick *et al.,* "Private Psychiatric Hospitals. United States: 1983–84 and 1986," *NIMH Statistical Note* 191 (Rockville, Md: National Institute of Mental Health, October 1989).

13. Frank *et al.,* "Growth in Expenditure for Mental Health Services" (supra note 1).

33. Comprehensive EAPs: Reshaping the Behavioral Health Care System

Cindy Yoder-Brown

Faced with the same cost-control challenges as the entire health care system, the behavioral health care system requires reshaping in order to continue to provide quality, cost-effective care. Part of this reshaping should include the integration of employee assistance programs (EAPs) with the other elements of health care benefit programs, including managed care and benefits design. Comprehensive EAPs are the logical and positive next step in the development of health benefits programs that combine quality with economy.

Employee assistance program (EAP) professionals are becoming increasingly aware of their responsibility to the company and its needs. As health care costs continue to rise, companies are concerned with cost-cutting and competitive management.[1] In searching for ways to control health care costs, companies are looking to EAPs for leadership.

This article details the challenges facing today's EAPs in their concern for cost-effective, quality care for clients under the present behavioral health care system. It concludes with specific actions for reshaping the system through an integration of EAP, managed care, and benefits design functions into a single entity called the Comprehensive EAP.

BALANCING QUALITY CARE AND COST-EFFECTIVENESS

Quality of care issues complicate corporate America's call for responsiveness by EAPs. By definition, quality means conforming to requirements.[2] Yet the

Reprinted from *EAP Digest,* January/February 1992, with the permission of Performance Resource Press, Inc., 1863 Technology Drive, Troy, MI 48083.

provision and evaluation of behavioral health care is individualized and subjective, unlike the observable, specific science of medical/surgical care. Because personal problems often lack objective definition, measuring the quality of behavioral health services is difficult.

As costs are easier to measure than quality, EAPs are concerned that cost-effectiveness will be emphasized at the expense of quality care.[3] Excellent care and low cost are rarely compatible; with some exceptions, high quality services carry a high price. However, "cost containment without quality is only an illusion of cost containment."[4] Inadequate, ineffective, or inappropriate treatment is never cost-effective, no matter how expensive the service—the client's condition worsens and further costs (in additional care, increased absenteeism, lower productivity, and related medical care) accumulate. Consequently, if cost controls compromise quality, the company ultimately accrues even higher costs. This realization aids the increasing awareness that reducing behavioral health care costs is best achieved with a long-term, quality focus.[5]

The EAP profession's agenda for the 1990s features growth and change in their efforts to balance cost-containment with quality issues.[6] The challenge is to find the highest quality care for the lowest cost while refusing to compromise services that are in the client's best interest.[7] To meet this challenge, the behavioral health care system must be redesigned to satisfy both human and economic needs.[8] Also, roles and relationships at each level of the system must be redefined and realigned and a new "team approach" adopted.

PROBLEMS IN THE BEHAVIORAL HEALTH CARE SYSTEM

Before attempting to "fix" the behavioral health care system, problem areas must be addressed. These areas include:

- Lack of standard, objective measurements;
- Cost control procedures;
- Underdeveloped and inappropriate care technologies;
- Uninformed care recipients;
- Employers skeptical of behavioral health care;
- Faulty benefit package designs;
- Proliferation of fragmented, cost-cutting-focused managed behavioral health care (MBHC) providers; and
- Ambivalence and uncertainty in the EAP profession.

Lack of Standard, Objective Measurements

A significant problem is the limited and subjective nature of measurement. This problem greatly limits the EAP profession from realizing the fundamental goals of evaluating and ensuring quality care for clients, integration of services within the company, and evaluation of EAP services. EAP professionals also tend to devote insufficient time and attention to developing and exploring statistical data and analytical observations on which to base referral-related decisions. Consequently, politics, marketing, and convenience often influence practice decisions that should be based on standard, objective criteria.[9]

These issues are due, in part, to the nature of a subjective business. It is also due, in some instances, to individual EAP professional's and provider's disinterest and lack of initiative. EAPs have much to learn and much to do. Until standard, objective criteria with which to guide the profession and the behavioral health care system are developed, EAPs will continue to choose providers by questionable means. In addition, because the field lacks the criteria for evaluating its services and those of providers, EAPs are not in a strong position to demand that providers account for their activities and prove their effectiveness. Consequently, EAPs continue to be biased by marketing and personal attitudes and rely on qualitative client feedback and trial and error to determine provider effectiveness.

Cost Control Procedures Often Encourage Inferior Treatment

Many cost control procedures only foster inferior care by inferior treatment providers.[10] Questionable networking and marketing procedures contribute to this problem, further complicating the situation when considering cost-effectiveness issues. Quality providers are often the busiest providers, and therefore, least interested in fee reductions. On the other hand, less qualified providers often have more time for networking and marketing their services and are more willing to become involved in fee-reduction negotiations.[11] Therefore, EAP provider networks are often in danger of being comprised of treatment providers who may be the least expensive, yet also the least qualified.

Underdeveloped and Inappropriate Care Technologies

Many communities do not have enough treatment resources and/or lack an appropriate variety of resources.[12] Consequently, troubled individuals may go untreated or are inappropriately treated, leading to more problems for the individual and more costs for the employer. Treatment alternatives such as partial hospitalization, halfway homes, and in-home intensive family therapy are lacking in most communities. Furthermore, many individuals and families have problems for which no appropriate treatment technologies have been developed.

Recipients Are Uninformed of Their Care

Clients tend to be uninformed concerning appropriate services for specific problems.[13, 14] They also tend to seek treatment without much guidance. This often results in benefits and personal dollars going toward inappropriate, ineffective treatment.

Employers Are Skeptical of Behavioral Health Care

Employers often have little knowledge regarding behavioral health care.[15] As a result, these services have traditionally been missing from employers' benefits packages. This issue relates to the behavioral health care system's lack of specific cost-effective and quality data. Companies tend to be conservative in offering behavioral health benefits for fear of creating a demand for services of questionable effectiveness.[16]

Faulty Benefit Package Designs

Historically, benefits have been inappropriately, ineffectively, and unjustly allocated with regards to behavioral health care. Benefit structures are usually inflexible and impersonal and limit appropriate referral and treatment related decision making.[17] Traditional benefit packages penalize individuals for having behavioral health problems, operating as if these individuals can choose to be sick.[18] For example, a diabetic is usually allowed much fuller coverage than an individual with schizophrenia. As unresolved behavioral problems are often manifest in physical complications, this discrimination in the allocation of benefits often results in increased benefits utilization. consequently, money not spent for behavioral health care is often doubly or triply spent on medical treatment.[19]

Another aspect of poor benefit plan design is that employers often lack clear objectives for their plans.[20] Clearly, articulated objectives are crucial to evaluating benefits and providing an appropriate plan design. Behavioral health care benefits often favor more costly, often less effective hospitalization over alternative forms of treatment.[21, 22] Poor or limited plans result in treatment and service technologies that take advantage of benefit coverage rather than meet the client's treatment needs.[23] Therefore, providers receive financial rewards and employees often receive inappropriate and ineffective treatment.

These inherent problems in behavioral health care benefit design, along with the other faults, result in excessive costs. In response, employers shift more of the burden to employees and cap benefits to guard against further cost escalation. However, cutbacks in benefits are self-defeating; employee behavioral health problems remain as treatment needs go unmet. Eventually, this results in more problems and costs to the employees, the family, and the employer.

Proliferation of Fragmented, Cost-Cutting-Focused Managed Behavioral Health Care (MBHC) Providers

Other problems involve the roles of EAPs and MBHC providers in the behavioral health care system. MBHC providers were quick to respond to the business community's call for cost-effective ways of dealing with rising behavioral health care costs. With little planning and a financial focus, many MBHC providers developed quick-fix, fragmented programs that emphasize cost-containment at the expense of quality care.[24-26] Claiming to manage care by controlling access, MBHCs only add multiple layers between individuals seeking care and the appropriate resource.[27] The results are restricted access to care and a decline in quality.

Although controlled access plans (HMOs, PPOs, and indemnity plans with utilization review or precertification) set out to cut costs by controlling benefit plan abuse, they have, in reality, given rise to an abusive subsystem that denies care through exclusionary tactics.[28] As many MBHC providers excluded common diagnoses such as eating disorders, sexual abuse traumas, and gambling addictions from benefit plans, the results were turmoil and higher costs. The overly-restrictive approaches of many MBHC providers are often used as a guise to ration care rather than a guide for ensuring quality, cost-effective care.[29] Companies may realize great savings in the first quarter, but such approaches prove futile in the long-term as they fail to achieve permanent cost reduction.[30] On a positive note, one benefit to these approaches is the awareness that reducing the cost of behavioral health care is best achieved with a long-term, quality care focus.

Pronounced Ambivalence and Uncertainty in the EAP Profession

EAPs have inherent weaknesses that add to problems in the behavioral health care system. One major weakness is the lack of knowledge regarding benefits. Many EAP professionals have failed to guide employers toward proper objectives and requirements for design and use of benefits.[31] As proof, many have only recently questioned the magic of a 28-day hospitalization for chemical dependency treatment and acknowledged the importance of individualized care.

Corporate America is calling upon EAP professionals to be responsive to the behavioral health care system cost crisis. The field has accepted this challenge with an air of ambivalence and uncertainty. Many EAP professionals are caught up in attempts to justify their existence and are emphasizing cost-effectiveness over quality. Others refuse to budge from traditional assessment/referral roles. Still others are uncertain about the role of EAPs in managing cost and care in the behavioral health care system.

SOLUTION: COMPREHENSIVE EAPs

The solution to the field's ambivalence and uncertainty and the solution to getting the behavioral health care system back on track are the same. EAP professions must adopt a creative and proactive stance to redefine and expand their role and mission. This requires shaping both internal and external environments to achieve a more cost- and quality-effective behavioral health care system.

Incorporating Structured Managed Care Functions

EAPs can learn from MBHC counterparts. Although many MBHC providers have failed to keep a proper client- and quality-of-care perspective, they have brought into focus many core elements necessary for a proper response to the behavioral health care cost crisis. The principles of managed care have offered EAPs a means to better attain their goals, and many have accepted MBHC functions as essential components of their EAP.

The permanency of structured managed care functions in the EAP field is revealed through the Employee Assistance Professionals Association's recent revision of its program standards and guidelines.[32] "Maximizing Behavioral Health Benefits Value Through EAP Integration" is a segment of the program standards and guidelines that describes an EAP's unique core elements with integrated MBHC functions. In a broader context, EAPs have provided these MBHC functions for years. Yet MBHC providers were instrumental in redefining their application and promoting a structured plan for gaining some control over the behavioral health care system.[33]

The Employee Assistance Professionals Association defines an EAP with MBHC functions as a "Comprehensive EAP."[34] According to their program standards and guideline, the Comprehensive EAP includes the following functions: benefit consultation; financial incentives; case management systems; and quality assurance systems to track short- and long-term effectiveness.[35]

Many EAP professionals and MBHC providers conclude that the best way to serve the needs of employees and employers while balancing cost-effectiveness with quality care is through an integrated approach. While managed care efforts emphasize cost-containment, the EAP perspective is that quality care is never cost-effective if it fails to meet the client's needs. Consequently, in combining managed care approaches with the philosophy and practice of an EAP, the Comprehensive EAP can balance quality care with cost-effectiveness. The EAP is the cornerstone of the managed care subsystem due to its focus on long-term cost-containment through long-term care management.[36]

Benefits Coordination and Effective, Flexible Plan Design

A variety of Comprehensive EAPs exist; however, the success of any program depends on close coordination with the benefits department. This coordination is essential if Comprehensive EAPs are to shape the behavioral health care system and balance the quality/cost-effective care issue. Coordination is also essential because benefits and treatment patterns influence each other more so than any other sectors of the behavioral health care system.[37]

Traditional means of cutting behavioral health care costs (capping benefits, increasing premiums, and cost sharing) have not been proven in the best interest of the employer or employee. Evidence suggests that this cut-and-slash approach leads to increases in the use of medical/surgical benefits and lowers productivity.[38] Comprehensive EAPs can help benefits personnel make the most of their budget by helping to develop flexible benefits designs for alternative treatment services specific to an individual's situation.[39] The Comprehensive EAP must educate and consult with benefits personal regarding appropriate services, providers, and coverage; help benefits personnel articulate specific and measurable objectives regarding the plan; and promote flexibility and creativity in designing or redesigning how these objective are to be met.[40] Malone and Johnson describe this flexible and creative benefit package design as "user friendly."[41] It includes improved access to benefits through specialized alternatives and options that ensure needed flexibility for treatment referrals.[42] In addition, benefits should be expanded to include all levels of care and treatment environments. This flexibility provides for choice and individualized care which is more important in behavioral health care than medical services because treatment effectiveness is dependent upon a good client-provider match.[43] Although most options and limitations can be written into the benefit plan, employers must also be willing to go outside the plan for maximum efficiency.[44]

Financial Incentives for Comprehensive EAP Utilization

Important in the development of an effective benefit plan are financial incentives to motivate use of the Comprehensive EAP. Incentives help ensure that clients are professionally guided to the appropriate, quality provider. Such incentives include increased benefit coverage and reduced or waived copayments.[45]

INFLUENCING THE BEHAVIORAL HEALTH CARE SYSTEM

Comprehensive EAPs are a result of corporate America's push toward a single, integrated system of EAP, managed care and benefits coordination.[46] Besides being easy to communicate and administer, coordinating responsibilities into one system is also the best tool for ensuring efficient, quality services.[47, 48] The effectiveness of this system depends on a supportive team approach whereby all players work toward mutual goals. As EAP professionals are the point-of-entry to the behavioral health care system and experts in the behavioral health care field, they are in the primary position to guide the system and ensure its quality focus through the following means:

- Evaluating quality through research and development;
- Influencing treatment providers through referral, case management, and flexible benefit plan design;
- Developing alternative community resources; and
- Effecting change through traditional EAP roles and functions.

Evaluating Quality Through Research and Development

Through systems integration of EAPs, managed care, and benefits, a Comprehensive EAP has greater potential to effect change within the behavioral health care system. The EAP field's proactive, creative stance involves and depends on research and development. Standards for measuring and evaluating how well providers meet these quality requirements must be developed. Through formal quality assurance measurements, EAPs can reach consensus and make appropriate referral/treatment decisions so that purposeful, goal-oriented growth can occur.[49] Also, new intervention approaches must be explored so that innovative treatments can be developed.

Influencing Treatment Providers Through Referral, Case Management, and Flexible Benefit Plan Design

As the criteria for measuring provider effectiveness are not fully developed, EAPs continue to refer to providers without certainty that clients are receiving appropriate care. Comprehensive EAPs, however, have inherent controls with which to influence providers. The Comprehensive EAP introduces flexibility, coordination, innovation, and balance into the behavioral health care field and encourages a provider's attention to client needs.[50] EAP professionals must understand and act on this powerful control to direct change in the treatment provider subsystem.

Traditional service delivery subsystems have not rewarded the prudent, quality-care provider.[51] As EAP professionals begin to control a greater percentage of referrals, they can be more demanding in their expectation for quality assurance measures from providers.[52] EAPs no longer need to accept a providers' definition of quality; Comprehensive EAPs proactively influence providers through inherent controls and are now defining what constitutes quality. For example, case management ensures that the employee obtains the most appropriate, effective, and least restrictive level of care.[53]

Comprehensive EAPs also improve the behavioral health care system by rewarding quality, problem-focused, change-oriented providers through increased referrals and benefit coverage. EAP professionals are serving in a policing function to identify unethical, unprofessional practitioners. Providers who do not offer quality care are removed from the provider network, and those whose quality is consistent are rewarded. When EAPs finally develop the objective means to determine quality of service, their impact on the treatment provider subsystem will be that much greater.

It must be stressed that the relationship between providers and the Comprehensive EAP is not adversarial, but one of mutual trust and respect.[54] The goal is to develop a behavioral health care system that rewards quality providers who share the EAP professional's commitment to clients.

Developing Alternative Community Resources

The power of referral, case management, and flexible benefit plans also influences the development of alternative methods of treatment and services. Historically, benefit coverage has been inflexible, favoring more costly and restrictive hospitalization that has not been proven effective. Redesigning benefit packages to accommodate alternative community resources is essential. Only now are EAPs discovering that individualized and less restrictive alternatives are in the best interest of the client.[55] However, the reality is that many communities lack appropriate treatment alternatives.

The Comprehensive EAP must be proactive and creative in motivating the community to develop needed services.[56] Aiding the development of these resources enhances the potential for fulfilling a client's treatment needs. It also increases the potential for reaching a balance between cost-effectiveness and quality care, because adequate and appropriate community services—in conjunction with flexible benefits packages—limit a provider's ability to abuse the system for financial gain.

As benefit coverage is opened up to a comprehensive range of alternatives (e.g., group therapy, in-home intensive family therapy, crisis resolution therapy, half-way homes) and providers (e.g., marriage and family counselors, art therapists, addictions counselors), and as EAPs advocate for clients, communities will be motivated to develop appropriate alternatives. These alternatives will result in treatment that is individualized as better matches occur between the client and his or her treatment provider, treatment setting, and level of care. Therefore, greater potential for high-quality care will occur at often significantly lower costs.[57]

Effecting Change Through Traditional EAP Roles and Functions

The comprehensive EAP provides the controls necessary to influence positive change in the behavioral health care system. Yet EAPs must continue with their traditional roles to help influence the system. One important function is that of educating, informing, and training employers and employees so that they may make appropriate, healthy decisions. EAPs also must continue to focus on prevention and early intervention so that problems and costs are minimized and individual prognoses are improved. This includes consulting with supervisors, managers, and union stewards on identifying troubled employees at an early stage and guiding them to the EAP. Also, EAP assessments are imperative for effective referral or short-term counseling. Assessment is the foundation of the behavioral health care system; all aspects of service delivery hinge upon proper assessment. If assessments are not thorough and precise, all other controls of the Comprehensive EAP are futile. EAPs must also continue to be sensitive to social, cultural, and gender issues in directing clients to the best treatment provider match. Finally, EAPs must actively continue long-term follow-up to ensure that clients receive effective treatment and resolve their problems.

REACHING NEW, DESIRED HEIGHTS

Integrating EAP, managed-care and benefits systems should be viewed as a positive step in refining the EAP profession. The field is increasing in status; no longer do EAPs exist in a separate niche within companies. EAPs have become integrated into the ongoing functions of companies and are moving closer to the source of decision making. EAP services are recognized as instrumental to helping balance quality of care with cost-effectiveness and to helping corporate American back on track.[58]

Rapid changes are occurring as the profession becomes increasingly comprehensive and assimilated into the functions of organization. Consequently, many EAPs are fearful of losing their autonomy and ongoing mission. However, were EAPs not so pervasive and strong, MBHC providers and insurance companies would not be trying to buy or develop EAPs.[59]

EAPs may not have a choice of modernization, yet the path of innovation is exciting.[60] EAPs must maintain a humanistic foundation while integrating a business ideology. Helping companies address and pursue their cost-control concerns opens up responsibilities never before available. If active and creative in addressing these changes and directing their movement, EAPs can continue to shape their mission and destiny while evoking great change in the whole behavioral health care system.

1. D Bridwell, J Collins, and D Levine, "A quiet revolution: The movement of EAPs to managed care," *EAP Digest* 8527-30, July/August 1988.

2. L Wenzel, *Suggested Employer Criteria for Mental Health and Chemical Dependency Benefits* (unpublished monograph).

3. WN Penzer, "Toward measuring the quality of mental health services," *EAP Digest* 7(6):55-62, September/October 1987.

4. WN Penzer, "The realities of managed mental health care," *EAP Digest* 10(1):66-68, January/February 1990.

5. R Winslow, "Spending to cut mental-health costs," *The Wall Street Journal,* December 13, 1989, p. B1.

6. BK Googins, "Taking a proactive position," *Employee Assistance* 1(7):43-44, February 1989.

7. OF Jones, "Why insurance carriers are taking an interest in the EAP field," *The ALMACAN:* 26-28, November 1988.

8. Supra note 4.

9. WN Penzer, "Toward sustaining quality mental health services," *EAP Digest* 7(3):35-40, March/April 1987.

10. Supra note 4.

11. Supra note 9.

12. C Dainas, "The EAP role in influencing community care," (unpublished manuscript, 1988).

13. J Mahoney, T Murgitroyde, D Levine, DL Reynolds, and J Roth, "The synthesis of EAPs and managed care: Five synopses," *The* ALMACAN 18(5):26-28, 1988.

14. WM Mercer, *Managing Mental Health and Chemcial Dependency Expenses.* New York: Meideinger Hansen Inc., 1990.

15. Supra note 13.

16. S Sullivan, TJ Flynn, and ME Lewin, "The quest to manage mental health costs," *Business & Health:* 24-28, February 1987.

17. AR Rodriguez and JJ Maher, "Psychiatric case management offers cost, quality control," *Business & Health:* 14-17, March 1986.

18. Supra note 13.

19. WN Penzer, "When are we gonna be there?! *EAP Digest* 8(5):41-45, July/August 1988.

20. Supra note 7.

21. Supra note 7.

22. EL Bassuk and SK Holland, "Accounting for high cost psychiatric care," *Business and Health:* 38-41, July 1987.

23. Supra note 12.

24. PD Gotcher and DL Redfield, "Integrated managed behavioral health care: Road to success," *EAP Digest* 8(5):46-52, July/August 1988.

25. RM Yandrick, "Multiple choices: EAP professionals can further managed care objectives by exercising their full range of referral options," *EAPA Exchange* 20(8):34-36, August 1990.

26. C Parker, "From EAP to managed care: Which hat do I wear?" *EAP Digest* 9(4):18, 45-47, May/June 1989.

27. Ibid.

28. CS Schmidt, "Management by manipulation: The dilemma of managed mental healthcare," *Employee Assistance* 2(12):16-20, July, 1990.

29. K McClellan, "What's the bottom line?" *Employee Assistance* 1(7):75-78, February 1989.

30. Supra note 25.

31. L Wenzel, "Let's take credit for being the good case managers that we are," *EAPA Exchange* 20(7):16-17, July 1990.

32. RM Yandrick, "With the release of two hallmark documents, EAPA is helping to position our young profession for growth and development in the 1990s," *EAPA Exchange* 20(6):14-19, June 1990.

33. Id.

34. Id.

35. Id.

36. Id.

37. Supra note 14.

38. Supra note 17.

39. Supra note 25.

40. Supra note 12.

41. ER Malone and RB Johnson, "Designing benefits to flex around alternative forms of treatment," *EAPA Exchange* 20(7):15-16, July, 1990.

42. Supra note 25.

43. Supra note 2.

44. American Managment Association: Managing Health Care Costs, *An American Management Association Research Report,* New York: AMA, 1988.

45. R Lightman and J Bloom Wagman, "A working proposal for the EAP role in a managed care system," *The ALMACAN* 18(5):18-21, May, 1988.

46. J Dolan, "The development of MMHC services is an EAPs best bet for longevity," *EAPA Exchange* 20(7):15-16, July, 1990.

47. Supra note 2.

48. Supra note 14.

49. Supra note 9.

50. LS Sims, "Managed mental health care: What it is and how it works," *EAP Digest* 8(5):32-38, 63-74, July/August 1988.

51. Supra note 2.

52. Supra note 3.

53. Supra note 2.

54. Supra note 31.

55. Supra notes 25 and 41.

56. Supra note 12.

57. DM Bartlett, "Cutting costs, not quality," *EAP Digest* 9(3):21-24, March/April 1989.

58.   Supra note 6.

59.   Supra note 2.

60.   Supra note 7.

Part 7

IMPACT OF QUALITY ON COST CONTROL

34. Health Care Quality: Issues for Employers and Providers
John A. George

As the ultimate payors for health care, many employers have recognized the need to identify the quality of service being delivered by the providers supplying health care to their employees. Employers realize that by basing their health care spending decisions not only on price but on quality, they can foster healthy competition among providers—competition that will help control their health care expenses.

Many people believe that advances in the measurement of health care services and the proposed changes in financing the provision of those services will lead to a buyers' market for health care. This change becomes extremely important since the control will now shift from the provider to the purchaser. Those providers that are able to respond to this consumer orientation will clearly be the winners in obtaining market share. Those that do not respond appropriately and adequately will certainly lose market share and most likely go out of business.

How are providers responding to this new market orientation and what does this mean to the health care system? What are payors doing in their purchasing of health care services and how will this change the structure and response of the delivery system? What tools and techniques are available for the purchaser to measure the service outcomes, adequately determine what they are paying for, and compare it to what others are providing? These questions will be the subject of this article which is intended to explore what employers (the ultimate payors) are doing and what effects this will have on the health care system.

"There's nothing better in life than a head-on collision." —Lawrence Taylor

Some believe that health care providers and the payors are on target for a head-on collision. As control changes from the provider to the payor, major adjustments must be made in the system. The first adjustment is for the providers to begin measuring and reporting on their service outputs. These quality outcomes measurements will form the basis for the payor community to determine what they will buy and from whom. Not only are providers being told to do more, to do it better, and to do it for less, they are also being asked to explain what they are doing and how they are doing it.

What, then, are the specific issues that providers are being asked to report on? First and foremost, providers are being asked to define and measure the quality of the services they provide. Second, they are being asked to report on the effectiveness and efficiency of providing those services. Effectiveness may be defined as the clinical outcome of a service intervention.[1] In other words, did the patient get better? Was there a readmission? Was the service provided appropriate to the specific case? In measuring efficiency, we are looking at the costs of treating the patient and the resources utilized, including clinical diagnostic tests, lengths of stay, etc. Therefore, as we approach the measurement of quality, we look at the outcome of treatment in terms of its effectiveness and efficiency.

"The man who complains about the way the ball bounces is likely the one who dropped it." —Lou Holtz

Hospitals and other health care providers are in a position to take the ball and run with it, but if they do not respond and respond quickly to the marketplace, employers and the government will increasingly dictate how the ball should be carried. Many providers are taking the initiative to define quality, cost, and outcomes. However, they have been reluctant to share their data with the marketplace. For many years, hospitals have defined quality care and decided what data will be collected and how much of that data will be shared. Little, if any, attempt had been made to determine the payor and patient's perception of quality.[2]

This brings us to a further expansion of the definition of quality that should be used by payors. Quality comes in two forms, technical quality and perceived quality. Technical quality can be accurately and objectively measured through various and available tools. Perceived quality is the patients' perception of the care received at a health care facility, physician's office, or other location.[3]

This second type of measurement, although valid, does have inherent problems. A recent article on patient surveys, designed to measure perceived quality, showed that the public rated urban tertiary, teaching hospitals as better or higher quality. Other research shows that the public perceives patient relations, medical or nurse staffing, convenience, and technology as keys in defining quality in a hospital. While some of these variables—such as staffing ratios—can be associated with quality of care, others cannot.[4] Therefore, a patient's perception of quality cannot be the only measure used.

Perceived quality is based on how the patient felt he or she was treated. Was the food warm? Was the room clean? Did I see my doctor while in the hospital? Did my doctor explain the treatment that was being ordered? Did other problems arise that were not there before my hospital admission? Did I have to be readmitted for the same problem? Did I wait in the hospital all weekend when no tests or treatments were rendered? And, finally, did I get better?

Patients do not just buy health care; they buy expectations. Providers must be able to respond effectively and efficiently to patients who expect quality services. Information obtained by patient surveys is important and should be required of providers and used by employers. Data from patient surveys will tell employers where their employees want to be treated. This, along with the quality measure discussed next, will prove invaluable for employers in determining where to send their employees. As employers deal more with managed care companies, these evaluations become extremely important.

Technical quality evaluation, while more difficult to measure, is an extremely important tool. If quality can be achieved through consistent results, then this consistency in the provision of services is critical. How, then, is consistency established and measured?

One way that this can be accomplished is through the use of benchmarking. This means rating a hospital's practices and delivered service against the best in the industry. Benchmarking is a critical technique in comparative quality assessment. Hospitals have been known to say "we're unique" to explain poor morbidity and mortality figures, but benchmarking against the results of the best in the industry delivering a particular service minimizes the use of this defense by hospitals. There must be a combined focus on outcomes and process that force the provider to look at both ends of the spectrum—what care is delivered and how it is delivered. In order for employers to best evaluate what they are getting for their health benefit dollar, they must begin to use the tools for measuring technical quality that focus on both the outcome—the final result, including the cost—and the process by which that outcome was delivered.

Combining technical quality assessment with perception surveys will give the employer the information needed to effectively evaluate the health care community, and thereby determine where to direct their employees for health care. This redirection will then add competition to the health care delivery system.

"There are three types of people . . . people who make things happen, people who watch things happen, and people who don't know what's happening."
—John Madden

Health care providers are now being forced by employers and the government increasingly to be involved in evaluating and showing the quality of service that they produce. With the nation's health care costs well over $650 million, employers are saying that they now want to know what they are paying for and who they are paying. General Motors, Chrysler, Hershey Foods, General Electric, and many other large employers are funding studies to help to determine the value of their medical purchases. A program underway in Cleveland, Ohio, is seeking to rank hospitals in terms of the cost and quality of the service produced. The long-term goal, according to Dr. Paul Ellwood, president of Interstudy, is to develop an accounting system for Medicare.[5] What this would effectively mean is the development of standards by which companies could compare physician performance and judge medical care for themselves and ultimately determine where they will seek medical care.

Why are employers, the government and health care providers taking these steps in determining what type of health care is produced? The cost of health care is escalating at horrendous proportions. Consider the following situation: A study ordered by Pennsylvania's legislature on 35 Pittsburgh area hospitals found that treating dizziness costs from $1,620 to $5,085—*with no difference in results*. In late 1990, two of 73 patients admitted for heart failure at a leading research and teaching hospital died, while four of 31 died at a local community hospital. Yet the teaching facility charged $11,015 per patient versus $5,845 at the community hospital.[6] Year after year major national publications report that average health care costs increase at double digit rates, with no indication of slowing. Study after study suggests that a significant portion of current medical care is inappropriate. Estimates are that 20 to 30 percent of care that we are paying for is unnecessary and, in some cases, harmful. This waste persists despite efforts that have proven that quality care can be provided at a cost far less than the national average. The amount of inappropriate care is not explained by high or low rates of usage in a particular area, by the kind of health care facility, or by any of the usual physician characteristics such as age, specialty, education, or board certification. The most important factor seems to be the practice style of the individual provider. Given the proper data, practice style can be altered to emulate the best.[7]

While these statistics appear bleak, there are programs in place that definitely show that raising levels of quality will, in fact, help reduce the cost of health care. In addition, once the payors have been given the necessary data to determine who the quality, cost-effective providers are, they must be willing to redesign their health benefits plan that financially encourages their employees, the ultimate consumer, to use these providers. Only when we quit rewarding the inefficient providers will a competitive model finally work in helping not only to reduce the cost of health care but also raise the quality of service.

Before reviewing what employers are doing in helping to implement this structure, let's look at a case reported on in *Business Week* on how raising the levels of quality will, in fact, reduce cost.[8] In 1991, it was reported that a hospital in Salt Lake City looked to lower its rate of postoperative wound infections. Before this effort started, the rate of would infection was reported at 1.8 percent. By incorporating quality measures in the process of delivering antibiotics before surgery, the hospital cut the infection rate in half, to 0.9 percent. Since that time, the infection rate has dropped to 0.4 percent. The average postoperative infection adds $14,000 to the hospital bill. By reducing the infection rate and, therefore, increasing the quality of its service, the hospital has been able to effectively reduce the average hospital bill.

Other hospitals that have sought other ways of improving the quality of their programs have seen similar savings. In the same issue of *Business Week*, it was reported that a hospital that reduced waiting time to admit patients cut payroll and other costs by $260,000 per year. Where is this being accomplished and who are some of the employers doing this? Many state hospital associations are attempting to collect the data to objectively assure the quality of care provided by their members.

The Maryland Quality Indicator Project, as reported in *Hospitals*, has 600 hospitals participating in its project.[9] This program includes other associations like the New Hampshire Hospital Association and about one-third of the hospitals in Wisconsin are participants. Additionally, the Colorado state government, as well as more that 30 other states, have passed legislation mandating the collection of data for quality evaluation. State after state can be identified showing what government is doing to require data collection for the purpose of evaluating the quality of care delivered by their resident hospitals. The important point to keep in mind is that data are being collected to make it easier for payors to more effectively evaluate what they are purchasing.

At the payor level this information must be made a part of the purchasing decisions. Pennsylvania's Health Care Cost Containment Commission (HC4) collects severity adjusted data. Hershey Foods Corporation in Hershey, Pennsylvania uses the HC4 data to identify a network of providers and to develop centers of excellence in order to direct their own employees to the most effective and efficient providers. In addition, a project funded by the John A. Hartford Foundation will use the same HC4 data to evaluate hospital effectiveness. This information will be used by purchasing companies and for companies that rate hospital bonds.[10]

These projects are only a few examples of what is occurring across the country. As businesses direct their employees to specific providers, they see more of a need to identify the quality of service being delivered by the providers. As managed health care companies grow by helping employees to reduce the cost of their health care benefits, the need to measure the quality of care of these preferred providers becomes more apparent. The health care purchasing decision will be made not only on the basis of price but, more importantly, on the quality of the service delivered.

1. JK Iglehart, "Competition and the pursuit of quality: A conversation with Walter McClure," 7 *Health Affairs*, 1 (1988): 79-90.

2. VK Omachonu, "Quality of care and the new patient: New criteria for evaluation," 15 *Health Care Manage Rev* 4 (1990): 43-50.

3. JA Boscarino, "The public's perception of quality hospitals II: Implications for patient surveys," *Hospital and Health Services Administration,* Spring 1992.

4. Id.

5. JF Silar and S Garland, "Sending health care into rehab," *Business Week,* Oct 25, 1991: 111-112.

6. WL Mobraaten, JJ Burdge, E Donley, ME Gilliard, RS Saul, and AJ Sordoni, *Strategies for Pennsylvania business in the containment of health care* (Harrisburg, PA: Business Council of Pennsylvania Health Care Subcommittee, 1984).

7. RH Brook and ME Vaiana, *Appropriateness of care: A chart book.* National Health Policy Forum. (Washington, DC: The George Washington University, 1989).

8. Supra note 5.

9. M Burke, "Clinical quality initiatives: The search for meaningful—and accurate—measures," *Hospitals,* Mar 5, 1992: 26-38.

10. Id.

35. Outcomes Management Systems: Tools for Measuring and Managing Health Care Quality

Patricia A. Ball

Outcomes measurement is the system of determining and assessing the effects of medical care on the life of the patient. The Outcomes Management System described here tracks and analyzes outcomes data concerning issues of patient functionality and quality of life, which are the terms meaningful to patients. Providers and patients both need the information and insight that outcomes measurement provides in order to make the best and most cost-effective health decisions.

Several factors have shaped the restructuring of the American health care industry over the past two decades, including (to name just a few) market forces, various managed care arrangements, and the proliferation of group practices. One direct consequence is that consumers of health care now find themselves with greater power to influence the medical care they receive. However, these newly empowered purchasers of health care generally lack the information necessary to make the most beneficial decisions; at present, there is a significant lack of knowledge of how medical interventions affect patients' lives, making it impossible to appraise the true value of health services. In the late 1980s, InterStudy (a nonprofit health policy and research organization) began developing the Outcomes Management System (OMS), a patient-centered system for measuring outcomes, to bridge this information gap.

Since January of 1993, InterStudy's early role as developer and distributor of the OMS has been assumed by the Health Outcomes Institute (HOI). HOI is a Minnesota-based nonprofit organization engaged in the following:

1. Developing and refining data collection tools useful in assessing the effects on health status of treatments and other behavioral and social factors;

2. Disseminating those tools, advising users on implementation, assisting in the early interpretation of findings, and providing support to foster the collection and use of outcomes data;

3. Educating system developers, vendors, and consultants regarding outcomes measurement implementation issues, preparing them to support the ongoing collection and interpretation of outcomes data;

4. Encouraging the preparation of presentations and articles within the clinical, management, and academic literatures, demonstrating the value and opportunities for use of the OMS and other health outcomes measures; and

5. Helping to establish a national data repository for the voluntary pooling of outcomes information.

THE OUTCOMES MANAGEMENT SYSTEM

Outcomes management is a continuous process linking outcomes with the process of care through a feedback mechanism. It is "a technology of patient experience designed to help patients, payers, and providers make more rational medical care-related choices based on better insight into the effect of these choices on the patient's life."[1] The OMS builds an ongoing observational study into routine medical care by providing a mechanism for systematically assessing, tracking, and analyzing health outcomes that are important to patients. Traditional clinical and physiological data as well as patient-derived functional status and quality of life information are compiled using language and terms understandable by both patients and providers. Data are collected in a common format, using widely accepted and publicly available survey forms and protocols.

Users tracking the effects of ordinary medical care link OMS data with existing or evolving computerized medical records, claims processing, or hospital information systems. In combination with relevant financial records, a permanent database can be established and used in isolating the experience of individual patients (or aggregations of patients) by diagnosis, treatment, provider group, etc. The result will be a powerful tool for the management of clinical services, comparable in significance to existing financial management systems.

The OMS consists of a series of questionnaires and data collection protocols known as "TyPE" (Technology of Patient Experience) specifications. OMS data include general health status measures and other condition-independent core data, along with various condition-specific instruments.

General Health Status Measures

OMS core data are collected through a series of general purpose surveys. Data captured with these tools include individuals' personal identifiers (e.g., social security numbers), demographic information, health risks, comorbidities, functional status and well-being, and satisfaction with provider services. Factors such as age, health behaviors, and multiple disease states affect the outcomes of care, making it important to have these core data for each patient.

Adult functional status and well-being data are collected principally through the Health Status Questionnaire (HSQ). The HSQ is derived from the RAND 36-item Health Status Survey 1.0, itself based on work done as part of the RAND Health Insurance Experiment and the Medical Outcomes Study. The HSQ has 39 separate questions, assessing eight specific health attributes grouped under three major health dimensions:

1. Overall evaluation of health (health perception);
2. Functional status (physical functioning, social functioning, role limitations attributed to physical health, and role limitations attributed to emotional problems); and
3. Well-being (bodily pain, mental health, and fatigue).

In addition, the HSQ includes a measure of health status change and a screen for depression.

Condition-Specific Measures (TyPEs)

To supplement the general data collected on all patients (employers, employees, etc.), condition-specific data are also collected on patients presenting with specific diagnoses. The condition-specific data are used to describe and compare individual patients' diagnoses, therapies, and clinical outcomes. Simple sets of basic clinical and therapeutic data are collected from patients before, during, and after treatment. The TyPEs also specify patient-provided quality of life and functional status measures uniquely relevant to the condition being assessed. For example, patients diagnosed with cataracts are asked about vision-related restrictions on reading and automobile operation.

Condition-specific TyPE protocols are developed in a collaborative process involving clinicians and scientists experienced with each condition. Each TyPE has a user's manual describing the rationale for included data elements and recommended data collection procedures. There are 16 condition-specific TyPE specifications currently available and several others under development (see Table 1).

Table 1. Currently Available Condition-Specific TyPE Instruments

Angina
Asthma
Cataract
Chronic Obstructive Pulmonary Disease (COPD)
Chronic Sinusitis
Depression
Diabetes
Hip Fracture
Hip Replacement
Hypertension
Low Back Pain
Osteoarthritis of the Knee
Prostatism
Rheumatoid Arthritis
Stroke
Substance Use Abuse: Alcohol

THE USE OF OMS DATA IN HEALTH CARE DECISION MAKING

Once implemented, the OMS can serve multiple purposes. First, providers may use the data to assess and choose therapies, estimate resources expended on treatment, and establish standards of treatment for specific conditions based on outcomes. At St. Vincent's Hospital and Medical Center in Oregon, orthopaedic surgeons studied the functional outcomes of patients receiving alternative prostheses (i.e., cemented or uncemented) during hip replacement. Results from their study showed that both physical and social functioning of patients receiving uncemented prostheses were better than those who had received cemented prostheses.[2]

Second, purchasers may use the data gathered through OMS efforts to predict the cost of medical care, select from among the various sources of health care, and design health care benefits. In recent years, several employers have formed coalitions to study patient outcomes and to stimulate competition in the health care industry based on quality.

Lastly, patients can be better informed about treatment alternatives and their likely effects on quality of life over a longer period of time. John Wennberg, MD, of the Foundation for Informed Medical Decision Making based at Dartmouth Medical School, has created a series of interactive patient videos to serve this purpose. Wennberg's videos are designed to provide unbiased descriptions of treatment options and patient outcomes that will improve the patient's decision making abilities.[3] Accumulating OMS data will provide an important resource for the preparation of similar patient education materials on a variety of conditions and therapies.

Many efforts to collect and use OMS data in the management of health services are underway. Projects vary in their scope, depth, and objectives, but all early users appreciate the need to have comparable data on patient outcomes. Some early implementations and trials of OMS data collection and interpretation are described below.

MULTI-SITE COLLABORATIONS

Two OMS projects stand out in terms of their scale, range of participants, and precedent-setting status. In both projects data from various health care settings are being pooled and the results are providing useful insights to the participants and the HOI.

The Managed Health Care Association (MHCA) Outcomes Project

In 1990, a consortium of major U.S. employers and managed care organizations (MCOs) organized to explore the feasibility and usefulness of outcomes management in improving the quality and cost effectiveness of medical care. The outcomes management consortium emerged from discussions between the Managed Health Care Association (MHCA), a group of *Fortune* 500 companies committed to quality improvement in managed care, and InterStudy. This employer and MCO initiated project is unique both in its origins within the business community and its specific focus upon the use of outcomes information in an attempt to improve the quality of health services. The initial goals for this project include:

- Demonstrating the commitment of purchasers and the managed care industry to rigorous evaluation of health outcomes.
- Assessing and reporting on the economic, political, and administrative issues in implementing outcome-based evaluations.
- Contributing to the body of information linking the process and outcomes of medical care.

In collecting outcomes data, project participants are using the OMS. Their work to date shows that MCOs can collect outcomes data from both inpatient and ambulatory settings, pooling data from a variety of organizations for aggregate analysis. The project consortium is expanding, and participants in this unique collaboration will continue to collect and pool samples of patient-reported functional status and clinical information from doctors and hospitals.

In addition to providing information about the processes and resources needed for successful outcomes implementation, results from the initial phase of the MHCA project have been used to identify potentially significant questions about the organization and process of treatment of angina and asthma, the

Table 2. MHCA Project Pairings

Ameritech	Blue Cross & Blue Shield of Illinois
Ameritech	Community Mutual Blue Cross & Blue Shield (Cincinnati)
AT&T	The Travelers
Digital Equipment Corporation	Fallon Community Health Plan
Digital Equipment Corporation	Harvard Community Health Plan
Digital Equipment Corporation	Matthew Thornton Health Plan
Digital Equipment Corporation	Blue Cross & Blue Shield of Massachusetts
General Electric Aerospace	U.S. Healthcare
General Motors Corporation	Blue Cross & Blue Shield of Missouri/ St. Louis
General Motors Corporation	Kaiser/Cleveland Region
HealthTrust, Inc.	AEtna Life & Casualty
James River Corporation	AEtna Life & Casualty
Marriott Corporation	The Prudential Insurance Co.
Procter & Gamble Company	Metropolitan Life Insurance Co.
Promus Companies	Metropolitan Life Insurance Co.
Commonwealth of Virginia	Blue Cross & Blue Shield of Virginia
Xerox Corporation	Blue Cross & Blue Shield of the Rochester Area

conditions selected by the employer-MCO pairs for testing. Intended only as a preliminary test of data gathering and pooling methods, the work suggests that factors predicting patient outcomes can be identified. These data, gathered in everyday practice environments, will help organizations to improve the patient care process and its outcomes.

The MHCA Outcomes Project is now entering its next phase, and activities include increasing both the number of cases studied and the number of sites from which data are gathered. This next phase will focus on further evaluation of the operational feasibility and usefulness of OMS data, and spur development of methodologies for "feeding back" data to providers and managers. Current MHCA project participants are listed in Table 2.

American Group Practice Association (AGPA) Outcomes Project

During the past several years, the American Group Practice Association (AGPA) has sponsored several collaborative outcomes projects in conjunction with its member clinics. The AGPA is a membership organization representing over 300 single and multispecialty group practices. In November 1989, they organized a consortium of six prominent AGPA member clinics — Henry Ford Medical Group (Detroit), Cleveland Clinic, Scott and White Clinic (Temple, TX), Park Nicollet Medical Center (Minneapolis), Virginia Mason Medical Center (Seattle), and Eugene Clinic (Oregon) — to investigate the outcomes of total hip replacement. Data were pooled among the clinics to assess the feasibility of OMS implementation and to compare outcomes across the clinics.

Current activities have focused on the use of OMS data by physicians and practice managers. Results from this project show that it is feasible to collect reliable and valid outcomes data, and to integrate these data into medical decision making processes. A second consortium of nearly 40 clinics has been organized to track outcomes of patients with asthma, cataracts, diabetes, low back pain, and hip replacement using OMS condition-specific TyPEs.

OTHER OMS IMPLEMENTATIONS

Hundreds of other OMS implementations are underway in a variety of settings ranging from single physician practices to multihospital systems, to insurance companies. Some examples include:

Minneapolis Heart Institute: Provider's Perspective. The Minneapolis Heart Institute (MHI) has successfully collected health status data on over 500 preadmission testing patients with OMS instruments. Nearly 40 percent of these patients proceeded to have either a percutaneous transluminal coronary angioplasty or atherectomy. Six-month follow-up health status data are being collected on eligible patients (e.g., patients who had previously completed baseline measures) using a mailout/mailback version of the health status questionnaire. The scope of activities at the MHI recently expanded to include merging OMS data with other clinical information contained in an existing interventional database and various cardiac registries. The assessment of function and well-being is providing new insights into the effect of procedures commonly used on patients with coronary artery disease.

Institute for Lower Back Care: Provider's Perspective. In another Minneapolis-based specialty practice, the Institute for Low Back Care (ILBC), outcomes information is collected on patients presenting with low back pain. At ILBC, OMS data collection has been integrated with materials routinely mailed to all new patients prior to their first clinic visit. In addition to the general health status questionnaire, ILBC has added a subset of measures from the low back pain TyPE specification. These data are used to assess the severity of back pain and back associated dysfunction. Data collection began in July, 1992 with health status and low back pain profiles now available for over 2,000 patients. The ILBC recently began collecting six-month follow-up data on a subset of their patients. Preliminary results are providing ILBC staff with a greater understanding of health status profiles for back patients, and are supporting ILBC's existing new patient severity classification system.

Blue Cross & Blue Shield of Minnesota: Insurer's Perspective. Blue Cross and Blue Shield of Minnesota (BCBSM) has made an organizational commitment to outcomes management, and has been involved in a variety of outcomes related projects for quite sometime. Their experience with OMS began in the late 1980s with the BCBSM Foundation, Inc., funding OMS implementation at Park Nicollet Medical Center, a large, Minneapolis-based group practice. Insights gained from the Park Nicollet experience helped BCBSM expand to other OMS efforts aimed at demonstrating the flexibility of OMS implementation across a range of practice settings.

This feasibility assessment began in selected mental health settings within their statewide provider network. The first phase of the project focused on establishing data collection protocols and assessing data collection feasibility in day-to-day practice. BCBSM began by incorporating patient health status data for all new patients at in-take. Having shown the viability of the data collection process, the clinic and BCBSM are now entering into the second stage of this project, more directly focusing on the collection of data for a defined diagnosis, depression. With this they will be increasing the scope of collected data to include items from the depression TyPE specification.

In addition to their OMS work in mental health settings, BCBSM is using patient outcomes measures in their select transplant network. BCBSM is working with two large hospitals in Minneapolis on this project. They also plan to facilitate outcomes implementation in their newly formed cardiac network. One of their goals is to use accumulating OMS data from these latter projects to aid patients in making better informed medical decisions about the risks and benefits of procedures.

AT&T American Transtech: An Employer Perspective. American Transtech, a subsidiary of AT&T, recently completed a health status assessment of their employees with an automated data collection system allowing respondents to use the telephone keypad for indicating answers to questions.

Employees were asked to complete the HSQ as well as items screening for the risk of carpal tunnel syndrome. During a two-week period, the health status of over 1,100 employees was assessed using this system. The use of this system to collect HSQ data proved practical, and the responses collected were shown to be valid when compared with traditional data collection measures. In addition, the data have allowed American Transtech managers to profile the health status of employees, evaluate the effectiveness of work site interventions, reduce the risk of hand and wrist injuries, and identify the health needs of their workers.

HOI'S EFFORTS TO STANDARDIZE THE OMS

To establish meaningful health outcomes data that allow widespread comparisons, greater standardization of data collection and use across groups is required. The HOI is working with a wide variety of providers, purchasers, scientists, and system vendors to establish practical protocols for the wide scale implementation of outcomes data collection, analysis, and interpretation. Data obtained through a voluntary national data pool will support continuous refinement of data collection standards. In addition, OMS users will benefit from the opportunity to compare providers', patients', and employers' experience within a broader sphere. The HOI is presently working with a number of organizations in planning the establishment and operation of such a data center.

SUMMARY

The health care industry is undergoing careful scrutiny over the cost of services and the allocation of resources. Outcomes data (including information on pre- and post-therapy patient function) will provide all players — payers, providers, and patients alike — with the data needed to make informed decisions about health care. The OMS is designed to support clinical, management, and purchaser decision making, and the HOI will serve as a vehicle to ensure that continuing development of the OMS reflects the concerns of major user groups (providers, employers, insurers, etc.). Fostering development of "generally accepted accounting principles" for monitoring the effects of health services, the HOI represents an opportunity for the private sector to establish standards guiding the collection and use of data useful to providers, patients, and purchasers.

1. Paul M. Ellwood, "Shattuck Lecture—Outcomes Management: A Technology of Patient Experience," 318 *New England Journal of Medicine* 23 (June 9, 1988): 1549-1556.

2. David Lansky, JBV Butler, and Frederick T. Waller, "Using Health Status Measures in the Hospital Setting: From Acute Care to Outcomes Management," 30 *Medical Care* 5 (Suppl., May 1992): MS57-MS73.

3. Berkeley Rice, "Educate Your Patients Without Taking More Time," *Medical Economics* Oct 5, 1992: 92-105.

36. Minnesota HMO Launches New Cardiac Network

Jerry Fruetel   MaryAnn Stump

Blue Cross and Blue Shield of Minnesota has begun to form an integrated managed care delivery system to improve quality and cut costs for Blue Plus, its HMO affiliate. The first element of this system, a cardiac care network, is already in place saving lives and money while sacrificing little in member access.

In Minnesota, the average mortality for elective heart bypass surgery can be as high as 53 deaths per 1,000, depending on where the surgery is done. Members of Blue Plus, the HMO affiliate of Blue Cross and Blue Shield of Minnesota (BCBSM), however, are guided to one of ten hospitals in their cardiac care network where mortality for the procedure averages only 15 deaths per 1,000. Based on data it collects on treatment and outcomes at 31 hospitals, BCBSM determines where care is best and most efficient, and sends its members there.

A DIFFERENT WORLD FOR HEALTH CARE

The health care industry today is quite different from the one that spawned HMOs and other forms of managed care plans a little more than a decade ago. As health care costs continue to climb, purchasers and payers search vigorously for innovative ways to facilitate the delivery of affordable, high-quality health care. Today, the most promising managed care strategies are premised on the philosophy that improved quality can help control rising costs, strategies that include:

- The application of continuous quality improvement (CQI) methods;
- The use of outcomes measures to assess quality of care delivered; and
- The creation of select provider networks, sometimes called "centers of excellence."

In the past, these strategies have been examined independently, but have not been integrated within a managed care delivery system. Blue Plus's new cardiac network is one of the first efforts to conceptually and operationally link these strategies. Comprising ten hospitals and 14 affiliated cardiology and cardiac surgery groups, the cardiac network is the first of several select networks that will become part of BCBSM's Project *Health*Vision quality management program.

Project *Health*Vision is a significant step for BCBSM as it moves toward managed care products that rely on primary care physicians and quality-based specialty networks. Launched in January 1993, the Project *Health*Vision cardiac network is built on criteria that address provider quality, geographic access, and a long-term commitment to improving care. The network certainly merits close attention as a promising step in providing effective and efficient care by strengthening provider selection and partnership, quality, and treatment outcomes.

DEVELOPMENT OF THE CARDIAC NETWORK

As the first step in developing the project *Health*Vision health management program, BCBSM targeted the creation of a select cardiac care network. An important medical specialty with relatively high visibility and costs, cardiac care also was an area that specifically interested health care purchasers.

Planning for the network began in 1991 with the formation of the BCBSM/Blue Plus task force directed by Mark Banks, M.D., BCBSM senior vice president and president and chief executive officer of Blue Plus. The task force included company representatives from several areas, including quality improvement, medical affairs, provider contracting, provider services, and marketing. It set goals of improved health care quality, cost-effective application of technology, long-term partnerships with providers, provision of appropriate care, and attention to customers' needs and expectations.

Selection Criteria

The task force concentrated on selection criteria and procedures for the cardiac network and identified three primary criteria for applicants:

1. Demonstrated ability to deliver high-quality care;
2. Provider location and accessibility to members; and
3. Potential of provider to participate in a long-term partnership with BCBSM.

The task force first focused on the demonstrated ability of the provider to deliver high-quality care for the following five key elective, non-emergency cardiac procedures:

1. Catheterization;
2. Angioplasty;
3. Coronary artery bypass graft (CABG);
4. Valve surgery; and
5. Electrophysiologic studies.

The criteria emphasized both hospital and physician quality, and important factors included compliance with patient selection guidelines and minimum procedure volumes recommended by the American Heart Association and the American College of Cardiology; acceptable malpractice history; acceptable length of experience; physician board certification for cardiology or cardiac surgery; formal assessment of patient satisfaction; and acceptable rates of mortality, morbidity, and other adverse procedure outcomes. Minimum procedure volumes were an important consideration in the selection process because research indicates that higher surgical procedure volumes are associated with better treatment outcomes. As a group, the cardiac providers selected for the network scored higher than those not selected on various indicators. For example, hospital finalists for the network averaged 404 CABGs in 1991 and 20.3 years of experience with CABGs. Nonfinalists averaged 131 CABGs and 13.3 years of experience.

Another selection factor was geographic access. BCBSM networks serve members throughout the state and border areas. Thus, the cardiac network could not be limited to metropolitan Twin Cities providers. An effort was made to include facilities and providers in both the metropolitan and Greater Minnesota areas.

A final important selection factor was the potential of the provider to participate in a long-term relationship with BCBSM. This involved an assessment of the provider's commitment and ability to collaborate with BCBSM in CQI and outcomes assessment initiatives. Medical care, including cardiac surgery, is a highly complex phenomenon involving complicated disease processes, sophisticated diagnostic testing and procedures, a high degree of physician technical skills, and complex interactions between operating physicians, surgical team nurses, and support staff. Processes and outcomes can vary significantly among physicians, hospitals, and support staff, and even within the same group from patient to patient. Some of this variation is due to the inherent variability among patients and their disease conditions.

The goal of CQI is to analyze the processes of care to identify and reduce the sources of unnecessary variation that impair efficiency and treatment outcomes. It is estimated that each adverse outcome costs an additional $15,000. BCBSM is committed to assisting cardiac network providers in implementing

Project *Health*Vision Cardiac Network

Abbott Northwestern Hospital, Minneapolis, MN
  Cardiac Surgical Associates
  Minnesota Thoracic Group
  Minneapolis Cardiology Associates

Dakota Hospital, Fargo, ND
  Dakota Clinic

Fairview Southdale Hospital, Edina, MN
  Cardiothoracic Consultants
  Cardiac Surgical Associates
  Minnesota Thoracic Group
  Southdale Heart Clinic
  Hennepin Faculty Associates
  Affiliated Cardiovascular Consultants

McKennan Hospital, Sioux Falls, SD
  Midwest Cardiovascular Center

Methodist Hospital, St. Louis Park, MN
  Park Nicollet Heart Center

North Memorial Medical Center, Robbinsdale, MN
  Minnesota Thoracic Group
  Cardiovascular Consultants

St. Joseph's Hospital, St. Paul, MN
  St. Paul Internists (cardiology)
  St. Paul Heart Clinic
  Affiliated Cardiovascular Consultants
  Cardiothoracic Consultants

St. Mary's Medical Center, Duluth, MN
  Duluth Clinic

United Hospital, St. Paul, MN
  St. Paul Heart Clinic
  Cardiac Surgical Associates
  Affiliated Cardiovascular Consultants

University of Minnesota Hospital
  University of Minnesota Clinical Associates

CQI initiatives and has based network selection in part on providers' commitment to CQI.

Provider commitment to outcomes assessment also is important to the ultimate success of this network. Providers' rates of mortality, morbidity, and other adverse outcomes considered in the initial selection of network providers will also be used to measure network performance and help assess the impact of CQI initiatives. As with processes of care, treatment outcomes can differ significantly between physicians, hospitals, and even among the same physicians performing a procedure at two different hospitals. Outcomes assessment identifies differences that cannot be explained by statistical chance or differences in patient characteristics, but rather due to variations in processes of care that can be reduced through CQI initiatives. The Project *Health*Vision cardiac network allows Blue Plus to work more closely with network providers, sharing data on case mix and severity adjusted outcomes, and, most importantly, enlisting their help in enhancing current outcomes measurement methodologies. Over time, we expect these will include "episode of care" analyses, which will move us beyond single patient events (e.g., an inpatient encounter) and link together all clinically meaningful events (e.g., pre- and post-hospital care and multiple patient encounters) to provide more powerful insights into the patterns and outcomes of care.

Selecting the Providers

Once the BCBSM/Blue Plus task fore had identified and defined the network selection criteria, a formal request for proposals (RFP) was distributed in May, 1992, to hospitals and physician groups specializing in cardiology and cardiac surgery. The RFP focused on providers' qualifications, quality-of-care indicators, and procedure-specific volume, mortality, morbidity, and complication rates for their entire patient population. Responses were received from all 22 hospitals with cardiac programs and from 34 of their affiliated physician groups.

These applications were reviewed by a BCBSM selection committee, and a list of finalists was distributed for comment to Blue Plus primary care physicians. Site visits for all of the finalists were conducted during the last quarter of 1992 by BCBSM physicians and quality improvement staff, and the finalists were invited to submit financial offers. Contracts were then successfully negotiated and signed with ten hospitals and 14 of their affiliated cardiology/cardiac surgery groups. The cardiac network reduces the number of participating BCBSM hospital cardiac programs from 22 to 10. The largest reduction took place in the Twin Cities, which realized a decrease from 12 to 7. Most of the other decrease—from 11 to 3 hospitals—occurred in cities with more than one hospital cardiac program. Indeed, the network has hospitals in nearly every community that previously had a hospital cardiac program. Thus, the new network has not drastically impaired geographic access to cardiac services.

Consistent with its focus on partnerships, BCBSM is committed to developing long-term relationships with the selected providers. Blue Plus expects that network providers will demonstrate their commitment to CQI and outcomes assessments. Opening the network to new providers will be considered in the event that a network provider is unable to meet this commitment.

ADVANTAGES OF SELECT PROVIDER NETWORKS

In the near future, BCBSM will introduce other select networks as part of its Project *Health*Vision program. Like the cardiac network, these networks will integrate CQI and outcomes assessment to offer a number of advantages to health care providers, payers, and purchasers.

First, Blue Plus will be able to manage its Project *Health*Vision networks more efficiently than its larger network, thus reducing administrative costs. Furthermore, by emphasizing quality criteria in the initial selection of providers, BCBSM can reduce the need for costly case-by-case micro-management of care. Instead, Blue Plus can work collaboratively with network providers to develop and implement better systems for measuring treatment outcomes and improving the processes of care.

Second, select networks will assist purchasers is assessing the performance of the networks in their health plan. Currently, purchasers have little or no information on the quality of the networks they purchase. The rigorous selection process undertaken by BCBSM for the cardiac network should help reassure them that the network providers meet high standards. An inherent disadvantage for consumers in select networks is the reduction in the number of providers from whom they have to choose. However, a central premise underlying Project *Health*Vision provider networks is that the reduction in the number of providers will be offset by the improved quality and efficiency that select networks can offer consumers.

Third, the Project *Health*Vision networks should help limit the unnecessary proliferation of new medical technology. Due to reduced patient volumes, non-network providers should be less inclined to engage in what is sometimes called a "medical arms race." With network providers, BCBSM will be in a position to initiate collaborative discussions early on as new technologies emerge. Our goal will be to effect more rational dissemination of technology based on the health care needs of subscribers, rather than on the marketing considerations of providers. Mobile cardiac catheterization laboratories are an example of a new technology that is being examined carefully in establishing the cardiac care network.

Finally, by reducing the number of participating providers, these networks will concentrate patient volume among fewer providers. As noted, several studies suggest that higher surgical procedure volume may improve treatment outcomes—which would clearly benefit patients. In addition, improved outcomes can lower health care costs by reducing rehospitalizations and other expenditures associated with medical complications and adverse outcomes. Concentrating patient volume also may produce economies that could help control the unit cost of surgical procedures.

THE GROWING TREND TOWARD MANAGED CARE

Minnesota has been a leader in health care innovation, and BCBSM has been part of the growing trend in managed care. Since 1986, both the number and proportion of BCBSM members enrolled in such plans have nearly tripled. The managed care trend is likely to accelerate at BCBSM and nationally in years to come. The Blue Cross and Blue Shield Association—the coordinating body for the nation's 73 independent Blue Cross and Blue Shield plans—estimates that up to 80 percent of Blue Cross and Blue Shield members nationwide will be enrolled in managed care plans by the end of the decade.

Several factors are fueling the growth in managed care. Today, health care purchasers are increasingly seeking information about the quality improvement processes and treatment outcomes of the provider networks they purchase. Some private third party payers are beginning to recognize that they gain competitive advantage by anticipating and effectively responding to these concerns. Managed care products that include quality-based, select provider networks are one form this response is taking.

Another factor driving managed care is the health care reform movement. On both the state and national levels, there is a widespread perception of serious and persistent shortcomings in our health system: double-digit inflation, increasing numbers of underinsured and uninsured, and mediocre health status levels compared to other industrialized societies. Proposals for significant government intervention in the private health care financing system, including single payer systems, national health insurance, national fee schedules, and expenditure caps are gaining the attention of policymakers. This in turn has persuaded private sector purchasers, providers, and payers of both the opportunity and the need to demonstrate successful reforms before they are imposed legislatively. Quality-based managed care products are part of this private-sector reform strategy.

In Minnesota, public policymakers are increasingly recognizing the potential cost and quality advantages of managed care. Reform legislation passed by the Minnesota Legislature last year calls for the development of "centers of excellence." It also calls for increased application of health data in the development of clinical practice parameters and outcomes assessment.

Growing emphasis on select provider networks may seem to be a departure from tradition at BCBSM, which has long been known for its large open-access networks. The BCBSM AWARE network, for example, includes nearly every acute care hospital in the state and more than 9,000 physicians. Indeed, the integration of select provider networks, continuous quality improvement, and outcomes measurement do signal an important evolution in BCBSM corporate philosophy—one that recognizes the growing importance of managed care strategies in the delivery of health care in the 1990s.

BALANCING COST AND QUALITY

While the trend toward managed care is significant and growing, it does not signal the end of traditional broad access fee-for-service networks at BCBSM. Almost certainly, there will always be purchasers who place a high priority on access and choice of provider, and BCBSM will continue to respond to their needs.

However, a growing number of health care purchasers are turning to new strategies for managing both the cost and quality of care delivered to their employees. Health plans that effectively develop and implement such strategies will be the ones likely to succeed in the new health care environment. *Health*-Vision networks, including the new cardiac network, have been developed by BCBSM to meet the needs of these purchasers with a new partnership between payer and provider. Project *Health*Vision is poised to demonstrate that purchasers' health care dollars are buying care that is demonstrably higher in quality.

37.   The Power of Clinical Credentialing
Alfred B. Lewis

To boost employee morale and improve satisfaction, Southern New England Telephone replaced its entire preferred provider organization with a network that emphasized the thorough credentialing of every applicant.

Southern New England Telephone (SNET) had increasing concerns about employee satisfaction with its previous managed-care network and decided to make a change. The work force—rightly or wrongly—perceived a shortage of high-quality providers across many specialties and geographic regions.

In developing its new network, the Connecticut company had to erase this perception entirely. However, simply creating a new network with the goal of having it mach the average practitioner quality in the state would not have been sufficient: SNET needed to create a premier network in Connecticut that would search out and invite the best practitioners in the state to apply. Due to a lack of widely available, economical, and reliable outcomes-measurement tools for identifying the state's best providers, SNET assessed practitioner quality via independent verification of the quality of professional credentials.

NETWORK DEVELOPMENT

SNET hired InterStrategies to design a state-of-the art preferred provider organization (PPO), with each prospective applicant credentialed thoroughly to ensure that all representations made on the application had a basis in fact.

Reprinted with permission from *Journal of Health Care Benefits*. Vol. 2. No. 6. Copyright © 1993 by Warren Gorham Lamont, 210 South St., Boston, MA 02111. 1-800-950-1211. All rights reserved.

InterStrategies set up a network called Preferred Medical Choice (PMC) and contacted provider groups it targeted as most attractive to the network, based on geography, specialty, and reputation.

When a state-of-the-art credentials review was applied to those applications a number of discrepancies were revealed between representations on the applications and corroboration from primary sources. While some of the omissions or misstatements were inadvertent or inconsequential, overall, 10 percent of the providers who applied for membership did not gain admission to the network. Virtually all of these providers had privileges at one or more hospitals and belonged to one or more plans, indicating the likelihood that many plans and hospitals in Connecticut are staffed with practitioners whose substandard credentials represent a significant, utterly avoidable liability risk.

The providers who were not admitted were rejected for the following reasons (see also Fig. 1):

1. Lack of sufficient credentials to grant board certification equivalence status to non-board-certified specialists to enable them to be listed under their claimed specialty in the network. (The review process was even more stringent for non-board-certified physicians than for board-certified providers. For instance, their medical schools and residency programs were consulted for performance evaluations.) While these providers were rejected as specialists, some were eventually accepted as primary care physicians.
2. Applications were incomplete because applicants had ignored multiple requests for information to resolve questions of acceptability.
3. Applications contained misstatements that were discovered during primary source verification.
4. Malpractice history was considered by PMC's medical director to be sufficiently serious to merit rejection of the applicant.

The Process: Cooperative, Not Adversarial

One might surmise from the high percentage of nonaccepted applicants that this process was as arbitrary as it was thorough. However, no network developer tries to exclude as many providers as possible—just the opposite, because network size is a key selling point. InterStrategies worked closely with applicants to help them complete their applications in a way that would present them to their best advantage. With support from SNET, the PMC medical director spoke directly to every physician willing to talk to him about resolving any discrepancies. In addition, to make the application process less onerous, PMC assumed the responsibility of verification. The attitude pervading the development of the network was: "We would love it if you join us—and the other providers who meet our high standards." This approach was effective in winning the trust of the physicians and building goodwill (see sidebar).

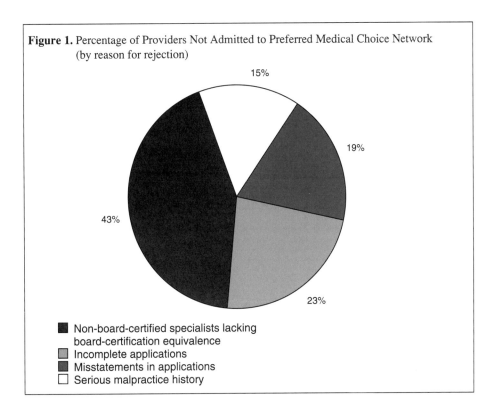

Figure 1. Percentage of Providers Not Admitted to Preferred Medical Choice Network (by reason for rejection)

- Non-board-certified specialists lacking board-certification equivalence
- Incomplete applications
- Misstatements in applications
- Serious malpractice history

BENEFITS OF THE SNET NETWORK

The PMC network that InterStrategies established for SNET has become the largest non-Blue Cross PPO in Connecticut. Additional employers have elected to join, and plans in neighboring states are negotiating arrangements for their members who live in Connecticut.

PMC was able to negotiate a 29 percent reduction in liability insurance for its own exposure, based largely on the quality of the credentialing process. Furthermore, PMC effectively expanded coverage to include other companies electing to use the PMC network, even though evolving case law indicates an increase in network liability in the credentialing area. More important, the coverage now includes claims arising from utilization review and provider selection/rejection.

Provider satisfaction with the network has consistently reached or exceeded 95 percent, despite the fact that providers must offer, on average, greater discounts than SNET's previous network providers. In addition, retention—excluding providers who retired, moved, or were dropped—was virtually 100 percent. Network satisfaction depends on a number of factors beyond the credentialing process. The makeup of the network is a critical success

---

THE GOODWILL FACTOR IN NETWORK DEVELOPMENT

To be successful, network development must be built on a trusting relationship between developers and providers. Failure to create trust can derail the entire effort, as Value-Care, a nonprofit corporation, discovered while forming a network in 1990.

With $1.4 million in funding from 19 employers covering an estimated patient population of 250,000, ValueCare's network had great potential—particularly given the generous proposed fee schedule. However, after initially cooperating with developers, the providers balked en masse, and only one-sixth of the anticipated 1,500 physicians actually signed up. The reason was a perceived bait-and-switch scheme that alienated the majority of providers. Following assurances that it would seek and weight provider input into utilization policy, ValueCare unilaterally selected a utilization management program operated by a well-known health care insurer and presented the plan to providers as a fait accompli.

The utilization management program itself was not an incitement to revolt, for it combined reasonably typical prior authorization requirements with an early and not especially constraining derivative of the industry-standard criteria for continued-stay review. In addition, on paper, ValueCare still offered higher fees (including many nondiscounted CPT codes), a less taxing application process, and a larger pool of patients than PMC. However, the imposition of the plan was perceived as a breach of trust. Providers felt that if the developers could act so arbitrarily at the outset, what might come later?

The ValueCare experience is enlightening. Many physicians distrust networks and, more often than not, joint to avoid losing patients rather than to gain them. Hence, their first choice may be to avoid networks altogether. In this case, a potential gain of 250,000 patients made moot that choice—until a single misstep galvanized the medical population into action. To avoid a backlash in this highly skeptical environment, network developers must build goodwill with providers continuously from day one.

---

factor in provider satisfaction. Providers appreciate the prestige and peer support that comes with being in a network with other good providers.

The credentialing process itself continues to pay dividends. PMC arranged for its borderline providers to be invited into another, non-competing network. Joining this network will help these providers to simplify their credentialing process by providing them with all the independent verification documents already on file, thus reducing the paper work from an eight-page form plus collaterals to a short addendum section.

SNET employees (by and large the same group who were unenthusiastic about the previous network) are highly satisfied with PMC. Perhaps the best measure of the satisfaction is the in-network provider utilization rate, which has risen 20 percent since the program's inception in 1990. Another indication of satisfaction is the fact that 85 percent of employees elected to stay with PMC after the first year. By contrast, health plan retention rates generally range between 70 percent and 75 percent.[1]

PMC's high retention rate is not a coincidence. Providers and their office staffs that are happy with a plan are more likely to communicate that satisfaction to their patients through prompt appointment scheduling, quickly returned telephone calls, and unrushed office visits, among other ways.

LESSONS FOR NETWORK EXECUTIVES

The lessons learned from SNET's experience all point to the importance of thorough credentialing. In fact, managed-care organization managers who view credentialing as just one more cost of doing business are taking unacceptable risks and missing tremendous opportunities.

Thorough Credentialing

According to PMC principal Douglas L. Elden, a managed-care attorney with a nationwide practice, "The case law is inexorably moving toward network derivative liability for torts committed by network practitioners where the practitioners were negligently selected, that is, where an investigation of the practitioner would have revealed inadequate credentials." In addition, Elden adds, "The day is approaching when employers will be held liable for the failure to investigate the credentialing and recredentialing of the networks they select."

Despite such predictions from experts, there has been little reaction within the network industry itself for one reason: Most plans are convinced that their own credentialing process is adequate if not exemplary.

However, consistent polls of credentialing seminar attendees show that very few networks actually turn down more than a few applicants and some have never rejected an applicant with privileges at an accredited hospital.[2] However, hospital privileges themselves are not proof of adequate credentials. Virtually all rejected applicants in the PMC plan had hospital privileges. In fact, most physicians with serious malpractice records have privileges somewhere. The relative insignificance of such affiliations is borne out by the fact that it is not an accepted defense in court.

While there is no magic-number quota for turndowns, experience shows that a nonacceptance ratio approaching 10 percent (including voluntary withdrawals of applicants and turndowns for board-certification equivalency) is a good indication of thorough credentialing.

No Guarantee Return on Credentialing Costs

A conscientious credentialing effort, if outsourced, can cost well over $100 per provider versus half that amount for a perfunctory effort. However, for two reasons, spending the greater amount does not guarantee reduced liability premiums or increased coverage. First, liability insurers, many of whom are unfamiliar with what a conscientious credentialing job entails, must be convinced that such an effort pays. Second, once the insurers are convinced that it pays, they must be willing to reduce premiums significantly. Neither task is easy. In the case of PMC, it took heroic negotiations, a few years' experience, and the threat of a competitive bid to earn the reduction. As actuarial experience builds and case law evolves, the gap in premiums between conscientious and perfunctory credentialing can be expected to broaden.

Network Endorsement

Plan selection is not without risk. When an employer select a network, it is tantamount to endorsing that network and to endorsing every provider who is a member. Even if networks did not carry the clear threat of employer liability, common sense would dictate the need for careful credentialing, particularly when the potential downside is mortality.

The strength of the employer's endorsement is a critical factor in encouraging employees to use network providers. Therefore, employer concern about the quality of credentialing will have a major impact on the buying power of the network. A well credentialed network will earn more accounts at a higher price over a shorter sales cycle.

Respectful Treatment of Applicants

Even in situations in which the market power clearly belongs to the network, it is important to treat potential physician applicants with respect and to communicate with them effectively and consistently. Such an approach may yield more qualified providers (and a more favorable fee schedule) than simply dictating terms. In addition, establishing a good rapport with providers early in the network development process will facilitate future fee scheduling and physician negotiations. By contrast, experience shows that even a highly favorable initial proposal will not maintain physicians' interest in an atmosphere lacking rapport and trust.

SPECULATION FOR THE FUTURE

As the disparity between plan credentialing efforts widens, some plans may gain a reputation for easy acceptance. As a result, those plans will be deluged with applications from practitioners who have been turned down by other networks, and quality providers will not want to remain in such a network. As a consequence, the high level of actuarial risk in such plans will, once recognized, seriously affect their insurability. This likely future scenario highlights the importance and potential benefits of credentialing in network development.

1. Commonwealth of Massachusetts, Insurance Division.

2. InterQual-sponsored credentialing seminars, Baltimore, Maryland, and Boston, Massachusetts, 1992.

Part 8

ADMINISTRATION, AUDITING, AND COMMUNICATIONS

38.   Health Care Fraud
James L. Garcia

Health care fraud currently drains some $80 billion in this country per year, and extends to all parts of our health care system. Fraud not only drives up costs for everyone, it can be a direct threat to patient health. Bringing this unnecessary, dangerous expense under control will require strong and concerted measures of deterrence, detection, and punishment, including consumer education, stiffer fines and penalties for fraud, and immunity legislation allowing information sharing among insurers.

Imagine that a product you needed had frequently doubled in price in the past eight years, and that its price was continuing to rise at a rate more than twice the rate of inflation. Then imagine that 10 percent of the cost of this product was due to dishonesty and fraud—a cost that was passed on to you as a consumer. You'd probably be outraged and demand a solution.

This scenario actually is reality when it comes to health care. We now spend more than $800 billion a year on health care in this country—nearly double what we spent in 1985. If the trend continues, this figure will double again, to $1.6 trillion, over the next decade.

Health care fraud is responsible for an estimated 10 percent of our nation's health care bill, or $80 billion. Fortunately now that health care costs in general are demanding a closer look, the cost of fraud is attracting some long-needed attention.

WHAT IS FRAUD?

By definition, fraud means that someone is trying to obtain something of value by intentionally deceiving, misrepresenting, or concealing. Health care fraud can take on many forms. In a non-legal sense, it encompasses a broad range of transgressions from "little white lies" to blatant falsification. It can be a doctor who occasionally bends the rules to serve the perceived needs of a patient. It can be a ring of clinics or labs that sets up an intricate scam to defraud insurance companies. It can be a patient who changes the figure on a bill to increase reimbursement.

Regardless of its form, health care fraud is a serious and growing problem that exploits patients, can threaten their health, and raises costs to us all unnecessarily.

Because of its multifarious nature, the health care system itself is vulnerable to fraud. Consumers generally aren't paying directly for the services they receive, and they often are easily intimidated by the medical process. Those paying the bills aren't receiving the services, and their attempts to share data are hampered by privacy restrictions. Compounding the problem is the fact that the system lacks an effective watchdog. Given its patchwork nature it's no wonder that so much fraud has crept into the health care system.

TYPES OF FRAUD

There are two main types of health care fraud: fraud committed by providers and fraud committed by consumers. Both are illegal, and both represent serious problems.

On the providers' side, only a small percentage of medical providers commit fraud, but that small percentage represents big dollars. The providers who indulge in fraud are not all back-alley schemers with ties to organized crime, although these, too, exist. Many well-respected physicians who have treated their patients effectively for years commit fraud. The acts are simple enough and, to an uneducated patient, seemingly harmless. Examples typical of this kind of fraud include the following:

- The physician performs a routine physical for a patient, but submits a claim for treatment of an illness to get insurance reimbursement for the patient.
- When treating a patient for obesity, the physician lists diabetes or hypertension as the cause to ensure reimbursement by the insurer.
- The provider agrees to forgo the copayment required for treatment, but inflates the bill submitted to the insurance company to cover costs.
- The provider bills for services not rendered.

Organized Fraud

There are also organized scams that grab headlines and rake in millions of dollars illegally. At Aetna, through our intensive fraud investigation efforts, we've uncovered a number of these scams and helped send dozens of perpetrators to jail. Some of those include:

- A California-based mobile lab scam, alleged to be the most massive health care fraud in the history of this country, totaled more than $100 million in claims for diagnostic tests. IN this case, two brothers aggressively marketed "free" medical testing services, conducting the tests out of mobile homes and at clinics, labs, and fitness centers. Although the tests were not medically necessary, those solicited were enticed to have them done—at no cost to them. Thousands of dollars in bogus medical claims were then submitted to insurance companies. Insurers eventually were awarded an $18 million default judgment in the case.

- Recently, a large California-based clinical laboratory pleaded guilty to submitting false claims to government health insurance programs and agreed to pay $110 million to the federal and state governments. The government claimed that, as part of its standard blood tests, the clinic automatically added charges for tests it knew were not reasonable or necessary for the treatment of an illness or injury.

- In Operation Goldpill, the FBI uncovered evidence of independent pharmacies filling prescriptions with generic brands but billing for more expensive brand names, billing multiple times for the same prescription, billing for fictitious prescriptions, and splitting prescriptions to obtain extra dispensing fees.

- In yet another case, a physician received $1.85 million from several large pharmaceutical companies for clinical studies he did involving experimental anti-inflammatory drugs. An investigation showed that he routinely falsified the results of these studies, providing the pharmaceutical companies and the FDA with clinical data that were useless and could have led to serious misjudgments concerning the safety and effectiveness of the drugs.

This last example demonstrates that beyond the financial aspects of these scams is the far more serious issue of quality of care. Even if no physical harm occurs as a result of unnecessary testing, some legitimate medical problems might go undetected while these providers focus on skimming money. Worse yet, some providers actually perform unnecessary surgery, not only defrauding employers and insurers, but also threatening the health and lives of patients.

In addition to provider fraud, we at Aetna are on the lookout for consumer fraud—patients who tamper with the health care reimbursement system to line their own pockets. As with provider fraud, we approach consumer fraud with a multi-step process that relies on education, detection, investigation, and deterrence to root out and prevent fraud.

The Detection Process

Although it would be counterproductive to analyze each claim for possible fraud, developing indicators of fraud probability can help claims processors isolate claims that warrant further scrutiny. The following fraudulent situations are most common:

- Unbundling of services in order to charge for individual parts of a procedure rather than for the procedure as a whole
- Billing for services not provided
- Joint efforts by providers to manipulate costs or services to enhance billings
- Billing more than one program or insurance company for the same service, or billing the insurance company more than once for the same service.
- Kickbacks and other arrangements between providers and vendors to enhance billings
- Billing for a higher level or more complex type of service than the actual service rendered
- Waiving coinsurance or deductibles so a patient won't question bills or disclose a fraudulent practice to the health care payor

Because patients are in the best position to detect fraud, they should be used as the first line of defense. At Aetna, we've taken a number of steps to promote the detection of provider fraud, and we're exploring others. Some of those steps include:

- Educating consumers via the news media
- Developing an educational brochure for distribution by employers
- Installing a hotline for reporting suspected fraud
- Including educational messages on the explanation of benefits (EOB) statement
- Providing financial incentives for insureds who report fraud

Investigation

When a potentially fraudulent claim is flagged, an investigation is necessary to gather the facts. The nature and scope of the investigation varies according to the type of claim and individual case circumstances. A review of group medical records or an interview may suffice in some cases, while extensive legwork and fact-finding may be necessary in others.

Generally, though, fraud investigations are tedious, painstaking, and can take up to two years to complete. A flash of investigative genius is rarely what resolves a case; rather, reams of claims and documents have to be reviewed before the truth can be obtained.

At Aetna, we have a team of 21 dedicated investigators in our home office who work with more than 60 fraud specialists in claims offices around the country. These fraud experts investigate more than 2,500 cases each year, working with appropriate law enforcement agencies such as the FBI, Drug Enforcement Agency, IRS, or U.S. Postal Service inspectors to pursue those cases.

Aetna also was one of the first insurance companies to use artificial intelligence in the fight against health care fraud. These systems, known internally as "Robot Cop" and "Radar," rely on advanced computer technology to assist investigators in identifying cases of fraud. We also rely on electronic claims submission to minimize the opportunity for fraud.

Deterrence

Deterrence is a key factor in fighting fraud. The health care industry needs to let the perpetrators of health care fraud know they are risking a criminal record, loss of livelihood, and possible payment in fines for more than the amount involved in fraud. Incidents of fraud are subject to a variety of administrative, civil, and criminal sanctions. Administrative sanctions include warnings, withholding of payments, and recovery of overpayments.

Fraud cases can be presented as criminal violations of the Medicare regulations or as violations of a number of sanctions of the U.S. criminal code, including statutes against conspiracy, mail fraud, racketeering, and obstruction of justice. Also, the health care industry has been successful in using different states' health care false claim acts. Some insurance companies have found the use of the Racketeering Influenced and Corrupt Organizations Act (RICO) of value in recovering losses and deterring future health care fraud activities.

Information Sharing

A major way to combat health care fraud is by exchanging information among health care payors, insurance companies, fraud units, anti-fraud organizations, and law enforcement officials. Insurance companies such as Aetna only represent a fraction of the health insurance business, and so can only detect a fraction of the total fraud being perpetrated.

The National Health Care Anti-Fraud Association (NHCAA) has recently launched information sharing programs in a number of states with corporate members. NHCAA represents a national cooperative effort by private sector health insurers and public sector law enforcement agencies to improve the detection, investigation, and criminal prosecution of health insurance fraud. The pilot programs will demonstrate the value of sharing information and its effect on obtaining prosecution.

Legislation enacting widespread immunity statutes is needed to permit insurance companies to freely share information, not only with law enforcement agencies, but also among themselves. Information gathered from insurance companies, when presented to law enforcement officials, increases the probability that a case will be prosecuted. These immunity statutes would provide immunity from civil liability for private insurance companies who share the same information.

Aetna has developed a model immunity statute that specifically provides protection for private insurance companies who share information regarding fraudulent insurance acts or omissions. This draft proposal is patterned in part after the model immunity statute proposed by the National Association of Insurance Commissioners.

We've also developed a model false claims act that would:

1. Make health care fraud a crime;
2. Provide a private right of action for insurance companies so they can recover the losses suffered as a result of health care fraud; and
3. Make health care fraud grounds for disciplinary action against health care professionals, regulated by the states.

The Employer's Role

As people become more aware of rising health care costs and the impact of health care fraud, employers and employees are taking a more active role in detection. But more remains to be done. In addition to the guidelines offered in the accompanying story (see box), larger companies that handle their own claims can use guidelines provided by insurance carriers to determine what constitutes normal frequency of treatment. Claims involving unusually frequent visits or expensive procedures should be reviewed by a medical consultant or outside review organization.

Other indicators of cases that warrant further review should also be identified. Claims processors should be alert to the many warnings signs such as strikeovers, erasures, or other alterations on a claims form, including adding extra digits to the figure claimed. Consecutively numbered prescription bills, photocopied bills, and bills dated on a Sunday or holiday also may be signs of fraud.

THE FUTURE

The future of our health care system lies in our ability to confront health care issues and major changes. Even reforming our health care system won't eliminate fraud; as long as people are part of the system, some amount of fraud is inevitable.

HOW EMPLOYERS CAN FIGHT FRAUD

Many employers take an aggressive stand on health care fraud. Aetna suggests its customers take the following steps to help their employees identify and handle suspected fraud:

1. Develop a written policy statement and enforcement guidelines.
2. Create general awareness of the problem through employee communications.
3. Establish a fraud hot line and/or a key "point person" on fraud.
4. Provide employees with accurate information to help them identify fraud. Here are some simple steps to fight health care fraud that employers can pass on to their employees:
   a. Be aware that health care fraud does exist and that anyone can be a victim.
   b. Become an educated health care consumer.
   c. Fill out, sign and date only one claim form for each covered medical service.
   d. Examine medical bills and explanations of benefits (EOBs).
   e. Call the health plan claim office with any discrepancies.

The National Health Care Anti-Fraud Association estimates that even though only about 2 percent of physicians routinely submit fraudulent claims, a higher percentage of physicians sometimes engage in fraudulent practices. And the problem seems to be getting worse. Companies engaged in health care anti-fraud activities report an increasing number of cases being investigated each year.

But just as we can control the rapid pace of rising health care costs, we can rein in the galloping cost of fraud. Through a committed effort to educate and communicate, and detect, investigate, and deter fraud, we can make progress on this critical issue. We cannot afford to let health care fraud continue. Trust and a sense of common purpose by all parties concerned is essential if we are to succeed in combatting health insurance fraud.

39. Third Party Administrators Consider Diversification

Nicholas J. Phillips   Steven P. Chase

As the sophistication of health care cost control possibilities increases, employers are looking for more and more value from their third party administrators. Many TPAs are responding by providing a wide array of new services including vastly improved claims management, data analysis and storage, provider negotiation and management, and even computer software and hardware leasing and sales. However, diversification generally means higher overhead costs, and TPAs have long depended upon low costs as their essential selling point.

Third party administrators (TPAs) once served primarily as claims processors, but today they are rapidly expanding their capabilities and range of services in response to plan sponsor needs. Health benefit plan administrative needs have exploded in complexity over the past decade, thanks to several factors:

- Employers have adopted a myriad of initiatives to control their plan costs.
- Employers have also added flexible benefits and other options to offer greater choice to an increasingly diverse work force.
- State and federal laws are adding further complexities, such as state mandated benefits, COBRA continuation requirements, and the recent family leave law.
- The Financial Accounting Standards Board (FASB), through rule SFAS 106, has forced employers to estimate and include on financial statements their current and future costs of retiree health benefits, increasing their concern about retiree health costs.

While these marketplace pressures are forcing TPAs to expand their capabilities, certain technological developments, such as more sophisticated computer applications, are making it possible for TPAs to serve more complex plans. The combination of increasing plan complexity, TPA capabilities, and above all, employer concern over rising health care costs, has led TPAs to focus on five functional areas of plan management:

1. Plan design;
2. Claims management;
3. Financial management;
4. Data management; and
5. Provider negotiation.

This article examines each of these areas and identifies some of the significant changes that these developments have created in third party administration of health plans. We also consider the emerging influences of 24-hour coverage (which combine health plan and workers' compensation administration), employer self-administration, and health care reform.

Sponsors of self-funded health plans that are evaluating prospective TPAs will need to consider which of these plan management issues are most important to them. They can then evaluate a TPA on the basis of how well it has adapted to the market changes that are most important to the plan sponsor.

PLAN DESIGN

The growth of managed care is the most significant development in health care plan design over the past ten years. It has caused TPAs to develop more sophisticated capabilities so they can administer features not present in traditional indemnity plans. For example, TPAs must:

- Simultaneously administer combinations of different benefit copayments, deductibles, and coinsurance. Increasing numbers of employers allow employees to choose between indemnity and managed care plans, and to elect differing coverages within those plans.
- Coordinate and monitor referrals for specialty care. They must keep track of whether plan participants obtained specialist treatment through their primary care physician's (PCP) referral, or whether the participant bypassed the PCP and self-referred to the specialist.
- Maintain a database of participating physicians and other providers, and integrate the database into the claims process.

CLAIMS MANAGEMENT

Claims management continues to be the core service that TPAs provide for their customers, but they must now cover a far greater breadth of claims management issues than ever before. As a result, plan sponsors can no longer simply measure TPA performance by claims turnaround time and processing and monetary accuracy. While these are still important considerations, a TPA's capabilities in the areas of analysis and intervention in health care delivery are also important.

For example, TPAs must often analyze and reinterpret the codes physicians and hospitals use in claim submissions. Specifically, this involves scrutinizing the four-digit codes used for diagnoses, called ICD-9 codes (for International Classification of Diseases, 9th Revision, Clinical Modification) and the five-digit codes for procedures, known as CPT-4 codes, (for Current Procedural Terminology, 4th Edition). This scrutiny and corrective action includes the ability to detect or analyze:

- Unbundled charges, where a provider bills for individual parts of a procedure rather than for one "bundled" procedure. For example, if a provider charges separately for each separate clinical procedure associated with surgery rather than charging under one consolidated CPT-4 code for the entire surgical procedure, this can add up to a more expensive claim.
- Upcoding or "code creep," where a provider classifies certain procedures under different but related codes that pay more. For example, a provider may bill for an extended visit or a full physical exam when only a brief visit or exam was necessary.
- Inconsistencies between ICD-9 diagnosis and CPT-4 procedural codes. For example, a procedural code charge for X-ray services when the diagnosis code is for a strep throat is an inconsistency.
- Churning, where a provider tends to see patients more frequently for a problem than necessary.
- ICD-9 diagnoses and/or CPT-4 procedures inconsistent with the patient's age or sex, such as obstetrical care for a male, and other, more subtle inconsistencies.
- Claims likely to mask a procedure not covered by the plan; for example, cosmetic surgery.

FINANCIAL MANAGEMENT

Before TPAs diversified their services, plan administrators often regarded claims services as a commodity and used price as the predominant consideration in selecting a claims payor. The TPA industry is now much more differentiated.

While one TPA may now charge $8 per month per employee, another TPA charging $10 per month per employee may actually provide a more cost-effective service. That is because the actual value of the TPA's services may depend on the quality and inclusion of other services it provides for that price. Factors affecting the value of a TPA's services include:

- The sophistication of its editing system in analyzing claims information and identifying and correcting irregularities. This includes how well it detects unbundled charges, upcoding, and ICD-9 diagnosis and CPT-4 procedure code inconsistencies, and whether it can perform edits online or whether it must perform them manually.
- The TPA's access to and use of physicians for medical consultation concerning nonroutine or suspicious charges.
- The sophistication and accuracy of the TPA's protocols for internal quality assurance audits.
- The nature of the TPA's performance guarantees. For example, while accuracy and turnaround guarantees are common, some claim payors also provide claims management performance guarantees, such as guarantees for savings through utilization review, and mental health and substance abuse management.

DATA MANAGEMENT

Employers are adopting increasingly aggressive cost control strategies that rely heavily upon data management. Consequently, they are demanding that their TPAs capture a broad range of data elements during the claim adjudication process and report that data in specified formats. Some of the data management services TPAs provide are:

- Retiree claim data sorted by age, for valuation of the employer's SFAS 106 liabilities. SFAS 106 requires companies to include on their balance sheets an estimate of their liabilities for providing retiree health benefits for current and future retirees.
- Data sorted by ICD-9 diagnosis and CPT-4 procedure codes to help employers evaluate patterns of health care utilization and identify groups with abnormal patterns of illness—such as a high level of heart or lung disease—that might be lowered through a preventive care plan.
- Data in a form the plan consultants and actuaries can use to measure the effectiveness of various cost control initiatives, for example, changes in plan design coverages or the addition of managed care options.
- Comparisons of an employer's health care costs and participant utilization with the average cost and utilization of similar population groups.
- Provider utilization profiling to assist employers in evaluating or developing managed care options. For example, if 50 percent of a plan's participants go to one hospital, the plan may want to negotiate an arrangement to pay the provider on a per capita rate in exchange for patient referrals.

Data storage, security, and ownership are other issues of growing in importance for health plans. The amount of health care data generated by plan administration is increasing, making storage more expensive, but as pressures to
control health care costs mount, accurate records and access to them become more
important.

Employers have a new reason to seek out TPAs that offer long-term storage
and data retrieval capabilities. In 1993, as part of a new "data match" program,
the Health Care Financing Administration (HCFA) sent out to employers bills for
services that it felt were improperly paid by Medicare in 1987, 1988, and 1989.
Although employers were given the opportunity to challenge the accuracy of
HCFA's bills, they had to have the time and ability to come up with documentation. HCFA may expand its recovery effort to request compliance and detailed
information from employers as far back as 1983.

As a result of this new employer need and growing problems with storage
space, TPAs may increase their capabilities and marketing of the following
services:

- Efficient storage and retrieval of data on microfiche or another space-saving
  medium, as opposed to paper or tape, to save space and costs.
- Ability to retain and retrieve data for a sufficient number of years to enable
  the employer to respond to HCFA information requests and billing.
- Data security protected by prudent backup and off-site storage procedures.
- Ability to analyze claims data and health care utilization patterns retrospectively.
- Guaranteeing the employer's ownership of its claims data, and its contractual
  right to obtain complete claims data, even after the termination of the TPA's
  services.

Incredible as it may seem, most claims are still prepared on paper. But
electronic claims filing and processing, known as electronic data interchange
(EDI), is finally starting to replace paper. The nation's largest claims payor, the
Department of Health and Human Services, is implementing an electronic health
care network to handle all billing for the Medicare and Medicaid programs. And
over 90 payors, including insurers and managed care organizations that insure
over 110 million lives, have joined a consortium known as the National Electronic
Information Corp. to handle their claims electronically. NEIC handled 20 million
claims electronically in 1992, and predicts it will process 35 million in 1993.

The pressures for payors and providers to adopt EDI are enormous. Paper
claims filing is costly, more prone to error, and relatively slow. HHS predicts it
will shave two weeks off the time it takes to pay claims as it moves from paper
claims to EDI.

The major commercial carriers, Blue Cross and Blue Shield plans, and the
Medicaid and Medicare programs are expecting to convert from paper to EDI
for:

- Enrollment reporting and verification.
- Claims submissions, payments, and explanations of benefit payments.
- Duplicate coverage inquiries.
- Precertification requests and authorizations.
- Claim status inquiries and responses.

As EDI usage becomes more prevalent, TPAs must also develop EDI and electronic funds transfer capabilities to remain competitive.

PROVIDER NEGOTIATION AND MANAGEMENT

TPAs are also diversifying into providing services similar to or in direct competition with managed care organizations, brokers, and consultants. TPAs already provide utilization review, precertification, and catastrophic claim management services, or aid employers in contracting for those services. The most significant strategic initiative for TPAs is diversification into provider negotiation.

If a TPA controls a large enough share of the patient market in a geographic area, it may have the leverage to negotiate PPO or EPO arrangements with health care providers on behalf of the plans it administers. While most TPAs lack the capital for network development, some may have access to capital through a parent company. They may be able to pursue network development profitably if they have sufficient market share to negotiate effectively and the ability to generate new revenue from network related growth.

Network development also requires expertise in developing provider selection criteria, credentialing providers, tracking outcomes, and other network management issues. TPAs that wish to develop a network may find the best route is to form a joint venture with a managed care organization that has network experience.

24-HOUR COVERAGE

Some TPAs provide administrative claims services for both workers' compensation programs and for medical benefit programs. Their diversification into workers' compensation will continue, and may progress into administration of integrated 24-hour plans. Once again, they will make this change in response to employer needs.

Workers' compensation has a purpose distinct from employee health benefits, and is governed by a different set of laws. Generally, it covers work-related or workplace injuries and is governed by state law. Usually, the plans have no deductible or coinsurance requirements, and employees have broad latitude in choosing their provider. In many companies, benefits managers have little to do with workers' compensation, which is typically handled by the company's risk manager.

These long-standing characteristics, however, are changing. Health care inflation has hit workers' compensation hard, sending costs skyrocketing even more quickly than benefit costs. A number of factors have contributed to these increases, including:

- Workers' compensation claimants generally can see any provider they want, and have little reason to limit their utilization. Elementary cost controls, such as utilization review and precertification, are limited if they exist at all.
- Claims under a benefits plan are often tightly managed, while those under workers' compensation are not. Providers who lose income by joining a managed care network have opportunities to shift costs to the workers' compensation plan.
- The more generous benefits under workers' compensation encourage patients to shift their claims from the benefits plan to the workers' compensation plan. For example, an employee with a back muscle strained on the weekend may delay seeking treatment until Monday and claim the injury occurred at work.
- As workers' compensation and health benefits are often managed by different areas of a company, administered by different TPAs, and insured by different insurers, the system is vulnerable to double dipping, where providers or claimants bill both the workers' compensation and benefits plans for the same treatment.

In response to the rising costs of workers' compensation, several initiatives are underway to change the system. For example, California has enacted legislation authorizing a 24-hour coverage pilot program in four counties, and several other states are also considering 24-hour coverage. The California program permits employers to contract with managed care organizations to provide both health care coverage under its benefits plan and coverage for occupational illness and injuries. Some companies have moved toward limited consolidation of their risk management and benefits departments, so they can at least share data to identify double-dipping.

The trend toward consolidated coverage, in whole or part, holds both opportunity and danger for TPAs. Those TPAs that can meet the challenge will seek to offer employers integrated or parallel benefit/workers' compensation administration, and assistance in integrating them into a single system. Those TPAs that cannot meet those challenges may find their potential client base, and maybe even their existing client base, shrinking.

SELF-ADMINISTRATION

Most companies contract with a third party administrator or insurance company to provide claims administrative services rather than taking on the task themselves. Some companies self-administer their claims, however, and that number may grow as medical costs become a greater cost of doing business, and the costs of software and hardware decrease. But as claims administration becomes more complex, even self-administering companies may have to change their administrative methods and rely more heavily upon TPAs.

For companies willing to take on the task, self-administration does offer a number of possible advantages, including independence from reliance on an outside vendor that provides poor service; possible savings on administrative costs; and service by the employer's own staff, who may be more diligent and understand the employer's own plan better. However, as plan administration becomes more complex, employers may find it prohibitively expensive to make continued investments in more sophisticated software programs and data management.

In response to the needs of self-administered employers, some TPAs have already diversified into software and hardware sales or leasing. This is an attractive option for companies that would find it too costly and time-consuming to build a system on their own. The TPA can provide equipment, software, online access to its central computer, administrative services as needed, and training. That allows companies to adopt self-administration through a "toe-in-the-water" approach, taking on more responsibilities gradually.

HEALTH CARE REFORM

The specifics of health care reform have not yet been resolved, but the most likely reform outcomes at the time of this writing would leave the system of employer-based health care benefits intact. Let us look at the these reform possibilities and how TPAs would fare under them.

Managed Competition

Managed competition would dramatically concentrate the supply of health care among a limited number of large health care organizations and funnel the demand for health care through health insurance purchasing cooperative (HIPCs), or health alliances (HAs). The market for most intermediaries, such as TPAs, insurance agents, and brokers, would decline in a managed competition environment. However, larger TPAs that have successfully developed provider networks may find new opportunities to market their networks through HIPCs or HAs. Also, since large employers may be permitted to continue to self-fund their own plans, the large TPAs that serve them may still retain that market.

State Reforms

Even if the nation adopts managed competition, the states will probably retain a major role in administering the system, and will have the flexibility to mandate additional reforms. If the nation does not adopt comprehensive reform, state health care reform efforts will probably accelerate. The variations in health care plan requirements at the state level would provide new opportunities for TPAs. Demand for TPA services will particularly grow if state efforts to dilute or eliminate ERISA's preemption exemption of state mandates begin to succeed.

Status Quo

It is quite possible that Congress and state legislatures will gridlock in their reform efforts, leaving employers to contend with the current system, unsatisfactory as it may be. In that case, employers will have to become more active in reducing plan costs. That will require more complex plan design and cost control efforts, which may create a greater demand for TPA services.

CONCLUSION

With the direction of health care reform uncertain, TPAs are poised at a crossroads. Generally, TPAs have lower overhead expenses and can respond more quickly to local conditions and networks than insurance carriers. Those TPAs that restrict their services to claims administration may be able to keep their administrative costs lower than insurance companies and more diversified TPAs, but if managed competition becomes a reality, they may see much of their market disappear. TPAs that expand their range of services to include claims and data reporting and analysis, consulting, provider negotiating, and software and hardware leasing may see less of their market disappear under managed competition, but risk raising their overhead expenses as they broaden their range of services.

It is also likely that some TPAs will consolidate, and some may even evolve into a new kind of organization by merging with the large managed care organizations that now offer a range of indemnity and managed care products. The resulting large benefits management companies would offer a broad menu of administrative, insurance, and health care services for employers to choose from, akin to the Section 125 cafeteria plans they already offer their employees.

40. Overcoming Obstacles to Effective Communication
Jane M. Lump

Benefits professionals charged with communicating today's complex plans and programs to employees are faced with obstacles ranging from shrinking budgets to changing work force demographics. By applying their creativity and a positive attitude, however, communicators can turn these obstacles into opportunities for improving plan participation and employee satisfaction with benefits, and saving benefits dollars.

It has been said naming something makes it so. Thus, communication obstacles like the diverse work force, reluctant management, or budget constraints might best be named opportunities for communicators rather than obstacles to communication. Such an attitude puts communicators in a better frame of mind for developing effective communications programs on a limited budget and selling these programs to management. And, perhaps most importantly, looking at tasks in a positive way frees the mind for creative thinking.

A COMMUNICATION OPPORTUNITY: DESIGNING FOR THE NEW WORK FORCE

Work Force 2000, published by the Hudson Institute in 1987, warned us to expect a work force shortage by the millennium and a force that will be considerably

"Overcoming Obstacles to Effective Communication," which appeared in the September 1992 issue, was printed with permission from the *Employee Benefits Journal,* published by the International Foundation of Employee Benefit Plans, Brookfield, WI. Statements or opinions expressed in this article are those of the author and do not necessarily represent the views or positions of the International Foundation, its officers, directors, or staff.

different from the present one. The shortage will encourage employment of more older, part-time, and contingent workers. Also, current patterns in demographics suggest the future work force will contain more women and minorities. Hispanics, the fastest growing minority, will make up to 27 percent of the net population growth by the year 2000. As a result, the traditional American worker, the native-born white male, will account for less than 20 percent of the 20 million people who will join the work force by the millennium. Thus, the work force of the 21st century will have a decidedly new appearance.[1] As they look to the mid-nineties and toward the 21st century, plan sponsors and human resource managers have begun to ask how they will meet communications challenges presented by this new work force.

Although sex, race, and ethnicity will have implications for communicating with the new work force, let us examine how to meet basic communication challenges caused by three changing worker characteristics—age, lifestyle, and literacy.

Older Workers

Although the work force history shows a tendency toward earlier and earlier retirement, as people take advantage of planned incentives, this trend is likely to reverse as the increasing demand for workers will keep or bring older workers into the work force. Understanding the physical changes in older people, especially in vision and hearing, will help when designing communications for them.[2] For example, older workers are likely to be:

- More farsighted and thus appreciate larger type sizes
- Slower to adjust to changes in light and thus need more time when shifting from dim to bright light
- Less precise in perceiving color and thus may find green and blue-violet difficult to distinguish
- Less able to hear high-pitched tones and thus may not hear all the tones in women's voices

More Contingent Workers

A dramatic gain in contingent workers—temporary workers, part-time workers, and the self-employed—occurred in the 1980s. By 1988 this contingent force accounted for 25 to 32 percent of the work force. Forecasters see this as a continuing trend, with more people working from their homes coming into the workplace on a contingent basis.[3]

Either pattern provides challenges in communication. Contingent workers may be hard to reach, for example. Communicators in multiemployer plans already know the challenges of working with plan participants who are not part of any one work force on a daily basis. But true contingent workers may have different value systems than others in the workplace. These workers may be part-time or contingent workers because they want to be at home with family during certain hours or because they want more freedom or autonomy. Thus, they may value different kinds of benefits and respond to different kinds of communication.

Decreased Literacy in the Working Population

Measuring national literacy, much less accounting for its decrease, is difficult. The population growth among the economically disadvantaged where literacy is traditionally lower and the growth in populations where English may not be the first language suggest there will be decreased literacy in the future work force.

To compound the result of lower literacy, the need for literacy skills is on the rise. Right now about 40 percent of jobs require low reading or computation skills. But by the year 2000 this percentage will drop markedly, requiring that almost three quarters of the work force be literate. According to the Department of Education, nearly all new service industry jobs will require at least an 11th grade reading level. Certainly this will present a great challenge to employers when the work force has shrunk and the proportion of English literacy has fallen. And certainly this will present a challenge to those who will communicate benefits and compensation issues to plan participants.

Are workplace solutions the answer? The International Foundation of Employee Benefit Plans published results of a survey that queried companies about their training and education programs. Of the responding companies, 47 percent say they currently offer basic skills training, and 26 percent say they will be in the year 2000. Although literacy programs are less common now, coming in at 19 percent, companies seem to be aware of the needs of their future workers since 31 percent of the respondents say they will offer literacy by the turn of the century.[4] This means perhaps about *half* of the companies will offer literacy training. But that, in turn, means that *half* will not.

Many publications describe how to conduct effective literary programs. Key elements include organizing the programs so that employees see the training as part of their jobs. Programs that are organized by job and simulate the work done on the job are best; and, of course, these work place students need frequent feedback and encouragement.[5]

WRITING FOR LESS ABLE READERS

Attractive Visual Aids

Since in-depth literacy courses are not an immediate solution, communicators will need to make print media as readable as possible to the greatest number of plan participants. For example, readability and retention increase when print is accompanied by visual aids like sidebars, charts, graphs, and pictures. *USA Today* clearly employs these techniques to attract less literate readers. Major news magazines demonstrate how charts and graphs become more understandable with graphic as well as numerical representations. Stacks of coins rather than lines, for example, can demonstrate investment growth to those with less reading ability or unfamiliarity with English.

Preview, Present, Summarize

When preparing print materials, follow a technique good teachers use: preview, present, and summarize. To preview the topic for readers, write headings that categorize the upcoming material. Use sidebars or quotes in a larger type to pull key ideas out from the text. These will help the reader anticipate the upcoming contents. A glance at *People* magazine shows how these techniques involve readers in the text. In fact, good preview aids allow readers to grasp the main points without even reading the text. Present main ideas and summarize them in a variety of ways. Sidebars that reinforce the main action or the angle of the story help readers understand main ideas.

Perhaps it is best to think of the communication process as a dart game. The messages or darts are aimed toward a target—the audience. We may have several choices to score, several chances to send the message. We plan, develop skills, and take careful aim. But no matter how careful the aim, the more arrows—or vehicles—we used to send the message, the better are our chances of hitting the bull's eye.

For example, the main body of print of a brochure describing your 401(k) plan could present the plan and explain how participants can join. To help readers visualize the benefits of saving, include a sidebar about a well-known retiree who enjoys a carefree retirement thanks to the savings plan, or samples of how savings could grow for three hypothetical participants. Thus, the communication summarizes the main ideas in several ways.

Text Appearance and Layout

When planning layout, remember that readability is affected by line length, justification, and font and type style. In general, these characteristics help the reader:

- Lines of no more or less than 50–60 characters
- Adequate type size—from 9 to 12 point

- Ragged right columns
- Serif fonts

White space is equally important in layout. Too much text on a page is intimidating, especially to poor readers. Generous white space creates a sense that the printed material can be easily grasped, that it is well organized.

Lively Style

Without readable style, even graphically excellent text falls flat. In general, readable style uses short words in short sentences that put people in action. In fact, these are the characteristics standard readability formulas use to assign reading levels. The Gunning Fog Index and Flesch formula count word length, line length, and numbers of multisyllable words. The higher the counts, the higher the school grade level a reader must have achieved to understand the material. While editing, a writer can apply these standards to lower the grade level of a passage. Short words—*use for utilize, pay for compensation*—are better than long ones. Sentences over 20 words should be used sparingly. Today, computerized grammar and style checkers like Gramma'tik or Right-Writer can quickly apply common readability formulas to text. They also have other features useful in working with readability.

Readers respond to action. To put people or things in action, use the active voice. For example, "In two weeks you will receive the registration card in the mail" is more lively than "The registration card will be received by mail in two weeks." In the first example, the sentence subject does the action of the verb and this makes the sentence more vivid and easier to understand.

ALTERNATIVES TO PRINT: VIDEO, VOICE RESPONSE, AND INTERACTIVE PC

Where the literacy needs of the audience are very diverse, alternatives to print like video, voice response, and interactive computers may be more effective. Video works best for creating excitement and explaining major concepts, not for covering every detail of a plan. It can use humor and summarize big concepts in a way that makes them memorable. But using video requires a well thought out implementation strategy. Videos work best when they are introduced by a meeting leader who is excited and knowledgeable about the program.

The interactive computer has the advantage of being a nonlinear communication. The user doesn't have to begin at a set point and move through to the end. Rather, the user selects each path. Thus, the interactive program is excellent for helping plan participants calculate individual retirement benefits. Once basic facts about salary, savings, and age are entered, the program

---

SUCCESS THROUGH READABILITY—
THE "YOU CAN DO IT" CAMPAIGN

A *Fortune* 500 company used a variety of ways of making print material less intimidating and more readable to attract more of its lower paid members to their savings plan. After members said they did not read the books the company typically used to describe benefits, we suggested a campaign for the savings plan that avoided books. To simplify the print material, the campaign, titled "You Can Do It," used five selling points, such as *you can borrow from yourself, you can save through easy payroll deductions,* and so forth. Since any one or two of the points might catch the potential plan participant's interest, it was not necessary to read all the points to be convinced. The selling points were printed on half sheets of paper folded in half, with a lightweight, "disposable" feeling paper. Each one had a clever graphic on it—little piggy banks climbed up investment rate returns, Uncle Sam pointed out tax advantages. A folded cardboard case held the flyers; when unfolded, each panel displayed the "Your Can Do It" message. Because no single page contained much print, the material was not intimidating to poor readers.

    Distribution of the flyers was carefully planned to be nonintimidating too. Since employees had expressed a dislike for meetings and formal videos, we used information booths with banners, tablecloths, and balloons. The flexibility of the materials allowed for variety in presentation methods among the company's 40 locations, so human resource managers could tailor methods that worked for their groups.

---

displays how much retirement income will be available at certain ages. To minimize the need for keyboard familiarity, the program can be touch-screen activated. Then the user need only touch appropriate parts of the screen for user-friendly information. For areas of high traffic or dust, the computer can be sealed in a kiosk so that only the screen shows.

A third nonprint medium, voice response, uses the telephone to present information. Although more limited than the PC, telephone voice response has several advantages. It requires no equipment investment and it is available 24 hours a day from home and work. Plan participants can use the voice response at a time and place convenient for them. Voice response programs can present information, conduct surveys, calculate benefits, and initiate transactions for a variety of benefit applications.

Telephone voice response surveys allow for immediate feedback. For example, if the user agrees with a statement, he or she may press 6. The voice response might tell him or her that 33 percent of the employees agreed with the response. This feedback encourages him or her to keep responding.

Voice response works best when introduced by print communication so that the user has an overview of what the program will do and is not put off when a computer voice rather than a live listener responds.

THE EMERGING GLOBAL WORKFORCE

The growth of multinational companies provides outstanding challenges—or opportunities—for communicators. More and more employers and plan sponsors are exploring how making employees feel part of a single organization, a shared culture, can impact multinational success. Developing strategies appropriate for various cultures and nationalities and finding ways to make media affordable for groups of 20 or 20,000 calls for creativity and innovation. For example, it may be cost effective to laser print materials for small groups and use traditional printing methods for large ones. Flexible packaging and modular video and slide components can help bridge the language and culture gaps. It may be useful to call on employees and plan participants with bilingual capabilities to assist in the communication effort. The key is to create a global strategy with enough flexibility for differences in local implementation: to think globally and act locally.

COMMUNICATION OPPORTUNITY: PERSUADING MANAGEMENT

Persuading management of the need for special communication efforts with plan participants often provides the most challenging opportunity for communicators. Because communication seems like such a basic and natural function, management often thinks it will take place with little effort or cost. Also, management may feel that its most important concerns will not be reflected in these communication efforts; a survey published in the *International Association of Business Communicators* (IABC) showed that CEOs' top concerns for the 1990s were almost never addressed in periodical in-house publications.[6] This experience with their in-house publications may affect their attitude toward the value of other communication efforts. For this reason, communicators need to be sure to include management in the communication strategy and to assign them a specific role in getting the message across.

The Age of Consent: Management Wants to Listen

As a result of a number of influences, managers are listening more to their employees and managing more by consensus. They are interested in letting plan participants help decide what should be in the benefits packages. This means finding out what they want. But how?

Communicators can use a variety of means to determine participant's needs and interests. Interviews, focus groups, and written surveys are possibilities. However, other means should be considered as well for collecting responses. For example, in some settings such as a university where groups don't often meet as

---

BOTTOM LINE RESULTS:
SAME BENEFITS, 59% INCREASE IN APPROVAL

To be wholly convinced, managers need to know how the communication effort will affect the bottom line. A case involving communicating benefit changes during an acquisition demonstrates how a communication strategy can affect employee attitude, a factor that almost certainly converts to a better bottom line.

A major producer of athletic wear planned to announce changes in its benefits immediately after the new benefits went into effect on July 1. Initially, management planned to simply shut down the sewing machines and announce the changes to large groups of employees. To make matters worse, employees anticipated very generous new benefits since the new parent company was known to be a good one. In reality, the old and new benefits were commensurate, so it was quite possible the employees would be disappointed with the changes. After careful planning and education, management was persuaded that the communication strategy could prepare the employees for the new benefits and show them how what they did on the job affected the performance of the company.

A series of newsletters was developed to cover the benefit changes *and* a host of broader issues such as how the parent company operates and treats its divisions and operating companies. Articles on the benefits explained how they worked, and educated employees about the cost of medical care and other key benefit and compensation issues. Managers were asked to review drafts, were given information before employees, and become better informed about the benefits. They were trained to conduct employee meetings and to become ongoing "local experts" for human resources issues. They become the key to effective delivery of the message.

The bottom line results of the strategy were impressive. Before the communication effort, benefits earned only a 27 percent acceptance level from employees on the company's yearly attitude survey. After the communication effort, benefits earned 86 percent acceptance. In reality, the benefits were not better, they were better communicated.

---

a unit, e-mail might be appropriate. Also some people like responding to nonprint media, like the PC and voice response systems discussed earlier, because they seem less permanent and more confidential.

A COMMUNICATION OPPORTUNITY: GETTING A REASONABLE BUDGET

To get a reasonable budget, we must remind management that communication with employees is a necessity. Without a strategy that invites involvement and understanding of the new plan, employees may be indifferent to management's reasons for the changes or downright resentful.

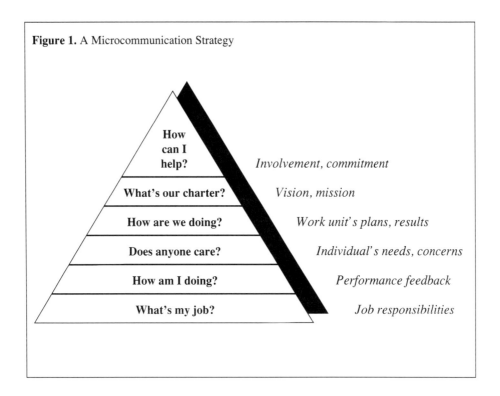

Figure 1. A Microcommunication Strategy

How
can I
help? — *Involvement, commitment*

What's our charter? — *Vision, mission*

How are we doing? — *Work unit's plans, results*

Does anyone care? — *Individual's needs, concerns*

How am I doing? — *Performance feedback*

What's my job? — *Job responsibilities*

To determine the most efficient use of communication dollars, design a corporate-wide strategy that includes management's concerns, the audience's needs and assessment. Good research and planning will lead to a strategy that includes all these components.

A HIERARCHY OF COMMUNICATION NEEDS

The most effective communication strategies are tied to management's overall strategic plan. Show management how the communication plan will *change the way employees behave*. If a CEO or plan sponsor has three new business strategies but does not convey them to the employees who make decisions on the line every day, does the company or plan *really* have a new strategy? However, if the strategies are translated to employees in terms of their own needs and interests, employees will make behavioral changes that can make the strategies a reality. One way to communicate such strategies to employees is to consider issues from an employee's viewpoint.

It is helpful to remember that communication needs are hierarchical. As the pyramid in Figure 1 shows, management can gain commitment to a strategy by helping an employee move from the fundamental question "What's my job?"

through "What's our charter?" to the significant question "How can I help?" Roger D'Aprix, who devised the model, comments, "As the employee ascends the pyramid, getting answers to other questions, he or she approaches an organization's ultimate goal for its people: commitment."[7]

Once individual needs are tied to corporate needs, the costs of communication is no longer viewed by head count level but rather from a larger perspective. For example, a video to introduce a new medical plan might cost $40,000—or $2,000 per employee. Of course this seems extravagant. However, if the new medical plan will save $1 million, the cost of the video is viewed differently. Therefore, when developing a communication plan, be sure to build in assessment to show how the net impact of a behavioral change will affect the bottom line.

1. Jerry J Jasinowski, "America's Work Force in the 1990s: Trends Affecting Manufacturers" (National Association of Manufacturers), 3-4.

2. Charles D Schewe, "How to Communicate With Older Adults," *American Demographics* (August 1991), 53.

3. Supra note 1.

4. "Nontraditional Benefits of the Workforce of 2000: A Special Report" (Brookfield, Wisconsin: International Foundation of Employee Benefit Plans), 10.

5. Patricia Dunn-Ranking and Drake Beil, "A Primer for Workplace Literacy Programs," *Training and Development Journal* (August 1990), 45-47.

6. Gary W Kempler, "Employee Publications: Are They a Poor Investment of Many Organizations?" IABC *Communication World* (April 1991), reprint.

7. Roger D'Aprix, communication consultant with William M Mercer, Inc., Boston.

Part 9

LEGAL AGENDA

41. Managed Care and the Courts: The Next Generation
Curtis Rooney

Managed care in various forms has been proven to save money and maintain quality, and has been implemented widely. The full legal implications of managed care programs, however, are still evolving. Employers that have or are considering managed care benefit programs need to be aware of issues ranging from ERISA preemption provisions and the possibilities of state and common law liability, to mandated benefits and anti-managed care laws.

Those concerned with providing quality employe benefit plans must be aware of the growing body of restrictions imposed on managed care. While policy-makers in Washington and in the states grapple with the issues surrounding comprehensive health care and ERISA reforms that may undermine current protections, employers must continue to look inward for methods aimed at controlling the rising costs of health care. It is therefore important that employers keep current with the legal context of managed care or with the latest managed care practices themselves.

The purpose of this article is to update *Managed Care and The Courts: An Overview,* published by the APPWP's Action Center for Quality Health Care in November of 1991, and to take another "snapshot" of the current state of managed health care law in the United States.

First, this article reviews the effects of ERISA's preemption provisions on employee benefit plans; second, it surveys the types of common law theories of liability employers may anticipate should a court find that a particular claim is not preempted by ERISA; third, it discusses the phenomena of state mandated benefits and anti-mandated benefits and anti-managed-care laws; fourth, it ex-

Reprinted with the express permission of the Action Center for Quality Health Care, Association of Private Pension and Welfare Plans, 1212 New York Avenue, N.W., Washington, DC 20005.

amines specific aspects of benefit changes and vesting with respect to employee
benefit plans; and finally, it concludes with a warning to employers that, while it
is still premature to draw conclusions, the evolving nature of the laws governing
managed care continues to change and therefore warrants a fresh and continuous
look at the next generation of managed care and the courts.

ERISA PREEMPTION

As state and common law theories of liability are extended to encompass the
various activities performed with respect to managed care entities, it is foreseeable that employers may also potentially find themselves in legal limbo. As
discussed below, the result of employers using the defense of ERISA preemption
has not been completely successful. Although the Supreme Court has not
delineated a "bright line" test, the Court has interpreted ERISA's complicated
preemption provisions in a number of cases and demonstrated that a cause of
action against an employer plan may be preempted under certain circumstances.
Several important preemption decisions have made it clear that ERISA should
preempt most claims against plans, plan sponsors, and plan fiduciaries when they
are based upon common law or state statutes that relate to an employee benefit
plan.[1] ERISA, with its broadly drawn preemption provisions, detailed reporting
and disclosure criteria, fiduciary requirements, and comprehensive civil enforcement scheme, demonstrates Congress's intent to strike a careful balance between
the need for adequate safeguards for plan participants and the public interest in
encouraging the formation of the private employee benefit system.[2] Not surprisingly, the framers of ERISA believed that the law's "crowning achievement" was
its preemption of state laws.[3]

For example, the Supreme Court held in *Pilot Life v. Dedeux*[4] (1987), that
ERISA preempted state common law causes of action, including the Mississippi
tort of "bad faith" arising in connection with the alleged improper processing or
denial of a claim for benefits by Pilot Life Insurance Co. under a plan it insured
under an agreement with Entex, Inc. The Court reasoned that a common-sense
understanding of the phrase "regulates insurance" does not support the arguments
that the Mississippi law of bad faith falls under the "savings clause." A common-
sense view of the word "regulates" would lead to the conclusion that in order to
regulate insurance, a law must not just have an impact on the insurance industry
but must be specifically directed toward that industry. Thus, state common law
claims for the denial of benefits and common law remedies such as punitive and
consequential damages should be preempted.

However, the Court has recognized that not every conceivable cause of
action that may be brought against an ERISA-covered plan is preempted. The
Supreme Court stated, "some state actions may effect employee benefit plans in
too tenuous, remote or peripheral a manner to warrant a finding that the law

'relates to' the plan."[5] It is a commonly held myth that only self-insured plans are ERISA plans that enjoy the full protection of that law's preemption provisions.[6] Employer-sponsored benefit plans that utilize an insurance product as its funding mechanism are also considered ERISA plans by the courts even though they are said to be "fully insured."[7] In addition, the Third Circuit recently held that a preferred provider organization (PPO) may be preempted under ERISA despite the fact that it has been designed to provide benefits for both insured and self-insured plans.[8] Thus, in terms of liability, the distinction between fully insured plans and self-insured plans may be less significant than whether the plan is considered an employee benefit plan and therefore afforded ERISA preemption protections.[9]

One significant distinction between self-insured plans and fully insured plans is that ERISA does not regulate the terms or contents of self-insured health plans,[10] whereas states may regulate the terms of the insurance products purchased by employers, thus indirectly regulating insured employee benefit plans.[11] ERISA does provide for the regulation of the procedural aspects of health and welfare plans, the plan's administration, the fiduciary conduct of those parties performing the administration of the plan, and the information available to plan participants.[12]

Despite the general success of ERISA's preemption provisions, the continuing health care debate has propelled ERISA reform onto the national agenda. In fact, the 102nd Congress of 1991 and 1992 saw the introduction of several proposals which would amend ERISA's preemption provisions. The proposals would allow for everything from providing for state law causes of action, including consequential and punitive damages, to granting waivers for states interested in accomplishing comprehensive health care reform, to the taxation of self-insured plans.[13] The debate regarding ERISA and health care reform will undoubtedly be even greater in the 103rd Congress.

THEORIES OF LIABILITY IN MANAGED CARE PROVIDER MALPRACTICE

Provider Malpractice

As stated in APPWP's *Managed Care and the Courts: An Overview,* one of the greatest concerns to employers and insurers who enter into managed care arrangements is the possibility of being sued for the alleged negligence of their managed care providers.[14] It is unlikely that ERISA would be found to preempt a state malpractice claim directly against the actual provider of medical services. However, the courts are split on whether or not a malpractice-type claim is always preempted by ERISA when the case concerns a state law malpractice claim related to the negligence of a contracting provider.[15]

A review of the cases suggests that ERISA may not provide all the protection employers may believe it does. While the courts have sided overwhelmingly with employers in a number of cases by finding that ERISA preempts state law malpractice claims against employer-provided medical benefit plans, not all courts have come to the same result, causing a split in legal authority.[16] For example, in *Independence HMO, Inc. v. Smith*[17] (1990), the court said that ERISA did not preempt "garden variety" malpractice cases despite the fact that the benefits were provided under an employee benefit plan. The court reasoned that the plaintiff's state tort claim for malpractice was not preempted because it was a "run of the mill" malpractice claim and had no connection to the plaintiff's denial of benefits under the employer plan.[18]

Following a similar analysis, the court in *DeGenova v. Ansel*[19] (1990), held that a plaintiff's state law claim did not "relate to" an employee benefit plan and thus was *not* preempted under ERISA. In that case, the plaintiff sued the insurer for the malpractice of the doctor the plan required the plaintiff to see for a second opinion. Upon going to the referred physician, the doctor went ahead with the procedure on his own in an allegedly negligent manner without consulting the insurer. The court reasoned that the plaintiff's claims, which were common law tort claims, did not "relate to" an employee benefit plan and thus were not preempted by ERISA. The pro-plaintiff court "reasoned" that if it were to find the plaintiff's claim to be preempted, the plaintiff would not be properly compensated under ERISA.[20]

Ostensible Agency

It is notable that in several recent cases, courts have found HMOs to be liable for the malpractice of physicians who are not employees of the HMO, using the negligence theories of apparent or ostensible agency.[21] Generally, courts have held that a party cannot be liable for the negligence of its independent contractors. However, under the theory of ostensible agency, if it can be shown that the allegedly liable party was an apparent or ostensible agent of another, the basis for imposing liability may be formed. Liability may arise where an agency relationship exists (i.e., an agency relationship may exist where one person acts as the legal representative or agent of another).[22] For example, in *Decker v. Saini*[23] (1991), the court held that an HMO could be liable for the malpractice of its participating primary care physician and a referral radiologist who were independent contractors. The court denied the HMO's motions to have the case thrown out of court on legal grounds, stating that the HMO held itself out as a provider by promising the best care available, and the plaintiffs, relied on those representations. The court held that an HMO could be found liable for the malpractice of its member physicians.[24]

While HMOs and employers are similar in that both participate in the financing of health care, the analogy should end there due largely to the fact that HMOs are, in addition, responsible for the delivery of health care services. This distinction should be enough for employer provided managed care plans to avoid liability under ERISA. Nevertheless, courts could follow a similar line of reasoning used in the above HMO cases to find that a network provider is an agent of the plan sponsor and thereby hold the plan sponsor liable.

Accordingly, plan sponsors will want to be careful in designing their health and medical benefit plans so as not to create the impression that they are also the providers of or maintain control over the actual providers of medical care. In addition, employers must be aware that if their plan design limits a member's choice of providers, the member is more apt to look to those providers within the network as being agents of the plan, if not the employer. Employers will want to make clear in their printed materials that the medical providers found in the network arrangements are independent contractors and thus, disclaim responsibility for the quality of care as dispensed by individual providers found in the network. Employers sponsoring managed care plans will also want to make it clear in employee communications that each employee is responsible for his or her choice of providers.

Corporate Malpractice

Several courts have held that hospitals and HMOs owe a "duty of due care" to others with respect to the selection and retention of physicians maintained on staff.[25] This means that hospitals and HMO's may be held responsible for the acts of their employees/doctors if they have not made a satisfactory effort to investigate their doctors' credentials, qualifications and backgrounds on an ongoing basis. It may follow that employers contracting with physicians in the arrangement of managed care panels may be liable for the malpractice of their physician-providers if their efforts to investigate the physician's credentials are inadequate. To prove liability on a corporate negligence theory, a plaintiff must show not only that the physician was negligent, but that the employer was negligent in its selection and contracting with that provider.

Therefore, to limit their potential exposure, employers will want to take precautions such as interviewing candidates, documenting the criteria used in their evaluation, and credentialing network providers to demonstrate that due care was taken in the selection process and that efforts were made to protect plan beneficiaries from foreseeable risks of harm.

Malpractice Due to Compensation Arrangements

Managed care arrangements often include incentives for members to use providers covered by the plans and for participating providers to be cost-efficient (e.g., prospective pricing, capitation financing, negotiated fees, and/or financial risk-sharing). In *Bush v. Dake*[26] (1989), the plaintiff sued the provider for malpractice and claimed that the financial incentives built into the plan caused "under utilization," thus delaying necessary treatment and causing harm to the plaintiff. The plaintiff in *Bush* alleged that the HMO's risk pool arrangement and capitation financing scheme developed under a contract with a physician group practice deferred testing and referral to specialists and postponed plaintiff's necessary treatment. The plaintiff alleged that but for the financing arrangement, her cancer would have been detected earlier. While the trial court allowed the jury to hear the plaintiff's malpractice theory, the case was settled prior to a verdict.

Had the case not been settled, the defendant would have undoubtedly wanted to show that either the plaintiff assumed the risk associated with the managed care arrangement by agreeing to participate in the risk pool, or that the plaintiff failed to seek the appropriate care on a timely basis and contributed to the risk associated with late diagnosis. To avoid liability, the defendant would have needed to show that the plaintiff knew about the financial arrangement with the physicians and did not object or that the plaintiff's own behavior contributed to her late diagnosis. Although employers finding themselves in similar circumstances will seek to argue that their actions are protected by ERISA, those employers developing like arrangements will want to make efforts to disclose such arrangements in their employee communications.

Negligent Utilization Review

Utilization review is a common element found in many managed care plans and includes controls such as preadmission certification, concurrent review, second surgical opinion, and case management. Utilization review affects the beneficiary's access to care by deciding what services are "medically necessary." Because of this limiting effect, several important cases have been brought to determine the responsibility of the plan or the plan's reviewer versus that of the patient's physician in the utilization review process. The managed care community was encouraged by the decisions in the *Wickline*[27] (1986) and *Wilson*[28] (1990) cases because of their pro-managed care results. However, the *Wickline* court did suggest in legally non-binding language that the negligent implementation of cost containment mechanisms such as utilization review could lead to liability. More recently, commentators have discussed their concerns regarding the court's opinion in the *Corcoran v. United HealthCare, Inc.*[29]

In *Corcoran,* the Fifth Circuit held that ERISA preempts a medical malpractice claim against a utilization review service found under an employer plan. Despite the positive result, some commentators have speculated that the court's decisions raises the specter of increased employer liability in certain circumstances, because, although the court found the state law claims preempted by ERISA, the court acknowledged that the utilization review firm "gives medical advice—but does so in context of making a determination about the availability of benefits under the plan."[30] It remains to be seen under what circumstances a court would find an employer liable for the implementation of cost containment mechanisms such as utilization review for injures of a plan participant or beneficiary.

Claims of Misrepresentation

State law claims of misrepresentation, fraud, and allegations of deceptive trade practices brought against an employer-provided plan may also be preempted by ERISA.[31] However, the question of liability for provider risk-sharing and the degree to which the failure to disclose these arrangements may constitute misrepresentation is less clear.[32] Employers will want to disclose such arrangements in their employee communications to ensure the best possible employee relations, as well as to protect themselves from potential liability.

Another related area of potential liability is for claims alleging breach of warranty. The marketing materials of employee benefit plans, which often suggest or imply that the plan will provide a certain level of "quality medical care," could lead an injured plaintiff to allege that the plan breached its warranty to provide for or arrange medical services.[33] Plan sponsors should take care to draft employee documents and materials to limit the risk of potential plaintiffs alleging liability on a breach of warranty theory.

Benefit Claims

Claims for benefits under a plan must be brought as federal claims for which ERISA provides its own specific statutory remedies.[34] In addition, because ERISA does not regulate the benefits within a plan or mandate a minimum level of benefits, claims to recover benefits not explicitly covered under the terms of the plan or included in the insurance contract should fail.[35] For example, in *Varol v. Blue Cross and Blue Shield of Michigan*[36] (1989), a federal district court dismissed, on the grounds of ERISA preemption, a claim brought under state law against a psychiatric managed care program, which included preauthorization and concurrent review and was offered under the General Motors health benefit plan and administered by Blue Cross and Blue Shield of Michigan.

In a once troubling case, the Third Circuit Court of Appeals recently rectified what could have been a disastrous result for the managed care community in the *Nazay v. Miller*[37] (1991) case. In *Nazay*, the U.S. District Court for the Middle District of Pennsylvania held that it was arbitrary and capricious and a violation of ERISA's fiduciary standards for a plan to impose upon its members a 30 percent penalty for failing to acquire precertification prior to hospitalization in a nonemergency situation. Fortunately, the Court of Appeals reversed this decision and permitted the plan to enforce the benefit reduction penalty. Precertification continues to be a basic practice of managed care and a fundamental cost containment tool for concerned employers. Nevertheless, plans may not find as sympathetic an ear when it comes to precertification cases involving experimental medical treatments.[38]

A question closely related to the issue of benefits claims exposure is the standard of review for benefit claims denials where a potential conflict of interest exists in a managed care setting. Generally, plan administrators have a fiduciary duty to discharge their obligations by acting "solely in the interest" of the plan's participants and beneficiaries.[39] The Supreme Court held recently that claims administrators should look to the plan document to determine the appropriate standard of review. Otherwise, the Court said that the appropriate standard of review regarding benefits claims is the de novo standard, which calls for a fresh look at the claim as if it had not been reviewed before, rather than the "arbitrary and capricious" standard which affords greater deference to the determinations by the plan administrator.[40]

Meanwhile, at least one lower court has held that where an insurer also acts as a plan fiduciary, an inherent conflict of interest exists, thus making the arbitrary and capricious standard inappropriate with respect to benefits determinations regardless of the plan documents.[41] This development has led at least one commentator to conclude that the "inability of an insurance company to be able to rely on the arbitrary and capricious standard of review makes it much more difficult to defend ambiguous [managed care] plan provisions. In observing some of the court decisions, it appears that ambiguity can be found in almost any plan provision."[42] Indeed, the Ninth Circuit Court of Appeals recently found that where the employer was also the plan administrator, a conflict of interest existed in a denial of benefits claim.[43]

Liability for Breach of Contract

Because breach of contract actions are generally state common-law causes of action, cases brought under this theory of liability will normally be preempted by ERISA if they are found to "relate to" an employee benefit plan. However, it is worth noting that in *Stelmach v. Physicians Multispecialty Group, Inc.*[44] (1989), the state appellate court upheld a verdict of $1.5 million against a physicians practice group on the theory of breach of contract with an HMO. The plaintiff successfully argued that she was a third party beneficiary of the contract, which was breached when the medical group failed to provide medical services of "good quality." Although reported cases against employers using a breach of contract theory for establishing provider networks are rare, because employers are so-called "deep pocket" entities, they can safely assume that this theory or liability will be used against them in future litigation.

STATE MANDATED BENEFITS AND ANTI-MANAGED CARE LAWS

State have become increasingly involved in mandating employee benefits and restricting managed care in recent years.[45] Currently, there are over 900 costly mandated benefit laws on the books across the nation.[46] In response to criticisms that these mandates unfairly burden employers' ability to offer health benefits, many states have sought to create so-called "bare bones" health packages. However, these packages have not sold very successfully and thus have not provided greater access to insurance; they usually include no managed care provisions.

In addition, many states have become more aggressive in their efforts to regulate managed care arrangements and entities within their states.[47] Fortunately, courts have struck some of these requirements down on the grounds of ERISA preemption. For example, in *Stuart Circle Hospital Corp. v. Aetna Health Management*[48] (1992), the United States District Court for the Eastern District of Virginia recently held that ERISA preempted Virginia's "any willing provider" statute as it appeared in Virginia's preferred provider organization law. The court stated that the law "goes to the sum and substance of employee benefit plans: the delivery of promised benefits," and was preempted despite the fact that some of Aetna's PPO network members are self-insured while others are fully insured.

BENEFIT CHANGES AND VESTING

One of Congress' express intentions in passing ERISA was to encourage the implementation of the voluntary private employer benefits system. To encourage companies to provide benefits to their workers, Congress wisely chose to allow plans to be modified where the plan reserved the right to do so. The Supreme Court has recently ratified this provision of ERISA in the case of *McGann v. H&H Music, Inc.*[49] (1992). Congress, in turn, has reacted by holding hearings to discuss the case and will undoubtedly consider legislation that would give plan participant and beneficiaries a "vested" right to existing benefit levels for the treatment of their existing illnesses.[50]

Regardless of the outcome of the ERISA vesting debate, employers considering changes in their health benefit plans to include managed care features will need to be mindful of the discrimination provisions of the recently enacted ADA concerning employee benefits. However, because implementation of the law for employers of 25 or more employees only began in July 1992, it will not be known for some time what the full effect of the ADA will be on employer health plans. As of December of 1992, the Equal Employment Opportunity Commission (EEOC) had reportedly received over 2,000 complaints under the new law (3.7 percent of those complaints concerned discrimination with respect to benefits), and many more complaints are expected to be filed as these cases wend their way through the litigation process as prescribed under the ADA.

CONCLUSION

The lines between traditional insurance and managed care programs have become blurred as the payment and the delivery of health care services have become increasingly integrated. Recent trends in litigation indicate that "deep pocket organizations" such as employers and insurers continue to be threatened by an onslaught of legal challenges. Employers also need to use caution when considering plan changes, taking the time to consider recently implemented laws such as the ADA, Congress' continued assault on ERISA, and state anti-managed care laws. Finally, because of the evolving nature of managed care, continued vigilance is warranted, as is an ongoing look at the next generation of managed care cases as they make their way through the courts.

1. *See Metropolitan Mut Life Ins Co v Massachusetts,* 471 US 724 (1985); *Pilot Life v Dedeaux,* 481 US 41 (1987); *FMC Corporation v Holliday,* 111 SCt 403 (1990); *Ingersoll-Rand Co v McClendon,* 111 SCt 478 (1990).

2. The Court held in *Massachusetts Mut Life Ins Co v Russell,* 437 US 134 (1985), that punitive damages and extracontractual damages, including damages for emotional distress, are not available to plan participants or beneficiaries in benefits claims actions. *See also Powell v Cheaspeake & Potomac Tel Co,* 780 F2d 419 (4th Cir 1985), *cert denied,* 476 US 1170 (1986). While federal courts have exclusive jurisdiction over all civil actions under ERISA (other than benefit claims cases), concurrent federal and state jurisdiction exists over benefit claims ERISA [502(e)(1)]. However, the Court in *Metropolitan Life Ins Co v Taylor,* 481 US 58 (1987), held that in benefit claims cases, the action can always be removed to federal court. Also, under ERISA § 502(g) attorney's fees and costs are available to either party in such actions, at the discretion of the court.

3. Representative Dent (D-PA), one of the original authors of ERISA, stated the case for the broadest possible preemption of state laws as follows: "Finally, I wish to make note of what is to many the crowning achievement of this legislation, the reservation to Federal authority [of] the sole power to regulate the field of employee benefit plans. With the preemption of the field, we round out the protection afforded participants by eliminating the threat of conflicting and inconsistent State and local regulation" (emphasis added).

4. 481 US 41 (1987).

5. The court in *Corcoran* quoting *Shaw,* thus, "run-of-the-mill state-law claims such as unpaid rent, failure to pay creditors, or even torts committed by an ERISA plan" are not preempted. *Shaw v Delta Air Lines, Inc,* 463 US 85, 100 n21 (1983). *See also Mackey v Lanier Collection Agency & Serv, Inc,* 486 US 825 (1988) (discussing these types of claims in dicta).

6. *See Managed Care and the Courts: An Overview* 5 (Nov 1991) ("A plan is self-fenced if the plan sponsor directly assumes the financial risk of providing medical coverage of its employees. A plan is insured if

the risk is transferred to a third party, such as an insurance company or an HMO. Under certain circumstances, a plan sponsor may, through the purchase of stop-loss insurance, shift a portion of the financial risk to a third party and still maintain a self-funded plan. There are two types of stop-loss insurance, aggregate and individual. Aggregate stop-loss insurance limits the total amount of plan benefits the employer must pay for the year. Individual stop-loss insurance, on the other hand, limits the amount of benefits the employer must pay on behalf of each individual or family for the year. In addition to entering into stop-loss insurance arrangements, self-fenced plans often contract with insurance companies to handle the plan's administrative needs. the insurance company processes claims for benefits, adjudicates disputed claims and issues benefit payments. If the third party administrator assumes no financial risk in its administrative function, the plan remains self-funded.")

7. Under ERISA § 3, 29 USC §§ 1102(1), (3), an employee benefit plan is any entity that meets the following definition: (1) The terms "employee welfare benefit plan" and "welfare plan" mean any plan, fund, or program which was heretofore or is hereafter established or maintained by an employer or by any employee organization, or by both, to the extent that such plan, fund, or program was established or is maintained for the purpose of insurance or otherwise, (A) medical, surgical, or hospital care or benefits, or benefits in the event of sickness, accident, disability, death or unemployment, or vacation benefits, apprenticeship or other training programs, or day care centers, scholarship funds, or prepaid legal services, or (B) any benefit described in Section 302(c) of the Labor Management Relations Act, 1947 other than pensions on retirement or death, and insurance to provide such pensions . . . the term "employer" means any person acting directly as an employer, or indirectly in the interest of an employer, in relation to an employee benefit plan; and includes a group or association of employers acting for an employer in such capacity.

8. *See Stuart Circle Hosp Corp v Aetna Health Management.* —F Supp— (ED Va July 22, 1992); *See also HCA Health Services of Virginia, Inc v Aetna Life Insurance Company,* No Civ Act No 92-574-A, US District Court for the Eastern District of Virginia, Oct 15 (1992); *But see Blue Cross and Blue Shield of Virginia v St. Mary's Hospital of Richmond v Blue Cross and Blue Shield of Virginia,* No 920146 (Va January 8, 1993). (Virginia State Supreme court held 'any willing provider' statute not preempted by ERISA.)

9. The term "employee benefit plan" includes both "employee pension benefit plans" and " employee welfare benefit plans." Health benefits are most often considered "employee welfare benefit plans" which is defined as a plan or program established by an employer to provide, among other benefits, employee medical care "through the purchase of insurance or otherwise. 29 USC §§ 1002(1), (3)(1988).

10. *See Shaw v Delta Air Lines, Inc,* 463 US 85 (1983) in which the Supreme Court observed in dictum: "ERISA does not mandate that employers provide any particular benefits, and does not itself proscribe discrimination in the provision of employee benefits"; *see also Moore v Metropolitan Life Ins Co* 856 F2d 488 (2d Cir 1988).

11. *See Metropolitan Life Ins Co v Massachusetts,* 471 US 724 (1985). The Court upheld a Massachusetts law requiring insurance companies to provide specified minimum mental health benefits in any health insurance plan offered in the State. The court held that states may mandate that insured health benefit plans provide certain benefits under the plan.

12. As discussed in *Managed Care and the Courts: An Overview, supra* note 6, ERISA imposes requirements on persons who are fiduciaries of pension and welfare plans. Any person who exercises discretionary authority, responsibility or control over the administration and operation of a plan may be a fiduciary [ERISA § 3(21)(A), 29 USC § 1002(21)(A)]. Fiduciaries who breach their obligations to a plan are subject to personal liability to restore to the plan any losses resulting from their breach of duty [ERISA § 409, 29 USC § 1109]. ERISA also contains specific claims processing requirements. Plan participants must be notified in writing, generally within 90 days, of the denial of any benefit claim. The plans must also establish an appeals process that affords participants an opportunity for a full and fair review of any adverse decision made by a plan fiduciary [ERISA § 503, 29 USC § 1133(1981); [29 CFR § 2560.503-1(1988)]. If benefits under a plan are provided or administered by an insurance company or service, such company may be designated as the appropriate fiduciary. The claims procedure of an HMO satisfies ERISA's requirements, provided the procedures satisfy Section 1301 of the Public Health Service Act, as amended, [42 USC § 300e(198)], and the regulations thereunder [29 CFR §§ 2560.503-1(c), (j)]. In addition, under

certain circumstances, ERISA requires group health plans to provide continued coverage under COBRA to participants whose coverage would otherwise cease as a result of a qualifying event [ERISA Title I, Part 6, 29 USC § 1161, *et seq*]. Finally, ERISA provides a comprehensive enforcement scheme that is primarily civil in nature, although criminal penalties may be imposed for violations of ERISA's reporting and disclosure, requirements or for coercive interference with a plan participants' rights.

13. *See* HR 1602, 102d Cong, 1st Sess. (1991); S. 794, 102d Cong., 1st Sess. (1991); S. 3180, 102d Cong., 2d Sess. (1992); S. 3232, 102d Cong., 2d Sess. (1992).

14. Association of Private Pension and Welfare Plan's Action Center for Quality Health Care, *Managed Care and the Court: An Overview* 11 (Nov 1991).

15. For an example of a court finding, the claim was not preempted by ERISA, *see Kohn v Delaware Valley HMO, Inc*, 14 Employee Benefits Cas (BNA) 2336 (Dec 20, 1991), *reconsideration denied*, 14 Employe Benefits Cas (BNA) 2597 No 91-2745, 1992 WL 22241 (ED Pa Feb 5, 1992), where the court recently held that a personal injury claim does "not relate to the benefit plan," and plaintiffs who alleged personal injury arising under an ERISA plan were allowed to sue without exhausting administrative remedies. The District Court in *Kohn* refused on a motion for reconsideration to dismiss the "ostensible agency" count for the negligence of the health care providers but held that the claim for punitive damages was preempted by ERISA. The court explained that the "malpractice claim did not arise out of the ERISA plan's contract," that is, it does not "relate" to the benefit plan. See also *Independence HMO, Inc. v. Smith*, 733 F Supp 983 (ED Pa 1990)

16. In *Altieri v CIGNA Dental Health, Inc*, 753 Supp 61 (D Conn 1990), the court found the claim was preempted by ERISA but did remand the case to state court to allow the plaintiff to pursue a "negligence" claim under state law. The court held that the plaintiff's claims against the dental plan were preempted because the central component of the claim arouse from the plaintiff's treatment under the employer provided dental plan. In *Rollo v Maxicare of Louisiana, Inc*, 695 F Supp 245 (ED La 1988), an HMO subscriber sued the physician that treated him and the HMO for damages arising out of the medical care provided. The court held that the plaintiff's claims were preempted under ERISA and noted that all of plaintiff's claims centered on the circumstances of his medical treatment as provided by the employer's medical benefits plan. The court reasoned that the general connection between plaintiff's claims centered on the circumstances of his medical treatment as provided by the employer's medical benefits plan. The court reasoned that the general connection between plaintiff's claims and the employer's health benefit plan was sufficient to conclude that the claims "related to" an employee benefit plan.

17. 733 F Supp 83 (ED Pa 1990)

18. *Id*.

19. 382 Pa Super 213, 555 A 2d 147 (1988).

20. *See also Pickett v CIGNA Health Plan of Texas, Inc*, 742 F Supp 946 (SD Tex 1990), where court ruled that ERISA did not preempt plaintiff's claim that three doctors covered through an HMO provided by an employer failed to diagnose and treat his cancer in a timely fashion. The court stated that the claim was not preempted because: 1.) The ERISA plan was not a party to the action, and plaintiff did not challenge the plan's administration; 2.) Plaintiff was challenging CIGNA's system of rotating doctors as an unreasonable medical procedure, and was not challenging its administrative procedures. Thus, CIGNA was being sued in its capacity as an HMO and not in is capacity as a plan administrator; and 3.) The court concluded that an ERISA plan itself is the only entity which may serve as a defendant in an ERISA case. This is an unusually narrow characterization of an ERISA suit as one which challenges the denial of benefits.

21. In *Boyd v Albert Einstein Medical Center*, 547 A 2d 1229 (Pa Super Ct 1988), a Pennsylvania HMO was sued for an allegedly negligent breast biopsy performed by a contracting physician which led to the death of the patient. Plaintiff's amended complaint alleged that because the HMO advertised that its physicians and medical care providers were competent and had been evaluate for up to six months before being selected, the HMO should be liable under an ostensible agency theory. Citing the statement contained in the HMO's marketing materials to the effect that the HMO "provided medical care," the court inferred that the plaintiff may have looked to the HMO rather than just its physicians for care.

22. *Black's Law Dictionary* 992 (5th ed, 1979) defines the term "ostensible agency" as an employed or presumptive agency, which exists where one, either intentionally or from want of ordinary care, induces another to believe that a third person is his agent, though he never in fact employed him. Elden & Hinden outline the factors looked at by a number of state courts when considering whether an ostensible agency relationship exists as follows: 1.) whether the provider is performing an inherent function of the defendant; 2.) the restriction on the patient's choice of provider; and 3.) the "holding out" of the provider as an agent. "Liability Issues of Managed Care Entities," *Medical and Hospital Negligence* § 22:11 (1990).

23. Dkt No 8-361788 NH (Mich Cir Ct, Sept 17, 1991).

24. *See McClellan v Health Maintenance Organization of Pennsylvania,* 604 A.2d 1053 (Pa Super Ct 1992); *Greely v Lipchin,* HCA No 90-0395 (Mar 2, 1992); *Jackson v Power,* 743 P2d 1376 (Alaska 1987). The Court in *Jackson,* found the regulatory scheme that controlled the defendant hospital justified the conclusion that the hospital's duty of care was non-delegable and therefore, the hospital was liable for the physician's malpractice. *See also Schleier v Kaiser Found Health Plan of Mid-Atl States, Inc,* 876 F2d 174 (DC Cir 1989), in which court held that an HMO can be liable for acts of non-employee consulting physician in view of HMO's ability to control the selection, discharge and performance of its doctors.

25. *See Darling v Charleston Community Mem Hosp* 50 Ill App 2d 253, 200 NE2d 149 (1964), *aff'd,* 33 Ill App 2d 326, 211 NE 2d 253 (1965), *cert denied,* 383 USZ 946 (1966); *Harrell v Total Health Care, Inc,* No WD 39809, 1989 WL 153066 (Mo Ct App Apr 25, 1989), *transferred to* 781 SW 2d 58 (Mo 1989).

26. Civ Act No 86-25767-NK2 (Mich Cir Ct Apr 1989).

27. *Wickline v State of California,* 192 Cal App 3d 1630 (1986), *review dismissed,* 239 Cal Rptr 805, 741 P2d 613 (1987).

28. *Wilson v Blue Cross of Southern California,* 222 Cal App 3d 660, 271 Cal Rptr 876 (1990), review denied, No S017315, 1990 Cal LEXIS 4574 (Cal Oct 11, 1990).

29. *Corcoran v United HealthCare, Inc,* 965 F2d 1321 (5th Cir 1992), *petition for cert denied,* 61 USLW 3435 (US Dec 14, 1992).

30. In *Corcoran,* the plaintiff, Mrs. Florence Cocoran, received health coverage under a self-insured plan provided by plaintiff's employer, South Central Bell Telephone Company which was administered by Blue Cross and Blue Shield with a utilization review feature performed by United Healthcare, Incorporated. Mrs. Corcoran was advised by her obstetrician to complete the final months of her difficult pregnancy with a regime of hospital bed rest in order to better monitor her condition. Her request for temporary disability benefits having been denied, Mrs. Corcoran contacted the utilization review firm to have authorized the recommended period of hospitalization. United refused to certify her request and instead authorized 10 hours a day of home nursing care. While the nurse was off duty, Mrs. Corcoran entered premature labor, and the fetus went into distress and died. Among the many state tort law counts brought was a wrongful death count against both Blue Cross and United Healthcare. The court held that the utilization review firm "gives medical advice—but does so in the context of making a determination about the availability of benefits under the plan," and therefore state law tort claims are preempted by ERISA.

31. *See Christopher v Mobil Oil Corp,* 950 F2d 1209, 1218 5th Cir 1992 (court held that common law fraud and negligent misrepresentation claims that allege reliance on agreements or representations about the coverage of a plan are preempted), *cert denied,* 61 USLW 3256 (US Oct 16, 1992)(No 91-1881).

32. *See Teti v US HealthCare, Inc,* Civ Act Nos 88-9808,88-9822, 1989 US Dist LEXIS 15644 (ED Pa Dec 29, 1989), aff'd, 904 F2d 6594 (3d Cir 1990), where members of U.S. Healthcare HMO filed a class action suit against the provider, alleging violations of RICO and state tort law. Based on the theory that the incentives between the HMO and certain physicians caused plaintiffs harm by not receiving the quality and amount of care as was represented in marketing materials, plaintiffs alleged that these "incentives and withholding" arrangements should have been disclosed to members of the HMO. However, because the court dismissed the RICO claim, the state law claims were not considered due to lack of federal jurisdiction and the case was dismissed.

33. *See Boyd v Albert Einstein Medical Ctr*, 547 A2d 1229 (Pa Super Ct 1988) (plaintiff's allegations that HMO's advertisements and marketing materials stated that its physicians were competent and highly evaluated, should render HMO liable under a theory of ostensible agency).

34. Under § 502 of ERISA, participants and beneficiaries may bring action to recover benefits due them under the plan, to enforce or clarify rights under the plan, or to recover civil penalties imposed for failure to provide certain information, including COBRA notice. Generally, the plan's internal remedies must be exhausted prior to bringing suit in court.

35. *See Makar v Health Care Corp of the Mid Atlantic (Carefirst)*, 872 F2d 80 (4th Cir 1989) (state claims, including claims for punitive damages, against HMO preempted by ERISA; however, action remanded with directions to dismiss without prejudice to plaintiff's pursuit of ERISA cause of action provided that plaintiff first exhausted her internal plan remedies, i.e., the HMO's grievance procedures); *Scullion v Travelers Health Network*, 720 F Supp 530 (WD Pa 1989) (ERISA governs plan participant's action against HMO seeking reimbursement of costs of in-patient substance abuse treatment that had been incurred at a facility not on HMO's approved list; HMO's denial of coverage withheld).

36. 708 F Supp 826 (ED Mich 1989). The court held that ERISA preempted the state law claims stating that to permit such claims "would gut the Plan and its essential purpose, preauthorization and concurrent review to enhance the efficiency and reduce unnecessary and excessive utilization."

37. 949 F2d 1323 (3d Cir 1991); *Nazay v Miller*, 768 F Supp 124 (MD Pa), *rev'd*, 949 F2d 1323 (3d Cir 1991).

38. *See Adams v Blue Cross & Blue Shield of Md Inc*, 757 F Supp 661 (D Md 1991), (court held the Blue Cross contract excluding as experimental those procedures "not generally acknowledged as accepted medical practice by the suitable practicing specialty in Maryland, as decided by us" did not grand Blue Cross ultimate discretion to determine whether a procedure was experimental). But see *Thomas v Gulf Health Plan, Inc*, 688 F Supp 590 (SD Ala 1988) (denial of claim on ground that procedure was experimental upheld, notwithstanding earlier precertification of procedure).

39. ERISA § 404 (a)(1) imposes five separate and distinct obligations on plan fiduciaries. A plan fiduciary must discharge his duties with respect to the plan in the following manner 1.) "solely in the interest" of the plan's participants and beneficiaries, i.e. the duty of "undivided loyalty"; 2.) for the "exclusive purpose" of a.) providing plan benefits; or b.) defraying reasonable expenses of plan administration; 3.) with the "care, skill, prudence and diligence" "that a prudent man acting in a like capacity and familiar with such matter would use in the conduct of an enterprise of a like character and with like aims" (courts often interpret this as the "prudent expert" rule); 4.) by diversifying the plan's investments to minimize the risk of large losses; and 5.) in accordance with the documents and instruments governing the plan insofar as those documents and instruments are consistent with ERISA.

40. Relying on general trust law principles, the Supreme Court held in *Firestone Tire & Rubber Co v Bruch*, 489 US 101 (1989), that *de novo* review is the appropriate standard for reviewing denial of benefits claims rather than the more general "arbitrary and capricious" standard unless the parties have agreed otherwise. *See also Newell v Prudential Ins Co*, 904d F2d 644 (11th Cir 1990) (court used arbitrary and capricious standard of review rather than *de novo* standard because plan gave Prudential sufficient discretion under the Firestone decision; *Boland v King County Medical Blue Shield, Inc of Alabama*, 798 F Supp 638(WD Wash 1992) (court stated standard of review when an ERISA plan administrator has both discretionary authority and is operating under a conflict of interest is more stringent than purely abuse of discretion, but less than *de novo* review); *see also Saah v Contel Corp*, 780 F Supp 311 (D Md 1991) (third-party administrator had a conflict of interest in processing hospitalization claims because of receiving financial incentives to keep the number of inpatient hospital days down, i.e. it received 25 cents more per claim processed if hospital days were kept below a set level. However, the court upheld the administrator's decision as reasonable.); *Salley v EI DuPont de Nemours & Co*, 966 F2d 1011 (5th Cir 1992) (conflict of interest is one factor in determining whether there has been abuse of discretion; here the court ruled against the plan on a question of medical necessity for mental illness hospitalization).

41. *See Brown v Blue Cross & Blue Shield, Inc*, 898 F2d 1556 (11th Cir 1990), *cert denied*, 111 S Ct 712 (1991), in which the Eleventh Circuit held that where an insurer also acts as a plan fiduciary the inherent conflict of interest in such dual roles makes the arbitrary and capricious standard of review inappropriate. The court in *Brown*, found that a conflict of interest arouse because Blue Cross served as a fiduciary in

deciding whether to pay benefits from its own assets. The court remanded the case to the district court, reasoning that blue Cross's profit-making role gave rise to a conflict in raising the issue of whether the benefit denial was in the best interest of the plan's participants and beneficiaries.

42.   Charles J Steele & Scott J Lardner, *ERISA Overview: Selected Topics* 20 (1992).

43.   *See Eley v Boeing Co,* 945 F2d 276 (9th Cir 1991).

44.   No 53906, 1989 Mo App LEXIS 852 (Mo Ct App June 13, 1989)

45.   *See Metropolitan Life Ins Co v Massachusetts*, 471 US 724 (1985). The Court upheld a Massachusetts law requiring insurance companies to provide specified minimum mental health benefits in any health insurance plan offered in the State. States may mandate that insured health benefit plans provide certain benefits.

46.   Blue Cross & Blue Shield Association, *Update on State Mandated Benefits,* (1992).

47.   *See State Barriers to Managed Care: Results of a National Survey of Blue Cross and Blue Shield, supra,* note 2.

48.   —F. Supp.— (ED Va July 22, 1992).

49.   *McGann v H&H Music Co,* 946 F 2d 401 (5th Cir 1991), *cert denied, Greenberg v H&H Music Co,* 61 USLW 3355 (US Nov 11, 1992) (No 91-1283) (section 510 of ERISA applies only to employer actions directed at specific participants, and does not cover changes in benefits that are made on a cost-benefit basis and that will be applied equally to all participants).

50.   HR 6137, 102d Cong, 2d Sess (1992).

42. AIDS, the ADA, and Health Benefit Plans: New Uncertainties for Employers and New Questions About Self-Insurance

George M. Kraw

With the passage of the Americans with Disabilities Act, employers that self-insure their health benefit plans may face greater liability exposure and higher compliance costs, particularly if their plans exclude coverage of specific illnesses such as AIDS. Although there is still a great deal of uncertainty about how the ADA will affect self-insurance, recent court decisions and EEOC regulatory guidelines have clarified many of the relevant issues.

Most large American companies now self-insure their health benefit plans, under the assumption that self-insurance provides the most effective means of controlling costs. The recent passage of the Americans with Disabilities Act (ADA),[1] greatly complicates the operation of such plans, and forces closer monitoring of plan operations to insure compliance with the statute.

In enacting the ADA, Congress made a specific finding that the disabled historically have been relegated to lesser benefits, jobs, and opportunities than the nondisabled. The primary purpose of the statute is the elimination of such discrimination, but this purpose can conflict with business efforts to restrain or reduce health care costs. The statute requires that workers with disabilities generally be given equal access to the same health benefits provided other employees. Employers cannot refuse to hire individuals with disabilities because of their potential effect on benefit costs.

NEW RULES UNDER THE ADA

Guidelines issued by the Equal Employment Opportunity Commission (EEOC) make the employer responsible for monitoring and proving that practices that discriminate on the basis of disability are justifiable under the ADA. These guidelines, known as the "Interim Enforcement Guidance," together with earlier EEOC regulations interpreting the ADA, will make it more difficult to exclude or limit coverage of specific illnesses such as AIDS or HIV infection from benefit plans. Plans that make such exclusions will have the burden of proving that they are not in violation of the ADA.

During the past decade, self-insured plans, since they were exempted from state law regulation by the Employee Retirement Income Security Act (ERISA),[2] have given employers greater flexibility in benefit design and plan operation. ERISA also protects self-insured employers from punitive or consequential damage awards. These advantages led some self-insured employers to adopt exclusionary policies that reduce benefits for certain illnesses, most notably AIDS. Specific exclusions were previously upheld by the Fifth Circuit in *McGann v. H & H Music, Inc.*,[3] and the Eleventh Circuit in *Owens v. Storehouse, Inc.*[4] However, neither case involved claims under the ADA.

The new ADA enforcement guidelines target benefit plans that exclude specific illnesses. EEOC personnel will follow these guidelines in investigating charges that a disability-based term or exclusion in a benefit plan violates the ADA. In fact, the day after the guidelines were issued, the EEOC filed suit against a multiemployer fund that had eliminated coverage for AIDS.

WHAT THE ADA FORBIDS

Under the ADA, the term "disability" means a physical or mental impairment that substantially limits one or more of the major life activities of an individual. It also includes anyone with a record of such impairment, or who is regarded as having such an impairment.

Employers cannot discriminate against a qualified individual with a disability with regard to hiring, compensation, or other terms of employment. Qualified individuals are those who, with or without reasonable accommodation, can perform the essential functions of the employee position in question. Discrimination includes the denial of equal benefits and the failure to make reasonable accommodations to known physical limitations, although reasonable accommodation is not required if the employer can prove that such provision would impose an undue hardship.

Section 501(c) of the ADA allows employers, insurers, and plan administrators to create "bona fide" health benefit plans that are based on underwriting or classifying risks consistent with state law. The EEOC regulations add that they are not intended to disrupt current insurance underwriting practices, and also state that they do not interfere with the current regulatory structure for self-insured plans. Employers can continue to sponsor and operate benefit plans that are not subject to state laws that regulate insurance.

However, the ADA forbids self-insured plans from being used as a subterfuge to avoid the purpose of the law. A self-insured benefit plan can still limit the amount, extent, or kind of coverage available to covered individuals, but cannot charge a different rate for the same coverage solely because of a physical or mental impairment unless the limitation is based on recognized actuarial principles or is related to actual or reasonably anticipated experience.

ACROSS-THE-BOARD REDUCTIONS ALLOWED

A benefit plan may reduce the amount of coverage for all employees, even if the reduction has an impact on employees with disabilities who are in need of greater medical coverage. The EEOC enforcement guidelines contain the example of a company that limits benefits for any health condition to a maximum of $25,000 per year. In this illustration, an employee files a charge of discrimination alleging that the $25,000 cap violates the ADA because it is insufficient to cover the cost of treatment for her cancer. The guidelines conclude that since the $25,000 cap does not single out a specific disability or group of disabilities, it is permissible so long as it applies equally to all employees.

However, in order to justify the exclusion of specific chronic illnesses, the employer must prove that the exclusion is not a subterfuge designed to evade the purpose of the ADA. Illnesses such as AIDS, HIV infection, cancers, heart disease, and diabetes all fit the ADA's statutory definition of disability.

SUBTERFUGE DEFINED

A plan provision may be a subterfuge in violation of the ADA even if the employer does not so intend. In enacting the ADA Congress specifically rejected the definition of subterfuge adopted by the Supreme Court in *Public Employee Retirement System v. Betts*[5] in interpreting the Age Discrimination in Employment Act. In *Betts,* the court held that a pension plan was not a subterfuge to evade the purposes of that statute unless it was intended to discriminate based upon age. (Congress overruled *Betts* in 1990 when it passed the Older Workers Benefit Protection Act.) The EEOC enforcement guidelines define subterfuge, without reference to intent, as a disability-based disparate treatment that is not justified by the risks or costs associated with the disability.

EMPLOYER BURDEN OF PROOF

Under the guidelines, once the EEOC finds that a challenged exclusion or term is disability-based, the burden of proof shifts to the employer. The guidelines provide a nonexclusive list of ways an employer can prove that a disability-based coverage exclusion or term is not a subterfuge. For example, the employer may prove that legitimate actuarial data or claims experience justifies disparate treatment. Similarly, the employer can justify disparate treatment by proving it is necessary to keep the plan financially sound. Disparate treatment is also permitted to prevent drastic increases in benefit payments or drastic reductions in plan coverage.

In order to justify a disability-based exclusion, the employer must show that no other change in the health plan would accomplish the purpose. If the employer's justification is based on actuarial data, the employer cannot rely on data that is seriously outdated or inaccurate. The guidelines specifically forbid reliance on data that is based on "myths, fears, or stereotypes" about the disability.

NEW CHALLENGES TO *McGANN* AND *OWENS* EXCLUSIONS

If the plaintiffs in *McGann* and *Owens* had brought challenges under the ADA, the results might have been different. In order to have avoided violation of the ADA, the employers in each case would have had to prove that the exclusions of coverage for AIDS were not a subterfuge designed to evade the purpose of the statute.

In *McGann,* an employee with AIDS so informed his employer shortly after learning of his illness. At that time, the employer maintained an employee health benefit plan through an insurer that provided lifetime medical benefits of up to $1 million for all employees. Shortly afterward, the employer became self-insured under a new plan, with the former insurer now acting as the plan's administrator. The new plan limited lifetime benefits for AIDS-related illnesses to $5,000, while maintaining the $1 million benefit for most other illnesses.

In ruling against the employee, the Fifth Circuit Court of Appeals in New Orleans found that the employer had an absolute right to alter the terms of medical coverage available to plan beneficiaries. Late last year, the United States Supreme Court let the Fifth Circuit decision stand.

Owens also involved a reduction of AIDS coverage after the employer was notified of the employee's illness. The employer provided a group hospital and medical benefits policy with a lifetime maximum of $1 million per employee. The employer, a retail specialty furniture store, received notification from its insurer of the latter's intent to cancel because of the high incidence of AIDS in the retail industry generally and among the employer's plan members in particular. At the time, 5 out of 160 full-time employees had been diagnosed with

AIDS. After negotiations, the insurer agreed to renew the policy, but only for six months. The new policy required the employer to remain self-insured for the first $75,000 in AIDS-related claims, as opposed to $25,000 for all other participants.

The employer, facing the possibility that at the end of the six-month policy it would be self-insuring claims up to $1 million, sought another carrier. The employer's insurance broker advised that the employer could obtain insurance only by placing a maximum lifetime limit on coverage of AIDS and AIDS-related illnesses. The employer then modified its plan to include a $25,000 cap on AIDS-related medical claims. An affected employee filed a claim under ERISA. The Eleventh Circuit upheld a lower court decision in favor of the employer, noting that it was "Congress' express intent that employers be free to fashion medical plans as cost, technology, and the marketplace dictate."

The *McGann* case presented a situation where the company acted on the basis of a perceived threat: the additional costs of an AIDS patient to its plan. It does not appear that McGann's employer could have provided legitimate data to support its position based on its own claims' experience, since this was the plan's first AIDS case. In *Owens,* the company's inability to obtain new insurance without restrictions might have been deemed sufficient cause for its actions. However, this would be a question of fact for the trial court.

Examples in the enforcement guidelines emphasize that an employer using disability-specific exclusions must justify them. The first is similar to the *McGann* case; a plan with a cap of $5,000 per year for AIDS benefits where all other physical conditions are covered up to $100,000. In the example, the self-insured employer has the burden of proof the AIDS cap is not a subterfuge. In the second example, an employer has an exclusion for preexisting blood disorders for a period of 18 months, but does not exclude other conditions. The employer here must prove that the disability-specific clause is not a subterfuge.

EEOC ENFORCEMENT ACTIONS

Even before the enforcement guidelines were issued, the New York District Director of the EEOC ruled that the Mason Tenders District Counsel Trust Fund violated the ADA by denying all coverage for HIV infections and AIDS-related conditions. After the ruling, the fund filed suit in a Manhattan federal court to overturn it, claiming that its financial circumstances necessitated the exclusions and that they were without any discriminatory intent. The fund also claimed the EEOC made its determination without any testimony from plan representatives or review of plan records, and that the ADA did not prohibit such discussions. Shortly after the EEOC issued its enforcement guidelines, it filed suit against the fund to enforce the New York director's ruling. The case indicates that the EEOC will aggressively enforce the requirement that employers justify discriminatory exclusions.

ALLOWED EXCLUSIONS

The guidelines allow certain exclusions that apply equally to a variety of conditions and to all employees. The EEOC does not consider such broad exclusions to be distinctions based on disability. For example, plans are permitted to set lower levels of benefits for mental conditions or eye care, as well as to create blanket exclusions of preexisting conditions. Other permissible exclusions include experimental drugs and treatments, and elective surgery. Benefit limitations that cut coverage across the board are also permitted. However, general coverage exclusions will violate the ADA if they are selectively applied. For example, employers cannot apply a neutral plan limitation on eye care to a beneficiary seeking treatment for a vision disability, but not to other employees.

Disability-specific exclusions are also permitted for treatments that have no medical value, although such exclusions may violate the ADA if the plan covers other treatments of no medical value. Such exclusions also cannot be applied differently depending upon the disability or the disease.

WHAT'S AN EMPLOYER TO DO?

The ADA will make many plan exclusions and limitations more difficult to justify. Denials based on lack of medical necessity are subject to challenge if the criteria are not equally applied. The approval of experimental or investigational treatments for cancer may make it impermissible for a plan to deny coverage for similar treatments for AIDS.

Employers who maintain disability-based exclusions in self-insured plans face uncertain standards for ADA compliance, and many employers will find this uncertainty an unacceptable risk in deciding whether to implement such exclusions. Some employers may conclude that the simplest and safest method of controlling their health insurance costs without risking violation of the ADA is to reduce plan limits. This is an effective method of cost containment that is specifically permitted by the EEOC. In all events, the ADA is likely both to create further animosity toward maintaining health care benefits, and to hasten calls for national reform.

1. 43 USC 12101, et seq.

2. 29 USC 1101, et seq.

3. McGann v H & H Music, Inc, 946 F 2d 401.

4. Owens v Storehouse, Inc, 984 F 2d 394.

5. Public Employee Retirement Sys v Betts, 492 US 158.

43. Lifestyle Discrimination: Health Care Cost Control and the Right to Privacy

Lewis L. Maltby

In their attempts to control health care costs through lifestyle modification, more and more employers are undermining the privacy rights of their employees, with negative consequences ranging from poor workplace morale to legal challenges. Policies that discriminate against the lifestyle choices of employees—for example, smoking—may seem at first like fair and straightforward ways of distributing the risks and costs of health benefits, but a longer look reveals that the issue is much more complex.

Privacy means different things to different people, but one widely accepted meaning is the right to be left alone and to be free from unauthorized and coerced intrusion into the parts of one's life not intended for public display. The framers of our Constitution and Bill of Rights certainly embraced this meaning, especially with regard to the sanctity of family life. In the employment setting, much of one's life is exposed to coworkers and supervisors. But activities away from the workplace that are not related to actual duties performed, or that do not affect one's ability to perform on the job, fall into the sphere of privacy and should not provide the basis for adverse employment action.

There is an emerging trend in the American workplace threatening to impinge on the right to privacy: Employers are beginning to adopt policies that discriminate against employees on the basis of their lifestyle choices. Some employers currently refuse to hire people whose private lives and hobbies are considered "unhealthy"; a few even fire current employees who do not change their lifestyles to meet new company demands. Other employers force workers who engage in legal activities that the company arbitrarily deems unhealthy to pay more for their health insurance, or provide a discount for employees who stop or do not engage in those same legal activities while away from work.

Several groups have been targeted by employers and subjected to discriminatory practices, both on the job and during pre-employment screening. Those most frequently targeted are smokers and people who are overweight. In 1989, an estimated 6 percent of employers would not hire someone who smokes, even though the smoking was done at home, and another 4 percent were considering implementing such a policy at that time. It is more difficult to quantify the number of companies that discriminate against overweight people because this is seldom an official corporate policy. Anecdotal evidence, nevertheless, suggests that such discrimination is at least as common. Other targeted groups are people with hypertension or high serum cholesterol levels, social drinkers, and sports enthusiasts (especially motorcyclists). In the future, people who are genetically prone to contracting certain debilitating diseases could face discrimination.

Instances of lifestyle discrimination have risen in recent years as employers turn to new methods to harness the rapidly increasing costs of health care benefits. According to some estimates, health care costs for many employers are rising at 10 to 30 percent per year. Employers who attribute rising health care and insurance costs to the lifestyle choices made by employees are looking for a quick answer to a very complicated problem. Few experts in the field of health care economics would claim that lifestyle choices are the prime contributors to this rising cost. Other factors, such as the cost of technology, the aging of the population, and unnecessary use and abuse of the health care system, have all been cited as major contributory factors in rising health care costs. In fact, the link between employee lifestyles and health costs is tenuous at best, and there is little basis to support the assumption that employers will save money by policing the private lives of their employees. Rafael E. Castillo, risk manager at the Coors Brewing Company in Golden, Colorado, notes that it is difficult to measure the success of so-called wellness incentives because "no one can say with authority how much poor health and unhealthy lifestyles actually cost the employer."

Furthermore, there is widespread disagreement among employers themselves on which behaviors affect costs and which they have a right to penalize. One company, for example, discriminates against smokers but not against those with high cholesterol levels, since it feels there are too many factors, including genetics, that affect cholesterol levels. Refusing to hire (or firing) people for reasons unrelated to job performance often prevents a company from hiring (or retaining) the best qualified individuals. For example, the Ford Meter Box Company of Wabash, Indiana had offered an employee named Janice Bone a promotion, but when the required urine test revealed nicotine in her system, the company dismissed her, causing it to lose an employee it originally desired to promote.

More importantly, virtually every decision a person makes has some impact on health, from having a cup of coffee in the morning to the amount of sleep that person gets every night. Eventually an employer would have to police every aspect of an employee's life that affects his or her health, from what he or she eats to the highly private decision to have children.

Many people cannot imagine that employers would go so far. But where do we draw the line as to what off-duty, legal behavior an employer can regulate? Should they have the right to tell employees they cannot sunbathe on a Saturday afternoon because of the increased risk of skin cancer? The real issue here is the right of individuals to lead the life they choose. It is inappropriate for employers to regulate the lives of their employees 24 hours a day, seven days a week.

The profound threat to privacy inherent in such arbitrary employer decisions is obvious. If discrimination against employee lifestyles becomes acceptable, capable people will be effectively banned from jobs regardless of their ability, preventing them from providing for themselves or their dependents. Some critics see lifestyle discrimination as analogous to charging an unsafe driver more for his or her automobile insurance, but this only raises the obvious question: To what extent are employees' off-duty activities equivalent to other means of distinguishing among people as insurance risks? An unsafe driver may be required to pay more for insurance based on actuarial data, but that same unsafe driver can still drive a car. An employee whose employer deems him or her unhealthy or at risk may very well be out of a job.

It is unclear if employers can achieve significant savings through the regulation of off-duty legal behavior, but even if they could demonstrate substantial savings, sacrificing the private lives of working Americans is too high a price to pay. Just ask Janice Bone —although she never smoked while at work, Ford's policy barred her from smoking at all. "I was shocked. It's devastating when this happens to you," she said. In spite of the ban, the company allowed employees hired prior to 1987, when the policy was first adopted, not only to continue smoking at home, but also to smoke in designated areas in the workplace. Arbitrary rules, like Ford's, have an inequitable impact on employees, affecting everyone's morale, not just those directly injured by the rule.

According to an Administrative Management Society survey in 1988, 6 percent of employers (over 6,000 companies) were discriminating against both current employees and applicants based on their legal activities during nonworking hours. That figure has almost certainly risen over the past few years. The implications of employers regulating the non-working hours of their employees are disturbing: at risk is our essential right to privacy, and to live our off-the-job lives the way we see fit. It is imperative that we preserve the distinction between company time and our private lives.

The methods used to enforce these policies raise serious civil liberties concerns. Most companies currently accept an employee's word that he or she is not violating the rules for off-duty behavior. As this type of discrimination becomes more common, however, it may become increasingly difficult for targeted individuals to simply avoid companies that maintain such policies. People will take jobs, not reveal their lifestyle, and hope that the employer does not find out. When this occurs, employers will be forced to employ other methods of verification, such as hiring company detectives to follow people away from work or requiring frequent universal medical testing such as urinalysis. Cardinal Industries, for instance, boldly asserts that it only hires nonsmokers, requires every applicant to take a urine test, and will fire those who claim they have quit but have not.

While the number of cases of employers who use smoking during nonwork hours as a criterion for hiring, firing, and promotion decisions is on the rise, a growing number of employers are also asking smoking employees to bear a larger proportion of their health care costs than nonsmoking employees. Lutheran Health Systems, a hospital and nursing home chain, for example, charges smokers 10 percent more than nonsmokers for insurance because the company says smokers' health claims are higher. According to Lutheran's benefits manager, the higher premium also applies to employees whose dependents smoke, even if the employee is a nonsmoker.

There are two fundamental problems with such a policy. First, even where a given behavior clearly causes a measurable increase in health care costs, it is not necessarily true that those costs will be borne by the employer. Employers are essentially penalizing certain individuals for costs that they have not yet incurred, and may never incur. Second, there is no actuarial data to suggest that people who engage in a certain behavior cost specific employers, such as Lutheran Health Systems, an extra 10 percent (or any other amount) on health care. Civil libertarians find this practice arbitrary and unfair. If, on the other hand, an employer were able to justify a surcharge imposed on an employee whose lifestyle was deemed unhealthy by demonstrating that the behavior increased the employer's health care costs by a specific, measurable amount, the employer should also be required to show that the surcharge does not have a disparate impact on any group protected from job discrimination under federal or state law.

Many employers have also targeted overweight employees for similar discriminatory treatment. In addition to charging smokers more for their health insurance, U-Haul, for example, pays employees who do not maintain a "proper weight" less than employees who keep their weight within company limits. A significant number of employees have also been fired or otherwise denied jobs solely due to their obesity. Companies that discriminate against overweight applicants and employees use the same justification for their obesity policies that they use for their off-duty smoking policies: unequal treatment is justified because of the added costs these individuals could place on their health plans.

Over the past decade, employees have drawn attention to lifestyle discrimination by bringing, and in some cases winning, lawsuits against employers under state and federal civil rights legislation. In 1985, for example, the New York Court of Appeals ruled against the Xerox Corporation, which had denied a woman employment solely on the basis of her obesity. In its decision, the court ruled that employers could not deny employment on account of a perceived undesirable effect a person's employment would have on its insurance benefits programs. The recently enacted Americans with Disabilities Act may also protect certain individuals from weight and other forms of lifestyle discrimination.

Some employers have gone even further in their attempts to control the off-duty activities of their personnel. The American Civil Liberties Union has received reports about companies who have refused to hire people who are occasional social drinkers, who ride motorcycles, or who play contact sports; other companies penalize people who have a high serum cholesterol level. Coors, for instance, offers employees who can prove they are "not at risk" a 10 to 15 percent discount on their health insurance. Coors uses cholesterol level as one measure of health risk, and subjects not only employees, but their spouses as well, to cholesterol testing in order to qualify for the insurance discount. This form of discrimination is particularly insidious because it is the company that chooses what criteria put employees at risk (often based on the findings of studies that have not been universally accepted), which in turn subjects employees to privacy violations at the whim of their employer.

It is clear that the majority of Americans believe that what they do in the privacy of their own home is none of their employers' business, unless their behavior interferes with job performance. According to a 1992 National Consumers League poll, 84 percent of Americans believe that an employer has no right to refuse to hire a fat person, and 93 percent think that an employer has no right to base an employment decision on whether an employee smokes after work.

A concerted effort on the part of a variety of civil rights and labor organizations has been launched to protect the privacy of every working American. Twenty-eight states and the District of Columbia have already passed privacy protection legislation. The majority of these protect only smokers, but several are broader, covering the off-duty use of lawful products; Colorado, New York, and North Dakota ban discrimination based on legal off-duty activities. This broader type of privacy legislation is an important step on the road toward ensuring the individual right of American workers to lead their lives as they choose.

Part 10

WORKERS' COMPENSATION

44. The Savings Potential
of 24-Hour Coverage
Taylor Dennen

Combining elements of workers' compensation with group health benefit programs, 24-hour coverage plans are designed to save money by cutting administration costs and eliminating double-filing fraud in workers compensation cases. While some stories suggest that using 24-plans may result in large cost savings, their use is still mostly in the experimental stage. Even if instituting such plans fails to prove cost-effective, the principles behind 24-hour coverage may be instructional—for example, the adaptation of managed care techniques to workers' compensation may be beneficial to some employers.

In today's business environment, many organizations are grappling with both the exorbitant costs and administrative difficulties associated with maintaining health care plans and workers' compensation. However, a novel approach to this problem has recently been developed and is being widely discussed — the concept of 24-hour coverage. Generally, 24-hour coverage plans are aimed at integrating workers' compensation insurance with employer health benefits programs; the idea is to create one insurance program that covers both on-the-job and non-work-related illnesses and injuries. Many claim that such plans will provide large savings to companies that implement them. According to these claims, savings will primarily accrue from two sources: a reduction of payments on duplicate billings from health care providers to both programs, whether those duplicate bills arise from fraud or aggressive billing practices, and a decrease in the excessive utilization of health care services by beneficiaries through coordinating case management across the two programs.

Reprinted from *Risk Management*, "The Savings Potential of 24-Hour Coverage," by Taylor Dennen, September 1992.

Recently, stories have been circulating about how 24-hour plans could result in big savings for companies. But despite this anecdotal evidence, there is little concrete information about the actual overlap between workers' compensation and employee benefits programs. A study conducted by William M. Mercer Inc. of two large employers — a public sector organization with 140,000 employees and a manufacturing firm with over 200,000 employees—examined the relationship between workers' compensation medical expenses and claims submitted to health benefits programs. The study focused on three issues: the amount of overlap existing between employees obtaining paid medical services from both the workers' compensation and the health benefit programs, the degree to which overlap exists between health care providers receiving payments from both programs, and whether duplicate payments are being made from both programs for the same services.

For the public sector employer studied, medical payments from workers'compensation for a one-year period totaled $11.2 million. These payments were made on behalf of 5,914 employees who had active claims for work injuries and illnesses. On the health benefits side, payments totaled $195.4 million for the 109,643 active employees who filed claims; an additional $165 million was paid out for medical services to dependents of employees. Over 70 percent of the health care providers on the workers' compensation system appeared as providers to the health benefits program. The overlapping providers generated a substantial portion of expenses for each program — $9.1 million (82 percent) of workers' compensation payments and $121.6 million (62 percent) of health benefits payments.

For the manufacturing firm, workers' compensation-paid medical bills for a one-year period amounted to $16.5 million, as compared to health benefits expenses for employees (excluding dependents) of nearly $400 million. Just under 4 percent of employees had a workers' compensation medical bill during the year; a little over 60 percent of workers' compensation claimants did not make any health benefits claims at all. However, the 40 percent of claimants who did have medical bills on both systems had 60 percent more expenses for benefits. These overlapping claimants constituted 33 percent of workers' compensation payments, but only 2 percent of health benefits-paid claims.

The amount of employee overlap between the two programs is insufficient to generate large savings from coordinated case management. The large overlap in medical care providers, however, points to a significant savings opportunity. Specifically, insofar as state regulations permit, employers with aggressive cost containment efforts in place on the benefits side may find that preferred provider and managed care techniques can also be used in the workers' compensation area.

CUTTING COSTS

One effective cost cutting method is to extend hospital pre-certification and concurrent review programs to cover workers' compensation. To make such programs effective, the employer should work to create the understanding that all hospital admissions are covered by the inpatient utilization program. At the same time, utilization reviewers should be able to recognize if a particular admission is due to a work-related injury or illness, and should then implement the proper disability management procedures for these cases.

Increasingly, employers are implementing outpatient utilization review programs for high-cost or highly discretionary services such as positron emission tomography, magnetic resonance imaging, arthroscopic surgeries, physical therapy services, and chiropractic care. Therefore, employers should use the same utilization review program for both benefits and workers' compensation; these programs should be structured to appear to the worker and the health care provider as a single entity, oriented towards ensuring both cost-effectiveness and quality of care. However, as in the case of inpatient reviews, the employer must ensure that reviewers fully address and deal with the special disability and return-to-work issues that play such a major part in many workers' compensation cases.

Furthermore, employers who enter into preferred provider or preferred network arrangement should take care to ensure that all contracts and procedures cover both programs, even if a differential is required for workers' compensation to reimburse the allegedly greater costs incurred by providers for workers' compensation cases.

Employers can take additional steps to achieve coordination of the two programs. For example, employers should ensure that preferred pharmacy and mail order drug programs are structured so that any prescriptions written for an employee under the workers' compensation program are compatible with prescriptions written under the health benefits plans. And, as a condition for entering into a preferred arrangement with a preferred provider or network, employers should certify that preferred physicians understand the unique features of the workers' compensation system, and are willing and able to provide the appropriate medical management to patients suffering from work injuries. This understanding should extend to disability management issues; knowledge of the relatively poor prognoses and treatment interventions for certain work injuries; and the recognition of the importance of light duty opportunities for injured workers and the return-to-work goal, which are the objective of any good workers' compensation program.

A similar plan of coordination must be established with any health maintenance organizations (HMOs) that the employer uses. HMOs have tended to view workers' compensation as a lucrative fee-for-service billing opportunity. Therefore, whether through written contracts or ongoing oversight review, employers should ensure that the same managed care principles are applied to workers, regardless of whether the injury occurred at home or in the workplace; also, the special needs of workers' compensation cases must be addressed in a cost-effective manner.

One area where coordinating health plans and workers' compensation may result in significant savings for the employer is in administration. For example using only one utilization management program instead of separate programs for benefits and workers' compensation can reduce the amount of time a staff must spend on administrative functions. However, employers must ensure that such consolidation will still meet the particular needs of each program.

Moreover, employers will want to avoid some of the major pitfalls experienced by countries that have already integrated health benefits and workers' compensation. In the 1980s, for example, New Zealand created an integrated insurance system to cover accidental injuries, regardless of whether the injury was work-related or not. In subsequent years, disability and lost time costs soared as the well-known problems endemic to the workers' compensation arena—such as subsidized time off work—expanded into the area of non-work-related injuries. Thus, in order to avoid this perilous situation, employers need to coordinate the two programs without obliterating the distinctions between the programs in regard to disability issues.

COORDINATING CLAIMS

The Mercer study discovered that, for both the public sector organization and the manufacturing company, the level of duplicate payments between the two systems is small in terms of percentage; this is apparently due to the vigilance of the claims administrators for the benefits programs. Therefore, although not providing a rationale for integration, comparing paid bills between the two systems on a computerized basis may yield a positive return if done on occasion. Additionally, employers should coordinate claims audit activities for both their benefits and workers' compensation programs; ideally, the auditor should be able to audit the payment integrity for both programs. The auditor should focus on the ability of each program to avoid duplicating each program to avoid duplicating payments made to the other system. Given the small number of duplicate payments that are likely if the two systems are well managed, a random sample audit is unlikely to turn up duplicate payments; an automated, computerized cross-check may prove beneficial, however.

In summary, there are costs to maintaining separate systems to cover both work- and non-work-related injuries and illnesses; there are also significant costs associated with achieving coordination—if not integration—of the two plans. Overall, the financial data do not indicate that the overlap between workers' compensation and health benefits is of such magnitude as to justify integration regardless of cost; however, the data do suggest that judicious exploitation of opportunities to coordinate the two programs, especially in regard to managing health care providers, may generate significant savings.

45. Managed Care and Workers Compensation: Legal Considerations

Arthur N. Lerner

Adapting managed care programs to workers compensation coverage can present a number of legal difficulties and risks, some of which are still evolving. There are, however, ways to overcome the obstacles and to minimize the risks.

Managed care programs are becoming popular for an increasingly large number of employers and will eventually play a significant role in workers compensation coverage. Therefore, employers, labor groups, insurers, providers, and prepaid health care plans interested in the future of managed care in workers compensation should be aware of the legal obstacles and pitfalls involved.

This article identifies the basic legal strictures that can make the adaptation of managed care programs to workers compensation difficult, as well as the types of legislative and practical initiatives that may be attempted to overcome these obstacles.

Also outlined are some of the evolving legal risks faced by managed care plans, employers, and health plans seeking to combine managed care principles with workers compensation coverage. The focus will be on utilization review and quality assurance, along with a discussion of malpractice and contractual liability, and potential antitrust issues.

Managed care organizations could get involved as provider networks for employees and insurers, or as administrators for self-insured employers and employer groups. The most critical legal issues are different for each company, based on the goals an employer expects its managed care program to achieve. If a program is focused on health care cost savings through provider contracts, medical delivery legal issues will be more important. If the focus is on saving money by reducing the time workers are away from the job, these same real concerns may not be so important.

STATE LAW OBSTACLES TO MANAGED CARE IN WORKERS COMPENSATION

The states have regulatory authority over both insured and self-insured workers compensation insurance programs. The federal Employe Retirement Income Security Act (ERISA) preempts state laws regulating self-insured employee benefit plans.[1] State workers compensation laws are excepted from this preemption.

State law is generally flexible in permitting utilization review or case management techniques to control costs of care. In some states, there may be more difficulty in structuring managed care provider network programs within statutory confines.

State Laws Mandating Freedom of Choice Provider

Many state workers compensation laws require that the injured employee be permitted to select the health care provider of his or her choice. This blocks a classic closed panel or HMO-type program in those states.[2]

At times, these law require freedom of choice among physicians, podiatrists, psychologists, chiropractors and hospitals. In other cases, the scope is less broad.

Employers may still be able to designate which hospital must treat an injured worker. This could be used to arrange admissions to a hospital that has agreed to both a specific price and utilization review terms, but this may *not* be practicable if the patient's selected physician lacks privileges at that hospital.

State Laws Requiring that Cost of Care Be Paid in Full and/or that Providers Accept Workers Compensation Reimbursement as Payment in Full

States require that injured workers receive full medical coverage at no expense. This can frustrate the adoption of preferred provider model plans in which the injured worker would have incentives (such as lower copayments or deductibles, and no balance billing) to receive treatment from a preferred provider.

States that Permit Restricted Panel of Providers for Emergency Services

States may permit the self-insured employer or insurer to designate particular providers to use in the event of emergency.[3]

However, such a law permits introduction of managed care techniques only in the *emergency* component of patient care. Some HMOs and PPOs lack successful experience managing the costs or provision of emergency care.

States that Permit Limited Provider Panel

Some states permit the imposition of a limited provider panel by the employer or insurer. Some merely direct the employer to furnish care; others specifically require the employee to use providers selected by the employer with limited exceptions.

Iowa law authorizes the employer to choose the care provider. If the employee is dissatisfied with the care received, he may seek authorization to switch providers.[4]

Virginia law requires the employer to provide the employee with a list of at least three physicians, one of whom must be chosen to provide his care.[5]

Florida law is unclear. It specifically notes that the employer may maintain a list of service providers but bars the employer from coercing the employee into selecting a physician, surgeon, or other provider.[6] The state has enacted a new law authorizing managed care pilot projects that may be based on an HMO model.[7]

Ambitious new legislation has been enacted in Oregon. Managed care organizations may not contract with employers or workers compensation insurer to provide or arrange for health care to workers compensation beneficiaries.[8] This type of approach is relatively untested.

The Oregon law requires injured workers to obtain service through the managed care organization that the employer or insurer has contract with, except in a medical emergency. managed care organization are also required to permit injured workers to continue to receive care from a primary care physician who is not a member of the plan's network, but who maintains the worker's medical records and with whom the worker has a documented history of treatment, if the primary care physician agrees to refer the worker to the managed care organization for any specialized treatment, including physical therapy, and agrees to abide by all the rules, terms and conditions regarding services performed by the managed care organization.

Insurers or self-insured employers offering managed care organization coverage must make adequate disclosures to employees of the program's terms an operations. An insurer or employer may not be the managed care organization unless it is a health care provider. Managed care organizations *must* be certified by the director of the Department of Insurance and Finance.

The Oregon law also requires that the managed care organization not discriminate against or exclude from participation any "category of medical service providers." It must include an adequate number of each category of medical service providers to give workers adequate flexibility to choose such services. Some health plans may find this objectionable, insofar as they do not normally include chiropractors, for example, in their HMO networks.

Managed care organizations are also required to provide appropriate financial incentives to reduce service costs and utilization without sacrificing the quality of service. The law does not explain what practical constraints this is intended to place on managed care organization contracts with health care providers.

Efforts to Adapt to Legal Strictures Providing Freedom of Choice

Some employers seek to develop voluntary preferred provider programs, under which employees are encouraged to use providers under contract to the employer or insurer. Employee education encourages the patronage of plan providers. Employers may also seek to encourage managed care enrollment for their basic health benefit programs, anticipating that an injured employee will seek treatment from a participating provider.

Employees may generally be willing to seek treatment from preferred providers, since in the traditional workers compensation setting it is sometimes difficult for injured employees to secure service from desirable practitioners. The employer may not be saving money on the fees payable to the providers, given that workers compensation fee schedules are quite low in many states. However, savings can be achieved through reduced length of hospitalization, and perhaps more importantly, in a quick return to work. This lowers the amount of workers compensation payable in lieu of wages.

Also, the plan encourages workers to use providers with whom they have built up a relationship. It also may try to attract physicians with assurances of relatively hassle-free payment.

Another alternative is to provide additional benefits to injured workers who seek treatment from a plan provider. Benefits equal to a portion of the amounts saved might be made available to the employee in the form of an employer contribution toward additional like insurance or other fringe benefits.

If the extra benefit should alter the benefits afforded under an ERISA-regulated employee benefit plan, care must be taken to comply with the notice and documentation requirements under ERISA.

Additional Obstacles

Even where the workers compensation law does not require freedom of choice, managed care arrangements between employer and HMOs, or between payers and provider, may run into difficulty under other state law provisions.

First, use of capitation or other risk-sharing techniques with health care providers could be deemed to be the unlicensed business of insurance by the state insurance division or attorney general.

Second, various state laws require disclosures to patients where referrals are made to persons in whom the referring party has a financial interest.

Third, state laws may not permit an HMO to be a workers compensation insurer. The HMO involvement may have to be as a contractor to insurer or employer.

Fourth, insurers and contractors to self-insured groups should be wary of conflicts of interest. For example, if an insurer is the health insurer of an employer as well as the workers compensation insurer, there is a danger of impropriety or fraud if claims are mischaracterized and charged to the wrong program.

Fifth, if an intermediary is involved, it may be subject to state licensing requirements of third-party administrators, private review agents, and preferred provider organizations.

LIABILITY CLAIMS

Employers and insurers involved in managing the worker's use of health care resources should be aware of the evolving trend of malpractice claims against health plans. The line of cases could be extended to employers in some circumstances.

Some individual state laws contain immunity provisions for peer review, in general or in context of workers compensation. State-by-state review is required, but these laws may not cover the full range of risks faced in managed care contracting.

Negligent "Agent" Participating Physician

A patient injured by provider negligence may claim that the provider was the *actual or apparent agent* of the plan or employer. A principal can be held liable for the negligence of its agents.

A staff model organization that employs its own physicians will be liable for any malpractice committed by them.[9] The same rule could apply to an employer whose own medical staff provides care to injured employees.

A referral physician whose practice for an HMO enrolle is controlled by the HMO may be found to be the plan's "employee" (even though he is not an employee for tax or other legal purposes), so that the HMO will be liable for the physician's malpractice.[10]

An HMO may be liable for the malpractice of independent physicians who contract to provide services to HMO enrollees as apparent agents.[11] With only some stretching, the same approach could be used to assert a liability claim against the workers compensation insurer or self-insured employer that had contracted with the managed care provider network.

Negligent Credentialing and Quality Assurance

Managed care organizations could be liable for negligent credentialing or quality assurance programs.

The established law is that the hospital is liable where patient injury is caused by hospital failure in its duty to adequately credential physicians.[12]

One court has extended this doctrine to the HMO setting, finding that an HMO has a duty to adequately credential the physicians permitted to practice as participating providers, and may be held directly liable for the malpractice of an incompetent physician if it negligently fails to exclude such a physician.[13]

A similar theory could be extended to a workers compensation insurer or employer who was negligent in ether selecting network providers or in selecting a health plan or PPO that selected providers.

Negligent Utilization Review

If improper care is rendered to an enrollee, or necessary care is not rendered, as a proximate result of the insurer's or employer's negligent utilization review, the insurer or employer might be held liable for patient injury.[14]

Negligence Induced by Provider Compensation Methods

Compensation arrangements with participating physicians that create disincentives for necessary referrals or diagnostic tests could perhaps support malpractice claims against plan sponsors.

In *Bush v. Dake*[15] the plaintiff cancer patient alleged that physician group capitation and risk arrangement resulted in harmful delay of necessary tests and specialist referrals. The court ruled that the claim could go to the jury. The court dismissed the plaintiff's separate claim that the HMO's incentive payments system violated public policy and was inherently negligent, noting that the legislature had approved HMO utilization management and cost containment efforts.[16]

In *Teti v. U.S. HealthCare, Inc.*,[17] a class action suit was filed by U.S. HealthCare enrollees who challenged the HMO's withholding and incentive arrangements with its primary care physicians. The plaintiff class alleged valuations of the federal Racketeer Influenced and Corrupt Organizations Act (RICO), breach of contract, and state common law fraud. The plaintiffs claimed the risk arrangement reduced the quality and comprehensiveness of care to less than that represented by the HMO in its marketing materials and that the HMO should have disclosed the nature and existence of the incentive fund to members. The federal court rejected the RICO claim and dismissed the case, leaving the plaintiff free to pursue state law claims in state courts. No suit has been filed in state courts.

The new Oregon workers compensation law requires managed care organizations to "provide appropriate financial incentives to reduce service costs and utilization without sacrificing the quality of service."

INJURED WORKER CONTRACTUAL CLAIMS

Claim Based on Breach of Contractual Obligation to Provide Quality Care

In *Stelmach v. Physicians Multispecialty Group*,[18] the subscriber was found to be the third-party beneficiary of a medical group's contractual obligation to the HMO to provide or arrange quality health care. Medical group contractual liability to the HMO subscriber was found based on the negligent (i.e., "non-quality") care of the outside consultant physician. The HMO's contract with the outside group did not have a disclaimer of third party beneficiary effect.

Failure to Provide Promised or Statutory Required Services

Depending on how the documents are drafted, the employer or insurer could be charged with failing to provide services as opposed to merely-failing to pay for services.

Safeguards for trouble spots:

- Oversee your plan provider's compliance with referral protocols.
- Keep policies and contracts up to date with changing regulations and accepted standards of medical practice.
- Document the basis for claim denials.
- Put all managed care program requirements in proper documents for affected workers.

LITIGATION AVOIDANCE OPTIONS

The following options cold help you avoid litigation:

- Describe program requirements in detail in documentation provided to employees.
- Perform quality assurance activities described in program documents.
- Monitor underutilization as well as overutilization.
- Be wary of pushing employees back to work too soon if there is danger of further harm.
- Do not rely only on hospital privileges status when undertaking a credentials check; obtain, and where appropriate, verify specific credentials information regarding applying providers; periodically check the credentials of current providers; and obtain a report from National Practitioners Data Bank.
- Closely monitor risk-bearing capacity and the performance of capitated providers, if this mechanism is used.
- Review representations regarding the relationship with participating providers in program documents.

ANTITRUST CLAIMS BY EXCLUDED PROVIDERS

Antitrust laws prohibit agreements or concerted actions that restrain trade unreasonably. Unilateral activity is not barred, except for monopolization, which is rarely an issue for managed care programs.

Agreement may be found where the program is controlled by competing providers, where the credentialing or termination decision is controlled by competing providers, or where the plan plots with competing providers.

Unilateral refusals to deal or reimbursement decisions will not normally raise antitrust risk.[19]

Even if agreement is found, exclusions of individual providers are not suspect absent market power or anticompetitive purpose.[20]

The antitrust risk is significant if the plan is controlled by competing providers and excludes providers affiliated with other plans. However, if competing physicians control the plan, exclusion or limitations on the reimbursement of allied practitioners is not illegal *per se*.[21]

Provider conspiracies in dealings with managed care programs can raise serious antitrust problems, such as the conviction in Arizona of a group of dentists who conspired to force an increase in HMO patient fees.

Risk avoidance cautions:

- Employ contracts that give flexibility to deny or terminate participation
- Adhere to contractual terms
- Ensure that decisions serve the *program's* interest, not the private interest of some contracting providers

- Consider following the procedures of the Health Care Quality Improvement Act[22] (it provides limited qualified immunity for professional review actions) and comparable state laws.

1. 29 USC § 1144.

2. See, e.g., Ohio Rev code Ann § 4123.651 (the injured employee has "free choice" of licensed physician, surgeon, or hospital).

3. See Wis Stat § 102.42(2) (use of this flexibility by the employer may permit improvement in quality and cost savings).

4. See Iowa Code Ann § 85.27; also Ind Code § 22-3-3-4.

5. See Va Code Ann § 65.1-88(A)(1).

6. See Fla Stat § 440.13(2), (3).

7. Fla Stat § 440.135.

8. See Or Rev Stat § 656.245(5), as amended (1990).

9. See *Sloan v Metropolitan Health Council of Indianapolis, Inc,* 516 NE 2d 1104 (Ind App 1987).

10. See *Schleir v Kaiser,* 876 F2d 174 (DC Cir 1989) (the consultant physician was the "employee" of the HMO for purposes of legal liability because the HMO had some ability to control the physician's practice through referral practice patterns).

11. *Boyd v Albert Einstein Medical Center,* 547 A2d 1299 (Pa Super Ct 1988) (the marketing and advertising materials of an IPA-model HMO, its credentialing activities, and this referral practice patterns could lead an enrollee to reasonably perceive the HMO as health care provider, and the physicians as agents of the HMO).

12. *Darling v Charleston Community Hospital,* 33 Ill 2d 325, 211 NE 2d 258 (1965).

13. *Harrell v Total Health Care,* Civ A No WD 39809 (Mo App), *rev'd on other grounds,* 781 SW 2d 58 (Mo Sup Ct 1989) (the plan is immunized by state statutory malpractice immunity for nonprofit health services corporations).

14. See *Wilson v Blue Cross of Southern California,* No B040697 (Cal Ct App Jul 27, 1990); *Wickline v State of California,* 192 Cal App 3d 1630 (1986) (the court finds in favor of payer but warns that "payers can be held legally accountable when medically inappropriate decisions result from defects in the design or implementation of cost containment mechanisms. . ."). See generally *Hughes v Blue Cross of Northern California,* 199 Cal App 3d 958 (1988) (Blue Cross is liable where standard for determining "medical necessity" is at odds with the community standard).

15. *Bush v Dake,* no 86-25767 (Mich Cir Ct Apr 27, 1989).

16. But see *Pulvers v Kaiser Foundation Health Plan,* 99 Cal App 3d 560 (Cal Ct App 1980) (in which the court rejects the plaintiffs' challenge to HMO incentive arrangements with physicians, noting that incentive arrangements are supported by professional organizations and the federal HMO Act).

17. *Teti v US Healthcare, Inc,* Civil Action Nos 88-9808, 88-9822 (ED Pa Nov 21, 1989).

18. *Stelmach v Physicians Multispecialty Group,* Docket No 53906 (MO Ct App 1989)

19. See *Monsanto Co v Spray-Rite Serv Corp,* 465 US 752 (1984); *Wildenauer v Vlue Cross and Blue Shield of Minn,* No 3-88-0134 (D Minn Nov 2, 1989) (the plan's arrangements with an outside contractor to review chiropractic claims did not establish agreement).

20. See *Northwest Wholesale Stationers, Inc v Pacific Stationery and Printing Co* 472 US 284 (1985).

21. *Leone v Pierce County Medical Bureau,* 767 F2d 934, 472 US 284 (1985), cert denied, 474 US 1057
     (1986); but cf. *Hahn v Oregon Physicians' Service,* 860 F2d 1501 (9th Cir 1988), Petition for cert. filed
     (US Jun 29, 1989).

22. 42 USC §§ 11101-11152.

46. The Americans with Disabilities Act, Disability Management, and the Injured Worker

Brian T. McMahon   Donald E. Shrey

The passage of the Americans with Disabilities Act, which beginning in 1994 will extend to companies with as few as 15 employees, will have significant implications on workers compensation and disability management issues. Understanding the ADA is the key not only to avoiding legal problems, but to improving worker productivity, safety, and morale. The ADA may complicate matters in some ways, but it also represents an opportunity for American business to bring down workers compensation costs and to tap into the productivity of the 10 million Americans who are disabled.

The Americans with Disabilities Act (ADA) is unequivocally the most momentous piece of civil rights legislation since 1964. No single event or law has had a greater effect on the employment of persons with disabilities.

The estimated $100 billion wasted to subsidize some 10 million disabled Americans who are employable and eager to work prompted the enactment of the ADA. Also considered were the runaway costs of workers compensation premiums, the affordability of accommodations, and the proven cost-benefit of accommodating individuals when necessary.[1]

The purpose of this article is to delineate the implications of the ADA for the management of disability among injured workers.

Reprinted with permission from *The Journal of Workers Compensation*, Vol. 1, No. 4 (Summer, 1992).

WHO IS COVERED?

The employment provisions of the ADA are in effect as of July 26, 1992, for employers with 25 or more employees, and will apply to employers with 15 or more employees beginning July 16, 1994. Covered entities include private employers, state and local governments, employment agencies, labor unions, and joint labor-management committees.

There is little to draw upon in the ADA regarding injured workers' lack of motivation and financial provisions to work. The lawmakers appeared more focused on initial job applicants and currently employed individuals with disabilities. Subsequently, less attention was given to state-specific issues such as industrial injury. There appears to have been a presumption that most states had anti-discrimination laws that were consistent with workers compensation statutes.

Not all individuals with disabilities are protected by the employment provisions, which apply only to a "qualified individual with a disability"; i.e., one ". . . who meets the skill, experience, education, and other job-related requirements of a position and can perform the essential functions of a job."[2] The ADA specifically states that certain individuals are not protected by is provisions, including those who currently use illegal drugs or prescription drugs illegally; persons of varying sexual orientations without other disabilities; and persons with selected behavior disorders.

In the simplest terms, Title I of the ADA requires that *all employment activities be unrelated to the existence or consequence of disability.*[3] This prohibition applies not only to recruitment and selection, but to *all* aspects of the employment process, including the management of injured worker issues. Nothing in the ADA is intended to challenge or lower an employer's production or qualification standards, although the latter must be job-related and consistent with business necessity.

At this juncture in the evolution of the ADA, it appears to be well understood that one unlawful action which constitutes discrimination involves refusing to make a reasonable accommodation to the known physical or mental limitations of a qualified individual with a disability. Less understood are the six other unlawful activities, including the following:

1. Limiting, classifying, or segregating an employee because of his or her disability;
2. Participating in a contractual relationship that subjects a qualified individual with a disability to discrimination;
3. Denying employment opportunities to a worker who has a known relationship or association with a person with a disability;
4. Using qualification standards, employment tests, or other selection criteria that are not job related and necessary for the business and that tend to screen out an individual with a disability;

5. Failure to use employment tests in the most effective manner to measure actual abilities in relationship to persons with sensory, manual, or speaking impairments; and

6. Discriminating against an individual who has sought redress or attempted to enforce the provisions of the ADA.[4]

Numbers 2 and 4 above have obvious implications for the management of injured worker issues and may be explored further by a direct examination of 29 CFR 1630.5-12.

PROSPECT FOR ENFORCEMENT

Until recently, employers who questioned the aggressive enforcement of the ADA may have chosen to calculate the cost of compliance against the cost of prospective litigation. The Civil Rights Act of 1991, however, leaves no question for employers as to the prospects for enforcement of the ADA. Every compliance effort to achieve access and accommodation is well advised since the remedies for breach, or penalties for discrimination, where extended by this law in November 1991 to include compensatory and punitive damages up to $300,000 per incident *in addition* to corrective action and legal expenses.

Additionally, plaintiffs who bring suit may be entitled to a jury trial. While the proportion of plaintiff victories is high in employment suits to begin with (higher still when enjoined by the federal government), few employers wish to defend themselves (before a jury) against charges of discrimination brought by an individual with a disability, particularly if visible disabilities resulting form unfortunate circumstances are involved. In bench trials, it is often necessary and sufficient for the defense to be on the right side of the law. In jury trials, the perception of fair treatment to the employee becomes more important in verdicts and awards.

Both employers and risk managers might consider that good faith efforts to re-employ the injured industrial worker not only reduce the risks of such litigation but also the length of lost work time and the amount of temporary total disability benefits. Such "good faith" compliance is also likely to be perceived positively by the state workers compensation system.[5]

The EEOC states clearly that ADA requirements supersede any conflicting state workers compensation laws. The Technical Assistance Manual on the Employment Provisions (Title I) of the Americans with Disabilities Act offers this example:

> Some state workers compensation statutes make an employer liable for paying additional benefits if an injury occurs because the employer assigned a person to a position likely to jeopardize the persons's health or safety, or exacerbate an earlier workers compensation injury. Some of these laws may permit or require an employer to exclude a disabled individual from employment in

cases where the ADA would not permit such exclusion. In these cases, the ADA takes precedence over the state law. An employer could not assert, as a valid defense to a charge of discrimination, that it failed to hire or return to work an individual with a disability because doing so would violate a state workers compensation law that required exclusion of this individual.[6]

Finally, filing a workers compensation claim in no way prevents a worker from filing a charge under the ADA. "Exclusivity" clauses do not prohibit a qualified individual from filing a discrimination charge with EEOC, or from filing a suit under the ADA if the EEOC issues a "right to sue" letter. The ADA anticipates approximately 15,000 filings of employment discrimination during the first year after the effective date. Five out of six new federal government positions approved for 1992 have been allocated to the EEOC.

MANAGEMENT OF INJURED WORKER ISSUES

ADA's expectations regarding the evaluation and placement of injured workers are somewhat challenging because injured workers are often involved in an adversarial process that recently operates outside the human resource management system. This may not have been thoroughly considered by ADA lawmakers and regulators who, for example, encourage employers to consult with disabled individuals first regarding accommodations. How such consultations actually play out in the adversarial arena of workers compensation remains to be seen.

Not all injured workers are protected by Title I of the ADA because a given injured worker is not necessarily an "individual with a disability" in ADA terms, and even then, all "individuals" are not necessarily "qualified." For many, the implications of the ADA for injured workers appear to be misunderstood or, at the very least, understated. Only injured workers who meet the ADA's definition of "qualified individual with a disability" will be considered disabled under the ADA, even if they satisfy criteria for receiving benefits under workers compensation or other disability laws (*e.g.*, long-term disability, veterans benefits, or social security).

Many, but not all, insured workers will meet the ADA definition of disability, which has its origins in the Rehabilitation Act of 1973. A disability is defined as:

> A physical or mental impairment which substantially limits one or more major life activities; or a record of such impairment; or being regarded as having such an impairment.[7]

Specifically, it is intended that personnel actions involving employees with disabilities be managed on a fact-specific, case-by-case, individual basis, in relation to the specific employment requirements or personnel practices in question. Employer concerns about frivolous claims of disability cannot be justified by either legislative or human resources experience. Indeed, it is safe to assume that for every individual who frivolously claims to be disabled under the

ADA, thousands will choose not to disclose a hidden disability for fear of prejudice, stereotyping, or generalization.

Employers are provided with several protections related to the definition that are designed to apply the law to legally defined persons and minimize or eliminate frivolous claims of disability. First, limitations to a major life activity must be substantial, and must result from the *impairment*, not from old age or disadvantagement. Second, employees must be *qualified*. They must meet all job requirements (which are job-related and consistent with business necessity) and must be able to perform essential job functions when afforded accommodations (if necessary and reasonable). It is incorrect to state that a qualified employee must be able to perform the job; only execution of the essential functions is necessary.[8] Finally, employees may not represent a direct safety threat (significant risk of substantial harm) to themselves or other workers.

Many work-related injuries never result in substantial limitations to a major life activity. Injuries that are not considered disabilities under the ADA include those that cause non-chronic impairments that heal over a brief period of time with little or no long-term impact. The payment of workers compensation benefits or assignment of a high disability rating (in workers compensation terms) does not automatically convey coverage by ADA Title I. Most state workers compensation laws, which are designed for purposes quite separate from nondiscrimination, define disability differently than does the ADA. Thus injuries must be considered on a case-by-case basis to determine if a worker is protected by the ADA.

While the notions of "substantially limits," "qualified," and "direct threat" may serve to limit the number of injured workers who meet the ADA definition, the real figure is increased by the fact that individuals with a record of disability or who are perceived as having a disability are also covered.

Historically, discriminatory attitudes and actions toward those with a record of industrial injury is at the root of this broad definition. The precise number of injured workers who will meet the ADA's definition of disability is impossible to estimate. Such statistics will likely be affected by the attitude employers of the future will assume toward this population.

MEDICAL SCREENING AND THE DIRECT THREAT ISSUE

Some employers have focused on the direct threat issue as a way to screen out employees believed to compromise (even remotely) workplace safety. Such an assumption requires careful reconsideration for a number of reasons.[9] As stated in the Workers Compensation Outlook: "A human rights agency in Pennsylvania recently ruled that an employer who acts on the basis of a future risk must provide statistical evidence from the past to back up this claim. Future EEOC and court decisions may follow along the same lines."[10]

Direct threat, although based upon objective medical evidence, may be challenged by other objective factors, including non-medical evidence (*e.g.*, a long-standing record of worker safety in the same or similar occupation). It must also be demonstrated that the risk is significant. The specific risk factor must be identified and described in terms of likely duration and the nature, severity, likelihood, and imminence of potential harm. The risk must also be related to present levels of functioning, and not presumptions of future incapacity. Finally, the potential for eliminating or at least reducing the risk to acceptable levels by reasonable accommodation must be explored.

It is obvious that the direct threat defense does impose a significant burden of proof upon the employer. These regulations are intended to eliminate employment or re-employment decisions that are based upon subjective perceptions, irrational fears, patronizing attitudes, or stereotypes. The *Workers Compensation Outlook* goes on to state: "An employer's paternalistic concern for the disabled person's safety cannot be used to disqualify an otherwise qualified individual from the position."[11]

Attempts to identify predispositions to injury are discouraged by the ADA, while valid, objective and reasonable attempts to identify legitimate workplace safety risks are allowed. Such attempts and inquiries should be applied equally to all workers.

Despite unique considerations for accommodating injured workers' job performance, *all* personnel actions must be addressed by accommodation, if necessary. For example, employment testing, minimizing direct threat, and accessing training programs and information about internal job vacancies are all subject to accommodation. The ADA strongly suggests that individuals with disabilities be consulted first regarding the need for and nature of accommodation and that technical assistance be considered as a last resort.

There are three types of accommodations that have unique implications for injured workers. The first is job restructuring. It is imperative that employers distinguish between essential and marginal job functions, because essential functions need not be accommodated by job restructuring. Second, regulations have stated clearly that the use of personal assistants to perform job-related duties may be regarded as a reasonable accommodation. Third, regulations have clarified that reassignment to vacant positions is required only for current employees (*e.g.*, injured workers) and *not* for applicants "off the street," however qualified.

ADA does not require an employer to restructure jobs to create a light-duty position where no such position existed before. If a vacant light-duty position is available, reassignment of the worker to the vacant position might be a reasonable accommodation. If necessary, the reasonable accommodation of the worker in the new light-duty position must also be addressed.

It is strongly recommended that all light-duty jobs be specified as temporary and transitional. Because this is a sensitive issue for both labor and management,

---

A Process of Identifying a Reasonable Accommodation

- Look at the particular job involved. Determine its purpose and essential functions.

- Consult with the disabled individual to find out his or her specific physical or mental abilities and limitations as they relate to the essential job functions. Identify the barriers to job performance and assess how these barriers could be overcome with an accommodation.

- In consultation with the individual, identify potential accommodations and assess how effective each would be in enabling the individual to perform essential job functions. If the consultation does not identify an appropriate accommodation, technical assistance is available form a number of sources, many without cost. There are also financial resources to help with accommodation costs.

- If there are several effective accommodations that would provide an equal employment opportunity, consider the preference of the individual with a disability and select the accommodation that best serves the needs of the individual and the employer.

- If more than one accommodation would be effective for the disabled individual, or if the individual would prefer to provide his ore her own accommodation, the individual's preferences should be given first consideration. However, the employer is free to choose among effective accommodations, and may choose one that is less expensive or easier to provide.

- The fact that an individual is willing to provide his or her own accommodation does not relieve the employer of the duty to provide this or another reasonable accommodation should this individual for any reason be unable or unwilling to continue to provide the accommodation.

---

existing collective bargaining agreements should be reviewed in light of ADA requirements. The congressional suggestion that all collective bargaining agreements negotiated after July 26, 1992 contain a provision permitting employers to take all actions necessary to comply with the ADA will be helpful.[12]

The new remedies for breach or penalties for discrimination, which have been extended to include significant punitive and compensatory damages, cannot be understated. It is worth noting, however, that remedies beyond the traditional corrective actions will be markedly less likely to occur if employers follow the specific reasonable accommodation procedure outlines in the Technical Assistance Manual.[13]

This recommended procedure was championed by disability rights groups because it was perceived to be powerful enough to resolve the vast majority of accommodation issues without resorting to litigation. In other words, if employers reach an erroneous conclusion after following this procedure, the legal and financial consequences will be far less significant than if the procedure is abbreviated or ignored.[14]

The refusal to accommodate on the basis of undue hardship is also becoming difficult to justify. Regulations have clarified that if the hardship is financial, only the final net cost of the accommodation to the employer (after employee contributions and tax credits and deductions offset by consumer groups, rehabilitation resources, or foundations) will provide the basis for hardship.

Because 75 percent of all individuals will require no accommodation and 0 percent of all accommodations will cost less than $2,000 prior to such offsets, claims of undue hardship are not likely to represent a strong defense.

MODIFICATIONS REQUIRED IN MEDICAL EXAMINATION PROTOCOLS

The first consideration is given to medical examinations for newly hired employees. Second injury funds often require an employer to certify (at the time of hire) that an employee had a pre-existing injury. Following an offer of employment, however, an employer may inquire about a person's workers compensation history in a medical inquiry or examination that is required of all applicants in the same job category. The employer may use information from medical inquiries or examinations for a variety of purposes including:

- Verification of employment history; screening for fraudulent workers compensation claims;[15]
- Screening for direct threat to the health or safety of the employee or others (which threat could not be eliminated or reduced to acceptable levels by reasonable accommodation); and
- Providing required reports to second injury funds or state workers compensation authorities, as required by state laws.

Such medical inquiries or examinations may occur only *after* a conditional offer of employment, *before* a person begins work and if the same inquiry or examination is made of *all* applicants in the same job category. An employee who knowingly provides a false answer to a lawful post-offer inquiry about one's health condition or workers compensation history may have the employment offer retracted, or may even be fired.

There are other pertinent issues regarding employment-related medical examinations. The intent of the ADA guidelines regarding medical examinations is to change the function of the medical director from "gatekeeper" to that of "resource person" who facilitates proper placement and reasonable accommodations.

Like health-related inquires, medical examinations are illegal prior to an offer of employment, but may be conducted after a conditional offer of employment is made (preferably in writing, specifying the conditions). Medical examinations will eventually come to resemble functional capacity examinations, which are related only to the performance of essential job functions.

Medical recommendations to *not employ* an individual in a particular job will likely be rooted in the direct threat issue, which carries with it a stringent burden of proof.

There are three positive aspects to this issue from the employer's perspective. First, physicians are not limited in health-related inquiry in the same way that employment interviewers are. In examinating new hires, physicians may ask about medical and workers compensation claims history and hospitalizations. Using medical information relative to the employment decision, however, should be related *only* to matters of performing essential functions and to direct threat.

Second, drug testing is allowed at any point of the employment process, provided it is conducted in a manner consistent with the organization's drug abuse policy, and the policy is evenly applied.

Finally, fitness-for-duty examination and/or agility tests are not regarded as medical examinations for employment purposes and, therefore, are not restricted in the same manner, as long as such evaluations are job-related and consistent with business necessity. However, for an agility or fitness-for-duty examination to be legally distinguished from a medical examination, the direct involvement of the physician should be minimized.

Regarding current employees (including injured workers), employers are free to conduct *only* job-related medical examinations, not full physical examinations, as a condition of returning to work. Such examinations are restricted to the employee's ability to safely perform essential job functions. Refusal to allow an employee who has not fully recovered from an injury to return to work may *only* occur when such a worker is not qualified (i.e., cannot perform the essential job functions) and/or poses a significant risk of substantial harm that could not be eliminated or reduced to an acceptable level by reasonable accommodation.

Medical information will be helpful in determining when and how an individual can return to work, and what accommodations might be facilitative. The employer bears the ultimate responsibility for determining whether or not an individual is qualified, however, and such liability cannot be placed elsewhere due to the accuracy, thoroughness, or reliability of medical information.

DISABILITY MANAGEMENT: AN ADA IMPLEMENTATION MECHANISM

Since many injured workers will be included as a protected class under ADA, requirements to accommodate workers with disabilities have profound implications for disabled workers *and* employers. Title I of ADA, as it relates to issues regarding workers compensation, will also have a significant impact on rehabilitation practice.

There is no specific mention of workers compensation in the ADA. However, there is no language in the ADA that excludes protection among individuals with acquired industrial injuries and occupational illnesses. The ADA definition of "individual with a disability" is based, in part, on the individual being limited in a "major life activity" because of physical or mental impairment. The law specifically identifies work activity as an example of a "major life activity." Consequently, any individual with permanent physical, psychological, or intellectual limitations that prohibit a return to work will certainly fall under the protection of the act.[16]

The ultimate impact of the ADA on the employment of individuals with disabilities will be difficult to assess until dispute resolution processes and litigation have resulted in legal precedents and case law. This seems especially true when considering those injured workers covered under various state laws who also meet ADA's definition of "qualified individuals with a disability." However, the following facts seem irrefutable, based upon review of the act, the rules developed by the EEOC and the opinions of legal and other experts:

- Many injured workers and other employees who develop disabilities during the course of employment do fall under the protection of the ADA.
- Employers ("covered entities") will be bound by the provisions of Title I, Section 102 of the ADA, as well as the Final Rule as published by the EEOC, when evaluating an injured workers' readiness to return to work, when making decisions regarding the reintegration of an individual with a disability into the workplace, and in performing all of the other claims and personnel administration functions related to the employment relationship with an employee having an acquired disability.
- Failure to receive technical assistance will not be a defense under the ADA.

ADA AND THE WORKERS COMPENSATION CRISIS

The terms "workers compensation" and "crisis" have become synonymous to business and industry, insurance underwriters, and the government leaders. An estimated total of $45 billion in workers compensation premiums in 1989 is expected to escalate to $200 billion by the year 2000.[17] Some employers have been ravaged by 300 percent increases in injured worker medical costs during the past decade.[18]

Changing demographics in the workplace (in terms of an aging work force), will create additional financial burdens for employers, since increasing age and incidence of disability are positively correlated.[19] Longer courses of rehabilitation and associated costs often accompany chronic disability among older workers.[20]

Compliance with the ADA and controlling injury and disability costs are not mutually exclusive concepts. Unknowingly, many proactive employers have created an atmosphere of ADA compliance through the development of innovative and successful disability management programs. Effective disability management strategies and interventions typically include the development of functional job descriptions, making reasonable accommodations, and utilizing joint labor-management efforts in maintaining non-discriminatory practices. Indeed, the definition of disability management embraces the spirit of the ADA.

Disability management has been defined as an active process of coordinating the activities of labor, management, insurance carriers, health care providers, and vocational rehabilitation professionals for the purpose of minimizing the impact of injury, disability, or disease on a worker's capacity to successfully perform his or her job.[21] Disability management involves the use of services, people, and materials to minimize the impact and cost of disability to employers and employees, and encourages return to work for employees with disabilities.[22] Operationally defined, disability management is a proactive process that jointly empowers labor and management to exercise both control and responsibility as decision-makers, planners, and coordinators of interventions and service. Disability management includes prevention rehabilitation and safe return-to-work programs designed to control the personal and economic costs of workplace injury and disability.[23]

ADA COMPLIANCE THROUGH DISABILITY MANAGEMENT

Disability management interventions, as currently used in injured worker rehabilitation, are an effective mechanism for achieving employer compliance with Title I of the ADA. Typically, disability management programs in industry are designed to:

- Prevent lengthy work disruptions among employees with medical impairments that affect work performance,
- Promote a safe and timely return to work among employees receiving workers compensation or sickness and accident benefits.
- Accommodate disabled workers who are less than fully capable of performing full-duty work.[24]

Generally, these programs are designed to protect the employability of workers, whether they have job-related or non-job-related disabilities. ADA regulations, in effect, enforce the employer's obligations toward those workers protected under Title I. Additionally, disability management interventions and programs established for workers with disabilities also have important implications for other persons with disabilities who are pursuing employment.

Both injured workers and non-working persons with disabilities may require reasonable accommodations. Injured workers need an opportunity to transition back to work; non-working persons with disabilities often require an initial transition *into* work. The development of a successful worker-job fit is a function of both the capabilities of the worker and the requirements of the job. According to the ADA, job accommodations are required to enable the person with a disability to perform the essential job tasks.

In reviewing model disability management programs, we can see that many have relevance to the spirit and letter of the ADA. for example an article in *Business and Health* described several disability management programs in business and industry relating to the economics of ADA compliance. Consumer Power Company's program resulted in a 48 percent decrease in the number of workdays lost due to recordable lost-time injuries. Safeway Stores saved eight dollars for each dollar spent, and reduced back injuries and related costs by 50 percent. Marriott, with 20,000 employees in 50 states, reduced the number of workers compensation cases by 30 to 50 percent, saved four dollars for every dollar spent, and reduced litigated workers compensation cases by 50 percent.[25]

The General Motors Buick, Oldsmobile, and Cadillac metal fabrication and assembly plants in Lordstown, Ohio, have an estimated annual savings of three million dollars, including 50,000 saved by creating a non-traditional, light-duty recycling job.[26] The disability management program of Lockheed Missile and Space Company reduced worker visits for physical therapy and associated costs by 50 percent during the first year of its operation.[27] On-site disability management programs created for both public and private employers have been cited, including the city of Lansing, Steelcase Corporation, Walbro Corporation, Walt Disney World, Herman Miller Corporation, and Federal Express.

The following elements, which relate closely to the achievement of ADA compliance, are common among most successful disability management programs:

- Joint labor-management commitment and involvement;
- Employee education and involvement;
- Multidisciplinary interventions (*e.g.*, medical, vocational, psychological, ergonomics, engineering);
- Case management/case coordination;
- Effective disability prevention strategies;
- Utilization of employer-based and community resources;
- Early intervention and early return-to-work philosophy;
- Supportive policies and procedures to facilitate accommodations and jobsite modifications;
- System that ensures accountability of all parties; and
- Management information system for program evaluation.[28]

Specific disability management interventions having direct relevance to ADA compliance include:

- Evaluating the physical capacity of the individual;

- Developing functional descriptions of essential job duties; and
- Making reasonable accommodations.

Employers can become aware of disabilities among their workers through the benefit program evaluation and entitlement process (*e.g.,* workers compensation, short-term and long-term disability). Entitlement to these programs can bring a worker under the protection of the ADA. In such cases, it is essential to functionally evaluate both the worker and the job, and to coordinate a reasonable accommodation analysis in the absence of the worker's complete recovery.[29]

THE WORK-RETURN TRANSITION CONCEPT

"Transitional work" is any *job or combination of tasks and functions that may be performed safely and with remuneration by an employee whose physical capacity to perform functional job demands has been compromised.*[30] Many features of on-site work-return, transition programs for injured workers are relevant to ADA compliance. They encourage and support an injured employee's safe and timely return to work. They also provide accommodations to workers with disabilities, affording them an opportunity to gradually make the transition into an expanded range of essential job tasks through conditioning, safe work practices, education, and work readjustment.[31]

Work-return transition (WRT) programs are designed to reduce lengthy periods of work disruption among employees with disabilities, promote safe and timely return-to-work activities among employees receiving workers compensation or other insurance benefits, and accommodate disabled workers having compromised capacities to perform the full range of essential job functions.[32]

The principle of "occupational bonding" is instrumental to the creation of an effective WRT program.[33] This refers to establishing a mutually beneficial relationship between the worker and the employer. In order to resolve potentially adversarial relationships between workers and employers, it is important to clarify the employer's intentions as well as the worker's expectations. When both workers and employers value strategies that protect the employability of the worker, the occupational bond becomes strengthened. WRT programs serve as concrete evidence of the employer's intentions. Through proper education and orientation, the worker's expectations become less suspicious and employer attitudes become less cynical.

ADA AND CHANGES IN REHABILITATION PRACTICE

Theoretically, vocational rehabilitation and ADA compliance require an equally balanced focus on the individual and the work environment. Disability may originate as much from environmental barriers as from the worker's personal traits.[34] Various typologies of rehabilitation intervention strategies have generally classified these services as those that either transform the individual with a disability, or those that alter the person's environment.[35]

What may essentially be altered by the ADA is traditional rehabilitation practice, which has historically underutilized environmentally oriented interventions. The majority of individualized written rehabilitation plans developed for injured workers contain only services that consider the client as the primary target, with the objective of modifying the person in some fashion.[36]

Even during recent years, standard rehabilitation practice has continued to include physical conditioning, work hardening, medical and vocational assessment, vocational training, and job placement. Such services are based on the premise that the traits of the individual can be modified to the degree that reintegration into the work force is possible. Conversely, the ADA requires the use of environmentally oriented services (e.g., jobsite modifications or reasonable accommodations), and ADA compliance addresses the external (work) environment as the prime target for change (with the objective of sustaining work performance), while protecting the employability of the individual with a disability.

Rehabilitation and disability management practices embrace a philosophy that promotes independence for persons with disabilities while maximing human potential. The ADA will be a catalyst in the deinstitutionalization of America's injured workers. The past two decades have witnessed attempts to simulate the world of work in sterilized clinical environments. Hospital-based work hardening programs have been characterized as the fastest growing of clinical services. Exhibit halls at rehabilitation conferences have been flooded with fashionable (and expensive) functional capacity evaluation tools and work simulation equipment. Lengthy periods of clinical programming for injured workers often translated into even lengthier periods of work disruption, with little or no involvement from the employer or labor groups. Workers with disabilities generally performed simulated non-remunerative work (while segregated from co-workers and supervisors), with little or no opportunity to experience work adjustment through work site accommodations or work-return transition programs.

The ADA will usher in an era of transformation in rehabilitation practice. Clinical interventions will be taken to the world of work. Job accommodations will promote work adjustment through creative employer-practitioner interactions. Workers with disabilities will be enabled to perform "real," compensable, and meaningful work, which will result in significant reductions in lost time and associated medical/indemnity costs to the employer. More importantly, the occupational bond between the worker and the employer will be strengthened as the balance between the employer's intentions and the worker's expectations is clarified.

PROJECTED TRENDS RELATED TO THE ADA

Trends that are likely to develop in the aftermath of the ADA are somewhat speculative. However, disability management programming emphasizing worksite rehabilitation as the ultimate compliance and cost-containment solution is likely to expand.[37] Re-employment of the injured worker with the same employer, which has always been the primary objective of the job placement professional, is likely to increase at the expense of outplacement activity.[38] Technical assistance regarding accommodations will involve an extensive review of human resources policies and procedures, through management training, some restructuring of the selection program, and the derivation of essentialness in job descriptions.[39]

Widespread experimentation with accommodations will ultimately lead to productivity enhancements for all workers, as well as to the discovery and implementation of more disability prevention programs in industry. Positions such as "in-house accommodation specialist" or "ADA coordinator" may become commonplace.

CONCLUSION

Protecting the rights of injured workers is an important component of the ADA. Every year, thousands of workers become disabled through industrial accidents and occupational disease. Without the accommodations required by the ADA, workers with such disabilities risk discrimination just as other individuals with disabilities do.

The profound impact of the workers compensation crisis will be experienced by American business and industry throughout the next decade. Just as this crisis offers a challenge to industry, the ADA creates an opportunity. With a decreasing labor pool, an aging workforce, and increased worldwide competition, employers must focus on protecting the employability of the American worker. Work-return transition programs offer tremendous promise.

Employers providing transitional work opportunities for individuals with disabilities demonstrate a real commitment to the ADA. Work-return transition programs will continue to promote the ongoing labor force participation of persons with disabilities, while simultaneously reducing financial liabilities associated with work-related injuries. The ADA will continue to ensure that persons with disabilities who participate in transitional work will be enabled to minimize the economic, physical, psychological, social, and domestic losses related to discriminatory employment practices and accommodation barriers.

1.   FG Bowe, "Development of the ADA," and BT McMahon, and LR Shaw, "Considerations for the Rehabilitation Consultant," in *The Americans with Disabilities Act: Access and Accommodations.* N Hablutzel, and BT McMahon, (eds) Orlando: Paul M. Deutsch Press, 1992.

2. 29 CFR 1630.2

3. 29 CFR 1630.4

4. 29 CFR 1630.5-12

5. S Blumenthal, "Impact of the ADA on the Vocational Rehabilitation of Industrial Injured Workers Under Workers Compensation," *In the Mainstream*, Vol 17 No 1 1992, 19–22.

6. Equal Employment Opportunity Commission, *Technical Assistance Manual on the Employment Provisions (Title I) of the Americans with Disabilities Act (EEOC: 1992)*, ch 9.

7. 29 CFR 1630.2 (Employers concerned about the broad nature of this and other definitions should understand that such vagueness is by design.)

8. Essentialness is best arrived at by a professional job analysis that describes the results of tasks performed rather than prescribing the processes or behaviors involved in task performance.

9. Supra note 6, ch 4.

10. L Abate, (ed) *Workers Compensation Outlook*, vol 2, no 2, Nov 1991, 6.

11. Id.

12. L, Kessler "Americans with Disabilities Act: Focus on Insurers," Presented at Alliance of American Insurers Symposium, Washington, DC, 1992.

13. Supra note 6, ch 3.

14. Supra note 12.

15. An employer may rescind a conditional offer of employment if the inquiry reveals that a number of workers compensation claims have been made and denied in a short period of time.

16. D Shrey and R Breslin, "Disability Management in Industry: A Multidisciplinary Model for the Accommodation of Workers with Disabilities," *The International Journal of Ergonomics,* in press, 1992.

17. R Thompson, "Fighting the High Cost of Workers Comp," Nation's business, Mar, 1990, 20-26. G Farrell, S Knowlton, and Taylor, "Second Chance: Rehabilitating the American Worker: A Case Management Approach to Long Term Disability Can Result In Savings," *Journal of Private Sector Rehabilitation,* 4, 3&4, 1989.

18. D, Galvin "Disability Management: An Overview of a Cost-Effective, Human Investment Strategy, *in Workers Compensation: Strategies for Lowering Costs and Reducing Workers' Suffering.* E Welch (ed.), Fort Washington, PA: LRP Publications, 1989, 39–54.

19. S Nagi, "An Epidemiology of Disability Among Adults in the United States," *Millbank Memorial Fund Quarterly,* 51, 1976, 439-468. J McNeil, *Labor Force Status and Other Characteristics of Persons with a Work Disability*, Washington, DC: Government Printing Office, 1982. K Lewis, "Persons With Disabilities and the Aging Factor," *Journal of Rehabilitation*, 55, 4, 1989, 12–13.

20. J Myers, "Rehabilitation of Older Workers," *Rehab Briefs*, 4, 8, 1983.

21. D Shey, *Disability Management: An Employer-Based Rehabilitation Concept in Assessing the Vocational Capacity of the Impaired Workers.* Scheer, M.D. (ed), Aspen, CO: Aspen Publishers, 1990.

22. G Schwartz, S Watson, D Galvin, and E Lippoff, *The Disability Management Sourcebook,* Washington, DC: Washington Business Group on Health, 1989.

23. D Shrey and R Breslin, "Disability Management in Industry: A Multidisciplinary Model for the Accommodation of Workers with Disabilities," *The International Journal of Ergonomics, in press, 1992.*

24. D Shrey, *Disability Management: An Employer-Based Rehabilitation Concept. In Assessing the Vocational Capacity of the Impaired Worker,* S Scheer, M.D. (ed), Aspen, CO: Aspen Publishers, 1990.

25. P Taulbee, "Corralling Runaway Workers Comp Costs," *Business & Health*, 9, 4, 1991, 46–55.

26. L Avers, "Hard at Work," *Ohio Monitor*, 1989, 5–10.

27. S Patenaude, "Promoting Functional Ability in Industry," *Industrial Rehabilitation Quarterly*, 2, 1, 1989, 34, 40–41.

28. R Habeck, "Managing Disability in Industry," NARRPS *Journal and News*, 6, 3&4, 1991, 141–146.

29. P Owen, *The Americans with Disabilities Act—An Employers Perspective: Obstacle or Opportunity*, McMillan, 1990.

30. D Shrey and J Olsheski, "Disability Management & Industry-Based Work Return Transition Program," (book chapter) in *A state of the Art Review in Physical Medicine & Rehabilitation for Industrial Medicine*, Caplan, (ed.), Hanley & Belfus Publishers, 1992.

31. J Frieden, "Cost Containment Strategies for Workers Compensation," *Business and Health*, Oct 1989, 48–53.

32. D Shrey, *Disability Management: An Employer-Based Rehabilitation Concept in Assessing the Vocational Capacity of the Impaired Worker*, S Sheer M.D. (ed.), Aspen, CO: Aspen Publishers, 1990.

33. S Bruyerer and D Shrey, "Disability Management in Industry: A Joint Labor-Management Process," *Rehabilitation Counseling Bulletin*, 34, 3, (1991) 227–242.

34. D Hershenson, "A Theoretical Model or Rehabilitation Counseling," *Rehabilitation Counseling Bulletin*, 33, 4, 1990, 268–278.

35. M Scofield, D Pape, N McCracken, and D Maki "An Ecological Model for Promoting Acceptance of Disability," *Journal of Applied Rehabilitation Counseling*, 11, 1980, 183–187. D Shrey, Mitchell, "Disability Management Among Private and Public Employers: Models and Strategies for Rehabilitation Intervention," *Journal of Applied Rehabilitation Counseling*, 17, 3, 1986, 13–19.

36. G Wright, *Total Rehabilitation*, Boston: Little, Brown & Company, 1980.

37. S Bruyere, and D Shrey "Disability Management in Industry: A Joint Labor-Management Process," Rehabilitation Counseling Bulletin, 34, 3, 1991, 227–242. D Drury, "Disability Management in Small firms," Rehabilitation Counseling Bulletin, 34, 3, 1991, 257–273.

38. R Matkin, *Insurance Rehabilitation*, Austin, Texas: Pro-Ed, 1985.

39. BT McMahon, and LR Shaw, "Considerations for the Rehabilitation Consultant," and T Ziemba and BT McMahon, "Reinforcing the Need for Progressive Human Resources Practices," in *The Americans with Disabilities Act: Access and Accommodations*, N Ablutzel and BT McMAhon (eds), Orlando: Paul M. Deutsch Press, 1992.

47.   Hands-On Answers to Hidden Health Costs

Michelle Neely Martinez   Joe Lamoglia

Repetitive motion illness in the office is causing a dramatic rise in health claims.

Computers. They were designed to increase efficiency and productivity, yet they have added strain to the office worker and cost to the employer in worker's compensation claims.

Once limited to meat packers, poultry workers and plant manufacturing workers, repetitive motion illnesses, commonly known as cumulative trauma disorders (CTDs), have filtered into office settings and retail establishments because these jobs have become "keystroke dependent."

A pilot study sponsored by the National Institute of Occupational Safety and Health (NIOSH) lists secretaries, typists, telephone operators and cashiers as the most likely workers to develop CTDs. Cumulative trauma disorders most often occur as a result of three factors—force, frequency and posture—combining to exceed the ability of a specific body part.

David Thompson, professor emeritus of industrial engineering at Stanford University, told *The Washington Post* that the average keyboard typist uses eight ounces of force to depress each key. A clerk who types 60 words a minute can touch the keys 18,000 times in a busy hour, equalling 108,000 strokes in six hours. That adds up to 50,000 pounds, or 25 tons, pressed through the fingertips during one day of typing, he says.

Not only is keystroking a problem; repetition is another factor. The computer cursor that advances automatically to the return line in a small and simple example of repetitive movement brought about by technological improvements. With the manual typewriter, workers often shifted positions to change paper or moved to

Reprinted with the permission of *HRMagazine* (formerly *Resource*) published by the Society for Human Resource Management, Alexandria, VA.

the typing table located away from the desk area. Though less movement has increased efficiency, it has allowed more strain and injury.

CTD CASES RISE

A 1989 survey by the U.S. Bureau of Labor Statistics reported that of 283,700 occupational illnesses reported to the agency, nearly 51 percent of the cases involved some type of repetitive motion trauma—the most common being carpal tunnel syndrome, an injury to the hand and wrist that can require surgery to avoid permanent damage. Other common forms of CTDs are tendinitis, De Quervain's Disease and Degenerative Disc Disease (classically diagnosed as a slipped or herniated disc).

When Liberty Mutual applies is average cost per CTD case of $6,168 to the bureau's figures, the annual tab for medical expenses and lost wages is $907 million.

Statistics like these have led Barbara A. Otto, president of *9 to 5,* to believe that the information age and technological improvements have created the sweatshops of the '90s.

"Few people realize that a video display terminal can be dangerous. But 10 years from now, we'll look back in shock at workers who sat in front of VDTs getting systematically maimed," said Otto. "It will compare to a decade when we were surprised to learn that factory workers were unknowingly getting cancer from chemicals."

Today, 20 million office workers are employed in the United States. According to Otto, whose Cleveland-based advocacy group represents office workers, there was one workstation for every 100 workers in 1980. In 1990, two workstations accommodated every three workers.

"There's been no consideration given to this change," she said. "Technology changed but the worker design hasn't. If anything, we do more repetitious work faster, but we don't look at the physical effects."

In the general population, carpal tunnel syndrome mostly affects women near the age of 50. However, according to Gary Franklin, medical director of the Washington State Department of Labor and Industries, employees in their 30s (men nearly as much as women) are most likely to be affected. Carpal tunnel cases have been difficult to track because of the inconsistencies in various reporting codes and classifications, he said.

CTD-Related Back Problems

Classification problems with back injuries—the leader in worker compensation claims at $14 billion a year according to the Safety and Health Institute[1]—are also a problem, says consultant David Busse of Risk Reduction Realized in Burleson, Texas.

"Though 80 percent of back maladies are repetitive motion illnesses, the Occupational Safety and Health Administration (OSHA) arbitrarily decided that all back cases will be reported as injuries, and wrist problems are illnesses. In most cases, the back or wrist conditions are caused by the same thing—repetitive motion. It's just affecting a different part of the body."

According to physical therapist Joan Smithcline, the kind of sitting done at the office can damage the back over time. Based on her work at Stanford University Hospital, she said that pressure on the back increases almost 600 percent from reclining to sitting upright. Slouching increases the pressure by 740 percent.

WORKPLACE ISSUE

David Bussee predicts that the primary issues he'll be dealing with in the '90s are the health issues of workers. "In the past, there's been exposure to such maladies, but they were not considered to be work related. That trend is changing due to the publicity of the number of claims, the attempt to control claims and the need to reduce employer liability," he said. "We now can accept the fact that the trend is there, assume it's work related, and see what can be done to reduce the problem."

Although no legislation exists at the national level to force employers to analyze their workplace for computer-related or video display terminal (VDT) illnesses, local municipalities in New York, New Jersey, California and other states are creating legislation. Businesses will have to look at the issue and make ergonomic adjustments in the workplace. In December 1990, San Francisco became the first city to regulate the use of VDTs by municipal ordinance.[2]

The San Francisco law requires that private and public employers with 15 or more workers provide: proper lighting, anti-glare screens, adjustable equipment and ergonomically sound equipment by the end of 1994. Workers who spend more than 50 percent of their time at VDTs must be given paid, 15-minute breaks every two hours. Mandatory training sessions are required for employees who spend at least 20 minutes per week on VDTs. Businesses have 12 months to bring new equipment into compliance and 30 months to modify the existing workstations in cases in which improvements cost less than $250.

Dr. Roger Stephens, director of ergonomics at OSHA headquarters in Washington, D.C., predicts that the ergonomic-standards and rule-making process at the federal level will begin sometime this spring. In August 1990, Stephens issued "Ergonomic Program Management: Guidelines for the Meatpacking Industry." The meatpacking industry, in particular, has high incidences of CTDs. Therefore, OSHA issued these guidelines to prevent the illnesses and to guide the industry in developing ergonomic programs, which should contain four components: worksite analysis, hazard prevention and control, medical management, training and education.

Stephens said it's too early for program participants to tell the cost-saving results from implementing these programs. "Most organizations that have bought into the program have not reported savings in worker compensation costs, but have reported better relations between labor and management and less absenteeism," he said. "A lot of the companies are still piloting the programs, but will probably have some real-dollar results in another year. Ergonomic programs are something that have to be phased in," he warns. "They're definitely not something that changes overnight."

SOLUTIONS THAT WORK

In the plant setting, Bussee said, production-line automation may be the only solution to an ergonomic problem like CTD. "A trend we'll probably see is machines replacing humans," he said, "because that's what machines are good at, repetition, not humans. Other ergonomically sound solutions are purchasing 'off-the-shelf items' that are relatively inexpensive to solve the problem."

"Some office environments are being very proactive, because they are seeing a lot of claims attributed to these illnesses, especially in the service industry," said Edie Adams, ergonomist at The Joyce Institute based in Seattle, Washington.

"In organizations where there is a lot of turnover, they may not be seeing the effects of these repetitive illnesses," she said. "It's organizations where employees are staying for a longer period of time that are really recognizing the disorders."

Adams said that addressing only one area will not solve the problem of repetitive motion disorders. "Management must look at the whole work environment and how the work area is laid out."

Her approach to solving CTDs includes preventive exercise (see sidebar), rest breaks, training employees so they will feel better, and training managers so they will know what to look for. Though the public has become more sensitized to these types of illnesses, Adams said that the companies focusing on ergonomically designed work spaces are those "where one or two individuals were injured or an organization that is planning a new facility and they want to ensure that things are set up right from the start."

LOW-COST FIXES

In Adams' opinion, the best things to reduce repetitive motion disorders can be "done cheap," such as providing employees with the correct back support, a seat pad that is neither too high nor too low, and foot rests.

GETTING A HAND UP ON
CARPAL TUNNEL SYNDROME

TIPS FOR BEATING THE MALADY
OF THE INFORMATION AGE

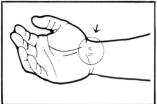

Carpal tunnel syndrome is a painful hand disorder caused by stressful and repetitive motions of the hand. Although the site of the injury is the wrist, pain is usually felt in the hand. Excessive movement of the wrists or holding the wrists in static positions for long periods of time can irritate the nerves, tendons, and arteries inside a narrow formation of ligament and bone at the wrist — the carpal tunnel.

If your work includes using a typewriter, computer, or other keyboard machine, be sure to practice proper body mechanics. Good keyboarding technique begins with good posture. Typing materials should be eye level so that you don't have to bend your neck over your work. Sit with the spine against the back of the chair, shoulders relaxed, elbows along the sides of the body, and wrists straight.

When using a keyboard or typewriter, move only the fingers — always maintain a straight-wrist position. If your keyboard has a pad at the bottom, use it to rest your wrists during breaks.

Before beginning a typing job and during breaks throughout the day, take time to do the following stretching exercises:

Rest the forearm on the edge of a table. Grasp the fingers of one hand with the other hand and gently bend back the wrist, stretching the hands and wrist. Hold for five seconds.

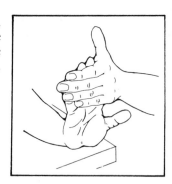

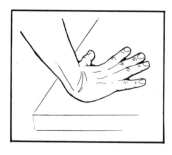

Gently press the hand against a firm, flat surface, stretching the fingers and the wrist. Hold for five seconds.

Strengthen the muscles along the wrist with the following isometric exercises:

Make a loose fist, palm up, and use the other hand to gently press down against the clenched hand. Resist the force with the closed hand for five seconds. Keep the wrist straight.

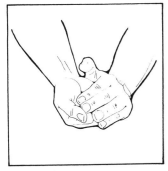

with the palm up,

the palm down,

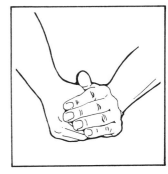

and with the thumb side of the fist up.

With the fist down, press against the knuckles of the closed hand. Resist for five seconds in each position. Repeat series five times.

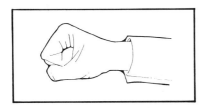

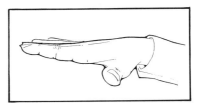

Clench fist tightly, then release, fanning out fingers. Repeat five times.

None of the stretches or exercises should cause pain or discomfort. If you have symptoms of carpal tunnel syndrome, consult a physical therapist or other qualified health care practitioner for an evaluation and individualized ergonomic and/or treatment plan.

For more information write or call the American Physical Therapy Association, 1111 N. Fairfax St., Alexandria, VA 22314, 703/684-2782.

Jeane Pollack, a partner with Chicago-based Wris Inc., agrees. "You don't have to spend thousands of dollars to fix the problem. I think there's this perception that if you don't spend a lot of money, the solution is not going to work."

Wris Inc.'s philosophy is that exercise programs are the most effective way to prevent cumulative trauma disorders. Based on the concept of "active rest," the programs Pollack designs are tailored to each employee depending on what job functions they perform daily. The exercises work an individual's larger muscle groups, which are often unused during work and strengthen the muscles involved in performing repetitive tasks.

"We go to the worksite and look at each individual job being performed, from sweeping to keystroking. We teach exercises that take five minutes, twice a day to perform—preferably in the morning and immediately following lunch" said Pollack. "The exercises we prescribe break connections or the signal from the brain that initiates the repetitive movement.

"For example, an employee does 10,000 keystrokes a day. One part of the brain tells the fingers what to do; another message makes the legs work which are shut down during the repetitive motion. Exercise prescribed for this person would stop the repetitive motion and light up the rest of the individual's board, so to speak."

Chicago-based Chas. Levy Co. implemented the active rest program within the last year and has reported a 43 percent reduction in workers' compensation claims. One of Wris Inc.'s newest clients is Allstate Insurance Co. An active rest program for its employees is currently underway.

PRODUCTIVITY AFFECTED

For productivity reasons only, more organization should consider ergonomically designed offices. A 1991 report by the NIOSH said that organizations who invest in ergonomically designed workplaces will experience a 24-percent increase in productivity.

"If people are having trouble doing their job because they're in pain," said Busse, "they're not going to do a good job, therefore quality decreases. They may also cause a production bottleneck which affects other employees," he said. "We need to educate professionals in other fields so they will consider the human factors in the workplace."

In the white-collar environment, the publishing industry was one of the first to experience the effects of cumulative trauma disorders. The *Los Angeles Times*, in particular, has had some serious problems with CTD injuries incurring workers' compensation costs of nearly $1.3 million between 1984 and 1991 despite CTD programs. *Newsday, The Fresno Bee* and other publishing houses have had similar cases of repetitive motion illness related directly to VDT usage. So far, litigation of CTD injuries in the white collar arena has been limited, but Rochester, N.Y.-based Eastman Kodak Co., parent company of Atex Publishing Systems, has had two suits filed against it by users of its newsroom computers who suffered CTD injuries.

Four 911 operators sued their employer, King County, Wash., and settled in January 1990 for $285,000. As part of the settlement, King County must install ergonomic furniture, limit job tasks and help injured workers find other jobs, if necessary.

At Gannett, publisher of *USA Today* and many local papers nationwide, efforts to control CTD injuries began in mid 1990. Gannett's health claims doubled between 1988 and 1989 and by late 1989, employees were worried about CTD injuries and had expressed their concern to management. Although claims doubled again between 1989 and 1990, the real catalyst for the program was the concerned employees.

Employees at branches across the country—mostly editors and writers—had learned the possible consequences of CTDs and were talking about it amongst themselves.

CTD "struck terror in the hearts of longterm workers at VDTs—they were looking at the potential loss of their career," says Chris Landauer, director of training and development. Those who were developing symptoms were "desperate people." In the worst cases "you can't feed yourself, let alone work." A feeling that Gannett was not responding fast enough was growing.

Employees were taking care of their injuries through their health insurance, not workers' compensation, and they were making considerable deductible payments—a growing part of the employee relations problem. Doctors, in most cases, did not think of CTD in terms of workplace activities—since some other activity, like gardening or crochet, often aggravated the condition—so neither the doctors nor the employees thought to file a workers' compensation claim and worse, treatment did not include a change of work habits. The average cost at that time was about $8,000 per claim.

Many employees feared that telling their managers they had CTD symptoms might negatively affect their careers. Landauer says one of the biggest problems was "overcoming a lot of resistance" from managers who said, "I spent my whole career working on a typewriter; what do you mean you can't type." Many "managers saw this as just malingering," she says.

The reality is that "serious cumulative trauma disorders occur among your best workers," because they spend the most time at their terminals and they are less likely to complain.

Soon after the program began, many employees did come forward with symptoms—just as some managers had feared. But Gannett wanted early intervention in all cases to lower costs. In addition, Landauer feels easing the minds of employees was a big step in restoring trust and well worth the extra time and expense. "Early intervention allows much more conservative treatments," she says. "We wanted to get out of the surgery loop . . . because of cost and because it's painful and doesn't always work."

"A big part of this kind of program is managing your insurance company," says Landauer. Gannett's answerer, Liberty Mutual, was "very receptive, but not knowledgeable" when approached about CTDs for computer users. Gannett found that their insurer's lack of knowledge was causing additional stress and improper care for those suffering from CTD injuries. Some employees suffering the symptoms of CTD were waiting two months for a second opinion or seeing doctors who didn't understand CTD.

Gannett did several things to improve the relationship among insurer, company and employee. First, they told their insurer to treat all CTD injuries as workers'-compensation covered, although several states did not recognize CTD as a worker's-comp injury. Gannett absorbed the extra cost.

Second, "We said to our insurer, you have six weeks to do all of our 80-plus newspapers; we want your most senior ergonomist to tell us" what needs to be done to eliminate the risk of injury. "After they gulped," she says, "they assembled a flying team of 20 people" who visited all the worksites and performed ergonomic evaluations of every VDT user's workstation and work habits. Gannett's insurer regularly visits industrial areas; they just never considered the office environment.

This process identified the high-risk users. Local management was instructed to make ergonomically correct, short-term solutions like swapping desks and using phone books as foot rests until proper equipment could be purchased. Gannet has spent considerable money on improvements— though less than they budgeted. They found, for instance that they didn't need to replace most of the chairs; many were adjustable. Teaching employees to adjust them properly was the solution.

Other solutions were equally inexpensive. Although Landauer is careful to point out that she's not an expert, she believes the simplest, least costly and most effective piece of equipment is a wrist rest. At less than $30 each "there's no company that can't afford them," she says.

Educational efforts also included written materials, such as guidelines for managers and a short video on CTD, proper posture and the importance of taking rest breaks and stretching.

Educating managers and employees seems to have worked. After the first 18 months of the program, Gannett has had "really dramatic and happily affirming results," says Ladauer. The cost per claim is now down to around $2,000—a quarter of what the average case cost less than two years ago.

Now, 20 percent of Gannett's cases have virtually no cost, they are caught early enough that a doctor's visit, some worskstation adjustments and exercises alleviate the problem—for a total cost of $200 to $300 according to Landauer. Although the number of claims has not diminished, Landauer believes they are heading into a declining curve.

Increased productivity has been another benefit of the program. The average time way from work for a CTD injury before the program was 8–12 weeks. Now, "only a handful are off the job for an extended period" she says, and "at least a third don't miss any work time."

Gannett has been fortunate. They did not have an employee completely disabled by CTD. This worst-case scenario would require a company to set aside a lifetime reserve of $2 or $3 million, estimates Landauer.

By the year 2000, OSHA and National Safety Council experts predict that 50 percent of all workers' compensation cases will be related to CTDs. Considered the health issue of the '90s CTDs won't go away. But the number of cases can be reduced and managed by employers who take these actions: determine whether they have ergonomic-related problems in their workplace; identify the nature and location of those problems; and implement measures to reduce and eliminate them.

1. See *NR News* Sept 1991, p A12

2. According to *The Wall Street Journal* (Feb 14, 1992) a California judge struck down the San Francisco law, saying such matter should be regulated by the state.

Part 11

WELLNESS

48.   The Most Successful Wellness
Programs Are Comprehensive and Integrated

John Erfurt   Don R. Powell   Andrea Foote   Max A. Heirich

Traditional wellness programs typically offer an uncoordinated array of services aimed at a variety of health risks, with no means of measuring their success. A new generation of wellness programs, however, combines the most successful wellness elements into one cost-effective whole. These innovative programs are comprehensive, fully integrated, and designed to be ongoing in their provision of services, and because they set measurable goals, their effectiveness may easily be determined.

Much is written about worksite wellness programs, but very little is said about how the structure and organization of a program can affect program outcomes. Indeed, many wellness program descriptions do not identify how the program will measure its effectiveness. Consequently, an analysis of these programs fails to describe the program configuration that leads to optimal success, or the measurements by which program success is evaluated.

The objective of this article is threefold: to detail the content of successful wellness programs based on available research data, to describe the way in which the components of the program interact to produce successful outcomes, and to review the outcome measures by which programs are evaluated. In doing so, we will discuss how program components are integrated to produce optimal success.

In carrying out this analysis, we will compare what we call "traditional" program models with more "innovative models. The traditional models, which comprise the overwhelming majority of wellness programs in America today,[1] lack comprehensiveness. Either they take only a single health problem, or their

Reprinted with permission from *Employee Assistance*, September, 1992.

component parts are segmented rather than put together in an integrated way. Innovative programs are comprehensive and fully integrated. They are long-term in their time frame and ongoing, with no expected end-point. Like employee assistance programs, these more innovative worksite wellness programs are continuous.

Many worksite wellness programs began with a concern about a particular health risk that needed attention. Employers offered smoking cessation or weight loss classes, for example, or installed a blood pressure monitoring machine that employees could use. Gradually policy makers and healthcare providers realized that individuals have a variety of health risks that need attention. Thus worksite wellness programs began to offer an array of services rather than focusing on a single health risk. A recent article suggested a number of program characteristics that need to be part of any comprehensive worksite wellness program.[2]

In the past several years, worksite wellness planners and evaluators have come to realize that presenting information that is relevant for health rarely is sufficient to motivate people to change pleasurable behaviors that put their health at risk, especially if that risk develops over a number of years before health deteriorates. Moreover, among people already motivated to attempt health improvements, relapse into more risky behaviors is common. Consequently, more innovative worksite wellness programs recognize that health improvement is a process that goes on over a considerable span of time, and that more information and inspiration at a single point in time is needed in order for worksite wellness programs to have long-term impact.

This article starts with the assumption that considerable agreement now exists about the various content areas for health improvement that should be available in comprehensive worksite wellness programs. It addresses the question of how to structure these services in order to meet the varied needs of individual employees, including how to assess those needs, how to engage employees in efforts at health improvement and how to motivate them to continue these efforts through time. It also deals with how to evaluate the effectiveness of a program and to improve it over time.

ASSESSING HEALTH RISKS

Many traditional programs rely on self-administered questionnaires to do a needs assessment of the target work force. This may be done by surveying employees' interests or through health risk appraisals (HRAs) which the employees complete. HRA results may then be used to produce a computerized summary of each employee's health risk profile.

Such an approach to needs assessment has two major disadvantages: self-administered questionnaires usually achieve low participation, and they rely on often inaccurate reports of physiological measures such as blood pressure and cholesterol. In addition, employees who smoke cigarettes are significantly less likely to complete a self-administered HRA than are non-smokers.[3]

The more innovative programs use trained professionals to obtain health risk information from the employees in the target work force during health risk screening. In the screening process, which takes approximately 20 minutes of the employee's time, screeners take multiple blood pressure readings, draw a fingerstick blood sample for a total cholesterol reading, obtain the employee's height and weight to determine the percentage over or under ideal weight and ask questions about the employee's former and current smoking status, current exercise levels, stress levels, and other relevant information.

After the screeners have obtained this information, they are able to make appropriate referrals for further evaluation and possible treatment for elevated blood pressure and/or blood cholesterol. These referrals are made in the employee's interest to various health improvement programs such as nutritional programs for cholesterol reduction or weight loss, smoking cessation, exercise and physical fitness, and stress management. Finally, the screeners encourage the employees to sign up for the health improvement programs in which they are interested.

The information recorded on the screening form can be used to produce a computerized HRA that can then be mailed to the employee. However, this is not crucial to the success of the programs. Studies have not been able to demonstrate that computerized HRAs make a significant difference in altering the health behavior of program clients and reducing their health risks.[4]

Health risk screening includes five waves of activities, which have been described elsewhere.[5] When all five waves of screening are carried out, the program can expect up to 95 percent participation among work forces in large worksites and 100 percent in medium and small worksites.[6]

HEALTH IMPROVEMENT INTERVENTIONS: PROVIDING OPTIONS

After attempting to assess employees' health risks, traditional programs generally rely on heath education classes, brochures, and newsletters to provide skills and information about health promotion. These are important program components, but they are not sufficient.

Without additional program options, class cancellation is a common event. If fewer than eight or ten employees show up to take, for example, a smoking cessation class, the class is often canceled. The few employees who have come may be urged to find additional smokers to participate and the class then has to be rescheduled. This situation can have deleterious effects both on the program clients and on the program itself. Smokers who have gotten themselves motivated to participate in a smoking cessation program only to have it canceled can be easily discouraged from the entire venture. Eventually, the program suffers because cancellations are interpreted by the work force as failures. We have had many companies who tried the traditional approach to wellness programming tell us that they "tried wellness, but it doesn't work."

In contrast, innovative, comprehensive programs provide a menu of options, so that all employees have opportunities to participate in health improvement ventures. These options include one-to-one guided, self-help intervention, and mini-group sessions (2 to 7 employees). Mini-groups are provided when not enough people are available to fill a class, so that scheduled classes are never canceled. In addition, many employees want to make health improvements, but do not want to participate in a group venture. They prefer to do it on their own. The innovative program enrolls them in a one-to-one guided self-help program provided by the on-site wellness counselor. More than 50 percent of the employees in our studies who began health improvement ventures chose the one-to-one guided self-help program provided by the on-site wellness counselor. More than 50 percent of the employees in our studies who began health improvement ventures chose the one-to-one option.[7] By offering the menu approach to health improvement programming, innovative programs can get five to seven times more participation than traditional programs.

ACHIEVING HIGH PARTICIPATION AND PREVENTING RELAPSE

Rather than relying on brochures and newsletters to reach out to employees after health risk screening has been carried out, the innovative program implements the most important component in the repertoire of wellness programming—outreach and follow-up counseling with all employees at risk, and sometimes with all of the employees at the worksite.[8]

Persistent but loving outreach is conducted with employees who have health risks, to assist them in finding treatment or health improvement interventions that will help reduce their health risks.[9] Once they are reached, 20-minute follow-up counseling episodes are conducted in order to

1. Monitor the employee's health risks and record any progress that the employee has made to reduce those risks,
2. Encourage the start-up of recommended treatment or health improvement programs,
3. Ensure long-range compliance with such treatment and completion of health improvement ventures,
4. Prevent relapse from newly acquired healthy lifestyle changes, and
5. Promote long-range health promotion and health risk reduction.

There are typically eight waves or modes of follow-up which have been described elsewhere.[10] When all eight waves are carried out, the program can expect to reach and follow more than 90 percent of its target employee population. Since program follow-up powers the success of the program and ensures the success of the other program components, reaching the majority of employees produces a truly effective program, reducing employees' health risks and ultimately preventing morbidity and premature mortality.

In order to attract worksite attention and program participation, traditional programs often rely on media promotion and one-shot health fairs. Health fairs are worksite-wide events that invite various wellness providers to come to the worksite, set up tables or booths, and display their wares or their services to the employees who participate in the event. There is nothing wrong with health fairs, *per se,* but by themselves they have little long-term impact.

On the other hand, when they are integrated with other services in innovative programs, health fairs can be useful as methods to help organize the workplace to support good health. Along with health fairs, the comprehensive wellness program organizes activities such as weight loss contests, walking contests, cigarette smoke-outs, etc. In addition, the program establishes "buddy systems" among employees to provide mutual support in their health promotion and risk reduction efforts.

Also, the innovative program works with the company to review health-related policies. They may consider such options as "well days" for employees who use few sick days, tuition assistance for wellness programming to discourage company-paid three-martini lunches, and so on. Cafeteria and vending machine personnel are consulted to ensure that health food choices are available through worksite food services. Smoking policies are reviewed, including designation of smoking and no-smoking areas and presence of cigarette vending machines.

The program utilizes a worksite wellness committee, comprised of key representative employees, including labor and management representatives and, where present, representatives from medical, ergonomics, employee assistance, health and safety, food services, and other relevant units. The program staff works with this committee to plan to carry out the various components of the program. This committee is very important in helping the program to produce changes in the corporate culture that lead to better health.

EVALUATING THE PROGRAM

A final difference between traditional and innovative programs relates to program evaluation. Traditional programs are seldom able to provide information about how effective they are in lowering health risks. Some proponents of traditional programs view program evaluations as "research," and argue that evaluation is too costly in addition to the services provided.

In contrast, innovative programs build program evaluation into the information systems, so that evaluation efforts are not separate from the provision of program services, but an essential part of those services. The most obvious example is the relationship between follow-up procedures and program evaluation. Because routine follow-up contacts are made with most or all of the employees at the workplace, the program requires an information system that assists in caseload management and that provides a method for recording changes in risk factors for the employees followed. When doing periodic program evaluation, the wellness counselors need only push a few buttons on their personal computer to summarize this information, and statistical reports can be produced summarizing these changes in health risk factors for the program as a whole.

Thus the program evaluation component is intrinsically interwoven into the service delivery parts of the program via a computerized information system. This also facilitates interrelating other components of the wellness program, rather than being unrelated and segmented as tends to be the case in traditional programs.

DIFFERENCES BETWEEN TRADITIONAL AND INNOVATIVE PROGRAMS

Traditional programs tend to segment their component services—fitness programs are done separately from blood pressure and cholesterol screening programs and often blood pressure screening is done at a different time than cholesterol screening. Smoking cessation courses are carried out apart from nutritional counseling sessions. Frequently, different program providers will offer these different services—a fitness company might set up and run a physical fitness center, a health promotion group might provide smoking cessation classes, and a local hospital might provide blood pressure or cholesterol screening.

In contrast, innovative programs try to avoid segmentation in the delivery of program services and in various content areas of wellness programming. While specific services such as smoking cessation interventions are offered, the interventions are designed to support and integrate with other interventions such as weight loss or stress management. Clients are treated in a holistic manner, dealing with the whole person's needs and risk reduction requirements.

The various components of an innovative program are linked together and interrelated. None of the activities of the innovative program is done in isolation from the other activities. All of the various activities are coordinated by the wellness counselor, who works with the worksite wellness committee.

Finally, the proof of the pudding is in the eating and the proof of the effectiveness of a wellness program is in the results—in the outcomes that such a program produces in the long-run. The two models produce strikingly different results.

Research has shown that traditional programs of the kind just described draw low participation, generally only 10 percent to 20 percent of the target employee population, and have little long-term impact on the reduction of health risks.[11]

Long-term health improvements are usually seen in only 3 percent to 5 percent of the workforce.[12] Cost-effectiveness is low—with costs averaging over $7 per employee per year for each additional 1 percent in health improvement.[13] In terms of cost-benefit these programs have been found to yield up to $3 returned for each dollar invested, due to decreases in health care claims.[14–18]

Innovative programs can be carried out in any work environment, in any size worksite, with all types of employees (blue collar, white collar, and pink collar), and for centralized or dispersed employee populations. Large corporations have adopted innovative programs, including some 82 UAW-Ford Motor Company locations, altogether composed of some 170,000 employees.[19] The smallest worksite with such a program may be Fred's Service Station in downtown Ann Arbor, Michigan with only four employees.[20] These worksites, both large and small, receive comprehensive wellness services and there is no appreciable difference in the quality of services nor in the results of the program activities.

At small worksites, a wellness professional comes periodically to provide all of the wellness services. The type of professional is rotated, so that the worksite has access to a variety of experts. sometimes a registered nurse comes, sometimes an exercise physiologist, sometimes a dietitian, sometimes a counselor. The services include screening, routine monitoring of the health risks of each employee (and sometimes the employee's spouse), guided self-help interventions to address each person's health risk, and consultation with the group about issues like regular exercise and getting health foods for lunch.

What makes the innovative and comprehensive program so effective and cost-effective? It screens employees for health risks using trained professionals, rather than relying on self-administered questionnaires. It offers a menu of options, rather than health education classes alone. It reaches out to employees, rather than dealing only with those who are already motivated to change. It organizes the worksite to support health promotion.

Because of its evaluation component, the innovative program is able to make constant improvements. The program can be done mostly on employees' own time, reducing concerns about lost productivity. The program is powered by persistent, loving inducement, but without coercion. While the program is entirely voluntary it is continually offered to each employee and participation is always encouraged. Employees who choose not to participate in the first year often decide to accept services in subsequent years. Because the innovative program is ongoing rather than short-term, it identifies new health risks as they are developed, helping employees to become risk free.

In conclusion, from the information in this article it is clear that we must be more innovative with our wellness programs.

The traditional programs that have predominated in the past are not effective nor cost-effective. These programs need to be replaced by a new generation of programs that are both comprehensive and integrated.

1.   JE Fielding and PV Piserchia, "Frequency of Worksite Health Promotion Activities." *American Journal of Public Health* 79:16-20;1989.

2.   DR Powell, "Five Characteristics of Successful Wellness Programs." *Employee Assistance* 4(6):36-38;Jan 1992.

3.   DS Nice, SI Woodruff, "Self-Selection in Responding to a Health Risk Appraisal: Are We Preaching to the Choir?" *American Journal of Health Promotion* 4(5):367-372;1990.

4.   A Foote, MA Heirich, "Health Risk Appraisals vs. Health Screening," *Employee Assistance* 3(6):22-26;Jan 1991.

5.   JC Erfurt, A Foote, MA Heirich, and W Gregg, "Improving Participation in Worksite Wellness Program Through Their EAP. *Employee Assistance* 2(6);41-44:Jan 1990.

6.   JC Erfurt, K Holtyn, "Health Promotion in Small Business: What Works and What Doesn't Work. *Journal of Occupational Medicine* 33(1):66-73;1991.

7.   JC Erfurt, A Foote, MA Heirich, and W Gregg. "Improving Participation in Worksite Wellness Programs: Comparing Health Education Classes. A Menu Approach and Follow-up Counseling. *American Journal of Health Promotion* 4(4):270-278;1990.

8.   Supra note 6.

9.   W Gregg, A Foote, JC Erfurt, and MA Heirich, "Worksite Follow-up and Engagement Strategies for Initiating Health Risk Behavior Changes." *Health Education Quarterly* 17(4):455-478;1990.

10.   Supra note 5.

11.   Supra note 7.

12.   JC Erfurt, A Foote, and MA Heirich, "Worksite Wellness Programs: Incremental Comparison of Screening and Referral Alone, Health Education, Follow-up Counseling and Plant Organization. *American Journal of Health Promotion* 5(6):438-448;1991.

13.   JC Erfurt, A Foote, and MA Heirich, "The Cost-Effectiveness of Worksite Wellness Programs for Hypertension Control, Weight Loss, Smoking Cessation and Exercise." *Personnel Psychology* 45(1); 1992.

14.   A Foote and JC Erfurt, "The Benefit to Cost Ratio of Worksite Blood Pressure Control Programs." *JAMA* 265(10):1283-1286;Mar 13, 1991.

15.   DW Bowne, ML Russell, JL Morgan, SA Optenberg, and AE Clarke, "Reduced Disability and Health Care Costs in an Industrial Fitness Program." *Journal of Occupational Medicine* 26:809-816;1984.

16.   RL Bertera, "The Effects of Workplace Health Promotion on Absenteeism and Employment Costs in a Large Industrial Population." *American Journal of Public Health* 80:1101-1105;1990.

17.   JO Gibbs, D Mulvaney, C Henes, and RW Reed, "Worksite Health Promotion: Five-Year Trend in Employee Health Care Costs." *Journal of Occupational Medicine* 27:826-830;1985.

18.   JL Bly, RC Jones, and JE Richardson, "Impact of Worksite Health Promotion on Health Care Costs and Utilization." *Journal of the American Medical Association* 256:3235-3240;1986.

19.   Supra note 5.

20.   Supra note 6.

49.   Benefits on a Shoestring: Wellness

Wellness programs don't have to be expensive to save money. This article provides step-by-step instructions for setting up an effective wellness program that doesn't require a large amount of time or money.

Companies that don't already have an employee wellness program shouldn't give up on the idea—wellness doesn't have to cost a fortune. We're going to show you how to design a low-cost program that can help your company achieve most of the benefits of a much more expensive plan—at a fraction of the expense.

It's important to understand what works and what doesn't. Nobody has ever proven, scientifically, that wellness programs pay off, but there's some evidence that they can make employees more aware of health issues, possibly reduce some high-risk behavior, and reduce absenteeism. They also appear to cut average claims slightly and boost productivity.

Health promotion probably has direct cost benefits in addition to the indirect cost-effectiveness benefits most often measured, according to Joseph Opatz, David Chenoweth, and Robert Kaman. Employee wellness programs are being studied by academics, and the Optaz team presented a fascinating paper to a 1990 symposium sponsored by the Association for Fitness in Business.

"Of the studies conducted to measure financial impact, most have focused on the cost-effectiveness (non-monetized) benefits of health promotion. These studies have *all* shown positive outcomes," wrote the authors. "Those few studies performed to date on the cost-benefits (monetizing both costs and benefits) of health promotion are strongly suggestive of a positive financial impact."

Employers have mostly focused on long-term, elusive goals: changing bad eating habits, educating people about high blood pressure, monitoring their cholesterol, etc., reasoning that risk reduction will eventually pay off. But most employers don't look at direct cost benefits: the paper by Opatz *et al* suggests that some easily measured numbers, such as days absent, may prove the benefit of health promotion (see Exhibit 1).

NOT EVERYTHING WORKS

If you're starting a wellness program on a shoestring, it makes sense to focus on components that are inexpensive and known to be effective.

A positive approach, possibly incentive-based, encouraging workers to develop good habits is far more cost-effective than a more negative drive aimed at eliminating bad habits. Pushing employees to make changes is a lot more work—and far less effective—than luring them into a positive program.

One reason for the lower cost-effectiveness is that "push" programs are less effective, in general, with human behavior; another is that these programs cost more, in the absolute and in terms of recidivism. It is generally better to substitute something positive rather than just stop something that is negative.

Smoking cessation and weight loss drives are two excellent examples of "push" programs that may not be effective. There's ample evidence that workplace smoking cessation programs don't pay (academics have proved that only a tiny fraction of a typical company's smokers actually quit through such programs). Weight loss programs are difficult to administer and, conceivably, could cause problems with the Americans with Disabilities Act.

On the other hand, some program components are almost undoubtedly effective. There is strong evidence from other fields (medicine and psychiatry) that exercise raises individual's productivity and self-esteem and reduces depression and susceptibility to illness.

Well-designed exercise programs are a good example of the positive incentive approach. They can do as much or more than weight loss drives to encourage employees to adopt healthful, long-term eating habits. They motivate some people to lose weight. They may also motivate others to give up smoking.

Encouraging employees to exercise is probably the single most effective step a wellness-minded employer can take. If you've been reading about gleaming corporate facilities and have given up on the idea because there's no money, take heart. There's a vast spectrum of successful employer exercise programs and they don't have to be expensive or elaborate.

Exhibit 1. Wellness may—or may not—pay off

Area studied	Short-term potential economic impact	Long-term potential economic impact	Benefit range per employee
Absenteeism	Moderate to strong	Inconclusive	One to two days fewer absences
Employee health behavior	Moderate	Inconclusive	Not quantified
Healthcare costs	Moderate	Inconclusive	Annual reductions of between $61–$851 per employee
Productivity	Moderate to strong	Inconclusive	From 4% to 25% increased productivity

MINIMUM WORK, MAXIMUM PAYOFFS

In addition to exercise, some of the most helpful components of elaborate corporate wellness programs are available at low or no cost to most employers.

Some of these take almost no time or money to administer and offer potentially huge (although hard to measure) paybacks—mostly in reducing future claims. All employers should consider implementing them, particularly when they relate to vital health issues.

A good example: high blood pressure education. The National Heart, Lung and Blood Institute offers an almost free, well-designed workplace program that you can administer yourself, with suggestions for tapping local health resources. High blood pressure increases the risk of strokes and heart disease, and if your small investment helps an individual prevent or detect a condition early, it's worth it.

Another example: maternity education. It's very inexpensive, and probably pays for itself many times over by reducing the incidence of small or unhealthy newborns.[1]

Screening for diabetes and colon cancer costs very little, especially when done in volume. Your local hospital can tell you how to accomplish this, *en masse;* if it sounds expensive, try another hospital. (For diabetes screening information, you can also call your local chapter of the American Diabetes Foundation.)

AS FORMAL, OR INFORMAL, AS YOU WANT TO MAKE IT

Exhibit 2 is a flow chart prepared by David Chenoweth, one of the authors of the paper we mentioned, that gives step-by-step instructions for starting a wellness program.

Exhibit 2. Worksite Health Promotion Planning Guide

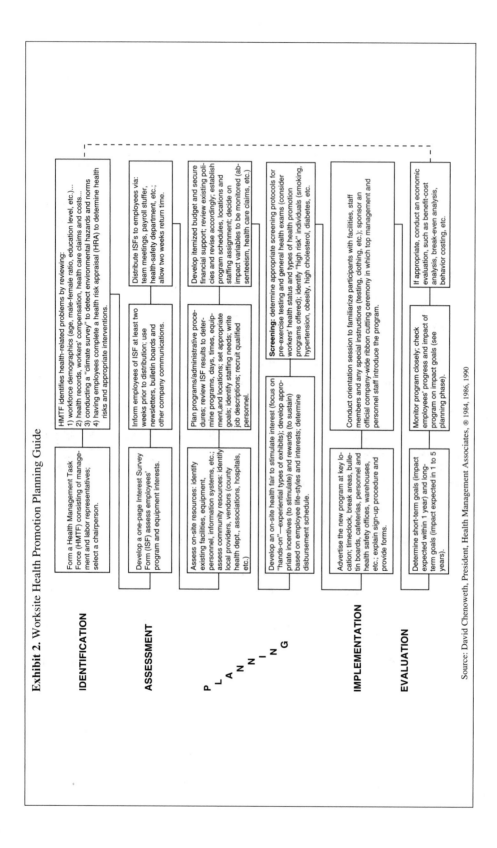

Source: David Chenoweth, President, Health Management Associates, ® 1984, 1986, 1990

If you want to be formal, start a task force. If you go this route, you should ask your CEO, human resources department, labor representative, medical staff, and communications department to participate or to name a representative, in addition to drafting some employees.

Even if you're doing a less formal program, or are all by yourself, it's a good idea to read the flow chart; a number of steps will be equally appropriate. We'll walk you through them.

Identification

If you've got a medical staff, the identification step is easier to perform and the formal steps on the chart will be easy to accomplish. Your medics can examine demographics and health records and conduct a health risk appraisal.

If you don't have a medical staff, look at workers' compensation claims and claims data—do you have a lot of stress-related claims? or lower-back claims? This is useful, if you're going to get outside help, to pinpoint what kind of a expertise you need to hire. Or there may be a local non-profit organization, such as a hospital or public health school, that can help conduct health risk appraisals.

You can analyze the demographics of your workforce yourself to get some guidance. If your workforce is mature, you may want to concentrate on general health maintenance through nutrition and mild exercise classes. If you've got a lot of young workers, disease prevention, maternity education, and life-style classes maybe appropriate. If you've got stressed employees, maybe you should think about ways to help them reduce stress or boost their mental health.[2]

Be sensitive to the fact that people aren't perfect, and for a variety of reasons. For example, some workers may eat poorly because of lack of education, others because they're going through problems. Some employees may not exercise because of lack of opportunity, others because of lack of interest.

Assessment and Planning

The chart discusses employee interest survey forms. If you have medical staff or are working with a hospital, surveying is easy to accomplish. Similar assessment may also be performed by local health associations, mental health associations, etc.

If you're working on a less formal basis, skip that step and go directly to assessing your resources. You have more of these than you think. Our resource list identifies several excellent sources of low- or no-cost programs, education, and services. As the chart says, vendors can include your county health department, association, hospitals, etc.

Practical Notes

Once you know what you want to do (and perhaps more important, how much you can do on your budget), decide when and where to do it. Depending on how formal your program is, you may want some kind of enrollment—it's good to keep this simple. Think about what reasonable goals are attainable: higher productivity, increased morale, less stressed employees, and anything else that you can afford.

Specific and obtainable goals aimed at worker behavior are easier to measure and keep track of than vague, ambitious targets concerning employee health. When your goal is "to increase the general health of the employees of this company" it's harder to achieve than "to get 25 percent of our employees earning a $10 bonus each month for walking at least three times a week."

It's also a good idea to design your program so people can enroll at any time. Make it as easy as possible for non-motivated individuals to participate: you don't want them to "miss" the enrollment deadline and wait another three months to get in.

Get department managers involved; if they're enthusiastic, scheduling is less problematic. Employees need to know that management is supportive of the program. Supervisory and managerial participation provides good role models for employees, and it shows a total organizational commitment to the success of your program.

Implementation

The first step is announcing the new program. It's best to have your CEO make the initial announcement, which provides corporate endorsement and keeps top management supportive. This communication should launch the program and inform workers that details will follow.

Then, start communicating the new program to employees. In addition to the ideas mentioned on the chart, you can use electronic mail, public address announcements, manager meetings, and the newsletters.

Here's where it pays off having the support of the communications department, which may be able to accomplish much of your promotion for you. Communications staffers may be able to help you with posters, fliers, etc. You, in turn, should offer to do a regular column about the program for the company newsletter (make it clear that the sponsors don't have to run it).

Evaluation

If your program is formal and involves medical staff, your advisors can suggest the best way to monitor its health effects.

At whatever level, you can look at claims levels and absenteeism before and after; the less specific your measurements, the less likely you are to measure a difference. If possible, collect data, before and after, about groups that participate in the program.

Be sure to measure worker input and output. You may be able to gauge more positive feelings about your employer, collect anecdotal evidence ("I feel more energetic"), or find out that employees feel less stressed.

Employee feedback can also help you fine-tune the program: be sure to ask workers about accessibility, location, time, etc. Find out why workers are participating—and, possibly more important, why they're not.

LOW EXPECTATIONS, BIGGER PAYOFF

It's ironic, but true: the less you expect out of wellness programs, the happier your company will probably be.

When you expect more, the pressure rises for definite, quantitative paybacks. But measuring the impact of health promotion is difficult even for academic researchers and may be impossible for the lone benefits manager.

That's a good argument for trying a variety of low-key, inexpensive approaches. Some of them are bound to help some workers, and you won't have staked a huge investment of time and money in something you can't prove is justified.

Our ideas for low-investment wellness can provide a program with many of the benefits, but far fewer potential corporate and departmental problems, than many huge programs. And, in this economic environment, low-investment wellness is much easier to sell to management than its higher priced counterpart.

RESOURCE LIST

American Cancer Society, 1599 Clifton Rd., NE, Atlanta, GA 30329, (404) 329-7984. Can refer you to local units, which sponsor worksite cancer education and screening. The national office also has information about multi-state programs.

American Diabetes Association, 1660 Duke St., Alexandria, VA 22313-3447, (703) 549-1500. Has information about workplace diabetes screening programs.

American Heart Association, 7320 Greenville Ave., Dallas, TX 75231, (214) 706-1363. Local chapters can conduct worksite cardiovascular health programs; the national office has information about national programs.

American Red Cross, 430 17th St. NW, Washington, DC 20006, (202) 737-8300. Has excellent worksite AIDS education program; local chapters may offer worksite efforts.

Association of Fitness in Business, 310, North Alabama, Indianapolis, IN 46204, (317) 636-6621. This group consists of a variety of interdisciplinary professionals. Its *Guidelines for Employee Wellness Programs* costs $25, prepaid.

March of Dimes Birth Defects Foundation, 1275 Mamaroneck Ave., White Plains, NY 10605, (914) 997-4466. Local chapters conduct *Babies and You*, the most common workplace maternity education program (see our May 1990 issue, p. 24). The national office has information about multi-state programs.

National Health Information Center, P.O. Box 1133, Washington, DC 20013-1133, (800) 336-4797. Will send "Healthy People 2000 Resources Lists," which are great guides to finding more information.

National Heart, Lung, and Blood Institute, Education Programs Information Center, 7200 Wisconsin Av., Bethesda, MD 20814, (301) 951-3260. The institute's workplace initiative offers materials and limited consultation in establishing cardiopulmonary disease risk reduction programs and high blood pressure programs. Will send a single copy of the "NHLBI Kit," which is a terrific set of fact sheets, brochures, posters, and materials.

National Institute of Mental Health; Depression Awareness, Recognition and Treatment Program (D/ART) National Worksite Program, 5600 Fishers Lane, Room 10-4140. A variety of educational materials that will help employers reduce the personal and economic costs of depression by enhancing awareness.

National Resource Center on Worksite Health Promotion, Washington Business Group on Health, 777 North Capitol St. NE, Washington, DC 20002. Sells a variety of reasonably priced titles, all directed towards employers, about depression, disability management, community-based health promotion maternal health, and more. Examples: *Directory of Worksite Health Promotion Resources* ($5.00, prepaid) and *Directory of State Health Promotion Resource for Employers* ($15.00 prepaid).

President's Council on Physical Fitness and Sports, 450 5th St., NW, Washington, DC 20001. Will send *Fitness in the Workplace: A Corporate Challenge and Building a Healthier Company,* both free.

Wellness Councils of America, 1823 Harney St., Suite 201, Omaha, NE 68102, (402) 444-1711. This organization provides direction and support services to community-based wellness councils. Publications include *Healthy, Wealthy, and Wise: A Practical Guide for Health Promotion Managers* ($25, prepaid) and *Healthy People at the Worksite 2000* ($5, prepaid).

1. For a complete discussion of how cost-effective maternal education is, see *Benefits,* Aug 1990: 24.

2. See *Benefits,* Aug 1990: 7.

50. Retiree Health Cutbacks: Responding to Lessons Learned From Recent Court Developments

Judy Bauserman   Anna M. Rappaport

As employers attempted to control retiree health care costs by cutting back on benefits and insisting that retirees share the cost burden, they were confronted by lawsuits. Employers have recently learned from these lawsuits that they must explicitly describe their rights to amend or terminate retiree health benefits. Even so, these so-called termination clauses are fraught with ambiguity, leaving employers at risk for providing lifetime benefits.

Employer-initiated cutbacks in employer-provider health benefits for retirees, either by increasing retiree premium contributions or reducing coverage, have been the subject of frequent misunderstanding and litigation. In reaction to a cutback, retirees often claim that their employer promised "lifetime" health coverage, while the employer will typically insist that it had reserved the right to change the plan. As more employers are considering cutbacks to control their retiree health costs and limit their FAS 106 liabilities, the issue has become much more important. For many of these employers, benefits for existing retirees represent such a large share of total liabilities that changing benefits only for future retirees is inadequate to solve their cost problems.

A general background on the employer environment and the legal approach courts use in determining whether an employer may cut back its retiree health plan for current retirees is necessary in order to offer a positive approach to dealing with communication for retiree health plans. Using such an approach should assist an employer both in *creating* and *maintaining* a positive

Reprinted from *Compensation & Benefits Management,* Vol. 9, No. 2, Summer 1993. A Panel Publication, Aspen Publishers, Inc.

relationship with its retirees, which, in turn, will enhance the employer's flexibility.

HISTORICAL PERSPECTIVE

In the 1960s and 1970s, employers frequently offered retiree health benefits as part of an effort to facilitate retirement, and to attract and retrain employees. At the time, medical costs, in general, were a much smaller budget item than they are today, and Medicare paid a significant proportion of retirees' medical costs. Employers often simply continued to cover retirees under the active employee health plan. Little thought was given to the future expenses associated with these retiree health benefits, and employers assumed they would be free to modify the benefits at any time. The economy was growing, the standard of living was rising, and the expectation was that the total funds available for benefits would continue to increase.

During the 1980s, these conditions began to change. Health care costs increased dramatically. Congress reduced Medicare benefits. Some industries, notably the U.S. steel and auto industries, lost business to overseas competition, and employers in those industries were forced to reduce the size of their workforces. Early retirement windows became a common tool used to implement downsizing programs. The issues raised in auto and steel companies were, to a lesser extent, found in other industries as downsizing and restructuring became more commonplace. As the number of active employees decreased, the ratio of retirees to active employees increased. Nevertheless, the shrinking revenues generated by this smaller pool of active employees were needed to support the costs associated with a growing pool of retirees. These factors caused the cost of retiree health benefits to consume an ever-growing proportion of corporate revenue.

As employers attempted to control retiree health costs by cutting back on benefits and insisting that retirees share the burden of their rising costs, they were confronted by challenges. Retirees claimed, often successfully, that their employers had legally promised to provide lifetime health coverage and thus were prohibited from main cutbacks. Also, the publicity that surrounded the cutbacks, regardless of the existence or the outcome of the lawsuits, was damaging to the employers' reputations. Unfortunately, there was much less clarity in the legal requirements that apply to retiree health benefits than in the requirements that apply to pension benefits. The legal framework was based on a combination of contract law, ERISA, and collective bargaining law, as patched together by the courts. However, different courts viewed what appeared to be similar situations differently. For example, some courts have followed documents literally, whereas others have relied more on verbal statements and other information.

Exhibit 1. Commonly Used Communication Vehicles

Types of Communications	Normal Retirements	Early Retirement Windows
Plan Document	X	X
Summary Plan Description	X	X
Benefit Handbooks	X	X
Computer Modeling	X	X
Group Retirement Counseling Sessions	X	X
Individual Retirement Counseling Sessions	X	X
Descriptions of Early Retirement Windows		X
ADEA Waivers		X
Collective Bargaining Agreements	X	X

More recently, employers have learned from these lawsuits that they must explicitly describe their rights to amend and/or terminate retiree health benefits in the plan documents, Summary Plan Descriptions (SPDs), and collective bargaining agreements that govern the benefits. However, many of these amendment/termination clauses are fraught with ambiguity that leaves employers at risk for providing lifetime benefits.

THE COURTS' PERSPECTIVE

Non-Collectively-Bargained Plans

In attempting to resolve disputes under EIRSA over the precise parameters of an employer's promise for retiree health benefits in a non-collectively-bargained situation, courts first analyze the terms of the plan document and SPD, if such documents exist,[1] to define the promise. If a plan document and SPD do not exist or are unclear, the courts look to informal communications to define the promise. Informal communications may include booklets or brochures summarizing a company's benefit programs; individual benefit statements or election forms for a particular plan; interactive computer modelling that projects an employee's financial needs at retirement; employment contracts; or oral statements, especially in connection with an exit interview, of managers and supervisors, human resource personnel, or plan administrators and trustees. Exhibit 1 summarizes the types of communication vehicles commonly found in normal retirement situation and early retirement windows.

If the plan document and SPD do exist, the courts will focus on whether they clearly and consistently reserve to the employer the right to unilaterally amend or terminate the plan. If they do, then courts will generally disregard any inconsistent informal communications that imply lifetime benefits and thereby will find in favor of the employer.[2]

In general, a court will find that a plan document and SPD are not clear and consistent either because they ambiguously address the employer's amendment/termination rights or because their provisions contradict one another. Ambiguity can arise in several contexts—e.g., when the relationships among separate plan provisions are unclear, when a provision is simply subject to different interpretations, or when an employer intentionally makes plan provisions vague or discretionary. Contradictions in retiree health cases commonly result from the omission of the employer's right to amend or terminate the plan from the SPD, or the language of the amendment/termination clause is susceptible to different interpretations.

If the plan document and SPD are not clear and consistent with each other with regard to the employer's amendment/termination rights, the employer can lose control of its promise—a court will likely give informal and often inconsistent communications greater importance in determining whether the unintended lifetime promise has been made.[3]

However, even when the plan document and the SPD appear to clearly and consistently reserve the employer's right to amend the plan, if a court finds that a retiree received and reasonably relied to his detriment on other communications that indicated that the retiree health benefits would be permanent, the court may work to develop an alternative theory to prevent the employer from cutting back the benefits. For example, a court might work extra hard to find that the plan and SPD are not as clear and consistent as one might have believed. Alternatively, a court might conclude that, under a communication independent of the plan document and the SPD, the employer had created a separate retiree health plan for the affected retirees and, in so doing, had not reserved the right to amend the separate plan.

An example of the *separate plan* theory can be seen in current litigation involving General Motors Corp. (GM). In 1988, General Motors imposed health benefit co-payments and deductibles on its nonunion retirees. GM's action provoked the 84,000 retirees to sue GM on that claim that GM had promised them free lifetime health benefits. In 1991, the district court dismissed the claims of over half of the retirees because the plan document and SPDs clearly reserved GM's right to modify the plan. However, 40,000 early retirees were allowed to pursue their claim that the individual early retirement agreements that they signed contractually bound GM to continue free lifetime benefits. These agreements, in which the employees waived certain legal rights, including the right to sue for age discrimination, in exchange for GM's promise to provide certain benefits,[4] were signed in conjunction with a series of early retirement window incentives. A full trial on the precise terms of the individual agreements is scheduled to begin this year.

Thus, although the plan document and SPD governing GM's retiree health plan clearly allowed GM to unilaterally change the plan, GM may have created 40,000 individual benefit plans in the process of encouraging some of this employees to retire early. It is unlikely that the early retirement agreements themselves contained any mention of GM's rights to amend or terminate the retiree health benefits.

Collectively Bargained Plans

Retirees are not considered employees under labor law. Consequently, an employer is not obligated to bargain with a union regarding the health benefits of current retirees. However, if an employer has agreed to provide health benefits to current retirees through negotiations with a union, then it must abide by the collective bargaining agreement it has signed. Any subsequent negotiations a union conducts on behalf of current retirees are not binding on the retirees; the retirees, either separately or as a class, can sue the employer to enforce the terms of the original agreement.

When an employer is challenged under ERISA for cutting back a collectively bargained retiree health plan, whether the employer will be liable for permanent retiree health benefits will turn on whether the plan, SPD, and collective bargaining agreement clearly and consistently reflect that the employer has the right to amend or terminate the plan. However, retirees who were promised health benefits under a collective bargaining agreement may also sue an employer that attempts to modify those benefits under the Labor Management Relations Act (LMRA) for violation of the collective bargaining agreement.

Although a complete analysis of how retiree health promises are interpreted under the LMRA is not discussed here, courts apply principles similar to those employed under ERISA—they look to the terms of the collective bargaining agreement to asses whether the employer reserved the right to amend or terminate the plan, and look to informal communications to resolve ambiguities in the agreement. However, unlike ERISA cases in which silence on the employer's amendment/termination rights within the plan document and SPD is usually treated as ambiguity, to be resolved by looking to informal communications under the LMRAS, courts may use other theories to determine the extent of an employer's retiree health promise.

Whether an employer's commitment in a collective bargaining agreement to provide retiree health benefits extends beyond the expiration of the agreement is a major issue. In these cases, some courts apply the labor law principle that presumes that the terms of a collective bargaining agreement (and thus the requirement to pay retiree health benefits) expire at the end of the contract unless the agreement *explicitly* provides otherwise. This reasoning was recently used to permit United Dominion Industries to cancel its retiree health plan. In a series of collective bargaining agreements adopted from 1975 through 1984, United Dominion agreed to provide health coverage to its retiree. Specifically, the agreements provided that "the Company will continue for retired employees, the [health plan]." An SPD prepared by the company in 1985 and a collective bargaining agreement adopted in 1986 specified that the terms of the bargaining agreement expired at the end of the current bargaining agreement term. In 1988 when the contract expired, United Dominion ceased to provide retiree health benefits.

The district court in the United Dominion case initially found that the language "will continue" was ambiguous. Whether the parties intended that the benefits would continue for the lifetime of retirees who retired under the terms of the contract or only for the duration of the contract was unclear, and informal communications demonstrated that the company had intended to promise lifetime health benefits to its retirees. As a result, the district court ordered the company to reinstate the health plan.

On appeal, a three-member panel of the Seventh Circuit ruled that the language was not ambiguous. According to earlier decisions in the Seventh Circuit, the terms of a collective bargaining agreement generally do not survive beyond the duration of the agreement. The court thus said that it takes more than a statement that welfare benefits "will continue" to create an ambiguity about whether the benefits would continue: "for the logical interpretation under our rule is that benefits 'will continue' for the duration of the contract." As a result, the Seventh Circuit upheld United Dominion's right to terminate the retiree health benefits.[5] However, a year later a full panel of the Seventh Circuit ruled in a similar case that the collective bargaining agreement need not *explicitly* state that the retiree health benefits are to be provided beyond the term of the collective bargaining agreement in order for a lifetime promise to exist.[6] It ruled that the agreement only needed to create the possibility of lifetime benefits. According to this decision, once ambiguity is present, the court is free to review extrinsic evidence to clarify the employer's intended promise.

Other courts, primarily those in the Sixth Circuit, apply a competing principle to resolve whether, absent an explicit provision in the agreement, a collective bargaining agreement binds an employer to provide retiree health benefits just for the term of the contract or for the life of the retiree. Under this principle, an inference exists that retiree health benefits are status benefits that will continue as long as the retiree remains in the retired status.[7] This principle was developed in the early 1980s and has been rejected by most circuits, but has not been completely repudiated by the Sixth Circuit.

MANAGING COMMUNICATION

As we have seen, the precise wording of the plan document and SPD (and, in some instances, the collective bargaining agreement) is of crucial importance to an employer that wants to manage the communication of its retiree health promise in order to avoid a lifetime commitment to provide benefits. An employer that wants to properly manage its communication process will first acted to assure that the amendment/termination rights set forth in these documents are clear and consistent, and will then act to assure that informal communications consistently communicate this right to employees. An employer that manages its retiree health communication process in accordance with these guidelines will, in addition to improving its chances of success in the event it is sued, avoid creating the type of false expectations among its employees that leads to lawsuits.

THE PLAN

ERISA requires that an employer have a written plan document. An employer may be prohibited from amending or terminating the plan unless it defines its right to do so, and the procedures for doing so, in the plan document and SPD.

Although it may seem obvious that a plan document should exist for each plan, some plan sponsors overlook this requirement. An employer may simply continue to cover its retired employees under the health plan that it maintains for its active employees. A general amendment/termination clause in such a document may not address whether changes can be made to the benefits of the retirees only.

For example, Moco Thermal Industries recently tried to terminate the health benefits of its retirees. The retirees were covered under the same Blue Cross/Blue Shield contract that covered its active employees. The Sixth Circuit upheld the lower court's decision that the termination clause authorized terminating the benefits of the "group" as a whole, but not for a portion of the group only. Moco was ordered to continue to provide health benefits to its retirees while the lower court reviewed informal communications to determine whether a lifetime promise had been made.[8]

An employer that has a retiree health plan document may be no better off than an employer with no plan document, if the document does not currently contain a provision that reserves the employers' right to amend or terminate the plan, or does so only ambiguously. An employer with a plan document that is silent regarding amendment/termination rights should consider adding the rights to the plan now. Adding such language to the plan will make it clear that the employer has the right to make changes to the benefits of future retirees. Whether adding such language will enable an employer to make changes to the benefits of individuals who had already retired at the time of the amendment is an open legal issue.

It is likely that courts would interpret a plan's silence regarding an employers' amendment/termination rights as an ambiguity to be resolved by looking at the informal communications and the employer's past practice. Thus, the court would review whether the employer ever told the retirees that their benefits were subject to change, and whether the employer had, in fact, changed benefits in the past. (However, as discussed above, in a union context, a court may decide that an employer has the right to change the plan at the end of the term of the collective bargaining agreement.) Alternatively, a court may conclude that silence on the issue prevents the employer from ever making changes to the plan.

Litigation involving Campbell Soup's retiree health cutbacks may give the courts an opportunity to address this difficult issue. Effective January 1992, Campbell Soup changed the Medicare coordination procedures under its retiree health plan so that reimbursements to retirees are reduced. The cutback affects 8,600 former employees, including 4,900 former union employees, who retired with 10 or more years served. The United Food and Commercial Workers Union (UFCW) has protested the change, and class action suits are currently pending in three separate federal district courts.

Campbell has asked the court to declare that it has the unilateral right to change its retiree health plan under ERISA and the LMRA. Campbell asserts that none of the relevant collective bargaining agreements, plan documents, or SPDs ever promised lifetime benefits at any particular level. However, a provision detailing Campbell's amendment/termination rights was not added to the documents until 1992, concurrent with the benefit cutback.

The unions charge that the plan modification is a breach of the collective bargaining agreements under which the former employees retired and of the SPDs. According to the union complaint, none of the bargaining agreements, plan documents, or SPDs explicitly reserved Campbell's right to amend or terminate the plan and, therefore, Campbell should be precluded from making these changes.

THE SPD

Once an employer has defined its intended retiree health promise in the plan document, ERISA requires that to be communicated to the participants in an SPD that reflects the plan document.

As noted above, ERISA treats the SPD as a formal representation of the employer's promise, so that the conflicts between the plan and SPD will be resolved in the participant's favor. Thus, an employer must be certain that it clearly and consistently expresses the intended promise in the SPD, including the fact that the plan can be changed or terminated at any time.

If the SPD does not now contain an amendment/termination clause but the plan document does, the language should be added to the SPD as soon as possible. At least one court says that the absence of an amendment/termination clause in an SPD does not negate such a clause in the formal plan document as long as it is added to the SPD before any changes are adopted.

Security Trust Life Insurance Company established a retiree health plan in 1978. The plan document clearly reserved the employer's right to amend or terminate the plan. The first SPDs were distributed in 1980, but they did not mention the employer's amendment/termination rights. In 1984, revised SPDs were distributed that clearly described the employer's amendment/termination rights. In 1988, Security Trust amended the plan to require retirees to begin contributing to the plan in 1989.

The retirees argued that, because the 1980 SPD did not inform them that the plan was subject to change, they had vested rights to employer-paid lifetime benefits. Because courts have consistently held that the terms of the SPD govern when a plan and SPD conflict, and the SPD is more favorable to participants, the retirees argued that the lack of amendment/termination language in the SPD was an affirmation that the benefits were intended to be permanent. They argued that the permanency implied by the SPD conflicted with the plan document and that the SPD should control. The district court agreed with the retirees and ordered Security Trust to pay for the retirees' benefits. Security Trust appealed.

On appeal, the Fourth Circuit ruled that, although the first SPD did not discuss the employer's amendment/termination rights, the plan document had always contained the provisions. And since the language was added to the SPD well before the employer made any changes to the plan, the court felt that participants were adequately notified that the employer might change the plan. Accordingly, the court rejected the retirees' argument that their benefits had become vested under the terms of the 1980 SPD. It thus reversed the district court ruling and held that Security Trust was free to implement the changes to its retiree health plan.[9]

The court does not discuss how much advance notice to participants of the potential for change is necessary, and the ruling implies that significant lead time is not required. As a practical mater, however, the longer a retiree has been on notice that his benefits could be changed, the less sympathetic he will appear to a court and the more likely it becomes that the court will rule in the employer's favor.

A common danger for a retiree health plan sponsor is that, in attempting to minimize the negative implications of an amendment/termination case described in an SPD, an employer will create ambiguities in the SPD. For example, American Can Company said the following in its retiree health SPD:

> The Company expects to continue this Plan indefinitely, but necessarily reserves the right to amend, modify, or discontinue the Plan in the future in conformity with applicable legislation.

When the company's successor tried to increase retiree contributions to the plan, the retirees argued that changes could be made only if required by legislation. The court is now reviewing informal communications and the past practice of American Can to determine if it promised lifetime health benefits to its retirees.[10]

The risk of a court determining that the SPD is ambiguous is particularly great when a retiree has reasonably and detrimentally relied on informal communications that imply the plan is permanent, thereby presenting the court with a sympathetic plaintiff.

INFORMAL COMMUNICATIONS

After confirming the plan documents and SPDs clearly and consistently describe the employer's rights to amend or terminate the plan, an employer must tackle the more difficult task of managing all other forms of benefit communications. As noted earlier, the effort is crucial because fewer misleading and incorrect informal communications means that there will be fewer false expectations and fewer sympathetic plaintiffs. And without sympathetic plaintiffs, courts are less likely to work to find conflicts and ambiguities in plan documents and SPDs and thus to find that informal communications have created lifetime commitments to provide benefits.

Of course, informal communications, such as newsletters and individual benefits statements, are created with much more frequency than are plan documents and SPDs. And oral responses to participant inquiries may occur daily. There is a significant risk of misleading statements and errors in these informal communications. Employers often use these informal communications to emphasize their benefit promises in an attempt to enhance employee appreciation; constant reminders that the plan may be changed, or even canceled, are not consistent with this objective.

Thus, a key to ensuring accuracy in informal communications is to clearly identify those individuals who have the authority to communicate the terms of the plan. The identity and role of these individuals should be communicated not only to the individuals themselves, but also to all plan participants and beneficiaries. Participants and beneficiaries should also be provided with examples of who is not authorized to communicate the plan.

In addition, these responsible individuals must be educated regarding their responsibilities and the terms of the benefit plans. In particular, they must be cautioned to avoid describing the retiree health benefits as *permanent* or *lifetime*. Even saying to an employe on the verge of retirement that his health benefits will continue after his retirement can create an inference that they will continue indefinitely.

Particular problems can arise when companies conduct retirement counseling. Counseling sessions are often used to acquaint employees near retirement with the full array of benefits that they will receive after retirement. This means that the employees' *permanent* pension benefits will be discussed in conjunction with the retiree health benefits that are subject to *change at any time*. It is crucial that the difference in the permanency of these two types of benefits be explained.

Miscommunications can be minimized by *formalizing* informal communications. An employer can create form letters for many of the common pre- and post-retirement inquiries. Similarly, the employer can develop scripts for retirement counseling sessions to help ensure that a consistent message is communicated. Larger employers may want to consider the use of modern technology, such as video presentations and voice response phone systems, to standardize many informal communications. Legal advisers can review these informal communications in advance and eliminate any dialogue that implies an unintended permanency to the retiree health benefits.

Employers should be especially cautious of making unintended promises if the promise is being used to induce the employee to take some action, such as retire early. When an early retirement incentive program is implemented, oral and written communications that would be considered *informal* with respect to a retiree health plan may be treated as formal plan documents or SPDs, if they are seen as creating a separate plan with respect to a retiring individual. Employers should take care to cross-reference all mentions of retiree health benefits to the larger retiree health plan, and should explicitly say that any changes made to the larger plan will apply to the early retiree. In particular, in the early retirement agreement, the employer should clearly reserve the right to amend or terminate the health benefits.

COLLECTIVE BARGAINING NEGOTIATIONS

Many lawsuits have arisen over whether a collectively bargained retiree health promise was intended to last for the lifetimes of current retirees, or only the life of the bargaining agreement. An employer can avoid this conflict with regard to future retirees by explicitly resolving the issue through collective bargaining in future negotiations. It can make sure that the collective bargaining agreements, plan documents, and SPDs clearly state what rights the employer has to unilaterally modify benefits, and whether the duration of the benefit promise extends beyond the term of the collective bargaining agreement.

Unions typically have little incentive to negotiate cutbacks in the health benefits of individuals who have already retired, particularly if a company has already contracted to provide lifetime benefits. In some instances, a union may agree to negotiate over the level of benefits, but it is unlikely that any union would agree to limit the duration of the benefits. The United Auto Workers (UAW) has recently shown some willingness to negotiate cutbacks in the retiree health benefits, but only because the employer was in obvious financial distress and forced the issue though the courts.

Farley Inc., an auto parts maker operating under Chapter 11 bankruptcy, and Navistar International (formerly International Harvester), on the verge of bankruptcy, took a novel approach to determining whether they could legally cut back their retiree health benefits. Each asked a federal district court to review the plan documents, SPDs, and collective bargaining agreements to affirm their ability to modify their retiree health plans. However, the courts never had to rule on the issue; the UAW represented the retirees whose benefits were at stake in each case and agreed to settlement negotiations. The UAW said that it agreed to negotiate with Navistar only because it was clear that failure to modify retiree health benefits would drive the company into bankruptcy. It seems unlikely that any union would engage in similar negotiations with a financially healthy company.

CONCLUSION

Past litigation has made it clear that an employer that wants to protect its ability to make future changes to its retiree health plan must clearly reserve its right to do so in the plan document and SPD. However, many employers that have existing retiree health plans do not have the benefit of hindsight to clarify rights defined years ago. But going forward, employers should take care in their formal documents and their informal communications not to make unintended promises. An employer attempting to clarify the bounds of its past retiree health promises and maximize its flexibility with regard to future changes may find the checklist shown in Exhibit 1 a useful tool for identifying the sources of its promise.

Other employers may take action similar to Farley, Inc. and Navistar and ask a court to clarify their rights, but an employer that does not want to resort to court proceedings to clarify the extent of its ability to modify the health benefits of existing retirees should at least take steps to review and clarify its plan documents and SPDs now. Those responsible for communicating the benefits to retirees should be cautioned not to imply that the benefits are permanent and, in fact, to be clear about the employer's right to change them. These actions will make it less likely that future changes come as a surprise to retirees so they will be less inclined to protest the change. Some employers will also choose to soften the impact of changes by treating retirees in different groups differently, so that retirees before a certain date are treated as grandfathered, and those after are subject to change.

1. A promise of employee benefits can be a plan subject to ERISA even if the sponsor has not complied with ERISA requirement that each plan be put in writing.

2. See, e.g., Moore v Metropolitan Life Ins Co, 856 F 2d 488, 9 EBC 2685 (2d Cir 188); Musto v American General Corp, 10 EBC 1441 (6th Cir 1988), *cert den* 10 EBC 2328 (1989); and Alday v Container Corp of America, 906 F 2d 660, 12 EBC2211 (11th Cir 1990), *cert den* 111 S Ct 675, EBC 1384 (1991).

3. See, e.g., Eardman v Bethlehem Steel Corp Welfare Benefit Plans, 607 F Supp. 196, 5 EBC 1985 (WD NY 1984), *appeal dismissed,* 755 F 2d 913 (2d Cir 1985); and Alexander v Primerica Holding, Inc, 15 EBC 1881 (3d Cir 1992).

4. Sprague v General Motors Corp, 13 EBC 2678 (ED Mich 1991).

5. See Senn v United Dominion Industries, 14 EBC 2238 (7th Cir 1992), *petition for rehearing den,* 15 EBC 1415 (7th Cir 1992) *cert den,* 509 US (1993).

6. Bidlack v Wheelabrator Corporation, 16 EBC 2217 (7th Cir 1993).

7. UAW v Yard-Man, Inc, 716 F 2d 1476, 4 EBC 2108 (6th Cir 1983), *cert den* 465 US 1007 (1984).

8. Gill v Konczalski & Moco Thermal Industries, Inc, 1991 US App LEXIS 29792 (6th Cir 1991). Opinion marked not for full text publication under Sixth Cir Rule 24.

9. Pierce v Security Trust Life Ins Co, 15 EBC 1873 (4th Cir 1992).

10. Alexander v Primerica Holdings, Inc, 15 EBC 1881 (3d Cir 1992).

Part 12

INSURANCE ISSUES

51. Marketers' Guide to Managed Care Networks

Louis Bodian

Employers or their consultants must compare different managed care networks and products in order to make decisions about health benefit purchases. Understanding the features of managed care and knowing which questions to ask network providers are the keys to identifying the best products, as well as the basis for effective communication of managed care plans to employees.

How well do managed care networks perform in reducing health care costs? By comparing the networks offered by various carriers, health care marketers can evaluate different products and make appropriate recommendations.

Based on the results of these comparisons, a solid communications effort must be conducted so that prospective members (employees and their families) can be advised of the quality of the physicians within the network. This will enable employees faced with choices among health insurance alternatives to better rationalize a decision to select a managed care offering, even though freedom of choice in selecting providers at time of treatment would be limited.

Because of the critical role that primary care providers (general and family practitioners, pediatricians, internist, and obstetricians/gynecologists) play as gatekeepers to the entire medical care system, it is the primary care panel that must be reviewed most closely.

A number of criteria can be used to judge the quality of providers within a network and communicate such quality to prospective marketing targets. These

Reprinted with permission from *National Underwriter*, ©1993, The National Underwriter Company; *National Underwriter, Life & Health/Financial Services Edition*, September 7, 1992.

criteria range from factors involving how well a doctor is prepared to deliver medicine (e.g., board certification, office management procedures, malpractice history, and practice limitation) to how well the network selects physicians to participate (e.g., credentialing criteria and process, hospital affiliation, utilization patterns, geographic and specialty adequacy, and physician turnover history). In this way, competing networks can be measured and compared against each other and what is prevalent in the region. It is not unreasonable to ask the network managers to compare their physicians network against community standards.

Board certification. Perhaps the first criterion is the extent to which physicians are board certified. Only those physicians who meet the very strict standards of their specialty are granted certification and thus can be "board certified." An important consideration would be the percentage of physicians possessing board certification versus the total number with that designation in the region. You would want to ensure that a good cross sampling of local physicians has been recruited.

Hospital affiliation. A critical consideration is whether the physician has admitting privileges at a hospital included in the network. The result of not having admitting privileges should an admisssion be required would be either to have reimbursement reduced or denied, or to be admitted to a network hospital where your primary care physician cannot care for you.

Utilization patterns. The power of managed care networks to reduce medical care costs rests with the ability of the network physicians to use sense in rendering and ordering medical treatment. Networks need to employ physicians who use judgment in prescribing laboratory or X-ray tests to assist in making diagnostic evaluations. To determine who are the efficient physicians, normative data on referral, treatment, and diagnostic patterns need to be used. Each physician needs to be compared to other physicians within his or her area and specialty to determine effectiveness. This analysis must be done by the organization putting together the network. Consultants and employers should assess the effort that has gone into this step in the physician recruitment process. As well, consultants should require network management to disclose all credentialing creiteria and the process used to screen potential providers.

Geographic and specialty adequacy. No matter what the quality of the physicians in the network, one has to ensure that an adequate number of providers has been signed up to deliver services. Among the measures commonly used are average number of miles those joining the program will need to travel to reach primary care and specialist physicians. A common standard in major metropolitan areas is that at least 55 percent of enrollees can travel 15 minutes or less to reach a primary care doctor, and not more than 30 minutes to reach most specialists.

Physician turnover history. All networks will experience some degree of physician turnover. Some of it will be positive, as networks need to prune those physicians who do not follow appropriate protocols or encourage excess utilization. Other turnover is unavoidable due to physician deaths, those moving away from the area, or switching to a more specialized practice. Excessive turnover due to physician dissatisfaciton with the network should be carefully reviewed.

Post implementation reviews. At selected points after a managed care network has been up and running, a review needs to be made so that poorly performing physicians are removed form the network and areas of weakness are improved. The most critical evaluations will come from those who are using the network—employees and their families. Telephone or mail surveys—questioning the length of time to get an appointment, office waiting time, accessibility of the physician for telephone consultation, and patients' perception of the competence of both the physician and the office staff—need to be undertaken. Additional reviews to be undertaken by the network management include the frequency of patients switching their choice of primary care physician, analysis of actual utilization patterns, chart audits to determine whether the network physicians are following appropriate medical protocols, review to ensure that precertification protocols are being adhered to, examination to determine the appropriateness and frequency of referrals and an audit of member grievances.

Other considerations. Potential members best assess the quality of the network by the network directories, which are distributed by the organizations offering the network product. It is imperative that such organizations include as much information as possible. At a minimum, in addition to the doctors name, information should include a complete street addreess, telephone number, whether evening and weekend office hours are available, what hospitals the physician is affiliated with, whether the physician is accepting new patients or limiting participation of existing patients, and whether the physician is board certified or board qualified. Additionally, the physician network directory should be updated frequently to reflect the inevitable changes that will and should occur.

In "Independent Practice Association" types of plans, it is not uncommon for a physician to limit his or her participation in a managed care network. Most often, limitation takes the form of whether the physician will accept new patients, or only participate for existing patients already seen by his practice. There should be an adequate selection of physicians for those employees seeking to enroll in a managed care plan.

How well does the physician maintain his or her office practice? Some investigative work needs to be done by the network manager. To what extent does the physician offer evening or weekend hours? It is also incumbent on insurers and managed care providers to incorporate information on office hours in their provider directories.

Patients searching for primary medical care professionals often ask what arrangements the physician has made for backup care when not available. So too should this be a consideration in selecting a provider under a managed care program. Many quality programs require adequate backup when the primary care physician is not available. This alternative provider should likewise be a member of that managed care panel, or should have a financial arrangement with the primary care doctors, so that patients are held harmless.

Recent news reports have indicated the ease with which one can enroll in certain foreign medical schools without serious review of undergraduate records or even whether an undergraduate degree was even obtained. While not condemning all such foreign schools, it is quite common for aspiring doctors not able to obtain admission to an American medical school to seek admission to foreign school, particularly in Mexico, Italy, and the Caribbean. The extent to which those participating in a network have earned their medical degrees outside the United States provides an indication of the general quality of the network.

A physician's malpractice history and level of coverage needs to be reviewed before admittance to the network. Of particular interest is a comparison of medical malpractice claims versus other doctors in the same specialty and geographic area. Some specialties (e.g., obstetrics) incur more claims than others due to the tragic consequences involved and the desire of insurance companies to settle out of court rather than risk a jury trial and potential large damage award. The level of effort exerted by the managed care organization needs to be reviewed to ensure that this criterion, in relation to the norm, is being used in credentialing physicians. In some networks, medical malpractice insurance is arranged by the carrier.

Just as it would be prudent to know if your personal physician has ever faced disciplinary action by the state or federal authorities, it is imperative on the part of network managers to determine whether physicians enrolled in a managed care panel has been subject to disciplinary actions. Consult the book "Questionable Doctors: Doctors Disciplined by States or the Federal Government."

In offering a managed care product, employers neeed to know whether the networks where employees and their families will be receiving medical care are capable of delivering the best possible health care services. Equally, employees increasingly faced with this critical need to know what kind of care they can expect. Asking questions and demanding straightforward answers is both proper and essential.

52.   Point of Service Products: Not Just Another Managed Care Fad

Stephen George

Point of service plans offer the strengths of HMOs—good benefits at a reduced cost—without their characteristic inflexibility. Their advantages include employee provider choice and easy plan customization for the needs and desires of specific employees. These strengths will be further enhanced as technology improves and deregulation occurs, ensuring that point of service products will continue to be important in the future of managed care.

Point of service plans, perhaps the fastest-growing product in the group health insurance market today, are not merely a fad but rather the product of the future. Managed care programs became part of the health care benefit marketplace during the past decade in an effort to better control insurance premiums for employers and, ultimately, overall health care costs. Results have been promising.

A recent report by benefits consultant Towers Perin says companies that urge employees to get medical care from organized networks of hospitals and doctors have reduced growth in health costs by one-third—to an average of 12 percent in 1991. At the same time, the report found that in 73 percent of the companies, employees who join networks are at least as satisfied with their benefits as under traditional fee-for-service plans—even though networks of ten require them to change doctors and limit their choice of specialists.

The traditional portfolio of managed care product offerings represents a continuum of choices that trade off limits of choice against cost and medical

Reprinted from *HealthSpan*, November 1992, Vol. 9, No. 10, with the permission of Prentice Hall Law & Business.

management performances. Now we have point of service (POS) plans, positioned some where in the middle of the spectrum of managed care products between the traditional health maintenance organization (HMO) and preferred provider organization (PPO) offerings. POS offers medical management and cost containment (which cannot be achieved with PPO products), as well as freedom of choice for employees, making them a popular option.

Approximately 11 percent of employers offered point of service plans in 1991, up from 10 percent in 1990, according to a survey by A. Foster Higgins & Co. Inc. In addition, another 7 percent intend to offer a point of service plan within the next two years, the survey found. Because of this and the advantages point of service products offer over traditional and other managed care products, they are the product of the future.

WHAT IS POINT OF SERVICE?

Point of service plans give employers tighter management of health care dollars, while giving employees freedom of choice. The product is called "point of service" because employees have the freedom to choose the level of benefit they receive at the time they seek service. Further, they can choose a different level of benefit at different times—they don't have to make a choice at the beginning of the year and be stuck with it throughout the year.

Employees generally can choose between two options of benefits and services. One is an HMO-sponsored plan in which the employee has a dual choice—HMO or a traditional indemnity benefit. The other option is a PPO-sponsored plan in which the employee has three choices—HMO, PPO, or indemnity. Employees may use non-network providers if they so choose, although this will result in a higher out-of-pocket cost.

Point of service products vary throughout the industry because product initiatives have emerged from two different vantage points—the HMO and the self-insured employer under an administrative services only (ASO) agreement with a carrier. Although they vary in the industry, POS products share certain characteristics.

These are:

- An HMO-type enrollment process in which employees and dependents enroll or are assigned a primary care physician.
- An aggressive plan design that uses disincentives to discourage out-of-network care.
- A higher percentage of co-insurance differential between in- and out-of-network care. For example, point of service products traditionally use a combination of co-insurance, co-pay deductible and out-of-pocket expense limits to achieve a 20 to 30 percent differential between in- and out-of-network care.

PPO plans traditionally have only 10 percent differential between PPO and non-PPO benefits.

- More choice that allows employees to select the type of service they want each time they seek medical care.

WHY POINT OF SERVICE?

Employers are interested in plan costs and employee choice—objectives that can be supported under the point of service product. In addition, health care benefit managers have very different attitudes, objectives, strategies, and philosophies that vary according to the industry, the company, and even the region of the country in which they are located.

While employers will continue to put a high priority on cost, they also will remain sensitive to the employee's freedom of choice. A 1990 survey conducted by Louis Harris and Associates confirms that freedom of choice is important to employees. According to the survey, consumers strongly oppose restrictions on their freedom to choose a provider—43 percent of 1,250 respondents say that such limitations are "not at all acceptable."

In today's group health area, benefit managers are facing progressively difficult challenges as they strive to maintain high quality, cost-effective benefit programs and favorable employee relations. Historically, benefits managers were more concerned with the type and level of benefits than with the cost, but with rising health care costs they must now address the cost and the resulting personnel and administration issues. A POS product allows employers to provide good benefits at a reduced cost and still give the employee a voice and choice in the process. Further, POS allows employers to customize plans, and to decide which benefits are covered and to what degree employees should pay, thereby shifting a greater part of the cost to employees.

HOW POINT OF SERVICE EVOLVED

Point of service products emerged from the desire to blend the benefits of an HMO with more freedom of choice. Employers wanted a plan that manages costs while offering employees flexibility. Of particular concern to employers in an HMO is the annual member lock-in where benefits are not covered unless authorized by the primary care physician. To prevent employee dissatisfaction, some HMOs began designing point of service products that enhanced choice while meeting the needs of the employer.

On the other hand, the indemnity carrier and the employer usually want to limit the number of HMO's in their plan. They also may want to control or manage some of the adverse selections that HMOs can create against an employer's group experience. In addition, some employers want to get back to whole case under-writing which has an aggregate risk under one umbrella, as opposed to under-writing the HMO and indemnity plans separately. Point of service may present an alternative to the separate HMO and indemnity offerings.

ADVANTAGES OF POINT OF SERVICE

What makes point of service so attractive to employers? Point of service products offer the strengths of the HMO—the enrollment process, the primary care physician, aggressive plan design, blending of the co-payment deductible and co-insurance cost sharing—without the inflexible restriction of freedom of provider choice. In addition, point of service products, as opposed to traditional HMOs, can be offered with all financial alternatives, including conventionally funded, minimum premium, or administrative services only programs.

Another distinct advantage is the fact that the primary care physician plays a central role in controlling costs. Recently, a Health Insurance Association of America (HIAA) study concluded that adding a primary care gatekeeper to a PPO shaves off an additional 6.5 percent on claim costs. The study also noted that in PPOs that had up to 90 percent in network utilization, the primary care savings were as high as 15 percent.

The gates to the different benefit options within a point of service product drive access and continuity of care through the primary care physician. The objectives of this are to:

- Encourage primary care triage and surveillance of employees' health care.
- Maximize in-network utilization.
- Achieve optimal quality and patient outcomes without rigid limits imposed by a restricted health care system.
- Facilitate employee participation in health benefit purchasing through em-phasis on member education, price-to-value tradeoffs, and meaningful plan design features.
- Achieve employer financial objectives through controls on adverse selection and rationing of plan administrators, and employee-driven acceptance of managed care.

Point of service can be used as a transitional product by allowing employers to move employees and their dependents into a more intensive medical manage-ment or managed care environment at a pace that's comfortable to the employees.

WHY IS IT THE FUTURE?

The future of point of service is certainly a current topic of debate. However, point of service will be an essential product through the next decade with both transitional and permanent value. The desire for employee choice providers and the differing priorities among employers dictate that these products are here to stay. In addition, point of service allows employers to customize plans, decide which benefits are covered, and determine to what degree employees should pay. Ultimately, total plan costs and annual trend factors will become the central performance measures. Point of service design will facilitate attaining these objectives by aligning the competing needs of the employers, the employee, and the provider.

Certain trends will converge over time to increase the growth and permanence of point of service within the portfolio of managed care products. One trend—technology advances—will make point of service products more efficient and easier to administer. These technology advances include electronic enrollment, smart card/electronic data interchange, and database architect and expert system cooperative processing. Other trends include experience curve effects on administrative costs; deregulation of state barriers; and visible public sector support through introduction of a Medicare point of service product offering.

The point of service market is likely to double in size in the next five years and will grow rapidly through the year 2000. Point of service will be to the '90s what PPO's were to the '80s. It's been said that managed care is the wave of the future in group health insurance. If that's true, then point of service products are the crest of that wave.

53. Empowering the Demand Side: From Regulation to Purchasing

Richard Kronick

In theory, free market competition among private insurers will lead to quality and economy in the provision of health care. In practice, however, this theory has failed miserably because of the way insurers are regulated. This article argues that a new system of regulation based on an active purchasing authority would empower the demand side of the health insurance equation, creating an environment of managed competition that rewards those provider groups able to offer high quality economical care.

An emerging debate in Washington asks how best to regulate the private insurance industry—what sorts of regulation are desirable, and what role, if any, should the federal government have in the regulation of insurance?[1] This paper addresses the question of how the private insurance industry should be regulated. What functions do we want regulation of private insurance to accomplish? What mixture of state and federal regulation will best accomplish these functions?

The first section of this paper describes the ways health insurance is currently regulated. Regulation of health insurance is focused on ensuring that insurers have the financial ability to fulfill the promises they make, and that there is no fine print in these promises that deceives the consumer. And naturally enough, it is focused on the market for health insurance and not the market for health care services.

The second section of the paper reviews a variety of rationales for supporting the existence of private, as opposed to public, insurance.[2] I conclude that the major economic, as opposed to political, rationale for the existence of private insurance is the hypothesis that multiple, competing private insurers will foster an environment in which providers will make better decisions on the use of resources than they would under a public insurance system. In a well-managed system of competing private sector health plans, a health plan that does a poor job of planning how many resources are needed to take care of its enrollees or that uses available resources inefficiently will lose members to a competing system that does a better job at health planning or resource utilization. This dynamic will encourage health plans (which are primarily groups of providers together with a fiscal and administrative management structure) continually to do a better job of planning and using resources, and responding to the preferences of their members. A well-managed system of competing private health plans can serve diverse consumer preferences on dimensions such as level of amenities, amount of freedom of choice of provider, length of waiting time for nonemergency appointments, and aggressive versus conservative practice styles.

However, the market for health plans is not naturally efficient; to achieve the hypothesized advantages of competition, active and intelligent management (regulation) of the interaction between consumer and health plans is required. In the third section of this paper. I argue that for a system based on competition among private insurers to create an environment in which providers will strive to improve the quality and economy of care, stronger and differently focused regulatory activity is required than exists currently. A new regulator—which might be called a Health Insurance Purchasing Corporation (HIPC)—should be established in each geographic area to manage competition among private insurers and to concentrate purchasing power on the demand side. If we maintain a primarily employer-based financing system, HIPCs should contract with insurers on behalf of small- and medium-sized employers, and individuals not covered by either a public program or employer-sponsored health insurance.[3]

If HIPCs were established as the exclusive purchasing agent for employees in small- and medium-sized businesses, then these employees could purchase only HIPC contracted products. This restriction on the potential interactions between insurers and small employers (and their employees) will upset many who support, in principle, the free market. However, in the absence of strong regulatory action, there is no chance that the hypothesized advantages of competition among private health plans will be realized. The major current proposals for small group market reform will not be sufficient to create a market that rewards quality and economy in the delivery of care, or that provides consumers with meaningful choice about how aggressive they want their providers to be in interpreting the phrase "medically necessary care." Unless we are willing to support strong action to empower the demand side—such as the creation of HIPCs—there is little reason to support the continuation of private insurance.

REGULATION OF HEALTH INSURANCE

The earliest efforts in the United States to protect against financial uncertainty were the informally organized "mutual aid" and "friendly" societies of the colonial era. These early forms of insurance were unregulated by the government. As the corporate business of insurance grew throughout the 19th and 20th centuries, regulatory activities grew as well, with the emergence of modern forms of insurance regulation dating from the progressive era at the beginning of the 20th century.

The regulation of insurance is intended to achieve a variety of purposes, but the major rationale for regulation is to ensure the solvency of insurers. Insurance is a contract in which the insurer accepts premium dollars today and makes a promise to deliver benefits in the future: the state regulates insurers to increase the likelihood that they will have the capacity to fulfill the end of the bargain. In the late 1800s, it was common for large numbers of insurers writing fire insurance to fail following major fires.[4] Insurance regulators in some states were granted the authority to require insurers to file financial statements, but few consumers could make sense of these filings, and regulators had no recourse against thinly capitalized insurers. Insurers attempted to collude to set minimum fire insurance rates, but barriers to entry were low, and those attempting to collude were unable to prevent competitors from offering lower rates.

Following the San Francisco earthquake of 1906, large numbers of fire insurance companies went bankrupt, repeating the common pattern. Many insurers agreed with their progressive critics that the free market encouraged some companies to compete for business by quoting unrealistically low rates. Companies that sold at low rates could be profitable in the absence of a major conflagration, but could not meet their obligations following an extensive fire. New York state responded by passing a law that allowed the superintendent of insurance to require prior approval of rates. The superintendent used this statute to authorize, and essentially require, insurers to collude in rate setting: an insurer who attempted to sell policies at less than the standard rates would be prevented from doing so on the grounds that the rates were unfairly discriminatory. This state regulatory action, adopted in many other states as well, gave official sanction to an insurance cartel in the property and casualty business, and significantly improved the profitability and stability of the industry. These regulations also benefitted consumers by increasing the likelihood that an insurer would be able to pay claims made against it, but such protection might have been possible through regulation of insurer solvency and investment decisions without official sanctioning of a rate-making cartel.

In contrast to the official sanction given collusive rate making in the fire insurance industry, progressive era regulation of life insurance focused on ensuring adequate reserves and sound investment policies,[5] ensuring policyholder control of mutual companies, approving policy forms (to prevent the sale of policies with fine print that might prevent "legitimate" claims from being collected), and curbing abusive practices of salesmen. Some of these regulations (particularly those restricting the practices and compensation of salesmen) improved the industry's profitability. Others (such as the regulation of policy forms) may have led to short-term losses for some companies, but no doubt led to long-term gains for the industry by improving the public's confidence in it.

The general patterns established in the regulation of life insurance were applied as well to the sale of health insurance. Regulation of health insurance is primarily directed at ensuring that insurers have the financial capability to fulfill the promises they make, and that consumers are protected from being sold policies without value and from overly aggressive tactics of insurance salespeople. State regulation of health insurance has a variety of other functions as well, including: mandating that all insurance includes a set of specified benefits; collecting premium taxes from commercial insurance companies; and requiring that health maintenance organizations (HMOs) demonstrate that they have made adequate arrangements for the health care of their members. However, with a few exceptions, insurance regulators do not regulate the prices charged to subscribers or the financial arrangements between insurers and providers. Regulatory activity in each of these areas will be briefly reviewed here.

Regulation of health insurance, like regulation of other lines of insurance, is almost entirely the responsibility of state governments. However, approximately 50 percent of the privately "insured" population works for an employer that is self-insured,[6] and these "insurance" plans are exempt from state regulation under the Employee Retirement and Income Security Act of 1974 (ERISA). The exemption of self-insured plans from state regulation creates some limits on the ability of state governments to use the regulations of insurance to accomplish public policy goals. However, with minor exceptions that I will discuss, these limitations are more theoretical than practical. It is not likely that regulatory activities or goals of insurance commissioners would be much changed even if the ERISA preemption were removed.

Capitalization and Solvency

In every state, an insurance company is required to show an adequate level of reserves to obtain a license to sell insurance (the required level varies by state, by line of insurance, and by the amount of insurance sold). Insurance regulators also prescribe permissible categories of investment in an attempt to prevent insurers from investing assets in overly risky ventures. In lines of insurance with long tails (such as whole life insurance), the insurer collects premium dollars today and makes a promise to make payments many years in the future. Left unregulated, insurers who were allowed to invest in overly risky ventures might be unable to make good on their promises.

Health insurance premiums account for less than 15 percent of the income of commercial insurance companies[7] and the emphasis in many departments of insurance on ensuring solvency is focused more on lines of insurance other than health insurance. Health insurance has a short claims tail and relatively small variance of actual compared to expected claims (for large numbers of covered lives). Compared with property insurance (in which large reserves need to be accumulated so that claims can be paid following a major fire or a hurricane) or whole life insurance (with a long period, on average, between premiums paid in and benefits paid out), health insurance companies have little need for large reserves. Nevertheless, regulation of reserve requirements and investment policies in health insurance has no doubt protected some consumers from unexpected loss. A small number of thinly capitalized "insurers" have been able to escape state regulation by claiming that they were self-insured multiple employer trusts exempt under the ERISA statute, have sold insurance to small businesses, and then have been unable to pay claims.[8] If all insurers were allowed to operate without minimum reserve requirements, more such failures might be expected.

Mandated Benefits

All statutes have laws that require insurers to include specified sets of benefits in any health insurance policy sold in the state.[9] Although these laws cover a variety of aspects of insurance policies, the most controversial mandates are those that specify the types of services that must be covered—for example, inpatient treatment for alcoholism, outpatient mental health treatment, podiatry, chiropractic services, or in-vitro fertilization—and those that specify the types of providers that must be paid for those services—for example, psychologists or marriage and family counselors.[10] The number of mandated benefits expanded rapidly in the decade from 1975 to 1985, and has been expanding more slowly since.

Many mandates have been enacted following extensive lobbying from the provider group that would benefit from the mandate, with little evidence of careful consideration of the advantages and disadvantages of enactment. Most provider mandates are opposed by insurance commissioners, insurers, and employers; however, the concentrated benefits that these mandates bring to provider groups often carry more weight in the political arena than the diffuse costs to payers. Large employers operating self-insured plans covered under the ERISA statute are exempt from mandated benefit laws, and this probably marginally decreases the strength of the political coalition opposing mandates. More recently, a number of states have enacted laws requiring a formal cost/benefit analysis before new proposals for mandates are considered, and this may have contributed to a slowdown in the growth of mandates. Further, a variety of proposals for small group market reform include a provision exempting insurance products sold to small employers from state mandates.

The area of mandated benefits is an exception to the general pattern in the regulation of health insurance; in most respects, the regulation of health insurance poses few constraints on the behavior of insurers that are injurious to the short-run interest of large insurers. Insurers would, however, be better off if they were not subject to the variety of provider and service specific mandates, since mandates raise the cost of insurance and decrease the number of people willing to purchase coverage.[11] Many aspects of the insurance market lead one to expect insurers to be quite successful in persuading regulators to adopt policies beneficial to the industry: many of the regulatory issues are highly technical; salience of many issues is low; the industry has substantial economic resources at its disposal and on many issues is highly unified; also, on many issues, organized opposition to industry interest is weak.[12] In the area of mandated benefits, however, there is strong organized opposition to the interests of insurers, and in many cases this opposition has been successful.[13]

Regulation of Price and Underwriting Practices

The sale of health insurance is subject to little regulation of price or underwriting decisions. Insurers, for the most part, are free to decide to whom they want to sell coverage and for what price they are willing to sell it. Insurers selling in the group market are free to accept or reject entire groups, accept some members of a group while refusing to write coverage for others, and/or impose preexisting condition exclusions in which coverage is denied for conditions that existed prior to the purchase of insurance. Similar latitude on coverage decisions is allowed in the nongroup market.

Insurers also have wide latitude on pricing practices. More than 90 percent of the under-65 privately insured are covered by group insurance, and in the group market insurers have virtually complete discretion on pricing decisions. For individual policies (in both the under-65 and the Medicare supplemental markets), the extent of regulation varies by state and by type of company, with Blue Cross and Blue Shield plans generally subject to greater restrictions than commercial insurers (particularly in the Northeast, where the Blues' market share is on average higher than elsewhere, and where the statutes tend to give them a variety of competitive advantages relative to commercial insurers). Nongroup commercial insurance policies in many states are subject to minimum loss ratio requirements, but few other regulations concerning price.[14] As part of enabling legislation establishing Blue Cross and Blue Shield plans, some plans are required to offer non-group policies in the under-65 market, Medicare supplemental policies in the Medigap market, and to obtain prior approval from the state commissioner of insurance before rate increases can go into effect. In some of these prior approval states, such as New York and Massachusetts, rate filings are carefully scrutinized by the commissioner of insurance, and the commissioner and the Blue Cross and Blue Shield plans engage in ritualistic arguments about the reasonableness of the requested rate, the efficiency of the plans' administration, and the adequacy of the plans' efforts to control health care costs. These arguments often result in delays or reductions in requested rate increases, and may result in some cross-subsidy between group and nongroup lines of business. However, over the medium term, nongroup premiums increase approximately at the rate of growth of claims costs plus the growth of administrative costs, and there is no evidence to suggest that department of insurance regulatory activity substantially affects either growth rate.

In summary, regulation of health insurance is directed at ensuring that insurers have the financial capability to fulfill the promises they make and that they make "reasonable" promises (that is, that there is no fine print in insurance contracts that would be deceptive to the insured), and at a variety of tangential functions, such as enforcing mandated benefits laws and collecting premium taxes. With the exception of mandated benefit laws, and the partial exception of regulation of HMOs and utilization review, insurance regulation is not concerned at all with regulation of interactions between insurers and providers.[15] In the few instances in which regulation does significantly constrain the interactions of insurers and providers, the regulation often favors the interests of providers over the interests of insurers and consumers. The separation between the regulation of insurance and the regulation of providers is exemplified by the fact that in those few states that have chosen to regulate hospital prices (New York, Massachusetts, New Jersey, and Maryland), regulatory activity is, in every instance, not vested in the department of insurance, but in a separate agency. Insurance regulation is directed at making sure that the market for insurance functions well, and is almost wholly unconcerned with the market for health care service.

ERISA

The Employee Retirement Income Security Act of 1974 was enacted primarily to solve a variety of problems that existed in the private pension arena. ERISA requires employers to adequately fund pension promises and to comply with a minimum set of requirements for vesting benefits; the purpose of these and other features of the ERISA statute is to ensure that employees actually receive the pension benefits promised to them.[16] In addition to its primary purpose of regulating pension plans, however, ERISA preempts state regulation of any health care plan established by an employer under ERISA guidelines. This preemption allows employers who self-fund their health care plans to avoid state regulation. Self-insurance allows employers to avoid premium taxes and mandated benefit laws. In addition, self-insurance allows employers to maintain control of their money until the moment that claims must be paid. and to avoid insurance company charges for risk. Health plans operating under ERISA guidelines are loosely regulated by the U.S. Department of Labor: these plans are required to publish a description of plan benefits but are subject to few restrictions on their operation.

The ERISA preemption leads to significant fragmentation in the regulation of health "insurance," but it does not seem likely that ERISA is the key factor preventing states from achieving significant policy goals. While ERISA does make coherent regulation of health insurance at the state level more difficult, the key obstacles to effective regulatory policy at the state level are political, and not the preemption features of ERISA. For example, while it is true that ERISA prevents state governments from requiring all employers to provide health insurance to their employees, states could accomplish nearly the same goal by requiring employers that do not provide health insurance to pay a tax instead.[17] The fact that no state has yet implemented a "pay-or-play" tax is primarily a result of lack of political agreement to do so, and not due to ERISA.

Similarly, recent reports have highlighted examples of self-insured employers operating ERISA-governed health plans who have cut off benefit for victims of AIDS, and have suggested that these actions would not be possible if state insurance laws had governed the plans.[18] However, while some state insurance laws prohibit insurance companies from discriminating against persons with AIDS, they do not require employers to include persons with AIDS (or with any other illness) in the group covered by employer-sponsored insurance. Health benefits are a matter for private negotiation between employer and employee; even an employer offering a group insurance policy regulated under state insurance laws would be allowed to exclude some employees from coverage under that policy. States may be inhibited from trying to regulate employer behavior regarding the offering of health plans by the knowledge that such regulations would not apply to employers offering self-insured plans covered by ERISA; in this sense, ERISA does increase the difficulty of enacting policies at the state level that guarantee coverage for all, or that ensure that those who think they are covered are in fact covered.

These difficulties notwithstanding, since there is so much that state governments could do to increase the number of employers offering health insurance and/or to increase the "fairness" of the terms on which insurance is offered without running afoul of ERISA, the fact that states have not taken the actions available suggests that political considerations, and not the legal preemptions created by ERISA, are the main obstacle to change.

Small Group Market Reform

There has been an increasing volume of complaints during the last four to five years about the functioning of the health insurance market for small businesses. Some of the complaints are old ones. Small businesses have always been forced to pay more for health insurance than large businesses. It costs more (as a percentage of claims) to sell and service policies for small than for large businesses. Further, small businesses are more likely than large ones to go out of business (further increasing insurer administrative costs), and more likely than larger firms to switch insurers, again increasing administrative costs. Most significantly, insurers suffer from adverse selection in the small group market—a small group with relatively healthy employees will be less likely to purchase coverage than a small group with relatively unhealthy employees, and this raises the price of coverage for all small firms.

Some of the complaints are newer and stem from changes in the underwriting and rating practices of insurers. According to these complaints, insurers are increasingly likely to refuse to renew a small group policy if one or more members of the group has an illness requiring extensive treatment; to require extremely large premium increases if they agree to continue coverage for such a group; and to refuse to initiate coverage for small groups with members who are either sick or perceived to be higher than average risks. Increasingly, according to these complaints, small employers cannot purchase real insurance against financial catastrophe—if an employee gets sick, he or she may be protected for the remainder of the contract year, but subsequently will lose protection.

Although there are enough anecdotes to persuade most that insurance practices have changed, there is not good evidence about the extent of change or a convincing explanation of why such changes have occurred. The most likely hypothesis to explain any change that has occurred points to the effects of the shrinking market for insurance among medium- and large-sized employers as the number of self-insured employers grew during the 1980s. With the growth of self-insurance, a variety of insurers who had concentrated in the large group market entered the small group market, and increased competition in the small group market may have forced insurers, including Blue Cross and Blue Shield plans, to move further away from community rating and adopt more stringent underwriting practices.

Regardless of the causes of change or the magnitude of change, a variety of solutions have been proposed. Although the proposals vary, most have some version of guaranteed issue (insurers must issue a policy to anyone who applies); guaranteed renewability (insurers must renew a policy once in force); limitations on medical underwriting and preexisting condition limitations for people who have been continuously insured (even if they change jobs); limitations on the extent of deviation from community rating (although many proposals do allow for quite substantial deviations from community rating); and the establishment of private reinsurance systems to protect individual insurers from being harmed by these changes. Many small group market reform proposals would exempt insurance products sold to small groups from state mandated benefit laws.

The Health Insurance Association of America is actively supporting some versions of these proposals, and has been working with the National Association of Insurance Commissioners to persuade state legislatures to adopt the reforms.[19] The private health insurance industry is under attack from many sides, and insurers recognize that the difficulty small employers and their employees have in purchasing multiyear protection increases the vulnerability of insurers to charges that they serve no useful purpose. Although the reforms are likely to increase insurance prices for currently insured small groups with healthy employees, they will also increase the value of the protection these groups are offered. Compared to most other health care financing reform proposals, these have the aura of motherhood and apple pie.

Within the insurance industry, small group market reforms are supported more strongly by larger insurers than by smaller companies. Smaller insurance companies have historically had a larger presence in the small group market than in the large group market; thus, smaller insurance companies have more to lose by a change in the rules. Due to greater experience with the small group market and, perhaps, greater willingness to exclude poor risks, many smaller insurance companies will be disadvantaged if they are prevented from competing based on their ability to select good risks. Further, supporters of small group reform hope that the reforms will increase the rewards to those insurers who sponsor effective managed care products, and larger insurers have been able to invest more than smaller insurers in the development of such products. As I will discuss here, however, despite the hopes of advocates, small group market reforms, even if enacted, will not be nearly sufficient to structure a market that will strongly encourage the provision of high quality, economical care.

WHY HAVE PRIVATE HEALTH INSURANCE AT ALL?

The existence of a large number of private health insurers has a variety of disadvantages: administrative costs are much higher than they would be in a system of publicly provided insurance; the private insurance system is failing in its historic mission of spreading risk; there are some people who cannot purchase coverage on what is perceived to be "fair" terms; and some people who think they are insured find that they are uninsured when they become sick. A question that many analysts ask, then, is, "Why have private health insurance at all?"

The usual rationale for private markets is that they lead to optimal allocations of resources. The existence of competition among producers for labor and capital, and the ability of consumers to choose freely to whom they provide their labor and how they allocate their consumption encourages the productive use and development of human and physical capital. A comparison of the performances of the agricultural sectors in the former Soviet Union and the United States provides an example of the advantages of private markets.

However, the mere existence of private markets for health insurance does not result in the efficient production of health care. Private insurance, like public insurance, primarily pays health care providers on a fee-for-service basis. Providers are paid more for providing more service, without regard to whether more is necessary or appropriate. If most treatment decisions were clear cut, fee-for-service payment would not be problematic—well meaning providers, acting as agents for patients, would provide only medically necessary care, and the techniques of third-party utilization review could be used to deny payment to those few providers who abused the principal-agent relationship. However, much of medicine is art and not science, and many treatment decisions are made under conditions of substantial uncertainty. This uncertainty, combined with third-party, fee-for-service payment, leads to the production of many services that do little to improve health outcomes or patient satisfaction. All could be made better off with none worse off, if these services were not rendered, and providers were paid to go on vacation.[20]

If we want to gain the efficiency-enhancing advantages of private markets in the purchase of health care services, we must shift our focus from competition among health insurers to competition among health plans. A health plan is a group of providers—primarily physicians, ancillary personnel, and hospitals—who are linked by some sort of administrative and management structure, and who have the financial and medical care capability to promise to take care of us when we get sick and to provide preventive services when we are well. We have many examples of health plans—health maintenance organizations (including prepaid group practices, network models, and independent practice association models) are health plans. Preferred provider organizations are health plans, although the extent of accountability for both cost and quality is weaker than in closed panel plans. Even old fashioned fee-for-service indemnity insurance can be counted as a health plan under the definition just offered, although with little ability to influence cost or quality. Commercial insurers and Blue Cross and Blue Shield plans can and do create health plans; other health plans (such as Kaiser or Harvard Community Health Plan) are not linked to a traditional insurer.

As developed by Enthoven,[21] the theory of managed competition posits that an environment of competing health plans can create incentives for physicians and hospitals to figure out how to make better use of resources than they do in our current fee-for-service payment system, or than they would in a public insurance system with extensive public sector health planning. In an environment of managed competition, doctors, hospitals, and health plan administrators would figure out how many resources are needed to take good care of an enrolled population; doctors in one specialty would challenge the protocols of doctors in other specialties; physicians would seek to understand the reasons for small area variations in utilization and expenditures, and to reduce utilization in high-use areas where appropriate. In an environment of managed competition, physicians would have strong incentives to work with terminally ill patients and their families to develop realistic expectations about prognosis, and to reduce the utilization for sources in circumstances in which there is no hope of prolonging a life of quality. In such an environment, physicians would be motivated to seek out and adopt the best information available on practice guidelines and would have the capability and support for implementing an outcomes monitoring system.

There are two necessary conditions to create an environment in which providers are rewarded for quality and economy. First, consumers must be cost and quality conscious when choosing among plans (that is, they must pay more if they choose a more expensive plan, less if they choose a less expensive plan; and they must have some information about health outcomes and consumer satisfaction in competing plans). Second, active and intelligent sponsors must work at dividing the provider community into competing groups, guarding against (and adjusting for) risk selection and making information available to consumers. Despite a decade in which rhetorical support for the competitive model was voiced in many quarters, we have done relatively little to implement such a model—many employed persons have no choice of health plan, many of those who do have a choice do not face a fully cost-conscious choice, and few of those with a cost-conscious choice have an active and intelligent sponsor managing competition among plans.

Dramatic changes would be needed in the market for health insurance to achieve an environment of managed competition; the sorts of changes required are discussed in the third section of this paper. Before considering how to create an environment in which the existence of competing private insurers will create incentives for providers to improve the quality and economy of care they deliver, it will be useful to examine other reasons that are sometimes advanced for maintaining a system of private insurance.

One rationale for private markets is that they cater to diversity in preferences and endowments, while public systems tend to be "one size fits all." For example, if the public sector used tax revenue to pay for housing for everyone in the United States, we would probably end up with most people (except for the politically favored few) living in very similar housing units. This would be inefficient— those with greater resources would prefer to spend some of them on bigger (and/or better quality) housing; those with relatively few resources might prefer to have less housing, and more money left over for food and clothing.

Similarly, to a limited extent, a system based on private health insurance can cater to diverse preferences in ways that would be difficult, if not impossible, for a public insurance system such as Canada's. People who are willing (and able) to pay money to reduce waiting time in physician offices, or to receive better quality hotel services in hospitals are better able to do so in a private than in a public insurance system. Some people may want (and be able and willing to pay for) medical treatments that, many physicians would agree, will do little (if anything) to improve health—an MRI for a splitting headache, or an angiography each time they have chest pain. Those with preferences and resources for a greater amount of "flat-of-the-curve" medicine than the norm will be more satisfied in a private than in a public insurance system.

However, in either a public or a private insurance system, the great bulk of medical care (and the preponderance of expenditures) will fall in the big black box labeled "medically necessary care," and patient preferences for health care relative to other consumption will have relatively little influence on the level of resource consumption. No patient would be willing to agree explicitly to purchase an insurance policy that covered only a limited number of hospital days (e.g., 30), and then required the provider to discharge the patient even if the patient would almost certainly die as a result of discharge (and no provider would be willing to practice in such an environment). Similarly, while private insurance (like public insurance) may refuse payment for procedures that are labeled "experimental," there would probably be little interest in an insurance policy that explicitly refused to pay for big-ticket services generally conceded to be likely to improve significantly quantity or quality of life; one cannot, for example, purchase an insurance policy that excludes coverage of coronary artery bypass graft surgery.[22]

While private insurance is likely to be superior to public insurance in accommodating diverse preferences for health care versus other goods and services, the range of preferences that can (and need to) be accommodated is much narrower than in many other sectors of consumption. In housing, for example, many upper-middle-income persons might prefer (and be willing to pay for) housing that is three or four times more expensive than a publicly provided average would be, while some lower income persons might prefer having housing only one-half to one-third as expensive as the average, assuming they were given the extra money to use for other consumption.[23] In health care, however, everyone wants to be assured of receiving "medically necessary care" when they are sick: the well-off may want to purchase more amenities or more flat-of-the-curve medicine than average, but it would be extremely rare for them to want care that is three or four times as expensive as average; the poor might be willing to accept fewer amenities, perhaps less well-trained providers, and a more circumspect definition of medical necessity in exchange for additional income, but again this is not likely to result in resource consumption that is one-half (or less) of some publicly provided norm.

Further, while private insurance can and does cater to diverse preferences on such dimensions as amenities, waiting time, and free choice of provider, the current market for private insurance provides little choice on the crucial dimension of how much flat-of-the-curve medicine the consumer desires. As argued by Havighurst, health insurers' (and health plans') offerings primarily accept the amorphous standard of "medical necessity" created in the fee-for-service environment, and a consumer willing to accept a more circumspect approach often is denied the opportunity to purchase such coverage.[24] One potential argument for private insurance—that it accommodates diverse preferences—has some strength. However, unless a market for health plans is created in which consumer preferences for aggressive versus more conservative practice styles are translated into the existence of health plans with aggressive and conservative styles, one of the major potential advantages of private markets will be unrealized.

Some might argue that a system based on private insurance is preferable to a public insurance system because the public system will require greater amounts of income redistribution, higher marginal tax rates, and will reduce the incentives for people to work hard. Without entering here into the equity/efficiency debate, this potential argument in support of private insurance can be disposed of easily: if our goal is to achieve universal access, then it is simply not true that a public insurance system requires more income redistribution than a private insurance system. The question of how money is raised (that is, who pays for health care) is largely independent of how money is spent; financing health care in a public insurance system can be just as regressive (or progressive) as in a private insurance system.

Some might argue for private insurance because they are concerned that a system based on public insurance (such as Medicare for all) would, in the long run, starve the health care system of needed resources. Although there are many different varieties of public insurance systems, in each the government makes decisions about the total amount of resources devoted to health care. Politicians are reluctant to raise taxes, and this reluctance might cause them to constrain health care resources inappropriately. Elections are blunt mechanisms of translating individual preferences into social outcomes, and as Arrow shows, no social choice mechanism can "perfectly" translate individual preferences into a social choice.[25] Thus it is possible that the outcome of a political decision-making process would be too few resources devoted to health care relative to some optimum. The opposite concern is expressed by some who fear that provider groups would dominate the political decision-making process, and too many resources would be allocated to health care. While these are legitimate concerns, the private insurance market, in anything like its current incarnation, provides no coherent mechanism for translating individual preferences for the volume of health care into a social choice; there is no reason to imagine that a political decision-making process would be worse, and many reasons to expect it would be somewhat better.

Regardless of the substantive merits of maintaining a private health insurance industry, private health insurance is the status quo, and the status quo contains strong inertial forces. It would take a sea change in political attitudes to imagine the American public supporting a $300 billion (or so) tax increase and a program of "Medicare for All," especially in the face of vehement opposition from many physicians, some hospitals, insurers and their employees, and insurance salespeople and brokers. However, at least for the purposes of this paper, political expediency is not a sufficient answer to the question of why we should have private insurance at all. In any case, in the absence of substantive reasons to support private insurance, we should expect that eventually some entrepreneurial politician will be able to win votes by advocating its demise.

To summarize, the primary justification for private insurance is the hypothesis that a health care delivery system in which competing health plans vie for patients will cause physicians and hospitals to make better decisions regarding resource consumption than would a system in which the public sector makes direct payments to providers. In a public insurance system, the allocation of resources within the health care industry will be politically determined, and may be only weakly influenced by considerations of how best to improve health outcomes. In deciding which new technologies to invest in or which hospitals to allow to rebuild, the government may well make poor decisions. The credo of politicians, like that of physicians, is "Do no harm," and this is likely to result in rigid allocations, so that the health care system 20 years from now may look much as it does today. This is likely to be a larger problem for the American political system, with a variety of institutional arrangements that increase the responsiveness of government to well-organized special interests, than for parliamentary systems such as Canada's[26] Careful attention to a variety of institutional design features can potentially improve the performance of a political allocation system. However, in a heterogenous society, full of intense conflicts among and between provider groups and among diverse parts of the citizenry, it is likely that any political allocation system will result in substantial inefficiency and deadweight loss in the provision of health care. There is at least the potential that a private insurance system may do better.

CREATING AN ENVIRONMENT IN WHICH EFFICIENT, HIGH QUALITY PROVIDERS ARE REWARDED

If the primary justification for maintaining a private insurance market is to create an environment in which physicians and hospitals are rewarded for the provision of high quality, economical care, it has to date been a miserable failure at achieving this goal. In this section of the paper I argue that active and intelligent management (regulation by another name) of competition among health plans is required to achieve the goal. This regulation of the interactions between consumers and health plans should require consumers to make cost-conscious choices, should limit the choices available to consumers to a subset of those that might be offered in a "free" market, should collect and publicize information on health plan performance, and should pursue a variety of strategies to minimize the ability of health plans to prosper through favorable selection of risks and instead ensure that those plans that do a good job of keeping enrollees healthy and taking care of them when they get sick will be rewarded.

The regulatory tasks required to create an environment in which providers are rewarded for quality and economy are quite different from the tasks currently within the purview of state departments of insurance. Although I have not taken a survey of commissioners of insurance (or their deputies in charge of health insurance), I would be quite surprised if many saw it as part of their job to create an environment that rewards efficient health care providers. As demonstrated in the first section of this paper, insurance regulation is focused on the market for insurance, not the market for health care services. This focus must change if the existence of private health insurance is to have any chance of creating an environment that rewards quality and economy. Although in theory these changes could occur through transformations within departments of insurance, in practice it probably makes more sense to establish new organizations—Health Insurance Purchasing Corporations (HIPCs)—with primary responsibility for regulating the sale of health insurance.

Need for Management/Regulation of Competition

The theory of managed competition in health care asserts that it is possible to create a marketplace in which health plans—that is groups of physicians, hospitals, ancillary personnel, and health plan administrators—will strive continuously to figure out how to better utilize health care resources, and will act as the reasonably faithful agents of their members in making decisions on the adoption of new technology and the utilization of existing technology. This theory has been extensively developed by Enthoven and will be only briefly reviewed here.[27]

There are two necessary conditions for the creation of such a market: first, there must be large numbers of cost and quality conscious consumers making choices among competing health plans; and second, there must be active and intelligent sponsors regulating the interactions of consumers and health plans—continuously providing information and adjusting the marketplace to assure that high quality, economical provider groups are rewarded. The need for cost and quality conscious consumers should be clear: if consumers are not asked to pay more if they choose a more expensive health plan, there is no reason to expect doctors and hospitals to exhibit restraint either in salary expectations or in the use of resources.

Active and intelligent sponsors (or regulators) are needed to ensure that the market rewards quality and economy, rather than felicity at favorable risk selection or other anticompetitive behavior. The market for health plans is not naturally competitive. Left unmanaged, we would expect health plans to attempt to avoid poor risks and enroll healthy people. Health plans have many strategies available to achieve these ends: tailoring of benefit packages to appeal to the healthy; providing biased information on coverage; selective marketing to healthy patients; placing subtle pressure on patients to disenroll once they become sick. Further, health plans can attempt to attenuate competition by segmenting the market through attention to benefit design and location of practitioners;

market segmentation reduces the price elasticity of demand, and reduces the incentives for provider groups to strive for quality and economy.

In unmanaged markets, health plans that contain large subsets for the doctors and hospitals in town may well be more attractive to consumers, in the short run, than health plans that divide the provider community into competing groups. However, competition among a set of health plans with largely overlapping provider lists will do little in the medium to long run to encourage providers to strive for quality or economy. Concerned action by a sponsor is likely to be necessary to ensure that a set of health plans emerges that divides the provider community into competing groups. Further, reliable information that can be compared across plans on patient satisfaction, quality of care, and health outcomes is a necessary condition for the creation of a market that rewards quality and economy; this information will not be produced in the absence of a "sponsor" or "regulator."

A free market in which cost conscious consumers made choices among competing plans would not result in improved quality or economy; a third party, or regulator, is required to constrain the interactions of consumers and health plans if a healthy marketplace is to be created. This regulator should engage in the following types of strategies: standardizing the benefit packages available to consumers, to remove the ability of health plans to tailor their benefit packages to segment the market and select good risks; managing the enrollment process to minimize opportunities for risk selection; monitoring the disenrollment process to determine if a health plan is extruding its sickest members, and require corrective action if it is; prohibiting health plans from terminating the contracts of people who become sick; and requiring health plans to provide standardized information on quality and health outcomes. A regulator is also needed to generate movement toward a scenario in which the set of health plans available in a geographic area divides the provider community into competing groups, rather than offering a set of health plans with largely overlapping provider lists.

There are three reasons to encourage the formation of plans that divide the provider community into competing groups. First, the sponsor should encourage health plans and the providers in them to work creatively at figuring out how many health care resources are needed to take care of the population being served; the ability to match the supply of resources to needs is limited if there are many health plans, each accounting for a small part of providers' patients. Second, the sponsor should encourage health plans and the providers in them to work creatively at figuring out how to improve the quality and economy of care provided; if each provider is a member of many health plans, there will be little incentive (for either the provider or the plan) to improve quality or economy and limited ability to do so. At the extreme, if each provider were a member of each plan in a community, the providers would have no incentive to lower their prices or restrain utilization levels. Third, the sponsor should encourage the formation of health plans in which providers see their own success tied to the success of the plan—if providers and health plans are, primarily, adversaries, there will be limited ability to improve quality or economy in the delivery of care.

The sponsor should encourage the formation of health plans that divide the provider community into competing groups by, for example, refusing to contract with largely overlapping independent practice association model HMOs, but health plans would not be required to have exclusive arrangements with providers. Specialized tertiary facilities would almost certainly be affiliated with multiple plans, as would some highly specialized physicians. It is not clear, *a priori,* how much overlap of provider lists among health plans is acceptable in the long run; at a minimum, competing health plans should have largely separate groups of primary care physicians.

In addition to regulation of health plan behavior, regulation is needed to ensure that individuals are not allowed to opportunistically decide to purchase insurance only when it appears likely they are going to need health care services; some third party must provide a large enough subsidy to individuals so that both the healthy and the sick will find the purchase of insurance attractive (or, alternatively, simply require all individuals to purchase coverage). Further, if despite all attempts at restricting the ability of health plans to enroll a favorable selection of risks, the risk mix of enrollees differs significantly across plans, the sponsor should risk-adjust the sponsor's contribution toward the premium so that health plans with sicker enrollees are not competitive disadvantages.

Although the 1980s were a decade in which creation of a health competitive marketplace was supported rhetorically by many government and industry leaders, we are still very far from an environment that rewards high quality, economical providers. Neither of the two necessary conditions for the creating of a healthy marketplace has been satisfied. More than 50 percent of workers with employer-sponsored health insurance have no choice of health plan, and many of those with a choice are not required to pay more if they choose a more expensive plan.[28] Even among the minority of workers facing a cost-conscious choice, few have the benefit of an active sponsor, or regulator, who is structuring the interactions of consumers and health plans.

The main reason we do not have cost-conscious consumers or active sponsors is that employers and individuals are faced with a collective-action problem: even though all would (arguably) be better off if all consumers were cost conscious and had the benefit of an active sponsor, any single employer and group of employees receive little benefit from converting to a system of managed competition. If providers are selling to a small number of consumers who reward quality and economy and a large number who do not, there is no reason to expect that providers will respond to the incentives created by the few rather than those of the many. If only one employer in a community pays the costs to manage competition, provider behavior will not be affected, and health care costs will continue to escalate without being matched by quality increases. Faced with the choice of converting to a system of managed competition and getting nothing for it, or not adopting a system of managed competition and avoiding the short-term labor relations difficulties and ongoing administrative costs, the decision for most employers, both large and small, will be clear. An environment in which providers strive for quality and economy has the characteristics of a public good—the benefits of this environment cannot easily be limited to those who contribute to its production.

Creating Health Insurance Purchasing Corporations: Concentrating Purchasing Power on the Demand Side

The collective-action problem can be solved if rules of the game are established that require large numbers of consumers to be cost conscious at the time of health plan choice and if a sponsor (or regulator) is established whose primary function is to actively manage competition among health plans on behalf of large numbers of consumers. This regulation can be accomplished by establishing one or more HIPCs in each state.[29] Each HIPC would contract with a set of health plans, just as the employee benefits manager of a large employer does today. The HIPC would manage competition among plans and ensure that consumers were cost conscious in their choice of plan; manage enrollment and monitor disenrollment; make information available on satisfaction and quality; standardize benefit packages; and risk-adjust sponsor contributions.

To be successful, the HIPC must be managing competition on behalf of a large number of subscribers—a large enough part of the market that providers will respond to the incentives created. One sensible approach is to require that any small- or medium-sized business that offers a group policy to its employees must offer the policies under contract to the HIPC.[30] The employer offering a group policy would be required to make a fixed contribution toward insurance; the employee would chose a plan and pay the difference between the employer contribution and the price of the plan chosen.[31] Just as most large employers do not accept preexisting condition exclusions in their contracts with health plans, HIPC contracted health plans would be required to accept any qualified employee who wanted to join without underwriting restrictions.

If all businesses with 100 or fewer workers were required to offer HIPC-contracted health plans to their employees, in many states the HIPC would be contracting with health plans on behalf of 50 percent of the population. (This assumes, as I will discuss, that the HIPC also contracts with health plans on behalf of persons who are not offered health insurance by their employer.) This concentration of purchasing power and the existence of large numbers of cost and quality conscious consumers would dramatically alter the incentives faced by providers. It is likely that virtually all providers would join or create a health plan that attempted to receive an HIPC contract—being shut out of a large part of the market would be disastrous for most providers. Further, since large numbers of consumers would be required to pay more if they chose a more expensive plan, health plans would have strong incentives to attempt to restrain premium growth. With HIPCs guarding against underservice, making information available to consumers on satisfaction and quality, and restricting the ability of health plans to select good risks or segment the market, restraining premium growth will require providers and health plan administrators to do the hard work of matching resources to needs (including, most likely, increasing the number of family practitioners and generalists and reducing the number of specialists) and examining and modifying practice patterns.

I assume that HIPCs would be operating within a system of universal health insurance coverage. If the financing of health insurance remains primarily employer based, achieving universal coverage will require either an employer mandate or a "pay-or play" tax approach. With either an employer mandate or a pay-or-play approach, individuals not offered health insurance by their employer should be required to choose one of the HIPC contracted products, with all, except for the poorest, paying the difference between the premium of the plan chosen and a fixed subsidy made available by the HIPC. Some method must be found for raising the subsidies that would be required for low-income persons not covered through employment. As suggested by Enthoven and myself elsewhere, revenues for these subsidies might be raised by limiting the amount of tax-free employer contribution to health insurance, taxing the income of self-employed persons, and taxing the wages of part-time workers.[32] As an alternative to the employer mandate or pay-or-play approaches, the government could raise large amounts of new tax revenue and provide a fixed subsidy to all members of the population (not covered by Medicare or Medicaid), and each person not covered by a public program would choose from among the HIPC contracted health plans. An approach similar to this has been proposed by John Garamendi, the California insurance commissioner.[33]

It would be desirable eventually to have the HIPCs contract with health plans on behalf of those currently covered by Medical and Medicare as well as the uninsured and those now covered by private insurance. A universal system would send clearer signals to providers than would a system in which providers would continue to be paid more for doing more for many patients with little regard for whether more is necessary or appropriate. A universal system would help create both the perception and reality of equity and fairness. Medical recipients would likely be better served in mainstream health care systems than in the largely separate health care settings that serve them today. However, in the short run, for both political and administrative reasons, it may make more sense to leave Medicare and, perhaps, Medicaid, unchanged.[34]

One of the many controversial features of this proposal is the suggestion that the HIPC should contract with providers for a standard benefit package. The contents of the benefit package would most likely be specified in the legislation establishing HIPCs, although the legislature might well choose to leave some discretion to the HIPC. There are two reasons to push toward standardization of benefits across plans. First, allowing health plans to offer substantially different benefit packages is an invitation to risk selection: it allows plans to tailor their benefit packages in an attempt to avoid poor risks. Second, allowing substantial variation in benefit packages will lead to segmentation of the market and attenuate competition among plans: if only one plan offers good mental health benefits, for example, then people who think they may need extensive mental health care have only one good choice, and their choice of plan will be price inelastic.

Although contracting for a standard benefit package will be opposed by some as an unnecessary limitation on the freedom of consumers to choose the benefits they value, it is a limitation that many employees of large employers currently accept and, apparently, do not suffer greatly from. Many large employers currently contract for similar benefits with each health plan under contract, without large loss of welfare for their employees. The HIPC is not a perfectly analogy to the large employer. Workers can, to a limited extent, shop around for an employer that offers a benefit package they value, and employers who contract for a package of benefits not highly valued by potential employees will be disadvantaged in the labor market. In contrast, people who are unhappy with the benefit package contracted for by the HIPC will have no effective options. To ameliorate this problem, it might be feasible for the HIPC to specify a small set (e.g., three) of benefit packages, and require each health plan desiring a contract to submit a premium quote on each of the plans.

Governance and Funding of HIPCs

HIPCs, as powerful entities, will be pressured by many interest groups for favorable decisions. HIPCs will be choosing the health plans with which to contract and the terms of those contracts, will be gathering and publicizing information on quality and consumer satisfaction, managing enrollment and monitoring disenrollment, and risk-adjusting sponsor contributions. We should expect health plans and providers who are unhappy with the HIPC decisions to work hard to obtain more favorable decisions. Similarly, organized groups of consumers (e.g., those with a specific illness or those who live in the neighborhood of a hospital that is threatening to close), health sector employees (e.g., nurses), and providers (those who provide a particular service) will pressure for favorable HIPC actions.

The rationale for establishing HIPCs is to structure the market so that health plans that do a good job of providing high quality, economical care prosper. As students of regulation and government activity are painfully aware, however, simply passing a law establishing HIPCs and charging them with creating an environment that encourages the delivery of high quality, economical care does not ensure they will perform as intended. In establishing HIPCs, we should be mindful of three goals. First, HIPCs should have the organizational capacity to carry out their tasks. HIPCs will need substantial administrative budgets that should not be subject to the vagaries of state or federal budgetary policy. This might be accomplished by funding the administrative costs of HIPCs through a dedicated tax on health expenditures, rather than requiring administrative funds to be annually appropriated by a legislature.[35] HIPCs must be seen as an attractive place for capable and experienced people to work—which means they must offer competitive salaries, opportunities for accomplishment and advancement, and interesting and challenging work.

Second, HIPCs must have enough independence from the short-term reelection imperatives of political executives and legislatures that the HIPC is capable of withstanding at least some pressure from well-organized interests. Like the governors of the Federal Reserve Board or the commissioners of the Securities and Exchange Commission, the directors of HIPCs should not serve at the pleasure of the executive branch, but rather be appointed for fixed length terms; the terms should be fairly long with staggered end dates, so that a new political executive cannot summarily make wholesale changes in HIPC management.[36]

Third, and most importantly, HIPCs must be held accountable for their performance in structuring a market that restrains health care cost growth and improves quality and consumer satisfaction. A well-funded consumer advocate may provide a partial counterweight to well-organized provider interests in presenting information and arguments to the HIPC; further, a consumer advocate may particularly be able to protect the interests of low-income persons, which are often excluded from regulatory processes. Accountability can also be enhanced by providing for systematic measurement and publication of a variety of outcome information: risk-adjusted measures of health outcomes for subgroups of the population; measurement of changes in overall health status of the population; changes in consumer satisfaction with care received; and measurement of changes in health expenditures.

None of those suggestions for HIPC governance and funding will guarantee that HIPCs will be diligent in attempting to accomplish their intended task of structuring a market that rewards quality and economy. HIPCs could well be "captured" by one or another interest group, sink under the weight of bureaucratic inertia, or might simply be unable to intelligently adjust the health care market in response to changing conditions and health plan strategies. However, we have examples of government agencies that do a reasonably good job of structuring markets to protect consumers and reward good performers—the Securities and Exchange Commission—and we have examples of government agencies that purchase health benefits for state employees. The sorts of tasks envisioned for HIPCs are tasks for which there are good reasons to expect a public sector agency to perform well.

Many advocates of private insurance will be understandably nervous about concentrating purchasing power in a central agency, and will prefer instead to support some version of the small group market reform proposals being advanced by the insurance industry. However, while it is unclear whether HIPCs could successfully structure the market to reward quality and economy, it is quite clear that proposed small group market reforms, if enacted, would do little to affect the rate of growth in health expenditures or to increase the value we receive for those expenditures. These proposed reforms: could not prevent insurers from selective marketing to groups expected to be healthy; would provide no mechanism for assuring that employees were cost conscious when choosing among plans; would provide no dynamic for moving toward a set of competitors that divided the provider community into competing groups; would allow substantial variations in benefit packages that could be used to segment the market (reducing price elasticity) and to select good risks; would encourage reinsurance mechanisms, and thus reduce the incentive for health plans to balance resource use with expected benefits for exactly the set of patients likely to receive the most resources; and would create no mechanism for the systematic production and dissemination of useful comparative information on health plan performance. Small group market reform would make the terms on which small employers purchase insurance look more similar to the terms on which large employers purchase insurance; however, these changes would not organize and empower the demand side sufficiently to overcome the many economic and political causes of failure in the market for health services.

Roles of Federal and State Governments

Creating a financing system to achieve universal health insurance will almost certainly require concerted action by the federal government. As states recover from the current recession and the strains on state budgets lessen, some states may begin to experiment with pay-or-play tax systems and with subsidized insurance programs for persons not covered through employment. However, concerns about the effects of such proposals on the ability of states to attract new small businesses, and concerns about in-migration of sick persons in search of subsidized insurance programs will likely limit the extent for such experimentation. In addition, ERISA preemptions increase the obstacles state governments face in attempting to craft a universal health insurance system. Federal government action that either directly creates a financing system guaranteeing universal coverage or that creates strong financial incentives for states to create such a system will be required to achieve this goal.

Similarly, federal government action is likely to be necessary to empower the demand side of the health care marketplace in many areas of the country. State governments could establish HIPCs as the exclusive purchasing agents for small- and medium-sized businesses without enabling legislation from the federal government. State governments have the right to regulate the sale of insurance, and could require that the only insurance products sold to employees of small- and medium-sized businesses (and to individuals) be those products under contract to the HIPC. Without changes to ERISA, self-insured employers could not be prevented from purchasing insurance independently from the HIPC, but few small employers are self-insured. State governments have the authority to empower the demand side of the health care market, and some states may decide to do so; however, many states are unlikely to take such action unless prompted to by the federal government.

The political prospects for greatly increased regulatory authority over the sale of insurance are mixed. Strong opposition would be expected from many small insurers who will be unlikely to have products that HIPCs will be interested in contracting with. In many large metropolitan areas, there will be somewhere between three and eight health plans—that is, three to eight groups of doctors and hospitals organized to take care of enrollees' health care needs. In addition, one or two more open-ended PPO or "managed indemnity" products might be under contract to HIPCs in each area. This greatly restricts the potential market for insurers, and it is likely to be difficult to generate industry support for such proposal. However, some insurers will maintain a presence in the health insurance market, and, depending on insurers' assessments of their alternatives, HIPCs may be an attractive proposal. HIPCs are less attractive for insurers, certainly, than existing small group market reform proposals, but these proposals, even if enacted, will do little to improve quality or economy of health care delivery and will only slightly ameliorate the hue and cry that insurers do not add value to health care system. Certainly HIPCs will be seen by insurers as preferable to entirely publicly provided insurance.

Small- and medium-sized employers and their employees might be expected to have mixed reactions to this proposal. HIPC contracted products will have a better price-to-value ratio than currently available products or those that are likely to be available after small group market reform. More importantly, if HIPCs are successful in restraining expenditure growth and increasing value for money, the viability of small businesses will improve. On the negative side, small employers will have fewer choices of product and benefit packages (or at least the potential for fewer choices), and this will cause real losses for some and the fear of losses for many more. Some small employers will be uncomfortable with a system in which a central purchasing agency is able to determine what products the employer can purchase.

Many providers will prefer HIPCs to a public insurance system and may find them preferable to a continuation and growth of private insurance arrangements in which they are increasingly hassled by third-party payers in an attempt to micro-manage the delivery of health care. Successful health plans will gain the loyalty and commitment of their providers and will control costs through constraining resource availability and creating an organizational culture supportive of continuous quality improvement, rather than by looking over the shoulder of physicians and second-guessing treatment decisions.

In the absence of any well-organized constituency leading the fight for the creating of HIPCs, the prospects for achieving empowerment of the demand side must be viewed as mixed, at best. However, there may well be an opportunity for a political entrepreneur to assemble a coalition in support of such empowerment.[37] The Washington Business Group of Health has endorsed the idea of creating HIPCs, as the purchasing agent for small and medium-sized businesses.[38] Many others who support private insurance may become convinced that it provides few benefits and ultimately will be replaced by government-sponsored insurance, unless the demand side is organized and empowered.

Many reasonable people will argue that managed competition is nothing but a theory, and that as a practical matter it may be impossible to successfully create an environment in which providers strive for quality and economy. One alternative is to continue muddling through, allowing larger and larger parts of our income to be turned over to health care providers, without getting much increased value for the money.

A second alternative is to control the budgets to hospitals directly and to use fee schedules and expenditure targets to control physician reimbursement. In sparsely settled, relatively homogenous states, this may work reasonably well. A public sector agency could allocate capital and budgets to hospitals, and the community of providers could use information provided by the public agency and work more or less cooperatively to figure out how best to use available resources. Managed competition will not work in a sparsely settled place—if there is a need for only one hospital and one group of physicians in town, it is neither desirable not possible to have these providers compete on the basis of price and quality.

However, in industrialized states with densely settled urban areas, large numbers of tertiary and community hospitals, conflicts among and between groups of providers, providers sharing few common ties, and political divisions within the population along class, racial, and ethnic lines, a public sector resource allocation model is not likely to lead to resources being put to their best use, and will likely leave in place substantial inequities in the delivery of services. Empowerment of the demand side can lead to better outcomes—but only if regulation of health insurance as currently practiced is replaced with active and intelligent contracting with competing health plans. Those who are content with simply buffing up the edges of existing regulatory schemes will likely be faced with an increasing crescendo of demands for the abolition of private insurance entirely.

The author is grateful to Amy Bridges and Jack Hadley for helpful comments on earlier drafts of this paper. Many of the ideas in the paper have been developed and refined in discussions with Alan Enthoven. All conclusions and, of course, errors are the responsibility of the author.

1. Sen. Lloyd M. Bentsen and Rep. Dan Rostenkowski have each introduced bills that would apply federal regulations to all insurance sold in the small group market. The Health Insurance Association of America has opposed such legislation, arguing that state regulation is preferable, and is working with the National Association of Insurance Commissioners to draft model small group insurance legislation and to lobby state legislatures to adopt such models. (See Hall, note 19.)

2. By private insurance, I refer to a system in which some financial intermediary, at least partially at risk, accepts premium payments from consumers and then makes payments to health care providers. The consumers can be individuals, employers, or government agencies (e.g., the Federal Employees Health Benefit Plan purchases "private insurance," as does Medicare when it contracts with HMOs on a risk basis). However, although the Medicare program (and many state Medicaid programs) uses fiscal intermediaries to pay health care providers, they are not at risk and thus are not in the business of selling private insurance.

3. If we adopt a publicly financed system for health insurance, as has been proposed by John Garamendi, the California Commissioner of Insurance, then HIPCs would contract with health plans on behalf of all those not covered by other public programs. (See Garamendi, note 32.)

4. KJ Meier, *The Political Economy of Regulation: The Case of Insurance* (Albany NY: State University of New York Press, 1988).

5. Regulations of investment policies were aimed at both preventing investment in risky ventures and requiring funds to be invested in the state in which premiums were collected, rather than being repatriated to the home state of the insurer. [K Orren, *Corporate Power and Social Change* (Cambridge MA: Harvard University Press, 1974)]

6. CB Sullivan and T Rice, "The Health Insurance Picture in 1990," 2 *Health Affairs* 10 (1991): 104–115.

7. US Bureau of the Census, *Statistical Abstract of the United States*, 11th ed (Washington DC: US Government Printing Office, 1991).

8. US House of Representatives, Committee on Education and Labor, "Oversight Investigation of Certain Multiple Employer Health Insurance Trusts (METs) Evading State and Federal Regulation," Hearing before the Subcommittee on Labor-Management Relations, Mar 5, 1982 (Washington DC: U.S. Government Printing Office, 1982)

9. JR Gabel and A Jansen, "The Price of State Mandated Benefits," 4 *Inquiry* 26 (1989): 419–431.

10. As classified by G. Scandlen, "The Changing Environment of Mandated Benefits," Employee Benefits Notes, 1987, mandated benefits laws also specify who must be covered (e.g., family policies must cover adopted children) and when services must be covered (e.g., insurers must allow employees who have been terminated from a group the option to continue their coverage or convert to a non-group policy). In one of the few federal intrusions into the thicket of state regulation of insurance, the Consolidated Omnibus Budget and Reconciliation Act of 1985 requires continuation options for most employees who lose their group coverage.

11. Supra, note 9.

12. For an explication of the "capture" theory of regulation, see GJ Stigler, "The Theory of Economic Regulation," 1971 *Bell Journal of Economics and Management Science* 2 (Spring): 3–21. For revisions to this theory, see S Peltzman, 'Toward a More General Theory of Regulation,'" 1976 Journal of Law and Economics 19 (August: 211–240; and RG Noll and BM Owen, *The Political Economy of Deregulation* (Washington DC: American Enterprise Institute, 1983).

13. The influence of providers is evident in other areas as well. Until the early 1980s, many states had laws that prohibited insurers from offering preferred provider products by prohibiting selective contracting

between insurers and providers. More recently, provider groups have supported attempts in a variety of states to regulate the utilization review activities of insurers.

14. In response to abuses in the Medicap market. Sen. Max S. Bacus introduced a bill passed by Congress in 1980, which created incentives for states to comply with a set of minimum standards in the regulation of Medigap products. These standards specified that individual Medigap policies should have a minimum loss ratio of 60%, and group Medigap policies a minimum loss ratio of 75%.

15. Regulation of HMOs generally requires demonstration that adequate capacity is available to take care of enrollees, that minimum capital requirements be met (usually less stringent than the requirements for indemnity insurance), and that the HMO has established quality assurance and grievance procedures. In most states, HMOs are exempt from the premium taxes paid by commercial insurers.

16. Congressional Research Service, *Health Insurance and the Uninsured: Background Data and Analysis* (Washington, DC: US Government Printing Office, 1988).

17. Whether a pay-or-play tax would be upheld in the face of an ERISA challenge is not completely clear, but carefully crafted pay-or-play legislation at the state level may well be consistent with ERISA language.

18. Freudenheim, "Employees Winning Right to Cut Back Medical Insurance," *New York Times,* Mar 29, 1992.

19. MA Hall, "Reforming the Health Insurance Market for Small Businesses," 8 *New England Journal of Medicine* 326 (1992): 565–570.

20. To the extent that services are provided that produce some value for patients, in order to make all better off with none worse off, patients must keep a little of the money that would otherwise have been paid to providers (enough to compensate for the marginal value of the services); the rest of the money could be donated to providers, whose gross moeny income would decline marginally, but who would, on net, be better off if they value leisure.

21. A Enthoven, "Managed Competition in Health Care and the Unfinished Agenda," *Health Care Financing Review,* Annual Supplement 1986: 105–119

22. The proposed Oregon Medicaid experiment is a partial exception to this statement. Oregon is proposing that the Medicaid program should refuse to pay for treatment of some conditions for which treatment has been judged to be lower priority than treatment of other conditions, even though in some cases, in theory, professional judgment might consider the excluded treatment "medically necessary." However, the initial line has been drawn at condition-treatment pair 587, and few providers would argue that there is much treatment currently provided in well-managed settings for conditions that are "below the line." Private insurers in Oregon are making plans to market policies that would exclude coverage of conditions "below the line": although they might well be successful in marketing these policies, it is extremely doubtful that they would be successful if the line someday moved up to a point at which many providers would argue that treatments below the new line were likely to confer substantial health benefits. Similarly, if the Oregon experiment is allowed to move forward, it will be an interesting political experiment to see whether the state government would be willing, in the face of the inevitable budget pressures in the future, to move the line up to a point where apparently beneficial and nonexperimental procedures would be denied.

23. The range of preferences would be even wider in many other areas. For example, many upper income persons choose to purchase life insurance that is at least an order of magnitude more costly than the life insurance purchased by lower income persons.

24. C. Havighurst, "Why Preserve Private Health Care Financing?" presented at American Health Policy: Critical Issues for Reform (Washington DC: American Enterprise Institute, 1991).

25. K Arrow, *Social Choice and Individual Values* (New York: Wiley, 1951).

26. Features such as divided responsibility between executive and legislative branches, weak political parties, decentralized decision-making in legislatures, and a relatively weak permanent civil service give well organized "special" interests multiple points of access in the United States.

27. Supra note 21; and A Enthoven, *Theory and Practice of Managed Competition in Health Care Finance,* (Amsterdam: North Holland, 1988).

28. R Krnonick, "Managed Competition: Why We Don't Have It and How We Can Get It," presented at American Health Policy: Critical Issues for Reform (Washington, DC: American Enterprise Institute, 1991).

29. In states with multiple HIPCs, each HIPC would be responsible for health plan contracting in a particular region of the state.

30. A voluntary approach, in which employers that wanted to could purchase through the HIPC while those that did not want to could purchase directly from insurer should not be successful for the same reason that many Multiple Employer Trusts fail—that is, adverse selection of high-risk employer groups into the HIPC pool, and segregation of good risks outside the HIPC. A potential alternative to prohibiting the sale of insurance to small employers outside the HIPC structure would be to provide strong financial incentives for purchase through an HIPC—for example, conditioning the availability of tax-free employer contributions to health insurance on purchase through an HIPC.

31. If some health plans serve a sicker mix of enrollees than others, the HIPC would risk-adjust the employer contribution—increasing it on behalf of health plans with sicker enrolles, and reducing it if the employee chooses a health plan with healthier than average enrollees.

32. A Enthoven and R Kronick, "A Consumer-Choice Health Plan for the 1990s," 1 *New England Journal of Medicine* 320 (1989): 29–37.

33. J Garamendi, *California Health Care in the 21st Century* (Sacramento: California Commissioner of Insurance, 1992).

34. Many of the elderly will fear uncertainty and change, and as unhappy as some are with Medicare, they might be more unhappy if it were to change significantly. On the administrative side, establishing well-functioning HIPCs will be a difficult enough task; if they also must be involved with adapting and modifying Medicare and/or Medicaid rules and procedures, the difficulty of the task will be increased. Further, in many states, bringing Medicaid recipients into mainstream medicine will raise expenditures; as part of a general set of health care financing reforms this may be acceptable, but holding universal coverage hostage to large-scale income redistribution is a dangerous strategy. A phased approach in which Medicaid and Medicare are brought under the public of the HIPC over time may be more sensible.

35. A straight percentage tax on health expenditures would not be desirable, since this would allow the funding stream for HIPCs to grow at the rate of health expenditures, and would cause administrative funds to vary inversely, rather than directly, with the success of HIPCs at restraining health expenditure growth. Alternatives to straight percentage taxes on health expenditures are more desirable.

36. Enthoven [*The 21st Century American Health System: Market Reform and Universal Coverage* (Jackson Hole Group, 1991)] and the Washington Business Group on Health (see note 38) have suggested that directors of HIPCs be elected by the small employers and self-employed persons who purchase coverage through the HIPC. While this might help protect the HIPC from the political influence of providers and insurers, these would likely be low salience and low turnout elections and it is quite possible that providers would be able to maneuver the election of supportive candidates. (Elections of school boards by parents of school children do not prevent teachers from having a strong influence on school board composition in many cities.) Further consideration of the method of governance of HIPCs is required to resolve this important issue.

37. John Garamendi, the elected insurance commissioner in California, is attempting to construct a winning coalition by proposing a system based on public financing and the establishment of HIPCs to contract with health plans on behalf of the entire population not covered by Medicare or Medicaid. Sen. Jeff Bingaman has drafted a bill that would provide federal seed money to states that established HIPCs as the exclusive purchasing agents for small employers.

38. Washington Business Group on Health, "Position of the Washington Business Group on Health on Restructuring the Small Group Insurance Market" (Washington DC: Feb 20, 1992).

Index